Gender, Sexuality, and Intimacy

A *Contexts* Reader

Sara Miller McCune founded SAGE Publishing in 1965 to support the dissemination of usable knowledge and educate a global community. SAGE publishes more than 1000 journals and over 800 new books each year, spanning a wide range of subject areas. Our growing selection of library products includes archives, data, case studies and video. SAGE remains majority owned by our founder and after her lifetime will become owned by a charitable trust that secures the company's continued independence.

Los Angeles | London | New Delhi | Singapore | Washington DC | Melbourne

Gender, Sexuality, and Intimacy

A *Contexts* Reader

Edited by

Jodi O'Brien
Seattle University

Arlene Stein
Rutgers University

with
Madelyn Glasco
and
Alexandra Maher

Los Angeles | London | New Delhi
Singapore | Washington DC | Melbourne

FOR INFORMATION:

SAGE Publications, Inc.
2455 Teller Road
Thousand Oaks, California 91320
E-mail: order@sagepub.com

SAGE Publications Ltd.
1 Oliver's Yard
55 City Road
London EC1Y 1SP
United Kingdom

SAGE Publications India Pvt. Ltd.
B 1/I 1 Mohan Cooperative Industrial Area
Mathura Road, New Delhi 110 044
India

SAGE Publications Asia-Pacific Pte. Ltd.
3 Church Street
#10-04 Samsung Hub
Singapore 049483

Publisher: Jeff Lasser
Editorial Assistant: Adeline Wilson
Production Editor: David C. Felts
Typesetter: C&M Digitals (P) Ltd.
Proofreader: Pam Suwinsky
Cover Designer: Anupama Krishnan
Marketing Manager: Kara Kindstrom

Printed in the United States of America

Library of Congress Cataloging-in-Publication Data

ISBN 978-1-5063-5231-2

This book is printed on acid-free paper.

17 18 19 20 21 10 9 8 7 6 5 4 3 2 1

CONTENTS

SECTION II. SEXUALITY

Introduction: Navigating Sexuality   138

Focus Point: Slut-Shaming Romance Writers by Nicole Bedera   145

Navigating Sexuality   146

Sexual Knowledge   173

SECTION III. INTIMACY

Introduction: Mapping Intimacy 228

Focus Point: An Unexpected Box of Love Research by Michelle Janning 233

Locating Intimacy 235

Marriage 261

Reproduction 290

PREFACE

For three years, beginning in 2012, we served as the editors of *Contexts*, a hybrid journal-magazine that translates sociological research to popular audiences. Published by the American Sociological Association, *Contexts* articles make cutting-edge social science research available to general readers, offering up-to-date information and analysis on contemporary social issues. In recent years, several *Contexts* articles have been compiled into readers for use in introductory sociology classes (*The Contexts Reader,* First and Second Editions, W.W. Norton). Students and instructors appreciate these readers for breadth of coverage and engaging writing about current topics.

During our editorship, we published many articles on gender, sexuality, and intimacy. Although we're general sociologists, our scholarly expertise is in these areas. Many potential authors therefore viewed our editorship as an opportunity to publish research that has historically been less visible in mainstream sociology. These days, gender, sexuality, and intimacy are robust research areas in sociology. They are also pivotal topics in contemporary media, politics, sports, and most other aspects of social life. As sociologists teaching and studying these complex subjects, we are often dismayed at the misinformation, stereotypes, and prejudices that characterize everyday conversations and experiences around such intimate aspects of our lives. As a society we are saturated with sexual imagery and contentious debates about gender and family, but we lack coherent, thoughtful frameworks for making sense of it all. *Contexts* is a venue for bringing newly emerging research into public conversation.

We conceived of this *Contexts* reader on gender, sexuality, and intimacy as a way of lifting debates around sensitive and sensational topics to a higher ground. The articles in this book provide points of reference that are grounded in empirical evidence and critical analyses. Our hope is that this material will not only lead to richer, better-informed discussions, but that an expanded, contextual perspective will leave readers feeling more encouraged and less anxious about their own life experiences.

acknowledgments

The readings in this book are from 2009–2015 and include material that was published under the editorships of Douglas Hartmann and Christopher Uggen (2009–2011), and Syed Ali and Philip Cohen (2015–current), as well as from our editorship. We are especially grateful to our fellow editors for their keen, incisive eye in encouraging manuscript submissions in the areas of gender, sexuality, and intimacy, and for shepherding many of these articles through the publication process. *Contexts* is a team effort involving the hard work and expertise of many people, including managing editors Letta Page, Carly Chillmon, Margaret Austin Smith, Jennifer Hemler, and Jessica Streeter and numerous department editors and design editors across the years. Kirsten Younghee Song (Rutgers University) was our initial research assistant on the project and compiled the first table of contents. Research assistants (Seattle University) Madelyn Glasco and Alexandra Maher deserve co-editorial credit for their work in updating the table of contents, brainstorming various thematic organizational schemes, and providing the reading annotations and discussion questions. We particularly appreciate Jennifer Hamann's keen editorial eye and production assistance. We are also thankful for the support and collaboration of the American Sociological Association (especially Karen Gray Edwards, director of publications and membership) and SAGE Publications (Jeff Lasser, sociology editor) in recognizing and promoting the value of this project. The SAGE production staff, led by production editor David Felts, has been hugely helpful and innovative in working with us to maintain a *Contexts* magazine look for this book and in moving it expertly through every step toward publication. A special shout-out to Claire Garoutte (Seattle University Photography faculty) who introduced us to cover photo artist Molly Landreth, and to Molly who so generously gave us permission to use a photo from her amazing series, "Embodiment: A Portrait of Queer Life in America."

Jodi: I am enormously grateful to my friend, colleague, and co-editor Arlene Stein who persuaded me that, yes, we really did want to take on something of the magnitude of *Contexts*. Despite how crazy it seemed at the time (and it was an incredibly steep learning curve), it's been one of the most fun and rewarding chapters of my professional career. This book project is a fitting epilogue.

Arlene: I could not have asked for a better partner in crime than Jodi O'Brien, whose smarts, organizational skills, and sense of humor made editing *Contexts* fun and exciting. I am very pleased that with the publication of this book, many of the articles we helped to shepherd to publication will enjoy greater visibility and longevity.

Jodi O'Brien (Seattle University)
Arlene Stein (Rutgers University)

GENDER

introduction
where is gender?

jodi o'brien

> **For awhile I thought it would be fun to call what I do in life *gender terrorism*. Seemed right at first—I and so many folks like me were terrorizing the structure of gender itself. But I've come to see if a bit differently now—gender terrorists are not the female to male transsexual who's learning to look people in the eye while he walks down the street. Gender terrorists are not the leather daddies or back-seat Betties. Gender terrorists are not the married men, shivering in the dark as they slip on their wives' panties. Gender terrorists are those who bang their heads against a gender system which [they think] is *real* and *natural;* who then use gender to terrorize the rest of us. These are the real terrorists: the Gender Defenders.**
> **—Kate Bornstein (1994:71)**

Where is gender? Is it in your body? In your mind? In your fashion choices? In your choice of lovers? In society? All of the above? None of the above? In her 1994 book, *Gender Outlaw: On Men, Women and the Rest of Us;* performance artist, author, and activist Kate Bornstein popularized a radical idea that was shared by many gender scholars: gender roles were not a reflection of naturally occurring sex differences, they were a cultural construction. Drawing on the research of gender sociologists Bornstein sketched a set of "gender rules" that operate as a taken-for-granted cultural template for who we can be and what we can do. These rules include:

- There are only two genders (female and male)
- Gender is invariant
- Everyone must have a gender
- Genitals are the essential sign of gender (vagina or penis)
- Exceptions are a sign of pathology (or a joke)
- The male/female dichotomy is "natural"
- Membership in one gender or another is "natural" (i.e., no one, including you, can decide what you are—it's up to nature) (1994: 46–50).

For Bornstein and the sociologists studying gender, these rules are one of the central belief systems of contemporary Western society. Gender rules shape everything around us – we gender professions (masculine military, feminine nursing, etc.) and even objects and concepts [mother earth, father time]. Sociologist Judith Lorber proposes that this makes gender a social *institution*, rather than an individual trait. She explains that because gender beliefs are so common and presumed to be natural, we're not even aware of them, like fish unaware of the water they swim in. Throughout the 1980s and '90s, self-described gender outlaws such as Bornstein made it their mission to show how unnatural these beliefs really are by disrupting everyday gender expectations and highlighting the ways in which gender is a social performance.

Fast forward to the present moment. From RuPaul's *Drag Race* to Caitlyn Jenner, popular media is saturated with stories and images that blur conventional gender lines. Transgender and gender queer identities are increasingly recognized in official school and work settings. Student activists promote gender fluidity and mental health professionals are increasingly acknowledging gender nonconformity in children as a normal manifestation of a gender spectrum rather than a form of pathology. Belief in the supposedly natural gender binary is on the wane, or so it might seem. But is it really?

nature/nurture binary

One of the most pervasive gender beliefs is that gender is natural and manifest through the genitals. The exclamation "What is it?" in reference to a new baby is commonly understood to mean "Is it a boy or a girl?" Through the use of ultrasound technology many expectant parents now celebrate a "gender identification day." Presence or absence of a penis is used to make a *sex assignment* and launch the unborn child on a gender journey. Sex assignment is presumed to indicate an innate gender that aligns with specific *gender roles* (tough boys, nurturing girls) and a corresponding *gender identity* (I am a boy; I am a girl). Additional beliefs embedded in this cultural script include: biological reproduction is the primary basis of human sexuality, and observed secondary sex differences (penis/vagina) line up with primary sex characteristics (testes/ovaries) to determine not only reproductive capacity but sexuality (see the next section for elaboration). Finally, chromosomal and hormonal structures are seen to align with the sex characteristics. Thus, any variation in gender identity and expression (including preference for same-gender sex partners) is "unnatural."

Gender and sexuality scholars have successfully critiqued the notion of natural gender roles and identities by pointing out that most of the behaviors associated with these identities and roles are culturally specific and socially constructed. Gender expectations are maintained largely through the ongoing social policing. Feminist biologists have contributed to this debunking by mapping out the range of variation within and across species. For instance, not all species share the XX or XY chromosomal structure associated with human sex characteristics. Even in humans there is not a binary on this dimension as is commonly assumed.

Biologist Anne Fausto-Sterling is an expert on gender development. She is especially interested in gender variance. She researches the many variations that exist among individuals who are trying to fit into a system that offers only two gender choices (female/male). Biologically, there is ample evidence that people vary along a spectrum: there are variations on chromosomal structures. Rather than the presumed XY and XX, there are at least five documented variations (e.g., XXY, XYX). Do you know what your chromosomal structure is, or do you just assume it matches the gender you consider yourself to be? From a biological perspective, nature may be "hinting" that the penis/vagina gender binary we assume to be natural (as rooted in reproductive propensity) is insufficient to account for the full range of natural possibilities. For Fausto-Sterling, "sex and gender are best conceptualized as points in a multidimensional space."

The emerging field of transgender studies offers a rich mosaic of gendered bodies, expressions, and identities throughout history and across cultures. This remarkable variation indicates that, biologically, there is a wide range of gender possibilities in nature. If this is the case, then why don't we see it that way? Recall that one of the gender beliefs is that the gender binary is natural. This is a belief, not a scientific fact, but given the persistence of these basic gender beliefs, historically many scientists and physicians have discounted gender variation as an anomaly or something out of order, even pathological. They're looking through the same gender binary lens as the rest of us and, accordingly, they see what they expect to see—two genders.

Imagine you had a box of blocks with at least five or more shapes and you were required to sort them all into two piles. What would you do? Most likely you'd find a particular characteristic and use that as your sorting rule. Perhaps some of the shapes look more roundish to you and some seem squarish. You can sort them into two piles of roundish and squarish, but you will still see the variation within each pile. For instance, where did you decide to place the star-shaped block? Over time, and the more you emphasize the binary you've created, the more likely you will come to see it that way (and to overlook the variation). You may even forget that you originally determined this categorical scheme yourself and come to see it as something "natural." Similarly, the historical practice has been to shoehorn potential gender variation into one of two gender boxes. For some people the fit is just fine; for others, it can mean a lifetime of feeling out of place. Cultural institutions such as medicine and psychiatry have perpetuated this natural gender binary myth with diagnostic categories such as "gender dysphoria"—a term for someone, often a child, who does not identify with their birth sex/gender assignment.

Paradoxically, one of the most intriguing gender debates to arise in recent years is a resurgence of the nature/nurture binary argument—but from an unlikely source. Many transgender and gender nonconforming people are resistant to the idea of gender as socially constructed and are (re)turning to naturalist arguments as a way of understanding their own experiences and of getting the medical and social resources they need. For these people, as well as family, community, and the church members and social service agencies they interact with, the idea that gender is socially constructed implies a choice. Given that this choice is often considered to be socially disruptive, the gender nonconforming person is typically pressured into reparative therapies and other programs and social engagements intended to bring about conformity. Conversely, the idea that one's gender expression is not a choice but a manifestation of nature provides gender nonconforming people with a strong rationale for gaining legitimacy and getting support. Notice that this logic is more or less consistent with the gender rules described at the beginning of this essay, with the exception of revision of the rule that genitals determine gender. Certainly this is radical shift in a pervasive cultural belief system, but sociologically it's important to remember that the nature/nurture debate is also a false binary.

Researchers in fields such as biology, evolutionary psychology, evolutionary linguistics, and neurology are increasingly exploring the dynamic interplay between the physical body and the cultural scripts that we use to understand, guide, and direct our bodies. Some of the best contemporary scientists and social scientists agree that it's neither nature nor nurture: it's both. For these scholars, among whom we include ourselves, this is a new frontier with much promise toward understanding the richly complicated connections between bodies and social processes. Fausto-Sterling describes the relationship between nature and nurture as a "dynamic system." In her words, "I believe that both sex and gender are in part social constructs. But they take place in the body, and so are simultaneously biological. Dynamic systems theories link the social—which impinges on the developing body—to the body itself. Cultural experience has physiological effects." In other words, we are not merely blank slates, we have bodies and we experience the world through our bodies. At the same time, our bodies do not arrive pre-formed: rather, the body "*acquires* nervous, muscular and emotional responses as a result of a give and take with its physical, emotional and cultural experiences."

Think for instance of the experience of wearing high-heeled shoes. The musculature and gait of people who regularly wear high-heeled shoes will develop accordingly. Although a bit trite, this example illustrates the dynamic between social behavior and the experience of our bodies. More sophisticated research looks at the ways in which repeated cultural experiences form neural networks that shape our perceptions and emotional responses. For example, from the moment they are born, infants are exposed to cultural gender expectations: they are dressed in particular colors and fabrics, offered gender-specific toys, and, perhaps most notably, encouraged when they behave in ways that are consistent with cultural gender rules. Much of this cultural "coaching" is unconscious but so pervasive that even the most gender-aware parents have difficultly avoiding culturally imposed gender expectations. As an experiment, spend a day doing something very minor that is gender atypical for you, for instance, sit with your legs spread wide apart, or cross your legs (opposite of your usual behavior), and pay attention to how you feel in your body.

gender scripts

For the sociologist it's clear that the range of *gender expression* is broadening significantly. At the same time, traditional gender defense is also on the rise. Take for example the rush in many states to enact "bathroom"

laws that would require people to use the bathroom associated with their birth sex assignment. Is this something we really want to be policing in the 21st century? Sociologists are curious about the reasons for this deeply emotional defense. These so-called gender wars are more than just a cultural battle over fashion and the right to pee in peace. The battles indicate just how deeply entrenched gender is as a *social institution*. Gender rules are a kind of social script that tell us who we can be, what we can do, and how to engage with those around us. Social scripts in general provide us with rules of engagement—without them, we can't make sense of ourselves, of one another, or the situations we find ourselves in. In answer to the question where is gender? the sociologist would reply it's in our bodies, minds, and social interactions, but specifically in the *gender scripts* we have for making sense of our bodies, our feelings and actions, our relationships with others, and society.

Whether you consider yourself to be more comfortable with emerging ideas about gender fluidity or with traditional gender binaries, it's important to closely examine the ways in which the gender rules described by Bornstein and Lorber reflect culturally specific gender scripts that shape your behavior and beliefs, often unknowingly. As a consequence, your behavior and experiences can be both gender conforming and nonconforming simultaneously. Consider the bathroom example. Although public gender-neutral bathrooms are increasingly common, it's usually the case that they are one-stall spaces. If the sign indicates all genders, then most people feel comfortable using the bathroom. In public spaces with one-stall bathrooms that are designated by gender (female/male), I often find lines of women waiting to use the signed "women" bathroom even though no one is in line for the bathroom marked "men." Occasionally some of these women will team up and someone will say, "Why don't you use that one, I'll watch out for you." I've often wondered what that means: "I'll watch out for you" in reference to using the man-signed bathroom. It's as if, in the moment, we're deciding to clamber over some gender fence and need back-up support. In contrast, imagine putting up signs in your own home for men/women. Although the example may seem trivial, the contextual emotional response is not. When we use the bathroom in someone's home it is ungendered. In public spaces, the mere presence of a gender sign invokes the power of gender scripts to make us feel as though we may be transgressing, regardless of how personally gender nonconforming we consider ourselves to be. In other words, *gender scripts come into play contextually and interactionally.*

Most of us don't wander around constantly thinking about gender; in fact, we're most likely to notice it when something doesn't fit the expected script for the context.

Consider the rules above about the gender binary. When we encounter someone we can't readily gender, we search for more clues (presence or absence of breasts is common). This activity is cognitive and typically mindless. Once the breasts are noted we slot the person into "female" and continue on our way. But wait! Is that a beard? Breasts and a beard? In some contexts, the contemporary expansion of gender scripts provides a cognitive basis for making sense of this anomaly and we can look for additional cues to fit a trans or gender nonconforming category. But how we react to this gender transgression is also contextual: is the person just a variation on the gender theme or some kind of freak? The context frames our interpretation and resulting feelings (e.g., lively urban setting with a queerish vibe versus buttoned-up office place). But note that even with the expansion of possible scripts beyond a gender binary, most of us are still strongly inclined to want to gender the person – the "everyone must have a gender" rule is still firmly in place in most settings.

pondering gender

Sociologists have noted that gender is one of the primary features we use to know how to interact with someone—our social scripts are so deeply gendered that if we don't know someone's gender, even if it's non-binary, we don't know how to engage with them. Consider the plausibility of this as you read this book and think about the situations in your own life. When does gender come into play? When do you feel most conscious of your own gender? When are you most comfortable/uncomfortable? Pay attention to contexts in which you feel you're "pushing out" or emphasizing your gender and consider why this is. These small activities illustrate the contextual, interactional aspects of gender—what some gender scholars call the "performativity" of gender.

So where is gender? As you reading through the selections in this book, consider the following as compass points for locating the always shifting, continually unfolding landscape of gender:

- We experience the world through bodies, but
- We use cultural scripts to classify and make sense of bodies (especially classifications such as gender, race, and age).
- In this society we are born into a culture that immediately groups infants into one of two genders according to specific gender rules.
- These rules are shifting but still consist of unexamined assumptions, especially about what is "natural."
- These categories do not necessarily represent the full variation that exists in nature.
- Our bodies are not entirely pre-formed, but develop in relation to socio-developmental categories, processes, and experiences.
- Gender socialization is what Fausto-Sterling calls a "dynamic iterative process." The small cumulative events of everyday life – how we move, talk, and dress, and how we feel about and judge ourselves and others day in and day out - have large effects on stabilizing binary forms gender expression.

The current battle over bathroom access is evidence that gender binary expectations are constructed and socially enforced. If this was a natural binary with associated naturally occurring behaviors we wouldn't have to mark gender with clothing and related expressions. And we certainly wouldn't have to monitor bathroom facilities.

recommended resources

Bornstein, Kate. 1994. *Gender Outlaws: On Men, Women, and the Rest of Us.* New York: Routledge.

Fausto-Sterling, Anne. 2013. *Sex/Gender: Biology in a Social World.* New York: Routledge.

Lorber, Judith. 1994. *Paradoxes of Gender.* Princeton: Yale University Press.

O'Brien, Jodi. 2016. "Seeing Agnes: Notes on a Transgender Bio-Cultural Ethnomethodology," *Symbolic Interaction 39*:306–339.

learning to parent transgender children

nicole bedera

spring 2015

Over the past few years, stories of transgender children celebrated by their parents have flooded the Internet. But how do these parents come to be supportive of their gender-variant kids? In a recent article in *Gender and Society*, Elizabeth Rahilly tries to answer that question. Her interviews reveal that instead of entering parenthood with gender-progressive ideologies, supportive parents learn to accept their child's gender-variance after their child's persistent urging. Together, parents and children develop methods to reaffirm the child's gender identity and combat the gender binary.

Rahilly identifies three common techniques that indicate a shift in parents' perspectives on how best to raise their gender-variant children. In this study, "gender variant children" refers both to children who identify as a different gender than they were assigned at birth and who more casually cross traditional gender boundaries. In responding to their gender variant children, parents first use what Rahilly calls "gender hedging," or the creation of boundaries for their child's gender variance. A gender hedging parent might allow their male child to wear pink socks, but not a pink sweater.

Gender hedging allows both children and parents to explore gender nonconformity and begin to question the legitimacy of the gender binary. This questioning leads parents to seek out information about gender-variant children, connecting them to online materials that accept and normalize gender variance.

Then parents participate in "gender literacy," or active education of their children about issues of gender variance. Rahilly argues that gender literacy permits parents to actively resist the gender binary and demonstrate acceptance of their own children. Finally, parents adopt a practice of "playing along" with the gender binary according to boundaries set partially by their children. For example, a parent may not correct a stranger who mis-genders a child in a grocery store if a child requests their silence, but will address a teacher who mistreats the child.

Ultimately, Rahilly found that supportive parenting of gender-variant children is largely child-driven. Neither parents nor children are driven by ideologies that encourage gender variation, such as feminism or gender-neutral parenting. Instead, accepting parenting practices develop directly in response to the children's interpretations of their gender and corresponding understanding of their needs.

locating gender

overview

We commonly believe that gender resides in the body—in one's genes and genitals. The way one moves is also frequently coded as feminine or masculine—hence the phrase "throwing like a girl." But gender is so pervasive that it permeates most—if not all—aspects of social life.

Our knowledge and experience of gender are deeply rooted in social contexts. In "Boys vs. Girls," Debra Rigney examines the ways children learn rules about what is masculine and what is feminine, locating gender in physical objects such as clothing and toys and in physical behaviors such as fighting and crying. Gender also shapes personal relationships and interactions. In "The Hearts of Boys," authors Niobe Way, C.J. Pascoe, Mark McCormack, Amy Schalet, and Freeden Oeur examine boys' intimate friendships with other boys. Since emotional intimacy is seen as a feminine trait, boys must figure out how to forge intimacy while maintaining manliness.

Gendered expectations are also bound up with race, as we see in the example of sports. In "Jeremy Lin's Model Minority Problem," Maxwell Leung addresses an intersection between race and gender. While boys in general are expected to enjoy sports, masculinity expectations differ across race and ethnicity. In this case, Black men are expected to be good at basketball while Asian men are not.

Gender is deeply coded in the body. But what happens when one's body does not conform to one's gender identity? In "Transitioning Out Loud and Online," Arlene Stein looks at how young transgender men use social media to share information about body modifications.

Gender does not reside only in bodies, of course; it is also a part of organizations. For example, some professions are coded as "male" and others as "female." In "A 21st Century Gender Revolution," Sangyoub Park delves into the world of women in higher education and historically male-dominated fields. Donna Gabaccia looks at the gendering, and feminization, of immigration.

things to consider

- Take a moment to consider where you experience/feel/see/express gender in your own life. You might consider your favorite television show, your extracurricular activities, or perhaps your morning routine, and how it may reflect gender difference.

- Think back to your childhood. Can you list five instances where you received direct or indirect messages about you assigned gender? These messages may be in the form of gendered gifts, toys, bedtime stories, or chores.

- In discussions of gender, femininity is more commonly discussed than masculinity. Consider the stereotypes associated with the concept of manliness, and the relationship between masculinity and the expression of emotions.

- Gender intersects with race and ethnicity. How does gender shape athletics, and notions of strength and competence? How is athletic success gendered and racialized? How might gendered expectations affect the lives of recent immigrants?

- How has the increased presence of technology in our everyday lives affected how you view and express your gender?

- Can you list or discuss five different professions that are still coded "male" or "female"? How might we work to dismantle this coding?

boys vs. girls

debra rigney

fall 2011

If you have children or work with them, you've probably heard statements like "Dolls are for girls" or "A fire truck is a boy's toy." At just three years old, how do children know if they are girls or boys? How do they find out their gender? The answer to this question is in some ways simple: gender socialization. In my introduction to sociology course, I learned to approach this concept first by splitting up the term.

So, sociologist Joan Ferrante describes gender as a social distinction based on culturally conceived and learned ideals about appropriate appearance, behavior, and mental and emotional characteristics for male and female. This differs from sex, because sex is a biological distinction, whereas gender is a social characteristic. Socialization, Ferrante writes, is the process by which people develop a sense of self and learn the ways of society in which they live. Therefore, gender socialization is the process of learning the norms of your specific gender.

This concept was on my mind when I recently started a new job at a daycare, and, in the past few weeks, I have been observing the children's gender socialization to see what they say to others and how they react to what others tell them about gender. The first day I observed, I was with the three- to four-year-old class. Damarion, a younger boy who doesn't attend preschool, wanted to wear a tutu. A four-year-old preschooler, Rhys, came up to him and politely said, "Damarion, skirts are

for girls," just before he went to the kitchen area to play with the dolls. When I followed to ask Rhys where he had learned the "skirt rule," he simply said, "My teacher only allows the girls at school to play dress up with skirts. She tells us that they are for girls," What was I supposed to say to that? I didn't know how to explain to Rhys that it was okay to wear a skirt as a boy without messing up what his preschool teacher had been teaching him. So, I only aksed, "So, if you think skirts are for girls, then don't you think that dolls are for girls, too?" Rhys corrected me, saying, "NO! Boys can be daddies and the girls can be the mommies." He then went on with his day. What I took from this interaction was that Ryhs has been learning at school that skirts are for girls, and Damarion hasn't. Therefore, Damarion, since he hasn't been told otherwise, thinks wearing skirts is perfectly normal for a young boy.

Another aspect of this interaction that stuck out to me is who had taught Rhys the "skirt rule." His teacher clearly isn't just teaching counting and the alphabet, she is acting as an agent of socialization. Ferrante defines agents of socialization as significant others, primary groups, in-groups and out groups, and institutions that shape our sense of self or social identity, teach us about the groups to which we do and do not belong, help us

> **Barbie shows girls what they should look like and what they can grow up to be, just as action figures do for boys.**

to realize our human capacities, and help us negotiate the social and physical environment we have inherited. In these ways, Rhys's teacher is socializing him to know the social norms of his gender. She is essentially teaching him how to "be" a boy.

On my second day of observation in the daycare center, I was with the five- to six-year-old group on the playground. During "free-play" I noticed Ethan, a kindergartener with four older sisters, crying. I went over to ask him if everything was alright. That was when I overheard another child, Dylan, saying "Ethan plays with Barbies. He must be a girl!" As Ethan began to cry harder, he tried to explain to Dylan that his sisters made him play with Barbies but he wasn't a girl. Dylan just laughed and walked away. I calmed Ethan down and put Dylan in time out. Dylan protested, "I shouldn't be here. I was just letting him know that he can't play with dolls or everyone will think he is a funny bunny." Dylan then explained that this is what his father said if he caught Dylan playing with Barbie dolls. "I was mainly looking out for him. If he keeps this up, everyone will think he's a girl, and he doesn't want that." When older children like Dylan do things that seem out of the social norm, like playing with dolls when they've been told that only girls do that, they can be made fun of. I believe that kids think this is the only distinction between girls and boys—what they play with or how they dress.

It seems that, above and beyond teachers, the most influential people in a child's gender socialization process are their parents. I know from experience that my parents influenced me and my brothers in many ways. My dad once told me "Sis, you can't be fighting with these boys, you will end up getting hurt." The sad thing is, I could keep up with them. And my mom used to ask, "Don't you want to stay home and practice your cheers instead of going with those dirty boys?" But then she would say things like "Black his eye!" or "Do a wheelie!" to my brother. I remember being about seven years old and beating up a little boy in the neighborhood because he was picking on my brother. My mom and dad were proud of me . . . and mad at the same time. My dad could only say, "Girls don't act like this." My response was "Well, Dad, if Bubby [my brother] didn't act like a girl, he could have beaten him up hisself. Is he even a boy?" In these situations and others, my parents taught me the social norms of being a girl.

As a daycare teacher, I, too, am an agent of socialization. We at the center are supposed to show all of the children the same amount of attention and console them in the same ways. During observation, though, I realized that this was not the case, even for me. I observed how differently all of the teachers reacted to similar cases. One of my first times in the toddler room, a little girl smacked another little boy, and the little boy hit her back. I went to the little girl to make sure she was okay and to calm her down. I then put the little boy in time out, and scolded him without even asking if he was okay. Why? Because most people believe that girls are more "sensitive," but if you "coddle" boys, they will grow up to be mama's boys (and nobody wants that).

One other big part of socialization deals with mass media and children's toys. Think about it: have you ever seen a boy dressed like a girl on television? The primary characters on television—intentional or unintentional role models—are gender-specific. If you turn on the Disney channel, you're going to see Disney princesses and princess merchandise targeted to female viewers, and it's effective. All of the girls at daycare want to grow up and be princesses. When I asked a group of three-year-olds what they wanted for Christmas, the girls wanted things like Barbies, various princess dolls, and "big girl make-up." Why? Because Barbie shows little girls what it's like to be grown up, and princess dolls are presented as the perfect portrayal of what a little girl wants to grow up to be. Have you ever seen a Barbie that dressed as a tomboy? Have you ever seen a fire fighter doll depicting what it's like to be a "girl"? Barbie shows and teaches girls what they should look like and what they can grow up to be, just as action figures do with boys. The problem is, action figures like those on the *Power Rangers* are often more imaginative and show boys that they can grow up to be big and strong, they can fight for what they believe in (or just to fight).

Between the influences of mass media, parents, teachers, and other kids, gender socialization takes hold early. These are just a few reasons why the children I observed "know" their gender and its appropriate social norms at such a young age.

Between the influences of parents, teachers and other kids, gender socialization takes hold early.

the hearts of boys

niobe way, c.j. pascoe, mark mccormack, amy schalet, and freeden oeur

winter 2013

Boys are interesting creatures in the American public imagination. They start off all "slugs and snails and puppy-dogs' tails"—cute!—but then they hit puberty and become lazy, sexual, carefree, violent, detached, and irresponsible. They become scary. We fear teenage boys, in part because they are in-between—neither children, nor adults—and they seem to be beyond our control.

boys as human

by niobe way

The popular stereotype is that boys are emotionally illiterate and shallow, they don't want intimate relationships or close friendships. In my research with boys over the past two decades, however, I have discovered that not only are these stereotypes false, they are actively hurting boys and leading them to engage in self destructive behaviors. The African American, Latino, Asian American and White teenage boys in my studies indicate that what they want and need most are close relationships—friendships, in particular—in which they can share their "deep secrets." These friendships, they tell us, are critical for their mental health. But, according to the boys, they live in a culture that considers such intimacy "girly" and "gay" and thus they are discouraged from having the very relationships that are critical for their wellbeing.

> *A central dilemma for boys growing up in the United States is how to get the intimacy they want while still maintaining their manliness.*

My longitudinal studies of hundreds of boys from early to late adolescence indicate that a central dilemma for boys growing up in the United States is how to get the intimacy they want while still maintaining their manliness. Boys want to be able to freely express their emotions, including their feelings of vulnerability; they want others to be sensitive to their feelings without being teased or harassed for having such desires. They want genuine friendships in which they are free to be themselves rather than conform to rigid masculine stereotypes. As Carlos said: "It might be nice to be a girl because then you wouldn't have to be emotionless."

During early and middle adolescence most boys, according to my research, do have close male friendships in which they can share their "deep secrets." It is only in late adolescence—a time when, according to national data, suicides and violence among boys soar—that boys disconnect from other boys. The boys in my studies begin, in late adolescence, to use the phrase "no homo" when discussing their male friendships, expressing the fear that if they seek out close friendships, they will be perceived as "gay" or "girly." As a consequence, they pull away from their male peers and experience sadness over the loss of their formerly close friends.

Michael, a participant in one of our studies, told his interviewer that friendships are important because, "if you don't have friends, you have no one to tell your secrets to. Then it's like, I always think bad stuff in my brain 'cause like no one's helping me and I just need to keep all the secrets to myself." Asked why friends are important, Danny said to his interviewer, "you need someone to talk to, like you have problems with something, you go talk to him. You know, if you keep it all to yourself, you will go crazy. Try to take it out on someone else." Kai implicitly concurred in his interview: "without friends you will go crazy or mad or you'll be lonely all of the time, be depressed. . . . You would go wacko." Asked by the interviewer why his friends are important, Justin said, "'cause you need a friend or else, you would be depressed, you won't be happy, you would try to kill yourself, 'cause then you'll be all alone and no one to talk to.' Faced with the prospect of having no close friends, Anthony said to his interviewer, "who you gonna talk to? Might as well be dead or something. I don't mean to put it in a negative way, but I am just saying—it's like not a good feeling to be alone."

Over the past three decades, studies, such as those done by epidemiologists Wilkinson and Pickett, have found that adults without close friendships are more likely to experience poor mental and physical health and live shorter lives than those with close friendships. Despite the growing body of data that underscores the importance of close friendships for everyone, harmful stereotypes that ignore boys' social and emotional needs and capacities abound. According to the boys themselves, these stereotypes significantly contribute to their isolation, loneliness, and depression. As they get older, boys get stripped of their humanity. They learn that they are not supposed to have hearts, except in relation to a girl, and then it should be a stoic heart and not too vulnerable.

We must allow boys to be boys in the most human sense of the word, nurture their natural emotional and social capacities, and foster their close friendships. We need to make relational and emotionally literacy an inherent part of being human, rather than only a "girl thing" or a "gay thing." The boys and young men in my studies know that what makes us human is our ability to deeply connect with each other. We must figure out how to help boys and young men strengthen rather than lose these critical life skills. Only then we will be able to address the psychological and sociological roots of this crisis of connection and the negative consequences associated with it.

homophobia in boys' friendships

by c.j. pascoe

According to media reports, we are in the midst of a bullying epidemic whose primary victims are gay kids. But young people's homophobia is more complex than such popular views suggest. Much of it is perpetuated by and directed at straight-identified boys. As the school resource website Teach Safe Schools, documents, 80 percent of those on the receiving end of homophobic epithets identify as heterosexual. While GLBQ youth are certainly harassed in school settings, these homophobic insults also play a complex role in heterosexual boys' friendships.

Researching teenage boys over the past decade, what I found is that boys' homophobia is not *only* about sexuality, or about pathological bullies going after gay boys; their homophobia is as much about making sure that boys act like "guys" as it is about fear of actual gay people. Through homophobic banter, jokes and harassment, straight boys define their masculinity in ways that are hostile both to gay boys and to straight boys who don't measure up to a particular masculine ideal. Insulting each other for being un-masculine, even for a moment, reinforces expectations of masculinity and also provides space for straight boys to forge intimate ties with one another, while affirming to themselves, and to each other, that they are not gay.

Homophobic insults, talk, and jokes—or what I call "fag discourse"—permeates boys' relationships. Different behaviors or attitudes, such as being too touchy, too emotional, dancing, and caring too much about clothing, can trigger this "fag discourse." Boys try fervently to escape the label of "fag" by avoiding these behaviors or directing the epithet toward someone else. "Fag" is likely to be the most serious insult one boy

Boys' homophobia is as much about making sure that boys act like "guys" as it is about fear of actual gay people.

can level at another. As Jeremy, a high school junior, remarked, "To call someone gay or fag is like the lowest thing you can call someone. Because that's like saying that you're nothing."

For many boys, calling someone a "fag" does not necessarily mean that they are gay. As J.L., a high school sophomore, explained, "Fag, seriously, it has nothing to do with sexual preference at all. You could just be calling somebody an idiot, you know?" Furthermore young men who engage in fag discourse often simultaneously support the civil rights of actual gay men, and condemn those who would harass them. Jabes, a senior, said, "I actually say fag quite a lot, except for when I'm in the company of an actual homosexual person. Then I try not to say it at all. But when I'm just hanging out with my friends I'll be like, 'Shut up, I don't want to hear you any more you stupid fag.'" Simple homophobia is too crude a concept for characterizing what is going here, because these insults seem to coexist with rising support for gay rights.

If these epithets are simultaneously reducing boys to "nothing," and are not necessarily about homosexuality, what are these boys talking about? The answer lies in high school senior David's statement: "Being gay is just a lifestyle. It's someone you choose to sleep with. You can still throw a football around and be gay." In other words, a gay man can still be masculine. What boys are doing as they lob these epithets is reminding one other that to be acceptably masculine is to be dominant, powerful, and unemotional. Violating those expectations can trigger a round of "fag discourse."

> " What boys are doing as they lob these epithets is reminding one other that to be acceptably masculine is to be dominant, powerful, and unemotional.

Thus, homophobia in boys' friendships is not only about some global fear of same-sex desire (though certainly, for all of the protestations about equality, fear, disgust, or loathing of same-sex desire between men still exists), it is also a way in which boys define themselves and others as masculine. When we call these interactions between boys homophobic bullying and ignore the messages about masculinity in these insults, we risk divorcing these interactions from the way they perpetuate restrictive and sexist definitions of manhood. We also fail to appreciate how boys carve out moments of intimacy, and that complexity, beauty and complicated ideas about masculinity lay at the heart of many of their friendships.

embracing intimacy

by mark mccormack

When we think of boys' friendships, we tend to think of rough and tumble physical energy. But research conducted over the past three decades warns that rough and tumble play often leads to aggression and violence, and that shallow friendships have resulted in boys being emotionally stunted. Another pernicious element of boys' friendships has been virulent homophobia. Given the cultural conflation of masculinity with heterosexuality, where acting feminine is perceived as being gay, boys go to great lengths to act "manly" and avoid homosexual suspicion. Homophobia prevents boys from expressing emotion, and makes them keep considerable physical distance from each other.

The centrality of homophobia to this damaging dynamic of friendship implies that as attitudes toward homosexuality change, so will the ways boys interact. I found this to be the case in ethnographic research that I conducted in high schools in England. Several studies indicate that homophobia has decreased at a greater rate in England than in the United States. For example, the most recent data from the British Social Attitudes survey show that only 29 percent of adults think same-sex relationships are wrong, down from 46 percent in the year 2000. Research from 2007 also finds that 86 percent of the population would be comfortable if a close friend was gay. Comparing BSA data with the American General Social Survey, in his book *Inclusive Masculinity*, Eric Anderson showed that American attitudes are approximately 20 percentage points less favorable than British ones, and that young people have the most progressive attitudes toward homosexuality.

In the three government-run schools I studied, heterosexual male students—aged 16 to 18—espoused pro-gay attitudes and condemned homophobia. They often had openly gay friends; some criticized their schools for their lack of openly gay role models. This inclusive culture has led teenage boys to redefine masculinity; as a result, their understanding of friendship is quite different than what one might expect.

The male students at these schools were proud of their close friendships and frequently demonstrated that publicly. For example, Jack had been away for the weekend and upon seeing his best friend Tim, he shouted, "Timmo, where were you all weekend, I missed ya!", and exuberantly kissed Tim on the top of his head. Then they talked about their weekend in a style best described as gossiping.

More frequent than this kind of boisterous demonstration of friendship, though, were the touching behaviors that occurred during quiet conversations. Here, boys used physical touch as a sign of friendship. Ben and Eli, for example, stood in a corner of the common room, casually holding hands as they spoke, their fingers gently touching one another. Halfway through the exchange, Ben changed his embrace, placing an arm around Eli's waist and a hand on his stomach. This kind of behavior was commonplace among the majority of boys; hugging was a routine form of greeting in these schools.

The boys also valued emotional support. Tim said, "I talk to my best friends about everything, if I've got girlfriend trouble, or when I'm upset or stressed. It's really important for me to be able to do that." Boys also openly recognized the closeness of their friendships, sometimes addressing each other as "boyfriend" or "lover" as a way of demonstrating emotional intimacy. Phil said, "Yeah, I call him boyfriend and stuff, but that's just a way of saying he's my best mate." Similarly, Dave commented, "I'll sometimes call my best mates 'lover' or something similar. It's just a way of saying, 'I love you,' really."

The friendships and social dynamics of the boys from my research are also evident in popular culture. Youth TV shows in the UK, such as *Skins* and *Hollyoaks*, show similar displays of physical and emotional intimacy between boys, and the latest boy band sensation, One Direction, models this new youth masculinity. While there are variations according to class, ethnicity, geography and other factors, the friendships I documented signify that a profound social change is occurring. Teenage boys are embracing once feminized traits of emotional openness and physical intimacy, rejecting the homophobia and violence that once characterized male friendship. This is directly related to a decline in homophobia, and boys no longer caring if they are socially perceived as gay. This has enabled them to redefine masculinity and friendship for their generation. It is something we should celebrate.

love wanting

by amy schalet

Michael, a high-school senior, is not a fan of commitment. His ideal is "more than one girl, basically." Proud of his own sexual experience, he's excited that his current girlfriend is a virgin: "It's cool to be the first one . . . it probably feels better too."

Tall, athletic and a "little rowdy," Michael would appear to epitomize the American teenage male.

Except that he doesn't. In my research on attitudes and experiences of sex and romance among high-school aged White middle-class American and Dutch boys, I found most American boys, like Dutch boys, want more than just sex; they want meaningful intimate relationships.

My findings are echoed in other studies that have surprised researchers. For instance, the *National Campaign to End Teen and Unplanned Pregnancies* found that when asked to choose between having a girlfriend and no sex, or sex but no girlfriend, two-thirds of American boys and young men surveyed choose the girlfriend over sex. A large-scale study published in the *American Sociological Review* in 2006 found that American boys are

as likely as girls to be emotionally invested in romantic relationships—but feel less confident navigating them.

Boys in the United States and the Netherlands face very different cultural environments in which to make sense of their romantic feelings. For Dutch boys, falling in love is normal—something everyone experiences while growing up. In the Netherlands, the notion that everyone falls in love is so taken for granted that in a 2005 national survey on youth and sex, researchers thought nothing of asking boys, ages 12 to 14, whether they'd been in love—finding that 90 percent said yes.

Teenage boys are embracing once-feminized traits of emotional openness and physical intimacy.

But in the United States, even if most boys do want romantic relationships, their romantic stirrings are culturally coded as feminine. Boys are seen as motivated by "raging hormones," not by a desire for intimacy. As one American father puts it, "teenage boys want to get laid at all times at any cost."

The popular stereotype of boys as acting only from hormones eclipses their desire for emotional intimacy as a normal part of maturation and masculinity. When boys do want or feel love, they think they're alone. Sixteen-year-old Jesse says his first priority in life is being in love with his girlfriend and "giving her everything I can." But he imagines these feelings make him very different from "most teenage boys" who "are pretty much in it for the sex."

To counteract stereotypes about them, American boys sometimes distance themselves not only from other boys, but also from their own sexual desires. Patrick, for instance, says, "if you really care about someone, you don't really care if you have sex or not," echoing a theme from American sex education curricula that teach youth to separate love from lust.

Unlike American culture and sex education, Dutch sex education curricula, with titles like "Long Live Love," encourage boys to view love and lust as intertwined. The Dutch boys I interviewed readily acknowledged being interested in sex, but they also connected physical pleasure closely to emotions and relationships. About the excitement he felt going through puberty, Gert-Jan says: "It also has to do with having feelings for someone. . . . You're really in love."

It's not just in school that cultures diverge, it's also at home. American boys are typically taught to view their sexuality as something symbolizing and threatening their freedom—for instance with an unintended pregnancy. While boys may receive tacit approval to pursue sexual interests away from home, most parents draw firm boundaries between the family and the exploration of sexuality, and rarely permit high-school aged boys to spend the night with their romantic partners at home.

Dutch culture, by contrast, places a premium on *"gezelligheid"* or *"cozy togetherness,"* which validates their enjoyment of platonic and sexual relationships. In the Netherlands, teen boys and girls are typically allowed to have sleepovers in their parents' house. This interweaving of sexuality and domestic life teaches boys that physical pleasure and emotional intimacy—familial and romantic—are not at odds. As eighteen-year-old Ben says about his girlfriend sleeping over in his room, "if my mother thinks it's *gezellig*, then why not?"

> *Most American boys, like Dutch boys, want more than just sex; they want meaningful intimate relationships.*

Still, Dutch masculinity does constrain boys in some familiar respects. For instance, national surveys of youth show that Dutch boys face, and engage in, more strictures against same-sex sexual behavior than do Dutch girls. But Dutch boys receive more support at school and home to integrate different aspects of themselves that American boys are often encouraged to separate—love, lust, participation in family life and sexual exploration.

Much of the debate around teenagers and sexuality in the United States focuses on what we should teach them about their bodies. Access to accurate information about anatomy, pleasure, and contraception—the usual hot-button topics—is critical. But just as important are the conversations about intimacy and emotions, and the question of how we can define and model manhood so those on its cusp might feel more empowered and equipped to love.

time to bloom

by freeden oeur

In the United States today, single-sex classrooms and schools are increasingly making their way into public schools. Nationally, about 560 K-12 public schools offer some single-sex academic classrooms, and about 80 more are entirely separated by sex.

Debates over single-sex schooling usually center on questions of gender equity. Supporters claim that they accommodate boys' and girls' different learning styles; critics charge that they perpetuate gender stereotypes. My own ethnographic research shows that in schools that serve predominantly poor young Black men, the relationships boys have with one another, and with adult male staff members are key. A school I call Perry High—one of the schools in an East Coast city where I conducted my research—serves a predominantly poor and Black student population, grades 7 through 12. Led by an administration made up of nearly all Black men, the staff has made it a priority to cultivate more positive notions of manhood among the students.

Perry administrators believe that a school where Black men care for Black boys can be empowering. At Perry High, some of the boys assumed that being "put with other boys," as seventh grader Lenny told me, meant they were in trouble. Mass incarceration of African Americans led these boys to fear all-male institutions—prisons, along with the city's disciplinary schools, where boys who commit major offenses are sent. Administrators and teachers focused on earning the trust of their students, and on strengthening relationships among men and boys.

A common stereotype of young Black men is that they resist authority. But at Perry High, many boys were open to having close relationships with men, especially if the men first opened up to them. The boys believed they needed those relationships in order to thrive in school. Referring to the adults in the building, Dante, a 12th grader, told me: "We need you. You don't need us." The youngest boys, from 12 to 14 years old, particularly doted on male teachers, shadowing them throughout the building and sticking around after school just to hang out. Groups of young boys were eager to connect with teachers who were willing to teach them a new hobby like playing the guitar, or spoken word poetry.

Mr. Westbrook, an administrator, remarked, "I see a lot of kids, especially the younger kids, who really cling onto certain adults for attention, and you become that surrogate father that so many of them are looking for." Male staff members used this as an opportunity to share visions of responsible adulthood. Gerald, an eighth grader, observed that what it meant to be a man was "to have a job and to be able to do important stuff like taking care of a family."

To instill a sense of responsible adulthood, a new mentoring program matched male adult professionals in the community with ninth graders. The organizers targeted this group because of the high dropout rates among Black boys after ninth grade. At a meeting of mentors and mentees, Raymond spoke eloquently about how the program had impacted him and his peers. Usually when male visitors came to the school, they aggressively relayed the message that the boys should avoid heading down a "dead-end street," he said. But Raymond appreciated that the mentors were not trying to scare the boys. Instead, they helped the boys to create positive visions of themselves: going to college or vocational school, contributing to the community instead of being a threat to it. Speaking directly to the male mentors in the room, he asked for their continued guidance and patience. "We're still learning how to be men and we need your help," he said. "Give us some time to bloom."

The mix of boys, encompassing six grades, meant that younger and older boys had opportunities to interact that they may not have had outside of school. The older boys felt the need to respond to seventh and eighth graders who were aching for male guidance. The younger boys tried to "play off," or imitate, older boys. Just as they did with male teachers, groups of young boys followed boys much older than them around the school. The older students took the younger students under their wing, looking after them as though they were their own siblings.

At this unique all-boys public school, rather than forge relationships of fear, older boys and men took responsibility for and invested in the lives of the younger boys. In this environment, young Black boys are able to envision themselves, in turn, as responsible men who will one day hold steady jobs and care for boys who need them. Should more of these single-sex schools open, we're likely to find that it's for reasons that go beyond that of gender equity, reasons such as the opportunity to foster caring, mentoring relationships.

At this unique all-boys public school, rather than forge relationships of fear, older boys and men took responsibility for and invested in the lives of the younger boys.

jeremy lin's model minority problem

maxwell leung

summer 2013

By the time the New York Knicks and Los Angeles Lakers faced off in New York in February 2012, breakout star Jeremy Lin had led the Knicks to a phenomenal three-game winning streak. Less than four minutes into the first quarter, the Knicks were leading 7–4, and Lin threw a perfect half-court pass to Tyson Chandler for an easy 2-point slam. As fans in Madison Square Garden cheered the offensive attack, Lin mouthed the words "Come on!" The Knicks pressed their defensive attack, and a player from the Lakers dropped the ball.

The crowd sensed another quick score. Lin scooped up the ball and drove in for an easy lay-up. The Lakers called a time out and the fans erupted. Less than five minutes in, the Knicks had an uncontested 10-point run. Lin already had 9 points and 2 assists.

For a brief moment, NBA star Jeremy Lin offered Asian Americans a different way to imagine themselves—while affirming many longstanding myths about immigrant success.

That night, a thousand miles away at Grinnell College in Iowa, I joined students from the Asian and Asian American Alliance to cheer on Jeremy Lin. Although we were unaware of it at the time, the game against the Lakers was one of the high points of what came to be known as "Linsanity"—the global cultural phenomenon that accompanied Lin's meteoric rise from an unknown player to an international star.

The excitement began with Lin's first game as a Knick in February 2012 and ended with the announcement of a season-ending knee injury only a month later. Since, Lin has left the Knicks to join the Houston Rockets and has struggled as a player. The national adulation that surrounded his breakout performance has largely faded.

The story of how Jeremy Lin became an NBA star is one of denied opportunities, enduring racism, and barrier-breaking in professional sports. Although his star has dimmed, Lin's story is worth our attention.

the model minority—again

Jeremy Lin's success in the face of daunting obstacles both challenges the prevailing racial narrative of basketball and reinforces it, offering Asian Americans the chance to see themselves as something other than doctors, engineers, or accountants, while also affirming the belief that they are high achievers. In effect, Linsanity affirmed the myth of Asian Americans as the "model minority." Through hard work and perseverance, Asian Americans supposedly show how any minority can overcome institutionalized inequality. At the same time, Lin's achievements alone could do little to undo understandings of Asian men. For a brief moment, nba star Jeremy Lin offered Asian Americans a different way to imagine themselves—while affirming many longstanding myths about immigrant success. 54 contexts.org exemplified by the docile honor student, that are at odds with male achievement in sports.

The model minority trope is taken for granted in U.S. media. In June 2012 the Pew Research Center released a report titled "The Rise of Asian Americans," and it was big news. The report *should* have given Asian Americans—who comprise nearly six percent of the national population—a reason to celebrate. Sampling more than 3,500 people from six of the largest Asian ethnic groups (Chinese-, Filipino-, Indian-, Vietnamese-, Korean-, and Japanese-Americans), Pew's report portrayed Asian Americans as an immigrant group that has successfully broken many social, political, and economic barriers. On the whole, Pew found, Asian Americans are highly educated, possess an admirable work ethic, and earn higher-than-average incomes.

The report goes on to describe Asian Americans' strong family ties and high levels of happiness: "Most Asian Americans feel good about their lives in the U.S. They see themselves as having achieved economic prosperity on the strength of hard work, a character trait they say is much more prevalent among Asian Americans than among the rest of the U.S. population. Most say they are better off than their parents were at a comparable age. And among the foreign born, very few say that if they had to do it all over again, they would stay in their home country rather than emigrate to the U.S."

Scholars, Asian American organizations, and advocacy groups—from the Japanese American Citizens League to the National Council of Asian Pacific Americans—criticized the report as "one-dimensional," "exclusionary," and full of "overgeneralizations" that portrayed Asian Americans as the torchbearers of American exceptionalism. California Congresswoman Judy Chu, who chairs the Congressional Asian Pacific American Caucus stated, "I would strongly caution against using the data [in the report] to validate the 'model minority' myth." As she pointed out, "Our community is one of stark contrasts, with significant disparities within and between various subgroups."

For example, another recent report, this time from the Asian American Center for Advancing Justice, showed that while Asian Americans are successful in terms of educational achievement compared to Whites, specific ethnic groups (such as Hmong, Cambodian, Laotian, and Vietnamese Americans) have high school graduation rates as low as 61 percent

and even lower rates of college graduation—numbers comparable to Latinos and African Americans. The Pew Report had lumped all these groups together as "Asian American," ignoring some of the most distressed communities and the economic, health, and other challenges they face.

When research and portraits of Asian Americans are consistently framed this way, Asian Americans are almost always seen as superior to other minority groups in terms of educational achievement, economic stability, and social acceptance. Supposed exemplary Asian cultural values—hard work, perseverance, strong family traditions, a reverence for education, self-reliance, even self-sacrifice—are portrayed as unique among ethnic groups. As this story goes, even when Asian Americans face cultural and linguistic barriers, institutional racism, and other dramatically unequal treatment, they will not only overcome the obstacles, but do so without protest or complaint.

Popular culture has long portrayed Asian American men as geniuses, overachievers, computer geeks, or nerds. They're shy and docile, humble and passive. If Asian American women are presented as exotic and hypersexualized, men are rendered effete, weak, and physically and sexually inferior. Examples range from the insufferable Long Duk Dong in the 1984 film *Sixteen Candles* to William Hung, famous for his cringeworthy rendition of "She Bangs" on *American Idol* in 2004. The character Raj on the hugely popular sitcom *The Big Bang Theory* is the most recent example of an image of a socially dysfunctional Asian American man. Such representations leave Asian Americans to struggle against broad stereotypes that are as inaccurate as they are negative—especially in a culture that prizes traditional masculinity.

Jeremy Lin's breakout success gave Asian American men a striking respite from these oppressive images. Lin is tall, strong, aggressive, and physically gifted. Far from shy or quiet, he's a powerful player in a physically demanding sport, displaying style Just one of the many books written about Lin in 2012 and 2013. and swagger on a huge media stage. The Linsanity phenomenon Summer 2013 contexts 55 marked more than just the international embrace of a spectacular new Asian American sports star—it posed a challenge to emasculating stereotypes.

At the same time, Lin could be the poster child for the Pew Report. He was smart and driven, but overlooked by college recruiters and the NBA draft, and he bounced from team to team. His hard work and focus—model behavior—paid off in the form of a phenomenal ascent to the upper echelons of a multi-billion-dollar sport.

invisible man?

The myth of the model minority is central to understanding the story of Jeremy Lin's encounter with discrimination and his subsequent success as a professional basketball player. Likely because he did not fit expectations about what an elite basketball player looks like, Lin was a talented player but flew under the radar. The fact that many college coaches and recruiters later admitted that they'd failed to recognize Lin's talents suggests they couldn't see "past" his Asian features.

> *Lin offers Asian Americans the chance to see themselves as something other than doctors, engineers, or accountants, while also affirming the belief that they are high achievers.*

As Lin himself said in an interview with EPSN in 2012, "I was very disappointed, discouraged. I'm undrafted, I'm out of Harvard. 'Asian American.' That was kind of the perception everyone had of me and that was kind of the perception I had of myself. And when everyone thinks that, then it's hard to break that."

Yet Asians and Asian Americans who play basketball are not a wholly new phenomenon. There have been Asian players in the NBA—most notably Yao Ming of the Houston Rockets and Wataru Misaka, the first Japanese American to play professional basketball with the New York Knicks in 1947. There have also been standout Asian American college players such as Raymond Townsend, part-Filipino, who played for UCLA in the 1970s; Corey Gaines, part-Japanese, who played for Loyola Marymount University in the '80s and Rex Walters, part-Japanese, who played for Kansas in the early '90s.

As Lin's remarks on ESPN and in a more recent television interview suggest, he is the first professional basketball player to deliberately and comfortably claim his Asian American heritage and be acknowledged as such by his fans. He has directly confronted the experience of social invisibility he experienced on his way up. And yet Lin's success as a Knick is still couched in the default language of the model minority: he worked very hard to get to the top. He's got intelligence—not just talent. If African American point guards are the norm in basketball, then Jeremy Lin is an anomaly whose existence almost demands explanation.

> *The Linsanity phenomenon posed a challenge to emasculating stereotypes.*

In his second career appearance against the Houston Rockets, Lin had an impressive showing, even though his Knicks trailed throughout the game and eventually lost. Late in the third quarter, one of the television sports show hosts commented about Lin's overall performance: "He's a hustler; he runs the show. Very intelligent player. Does the fact that he went to Harvard help that? Absolutely!"

But what *does* Lin's intelligence or Harvard degree have to do with his basketball skills? One could say that all professional athletes need intelligence to perform exceptionally. One might also observe that playing point guard requires especially intelligent play—a successful player in this role must read defenses, make plays, and provide assists. But in relation to race, "intelligence" is a loaded word.

According to sociologist Douglas Hartmann, "because of sport's *de facto* association with bodies and the mind/body dualisms . . . African American athletic excellence serves to reinforce racial stereotypes by grounding them in essentialized, biological terms." He continues: "Athletic prowess is believed to be inversely associated with intellectual and/or moral excellence." Reporting and commentary about Black basketball players, for example, often refers not to their formal education, but to an "urban experience" of playing basketball in the streets.

In contrast, Lin's "intelligence" on the court was tied explicitly to his Ivy League education, even though Lin began playing the game at his local YMCA and on neighborhood playgrounds in Palo Alto, California. It's the model minority discourse at work: educational achievements are primary, and the physical experience of playing ball is less central.

In the Lin narrative, basketball is a meritocracy based on skill, and those who rise to the top earn their rewards. This reaffirms the classic American story that those "who work hard and possess the right stuff will always prevail"—and deserve to, according to sociologist of sport Susan Birrell. Conversely, those who try and fail? They didn't work hard enough.

trying to flip the script

Despite the Asian American basketball players who came before Jeremy Lin, his stunning performance on the national stage confirmed something Asian Americans know, but had rarely witnessed: We can jump, drive, and shoot the ball. According to sociologist Oliver Wang, Linsanity made Asian Americans playing professional basketball "a national concept." Lin's triumph resonated with Asian Americans and many others, and it led some to believe Lin could present a real challenge to long-standing stereotypes.

Not only do Asian Americans hope that Lin is the real deal, a truly talented basketball player of NBA caliber, we also want to see the devotion he has generated translate into real changes in perceptions of Asian Americans. For us, it is hard to overestimate the pure euphoria of seeing this man lead on the court, outmaneuver defenders, and make clutch plays—all with confidence, bravado, and off-court dignity.

This year, the documentary *Linsanity*, directed by Evan Jackson Leong, premiered at the Sundance Film Festival and opened San Francisco's Center for Asian American Media's annual film festival. Audiences cheered, giving it a standing ovation. An inspirational basketball story told through Jeremy Lin's eyes, the film documents his rise to stardom.

Although Linsanity lasted just three glorious weeks, Jeremy Lin still offers a powerful new image of Asian American male sport prowess that both challenges and reaffirms the model minority myth. His success offers a critical commentary on how we understand the contradictory and often frustrating place of Asian Americans in American culture.

In March 2013, *Wall Street Journal* columnist Jeff Yang, discussing the Leong documentary, told eager readers: "Keep your eyes peeled, sports fans. Linsanity may well end up having a sequel." Although Jeremy Lin has faded from basketball stardom, his story, by reaffirming some stereotypes while calling others into question, gives us a way to understand Asian American's complicated relationship to American cultural values.

recommended resources

Carrington, Ben. 2010. *Race, Sport and Politics: The Sporting Black Diaspora.* London: Sage Publications. Using postcolonial theory, cultural studies, and poststructuralist theory, Carrington's work interrogates how race and racial difference is made through the spectacle of sport.

Chou, Rosalind S, and Feagin, Joe R. 2008. *The Myth of the Model Minority: Asian Americans Facing Racism.* Boulder, CO: Paradigm Publishers. Chou and Feagin's study of subjects from different nationalities and geographic locales reveals the extent, reach, and penetration of the model minority stereotype.

Fong, Timothy. 2008. *The Contemporary Asian American Experience.* Upper Saddle River, NJ: Prentice Hall. Fong's work surveys key contemporary issues impacting Asian Americans and includes a special section on sports.

Hartmann, Douglas. 2000. "Rethinking the Relationships Between Sport and Race in American Culture: Golden Ghettos and Contested Terrain," *Sociology of Sport Journal* 17:229–253. A key article that helped problematize the racial spectacle of sport as a hegemonic formation while at the same time acknowledges the potential for racial resistance and change.

Yep, Kathleen S. 2008. *Outside the Paint: When Basketball Ruled at the Chinese Playground.* Philadelphia: Temple University. A historical book on the development of Chinese American men's and women's basketball leagues in San Francisco Chinatown from the 1930s to 1940s.

transitioning out loud and online

arlene stein

spring 2016

Kye dreams of having a masculine chest one day. "A big chest is extremely dysphoric for a lot of transguys," he says, using the psychiatric term signifying estrangement from one's sexed body. Though the 16-year-old has small breasts, wearing a bra "enhanced them and made them look bigger," so he started binding them in order to minimize their appearance.

In a four-minute YouTube video, he displays his flattened chest and instructs others on how to achieve a similar effect; over 75,000 viewers have seen it. "I'm a real boy!" he proclaims in the video, which was shot on his computer in his bedroom, poised in front of a dinosaur crossing poster, a series of handdrawn animal cartoons, and the cover of a Broadway playbill.

Kye is among a growing number of transgender men (female-assigned-at-birth who identify as male) who are coming out of the shadows, at younger ages—and online. In YouTube videos, transmen are documenting their decision to assume a male gender, disclose to family and friends, and undergo surgical and non-surgical body modifications. (In the following, I refer to individuals using male pronouns, in accordance with how they wish to see themselves.)

Over the course of three years, Kye posted 20 videos on subjects ranging from "How Do You Know You're Trans?" to an interview with his girlfriend: "How to Date a Transman." People have viewed his YouTube channel, which has over 1,000 subscribers, over 145,000 times. His is one of thousands of video blogs, or vlogs, produced by young female-to-male (FTM) individuals on the Internet.

While the very public gender transition of Caitlyn—formerly Bruce—Jenner dominates the television airwaves and tabloid pages, hundreds, perhaps thousands, of young people are utilizing YouTube, Instagram, and other social media sites to publicly narrate their gender transitions, creating videos which are buried in plain sight among clips of adorable cats, high school girls mugging to Miley Cyrus songs, and do-it-yourselfers instructing people on how to change a flat tire or fix a toilet.

Stumbling upon these videos while doing research on transgender men's lives, I became intrigued by the ways these young people are using YouTube to connect with others. What do they talk about? Who are they talking to? And how do they negotiate questions of privacy in such a public forum? To find out, I first conducted a content analysis of 50 randomly chosen transmale vlogs on YouTube, and then narrowed my search, focusing upon videos which document a particular aspect of the transition process: chest binding.

What I found is that by producing and consuming YouTube vlogs, young transmen are producing a visual record of the transition process and creating what Internet researcher Danah Boyd calls "networked publics"— spaces that are structured by networked technologies for people to "gather, connect, and help construct society as we understand it." If feminists in the 1970s formed small groups to speak the truth of their lives, blurring the boundaries of private and public, today's gender dissidents are more likely to do so online.

networked publics

A young transman in rural south central Kentucky told media scholar Mary Gray, when she interviewed him nearly ten years ago, that he documents his own transition on YouTube in order to "'think out loud' to himself and mull through his own anxieties about gender reassignment surgery and what it would be to become the boy he felt he had always been."

For millennials—the vast demographic group born between 1980 and 2000 who are the first generation of so-called "digital natives"—growing up online is normal and natural. Queer millennials, transpeople among them, have been particularly enthusiastic users of social media. If not for the Internet, many of them, particularly those who live in rural areas, or who are particularly young, would have little or no access to others like themselves. Many utilize YouTube, the video-sharing website, to find other trans masculine individuals with which to share their stories.

"When it comes to real life stories, how we feel about our bodies and how we identify, documentaries are generally not made by trans people. They're made about transpeople for nontransgender people," says Warren, a transman in his early 20s. YouTube, he says, offers transmen a forum for discussing "everything from the initial coming out, to ten years posttransition what's going on in their lives."

Warren continues: "Seldom do we see the telling of a story the way that we would tell it ourselves, or tell another person who has gone through something similar. That's what's really interesting about YouTube. There are hundreds of transpeople on YouTube sharing their story." The beauty of vlogs, says Warren, is that "you get invested, and you make friends, and you get to see where each other's lives go and evolve over time." The vlog format is particularly well suited to narrating processes over time.

In 2000, a cisgender (normative, or non-transgender) man by the name of Adam Kontras posted a video alongside a blog entry to inform his friends and family of his cross-country move to Los Angeles to try to break into show business, documenting his adventures. It is thought to be the first vlog. Many vlogs are, in effect, interactive diaries. Communication is asynchronous: someone posts a video, and others may view it days, weeks, and sometimes months or years later, posting comments, thanks, and sometimes questions.

Transgender males, who often speak of the process of changing gender as a "journey," use vlogs to document aspects of the transition process: the decision to

> **By narrating their life stories and sharing information, young transmen are building emotional bonds with one another.**

move away from their assigned gender, bind their breasts, change their pronouns, pass as male, and often, undergo chest surgery—along with the emotional challenges such choices pose.

sharing information, creating intimacy

Since breasts are such a central marker of femaleness, a key part of the FTM transition process involves refashioning one's body to minimize or conceal the appearance of having them. Like Kye, many transmen hope someday to have "top" surgery, but typically they must wait at least until they are 18 to do so. In the meantime, many bind, or flatten, their chests.

"If a transman can walk down the street in a way that does not call any attention to the way he is self-consciously producing gender," write anthropologists Ryan Pils and Evelyn Blackwood, "that gives him greater confidence." Little wonder, then, that binding techniques are a popular topic of discussion on transmale vlogs. (Searching for the terms "transgender men" and "chest binding" on YouTube yielded over 4,000 videos.)

"Wearing sports bras are better than nothing," says Kye in a video post, but "binders are what transmen need to start passing as men"—that is, to be seen by others as male. Kye, who lives in Illinois, can't afford commercially made binders, such as undershirts which have two or three layers of spandex, so he affixes Ace elastic compression bandages tightly across his chest with a safety pin, cautioning viewers of his vlog: "when wrapped too tightly, they can do damage." Many transmen bind their breasts for months, even years, often as a prelude to undergoing "top" surgery.

In his videos, Kye thinks out loud, figuring out ways of minimizing the social tension that occurs when gender presentation raises questions in public, and sharing what he's learned with others facing similar challenges. He's trying out a different body, helping others to do the same, and building an intimate community with other young transmen.

For young transmen, these opportunities for public self-reflection are particularly important as they contemplate gender transitions, frequently while they are still living in the liminal space of their family homes. Being out in public is difficult, if not dangerous. By narrating their life stories and sharing information they are creating a networked public comprised of young transmen, building emotional bonds with similar others.

In the first of over 40 videos documenting his transition, a young transman named Connor introduces himself: "The name is Connor and like many other people in the world I am transgender. I know there are a million videos that you can watch about trans stuff but now you have another one. I am here to help and to entertain. DUUHH! A'ight so love you my friends. Enjoy the page."

> **If feminists in the 1970s formed small groups to speak the truth of their lives, blurring the boundaries of private and public, today's gender dissidents are more likely to do so online.**

One video in his vlog "Journey to Connor" is entitled a "Moment of Major Dysphoria." Here Connor grapples with his estrangement from his natal body, and others' inability to recognize him as the gender he feels himself to be. His room is dark, illuminated only by the glow of the computer. He discusses his desire to physically transition: "I really need to get it done. It's hard to wait. I want to get on t (testosterone). It gets better, I think. It just takes time." He is crying.

In the vlog, he tells his viewers that when he went to work the other day, everyone called him by Connor, his chosen name, rather than his given female name, "which was really cool." A few people even "called me sir," he said, "but it doesn't fool me." He desperately wishes to be recognized by others for the gender he feels himself to be. "I want my parents to be ok with it, and I just want to get things done"—meaning he wants access to chest surgery and hormones. He addresses his viewers, other transmen, the "guys," with familiarity and affection, and describes "meeting buddies online," though they have never actually been in the physical presence of those they communicate with and probably never will be.

"Looks like some of you are watching," Connor says. "I hope everyone else who has this problem is hanging in there. Don't give up. Hopefully you guys are rooting for me, and I will root for you too. Peace and love, I'll talk to you guys soon." At one point, he appears on screen with his girlfriend, a gender studies minor, and tells viewers: "I'm going to be making some more videos soon." He

> **The allure of fame may drive some transmen to produce and post videos; the vast majority, though, are content sharing their story with like-minded others.**

invites others to comment and ask questions, and signs off: "I love you, talk to you soon."

To the outside observer, he and other young people seem extraordinarily willing to share the deepest aspects of their private lives—and even overshare, at times. When he first saw these videos on YouTube, sociologist Sal Johnston, who is a member of an earlier cohort of transgender men, admits that he initially feared that their publicness would invite voyeurism, disdain, and mockery. "Why would you do that?" he wondered.

But today's young people are living their lives online. Millennials who openly narrate their experiences online, even experiences that are at odds with the vast majority of those around them, are downright normal.

transitioning in the age of publicity

As a number of observers have suggested, young people's online and offline lives often blur into one another. Many millennials assume that the sheer volume of information available online means that only like-minded people will view their videos, and that those who lack a direct investment in such concerns will have little interest in them. In other words, those who enthusiastically share their intimate lives with those online often believe that disattention, in effect, protects their privacy.

While few barriers to public gawking actually exist, norms of mutual respect generally seem to operate on transgender vlog sites. "In networked publics, interactions are often public by default, private through effort," writes Danah Boyd. "What's at stake is not whether someone can listen in but whether one should." Even though transgender vlogs tend to be open for all to see, my content analysis of more than 50 videos revealed only a half dozen instances of negative feedback. In each of these cases, a member of the community, or an ally, came to the defense of those who were attacked.

So for example, when Ethan posted a vlog of his flattened chest, discussing the virtues of a particular type of chest binder, and was taunted: "If your [sic] a dude why can't you show your chest?" another viewer responded in Ethan's defense: "If you think it is wrong and/or nasty, then why would you search for it to begin with? Ethan is not a woman, he's a man . . . you deal with it."

Feedback is much more likely to be positive. Responding to one of Kye's videos, a viewer writes: "Ok so, I'm not FTM or MTF but my boyfriend is FTM and watching your videos has helped me. Thank you so much, and keep up the great Vlog." She adds: "PS. You're great for starting these to help people. Not just to bitch or try to get famous. You're an amazing guy, and I appreciate you!"

Another viewer writes: "You inspire me beyond belief. Maybe one day I can come out, too."

In theory, individual vloggers can control their privacy settings, deciding which videos to share and which to keep private. But creating boundaries around online spaces is difficult—and clashes with the goal of reaching as many viewers as possible. The greater the number of viewers, the less isolated vloggers feel, and the more information they are able to share. For those who participate in these networked publics, coming out online can be personally powerful.

In their everyday lives, transgender people must be acutely aware of how they appear to others, particularly when they use bathrooms and travel through public places. "Moment to moment, day to day, you have to be careful," Sal Johnston says. "It's an exhausting way to live." But by openly narrating their lives on YouTube, young transmen are throwing off their internalized shame and making a claim for attention in a world where attention-getting is key to self-making.

Growing up in an age of publicity, young people understand the search for attention as normal—and inseparable from our "brand culture," according to communications scholar Sarah Banet-Weiser. Brand relationships, she argues, have become cultural contexts for everyday living, individual identity, and personal relationships.

Indeed, many FTM transition vlogs are a mash-up of coming out stories, *Consumer Reports* product reviews, and reality television self-revelations. Short, personal, and informational, they are embedded in the commercial culture in which they have sprouted, appearing next to videos instructing viewers on "How to get a flat stomach in a week," or ads for Epson printers, exemplifying the freedoms as well as constraints of self-making with new media.

A vlogger called DemyDew reviews a chest binder that costs $34. "I'm a D38 and it gets me pretty damn flat," he proclaims. He shows off his chest, pleased that with the binder he looks like "a dude with a belly." "[The binder] pretty much flattens me out," he says. "Some binders look like you're wearing a bra, and that's not cool," he says. But this one doesn't have straps. "It just looks like I have man boobs because I'm a big dude anyways. I'm almost 200 pounds." Of the chest binder, he says, "Go get one, it's worth it, and thanks for watching."

In addition to consuming branded products, young people at times engage in the process of "self-branding," marketing themselves, in effect, as brands. Adrian, who has nearly 9,000 viewers, posts videos that are barely distinguishable from the commercials that surround them. In one, he touts an Underworks chest binder: "This is like the best thing ever." A Christmas tree sits in the

background, and banners for Black Friday sales and the Home Shopping Network drift across the screen. "The good thing about this is that it is low-cut, if you want to show some skin," he says. "My boobs are size C. They hold them back nicely."

Those who master the art of attention-getting have some potential to earn money by directing traffic to ads and becoming "content management partners." Brandon has posted 43 videos, and has 177 subscribers. He has started a YouTube channel of his own. "I have about four guys who are going to be doing videos," he says, "I'm still going to be doing videos here, and also on our channel. A 13-year-old is our youngest." He meets lots of his "buddies" online, he says, and plans "to get a couple more guys so that we can have a video every day."

Some young people have parlayed sizeable fan bases on Facebook, Instagram, and Vine into book contracts for Young Adult novels, television roles, and "micro-celebrity" status. Aydian Dowling, a 28-year-old weight-training enthusiast, activist, and entrepreneur from Eugene, Oregon, who became known in the transmale community through his online videos, was recently named a finalist in *Men's Health* magazine's "Ultimate Guy" contest, crossing over into the mainstream, at least for a brief moment.

But while the allure of fame may drive some transmale vloggers to produce and post videos, the vast majority are content sharing their story with like-minded others. A year after he began posting videos on YouTube, Kye underwent top surgery; his final video documents the effects of testosterone on his changing body. Today, Kye, an art student studying illustration, lives fulltime as male, and no longer posts videos online. But only a few years ago, his vlog was a lifeline, enabling him to publicly document his transition and help others to do the same.

recommended resources

Banet-Weiser, Sarah. 2012. *Authentic: The Politics of Ambivalence in a Brand Culture.* New York: New York University Press. For communications scholar Banet-Weiser, branding is much more than marketing or commodification: it defines our modern selfhood.

Boyd, Danah. 2015. *It's Complicated: The Social Lives of Networked Teens.* New Haven, CT: Yale University Press. A smart, accessible book on different aspects of teens online lives: their oversharing, their bullying, and how they form identities. The upshot: parents, dont panic.

Gray, Mary. 2009. *Out in the Country: Youth, Media, and Queer Visibility in Rural America.* New York: New York University Press. Young queer people living in rural areas may face many challenges, creatively using new media and other strategies to find one another.

O'Brien, Jodi. "Writing in the Body: Gender (Re) production in Online Interaction." In M. A. Smith and P. Kollock (eds.), *Communities in Cyberspace.* London: Routledge. An important early analysis that suggests that for lack of visual cues, people nonetheless seek out information about the "real" sex of those with whom they interact online.

Plis, Ryan, and Blackwood, Evelyn. 2012. "Trans Technologies and Identities in the United States." In Lenore Manderson (ed.), *Technologies of Sexuality and Sexual Health.* London: Routledge. Surveys varied techniques of gender transition, acknowledging the importance of online media as a key technology of change.

fashioning flawlessness
kelly kato
winter 2014

During New York's Fashion Week last September, patients of plastic surgeon Ramtin Kassir sashayed down the runway to model the latest in "surgical designs," including rhinoplasty, breast augmentation, and liposuction. The show ended with two beauty pageant winners, a mother-daughter pair, who strutted down the runway showcasing Kassir's handiwork.

The show was staged to coincide with the fashionista gathering in order to make a point: the fashion industry expects "absolute flawlessness," in the words of feminist media activist Jean Kilbourne. While we generally believe that these beauty standards derive from nature, models and beauty queens increasingly use plastic surgery and digital enhancements to achieve unattainable ideals in terms of body type, facial features, skin complexion and eternal youth.

A model's value depends on her ability to achieve and maintain flawless beauty. Sociologists Joanne Entwistle and Elizabeth Wissinger, writing in *The Sociological Review* in 2005, argue that since models' sense of identity and self-worth are closely linked to their value in the industry, those who deviate from any of these rigid standards are devalued both professionally and personally.

But in a beauty commercial parody that recently went viral, blogger Jesse Rosten said it best: the only way to look like a "real" cover girl is to use Photoshop.

a 21st century gender revolution

sangyoub park

winter 2011

Sociologists have long questioned whether the mass media reflects or shapes reality. Such questions are difficult to answer, especially when it comes to working women on television. Take, for instance, Kyra Sedgwick (playing a female detective in TNT's *The Closer*) and Archie Panjabi (portraying a female private investigator in CBS's *The Good Wife*) who won the Best Actress and Best Supporting Actress awards, respectively, at the 2010 Emmys. Their small screen dramas are among today's many popular shows featuring women in the roles of detective, lawyer, crime scene investigator, and police officer—and often showing their heroines as much more street-savvy than their male partners (see the franchises *CSI, Law and Order, Saving Grace, In Plain Sight, Castle,* and *Chase*). Are these depictions fact, fiction, or somewhere in between?

In 1994, Phyllis Moen described the steadily increasing numbers of women in the paid labor force as the "revolution in gender." Nearly 20 years later, Americans may be witnessing another, albeit slightly different, revolution in gender. Women are currently outpacing men when it comes to college graduation and labor force participation, and they are rivaling men when it comes to holding jobs in law, medicine, and other traditionally male-dominated professions. The Bureau of Labor Statistics (BLS) reports that 61 percent of all women were in the labor market in 2009 (compared to 40 percent in 1975) and that women outnumbered men in the workforce for the first time in 2010. According to BLS data, 64.2 million payroll employees were women (just 63.4 million were men) in January 2010.

What accounts for these patterns and whether they are a blip or a continuing trend? Some economists say that women now outnumber men in the labor force because the current recession has disproportionally struck male-dominated industries including finance, insurance, real estate, and construction. Pundits have even dubbed the economic climate a "he-cession" or "man-cession" to reflect the fact that 80 percent of the jobs lost in the downturn had been held by men. Still, though, many experts expect the trend to reverse or plateau once the recession passes.

Other observers counter that the trend of women outpacing men in the workforce is here to stay. A shift in educational attainment is the main reason behind the steady rise in women's employment. Since 1991, the percentage of young women both attending and graduating college has outpaced men; a greater proportion of women ages 25 to 34 have completed four years of college or more, relative to their male counterparts. And by 2009, about 36 percent of young women completed at least a four-year college degree, compared to 28 percent of young men.

This new gender revolution is increasingly visible on college campuses; according to the Census Bureau, 53 per-cent of college students in 2008 were women. Experts project that women will soon outnumber men on college campuses by a ratio of 1.5 women per every one man. The "degree gap" is more pronounced for racial and ethnic minorities, especially for Blacks. Black women outnumber Black men almost two to one in higher education. This striking trend suggests

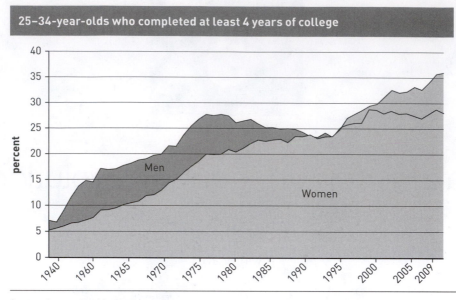

25–34-year-olds who completed at least 4 years of college

Source: Current Population Survey

Note: Data not available for each consecutive year prior to 1964

that women may become the majority of American workers, provided they are given the opportunities to blend work obligations with family responsibilities and female-friendly policies.

It's not just women's rates of overall employment that are remarkable, but the fact that women are steadily filing into occupations that were historically men's domains. I focus here on just three: detectives, lawyers, and physicians. Although the gender composition of these three occupational groups is not yet 50:50, the pace of change is very steep. The chart on the next page illustrates changes in these three occupations. You can see, for instance, how the percentage of all police officers and detectives who are women has increased steadily over the past 25 years.

Similar trends are evident for the highly prestigious and historically male-dominated professions of law and medicine. The proportion of all lawyers who are female more than doubled, rising from 15 percent in 1983 to 35 percent in 2008, and a virtually identical pattern emerges for medicine. While 16 percent of physicians were female in 1983, by 2008 this proportion increased to 31 percent. The fact that one third of doctors and lawyers are women reflects the considerable strides that women have made in education over the past three decades.

Experts anticipate that this pattern will continue; the entering classes of medical schools and law schools now include more women than men. According to

the Association of American Medical Colleges, female applicants to medical schools outnumbered male applicants in 2003 and women comprised nearly 50 percent of graduates of medical schools in 2008. The U.S. National Center for Education Statistics reported that half of those who earned a Doctor of Medicine degree in 2007 were women. (The chart above demonstrates this remarkable change in the proportion of women enrolled in medical schools.)

Further, 2009 marked the very first time American women earned more doctoral degrees than men, according to the Council of Graduate Schools. Women represented approximately 51 percent of awarded doctorates (although men continue to earn the majority of doctorates in traditionally male-dominated fields such as engineering with 78.4 percent and mathematics and computer sciences with 73.2 percent).

With more young women represented in higher education and the current recession, labor market analysts project that women will outnumber men in the labor force, at least for the fore-seeable future. This partly reflects the fact that the majority of women still are employed in recession-resistant (and female-dominated) fields such as education and health care. At the same time, an increasing number of women are making inroads into a wide variety of male-dominated fields beyond law, law enforcement, and medicine to fields such as technology and finance.

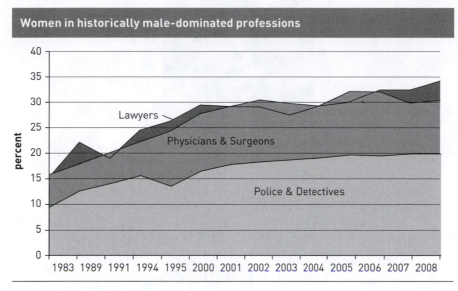

Women in historically male-dominated professions

Source: U.S. Census Bureau
Note: Percentage in Police & Detectives was estimated after 2002 due to changes in Census Bureau occupational and industrial classification systems.

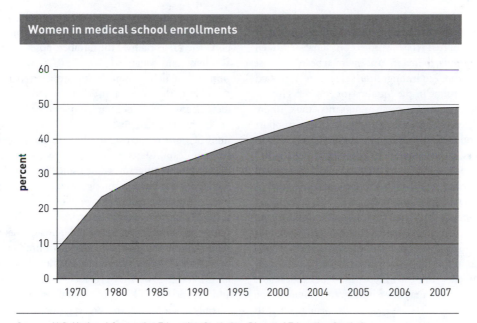

Women in medical school enrollments

Source: U.S. National Center for Education Statistics, Digest of Education Statistics

These strides do not necessarily reflect a wholly "good news" story, however. Women are still more likely than men to exit the labor market when they have children, and many face institutional obstacles as they strive to balance work and family. Although the gender pay gap is now at its all-time narrowest, where women now earn 82 cents per every dollar earned by a man, the declining gap is due to the erosion of men's earnings rather than an increase in women's pay. The true "gender revolution" will be achieved only when men and women earn equal and sufficient economic resources to support them-selves and their families.

the feminization of
american immigration

donna r. gabaccia

spring 2015

In 1984, when statisticians at the U.S. Department of Labor first reported that women outnumbered men among immigrants, their announcement appeared amidst growing fears that the immigration reforms of 1965 had precipitated a decline in the "quality" of America's immigrants. Critics claimed newer immigrants "took" more than they "gave." There was little evidence to support such fears, but the momentum increased and eventually Congress passed the Illegal Immigration Reform and Immigrant Responsibility Act of 1996, which ended most social services to America's foreign-born, whether or not they possessed green cards.

Scholars, politicians, and American citizens have long imagined immigrants as working-age men who built America through their hard labor. By contrast, immigrant women and children were long assumed to be economic dependents. The 1984 Department of Labor report showed, for example, that most immigrant women in the 1970s entered with visas facilitating family unification. Thus, the *New York Times'* decision to headline its article on the report "Men Only a Third of U.S. Immigrants" provocatively added fuel to the fire. It fed fears that adult immigrant women were no

Although many associate increased female migration with trafficking, scholarly studies all point toward family unification, the recruitment of female care-workers, and the admission of refugees as drivers of gendered dynamics of migration.

different from children: they all depended on men's support. The *Times* claimed the numbers upset "Conventional Wisdom" and suggested that the U.S. was unique in a world where other countries still attracted male workers.

In fact, the labor statisticians' report made none of these claims. On the contrary, it questioned the association of visa status with female dependency and showed that a third of women entering the U.S. to unify families listed an occupation. Other evidence showed that wage-earning rates among immigrant women since 1970 had been only slightly lower than rates among native-born women. What's more, many more adult women of both groups worked for wages both before and after marriage than in the past.

Family unification visas and female majorities also preceded the passage of the 1965 immigrant reforms by several decades. Restrictive immigration laws passed in 1921 and 1924 first provided for the entry of wives and dependent children of naturalized immigrant men. Already in the 1950s, the largest group of migrants entering the U.S. did so with visas for family unification.

Female majorities were equally long-standing. Women and girls had been only 34.9% of immigrants between 1910 and 1919. With immigration restriction, however, that percentage rose to 43.8% in the 1920s, 55.3% in the 1930s, and 61.2% in the 1940s. After the passage of the 1965 reforms—changes that undid many of the earlier restrictions—the percentage of female immigrants actually fell to 53% in the 1970s.

We now also know that the feminization of migration occurred globally; that is, it did not set the

U.S. apart as either unique or uniquely disadvantaged in its labor force. Many countries in Europe and Australia also had gender balanced migrant populations before 1960, and it became more common among immigrants in parts of Asia, Africa, and Latin America after 1960. Today, women are 50% of refugees worldwide and migrant men outnumber women only as asylum-seekers and as undocumented or clandestine labor migrants. Although many associate increased female migration with trafficking, scholarly studies all point toward family unification, the recruitment of female care-workers, and the admission of refugees as drivers of gendered dynamics of migration.

Most significantly, no study has *ever* documented negative consequences of gender balanced migrant populations. While the 1965 reforms of U.S. immigration policy certainly had unintended consequences and family unification provisions did encourage the multiplication of once-tiny Asian and Latin American migrations, the feminization of migration was not itself a consequence of immigration reform. Nor did women's use of visas for family unification render them economic dependents or "takers." Gender balance among immigrants—whether in the United States or elsewhere—is thus no cause for alarm and it provides no evidence to support either further restrictions or the stigmatization of recent migrants as undesirable.

fashion victims
aghil daghagheleh
fall 2015

Earlier this year, survey researchers at the University of Michigan questioned citizens of seven Muslim countries about how they think women should dress. They asked both men and women to select from among five styles of hijabs, or veils, or whether women should wear no hijab at all. They tried to reduce a multifaceted piece of clothing, embodying, a complex decisions, to a few simple choices, as shown below.

For one thing, the meaning of the hijab varies widely across the Muslim world. In Egypt, veiling is a personal choice, and can be an expression of virtue, personal style, or resistance to secularism, according to anthropologist Saba Mahmood (*Politics of Piety*, 2004). In Iran, where the hijab is mandatory, hijab styles are a sign of resistance against an Islamic government that sees itself as the guardian of women's bodies.

In addition, the hijab is not merely one piece of clothing, and encompasses many different styles. The intense competition among women's wear designers, Islamic fashion shows, and glossy hijab magazines showcase these variations—and their wide appeal for Muslim women.

What this tells us is that people's way of dressing is shaped by their social context, as the anthropologist Lila Abu-Lughod reminds us in her 2013 book *Do Muslim Women Need Saving?* After all, American women don't live in a world of free choice either. The "tyranny of fashion," in other words, is a challenge for women in many parts of the world.

scripting gender
media and culture

overview

We learn gender scripts—who to be and what to do and feel—from culture, especially social media. From "It's a Girl" balloons to playground shouts of "Don't be such a sissy," to television, movies, magazines, and the Internet—gendered scripts are pervasive in our lives. From these scripts children and young adults learn what it means to be boys and girls, women and men.

Many of our cultural scripts focus on celebrities. Rebecca Tiger looks at the gendered double standards by which we judge female celebrities. Another source of gender scripting, specifically for young women, are magazines such as *Cosmopolitan*, *Seventeen*, and *Teen Vogue*, whose glossy covers offer seemingly benign life advice. Amanda M. Gengler's article "Selling Feminism, Consuming Femininity" explores how these magazines use feminist language of "empowerment" while preaching that young women still need to constantly improve themselves to grab and maintain the attention of men.

American culture's double standard and gender scripting for the "ideal" woman and the female celebrity is not a modern phenomenon as Karen Sternheimer explains in her article "Enduring Dilemmas of Female Celebrity." Sternheimer's examination of the historical development of the concept of a female celebrity shows how the public popularity and fame of female celebrities is restricted by the their ability to balance their public work with traditional feminine roles of marriage, motherhood, and maintaining a home. Recently, we have seen the growth and public emergence of a new kind of celebrity script. As the lives of transgender folks become more public, there has been a rise in media coverage of transgender celebrities like Laverne Cox and even more recently Caitlin Jenner. D'Land Compton and Tristan Bridges comment on this in their piece "#callmecaitlyn and Contemporary Trans* Visibility."

Julia Ericksen explores the culture of competitive and professional ballroom dancing, which requires both women and men to conform to strict beauty regimes and gender presentations.

Finally, Black men of color are faced with the challenge of maneuvering in spaces which code them as dangerous. Nightclubs create dress codes which are designed to keep Black men out, according to Reuben A. Buford.

things to consider

- One theme in these readings is the prevalence in our media and culture of a double standard of gender. The demand that women be sexually available and also pure is particularly evident in reporting on the lives of female celebrities. Discuss how you might change this stereotypical coverage of femininity. Are there any double standards which surround media coverage of male celebrities?
- Take a moment to consider the gender scripts you experience and utilize in your own life. Where do they originate from?
- How are race and class also present in gendered messages within media and culture?

celebrity drug scandals, media double standards

rebecca tiger

fall 2013

In the past few years, two much-admired celebrities' drug use became the focus of media attention. Whitney Houston's death in February of 2012 prompted a spate of *New York Times* articles celebrating her musical talents and castigating her as an "addict" whose drug use damaged her "plush, vibrant and often spectacular" voice. Readers who commented in letters and online helped construct that dominant narrative—addiction as descent to rock bottom—lamenting the loss of a gifted singer who had squandered her talents by drug use. In this seamless morality tale, the star was eclipsed by the addict.

media double standards

Lance Armstrong's repeated drug use, on the other hand, provoked very different coverage. As the Armstrong story unfolded—and continues to unfold—the *Times* and its readers, in opinion pages, and columns by prominent *Times* writers, struggled over the meaning of his habitual use of erythropoietin (EPO) and other "performance enhancers." In this case, they've been slow to create a morality tale for Armstrong's repeated use of drugs banned by the cycling authorities—even after Armstrong publicly admitted to some of the U.S. Anti-Doping Agency's accusations.

Why has Armstrong's repeated use of banned substances received such ongoing and nuanced treatment while Houston's drug use was quickly dismissed through the familiar trope of addiction? The difference lies in the symbolic importance we assign to different drugs and to drug users of different races and genders. The two stories reflect long-standing cultural distinctions between

"good" and "bad" drug users, distinctions that are codified in public policy. Houston's narrative conforms to the historic frame of the degraded, irredeemably deviant addict, who is often pictured as Black and female. Armstrong, a White man, did a bad "thing," but because he is considered to be a hard worker who uses drugs to be more productive, he escaped stigmatizing labels. Armstrong is allowed multiple identities—cancer survivor, humanitarian, gifted cyclist—while Houston's identity as an addict eclipses her other accomplishments.

the "real" houston

While these two cases might seem incomparable, they reveal how centrally media portrayals of drug use and abuse are framed by race and gender. Take, for example, Jon Caramanica's article, "A Voice of Triumph, the Queen of Pain," immediately following Houston's death. Caramanica calls Houston "pure musical royalty," but argues that "maybe, beneath the old sheen [of stardom], she was always so messy," suggesting that the "early vivacity" that made her a star wasn't the "real" her. Her "troubled later life" was the "throne" she was meant to occupy. He refers to Houston as an addict and her death as a "cautionary tale," but never explains the moral we should take from it—he doesn't have to.

As I argue in my book *Judging Addicts*, society's construction of addiction as a medico-moral disorder—sickness and badness—is so widespread that it can be deployed and understood with little explanation. Most of the 487 *Times* readers who responded to Houston's obituary reflected this view, referring to her death as a "tragedy," "an example of what drugs can do," and a warning never to be "shackled with addiction." One reader's call to avoid "overdramatization" before "knowing the cause of her death" was ignored by hundreds of others eager to accept the "lesson" of "the ravages of drugs and alcohol" the newspaper encouraged. By casting Houston as, above all else, an addict and suggesting that this was her "real" self, the *Times* and its readership ignored the possibility that Houston may also have used drugs to enhance her acclaimed performances.

> **Armstrong is allowed multiple identities—cancer survivor, humanitarian, gifted cyclist—but Houston is just an addict.**

The *Times'* coverage of Houston's death quickly took on the distinct overtones of race that characterize most discussions of drugs in the U.S. Columnist Frank Bruni begins his article "Drinking and Drugging" with Houston's now-infamous quote, from a 2002 interview with Diane Sawyer, "Crack is wack." Bruni, like others, assumes that Houston disparaged crack to show that she didn't need "cheap [drugs] . . . with album sales like hers, you didn't have to suck on a pipe." But by immediately raising the specter of an African American woman using crack cocaine, Bruni cements the connection between Blackness and this much-demonized drug. As Harry Levine and Craig Reinarman argue in *Crack in America*, that connection—the result of the media's framing of crack as a "ghetto" drug, and powder cocaine users as White and wealthy—has contributed to harsher drug laws for crack, and racial inequity in policing and incarceration.

indulgences

And yet Bruni's references to crack are a gratuitous introduction to another topic of doubtful relevance to Houston's story: alcohol abuse. Bruni speculates that the "unconfirmed inventory of pills in her hotel suite" did not "represent the extent of her indulgences," and that

"by many accounts Houston also drank. More than a little." He argues that alcohol is as dangerous as all the other drugs he assumes Houston used, and that the United States needs to restrict its availability, marketing, and production, and tax it more heavily. He assures his readers that he's not arguing for prohibition, nor is he "about to abandon my white Burgundy or gin martinis." But he thinks we need "public discussion" about other people's drinking; his speculation that Houston drank herself to death is the catalyst for this conversation. Even as Bruni admits that "what killed Houston [was] still to be determined," he is ready to urge that we "not be too quick to edit drinking out" of her tale. In fact, the coroner's toxicology report did not include alcohol; Houston drowned to death, and traces of marijuana, cocaine, and prescription medicine were found in her body. There was never a correction that incorporated this new information. Moralizing is permitted—even when the facts run counter to the lesson we're supposed to learn.

Mining Houston's death further, the *Times* devoted one of its "Motherlode: Adventures in Parenting" columns to drug-using mothers. In "Whitney Houston, My Mother and Addiction," Paige Bradley Frost admits "we don't yet know the exact cause of [Houston's] death," but hopes that her death will awaken us to the "realities of drug and alcohol abuse . . . Mothers are not immune" to alcoholism, she says, in a culture that perpetuates the dangerous view that "drinking and motherhood are an acceptable mix." Again, Houston's death should serve a particular purpose: "Will Ms. Houston's death lead even one woman to look honestly at her drinking or drug use and ask for help?" asks Frost. "I hope so." Although "alcohol may not have killed Whitney Houston," Frost admits, "alcoholism and drug addiction are deadly diseases with the power to destroy relationships, families and lives." Eighty-six readers responded to her story, many thanking the writer for this "poignant," "amazing, powerful, courageous," and "beautiful, beautiful" post.

Some readers argued over the nature of addiction, asking: is it a disease or the result of bad choices? Yet most agreed that Houston was an addict, and drug users can't be good mothers. The one reader who suggested that "it would be more respectful to wait until the cause of death is determined before launching a personal cause from the pad of a public tragedy," was quickly admonished by others, one of whom saw "compassion and hope" in Frost's using Houston's death, combined with the story of her own mother's alcoholism, to lay bare the perils of addicted mothers. Frost and her readers claimed that she was shedding light on a hidden issue. Yet negative portrayals of African American mothers who use drugs, particularly in the media's coverage of the "crack-baby epidemic," are all too familiar. Two weeks after her death, the nation's leading newspaper set Houston's morality tale solidly within this frame, despite the fact that there was little evidence of what prompted her death.

"we are all culpable"

On October 22, 2012, Lance Armstrong was stripped of his seven Tour De France titles. The International Cycling Union decided not to appeal the U.S. Anti-Doping Agency's findings (based on over 1,000 pages of evidence, including testimony from teammates) that over many years, Armstrong used and required his teammates to use EPO, testosterone, human growth hormone, and other forms of blood doping. The 972 reader comments posted to the *Times* in the two days after the Tour's actions are remarkable for their diversity of opinion. A number of readers excoriated Armstrong for lying, but many also blamed a "sick" society where "cheating and greed are rewarded." Armstrong's staunch defenders called the investigation a "misguided witch hunt" and cited a lack of toxicological evidence. Others argued that since every other racer was doping, it was a "level playing field," making Armstrong the legitimate winner.

A debate emerged about what to call EPO and other so-called performance enhancers. When a few commentators referred to them as drugs, others disagreed, one explaining: "blood doping and EPO . . . are not 'drugs'" because they are "not detectable by post-event testing," a defining feature of "drugs" for several readers. Others, calling EPO a supplement or medicine, were quick to argue that athletes should be permitted to, as one put it, "maximize their performance and natural talents through performance-enhancing supplements."

beyond lance and whitney

As historian Caroline Acker shows in her book, *Creating the American Junkie*, the distinction between "medicine" and "drugs" relies heavily on the race of the user: White people take medicine and are managed by doctors, while people of color take "street" drugs and are criminalized. Though the coroner in Houston's case found traces of several legal pharmaceuticals (commonly called "medicine") in her body, that didn't change the fact that she had been labeled a drug-user whose actions carried the taint of immorality.

In a *Times* op-ed pegged to the Armstrong case, "A Drug to Quicken the Blood," Kathleen Sharp, author of *Blood Medicine*, defines EPO as an "anemia drug"

genetically engineered from a "naturally occurring hormone that stimulates the production of red blood cells." Explaining its appeal, she asks, "What red-blooded American doesn't crave more energy?" Of course, EPO has that in common with cocaine; both give users more energy and make them feel good. But op-ed writers and readers downplayed the par-

Many saw Armstrong as a hero, a cancer survivor and a humanitarian. They didn't want his doping scandal to undo all he did "to make the world a better place."

allel because they associate EPO with hard work and cocaine with indulgence. Sharp went on to divert blame from the EPO user by criticizing pharmaceutical companies that make EPO, doctors, and society at large—as well as demanding patients. She concludes that, while "it's too bad about Lance Armstrong . . . we are all culpable in this blood-doping scandal."

The media continued to frame Armstrong's actions as the consequence of pushing winning at all cost, with some readers seeing valor in the way Armstrong met that challenge and dismissing the degree to which his substance use contributed to his cycling victories. As one person explained, echoing similar sentiments, Armstrong's body is "in such [good] shape it's unbelievable . . . That did not come from blood packing . . . it came from getting on his bike and riding . . . How many of you couch potato critics have ever ridden a bike that far, once?" In other words, Armstrong's doping had simply helped him attain the kind of fit body achieved by behaviors— such as hard work and exercise—regularly lauded in the *Times*' "Fitness & Nutrition" section.

This framing of drug effects adds to the distinctions that were drawn between Houston's and Armstrong's history of substance use. If people misuse medicine, they are often cast as victims of the medical establishment, not to blame for drug use. But no one suggested that Whitney Houston was "just like us," in Sharp's terms, or that using drugs helped Houston cope in a profession— not unlike sports—where audiences demand perfection and unfailing energy is necessary to perform. Instead, Houston's drug use is cast as an individual failing, an indulgence, a reflection of her "real" identity. She is an addict, a victim of her own pathological impulses. In contrast, Armstrong was seen by many as a hero.

international icon

The idea that Armstrong should be admired, not condemned, was widespread among readers. The "Lance Armstrong phenomenon" as one reader explained, "inspired me to exercise . . . something to keep in mind with the health and obesity difficulties this country is facing." Even if he doped, he provided an unparalleled example of "fitness and health" that motivated many *Times* readers. Armstrong's history of testicular cancer gave him even more credibility. He was a guy "who looked cancer in the eye and did not blink," wrote one reader. He "inspired whole nations to persevere to overcome one of the deadliest obstacles known to mankind." And "by giving hope to a lot of people, [he was] heroic." While some labeled Armstrong a cheater, many others saw him as a hero, a cancer survivor, and a humanitarian. They did not see how the doping scandal could undo all he did "to make the world a better place."

It was precisely Armstrong's reputation as a humanitarian that led the paper to devote an "Ethicist" column to "The Lance Armstrong Conundrum." Columnist Chuck Klosterman dismissed the "debatable" ethics of using performance-enhancing drugs in favor of the question: "How to weigh the many bad things Armstrong did against the very good charity he created?" While Klosterman assumes that Armstrong "did bad things," he refuses to give him a label that might permanently taint his identity. He concludes: "there is no right or wrong way to feel about Armstrong" and that we must look at "the totality of his career."

By contrast, the *Times* never mentioned Whitney Houston's humanitarianism, that she supported a range of charities including the American Foundation for AIDS Research, the Children's Defense Fund, and the United Negro College Fund. They ran a morality tale that pathologized her as an addict and offered little room for complexity. Nor was her story complex enough to warrant expert analysis.

But the *Times*' treatment of Armstrong included a "Room For Debate" column where "knowledgeable outsiders," with expertise in sociology, public policy, corporate branding, and leadership and organizational psychology were brought in to help answer the question: "Does a Fallen Leader Crush His Cause?" We learn that "a brand is a promise," "brands are about creating trust," and that "leaders [are] extremely complicated human beings." Armstrong is called a brand, a leader, a philanthropist, and an icon. Although the article warns us to "be vigilant about would-be icons" and identifies the scandal as a "mentoring moment" to teach youth "what it means to be a strong leader," Armstrong becomes the basis for broader discussions that go far beyond the meaning of his

> While these two cases might seem incomparable, they reveal how centrally media portrayals of drug use and abuse are framed by race and gender.

drug use into a jargon-laden conversation among experts about heroes and leadership.

Three months after Lance Armstrong was stripped of his Tour de France titles, columnist Gail Collins queried her readers: "Right now, you're probably asking yourself: 'What can the Lance Armstrong scandal teach us as a nation?'" But even with the benefit of hindsight, Collins finds no serious or concluding "point" to deliver. Armstrong "isn't particularly lovable," she remarks. Yes, the Postal Service wasted $40 million in taxpayer money sponsoring Armstrong's Tour De France team. But, she ends flippantly, "We'll look for another moral. Maybe something about [Armstrong's ex-girlfriend] Sheryl Crow." She has no interest in the scandal as morality tale. Armstrong's privileged status means that his years as a regular drug user is eclipsed in favor of his identities as sports icon and humanitarian, however tarnished.

In his famous essay "White," film scholar Richard Dyer argues that "White people . . . are difficult if not impossible to analyze *qua* White. The subject seems to fall apart in your hands as soon as you begin." The "panic" over drug use by elite White men has yet to be set into an easily deployed frame. In drug panics, mainly White elites speaking through mainstream media distinguish themselves from those whom the rules are meant to govern. This dominant social group highly values what it sees as the end result of Armstrong's doping—triumph in grueling races and demonstrable physical prowess. His privileged status shields him from easy moralizing, and his transgressions, if they can even be called that, are subsumed by ongoing debates about their meaning.

The impression that Armstrong's and Houston's cases aren't parallel speaks to the power of the media to reinforce double standards. He was productive; she indulged. He "doped"; she was an addict. His role as a father was *rarely* questioned; she was quickly castigated as a bad mother. He enhanced his performance; she squandered her talent. Their stories reflect the enduring cultural distinctions we collectively draw between good and bad drugs and good and bad users—distinctions that, after a century of U.S. drug policy, are unlikely to change anytime soon.

recommended resources

Coomber, Ross. 2013. "How Social Fear of Drugs in the Non-Sporting World Creates a Framework for Doping Policy in the Sporting World," *International Journal of Sport Policy and Politics*. Argues that doping policy, while presented as separate from other drugs, actually reflects the broader social fears that have historically governed drug policy in the non-sporting world.

Derrida, Jacques. 1999. "The Rhetoric of Drugs." In Anne Alexander & Mark S. Roberts (eds.), *High Culture: Reflections on Addiction and Modernity.* New York: State University of New York Press. Argues that the word "drug" is not a scientific concept but the result of political and moral evaluations.

Gamson, Joshua. 1994. *Claims to Fame: Celebrity in Contemporary America.* Oakland, CA: University of California Press. A classic in the field of celebrity studies that examines the social significance, consumption, and production of celebrity in the United States.

Musto, David. 1999. *The American Disease: Origins of Narcotic Control.* London: Oxford University Press. Historical account of the development of drug laws in the United States.

Reinarman, Craig. 2005. "Addiction as Accomplishment: The Discursive Construction of a Disease," *Addiction Research and Theory 13*:307–320. Frames the disease model of addiction as an historical, cultural, and discursive "social accomplishment."

orange is mostly the same gender
adriana brodyn
winter 2015

People noticed *Orange Is the New Black* for its attention to gender and sexuality. The show features a transgender character, Sophia, which gives welcome representation to the struggle over transgender rights. But because of her transition through gender reassignment surgery, does the character actually reinforce binary notions of gender?

Writing in *Gender & Society* in 2014, Laurel Westbrook and Kristen Schilt explore how contexts play a role in the criteria used to determine gender, drawing on three cases: public debates over transgender employment rights, policies that decide eligibility for transgender people in sports, and proposals to remove the genital surgery requirement to change sex categories on birth certificates. From these cases, the authors identify two main ways gender is determined: through identity-based criteria or through biology-based criteria. Social context affects which criteria are used.

In gender-integrated spaces, the tendency is to use identity-based criteria, relying on cues people use to represent themselves. But in gender-segregated spaces—like the women's prison in which *OITNB* takes place—the tendency is toward biology-based criteria, such as genitalia.

So does *OITNB*'s Sophia challenge the prevailing sex/gender/sexuality system? Yes and no. Yes, there is an opportunity for the category "woman" to be expanded by trans representation. But mostly no, because Sophia is quickly reabsorbed into that system. For Sophia to belong, the audience is led to imagine that she has transitioned, importantly, removing anatomical markers of maleness. For example, when the prison reduces Sophia's dose of estrogen, there is a moment of gender-related panic: without the correct dose, is she a woman? This could have been a powerful moment of undoing, bringing into question gender and the problematic assumptions that police gender-segregated spaces. Instead, a flashback confirming that Sophia is in prison for committing fraud to finance her gender reassignment surgery dissolves the panic and reabsorbs her into an unquestioned gender binary.

selling feminism, consuming femininity

amanda m. gengler

spring 2011

Many women, even those of us now in our twenties, thirties, forties, and beyond, remember the thrill of coming home from school to the fresh, crisp pages of the latest issue of *Seventeen* (now in it's 66th year), hoping for guidance as we struggled to navigate the perils of adolescence. Today's girls consume an even wider range of "teen 'zines," both in print and online, and at increasingly younger ages. Their pages are filled with how-to pieces—how to style your hair in the latest fashion, give your lips an enticing shine, even how to kiss correctly. But beyond beauty tips, teen magazines also teach girls, at a basic level, *what it means* to be a girl today.

While we might have hoped traditional ideas about femininity had been relegated to the past along with typewriters and Burma shave, teen magazines are still saturated with them. In their pages, girls should focus on being pretty, pleasing men, and decorating men's spaces. Without the colorful modern layouts and contemporary actresses splayed across their shiny covers, one might mistake the glossies for dusty relics left on the shelf since the 1950s.

> **Without the modern layouts and contemporary actresses, these glossies might be relics from the 1950s.**

Indeed, recent covers offer little more than provocative teases about boys and beauty, such as "Where will you meet your next boyfriend?" or "Is school secretly making you fat?" Pieces that focus on substantive issues—drunk driving, careers, or politics—are rare. The overall message a girl receives, journalist Kate Pierce found in her study of *Seventeen* over time, is that "how she looks is more important than what she thinks, that her main goal in life is to find a man who will take care of her . . . and that her place will be home with the kids and the cooking and the housework."

Sociologist Kelly Massoni also studied *Seventeen*, finding that men held 70 percent of the jobs represented in its pages. Women were disproportionately shown either not working or working in traditionally feminine jobs, with a particular emphasis on modeling and acting careers. Advice on sexuality hasn't evolved much either. Sociologist Laura Carpenter explored the presentation of (almost exclusively hetero-) sexuality in *Seventeen* across the decades, and though she saw greater inclusion of sexual diversity and increased openness to women's sexual agency in recent years, these progressive messages were often presented alongside more traditional ones, with the author or editors emphasizing the latter. Girls might now learn they can "make the first move" or dress in clothing as risqué as fashion demands, but the subtext is clear: a hip young woman is more concerned with lipstick, boyfriends, and belly-button rings than books, politics, or careers.

So beside how-to features on hair styling, body shaping, and make-up application, there are explicit instructions for interacting with men and boys. While beauticians, personal trainers, actresses, or other women offer advice on beauty, fashion, and exercise, *men* (often adult men in their twenties) advise girls on how to support, entertain, and excite their boyfriends by cheering them on from the sidelines, doing personal favors, making them laugh, and "talking dirty." Despite a new millennium, much remains unchanged.

What *has* changed is the packaging: many of these messages are now couched in feminist language. Advertisers must convince young women that they are in need of constant improvement—largely to get and keep boys' attention—without threatening young women's views of themselves as intelligent, self-directed, and equal. Buzz words like "empowerment," "self-determination," and "independence" are sprinkled liberally across their pages. But this seemingly progressive rhetoric is used to sell products and ideas that keep girls doing gender in appropriately feminine ways, leading them to reproduce, rather than challenge, gender hierarchies. An ad for a depilatory cream, for instance, tells girls that they are "unique, determined, and unstoppable," so they should not "settle . . . for sandpaper skin." Feminist demands for political and economic equality—and the refusal to *settle* for low-wages, violence, and second-class citizenship—morph into a refusal to settle for less than silky skin. Pseudo-feminist language allows young women to believe that they can "empower" themselves at the checkout counter by buying the accoutrements of traditional femininity. Girls' potential choice to shun make-up or hair-removal disappears, replaced by their choice of an array of beauty products promising to moisturize, soften, and smooth their troubles away.

Everywhere, girls are flooded with messages urging them to see success, as achieved through beauty, just a purchase away. By some estimates, a ten-year-old is likely to spend $300,000 on her hair and face before she reaches fifty. In *Beauty and Misogyny,* Sheila Jeffreys catalogs the damage these beauty products, cosmetic treatments, and surgical procedures do to female bodies. Jeffreys argues that beauty practices normalized in Western culture—wearing high heels, for example—can injure women physically and socially. These practices are seductive, because we learn to take pleasure in them, but they also reinforce the underlying ideology that women's bodies are unattractive when unadorned and must be carefully groomed simply to be presentable.

On top of the advertising that accounts for around half of these texts' content, many articles that *appear* to be editorial—pieces comparing the merits of accessories,

fingernail polishes, or facial cleansers, for example— are advertisements in disguise, conveniently including brand names, retail locations, and prices. In her ethnography of teen 'zine consumption in a junior high, Margaret Finders noted that girls often failed to recognize these as marketing, interpreting them as valuable, neutral information instead.

This is not to say that all girls consume teen 'zines uncritically. Interviews by sociologists have shown that girls are often critical of airbrushed models and claim to ignore advertisements. Melissa Milkie, for example, found that girls of color were especially skeptical, viewing teen magazines as oriented primarily to White girls and including girls and women of color only when they fit White beauty ideals. For the most part, however, girls' critiques stop at body image, failing to question these texts' nearly exclusive focus on beauty and hetero-sexual romance. Dawn Curie found that 70 percent of her interviewees were "avid" readers, for whom the reading and sharing of these texts was a significant pastime. These girls spent hours devouring their content, and admitted that they turned to the magazines' "real life" pieces for "practical advice," and used the girls in the magazines as yardsticks by which to measure their own lives and experiences.

Teen girl magazines breathe new life into some very old ideas. Today's successful woman, they proclaim, orients her life around looking beautiful and snagging a man. Seemingly esteem-boosting "grrl power" rhetoric makes this message seem fresh, and provides marketers an appealing way to sell even independent-minded girls old-fashioned deference and subordination as "empowerment." Those of us who grew up with these texts can't deny that consuming them, along with the products they push, was often a lot of fun, even a rite of passage. But if feminist goals of equality are to be realized, girls need better options (*New Moon,* newmoon.org, is one attempt to offer an alternative to traditional girls' magazines). We can also teach girls to question the basic assumptions embedded in popular media and to become critical consumers (or non-consumers) of these texts and the culture of beauty and romance they peddle. We might even offer girls the more radical message, learned and lived by earlier generations of feminists, that true empowerment comes not through consumption, but solidarity, critical-consciousness, and collective action.

beauty beyond a size 16

amanda m. czerniawski

spring 2016

Plus-size models made headlines in 2015, signaling a shift towards greater size diversity in fashion. Robyn Lawley became the first plus-size model featured in a swimsuit issue of *Sports Illustrated*. Another (Ashley Graham) was featured in an ad in the same issue. Graham gave a TED Talk on body acceptance in the spring, was featured in Lane Bryant's #ImNoAngel and #PlusIsEqual campaigns, and debuted her lingerie collection at New York Fashion Week in the fall. In the design field, *Project Runway* made history when it crowned plus-size designer Ashley Nell Tipton as its season 14 winner.

> **Size bias is hanging on in the very sector of fashion believed to be immune to size discrimination.**

Both Lawley and Graham, along with a number of prominent plus-size models including Denise Bidot, Stefania Ferrario (who launched the #droptheplus campaign), and actress and now clothing designer Melissa McCarthy have used their recent successes to ignite a movement to encourage a fashion industry built around a thin body beauty ideal to include women of every size and eliminate the categorical system that segregates both models and consumers on the basis of size.

Are these successes part of a spectacle that will soon fade or, rather, the start of a fashion revolution? Developments indicate this is not a passing fad, as significant institutional changes have occurred within modeling agencies and designers are responding to a consumer-driven demand for a greater representation of larger models in the fashion landscape. However, as the plus-size sector works to expand the definition of beauty and unify the modeling market, it, too, is plagued by elements of thin privilege; there is still a commercial preference for models on the smaller end of the plus-size spectrum who have "thin" faces.

As I found while researching the fashion industry as a plus-size model for more than two years, size distinctions are starting to erode within modeling agencies. Jag Model Agency, founded in 2013 by the former directors of Ford Models' now-defunct plus-size division, formally began this trend. The agency represents models from size 6 to size 20. And unlike other agencies, Jag does not group their models based on size category. IMG Models (the world's top modeling agency) announced in the fall of 2013 that they, too, would no longer segregate models into different boards based on size. As it stands, the distinction between straight- and plus-size models is based solely on size—"plus size" is everyone above a size 8. The basic model requirement of proportionate facial and bodily features is standard among all models and, quite simply, the nature of modeling work is the same, no matter the model's size. Modeling agents saw little justification for the continuation of this division.

Still, modeling work is divided into different types (runway, commercial print, fit, etc.), and each requires a specific look and size of model. The commercial print world is dominated by a specific image of plus-size beauty. Modeling agencies that focus on commercial print work represent plus-size models who fit within a narrow range in size (from an 8 to a 16) because there is not enough work for models larger than a size 16. As one agent claimed, "that is what advertisers want," even plus-size ones. This rationale explains the increased visibility of models (like Lawley at a size 12 and Graham at a size 16) who inhabit the small end of the plus-size spectrum. Consequently, size 18 and up models are virtually absent in print, working predominately as showroom and fit models.

Plus-size fashion companies produce lines of clothing that range from a size 14 to 24. These companies usually build their lines from a pattern based on a size 18 fit model. Designers and clothing manufacturers hire fit models to try on garments at various stages of production to determine the fit and appearance of the pieces on a live person. When it comes to selling these garments, however, smaller models more often appear in the clothes. "Larger" plus-size models work behind the scenes in fashion while the "smaller" ones are out basking in the public's attention.

While the gradual elimination of separate modeling divisions and increased media presence of plus-size models like Lawley and Graham mark a progressive move by fashion to embrace larger bodies, more striking are developments involving Tess Holliday, a model who is revolutionizing the commercial definition of plus size.

The typical, commercial, plus-size model is tall (minimum height of 5'8"), wears a woman's size 10 to 16, and portrays a conservative style of appearance. Most casual observers would probably fail to identify these models as plus size. In sharp contrast, Tess Holliday is short, large, and tattooed.

In January, MiLK Model Management in London signed 5'5", size 22 Holliday, making it the first major agency to represent a model of that size. Since then, Holliday has become the face of a number of campaigns and made high profile appearances. She has led the Sea by Monif C swimwear campaign (the first model over a size 18 hired by the swimsuit line), Torrid's Photoshop-free spring 2015 campaign, and the #SimplyBekini summer body confidence campaign for the UK's plus-size brand Simply Be, and she has modeled for Benefit Cosmetics and *Vogue Italy*. Holliday even appeared on the June cover of *People Magazine* with the headline, "the world's first size 22 supermodel."

Holliday and her booming career are remarkable given the tendency of fashion to hide bodies over a size 16 in designer studios and showrooms, out of sight from consumers. But those consumers are starting to notice the absence of larger bodies.

Newer, web-based retailers have begun using "larger" plus-size models. For instance, one owner of an online boutique explained, "I prefer to use size 16 models so my customers can identify with them. I've had complaints in the past that our models didn't look plus-size enough. I actually used a size 22 for some pictures." Competing with national retailers who do not use models larger than a size 16, these newer brands do not want to risk alienating consumers. This concern prompted designer Monif Clarke to hire Holliday. "We've always featured size 14 plus models," Clarke explained to Yahoo, "But, we thought, 'How do we make this more compelling for our customer?' The feedback we were getting was, 'We love that you show women in size 14 and 18 but what about the 22s and 24s?'" The "larger" plus-size model, shunned by certain sectors of the fashion industry, is gaining visibility in a burgeoning virtual marketplace of e-commerce.

Ultimately, the distinction between "smaller" and "larger" plus-sizes reveals the continuation of thin privilege and size discrimination in fashion. It is not uncommon for size 10 and 12 models to advertise plus-size clothing lines they could not actually wear. It's not that they're too big, but too small. Many of these "smaller" plus-size models use body padding to effectively size up, because clients want a curvy body but a thin face.

This padding technique, which involves strategically inserting foam pieces underneath hosiery or shapewear, allows a model who may be in-between sizes or on the lower end of the plus-size spectrum to temporarily add to her dimensions and "size up" to meet client demands. "Whenever I get a call from my booker about a casting," one size 10/12 model confided, "I make sure to ask which size they [the client] want." Depending on the client, this model will either present herself as a size 12 or, with padding, a size 14.

These "fat pads," as fashion insiders call them, accentuate the breast, butt, and thighs while providing the illusion of a slimmer waist and face—that is, the "perfect" hourglass figure clients want of plus-size models. As another plus-size model explained: "They'll use padding to size a girl up. A girl may be a size 10/12 but the client wants a solid size 14. They like her thinner face but want a bigger body, so they'll make her wear foam padding under her clothes. It's a win-win situation for smaller models. The model gets the job and the client gets the look they want. Unfortunately, it hurts larger models." The model experienced this form of size discrimination firsthand when she lost a commercial print job to a "smaller" model while working for the client as a fit model. The irony was that the designer hired this model to shape the very garment used in the print advertisement—but not to sell it in a catalog spread. The designer did not deem her body (or face) desirable for commercial advertising.

> *It is not uncommon for size 10 and 12 models to advertise plus-size clothing lines they could not actually wear. It's not that they're too big, but too small. Many use body padding because clients want a curvy body but a thin face.*

Sharon Quinn, a veteran plus-size model with over twenty years experience, acknowledged this all too common practice of hiring "smaller" models in PLUS Model Magazine: "Look more closely at some of the current window display ads for some of the major plus sized stores. Notice anything off? It doesn't seem to matter that the models look like little girls playing in their mother's clothing—all that seems to matter is that their faces are slimmer." Even Lane Bryant, the nation's leading women's plus-size apparel retailer, admitted that the company used models in their commercial print campaigns who were sometimes "only size 14 on the bottom half of their bodies."

As a photographer who has shot for catalogs and a model who graced the runway for John Galliano and Jean Paul Gaultier, Velvet D'Amour asserts that advertisers rely on "smaller" plus-size models to boost sales, "If they put a size 11 girl in, and she's wearing butt padding and boob padding and they sell a muumuu with this girl in that outfit, they're going to get more sales having her in that outfit than they are me [at nearly 300 pounds]." D'Amour argues that the nature of media and retail fashion creates this size inconsistency in marketing: "They need to create the unattainable, because the unattainable is what drives capitalism. If everyone accepted themselves, just as they are, imagine how sales would go down the tubes." So the tactic of hiring "smaller" models and then padding them up and pinning them into garments for photo

> **Each of plus-size fashion's milestones has seen mixed reception: there is a persistent cultural stigma around fat.**

shoots is simply part of a larger process of image manipulation aimed at increasing sales. But such manipulations further distort our sense of what bodies should look like, creating ever-more impossible ideals. And they perpetuate thinness, albeit of the face, as an ideal component of beauty.

Given the persistence of thin privilege within the plus-size industry, it is quite an accomplishment for models larger than a size 16 to be in the limelight. As one of these "larger" plus-size women, model and photographer D'Amour highlights the importance of capitalizing on what seems a rare moment in fashion's spotlight: "I try to create opportunity for other people because I know that that opportunity is very limited . . . I think that the reason people admire me is because I give them that sense of possibility. I was able to do it. I was able to break through that barrier." "Larger" plus-size models work to expand the definition of beauty beyond not only a size 6 but also a size 16.

First, it was the "smaller" plus-size models like Lawley and Graham who made history (the latter appeared on the cover of *Sports Illustrated*'s 2016 swimsuit edition). Then, it was Holliday on the cover of *People Magazine* and size 18 Erica Schenk on the cover of *Women's Running*. Today, given the mixed reception each milestone received under the persistent cultural sigma of fat, "larger" plus-size models still have trouble establishing themselves as legitimate models. Their current celebrity status in the fashion industry is a statement and not the norm, but, ultimately, it serves as our wake-up call to size bias hanging on in the very sector of fashion believed to be immune to size discrimination. It reveals just how deeply our culture's narrowly constructed ideas about bodies and beauty go.

enduring dilemmas of female celebrity

karen sternheimer

summer 2011

A 2007 *Newsweek* article, "Girls Gone Bad," focused on the exploits of Britney Spears, Paris Hilton, Nicole Richie, and Lindsay Lohan, arguing that they were "oversexed." Sex, drugs, and body size are all subjects of heightened focus for female celebrities, each used as evidence of lack of virtue and self-control. While Spears, Hilton, and Lohan have remained tabloid staples, Richie's foray into motherhood and marriage seems to have allowed her to rehabilitate her image, reflecting historian Alice Kessler-Harris's observation that family is equated with virtue for women. Wedding rites, baby bumps, and motherhood are all central facets of covering female stars today. Ambivalence about women's proper roles in public life lingers in these glossy pages and beyond.

Celebrity has long held the potential to be both liberating and constraining; women who capitalize financially on their renown might create their own production companies and parlay fame into numerous business ventures. However, celebrity status is often rooted in regressive definitions of gender. There are notable exceptions—Madonna and Lady Gaga have famously played with these contradictions in their acts—but young women drawn to the allure of fame today will find much in common with the experiences of young women decades ago, walking a tightrope between celebration and condemnation.

During the silent era, when movie fan magazines were first published, *Motion Picture Story Magazine* (1911–1977), *Photoplay* (1911–1980), *Picture Play* (1915–1941), and others were subsidized by the studios as industry boosters. Unlike today's glossies, which reveal every detail of the lives of the rich and famous, these magazines initially offered little information about silent screen performers, known as "picture players." This was by design: early films carried no credits, since producers wanted the films themselves to capture the public's attention, and actors' anonymity protected their potential careers in the legitimate theater.

That all changed as readers—often women—began to write in requesting information, mostly about the female players. What is her name? How does she keep her hair so lovely? Is she married? A Christian? Movie mavens soon realized that selling its performers, particularly its female performers, could also help sell the fledgling industry.

As cultural sociologist Joshua Gamson notes in his study of fame, women had historically been excluded from positions of public renown, but gained ground as they increasingly became primary consumers of mass produced goods at the start of the twentieth century. Advertisers picked up on this trend and used silent screen stars in their ads for beauty products. Features soon

41

provided details of players' personal backgrounds (albeit often fabricated) and burgeoning careers. Most fan magazine writers were women, and issues with women on the covers tended to sell better too.

Thus, fan magazines reflected women's ambivalence about the change in their identities as they took on greater importance outside the milieu of home and family. As I found in my examination of nearly 600 issues of 8 different magazines for my latest book, *Celebrity Culture and the American Dream*, the articles and photos that made up coverage of female celebrities at once challenged and reinforced traditional notions of femininity in the Golden Age of Hollywood and beyond.

women's work

Not coincidentally, fan magazines first appeared at a time when women began entering the labor force in larger numbers, seeking a higher status in public life. As historian Alice Kessler-Harris observes, "Women are used in the workforce in ways that relate the ideological justifications of a whole society to its immediate labor needs." Leo Braudy, author of *Frenzy of Renown: Fame and Its History* further explains, "The history of fame is also the history of the shifting definition of achievement in the social world." Women would have more opportunity for public recognition at the start of the twentieth century than

> **In Hollywood's Golden Age, the promise of upward mobility was at once liberating and constraining.**

perhaps ever before. "The dream of fame in Western society has been inseparable from the ideal of personal freedom," Braudy notes. If fame connotes a degree of public admiration, increasing opportunities to achieve public acclaim reflect women's shifting status in society. At a time when women's involvement in the paid labor force would increase for all American women, female movie stars would be on the vanguard.

Film scholar Marjorie Rosen argues that "the birth of movies coincided with—and hastened—the genesis of modern woman." The growth of the movie industry in the early 1900s coincided with both rapid urbanization and women's suffrage; for young women seeking independence, moving into cities provided new possibilities, although mostly in low wage occupations.

According to the 1910 Census, three-quarters of employed women worked in agricultural, manufacturing, or domestic jobs. While many men experienced upward mobility within growing corporations, high-paying corporate positions were mostly out of reach for

women until the end of the century. The movie industry held the promise of less physically demanding work.

In her 1977 book *Men and Women of the Corporation*, sociologist Rosabeth Moss Kanter observed how corporate executives assumed women were too emotional for managerial positions. In the company she studied, women were pigeonholed into the roles of mother, seductress, non-threatening "pet," or "iron maiden." While these stereotypical images would limit women's advancement in midcentury corporations, actresses could parlay them into on and off-screen identities—and big paydays.

Of course not all actresses would get rich, but many did find careers. Movies offered only a lucky few on-screen roles, but other women found work writing scripts or writing for fan magazines, among other behind-the-scenes jobs. Lacking the prestige of the theater and thus initially less appealing to men, the early film industry provided women opportunities as creative workers.

According to Denise D. Bielby and William T. Bielby's study of Hollywood writers, women comprised about half of all screen writers during the silent era; when the industry gained clout and male-led studios dominated the production process that percentage dropped dramatically. (Female writers remain in the minority in Hollywood and earn about 20 percent less than their male counterparts today.)

In this Golden Age, the promise of upward mobility was at once liberating and constraining. A select group of women did achieve economic independence and public acclaim, but they also typically embodied traditional notions of femininity and a narrow definition of beauty. Like today's stars, their success likely lured thousands of women to the industry—and to the fabled casting couch—even as men continued to control production, financing, and the very nature of the work.

famous yet feminine

Beginning in the 1910s, fan magazines celebrated women's opportunities to rise from rags to riches in the movie industry, often highlighting women's working class backgrounds and "girl next door" virtue. Freedom from toil seemed possible for more women than ever in these articles that so effectively mirrored Horatio Alger's inspirational tales of the nineteenth century.

A February 1918 *Photoplay* article, "From Stenography to Stardom," for example, describes Virginia Valli's rags-to-riches story. The article vividly recalls how she walked past rotting food and animal carcasses to get to her stenography job in Chicago before making it big: "She would climb a long pair of dingy half-lighted stairs, go into a dingy, half-lighted office." The city was threatening, and every day Valli passed by the "voluble sons of Italy," unable to "keep herself neat and dainty, and she had to endure being ogled by express drivers and roustabouts." But persistent Valli visited a local movie studio, applied for a position, and went back three times until the director would see her. Her career apparently a reward for virtue and doggedness, Valli could now lead the "limousine life," no longer enduring the indecency of city life, framed as unfit for young women.

Plenty of other stories, too, gushed over women's newfound career success. A 1915 issue of *Motion Picture Classic* trumpeted "Women's Conquest in Filmdom," and a *Picture Play* piece from the same year detailed how the new movie industry had become an increasingly respectable outlet for "ambitious girls." Written by Kathlyn Williams, known then as the "Jungle Actress," the story described the bravery needed to work with animals in movies. The next year, the same magazine profiled "Girls Who Play with Death," the women performing risky stunts on film sets.

Even outside the movie industry, women were entering the workforce in larger numbers in this period. According to Census data, women's participation in the paid labor force more than doubled between 1890 and 1910. Many worked in expanding "female occupations" as sales clerks, telephone operators, stenographers, typists, and in other relatively new positions. World War I further hastened women's entry into the labor force; America's brief involvement threatened to create a male labor shortage. "The war has caused a tremendous shortage of salesmen—*women must be trained to take their places,*" a 1919 *Photoplay* ad for traveling saleswomen beckoned. Also during the war, *Motion Picture* featured a photo spread of silent movie actress Gladys Brockwell doing "men's work," appearing behind a movie camera, climbing a telephone pole, and driving a horse-drawn cart.

Profiles like these still revealed an underlying discomfort with shifts in the gender order in the years leading up to women's suffrage in 1920. Brockwell's foray into "men's work" was, to be sure, temporary: "It is the present crisis that inspired Miss Brockwell to discover just how many of the purely masculine jobs a woman could perform if it became absolutely necessary for men to leave for duty 'somewhere in France.'" The title of the article, "Gladys Brockwell Does 'His' Bit," reinforced the idea that she was crossing a gender boundary for the photo shoot, but it was fully expected that she'd cross back once the camera was gone. Still, the female reporter recognized the changes that had taken place for her generation: "It is a far cry from the simpering, languishing lady of Victoria's day," she observed.

The earliest fan magazines clearly celebrated women's opportunities to have exciting new careers, but even as they challenged Victorian notions of femininity and domesticity, the magazines reminded readers that the "new woman" was non-threatening. Historian Alice Kessler-Harris describes how independence and virtue were often viewed as incompatible in the first decades of the century; women who defined their public roles as tied to home and family were perceived as more virtuous. A 1918 photo spread in *Motion Picture*, for instance, featured silent screen performers doing household chores. Despite their high-profile careers, these women supposedly enjoyed scrubbing floors, doing laundry, cooking, and washing cars in their spare time. Perhaps the first true movie star, Mary Pickford—called "Little Mary"—embodied this nonthreatening femininity, playing a young girl in films even after she turned thirty.

the threat of upwardly mobile women

Some women responded to the promise of upward mobility by seeking their own acting career. As Marjorie Rosen notes, Census data indicate that the number of women listed as "actresses" rose between 1910 and 1920 (and was nearly as high as those who had earned bachelor's degrees), while the number of male actors declined.

While the aspiration rose, the *celebration* of these career opportunities was short lived. As women gained professional ground in Hollywood and got the right to vote, fan magazines more frequently framed independent women as fallen or morally bankrupt, heartless schemers threatening unsuspecting men. In the era of flappers, women's onscreen sexuality became more overt—and seemingly more dangerous. Fan magazine articles reflected this backlash against women's growing independence, suggesting that the shifts in the gender order had left men impotent. Ads for body-building products chided men as weaklings.

> **A handful of famous women symbolized the threat reflected by women's gains in an age of uncertainty.**

Photoplay ran a story in 1929 about female celebrities, rife with hand-wringing over the prediction that men might one day be little more than "excess baggage" on a woman's quest for fame—especially if they were less famous or less well-paid than their wives, as was increasingly likely after the start of the Great Depression.

During and after the Depression, women still slowly gained ground in the labor force: in 1920, 23 percent of all women age fourteen and over were working for wages, and by 1940, that proportion was up to a full quarter. Kessler-Harris observes, "It is noteworthy not that women gained few jobs in the 1930s, but that they lost so little." Also, marriage was less likely to signal a retreat from the labor force. In 1920, 23 percent of married women worked for wages, compared with 36 percent in 1940. Since women's labor was cheaper than men's, their employment prospects were sometimes better, shifting the gendered balance of power within their families.

In "Hollywood is a Woman's Town," a 1932 article, *Photoplay* claims "women decide how men shall spend their money and their leisure hours," and *Motion Picture's* "The Women Who Made them Famous" from the same year credits women with the success of stars like Clark Gable and Maurice Chevalier. These women emasculate men, according to the magazine, by pursuing men romantically, a "reversal of the age-old formula of boy seeks girl."

Some of the men in question spoke up. Actor Douglas Fairbanks, Jr., for one, expressed his displeasure about the growing status of female stars in a 1934 *Photoplay* article. He claimed he was quitting the Hollywood life because leading ladies got too much attention. "The best that any [male actor] can look forward to is the ignominy of finding himself cast opposite the woman star who is momentarily in the ascendant. And to submit to that sort of thing is too stultifying for most men." A handful of famous women symbolized the threat reflected by women's gains in an age of uncertainty.

Fairbanks had recently divorced Joan Crawford, whose celebrity was a direct creation of the fan magazine—her very name was the result of a 1925 *Photoplay* contest to replace her given name, Lucille LeSueur. Crawford embodied the good-time flapper before transitioning into the quintessential powerful woman, broad shoulders and all. But by the end of the 1930s, she and fellow actress Katharine Hepburn had been labeled "box office poison." Hepburn's independent image (both on and off-screen) directly challenged traditional ideas. RKO canceled her contract in 1938, and she did not appear in films for two years. Crawford had to take a pay cut to have her contract renewed.

Magazines came to offer morality tales about women who focused too much on their careers and alienated men. Stories like "Is the Devil a Woman?" (*Motion Picture Classic*, 1930) and "Are Women Stars the Home Wreckers of Hollywood?" (*Motion Picture*, 1932) warned that women who out-earned and outshone the men in their lives might find themselves permanently single. "The minute a male star weds a film beauty he finds himself in a subordinate role," according to a March 1939 *Motion Picture* story. A 1935 *Photoplay* cover teased the article, "Why Male Stars Marry Plain Girls." Apparently

even beautiful women could be undesirable if they threatened the gender order. If even rich and famous women had to maintain a delicate balancing act, the magazines' everyday readers must have been overwhelmed.

hollywood wants you

In another shift, independent women soon became invaluable as the U.S. entered World War II. Hollywood fan magazines no longer portrayed strong women as devils; instead, articles and ads reminded female readers of their important role as workers in the war effort.

"Your Country needs you in a vital job!" an Ipana toothpaste ad beckoned, encouraging women "to release more men for wartime duties." A Beautyrest mattress ad bore the caption, "She'll do a man-sized job tomorrow!" and will be well rested for her "full-time regular job, (and) her after-hours war work." "Every woman is a war worker today!" a feminine hygiene ad proclaimed. A tampon ad pictured a woman changing a tire. Female pilots could be powerful yet feminine, according to an ad for nail polish. "America's Smart Flying Women Choose Favorite Cutex Shades" pictures women in uniform wearing shades named "On Duty," "Alert," and "Off Duty."

Features now characterized actors like Rosalind Russell as advocates for their own careers; a 1942 *Photoplay* story called "Don't Be a Doormat!" detailed confrontations with male studio bosses to get prized roles. "Who said Women aren't Men's Equals?" asked *Photoplay*. Both Joan Crawford and Katharine Hepburn saw their careers rebound in the war years. Strong women were back in vogue, but not for long.

When the war ended, the independent woman disappeared from fan magazine coverage again. Now (presumably suffering from whiplash) she could only serve as a warning to female readers that they might lose the men in their lives. Coverage of elaborate weddings became more frequent, and as the baby boom began, celebrity stories came to feature the now-omnipresent photos of nurseries, newborns, and baby showers, as well as features about how stars got their figures back after giving birth. Women's virtue was once again linked primarily with home and family.

Female celebrities who put child rearing and their husband's careers first gained high praise in these pages. Just as the fictional Lucy Ricardo schemed to get into her husband's shows to launch her own career (and create sitcom mayhem), celebrity stories emphasized how women who refused to put their husbands and children before their ambition were sure to face marital failure.

A 1948 *Photoplay* story accused "ambitious Aphrodites" of marrying as a career move. "Hollywood's

Biggest Headaches" were wives who tried to become as successful as their movie star husbands, according to a 1953 *Motion Picture* article: "Happiness is only possible with his wife at home." "Till Work do us Part," a 1947 *Photoplay* story, suggests Judy Garland and Vincente Minnelli's marriage troubles were largely due to her work schedule.

If a good wife wanted a career, she could work to support her husband's. Alan Ladd's wife Carol Sue Ladd, for instance, served as his agent. Stars who "made him her life's work," as Lauren Bacall allegedly did with Humphrey Bogart, would give husbands "the kind of push a man needs to send him soaring," according to a 1952 *Photoplay* story. "The husband couldn't possibly be where he is today . . . if the little woman hadn't been right behind him," the article concludes. World War II pinup Betty Grable wrote "Rules for Wives" for *Photoplay* in 1949, recommending that women learn to accept their husband's criticism.

"We Applaud Mrs. Robert Taylor," a 1957 *Photoplay* story announced, citing her decision to make "his career more important than hers" and "for giving up 'sophistication' to be a housewife and mother." "Behind every top actor you'll find a woman—living in the shadows of success and giving freely of courage, love, and devotion," wrote Hedda Hopper in a 1949 *Modern Screen* article.

According to the Bureau of Labor Statistics, in 1950 about a third of women sixteen and over were part of the paid labor force. Although part of postwar lore, the domesticity celebrated in movie fan magazines did not necessarily reflect the realities of their readers—or even of the celebrities they featured. Instead, celebrity stories reflected an ever-shifting ideology and the fact that women were simply less necessary (or even a hindrance for men returning from war and looking for work) in the paid labor force of the postwar economic boom.

For nearly a century now, movie stardom has offered women financial opportunities rarely available elsewhere. From their first publication, fan magazines touted women's upward mobility via movies, reflecting celebration and concern about women's increasing numbers in the paid labor force. And now, while celebrity stories no longer routinely blame women's ambition for relationships that don't work out, young women's morality is still a major source of gossip and judgment. Male celebrities' behavior isn't, of course, immune from disparaging gossip—Charlie Sheen's springs to mind—but an emphasis on young women's virtue echoes coverage from a hundred years ago, and has expanded well beyond fan magazines. If the pressures to be successful screen actors, doting wives and mothers, and sufficiently virtuous examples of femininity continue to bedevil even the most famous and privileged among us, one wonders how the rest of us are to manage such a thing.

recommended resources

Bielby, Denise D, and Bielby, William T. 2002. "Hollywood Dreams, Harsh Realities: Writing for Film and Television," *Contexts 1*(4):21–27. A comprehensive analysis of the challenges writers face navigating careers in Hollywood.

Braudy, Leo. 1986. *Frenzy of Renown: Fame and its History*. London: Oxford University Press. An exploration of fame in history, including discussion of the Roman Empire, ancient Greece, religiosity, and the democratization of fame.

Gamson, Joshua. 1994. *Claims to Fame: Celebrity in Contemporary America*. Oakland, CA: University of California Press. A study of how celebrity is produced by the culture industry, offering historical analysis, ethnographic accounts, as well as audience reception analysis.

Kessler-Harris, Alice. 2007. *Gendering Labor History*. Champaign, IL: University of Illinois Press. A collection of essays about women's labor force participation in U.S. history.

Rosen, Marjorie. 1973. *Popcorn Venus: Women, Movies and the American Dream*. New York: Coward, McCann & Geoghegan, Inc. Uses movies from the silent era to the 1960s to analyze changes in portrayals of women in film.

#callmecaitlyn and contemporary trans* visibility

d'lane compton and tristan bridges

winter 2016

It seems the media is discussing transgender people more than ever. This has the potential to promote social justice using celebrity faces as potent symbols for gender diversity, transgender rights, and more. They bring awareness and help expand the public's vocabulary regarding greater gender possibilities.

Although this is good news overall, public attention and support must extend and translate into legislation and rights. Paradoxically, trans* celebrities may be bringing attention to trans* issues *and* obscuring diversity within trans* communities. Simply put, not all transgender people are being celebrated. (We use trans* to denote the diversity of trans identities.)

In May 2014, *Time* put a transgender individual, Laverne Cox, on its cover. Just under a year later, Caitlyn Jenner came out as a transwoman, featured on the June 2015 cover of *Vanity Fair* alongside a story titled "Call Me Caitlyn." Quickly, the hashtag #CallMeCaitlyn took social media by storm, and Caitlyn Jenner broke the record for fastest accumulation of one million Twitter followers (four hours, beating out President Barack Obama's @POTUS record).

Jenner's case is interesting precisely because of her achievements and notoriety as Bruce. As Bruce, she was a successful Olympic decathlete, a status cast as the pinnacle of human athleticism and masculinity. In fact, when Jenner won gold in 1976, there was no women's decathlon event. Now featured on the cover of *Vanity Fair*, Caitlyn has arguably been held up as a gold standard of femininity. One person has reached some of the greatest heights of gendered status as both a man and woman.

Jenner is also a cross-generation celebrity—known to previous age cohorts as a sports hero, and now popular as a member of one of the most visible and followed contemporary celebrity families in the U.S. Jenner's celebrity invites gossip, but it might also prove a powerful way to start a discussion regarding gender and social justice issues related to gender, bodies, and civil liberties.

Through Jenner's transition, the American public is becoming familiar with transgender people, problems, and politics. For example, in her reality show, *I Am Cait*, she not only shares her experience but also gives attention to the experiences and knowledge of others, including transgender youth and long-time activists like Kate Bornstein and Jennifer Finney Boylan.

Yet existing research primarily paints a bleak picture of the experiences and lives of transgender people. Transgender youth suffer from depression at rates much higher than the general population, and they are at a much higher risk of suicide, homelessness, and homicide. The National Transgender Discrimination Survey found that about 1 in 4 trans* people have lost a job due to bias and discrimination, 1 in 2 experience harassment at work, and 1 in 5 were evicted from or denied housing as a result of their gender identity. Those transgender people who are least likely to experience the most damaging consequences are those best able to approximate heteronormative, cisgender ideals. This often means demonstrating feminine and masculine beauty and body standards associated with being "cis," or having a gender identity that is consistent with the one assigned to them at birth. The cultural standards the transgender people we most readily encounter in the media are less easily achieved—and not necessarily desired—by everyone identifying as trans* gender.

Moreover, while #CallMeCaitlyn was trending, #Occupotty and #TransLivesMatter received much less attention. #Occupotty began in reaction to proposed "bathroom bills" seeking to legally mandate that individuals use the public restroom facility associated with their assigned sex at birth. Bathroom bills are most often proposed and justified by playing on inaccurate stereotypes of transgender people as sexually deviant and potentially violent. Indeed, they are generally proposed as safety measures, though transgender women and men are much more likely to be the *victims* than the perpetrators of harassment and assault. The fears these bills play on are manufactured, but powerful. Fear of deviant men invading girls' bathrooms, for instance, led a Houston gay rights ordinance to fail—by a wide margin—in a public referendum last fall.

The public celebration and recognition of transgender people is a start, but it has not yet been matched by achievements in gender equality and diversity. There are limits to what celebration can do. Now we must work toward the legal and institutional changes required to turn ideals into policy.

dancing the body beautiful

julia a. ericksen

spring 2012

In the professional Latin event at a ballroom dance competition, men wear dance pants with tight shirts open to the waist, showing bulging chest muscles. Their hair, which must stay motionless and shiny for the entire event, is glued back with gel and blow-dried with hair spray. Faces are tanned, and matte makeup makes the skin appear translucent and blemishfree. Men's high-heeled shoes are immaculate and usually black, as is the costume. Bodies are perfectly proportioned with no fat in sight.

Each handsome man frames an equally gorgeous woman, wearing a brightly colored skimpy dress that flares out with every move, embellished with hundreds of Swarovski crystals, glued by hand, as well as earrings, bracelets, and necklaces in matching stones. High-heeled, open-toed shoes are typically flesh-colored, to make legs look longer. Women's backs are bare and tanned, and faces are elaborately made up. Hair is long, swept up or in a ponytail. Not only are the bodies taut and muscular, but the heights and looks of each member of the couple are purposely matched.

While looks have always been important on the dance floor, they have become increasingly important in recent years, especially in Latin dance. Clothing has become more revealing and unforgiving of imperfections, and dancers' concern with appearance has intensified. Dancers' identities have become intertwined with the bodywork they do, and the bodies they produce.

I became interested in studying ballroom and Latin dance after my husband and I started taking lessons about 10 years ago. I had danced as an adolescent. My parents, like many members of their post-World War I generation, met on the dance floor (in Blackpool, in the North of England), on what is now a famous competition dance

floor. I abandoned ballroom when it fell out of favor in the 1960s. Recently, I became passionate about learning to dance, and also about competing.

Every weekend in America, students compete in "pro/am" (professional-amateur) dance, which means that they dance with their teachers. They compete during the day and watch professional competitions at night. Pro/am began in chain dance studios as a way for professional dancers to supplement their incomes and subsidize professional competition. It is now so popular and lucrative that professionals from all over the world come to the U.S. to teach and compete.

The over-the-top look of Latin dance used to puzzle me, but now I embrace it, along with the demands it puts on the performer. In addition to the pleasure of syncopated steps in time to sexy Latin music, I love the intimacy of the dance studio, and the permission it gives me to violate the rules about touching a man other than my husband. I like the fact that students view the professional dancers as their models for what a dancer should look like, and that well-toned older bodies in skimpy costumes are a common sight. It has made me interested in improving my body, and I am happy that at age 70 I have flexibility, balance, and strength.

As a sociologist, I became interested in how professional dancers—especially Latin—produce the bodies we see on the dance floor. My interviews and ethnographic research on top dancers suggests that bodywork has become increasingly important to Latin dance in recent years.

tsvetanka's story

A dancer in her late twenties, whom I call Tsvetanka, had been dancing since age four. Off the floor, most dancers look ordinary, but Tsvetanka is stunningly beautiful. She describes her look as the result of hard work, and puts constant effort into creating and maintaining her appearance. This bodywork begins with physical exercise. Tsvetanka takes gyrotonics classes—an exercise similar to Pilates and popular among dancers—twice a week, in addition to hours of dance daily. In the beginning, she worried that she might get too bulky, but found instead, she said, that her body "became longer, more stretched." In her late teens Tsvetanka had been "chubby, not chubby-chubby, but my thighs were bigger." Everyone noticed the change, after she started gyrotonics, because the exercise regimen elongated her muscles and "created more elegance." It also improved her flexibility, strength, and balance.

Tsvetanka was careful about diet. When she was younger, she and her partner would "eat whatever," but now they have a nutritionist who teaches them "what is good and what is bad," and "how to eat for energy." They eat nothing that is not part of their prescribed regimen. This is in marked contrast to earlier years in her home country, when they survived their first overseas competition by smuggling salami, bread and ketchup across the border, using the little money they had to buy stones for her dress. Their hunger did not matter, she said, because they finally had the chance to see the all-time Latin dance greats, Donnie Burns and Gaynor Fairweather. After that, said Tsvetanka, "We were hooked, we wanted to be like them, from the makeup to the dress, to everything."

In addition to creating her physical body, Tsvetanka spends countless hours planning her costumes. She keeps a "little board" beside the dining table and "everything I like, from the Oscars, from the Grammys, from the red carpet, I cut from the newspapers and magazines, and I put there." Every day, her husband/partner adds ideas, sometimes from other competitions, creating designs for her next dress. Even at mealtime, they are absorbed in bodywork. After her dresses are made, she spends hours decorating them with stones herself, and decorating Pavel's shirts to match hers. On the day of the competition, this appearance work intensifies. They put on their tans, and apply eyelashes and makeup. Since Tsvetanka is not particularly good with her hair, Pavel does it, as he has done so "since [they] were little kids," she says. Sometimes she helps him with his hair and makeup as well.

Tsventanka and her partner have compatible looks, which she believes is important. They are tall, dark, and slender with long legs. Tsvetanka believes that their similar shapes aid their dancing, as well as their appearance. "I've seen couples where both man and the lady are very, very good, but for some reason," she says, "the body structure, it's not as great." Having compatible body structures is important, she says, "if you want to have a great success." They coordinate their clothing to accentuate this similarity. (Tsvetanka's point about the importance of matching bodies is illustrated by the images of dancers Gherman Mustic and Iveta Lukosiute, pictured left. Like Tsvetanka, Iveta's semi-nude body reveals gleaming, tanned muscles, and her height matches that of her slender but muscular partner.)

While most professional dancers told me that the quality of the dancing should be the most important part of competition, they recognized that flawless beauty creates the appearance that they have a romantic relationship. "You have to be very well attached on the personal level," says Tsvetanka, who believes that relationships appear more genuine and passionate when those involved are beautiful. In Latin dancing, unlike other forms of dance, audience members call out the names of their favorite couples during competitions. Dancers like Tsvetanka exert great discipline and control to achieve bodies that look "naturally" sexy.

The cultural mandate of thinness is also evident on the dance floor. While ballet dancers must be waif-like, with no perceptible curves, Latin dancers are supposed to be curvaceous but slender—not as thin as ballerinas, but without an ounce of extra fat. The appearance work Tsvetanka performs, both as part of her regular routine and before a competition, makes performances more pleasurable for the judges, the viewers, as well as for the dancer and her partner. We are conditioned to enjoy looking at what we see as desirable, and to believe in the story beautiful dancers tell. But their beautiful bodies are the products of rigorous behind-the-scenes discipline.

This appearance work also naturalizes gender, making it visible and obvious. Bodies in Latin dance are strictly gendered, and while some of the men are openly gay, the performance is always heterosexual, facilitating audiences' fantasies of heterosexual romance. Though ballroom audiences are knowledgeable about dancing and about the work involved in creating an illusion, they respond to this romantic fantasy. Couples accentuate this by wearing matching outfits.

> *Dancers' identities have increasingly become intertwined with their bodywork.*

Gender scholar Susan Bordo, in her book *Unbearable Weight*, describes a culture in which slender, athletic bodies have come to represent the ideal woman in control of her appearance and destiny. Women are logically responding to the culture when they go to great lengths to monitor how they look. At the same time, fashioning their appearance also gives women power and pleasure. Historian Kathy Peiss, in her history of American beauty culture, *Hope in a Jar*, argues that the pursuit of beauty "has never been only a regimen of self-appraisal and surveillance." Women use clothing and makeup for many purposes: to declare adulthood, sexual allure, and to define themselves.

> " *This appearance work naturalizes gender, making it visible and obvious.*

Tsvetanka's attention to her body is an extreme example of Bordo's point, testifying to the satisfaction she achieves from looking beautiful on the dance floor. Her whole identity is bound up in dance, but also in the bodywork she undertakes. While Latin dancers like Tsvetanka take this idealization of beautiful bodies to a higher level than most Americans, now that I dance, I experience some of this, too. I take Pilates and gyrotonics and have become more flexible, and I have greater control over my core muscles. These abilities are important in dancing, but they provide an additional pleasure when one lives in a body that one has improved through hard work and discipline. These changes are not something I imagined were possible to achieve; I grew up in a world where you accepted the body you were born with.

no chubbies

In the past, men were taught to make their partner the focal point of the performance, using expressions like "the man is the frame and the woman is the picture." Today, this traditional obligation is weaker. Many men display themselves almost as much as they display their partners. For example, Pavel, Tsvetanka's husband and partner, is as involved in appearance work as his wife. Partners, he says, "have to match well, and they have to look beautiful, and they have to match the bodies." To accomplish this, Pavel works on every aspect of his body and its presentation. Because he does not want to be too "chubby" or too skinny, in addition to careful diet and practice and the many hours he spends coaching and teaching students, he takes gyrotonics classes, uses a Pilates machine at home, and has a personal trainer at the gym. He needs the personal trainer, he says, "because my legs are long compared with my torso." In order to be, "connected with the center [of your body], you get tired." He works on his upper body, and on general physical toning.

Pavel has a complicated routine before each competition. He eats, drinks coffee, and does pushups to engage his core, and then focuses on his appearance. He shaves and does his hair, as well as his partner's. As Tsvetanka puts on her makeup, he offers her constant advice, "Do more of this. Don't do that." Sometimes they fix their costumes, or experiment with something new. Finally, two hours before the competition, when they are happy with their looks, they warm up together, and get into the competitive mood by listening to music and talking quietly.

Pavel believes that their meticulous attention to detail pays off. "In the beginning," he notes, "when we didn't know how to dance so good—because we always dress well, we always did good." Some dancers, he adds, do not know this. "Sometimes you go to practice, and you see very good couples, and you're like 'Wow, damn, they're very good.' Then the competition starts, and they wear crap. The girl has such a gorgeous body, and, she puts so much stuff on her, she looks like a Christmas tree." Pavel believes that it is important to impress the judges and the audience with the right appearance and look before the dancing begins. Clothing should show dancers' best features and hide the flaws, he says.

One might contrast the story of these dancers, who are at the peak of their competitive careers, with a somewhat older dancer, Peter, who retired from professional competition at about the time that bodywork increased in importance. When asked about exercise, he pays lip service to the idea: "I should. I don't," he says. These days he notes, "couples coming up are doing exercise, they are going to the gym, they are getting bodies beautiful." However, he believes that dance itself is sufficient exercise: "When you're practicing every day, you're dancing, you're teaching people to do it the right way. You're exaggerating the movements; you're actually using a lot of resistance in your own body to show them." Peter adds, "I could always do more exercise, and I could always be fitter, and that would help, but I don't want to be so tired that I can't do anything." When asked about his diet, Peter smiles and says, "Before a competition I eat less ice cream." When he prepares for competitions, he adds, "the weight just drops off you." Though he might put a few pounds on afterwards, he is confident that it will come off.

Peter's account is typical of older dancers who put their energy into practicing and worried less about their appearance. Peter credits being "mentally strong on the competition floor" for his success. He never gives in; he describes his attitude as "a lot of sheer bloody-mindedness really." Every now and then, he turns over a new leaf by going to the gym for a few weeks. However he adds, "then I'm travelling or I'm teaching and suddenly I don't have the time." Peter believes that bodies can be improved through hard work, but it is not a priority for him as it is for younger dancers. His identity as a dancer is not as dependent on looks.

Still appearances matter. "When you're out on the floor, first impressions count," he says. This means having "the right costume, the right hair, the right makeup." Furthermore, he says, "it helps if you've got a beautiful girl; it helps if you have a handsome guy." Still, he believes "people who are not so good-looking, or bit of a funny shape" could overcome this if they dance well. He names past champions who did not have beautiful, matching bodies, suggesting that they overcame their body limitations through the force of their personalities, and through their dancing skill. Only a few years ago, the world champion, Bryan Watson, covered his belly with a long shirt that hung over his pants. His partner, Carmen Vicenji, was slender, but she was cavalier about her appearance, and wore her hair in a short, manageable bob. For younger dancers today, appearance is increasingly important.

the pursuit of perfection

The body project is not simply something that dancers *do*. Increasingly, it is who they *are*. Their identities are bound up not only in what they do on the floor, but also in how they look. Why this change has occurred is not entirely clear. Perhaps perfection appears to be more attainable today. As exercise and diet are pushed by the media and absorbed by the public, bodywork has become a generalized part of our culture. Every young dancer I interviewed believes that bodies are malleable, and that it is incumbent upon them to achieve their body's fullest potential. One Latin dancer says, "Your body is the only thing you ever truly own," so of course you should treat it carefully and work hard to improve it. The idea of "owning" something that is part of you is a perfect illustration of the ways the body has become a "project."

Having largely ignored the body, sociologists have recently become interested in how social systems create the bodies we inhabit, and how bodies limit and enable social forms. While our ideas about what is possible and what is beautiful arise from our culture, the physical body places limits on these expectations. Latin dancers have moved from a world where it is possible to enhance one's body, but only to a degree, to a world where the possibilities of perfection seem limitless and where, if these limits seem insurmountable, partners must change. Younger dancers like Pavel and Tsvetanka feel a moral imperative to perfect their bodies and their appearance, and to dance with a partner whose looks enhance their own. Savvy about creating a visual image of heterosexual romance, they offer an extreme example of the pervasive ways we are all encouraged to discipline our bodies.

> *The body project is not simply something dancers do; it is who they are.*

recommended resources

Bordo, Susan. 1993. *Unbearable Weight: Feminism, Western Culture and the Body.* Oakland, CA: University of California Press. The classic book on the tyranny of the body.

Ericksen, Julia A. 2011. *Dance with Me: Ballroom Dance and the Promise of Instant Intimacy.* New York: New York University Press. This is an account of the emotional connection between dancers of all levels and talents.

Featherstone, Mike. 1982. "The Body in Consumer Culture," *Theory, Culture, and Society 1*:18–33. This early essay in the sociology of the body describes the growing importance of bodywork in contemporary culture generally.

Marion, Jonathan S. 2008. *Ballroom, Culture and Costume in Competitive Dance.* Oxford: Berg. A detailed account of the clothing decisions of ballroom dancers.

discrimination and dress codes in urban nightlife

reuben a. buford may

winter 2015

It was Friday night and Terrence, an African-American college student, was looking forward to heading out to Figaro's—a popular nightclub in a midsize, predominantly White, college town I'll call Northeast, Georgia. Terrence knew Figaro's might have a dress code, so he pulled out a pair of new, relaxed-fit jeans, and a white, short sleeve, button down collared shirt, and brown loafers to complete his collegiate look. With his also carefully dressed African-American friend Calvin, Terrence arrived at Figaro's, where the bouncer, a tall White male, took one look at them and said, "I can't let you in with those baggy jeans. We have a dress code." The bouncer pointed to a sign over his right shoulder: "No baggy jeans or shirts, No tank tops, No gym shoes, No necklaces, No du rags, No white t-shirts, No hats turned sideways, No Jerseys. DRESS CODE STRICTLY ENFORCED."

"But there were two guys in front of me wearing the same kind of clothes and you let them in," Terrence protested. Calvin, sensing his friend's growing frustration, interrupted. "Come on man. Let's just go. You know why those other guys got in." Calvin left off the rest of the sentence: the other patrons were White.

Terrence's rejection seems to reflect an increasingly common experience for African-American men seeking access to popular nightclubs in places like Northeast. Media reports from cities like Chicago and New Orleans suggest that dress codes *are*, in fact, used in racially discriminatory ways. For instance, the owners of Original Mother's—a nightclub in Chicago's upscale Gold Coast area—reached an agreement with six out-of-town Black college students denied access. The students, visiting from Washington University in St. Louis, alleged that Original Mother's had used a dress code against baggy pants to racially profile them. As proof, they pointed out that they had switched pants with their White friends, who then promptly gained admittance. Same pants, different skin. Worse, at the Razzo Bar and Patio in New Orleans in 2005, Levon Jones, a student at Georgia State University, and his friend were denied admission because his friend purportedly did not meet the club's dress code. A fight broke out between Jones and the bouncers, and Jones was killed. Around the U.S., in privately owned but ostensibly public entertainment venues, dress codes have become an informal color line.

Few sociologists have explored issues explicitly related to race, class, and access in urban nightlife. Based on my participation, observation, and interviews with patrons of nightlife in Northeast, the implementation and use of

> *Around the U.S., in privately owned but ostensibly public venues, dress codes are an informal color line.*

dress codes against hip hop fashion are a major topic. In my work, I've found three distinct experiences among the African-American men of Northeast's nightlife: first, there are men who refuse to change their style, get rejected from the nightclubs, and accuse the owners of racial discrimination. Then there are African-American men who generally sport a middle-class, college student fashion, gain access to nightclubs, and do not feel that the dress codes target African Americans. Finally, there are the young men like Terrence, who anticipate the dress codes and adopt the "proper" attire, but still get rejected from the clubs. They feel targeted. Each groups' thoughts on dress codes illustrate how race and class are closely tied in racial discrimination and nightlife.

race, boundaries, and bouncers

Like Figaro's, many public entertainment facilities throughout urban America have dress code requirements. Since nightclubs are privately owned, they can legally impose dress codes as long as they can demonstrate consistency in the use and enforcement of those rules. Some high-status individuals may occasionally violate dress codes without reprimand, but, in general the dress codes provide a means by which owners can control who uses their facilities, limiting patrons to a preferred clientele.

Typically, dress codes are directed at men's attire. There are a number of possible explanations for why women's clothing is not the subject of dress code enforcement, but the most prevalent is that men, especially Black men, are considered a bigger threat and more prone to disorderly conduct than women. Indeed, in her study of an elite nightclub in Boston, Lauren Rivera found that bouncers used multiple cues to determine who might be trouble. The gatekeepers told Rivera they believed women were the least difficult patrons and worthy of less surveillance than men—particularly those men perceived to be potential "troublemakers" based on their attire.

Race and class clash at these clubs, many of which feature hip hop music but restrict the clothing styles associated with hip hop culture. Perhaps drawing on the iconography of rap as a subculture expressing the experiences of young, poor minority men, it's possible that nightclub owners see the musical messages as a sort of warning. Such owners contend that dress codes are a matter of public safety, citing fights at other nightclubs or police suggestions that the rules keep order. The unspoken part is that nightlife participants who wear hip hop clothing are seen as lower class and likely to threaten the enjoyment and pleasure of other club-goers.

An African-American male in fresh white sneakers or sporting a flashy gold chain—elsewhere signs of status and disposable income—becomes, irrespective of his economic class, education, or cultural sensibilities, a threat. At the very least, he *looks* like one to the people who make the rules.

When I spoke with a few owners and bouncers in Northeast regarding the disproportionate impact of dress codes on African Americans, they simply repeated that they were seeking to attract a certain type of clientele. It had nothing to do with race, they said. Then again, consider who was asking the questions: I am an African-American male.

One former nightclub manager, a White male, shared a different perspective, however. He said, "Yes, we had to institute dress codes, and to me the dress codes are discriminatory. But we started to have trouble with drugs and stuff. There were just too many problems going on there. That's one of the reasons I left." While he suggested a discriminatory tone to the dress codes, he justified their enforcement for public safety. Few managers, owners, or bouncers are likely to be so candid. Explicitly acknowledging the function of dress codes in African-American males' nightlife could bring anything from bad publicity to legal action.

> *Dress codes provide a means by which club owners can limit patrons to a preferred clientele.*

a night out in northeast

As an African-American male growing up in Chicago, I had been intrigued by the hustle and bustle of city nightlife. It was when I moved to the South, near Northeast, that I had the opportunity to study it in earnest. For three years, I made weekly visits to nightclubs. I soon saw that, although official dress codes specifically targeted clothing styles and not persons, African-American men were disproportionately affected. It's also when I started to realize that, among the young men I saw going out, there were three different responses to dress code enforcement.

As I described in the intro, some African-American men view the dress codes as racially discriminatory, while others see them as unfortunate, but not specifically related to race. Still others expressed frustration, arguing that bouncers were selectively enforcing the dress codes, even when club-goers had carefully dressed to meet the rules. These varied perspectives reveal a complicated relationship between race and social class and how each is policed in formal and informal ways.

The nightlife participants who saw discrimination based their conclusion on two observations. First, they pointed out that there was nothing particularly distinctive about the quality of clothing permitted or not permitted in the nightclubs (particularly apropos given that Northeast's nightclubs are less selective than large city nightclubs and rarely require an admissions fee). Second, they suggested that if observers were to consider the cost of clothing, they would discover that some of the African-American men's clothing was quite expensive. Although questions of dress aesthetics and style of dress can't be answered with price tags alone, as sociologist Pierre Bourdieu indicates, these African-American men, typically lower-class, local patrons, took the cost of clothing as a proxy for appropriate dress. Considering both observations, the men told me they could only conclude the rules weren't about their clothes, but about *them*.

> **One former nightclub manager said, "Yes, we had to institute dress codes . . . to me [they] are discriminatory."**

Joe, an African American, explains the paradox of policing hip hop style in a hip hop club this way: "The dress code policy or whatever is basically, no jean shorts, no athletic wear, no jewelry, no excessive jewelry. Anything that's like, in reference to the hip-hop culture is excluded. It's excluded from downtown, but at the same time they wanna play all the hip hop music, you know what I'm saying? But they don't want Black people in the club. It's like a contradiction. They can play the music, but we can't dress the part."

For patrons like Joe, playing hip hop without permitting its fashion is direct resistance to African Americans' participation in the nightlife. Such exclusionary practices resemble past eras when Whites have exploited the cultural products of Black creativity—like jazz and blues music—while excluding Blacks from full participation in enjoying those products. The White-owned nightclubs and music venues where the music was being played, in some instances by African-American performers, were as selective about admittance as Northeast's clubs are today.

> **Dress codes, race, class, fashion, and exclusion interact when African-American men step up to the bouncer.**

Interestingly, some White patrons are unaware of the dress codes. For instance, I asked Eric, a 22-year-old White male who frequents Northeast's downtown clubs in polo shirts and khakis, what he thought about the dress codes: "What dress codes?" he asked. "They have dress codes for bars in downtown Northeast? I didn't know." Either White patrons like Eric do not wear clothing subjected to the dress codes or their clothing is not as closely scrutinized as that worn by similarly dressed African-American men.

Thus, as you might expect, the African-American men I spoke with who had gotten into the clubs had been dressed like their middle-class, White, college student counterparts. They told me they saw the dress codes as the owners' prerogative and dressed carefully so as to get in. Derrick is typical: a regular at Northeast's nightclubs, he also frequents all-Black nightclubs in Atlanta. While neither of the two Black-owned clubs in Northeast uses a dress code, Derrick finds Black-owned clubs in Atlanta implement dress codes and they're enforced by Black bouncers. He commented, "The nightclubs are not racist. It's just insurance against letting the wrong kind of people in. You know, the kind of people that start fights and stuff." Like the nightclubs' owners, Derrick justifies the use and implementation of dress codes as a matter of safety, not racism.

Terrell, another downtown Northeast regular, views the use of dress codes somewhat differently. He has been rejected from nightclubs because he enjoys wearing hip-hop style clothes. Now he adapts: "They might have come up with dress codes that target clothes worn mostly by minorities, but if you wanna get in, you gotta conform. You gotta put on your collared, buttoned-down shirts. That's reasonable." For Terrell, it matters little whether the nightclub owners are motivated by race, because the code isn't unachievable. In his eyes, the dress codes are simply a condition of entry, no more inflammatory than a cover charge.

Although some African-American men gain access to the Northeast nightclubs, their experiences are complicated by the feeling that they are still not readily *welcomed*. Both middle- and lower-class African-American men in my study shared recollections that highlighted ways in which their behaviors, interactions, and movements on the streets and in the nightclubs were under constant surveillance. Other patrons, bouncers, and police cannot, or do not care to, readily distinguish between those African-American men who pose a threat and those who do not. For these observers, race is a proxy for threat.

Perhaps it is this overall sense of being unwelcome yet constantly watched that underlies the third group of African-American men's views. They believe the dress codes are actually race codes. They argue that, after they have intentionally selected their clothing to fit the dress code, they are still rejected. Recall Terrence's rejection from Figaro's at the opening of this article. For Terrence, the most troubling aspect of his experience is that there is no satisfactory answer to his implicit question: Why am I being shut out when I am following the dress code? Ostensibly, he is being rejected for failure to meet an objective standard. Yet White patrons get in. Maybe there is a subtle difference between what Terrence is wearing and what the White males are wearing that Terrence just cannot see. Perhaps the bouncer has unfairly evaluated Terrence's attire or simply missed the White males' violation of the dress code. Or maybe the White males are local celebrities with elevated status and so they do not have to comply with the dress codes. Terrence is befuddled. Whatever the potential explanations, Terrence can only conclude he is a victim of racial discrimination.

The velvet ropes separating in-groups from out-groups hold different meanings for these three groups of men. Dress codes, race, class, fashion, and exclusion all interact when African-American men step up to the bouncer.

worn down

Local civil rights commissions typically find dress codes defensible as long as nightclub owners can demonstrate that the codes are applied consistently and are not used to single out or refuse groups based on their racial or ethnic background—a point owners can easily make by demonstrating the mere presence of a member of that group in the nightclub. But the owners' practice of permitting a small number of African Americans or employing African-American bouncers to enforce the dress codes may simply mask the intentional use of dress codes to hinder African Americans' participation in the nightlife.

Whether nightclub dress codes are intentionally or unintentionally used in a racially discriminatory manner is a complex issue. Based on my conversations with African-American men in Northeast, Georgia, it is clear that many carry the burden of evaluating their experiences at the nightclubs against the backdrop of negative stereotypes.

There is little explicit "proof" of racial discrimination, but the African-American men's awareness that their attire will be thoroughly scrutinized and that they risk humiliation despite their efforts to meet the dress code make for a potentially troubling experience at the thresholds of nightclubs. Couple this possibility with African-American men's overall feelings that they are unwelcome and it's little wonder that many don't even try to gain access to popular urban nightclubs. In effect, if not by design, these men are constrained by race, even when it comes to a night out with friends.

recommended resources

Bourdieu, Pierre. 1984. *Distinction: A Social Critique of the Judgment of Taste.* Cambridge, MA: Harvard University Press. Investigates how social, cultural, and educational cues are used to communicate social status in society.

Grazian, David. 2007. *On the Make: The Hustle of Urban Nightlife.* Chicago, IL: University of Chicago Press. Explores the practices of nightclub owners, promoters, and nightlife participants as they engage in the cultural production of the nightlife experience.

May, Reuben A. B, and Chaplin, Kenneth S. 2008. "Cracking the Code: Race, Class, and Access in Urban America," *Qualitative Sociology* 31:57–72. Examines the significance of culture, tastes, race, and social class for African-American men's mobility in public spaces.

Rivera, Lauren. 2010. "Status Distinctions in Interaction: Social Selection and Exclusion at an Elite Nightclub," *Qualitative Sociology* 33:229–255. Shows how Boston's bouncers evaluate the status of potential nightlife patrons for inclusion or exclusion.

scripting gender
sport

overview

Through sports boys learn how to compete against one another, how to work in teams, and how to "be men." As girls and women become more involved in sports, they navigate scripts of femininity which may be at odds with the ideals of athleticism. The gendered scripts of sports shape athletes as well as spectators.

In her article, "Tiger Girls on the Soccer Field," Hilary Levey Friedman examines the scripts of femininity associated with afterschool activities for young girls. Some parents encourage their daughters to become involved in activities that stress characteristics typically associated with masculinity in order to help them succeed in male-dominated spaces later in life. These scripts are classed, too, and are based on who has access to these activities. Scott Melzer describes in his article, "Ritual Violence in a Two-Car Garage," how one group of men uses a Fight Club style form of violence to express and manage their emotions. In "The Sanctity of Sunday Football: Why Men Love Sports," Doug Hartmann describes the importance of sports in teaching boys about masculinity and offering men a way of relating to each other.

Cheryl Cooky and Nicole M. Lavoi look at the state of women's sports after Title IX and find that there are limited ways of being a female athlete. In "Muslim Female Athletes and the Hijab," Geoff Harkness and Samira Islam analyze the choice to wear or not to wear the hijab in order to understand the new gender scripts Muslim women athletes are creating. Finally, the photographic essay "Babes in Bikeland" by Bjorn Christianson explores the world of alleycat bike racing for women/trans/femme (WTF) cyclists. In a male dominated space, WTFs have been made to actively create space and scripts for themselves.

things to consider

- Organized sports are an important part of the socialization process for young children across the United States. Whether you participated in sports or not, what are some benefits of experiencing sports at a young age? Are any of these benefits stereotypically gendered?

- How are race and class also present in gendered messages within sports?

- Take a moment to consider how women in professional sports combat, embrace, or reject efforts to masculinize themselves and their bodies.

- Sports tend to be one accepted avenue for men and boys to safely express emotions, specifically anger and joy. What would need to change in sports culture to promote a more well-rounded vision of masculinity?

tiger girls on the soccer field

hilary levey friedman

fall 2013

Charlotte, age 9, told me about her experiences playing competitive soccer: "At recess I'm like the only girl playing soccer. Everyone else is doing something else. So usually they call me a tomboy because I'm playing with the boys. But I'm NOT a tomboy. A tomboy is somebody who like wants to be a boy and is like always being with the boys and stuff. I have dolls and I like pink. I really like girl things, like I painted my nails."

To Charlotte, being a tomboy is a negative label. She is more eager to identify with her femininity, pointing out how she paints her nails and wears pink. She wants a strong femininity, the kind that lets her be an aggressive soccer player, too. "We play soccer against boys sometimes because it's better for the girls to learn to be more aggressive," she told me. While Charlotte thinks girls can be just as good as boys at soccer, she thinks they'll only improve if they become as tough as the boys.

Her mom Marie agrees. Looking ahead, she sees competitive sports as a way for her daughter to become aggressive—not just in the athletic arena, but also in life. Marie told me, "We have no illusions that our daughter is going to be a great athlete. But the team element [is important]. I worked for Morgan Stanley for 10 years, and I interviewed applicants, and that ability to work on a team was a crucial part of our hiring process. So it's a skill that comes into play much later. It's not just about ball skills or hand-eye coordination."

"When I was interviewing job candidates at Morgan Stanley," Marie, a White woman with two Ivy League degrees, told me, "if I got a female candidate—because it's banking and you need to be aggressive, you need

to be tough—if she played, like, ice hockey, *done*. My daughter's playing, and I'm just a big believer in kids learning to be confidently aggressive, and I think that plays out in life assertiveness."

Many parents like Marie believe that being cut-throat and aggressive sets girls on a path to the corner office as a company executive. The higher up you go in the class hierarchy, the more likely you will encounter parents like Marie, who believe in teaching their daughters what I call "aggressive femininity." They are taught to be both physically and competitively forceful, actively subsuming aspects of their femininity; many of their parents define their daughters in opposition to "girly girls."

As Sheryl Sandberg, CEO of Facebook and author of the bestseller *Lean In*, declared that "Instead of calling our daughters bossy, let's say, 'My daughter has executive leadership skills!'" Girls today grow up in a world with an unprecedented set of educational and professional opportunities, and many look up to successful women like Sandberg. More girls will graduate from college and earn advanced degrees than ever before, and nearly all professions are open to them, even combat careers in the military.

Successful women want to raise daughters who share the qualities that have brought them success—qualities that some liken to bossiness.

nice girls competing

When I studied 95 families with elementary school-age children who were involved in competitive afterschool activities—chess, dance, and soccer—I met parents like Marie who saw their kids' participation in competitive afterschool activities as a way to develop certain values and skills: the importance of winning; the ability to bounce back from a loss to win in the future; to perform within time limits; to succeed in stressful situations; and to perform under the gaze of others—what I call "Competitive Kid Capital."

One of the most striking findings was that upper-middle class parents of girls often perceive a link between aggression and success in athletics, and are more likely to enroll their daughters in soccer or chess, rather than dance—activities that are deemed more cooperative and less competitive. Like Sheryl Sandberg, they believe that executive leadership skills can be effectively developed and honed on soccer fields and basketball courts, even when the competitors are wearing pink shoes and jerseys.

> **Many parents believe that being cut-throat and aggressive sets girls on a path to the corner office as a company executive.**

Malcolm, an African-American lawyer with three Ivy League degrees, believes that sports don't just steer his seven-year-old daughter toward assertiveness, they actively drive her away from more traditionally feminine pursuits. "She's a cute little girl, but I don't like her to be a girly-girl," he explained. "You know, I don't want her to be a cheerleader—nothing against that—but I want her to prepare to have the option, if she wants to be an executive in a company, that she can play on that turf. And if she's kind of a girly-girl, maybe she'll be a secretary. There's nothing wrong with that, but let her have the option of doing something else if she wants."

Malcolm thinks being a "girly-girl" means less desirable, more traditionally feminine occupations. The images he evokes related to being an executive, such as "play on that turf," suggests the importance he places on athletics to help his daughter follow a historically male career path. And he identifies cheerleading—which was once a male-dominated area and still has an athletic and competitive component, even as the athletes are now expected to wear make-up, curl their hair, and often bare their midriffs—as being too much of a girly-girl activity.

sports make the girl

Today, sports are an important element of American upper-middle-class culture and child-rearing practices. But as recently as a century ago, organized team sports were limited to males. Women and girls were generally seen as physically inferior and mentally unable to handle competition. Even when they were allowed to participate, competition was off-limits, and seen as damaging.

When New York City's Public Schools Athletic Girls League was founded in 1905, for example, the director was opposed to keeping records, arguing that girls could easily injure themselves if they got too aggressive or tried to break a record. All-girls' elite schools were among the first to break with this view of women and competition, though they called competitive organizations "associations" instead of "leagues," lest people complain a league was too masculine.

Much of this changed, along with social attitudes, after the passage of Title IX 40 years ago. With time, young women who had once been focused on the arts came, in the twenty-first century, to see athletics as especially important tools for development. Two recent studies, one by the Women's Sports Foundation and the other by the Oppenheimer Foundation, have found that 82 percent of executive businesswomen played organized sports in middle school and high school. Of female *Fortune 500* executives, 80 percent said they were competitive tomboys during childhood. The Oppenheimer study also found that, while 16 percent of all American women describe themselves as athletic, among women who earn over $75,000 annually, the number rises to about 50 percent.

These conclusions are consistent with the studies like those of economist Betsey Stevenson, whose work on Title IX finds that participation in high school sports increases the likelihood that a girl will attend college, enter the labor market, and enter previously male-dominated occupations. She suggests that sports develops such skills as learning how to compete and how to become a team member, which are both key as women navigate the traditionally male-dominated labor market.

But competition, athletic or otherwise, is still seen as a masculine attribute. In 2010, the journal *Sex Roles* published a study on high school boys and girls that found that even today, "boys are 'trained' from an early age to be competitive . . . Research suggests that girls are less comfortable than boys in competitive circumstances and that girls are socialized to mask overt competitiveness and aggressiveness more generally." David Hibbard and Duane Buhrmester, both psychologists, argue that a mentality of "competing to win" is at odds with the "nice girl" ideal. Girls who engage in head-to-head competition may have more social difficulties, even as they become prepared for a fast-tracked, upper-middle-class life.

pink girls and dancing queens

Parents of chess-playing girls also encourage their daughters to be assertive and competitive. As one chess mom explained to me, "We're raising her . . . to be feminist. And so she says she wants to be a Grandmaster or the President [of the United States]. She doesn't have any ideas about gender limitations and I think that's a good thing."

Chess girls don't have to be as assertive as soccer girls like Charlotte. Partly because it is not a physical game, chess allows girls to be what one mother of two sons described to me as a "pink girl": "These girls have princess T-shirts on," she said. They have "rhinestones and bows in their hair—and they beat boys. And the boys come out completely deflated. That's the kind of thing I think is so funny. That girl Carolyn, I call her the killer chess player. She has bows in her hair, wears dresses, everything is pink, Barbie backpack, and she plays killer chess."

That a winning girl can look so feminine has an especially strong effect on boys, and sometimes their parents. Another chess mom told me how a father reacted negatively when his son lost to her daughter: "The father came out and was shocked. He said, 'You let a girl beat you!'"

In competitive dance, it's more common to see girls win, if only because the activity is dominated by girls. Dance is a physical activity that, like cheerleading, "no girly-girls" dad Malcolm would like his daughter to avoid. Competitive dancers are expected to wear make-up when they compete. While this has a practical purpose—to make sure the dancers' faces are not "washed out" by the stage lights—lipstick, blush, and mascara also accentuate feminine features; their practices are among those sociologist C. J. Pascoe would identify as part of "normative femininity."

As I sat in the audience at dance competitions, I often heard teachers and parents remark, "Wow, she looks beautiful up there," or, "They look very good." In addition to make-up, girl's dance costumes featured sequins, rhinestones, ribbons, and other decorative embellishments, and, at most competitions, costume and appearance are evaluated as part of the final score.

In contrast, in chess and soccer, appearance matters little to the outcome of the competition. Although soccer girls' appearances are regulated, it is done in a way that de-emphasizes femininity. Soccer girls must remove all jewelry (for safety reasons), and coaches direct girls to make sure all of their hair is out of their faces. To keep their view unimpeded, girls pull their hair back in ponytails, using headbands or elastic bands. This has become a fashion and identity statement itself—perhaps a way to assert femininity in a less-than-feminine environment, and to keep shorter hair and bangs off the face. And, of course, female soccer uniforms are not easily distinguishable from male uniforms. Many traditional markers of femininity are absent from the pitch.

It is not surprising, then, that although both soccer and dance parents mentioned lifelong fitness and health as a motivation for their young daughters' involvement with these activities, only dance moms linked their kids' participation to obesity and appearance. Dance mom Tiffany told me about her concerns about her daughter's future body: "My short-term goal for her is to keep, believe it or not, physically fit. Because, she's an eater, across the board . . . [Dance] keeps her at a nice weight. You know what I mean? And she struggles with that [weight], that's going to be her struggle, I told her."

While 16 percent of all American women describe themselves as athletic, among women who earn over $75,000 annually, the number rises to about 50 percent.

gender scripts and classed lessons

Another set of scripts—those about femininity—helps explain how parents (especially dance and soccer parents) choose among activities for their daughters. I call the dance script the "graceful girls," the soccer "aggressive girls," and the chess "pink warriors." When dance, soccer, and chess parents draw from different gender scripts, they are shaped by class, producing classed lessons in femininity for their girls.

Though nearly all of the families I met are part of the broadly defined middle class, parents higher up in the hierarchy of the middle class promote a more aggressive femininity, as seen in both soccer and chess families. Dance mothers, who generally have lower status than the chess and soccer parents, promote a femininity that is less competitively aggressive and prioritizes physical appearance. Lower-middle-class and working-class families place a greater emphasis on traditional femininity.

Among the 38 families I met who had competitive young girls, the vast majority of soccer families were upper-middle-class. None of the dance families were upper-middle-class, and over a third were lower-middle class; dance was the only activity of the three that had any working-class participants. Chess families with daughters who compete tend to look the most like soccer families, as the majority of families are upper-middle-class.

These upper-middle-class families had at least one parent who has earned an advanced postgraduate degree and work in a professional or managerial occupation, and both parents had earned a four-year college degree. The lower-middle-class families have just one parent with a college degree; neither parent works in a professional or managerial occupation.

> Today, there are three times more female soccer players than Girl Scouts in the United States.

Recall Malcolm and Marie. The former is a lawyer, and the latter was an investment banker who recently stopped working to spend more time with her five children. Both attended elite universities, and were representative of the rest of the parents. Most of the soccer parents had similar occupations, or they were professors or doctors.

It is not surprising that these highly credentialed, competitive parents have similar occupational aspirations for their children, including their daughters. They are trying to impart particular skills and lessons to their daughters at a young age to help them succeed in the long term. As Malcolm made clear, upper-middle-class parents do not want their daughters to end up as secretaries, so participation in competitive activities, where aggression is inculcated, becomes a priority so the girls can maintain their family's status in the future.

bossy is best?

Today, there are three times more female soccer players than Girl Scouts in the United States. This trend is due, in part, to the fact that upper-middle-class families are trying to strategically maintain their family's class position, preparing their daughters to enter what are traditionally male worlds. Parents are choosing after-school activities that will give these girls an advantage in college admissions and beyond; they are more likely to have the resources to enable their daughters to travel and compete.

But aggressive femininity can come at a cost. A recent study of the long-term effects of sports participation on adolescent girls by psychologists Campbell Leaper and Elizabeth Daniels found that many girls "struggle to reconcile their athleticism with traditional standards of hegemonic femininity that emphasize maintaining a thin body ideal and adhering to a rigid definition of beauty." Aggressive and pink warrior girls, along with graceful girls, face what psychologist Stephen Hinshaw calls the "triple bind" of being supportive, competitive and successful—and effortlessly beautiful.

In her work on female litigators, sociologist Jennifer Pierce similarly found that successful women had to become either "very male" or "very caring." She describes this binary: "Whereas men are praised for using intimidation and strategic friendliness, women who are aggressive are censured for being too difficult to get along with, and women who are nice are considered 'not tough enough' to be good litigators." Women need to be aggressive to succeed, but not *so* aggressive that they get labeled bitchy. It's a delicate balancing act for women in the work force, and for parents who want to raise girls who can be the boss.

These classed gender ideals also have long-term implications for inequality. Girls from upper-middle-class families seem better equipped with the skills they need to succeed in more lucrative careers, and in leadership roles as adults. Better understanding of socialization practices at the upper end of the class structure may open up real opportunities for others as well.

Sheryl Sandberg wasn't a soccer player. She wasn't even athletic, in an aggressive sense, at all. She was once an aerobics instructor who succeeded by leading others in a silver leotard. Her story suggests that soccer and contact sports aren't a direct path to the corner office, and that dance and cheerleading don't shut the door on success.

The future is not cast in stone: Tiffany's dancing daughter may yet become an executive, and Malcolm's daughter may become her assistant. That doesn't stop many affluent parents from being convinced that leaning in while wearing pink cleats produces girls with executive leadership skills.

recommended resources

Daniels, Elizabeth, and Leaper, Campbell. 2006. "A Longitudinal Investigation of Sport Participation, Peer Acceptance, and Self-esteem among Adolescent Girls and Boys," *Sex Roles* 55:875–80. One of the few longitudinal studies to look at competition and sports among young people.

Hibbard, David R, and Buhrmester, Duane. 2010. "Competitiveness, Gender, and Adjustment among Adolescents," *Sex Roles* 63(5–6):412–24. An example of how psychologists look at these questions, with provocative conclusions.

Hinshaw, Stephan, and Kranz, Rachel. 2009. *The Triple Bind: Saving Our Teenagers from Today's Pressures.* New York: Ballantine Books. Focused on the pressures girls face today, this book provides suggestions on how to help them navigate academic and social pressures.

Pascoe, C. J. 2007. *Dude, You're a Fag: Masculinity and Sexuality in High School.* Oakland, CA: University of California Press. An important book on how gender matters among young people today, with good discussions of athletics and appearance.

Stevenson, Betsey. 2010. "Beyond the Classroom: Using Title IX to Measure the Return to High School Sports," *Review of Economics & Statistics* 92(2):284–301. The first study to look at the long-term impacts of Title IX on women's achievement outside of sports.

babes in bikeland
bjorn christianson
winter 2015

One of urban cycling subculture's most interesting rituals is the alleycat: a bike race on open streets, where the riders choose their route between multiple checkpoints as outlined on a manifest. The competitions started as proof of skill among bicycle messengers, whose workday the events mimic. As bicycle messenger culture began to bleed into popular culture in the 1990s, leading to the new bicycle boom of the early 2000s, alleycat racing grew in popularity.

Babes In Bikeland was created in 2007 by Kayla Dotson and Chelsea Strate, with the aim of providing a safe place for women to compete in this unique, generally male-dominated format of bicycle racing. Nine years later, with hundreds of annual participants, the event is a celebration of the women/trans/femme (in the event's parlance, "WTF") cyclists—and is a powerful tool for educating the cycling community about gender issues.

Minneapolis, Minnesota has long been a center of alleycat racing, playing host to one of the largest, longest-running of such events, the infamous Stupor Bowl, held each year since 1997 on the day before the American football event with a similar name. But alleycat racing and the culture surrounding it has been unwelcoming to WTF cyclists. From lack of prize equity to harassment, stories of WTFs being shut out of such events abound. Alcohol, ego, and a no-rules attitude often lead to uncomfortable or even dangerous situations for these riders.

At Babes In Bikeland, cisgendered males (men whose gender identity matches the gender they were assigned at birth) participate as volunteers at registration, running activities at checkpoints, or at the finish line. Each checkpoint has a captain, responsible for making sure that stop is a safe space. Riders, volunteers, and spectators are encouraged to know what a safe space is and feel empowered to enforce its boundaries, including no touching without both parties' "enthusiastic consent" and no questioning whether a racer "belongs" in the race. During the awards ceremony, men are encouraged to get to the back of the room: WTFs to the front.

15

ritual violence in a two-car garage

scott melzer

summer 2013

What attracts mostly suburban professionals, dads, and husbands to a fight club? For some, it's a lifelong interest in fighting and martial arts and a desire to test their skills and toughness. For others, it's a space to exorcise boyhood experiences of emasculation.
KICK ASS AND TAKE NAMES! You were **BORN** for violence my fellow MAN. Take up that stick knowing in your heart of hearts that every fiber of your being has either evolved through fighting and death or was simply created . . . to do . . . THIS.
—e-mail from Fight Club member two days
before my first fight

"Do not cripple your friends. Do not bring them to tears," says the organizer. "If it's your first time at Fight Club," he adds, turning to face me, "you fight first." He hands me a dulled, rounded 9-inch training knife, padded gloves, and a fencing mask. My opponent, Mike, is about the same size as me. He has a knife, too. Unfortunately for me, Mike actually knows how to use his. I have no fight training or experience, and it's about to be painfully evident.

I try not to think about the language in the release form I just signed. "I the participant, am knowingly risking injury, which typically includes bruises, bumps and scrapes but can include serious injury and death from either fighting or watching." Bruises. Bumps. Scrapes. Death? It's unlikely anybody will come close to dying today—at least not of anything more than humiliation.

Mike and I are fighting under the auspices of The Gentlemen's Fighting Club—a San Francisco Bay Area group formed in the late 1990s. In GFC's history, there have been few serious injuries. This fact, along with the thickly padded gloves and sturdy mask, alleviate most of my concerns. Still, I am tempted to repeat the pre-fight instructions to Mike: Please do not cripple me or bring me to tears. "Fighters ready?" the timekeeper asks. I tighten my fingers around the handle of the training knife and square off with my opponent. "Fight!"

It's Fight the Professor Day at GFC, a one-time gathering organized at my request. It's a comforting sign of the GFC philosophy that my original title—"Punch the Professor"—was rejected. While typical GFC novices fight in a suburban garage, this event is being held on a concrete patio and grass in a fenced-in backyard. First-timers and longtime members alike fight in a rotation of among five to ten people, usually friends and acquaintances, almost always only men. A few hundred people have fought at GFC, and most fight only a few times. Only a couple dozen were regulars at the club's peak, when they fought biweekly.

Almost all the men have a martial arts or fighting background. None are amateur or professional mixed martial arts (MMA) fighters. Sanctioned, refereed MMA fights are short, violent exchanges that typically end with a knockout or forced submission. GFC provides a more authentic combat experience than martial arts sparring and less risk of injury than MMA, as well as an especially varied and creative array of weapons. In addition to the grappling and hitting that is part of martial arts and MMA, these fighters use brass rods rolled-up into magazines, unopened soda cans or soap bars wrapped in pillowcases, small purses filled with buckshot, folding chairs, cookie sheets, computer keyboards, and even metal chains.

Fighters wear just about any protective gear they choose, or none at all. Bruises, cuts, blood, and pain are routine. Broken fingers happen. The stakes are higher than a schoolyard fight, but only rarely does someone get badly injured. They have to go home to their families and to work the next day, and they want their friends and foes to leave intact, so they can return to fight another day.

geek fight club?

They're crazy! It's fake! A Geek Fight Club!? More like cubicle jockeys desperate to feel something real.

When the media first discovered the Gentlemen's Fight Club, reporters, fighters, martial artists, academics, and others joined in laughter, scorn, and skepticism. What motivated these guys to take up arms and fight? To answer that question, I observed fights, participated in one afternoon of combat, and interviewed 13 GFC fighters on their own and three in a group setting. I found that these men fight to test their skills and toughness, to conquer their fears, and, in some cases, to restore a sense of masculinity and control they lost during experiences of boyhood emasculation.

GFC is a democratic institution. Occupation and social class aren't used as filters for entry. Although members joke about excluding "yuppie punchers" and the "Gentlemen" moniker harkens to upper-class British pugilists, no interested fighter has been turned away. Landscapers, marketers, police officers, community organizers, students, and even a couple self-identified gang members have fought at GFC. Social class and status disappear behind the headgear and weapons.

The media has portrayed the club as primarily for geeks—software engineers and computer programmers—trying to escape their cubicle existence. The high proportion of middle- and upper-middle class tech professionals

is primarily due to the Bay Area location, the founders (who came from those fields), and the members' own personal and work networks. More than their profession or economic status, it is a background in martial arts—and some frustration with the limits of their training—that draws men to GFC.

The fighters I chose to interview are a racially and ethnically diverse group in their 20s, 30s and 40s, single or with children, and mostly college-educated. Like most GFC regulars or visitors, they are unlikely to find themselves fighting in a bar or anywhere other than GFC. Of course, each fighter brings a different biography and life experience to the club. But they share a similar cultural upbringing: longtime American attitudes towards men's violence and combat that transcend divisions of class and race.

boys to men

American culture simultaneously expects, celebrates, and punishes violence in boys and men. Despite the contradictions, and without a formal rite of passage from boyhood to manhood as found in cultures throughout the world, our society produces the unofficial, nearly universal boyhood ritual of fighting. American educators, parents, and law-enforcement authorities have been trying to discourage fighting, violence, and bullying, now broadly defined to include physical and verbal intimidation.

But real-life fighting continues to be the way most boys prove themselves physically, testing themselves and one another. For some men, GFC is simply an extension of their lifelong fascination with fighting—from vicariously experienced cartoon violence to actual schoolyard clashes and martial arts training. Another inspiration for the GFC was the rise of mixed martial arts, in which fighters use all disciplines; the first Ultimate Fighting Championship was held in 1993.

It's unclear how many fight clubs exist. There are, of course, media stories about teenagers fighting in front of crowds of fellow teenage spectators. These fights may be staged for fun, for gambling, and sometimes to create homemade movies that are sold for profit. They have little in common, though, with the handful of adult fight clubs I discovered during my research. With the exception of GFC, the adult clubs were either no longer active or deeply underground, and they mostly mirror increasingly popular and mainstreamed mixed martial arts (MMA) events.

Gentlemen's Fight Club is the only club I located that uses weapons and holds regular fight nights. It is distinct from MMA and other groups in one other significant way: winning and losing is irrelevant. No one scores the fights or keeps track of the number of strikes landed. There's almost a team spirit, despite the one-on-one nature of combat. The fighters have an interest in helping each other build their skills, but they show no interest in ranking each other, playing out anger, or humiliating anyone. The fighters certainly deliver painful blows and cause injuries to opponents, but there's no intent to cause serious harm.

In one of my fights, my stronger opponent skillfully delivered painful strikes using rattan sticks, but he didn't bull-rush or grab me, pin me down, or pummel me. Stronger and more skilled fighters use the weapons to expand their own and their opponent's skills. They gain nothing by overwhelming smaller, less experienced fighters with brute strength. Winning is supplanted by skill development.

A couple of GFC fighters eagerly spoke of physically dominating their opponents, using aggression and overwhelming force. But as sociologist Michael Kimmel argues in his 2006 book *Manhood in America*, being a man isn't really about pursuing domination over others—it's about evoking a fear of being dominated and controlled. For many GFC fighters, it's gratifying just to participate, to put oneself at risk and survive, to experiment with losing and establishing control. All this is to say, asserting masculinity isn't necessarily about inflicting damage. It's about controlling others, and controlling one's own reactions and emotions—especially fear.

> **Fighting is therapeutic. Even when the men lose, they demonstrate an ability to withstand violence and reestablish masculinity.**

losing control

Many men are motivated to fight because they've arrived at adulthood without evidence (at least for themselves) that they've passed the "test." They want to know if their own strength and training would hold up in a real fight, if they have the courage to face an armed attacker. Can they overcome a sometimes paralyzing fear of injury and protect themselves and their families—maybe even kick a little ass if they have to?

One subset of this group wants to exorcise particularly painful memories of fear, humiliation, and defeat that continue to haunt them. Several men I interviewed—including Asher, Sammy, and Freddy—have met many of society's expectations for what men should be and do. Their college degrees, successful careers, and families offset some of the insecurities that arose from their physical shortcomings as boys. They aren't conquering their childhood demons by committing acts of violence in the streets or using alcohol and drugs to escape their memories. Yet they continue to define themselves in part by those boyhood experiences; these scars aren't easy to erase, even for men who measure up in most other areas.

Asher is 34, married, and a father. He has a lucrative career in the technology sector. Like several of the men I met, he was bullied and beaten up as a boy and considers those experiences formative: "I felt like a weakling most of my life." Asher's father enrolled him in martial arts classes, but he quickly quit and has long regretted not being better at "standing up for myself when I was younger."

GFC fighter Sammy, 44, spent years training in martial arts and sparring in dojos, but when he heard about GFC he was still asking himself, "Can I really fight?" He is slight of stature, which, not surprisingly, exposed him to more bullying as a child and teen in the occasionally violent and gang-ridden neighborhoods where he grew up. When threatened by gang members, he said, all of his options felt emasculating: crying for help, submitting by begging for mercy, or suffering the pain and failure of being beaten. He chose submission to avoid the physical pain. "Saying 'Sorry, sorry,' many times definitely hurts your ego," he told me, laughing ruefully. It was "powerful, because I was all cocky when I was young and then, 'Oh, fuck. A few guys come [at] you and then you're nobody. Definitely, this had something to do with getting me to try to practice [martial arts] and prove my manhood."

Freddy, one of the long-time GFC regulars, says he got into grappling and wrestling to get the feeling that he could control his own body and others'. Once, when he was in elementary school, two older neighbors pinned him down, stripped him of his clothes, and ran away, leaving him to try to sneak back into the house, naked, in front of some older women relatives. He'd not only lost control of his body, but was exposed, literally and figuratively. When he was in college, some "friends" tried to pull a similar stunt, grabbing him and attempting to strip him naked in a dorm hallway. This time, he says, "I kneed the first guy in the balls; I turned around and grabbed the other guy by the throat and threw him down."

fight therapy

For these men, Fight Club offers an opportunity to replace the psychological scars of bullying and submission with physical scars they can wear as trophies of manhood. Fighting is therapeutic, and it brings more than understanding. The fighters can confront their feelings of failure *directly*, as adults. And they restore a sense of control, paradoxically, by choosing to give it up, placing themselves at risk. Even when they lose, by demonstrating an ability to withstand violence, they are reestablishing their masculinity. A fight is a "situation where you just don't know what's going to happen," says Asher, "but now, I know what I can do and I know that I'm not going to lose my cool." It's not about eliminating fear, he says, "but knowing you're not a coward."

"After I got punched enough times [at Fight Club]," Sammy says, "I understand that I can definitely take a [big] punch and then I'll nail you one." Sammy doesn't expect to be bullied by gang members now that he's an adult, but if he finds himself in that situation, he now has the confidence to deal with it. He expected to reclaim his manhood by beating up his Fight Club opponents. Instead he came to believe that the "true power" was being able to withstand a beating. Getting hit is, in many ways, more important than hitting.

"So, sometimes losing is winning?" I asked him. "Losing is *definitely* winning," he said. He now invites and even embraces fights with men at GFC who are stronger and may subject him to countless strikes. The same confidence has helped him handle non-violent confrontations at work, he notes.

Freddy's extensive GFC experience has translated to an acute self-awareness and sense of control. "Now I think of myself as a hard target. I don't feel like a mark," he says. "Only *I* kill me." With the skills and confidence he has developed, he believes it's only his own mistakes that lead him to lose a fight.

Ronnie, another experienced martial artist, says he wanted definitive proof that fear could no longer dominate him. "What I get [from fighting at GFC] is the truth. [To know] that I could protect myself and I'm not scared in any situation." He wavers a little. "[Well] you get scared in a lot of different situations. But I feel, well, it gives me a level of confidence."

Social science research reveals that men who fall short on some measure of manhood often find other outlets to compensate for their perceived shortcomings. Young men living in poverty and denied access to good jobs may assert themselves through sports, sexual conquests, or risk-taking activities like crime. Adult men who fail as breadwinners are more likely to abuse their wives or girlfriends. Men with physical disabilities may highlight their decision-making skills and authority to offset their inability to live up to men's body ideals.

GFC offers at least one group of men a direct way to repair and bolster their masculine identities. This may help explain why they don't reject cultural expectations of physical toughness and control or embrace a different definition of manhood.

In place of recurrent memories of humiliation, some GFC fighters say they have daily fantasies or daydreams in which they are superheroes or doing heroic things. Some confess to harboring fantasies of violence—such as clearing a bar full of people when forced to defend themselves. Even after proving their courage, toughness, and ability repeatedly at GFC, some fighters return again and again, for months or even years. The ritual binds them.

New fighters may feel as if they are undergoing a controlled hazing ritual, but the regulars help create the best of a fraternal atmosphere—camaraderie and bonding—without fear of being judged by other men. The bond is evident in the post-fight hug, an authentic embrace of appreciation and respect. My afternoon of fighting ended, as they all do, with beer and laughter while watching recordings of the fights. (No copies of the videos are made or distributed.)

GFC may be unique in the way it cultivates the most visceral element of American manhood. Unlike MMA competitors, these garage fighters don't attempt to injure each other to win. And unlike middle school bullies, they don't try to physically humiliate each other. They push and challenge each other, encouraging everyone to grow as fighters—and as people. As one veteran explained as I prepared for my first fight, your fellow fighters are "there to bring you up, not beat you down."

Masculinity is elusive and tenuous, always capable of being undermined by a single failure. GFC gives men a venue where they can prove themselves physically, shielding them from the burden of trying to dominate others—and the fear of being dominated.

recommended resources

Canada, Geoffrey. 1995. *Fist Stick Knife Gun: A Personal History of Violence in America.* Boston, MA: Beacon Press. Describes boys' street socialization, unwritten rules about and informal training in fighting, and violence in tough, inner-city neighborhoods, before and after guns were prevalent.

Kimmel, Michael. 2006. *Manhood in America: A Cultural History*, 2nd Edition. London: Oxford University Press. Exhaustively documents and analyzes culturally ascendant and competing versions of American manhood throughout U.S. history.

Messerschmidt, James W. 1999. *Nine Lives: Adolescent Masculinities, The Body and Violence.* Boulder, CO: Westview Press. Examines young boys who have been physically and sexually abused, and who have attempted to overcome their victimization by committing these acts against peers.

Phillips, Debby. 2007. "Punking and Bullying: Strategies in Middle School, High School, and Beyond," *Journal of Interpersonal Violence 22*(2):158–178. Explains how boys use verbal and physical abuse to humiliate and shame other boys in an attempt to demonstrate their own masculinity.

the sanctity of sunday football

why men love sports

douglas hartmann

fall 2003

The American male's obsession with sports seems to suggest that the love affair is a natural expression of masculinity. But sociologists have found that, conversely, sports teach men how to be manly, and studying sports reveals much about masculinity in contemporary America.

My father, a no-nonsense grade school principal, had little time for small talk, contemplation, or leisure—with one major exception: sports. He spent Sunday afternoons watching football games on television, passed summer evenings listening to Jack Buck announce St. Louis Cardinals baseball games, and took me to every sporting event in town. He coached all the youth sports his children played, and spent hours calculating team statistics, diagramming new plays, and crafting locker room pep talks. Though never a great athlete, his high school varsity letters were displayed in his basement work area; just about the only surefire way to drag dad out of the house after a long day at work was to play "a little catch." Sports were one of the few topics he ever joked about with other men.

My father's fascination with sports was not unique. Though women are increasingly visible throughout the sporting world, more men than women play sports, watch sports and care about sports. Is it any wonder that corporate advertising campaigns, drinking establishments, and movements such as the Promise Keepers all use sports to appeal to men? Or that sports figures so prominently in many books and movies dealing with men and masculinity in America? Nevertheless, there is surprisingly little serious reflection about why this is the case. When asked why so many men are so obsessed with sports, most people—regardless of their gender or their attitudes about sports—say something to the effect that men are naturally physical and competitive, and that sports simply provide an outlet for these inherently masculine traits.

To sociologists, however, men love playing, watching, and talking sports because modern, Western sports—dominated as they are by men and by values and behaviors that are traditionally regarded as masculine—provide a unique place for men to think about and develop their masculinity, to make themselves men, or at least one specific kind of man.

where boys become men

Ask sports enthusiasts why they participate in sports and you are likely to get a wide variety of answers. "Because it is fun and exciting," some respond. Others say it is because they need the exercise and want to stay physically fit. Still others talk about sports providing them a way to relax and unwind, or about the thrill of competition—these responses are especially common for that large percentage of sports lovers whose "participation" mainly takes the form of being a fan or watching sports on television. These are important parts of sports' value, but they do not really explain why men are, on average, more likely to be involved in sports than women.

For many men, the love of sports goes back to childhood. Sports provided them, as young boys and teens, with a reason to get together, to engage with other boys (and men), and in doing so to begin defining what separates boys from girls: how to act like men. Barrie Thorne's study of grammar school playgrounds illustrates the phenomenon. Thorne finds that preadolescent boys and girls use recreation on the schoolyard to divide themselves along gender lines. How they play—for example, running around or quiet games—Thorne suggests, distinguishes male and female child behavior. As they get older, kids become more aware of these distinctions and increasingly use sex-segregated athletics to discuss and act out gender differences. Gary Alan Fine, in *With the Boys,* describes how much of the learning that happens in Little League baseball involves being tough and aggressive and dealing with injuries and other setbacks; and in off-the-field conversations young ballplayers learn about sex and about what it means to be a man as opposed to a "dork," a "sissy" or a "fag."

When Michael Messner interviewed retired athletes and asked them how they initially got involved with sports, they told him it had little to do with any immediate or natural attraction to athletics and was really based upon connecting to other boys and men. "The most important thing was just being out there with the rest of the guys—being friends," said one. Sports, according to Messner, "was something 'fun' to do with fathers, older brothers, uncles and eventually with same-aged peers."

Girls start playing sports for similar reasons, and children of both genders join in other activities, such as choir or community service, for social purposes, too. (Many boys and girls start to drop out of sports at about ages 9 or 10—when the sports they play become increasingly competitive and require them to think of themselves primarily as athletes.) What is distinctive about the experience of boys and young men in sports, however, is that the sporting world is organized and run primarily by men, and that athletic activities require attitudes and behaviors that are typically understood to be masculine.

Of course, not all boys play sports, and boyhood and adolescent experiences in sports are not uniformly positive. A great deal of the sociological research in this area focuses on the downside of youth sports participation. Donald Sabo, for example, has written extensively about the pain and violence, both physical and psychological, experienced by many boys who compete in athletics. And Harry Edwards has long argued that over-investing in sports can divert poor and minority youth from more promising avenues of upward mobility. But, despite the harsh realities, sports remains one of the few socially approved settings in which boys and men, and fathers and sons, can express themselves and bond with each other.

sport as a masculine enterprise

Once boys and girls separate in physical play, it does not take long for gendered styles of play to emerge. Study after study confirms what most soccer moms and dads already know: boys' athletics tend to be more physical and aggressive and put more emphasis on winning, being tough in the face of adversity, and dealing with injuries and pain. Even in elementary school, Thorne finds boys take up far more of the physical space of the playground with their activities than girls, who tend to play (and talk about their play) in smaller spaces and clusters.

People debate whether there is a physiological component to these differences, but two points are clear. First, parents, coaches, and peers routinely encourage such intensity among boys in youth sports. More than a few single mothers bring their boys to the teams I coach out of concern that their sons are insufficiently tough or physical because they lack a male influence. Messner writes about how he learned—against his inclinations—to throw a ball overhand with his elbow tucked in because his father did not want him to "throw like a girl." Stories about overly competitive, physically abusive coaches may be overplayed in the American media, but in many ways they are the inevitable consequence of the emphases many parents express.

Second, the behaviors and attitudes valued in men's and boys' athletics are not just about sports, but about

When Michael Messner interviewed retired athletes and asked them how they initially got involved with sports, they told him it had little to do with any immediate or natural attraction to athletics and was really about connecting to other boys and men.

Study after study confirms what most soccer moms and dads already know: boys' athletics tend to be more physical and aggressive and put more emphasis on winning, being tough in the face of adversity, and dealing with injuries and pain.

masculinity more generally. The inherent connection of sports to the body, physical activity and material results, the emphasis on the merit of competing and winning, the attention to rules, sportsmanship and team play, on the one hand, and gamesmanship, outcomes and risk, on the other, are not just the defining aspects of male youth sport culture, but conform to what many men (and women) believe is the essence and value of masculinity. Female reporters, homosexual athletes, and men who challenge the dominant culture of men's sports—especially in the sacred space of the locker room—quickly learn that sports are not just dominated by men but also dominated by thinking and habits understood to be masculine (in opposition to the more nurturing values of compromise, cooperation, sympathy, understanding, and sharing typically associated with femininity). If the military is the quintessential institution of Western masculinity, then sports is surely a close second.

The notion that sports is a masculine enterprise is closely connected with the development of modern Western sports. As historians have detailed, middle- and upper-class men used sports in the 19th and early-20th centuries to present and protect their particular notions of masculinity in both schools and popular culture (the classic literary expression being *Tom Brown's School Days*, a 19th-century English story of boarding school boys' maturation through hard-nosed sports). The media is a critical part of perpetuating sports' masculine ethos today, because most adults participate in sports as spectators and consumers. Not only are female athletes and women's sports downplayed by most sports coverage, but the media accentuates the masculinity of male athletes. For example, Hall of Fame pitcher Nolan Ryan's media coverage, according to a study by Nick Trujillo, consistently described him in terms of the stereotypical American man: powerful, hard-working, family patriarch, a cowboy and a symbol of heterosexual virility. Such images not only define an athlete's personal qualities but legitimate a particular vision of masculinity.

The authority of the masculine ethos is underlined by the fact that so many female athletes believe they can receive no higher compliment than to be told they "play like a man." Many feminists cringe at the irony of such sentiments. But they also realize that, while the explosion of women in sports has challenged their male dominance (2.5 million girls and young women participated in interscholastic sport in 2003, up from 300,000 in 1972—before Title IX's federal mandate for gender equality), women's sports have essentially been based upon the same single-minded, hyper-competitive masculine model. Not surprisingly, they are witnessing the emergence of the same

kinds of problems—cheating, physical and emotional stress, homophobia, eating disorders—that have long plagued men's sports.

sports and maintaining masculinity

As the men Messner interviewed became more committed to being athletes, they began to construct identities and relationships that conformed to—and thus perpetuated—sport's masculine values. Athletes are so bound up with being men that when, in his initial interviews, Messner inadvertently referred to them as "ex-athletes," his interviewees responded as if he were taking away their identities, their very manhood. A professional baseball player expressed a similar sentiment when I asked how he dealt with his time on the disabled list last summer because of a serious arm injury: "I'd throw wiffle balls left-handed to my eight-year-old son—and I had to get him out! Just so I could feel like a man again."

Of course, few men participate in sports with the intensity of professional athletes. Those who cannot move up the competitive ladder can still participate in other ways—in recreational sports, in coaching, and perhaps, most of all, in attending sporting events, watching sports on television, and buying athletic gear and apparel. Indeed, it is in being a fan (derived from *fanatic*) that the male slant of sports is clearest. While women often follow sports, their interest tends to be driven by social ends, such as being with family or friends. Male spectators are far more likely to watch events by themselves, follow sports closely, and be affected by the outcomes of games and the performance of their favored teams and athletes. The basic explanation is similar to the one developed out of sports activity studies: Just as playing sports provides many boys and young men with a space to become men, watching sports serves many men as a way to reinforce, rework, and maintain their masculinity—in these cases, through vicarious identification with masculine pursuits and idealized men. Writing of his obsession with 1950s football star Frank Gifford in *A Fan's Notes*, novelist Fredrick Exley explained: "Where I could not, with syntax, give shape to my fantasies, Gifford could with his superb timing, his uncanny faking, give shape to his." "I cheered for him with inordinate enthusiasm," Exley wrote, because he helped me find "my place in the competitive world of men . . . each time I heard the roar of the crowd, it roared in my ears as much for me as for him."

It was no accident that Exley chose to write about football. With its explicit appropriation of the rhetoric and tactics of combat, the sport supplanted baseball as the most popular spectator sport in the United States in the 1970s. Football's primary ideological salience, according to Messner, "lies in its ability . . . to symbolically link men of diverse ages and socioeconomic backgrounds. . . . Interacting with other men and interacting with them in this male-dominated space . . . [is] a way to assert and confirm one's own maleness. . . ." Being with other men allows males to affirm their masculine identity. Listen to today's sports talk radio. These programs are not only sophomorically masculine, many of them serve as little men's communities unto themselves: Tiger fan Jack; Mike from Modesto; Jay the Packer's guy—even teams' announcers have unique personalities and identities, fostering the impression that this is an actual club where all the guys know each other.

The salience of sports as a medium to validate masculinity may be best illustrated when it is taken away. Journalist Susan Faludi reported on what happened when the original Cleveland Browns football team left town to become the Baltimore Ravens. The mostly working-class men who occupied the section of seats in Cleveland called the "Dawg Pound" talked about the team's departure with an overwhelming sense of loss and powerlessness. As it often is for former athletes, it was as if they'd had their manhood taken from them. In tearful media interviews, John "Big Dawg" Thompson compared the team's departure to witnessing his best friend die in the hospital.

sports as "contested terrain"

Critics of sports' heavy masculinity (most scholars doing work in this area are critics) have focused on its neglect or even exclusion of women. The way that golf outings perpetuate the privileges men enjoy in the corporate world is a frequent example. Others have gone so far as to suggest that the powerful appeal of sports for men arises because sports provide them at least symbolic superiority in a world in which men's real authority is in decline. As columnist and former professional basketball player Mariah Burton Nelson put it in the deliberately provocative title of her popular 1994 book, "The stronger women get, the more men love football."

In recent years, sociologists of sports have also begun to identify tensions within the masculine culture of athletics. Looking at Great Britain's soccer stars, for example, Garry Whannel has studied how the hedonism of the "new lad lifestyle" (as represented by players like David Beckham) rubs up against the disciplined masculinity traditionalists perceive to be necessary for international football success. Messner, for his part, has shown how "high status" men (White and from middle-class backgrounds) and "low status" men differently

understood themselves as athletes. The former tended to transfer what they learned in sports about being men to pursuing success in other spheres, such as education and career. Men from lower status backgrounds saw sports as their only hope for success as a man—an accomplishment that the higher status men looked down upon as a narrow, atavistic type of masculinity. Expanding from this, some scholars have demonstrated that in popular culture the masculinity of African-American athletes is often exaggerated and linked to racial stereotypes about violence, risk and threat. Basketball star Dennis Rodman, for example, gained notoriety by playing on his persona as a "bad" ball player. While problematic in many respects, these images of Black masculinity can also provide African-American men with unique opportunities for personal advancement and broader political visibility (as I have suggested in my work on the 1968 Black Olympics protest movement).

Such research has led many scholars to see sports not only as a place where mainstream masculine culture is perpetuated, but also a place where it is challenged and possibly changed. These issues have played out clearly in the debates over the implementation of Title IX legislation for women's equal access to sports. While still hotly contested (as evidenced by the recent controversy surrounding the all-male Augusta National Golf Club, as well as speculation that the legislation may be challenged in court by the Bush administration), Title IX has transformed men's relationship to sports, to women, and even to masculinity itself. Sports' most vital social function with respect to masculinity is to provide a separate space for men to discuss—often indirectly, through evaluations of favorite players or controversial incidents—what it is to be a real man. And that space is increasingly shared with women.

Some scholars envision new, more humane or even feminine sports—marked less by an emphasis on winning, recordsetting and spectatorship, and more by open participation, enjoyment and fitness. Cross-cultural studies of sports show that these are real possibilities, that sports are not "naturally" and inherently masculine as Americans have long assumed. Sexism and homophobia, for example, have never been a real problem in Chinese sports, anthropologist Susan Brownell explains, because sports emerged there as a low-status activity that more powerful men felt no special compulsion to control or participate in. As a consequence, it is widely believed that a skilled female practitioner of kung fu should be able to defeat stronger but less-skilled men. At the same time, Brownell points out, the current proliferation of Western, Olympic-style sports in China seems to be contributing to the redefinition of gender roles there nearer the pattern of Western sports and masculinity.

playing deeply

In a famous paper on cockfighting in Bali, American anthropologist Clifford Geertz used the term "deep play" to capture the way fans make sense of such competitions as the cockfight, cricket or American football. As passionate and articulate as they may be, these enthusiasts generally do not attempt to justify their pursuits. Instead, they downplay the significance of sports as separate from the serious concerns of real life. We can learn a great deal from such play, Geertz said, if we think about it as an "art form" which helps us figure out who people really are and what they really care about. Similarly, American men who love sports may not be able to fully articulate and understand how it is part of their being men, but their passion for sports can certainly help us understand them and their masculinity.

This peculiar, "deep play" understanding of sports makes it difficult for most men to recognize or confront the costs and consequences that may come with their sports obsessions. But in many ways isn't this true of masculine culture in general? It makes male advantages and masculine values appear so normal and "natural" that they can hardly be questioned. Therein may lie the key to the puzzle connecting men and the seemingly innocent world of sports: they fit together so tightly, so seamlessly that they achieve their effects—learning to be a man, male bonding, male authority and the like—without seeming to be doing anything more than tossing a ball or watching a Sunday afternoon game.

recommended resources

Birrell, Susan, and Cole, Cheryl L. (eds). 1994. *Women, Sport and Culture.* Champaign, IL: Human Kinetics. A collection of feminist critiques of sport that includes several influential contributions on men and masculinity.

Brownell, Susan. 1995. *Training the Body for China: Sports in the Moral Order of the People's Republic.* Chicago: University of Chicago Press. The chapters on sex, gender, and the body offer a fascinating cross-cultural contrast, and provide an introduction to sports in the nation that will host the 2008 Olympics.

Burstyn, Varda. 1999. *The Rites of Men: Manhood, Politics and the Culture of Sport.* Toronto: University of Toronto Press. The most comprehensive treatment of the social, cultural, and historical forces that account for the relationship between men and sports in modern society.

Fine, Gary A. 1987. *With the Boys: Little League Baseball and Preadolescent Culture.* Chicago: University of Chicago Press. A pioneering field study from a noted sociologist of culture.

Kelley, Robin D. G. 1997. "Playing for Keeps: Pleasure and Profit on the Postindustrial Playground." In Wahneema Lubiano (ed.), *The House That Race Built.* New York: Random House, pp. 195–231. An ethnographically informed treatment of the opportunities basketball presents to inner-city African-American men produced by the country's preeminent historian of Black popular culture.

Klein, Alan M. 1993. *Little Big Men: Bodybuilding Subculture and Gender Construction.* Albany, NY: State University of New York Press. A vivid ethnography of competitive body builders on the West Coast that draws upon Robert Connell's seminal critique of the intersection of men's bodies, identities and sexualities in masculine culture.

Messner, Michael. 2002. *Taking the Field: Women, Men, and Sports.* Minneapolis, MN: University of Minnesota Press. The latest book from the leading scholar in the field. It exposes the ways in which men and women together use sports to define gender differences.

Pronger, Brian. 1990. *The Arena of Masculinity: Sports, Homosexuality and the Meaning of Sex.* London: St. Martin's Press. Pronger explores the problematic connections between gender and sexuality in sport, highlighting its libidinal dimensions.

playing but losing

women's sports after title ix

cheryl cooky and nicole m. lavoi

winter 2012

Title IX of the Educational Amendments to the Constitution states, "No person in the United States shall, on the basis of sex, be excluded from participation in, be denied the benefits of, or be subjected to discrimination under any educational program or activity receiving federal assistance." In the nearly 40 years since it passed, this provision has played an important role, both directly and indirectly, in girls and women's sport participation in the United States.

Title IX has dramatically increased the number of sport opportunities for girls and women in educational institutions. According to data collected by the National Federation of State High School Associations, in 1971 (just prior to the passage of Title IX), 294,105 girls participated in high school sports. By 2009–2010, that number had grown to 3,172,637. R. Vivian Acosta and Linda Jean Carpenter, authors of an ongoing, longitudinal study, found that female participation at the collegiate level has increased six-fold, from 30,000 in 1977 to more than 180,000 in 2010. In short, girls and women comprise nearly 40 percent of all interscholastic and intercollegiate sport participants.

Progress is also evidenced in other sporting realms not directly impacted by the Title IX mandate. Today, women are participating at the professional level in sports that seemed beyond reach 40 years ago—including professional football (the Independent Women's Football League). The growing popularity of the Women's National Basketball Association (WNBA) and the Women's Professional Soccer (WPS) league is an important phenomenon in itself. Indeed, the visibility and excellence of female athletes and women's sport have helped create a broader cultural context in which female athleticism has become "normalized," and in many cases, celebrated. Sport and female athleticism have become inextricably linked to the empowerment of girls and women—as in the "Girl Power" movement in the 1990s, which led to the proliferation of representations of strong, athletic women in popular culture.

Yet, despite this progress, we are far from a world of gender equality in American sport. Compared to their male counterparts, major inequities and shortcomings remain for female athletes—especially in terms of media attention and opportunities to coach and lead in the world of sport. In this article, we examine some of the sociological research that documents and helps account for these shortcomings. This work speaks to the multifaceted nature of an institution as large as sport, the persistence of sexism and male dominance, and the challenges entailed in making social change.

media

Fans of women's sports today find more social media sites with a primary focus on female athletes; they might, for example, look to WomenTalkSports.com, an online blog network. More media outlets broadcast women's sport and in higher broadcast quality than in the past. Research has shown that the production values (such as the number of camera angles, use of slow motion replays, graphics, and quality of commentators) have also improved dramatically over the past 20 years. Still, there is a lack of coverage of women's sport in the mainstream media.

Although televised broadcast coverage of female sport participation has improved in both quality and quantity, these gains have not translated into increased coverage in newspapers, magazines, or televised news and highlight shows. For example, in 2003 ESPN began broadcasting the entire women's NCAA basketball tournament on its sister station, ESPN2. However, in a longitudinal study released in 2010 by the University of Southern California's Center for Feminist Research, sociologists Michael Messner and Cheryl Cooky found that ESPN—the dominant sports network in the United States—dedicated 100 segments and over 3 hours on the men's tournament, and only 11 segments and 6½ minutes on the women's; most of the women's tournament coverage was relegated to a small, scrolling ticker at the bottom of the screen. Messner and Cooky also found that televised news media coverage of women's sport was at its lowest level in 20 years—it accounted for less than two percent of televised news coverage in 2009.

Perhaps even more problematic is that when female athletes do receive mainstream media attention, it is typically in sexualized ways that trivialize their athleticism. For example, one of the more disturbing trends that we have observed is the growing number of female athletes featured in "lad mags" like *FHM, Maxim*, and *Playboy*. Audiences are more likely to see a female athlete in her swimsuit lounging on the beach than in her uniform on the field. Since the early 2000s, *Sports Illustrated* has featured female athletes in the annual "Swimsuit Issue"—its best-selling issue every year. The issue has boasted top female athletes such as Serena Williams, Maria Sharapova, Danica Patrick, and Amanda Beard (and far more often than they've appeared in any other issue of *Sports Illustrated*). Racecar driver Patrick and Olympic swimmer Beard have also been in *FHM*, posing in ways that resemble soft-core pornography. And this past summer, the German U-20 women's soccer team showed up in the German edition of *Playboy*, just days before the 2011 Women's World Cup, to help "promote the sport." As sociologist Mary Jo Kane recently argued

in a column for *The Nation*, such images "sell sex" but do little to legitimize and promote female athleticism. Stereotypical representations of this sort would not be so troubling if media images of female athletic competence were commonplace.

There are certainly far more female athletes, professional leagues, and female athlete superstars today than there were 20 or 30 years ago. So, why does the media continue to silence, ignore, trivialize, and hyper-sexualize female athletes? Scholars argue that the ways in which male and female athletes are represented in the media maintain existing gendered hierarchies, uphold sport as a male preserve, and reaffirm the masculine norms and values that are dominant in the wider society. The ways female athletes shape their own images and representations are also part of the package, along with the choices of media producers, journalists, and audiences to produce and consume these images. All of these choices, of course, are made within a broader context—where ways of seeing privilege men and masculine ideals.

> *Major inequities remain for female athletes—especially in terms of media attention, distribution of institutional resources, and opportunities to coach and lead in the world of sport.*

Some argue that in order to combat the trivialized and hyper-sexualized images of female athletes, we need more women in positions of power within media organizations who could challenge embedded sexism and masculine ideals. Yet women are consistently underrepresented in such positions of power in mainstream media organizations—and beyond.

taking charge—or not

Many of those who fought for Title IX assumed that a rise in female sports participation would automatically translate to increased leadership opportunities for women in sport. This expectation has not been borne out. Despite the fact that female athletic participation is at a historic high at all levels of sport, women are a scarce minority in positions of power within sports organizations. For example, Acosta and Carpenter have shown that the percentage of women in coaching and administrative positions in women's sport has actually declined, from over 90 percent to roughly 40 percent, since Title IX passed—and this percentage is lower than at any time in history except in 2006. In fact, in the most visible and arguably most important positions in sport—head coaches, athletic administrators, and sports editors—women remain so marginalized they're essentially statistical tokens—that is, they represent less than 15 percent of the workforce population.

A by-the-numbers analysis paints a bleak picture. In February, 2011 the *Chronicle of Higher Education* reported that only five of the 120 athletic directors in women's Division I-A—the biggest and most prominent collegiate programs—are women. Only 19 percent of collegiate athletic directors across all divisional levels are female. These stats actually represent a sharp decline from the early 1970s, when over 90 percent of those who oversaw female athletics programs were women. And at the Associated Press, for instance, 94 percent of sports editors are men.

Although there is no national data on women in high school or youth sport leadership, Nicole LaVoi and Cindra Kamphoff, researchers affiliated with the Tucker Center at the University of Minnesota, suggest the trends at those levels are similar. An analysis of one state-level youth soccer association showed that women seldom occupy positions as head coach (15.1 percent) or assistant coach (18.9 percent). As in other sports, women are clustered in the less prestigious and less visible position of team manager, coach for younger age groups or coach at the lower competitive levels.

What factors explain why women are so poorly represented in positions of sport leadership? Scholars have uncovered many complex barriers that come into play. In order to gain credibility, female coaches and administrators often have to perform at higher levels than their male colleagues. They may feel pressure to conform to organizational norms in order to succeed, rather than challenge them. Women are also at increased risk for gender discrimination due to sexual harassment, wage inequities, and limited opportunities for promotion.

In one recent study, Messner interviewed women who were involved in an American Youth Soccer Organization (AYSO) league. He found that many women experienced informal negative interactions, including overt sexism and challenges to their authority by male coaches, parents, and the "old-boys network" at work in their league. These experiences, taken together, created a "glass ceiling" that influenced many women to "opt out" of coaching youth sport.

Similar dynamics also occur in other sport organizations as women "choose" to opt out of careers as head

When a female athlete receives mainstream media attention, audiences are more likely to see her in her swimsuit lounging on the beach than in her uniform on the field.

coach, athletic director, or sports editor, in part because of the informal interactions in these male-dominated and male-identified contexts. Women may also opt out of demanding, high profile, time consuming, and stressful positions, and instead choose to remain in supporting roles (such as assistant coaches, associate and assistant athletic directors, and assistant sports editors) in which work-life balance and quality of life is more possible to achieve.

At the higher, more competitive levels of sport, homophobia and heterosexism also impact female participation and career trajectories. Some lesbians remain closeted due to perceived threats to their job security and advancement, recruitment issues, and fear of discrimination and backlash. Heterosexual athletes and coaches—who must constantly "prove" their sexual identity, deal with persistent negative sterotypes, or defend their sport participation choices—are also affected. Despite increasing tolerance for gays and lesbians in mainstream society, research (and accounts such as coach and star athlete Pat Griffin's groundbreaking *Strong Women, Deep Closets*) suggest that the fears of female athletes, coaches, and administrators are not unfounded.

Surprisingly, men's professional sport—historically one of the most homophobic contexts—may be inching toward progress on this front. During the 2011 NBA playoffs, a public service announcement featuring NBA stars Grant Hill and Jared Dudley challenged NBA players (and, presumably, fans) to resist anti-gay name-calling. Athletes in other men's professional sports have also advocated for the rights of gay, lesbian, bisexual, and transgender individuals. Leading up to the 2011 Stanley Cup playoffs, National Hockey League player Sean Avery publicly endorsed gay marriage, and straight athlete Hudson Taylor formed a non-profit organization called "Athlete Ally" to take "proactive steps to end homophobia and transphobia in sports."

taking stock, looking forward

As athletes, girls and women have gained entry into the institution of sport. Still, sexism, masculine ideals, and homophobia continue to be reproduced within sport contexts at all competitive levels. In other words, the movement for gender equality in American sport is partial, the revolution incomplete.

There are well-documented health, social, and psychological benefits for girls and women who participate in sport. Sport is, to be sure, also one of the most important

American social institutions. Women's equal participation in sport can help change outdated stereotypes about women's capabilities and capacities. This isn't just good for girls and women: it's good for everyone.

Let there be no doubt: the institutional, societal, and cultural barriers standing in the way may be large and complicated, but gender equality in sport does have broad-based support in the United States. Indeed, a recent *New York Times* article concluded that most Americans approve of efforts to address gender equality, such as Title IX. Unfortunately, social change is slow and often difficult, and it requires multifaceted approaches. Legislative changes alone cannot address the sexism and homophobia that often undergird gender-based forms of inequality in institutional contexts.

The under-representation of women in positions of power is, of course, not unique to sport. And progress in social institutions is often re-articulated or re-appropriated in ways that defuse its progressive or liberatory potential. Though female athletes receive more broadcast media coverage than they did in the past (for example, when ESPN broadcasts the entire NCAA women's basketball tournament), news coverage, advertising, and popular cultural representations still highlight female athletes' heterosexuality and femininity over their athletic accomplishments, thus trivializing their sport experience.

So while we are optimistic about the future of girls and women's sport, we are uncertain about what the future holds. The current generation of girls and boys, who are coming of age in a world in which females are participating in sport at all competitive levels, will be the coaches, administrators, media producers, and sport journalists of tomorrow. Advocacy and educational programs are supporting gender equity among the "post-Title IX" generation; for example, the Fair Shot Project at Columbia College, Chicago is training high school girls in investigative journalism, Title IX, and gender and race in media analysis with the goal of educating and empowering girls to create positive social change in sport. Another promising program is Pat Griffin's Changing the Game: The GLSEN Project, which uses education and advocacy to address lesbian, gay, bisexual, and transgender issues in K-12 physical education programs. And the newly-formed Alliance for Women Coaches advocates for equal opportunities for all women in athletics, and provides ongoing support to women in the coaching profession. Programs such as these offer the potential for new generations to fully achieve gender equality in sport.

recommended resources

Acosta, Vivian R, and Carpenter, Linda J. 2010. *Women in Intercollegiate Sport: A Longitudinal, National Study* online at acostacarpenter.org. An ongoing, longitudinal study that tracks athletic participation rates, and coaching and administrative positions, in women's collegiate sport.

Griffin, Pat. 1998. *Strong Women, Deep Closets: Lesbians and Homophobia in Sport.* Champaign, IL: Human Kinetics Publishers. Examines homophobia through interviews with athletes, coaches, and sport administrators.

Hogshead-Maker, Nancy, and Zimbalist, Andrew. 2007. *Equal Play: Title IX and Social Change.* Philadelphia: Temple University Press. A comprehensive history of Title IX and its impact on sport and society.

LaVoi, Nicole M, and Kamphoff, Cindra. (in progress). "Females in Positions of Power in High School Athletics." An AAHPERD-funded longitudinal study that aims to reproduce Acosta and Carpenter's analysis of females in positions of power at the interscholastic level.

Messner, Michael A, and Cooky, Cheryl. 2010. *Gender in Televised Sports: News and Highlight Shows, 1989–2009* online at usc.edu/dept/cfr/html/documents/tvsports.pdf. A longitudinal study of the quality and quantity of televised news media coverage of sport.

18

muslim female athletes and the hijab

geoff harkness and samira islam

fall 2011

Just a cursory glance at recent headlines makes it clear that the role of women in the Middle East is undergoing rapid and vast transformation. Women have been key participants in the uprisings in Egypt, Tunisia, Bahrain, and elsewhere in the region.

"I'll never forget what I saw," journalist Lama Hasan wrote from Libya. "Mothers dragging their children along so they could witness history; girls who weren't shy about mixing with boys, standing shoulder to shoulder with them to fight for their cause; and the female volunteers who helped with security, day and night."

As these stories make headlines, a quieter gender revolution has been brewing in the arena of sports. For more than two decades, female athletic participation has been slowly rising throughout the Middle East, where it's often tied to larger trends, including modernization, educational reforms, and the influx of wealth from oil revenues. The Islamic Federation of Women's Sport was founded in 1991, with the goal of organizing female sporting events while retaining religious traditions, and in 1993, Iran hosted the first Women's Islamic Games, which included competitors from ten countries. By 2005, athletes from 44 countries were taking part in the event.

These changes have had a significant impact on female sport participation, which is now commonplace in most Middle Eastern countries. Women and girls from the region who want to play sports, however, encounter a unique set of challenges not faced by their Western counterparts. While female athleticism is widely encouraged in many parts of the world, in the Middle East it is widely

regarded as an affront to traditional Arab values. Female athletes in the Middle East face pressures that include family, religion, politics, and culture. These issues often take place over use or nonuse of the *hijab*, the traditional head covering for Muslim women. The hijab serves as a site of negotiation, resistance, and conformity.

"The reason I cover up is because of my religion," says Rima, a Pakistani member of her university's basketball team. "If [a game] is open to male spectators, then I don't feel personally comfortable, even if I have my hijab on. And also my family, they do not see this as appropriate or respectful."

Partly an expression of rebellion against post-9/11 Islamaphobia and partly because of a more general resurgence of conservative culture in the Middle East, wearing the hijab has increased over the last twenty-five years. Social scientist Symeon Dagkas and his co-authors assert that the hijab's comeback represents "an affirmation of religious identity. For many, the hijab is a symbol of honor connected to faith and respect for the Islamic requirement to cover their hair."

This has outraged some Western feminists, who view the hijab as the ultimate symbol of female oppression. Earlier this year, France banned public use of the *niqab*, the Muslim veil that covers every part of the head but the eyes, and threatened heavy fines for women who wore one publically and husbands or fathers who forced their wives and daughters to do so. French politician André Gerin declared, "The full veil is a walking coffin, a muzzle."

This probably wouldn't surprise sports sociologist Gertrud Pfister, who noted in a study of Muslim female athletes in Denmark that, "Headscarves provoke opposition among the mainstream population more than any other Islamic precept or interdiction." But it hasn't stopped a dramatic increase in the number of females wearing the hijab in Denmark and other European countries. "'Doing Islam' has become a widespread habit, in some cases almost a fashion," Pfister wrote.

The hijab's newfound chic, along with the rise in sports participation among Muslim females, has turned this piece of clothing into a cranial combat zone upon which culture wars are waged. Turkey banned the use of the hijab in competitive athletics outright, while other Middle-Eastern countries *require* Muslim women to cover their hair at public sporting events.

In their case study of a women's soccer team in Palestine, Petra Gieß-Stüber and her co-authors noted that use or nonuse of the hijab "varies considerably according to the country or region of birth, social class, level of education, the religious customs of the older generation and the location." An issue faced by scholars of the Middle East is that each country in the region has distinct values and beliefs regarding religion, culture, politics, and gender. Countries such as Lebanon are relatively progressive in their attitudes and policies towards women, while nations like Saudi Arabia and Iran are much more restrictive.

Middle-Eastern women are often lumped together as representing a collective whole, but this could not be further from reality. Indeed, many nations in the region are populated by expatriate women from other parts of the Middle East, as well as countries such as India, Sudan, and Ethiopia, making the notion of monoculture preposterous. A single sports team can include as many countries of origin as it has players, each of whom must decide how they will dress and whether or not to participate publicly.

Some of these female athletes have helped spawn a cottage industry devoted to the manufacture and sale of sportswear that conforms to Islamic standards. Web sites such as ahiida.com peddle the Burqini, a two-piece, full body swimsuit with attached "Hijood" head covering. "All eyes are on the appearance of Muslim women in sports," writes company founder Aheda Zanetti. "Their appearance should be modest and at the same time it should reflect a professional sporty appearance with pride." While these sartorial innovations skirt clothing regulations, they aren't always practical for aquatic activity. Egyptian athlete Sahar Elrefai swam competitively as a child, but gave it up after she began wearing traditional Muslim clothing at age 13. "You can't do professional swimming with [a Burqini] because it's just too heavy," she said.

Certain Middle Eastern nations (or athletic organizations within them) also require that sports be segregated by gender. Male spectators are not allowed at games that include female contestants. Others countries or organizations refuse to separate by gender, creating a quandary for conservative Muslim female athletes. More often than not, these young women refuse to take part in public sporting events.

"I don't play in front of mixed audience because of Islam," declares Maryam, a Palestinian woman who practices with her university's soccer team but declines to compete in official games because there are male observers in the audience. "I am fine playing in front of girl audiences but not mixed. When you're playing in front of mixed audiences, it's going to be violating [Islamic principles] because you are not dressed in the right way," she said.

> The hijab has become a cranial combat zone upon which culture wars are waged.

Maryam's teammate, Tara, is a practicing Muslim originally from Sudan. Tara wears a head covering in her everyday life, but she removes it to play soccer and ignores the male spectators. "I am more comfortable when there isn't a mixed audience, but it's not like it's a strong enough reason for me not to play in the game," she said.

According to the Pew Research Center, there are about 1.57 billion Muslims in more than 200 countries internationally. This represents about 23 percent of the global population, making Islam the world's second most practiced religion, and it includes professional athletes such as Fatima Al Nabhani, an Omani tennis player who eschews traditional Muslim garb during matches, and Bahraini sprinter Roqaya Al-Ghasara, who was fully covered and wearing a hijab when she ran in the 2008 Olympic Games in Beijing. Both women not only serve as role models for aspiring female athletes from the region, but also shatter Western stereotypes.

"I am hoping to be a good example of showing that, even though there are religious restrictions wearing the veil and some girls are not allowed to play in front of men, you can still carry on and play sports," says Sahar Elrefai, who is captain of the Texas A&M at Qatar women's basketball team. "You see these girls out running and they are not even covered up. That just defies what people think."

violence and transgression

overview

Acting out aggressive feelings through violence is at times a socially sanctioned response, particularly for men. How are institutions complicit in violence? How are men and women constructing new scripts that might sever the links between intimacy and violence?

Lisa Wade, Brian Sweeney, Amelia Seraphia Derr, Michael Messner, and Carol Burke ("Ruling Out Rape") investigate the culture of sexual assault in the institutional settings of college campuses and the military. Moving away from a focus on individual perpetrators and survivors, they examine the practices, policies, and cultures of institutions and how they influence the prevalence of sexual violence.

Kristen Barber and Kelsy Kretschmer thoughtfully examine the role of men in Slut Walk marches and in the larger conversation around sexual violence. "Walking Like a Man?" argues that men's position in feminist spaces can both challenge male power and reinforce it. Jennifer Dawn Carlson describes the ways women who carry guns ("Carrying Guns, Contesting Gender") understand their engagement in an activity that is generally coded as masculine.

In "Stealing a Bag of Potato Chips and Other Crimes of Resistance," Victor Rios examines raced and gendered expectations of young men of color living in East Oakland. For these young men, transgressing these gender expectations looks like small acts of resistance that do not always make sense to authority figures.

Finally, Shari Dworkin's interview with activist Dean Peacock shows how one man has fought against gender-based violence, transgressing gendered expectations that gender-based violence is a "women's issue."

things to consider

- Personal, interpersonal, and institutional violence is pervasive in our culture. But violence also spawns active resistance against gender scripts, norms, and expectations. How do you practice, or see gendered resistance in your everyday life?
- Can you think of some less obvious or non-physical forms of gendered violence and/or resistance after reading this section?
- Why is gender stereotyping, a form of gendered violence, more than a "woman's issue?"
- Discuss what you believe the role should be for men and masculinity in feminine and feminist activist spaces.
- In the past five years there has been an increasing amount of attention on instances of sexual assault and violence on college campuses across the country. After reading the articles in "Ruling Out Rape," what changes would you like to see enacted in institutions, and in our culture?
- In what ways are gendered and racialized violence connected? How might men of color experience violence differently than women of color or trans people of color?

ruling out rape

lisa wade, brian sweeney, amelia seraphia derr, michael a. messner, and carol burke

spring 2014

Sexual assault is epidemic in the United States. Recent media reports, public outrage, and activism have been focused on the institutional settings in which these assaults occur. Colleges and universities, as well as the military and athletic programs, have come under increasing scrutiny as settings that not only fail to deter, but possibly foster rape.

Vanderbilt, Notre Dame, Maryville, Steubenville, Florida State, and the University of Missouri, to name a few, are among the recent highly-profiled institutions in which student athletes allegedly committed rapes that were ignored or downplayed by school administrators. The victims in these cases were treated with hostility by the schools, police, and even their peers who considered the reports of rape to be exaggerated responses to a party culture where "everyone is just trying to have fun" and where "stuff happens." Some of these victims have committed or attempted suicide.

Social consciousness around putting the victims of rape on trial may be evolving, but are the environments that foster these assaults really changing? President Obama recently promised women who have been sexually assaulted in college: "I've got your back." Should we be guardedly optimistic that this message from the top signals change, or do policy trends indicate attempts to protect institutions at the continued expense of victims? In this *Viewpoints*, five experts weigh in on the question of situational factors and institutional accountability around rape.

Lisa Wade reviews what we know about who commits rape on college campuses and the conditions that support this behavioral profile. She asserts that campus officials need to understand the interplay of cultural, psychological and situational causes for rape in order to make viable policy decisions. Brian Sweeney highlights the connection between alcohol consumption and sexual assault. He argues that campus policies that address binge drinking are doomed to fail unless they take into account that, for many young people, drinking and casual sex are rewarding. Amelia Seraphia Derr focuses on federal policies for reporting campus rape. She notes that colleges and universities are beginning to take these regulations more seriously, but raises concerns that they may trend in the direction of a "culture of compliance," where the fear of litigation that drives policy making could be counterproductive for prevention and support programs.

Michael A. Messner turns the lens on rape culture among male college athletes and asks what can be done. He's not convinced that current reform programs that target individual men and men's sports teams will mitigate sexual violence. He suggests we need a deeper understanding of the link between sexual domination, and the ways we celebrate male athletes and their violent domination in sports. Writing about a different, though familiar context, Carol Burke examines recent rape scandals in the military. She chronicles the mounting evidence for a high-level official blind eye on sexual assault and the resulting outrage among congresswomen who are calling for accountability. Is change in the offing? Read on and see what these experts have to say.

understanding and ending the campus sexual assault epidemic

by lisa wade

College attendance is a risk factor for sexual assault. According to the U.S. Department of Justice, one in five women who attend college will be the victim of a completed or attempted sexual assault, compared to one in six women in the general population. Up to 90 percent of these women will know their attacker. Only about half will identify their experience as assault and fewer than 5 percent will report their experience to campus authorities or the police. Four percent of college men also report being sexually assaulted, overwhelmingly by other men.

> *If institutions of higher education want to, they have the tools to reduce rates of sexual assault. And, even if they do not make this a priority, they face increasing pressure to do so.*

Scholars have been working to gain a better understanding of the prevalence of rape on campuses, why it's infrequently reported to authorities, and what we can do about it. In a 2006 article, Elizabeth Armstrong and her collaborators point to cultural, psychological, and situational causes. In the effort to prevent sexual crimes, colleges and universities need to understand these interrelated causes and how they contribute to rates of sexual assault.

What are the psychological factors? A small number of men may be more predisposed to assault their peers than others. In a 2002 study by David Lisak and Paul Miller, 6 percent of male college students admitted to behavior that matched the legal definitions of sexual assault or rape. Of those men, two-thirds were serial rapists, with an average of six assaults each. Serial rapists plan their assaults, carefully choose their victim, use alcohol as a rape drug, and employ force, but only as a back-up. Lisak and Miller find that these men are more likely than other men to engage in other forms of violence as well.

What about context? Some men may be inclined to harm others, but whether they do so is related to their opportunities. The right context can offer these men an opening to do so. Peggy Sanday first recognized the role that context plays in facilitating sexual assault. Studying fraternity parties, she found that some are generative of risk and others are less so. Parties that feature loud music, few places to sit, dancing, drinking, and compulsory flirting are, she explains, "rape prone." In these more dangerous places, rape culture camouflages the predatory behavior of serial rapists—like plying women with alcohol or pulling them into secluded areas—making it look normal and more difficult to interpret as criminal.

And then there's culture. Rape culture narratives—those that suggest that rape is simply a matter of miscommunication, that "date rape" isn't "real rape," that women frequently lie about being sexually assaulted for vengeance or out of shame—make it difficult for bystanders to justify intervening and for some victims to understand that their experience was a crime. Rape culture also gives rapists plausible excuses for their actions, making it difficult to hold them accountable, especially if members of the campus administration buy into these myths as well.

Armstrong and her colleagues show that all three of these causal factors interact together and with campus policy. Strict penalties for drinking alcohol in residence halls, for example, especially when strongly enforced, can push party-oriented students off campus to less safe places. Rape-friendly contexts offer a target-rich haven for the small percentage of individual men who are motivated to use force and coercion to attain sex. Rape culture contributes to concealing the predatory nature of their behavior to victims, their peers and, all too often, their advocates.

Currently, we're in the midst of a transformation in how colleges and universities handle sexual assault. While our understanding is far from complete, we know more than ever about the interaction of situational, cultural, and psychological causes. If institutions of higher education want to, they have the tools to reduce rates of sexual assault. And, even if they do not make this a priority, they face increasing pressure to do so. A strong national movement now aims to hold institutions accountable for ignoring, hiding, and mishandling sex crimes. Thanks largely to Know Your IX, 30 colleges submitted complaints to the U.S. Office for Civil Rights in 2013, nearly double the number from the year before. We should expect even higher numbers in 2014. Praising these activists, President Barack Obama announced that he was making the end of men's sexual violence against women a priority. The combination of "insider" and "outsider" politics, and a sympathetic media, is a promising recipe for change.

drinking and sexual assault [kids just wanna have fun]

by brian sweeney

Getting wasted is fun, as is hooking up. In today's campus hookup culture, alcohol and sex often go together, and both can be rewarding experiences for young adults. Party culture glamorizes heavy drinking, making it seem less dangerous and, too often, causing students to dismiss the negative effects—whether getting puked on at a football game or being sexually assaulted—as "just stuff

that happens." But sexual assault is a predictable result of party subcultures characterized by extreme drinking and sexual double standards. A majority of college rape victims are drunk when attacked, and rapists use alcohol as a weapon to incapacitate their victims. Men—and other women, for that matter—may see overly drunk women as fair game, giving up their right to feminine protection because they have failed to be respectable and ladylike. Given the connection between intoxication and sexual assault, many ask, "Why not just tell women not to get so drunk?" But a mindset that places responsibility on women ignores the widespread attitudes and practices that encourage men's sexual predation and victimization of women in the first place.

To be clear, drinking, by itself, does not lead to sexual assault. Drinking heavily makes women more vulnerable, but it is overwhelmingly men who take advantage and rape. It is also men who stand by and watch their male friends ply women with drinks, block women from leaving rooms, and sometimes gang-rape women too drunk to walk home. Equipping women with "watch your drink, stay with your friends" strategies ignores both the fun of partying with abandon and the larger structures of domination that lead men to feel entitled to (drunk) women's bodies. Moreover, while rape-supportive beliefs are widespread, their influence over men's behavior is dependent on rape-supportive social and organizational arrangements—campus party culture and alcohol policy included.

> *In today's campus hookup culture, alcohol and sex often go together, and both can be rewarding experiences for young adults.*

Drinking subcultures have a long history on American college campuses, but since 1984 and the passage of the National Minimum Drinking Age Act, all 50 states have opted for billions in federal highway aid in exchange for passing Age-21 laws. As a result, many college campuses send mixed messages and endorse confused policies. Students are regularly fined and written up for drinking infractions but also educated about drinking responsibly. Students flock to so-called party schools and then spend most of their college years trying not to get caught—secretly "pre-gaming" with hard-alcohol in dorm rooms, hiding out in fraternity basements during party inspections, and nervously sweating as the bouncer checks for fake IDs. Alcohol becomes a coveted commodity, with many students seeking access to it and fortunate others wielding control of it.

Problems related to drinking exist, in part, because we have constructed a firewall between students and the adults who run universities—a divide that surely undermines our mission of creating safe and rich learning environments. We are allowing young people, unsupervised, to initiate each other into adulthood, often through rituals built around drinking. The campus pub is long gone at most schools, a relic of a bygone in loco parentis era when many professors lived among students and mentored them academically and socially. We could perhaps learn valuable lessons from a time when drinking was less illicit and student social life more open and watched over. Bringing drinking "aboveground" would disrupt some of the party scenes that sociological research has shown to be productive of sexual danger for women, would remove some of the constraints college administrators face in crafting effective alcohol education and policy, and would embolden sexual assault victims to come forward, reducing their fears of being punished for drinking violations.

Many schools are trying to get students to drink more responsibly. Since 2008, over 125 college and university presidents and chancellors have signed on to the Amethyst Initiative, which calls for "informed and dispassionate public debate" on Age-21 drinking laws. The supporters of the initiative, while not explicitly endorsing a lowering of the drinking age, believe Age-21 laws drive drinking underground, leading to dangerous binge drinking and reckless behavior among students. Five years after its inception, it is unclear if anything will come of the Amethyst Initiative. Federal and state government officials seem stubbornly unwilling to open discussion on Age-21 laws. And yet, because the initiative focuses on moderate and responsible drinking among students rather than abstinence, its ideas should have traction in correcting party cultures that, as they are currently organized, produce both fun and sexual danger. What is fairly certain is that sexual assault policies that ignore the collective, rewarding nature of drunken, erotically charged revelry will likely fail among many young adults.

a culture of compliance vs. prevention

by amelia seraphia derr

The under-reporting of campus sexual assaults has become a social problem. Students around the country are waging protests and demanding accountability from university administrators who have been accused of making light of alarming rates of sexual violence on college campuses. In 2011 the U.S. Department of Education Office of Civil Rights, in reaction to a Department of Justice report on the serious under-reporting of campus sexual assaults, and with the encouragement of Vice President Joe Biden, issued a Dear Colleagues Letter (DCL) on the topic of sexual violence. Specifically, the DCL emphasized and reiterated the legally mandated expectations for systems of reporting and adjudicating cases of sexual violence, for training staff, and for developing prevention and support programs.

Legislated reporting of sexual assault is the fruit of efforts dating back to the 1972 issuance of Title IX of the Education Amendments, which included sexual violence along with a variety of other forms of gender discrimination. In 1986 the Clery Act clarified and expanded the reporting requirements that were part of Title IX by establishing clear expectations for support services for students who are victims of sexual violence, and for the types of sexual violence-related reports that colleges and universities must file annually.

This legislative action intensified in 2011 when Bob Casey (D-PA) learned of Title IX violation complaints against Swarthmore College, alleging under-reporting cases of sexual misconduct, and took action. He introduced the Campus Sexual Violence Elimination Act (The SaVE Act), which became law with the passage of the Violence Against Women Reauthorization Act in August 2013. This act closes a serious gap in the existing law by requiring clearer and more publicized policies, education on student's rights, "bystander education" for the purpose of prevention, expanded reporting requirements, mandated prevention programs, and procedural rights for the accuser and accused.

This federal-level attention has created a sense of urgency in higher education, prompting university administrators to revisit policies on sexual assault to ensure compliance. But does it actually help change an organizational environment that is highly conducive to assault?

Institutionalizing accountability is essential; policies are a sustainable tool for addressing sexual violence on campuses. Evidence of the effectiveness of such policies can be seen in the fact that since the 2011 DCL there has been a steep increase in the number of Title IX and Clery Act complaints filed. According to the U.S. Department of Education, 62 Title IX complaints dealing with issues of sexual violence and harassment were filed between Oct. 1, 2012 and Sept. 30, 2013 alone.

However, a heightened regulatory environment may create a culture of compliance where the fear of litigation—rather than expert knowledge on prevention—drives policy-making. Institutional priorities and resources are directed differently depending on whether a university focuses on compliance-based reporting

> *Federal-level attention has created a sense of urgency in higher education, prompting university administrators to revisit policies on sexual assault to ensure compliance.*

"By going beyond traditional risk reduction alone and covering primary prevention, consent, bystander intervention and reporting options we will begin to change the culture of tolerance for sexual violence and the silence that surrounds it."

– S. Daniel Carter, formerly director of public policy for Security On Campus, Inc., wrote of the SaVE Act in a blog for The Huffington Post.

policy. The SaVE Act would require institutions to provide prevention and awareness programs for all incoming students and new employees.

"By going beyond traditional risk reduction alone and covering primary prevention, consent, bystander intervention and reporting options we will begin to change the culture of tolerance for sexual violence and the silence that surrounds it," S. Daniel Carter, formerly director of public policy for Security On Campus, Inc., wrote of the SaVE Act in a blog for The Huffington Post. Security on Campus is one of 29 organizations that has endorsed the SaVE Act. (Carter is now with the VTV Family Outreach Foundation.)

At least 75 instances of sexual assault were reported on college campuses in news articles within the first six weeks of the current academic year, according to a survey of media reports by The Huffington Post. That number reflects only a small percentage of the total instances, as few assaults make it into news reports and only a small percentage of sexual violence victims ever report their attack to school or law enforcement officials. According

policies or prevention and support programs (which also include reporting policies, but within a framework of victim advocacy rather than institutional protection). For example, the DCL states that "if a school knows or reasonably should know about a potential sexual assault it is required to take immediate action." Ambiguity about what this means may prompt universities to adopt a mandated reporting policy for adult-aged students similar to those in place for minors or other vulnerable populations in order to avoid litigation.

Duke University (along with University of Montana, Swarthmore, and several others) has instituted such a policy, naming almost all of its 34,000 employees as mandated reporters. When staff or faculty members realize that students are about to share a concern with them, they must inform the student that the information they share will be reported to the designated administrator, with or without the student's permission. Duke University states that reports have increased since this policy was adopted. However, some victim's advocates oppose the practice. They counter that campus policies that mandate reporting irrespective of the victim's desire perpetuate a campus environment of silence and isolation and limit victims' options for confiding in trusted sources. A student Resident Assistant (RA) at Swarthmore, where RAs are considered mandated reporters, was recently fired from her position because she refused to break confidentiality by identifying a victim. Critics warn that these policies could ultimately lead to decreased reporting from victims

who feel there is no safe space for them to turn in confidence. This is especially likely to be the case at a campus with few or insufficient survivor support services.

The real issue is how to move beyond a culture of compliance to a culture of prevention. In response to the requirements of the Campus SaVE Act, university policies should foreground survivor self-determination, provide strong perpetrator-prevention programs, offer robust victim support services, and promote increased dialogue about sexual violence with all members of the university community. These efforts will take us beyond the high visibility that reporting requirements have had, and into the areas of support and education required for true change.

can locker room rape culture be prevented?

by michael a. messner

Recipe for sexual assault: Assemble a group of young men. Promise them glory for violently dominating other groups of young men. Bond the group with aggressive joking about the sexual domination of women. Add public adulation that permeates the group with the scent of entitlement. Provide mentors who thrived as young men in this same system. Allow to simmer.

> ## "Sometimes it's not about football. Sometimes it's just about rape."
> - Patricia Carroll, **Lawyer**

> " **Sexual assault is embedded in the routine values and culture of silence in organizations.**

What have we cooked up? Horrendous sexual assaults on unconscious girls by high school football players in Steubenville and Maryville as well as an ongoing parade of sexual assault accusations against college football players, most recently at Florida State, Vanderbilt, and the United States Naval Academy. Do we over-emphasize cases of football player sexual misconduct because of their high profile? Perhaps. But research by sociologist Todd Crosset since the 1990s has shown that men who play intercollegiate sports are more likely than non-athletes to commit sexual assault—especially those in high-status sports that valorize violence.

Of course most football or ice hockey athletes don't rape women. Recently, some male athletes have even formed organizations to stop violence against women.

"Male Athletes Against Violence" has done peer education at the University of Maine for years. And since 1993, Northeastern University's Mentors in Violence Prevention program has created a template for a national proliferation of sports-based programs that deploy a "bystander" approach to violence prevention. These programs attempt to disrupt the ways that high status male groups—like sports teams and fraternities—layer protective silence around members who perpetrate violence against women. A bystander approach teaches men to intervene to stop sexual assaults before they happen—for instance, stepping in when seeing one's teammates dragging an inebriated woman to a back room. A good man, the bystander approach teaches, steps forward not only to keep a woman safe, but also to keep the team safe from public trouble.

The years of silence surrounding Penn State University football coach Jerry Sandusky's serial sexual assaults of children is one example of the absolute failure by high-profile university coaches and administrators to model the responsible bystander behavior they say their young athletes should engage in. This case showed that, rather than resulting simply from the actions of one bad man, sexual assault is embedded in the routine values and culture of silence in organizations.

A number of years ago, I assisted psychologist Mark Stevens—a pioneer in working with athletes to prevent sexual violence—in an intervention with a college football program after members of the team were accused of sexually assaulting a woman at an off-campus party. Before the first of two workshops, I asked Stevens if he really thought that a few hours of talk could change the culture of sexual dominance that so commonly cements football team members' loyalties while simultaneously

> " This case isn't about a YouTube video. This case isn't about social media. This case isn't about Big Red football. This case is about a 16-year-old girl who was taken advantage of, toyed with and humiliated. And it's time people who did this to her are held responsible. "
> - Marianne Hemmeter, **Prosecutor**

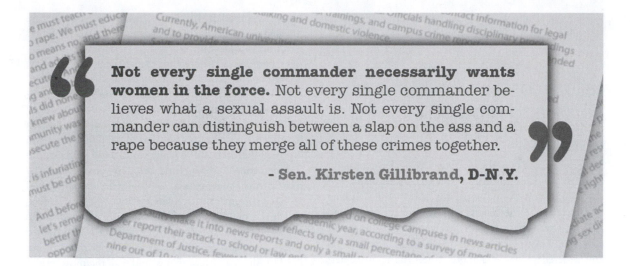

> **Not every single commander necessarily wants women in the force.** Not every single commander believes what a sexual assault is. Not every single commander can distinguish between a slap on the ass and a rape because they merge all of these crimes together.
>
> **- Sen. Kirsten Gillibrand, D-N.Y.**

putting women and vulnerable men at risk. Stevens answered no. "But," he added, "if we can empower one or two guys who, down the road, might intervene in a situation to stop a sexual assault, then our work will have made the world safer for at least one woman."

I still worry that such interventions do less to prevent acts of violence than they do to contain the public relations nightmare that sexual assaults create for athletics departments. Confirming that fear, a man I recently interviewed told me that he had been hired by a big-time college sports program to institute a violence prevention program, only to find it "incredibly disappointing" when he learned his employers had hired him mostly to work with male athletes of color to keep them eligible to play sports. "I thought that they were genuinely ready to do something, you know, make some changes . . . I got kind of duped. I had this particular background [in violence prevention] so

that was really enticing for them, and they had no intention of actually letting me do any of that work."

While some schools have adopted sexual assault prevention programs for some of their men's sports teams, we just don't know how well they work. We need good research that points to how, or under what conditions prevention programs within institutions like football (or the military) can actually succeed in mitigating gender-based violence. To have such an impact, I believe these interventions will need to confront how sexism is routinely intertwined with male entitlement and celebratory violence. To be truly successful,

> *Nowhere in America do we allow a boss to decide if an employee was sexually assaulted or not, except in the United States military.*

Sexual assaults by US military in Japan unlikely to end in prison

At US military bases in Japan, most service members found culpable years did not go to prison, according to internal Department of Def...

Rape victims say military labels them 'crazy'

By David S. Martin, CNN

The Military Has a Rape Problem and It's Not Just Women Who Suffer

The military says it's working to wipe out sexual violence in the armed for...

I suspect, such a program would render the game itself to be no longer football as we know it.

failure to serve and protect

by carol burke

Military scandals in the past two years have brought new attention to old problems: sexual harassment, sexual assault, and the potential for bias in the handling of these crimes. The general who commanded the 82nd Airborne was charged with forcible sodomy, indecent acts, and violating orders, and was issued a reprimand and ordered to pay a $20,000 fine. The commanders in charge of Lackland Air Force Base apparently didn't realize that, over a two-year period, 62 recruits were assaulted by 33 drill instructors. Even those tasked with preventing sexual assault were charged with the crimes they had pledged to thwart. A lieutenant colonel who headed the Sexual Harassment and Assault Response Prevention program at Fort Campbell, Kentucky, was arrested and charged with stalking an ex-wife and sending her threatening emails in violation of a restraining order. A lieutenant colonel in charge of the Air Force Sexual Assault Prevention and Response Program was charged with the sexual battery of a stranger in a parking lot. His alleged victim, according to witnesses, took justice into her own hands and after pushing away the drunken officer, ran after him and punched him in the face. At trial, the officer was acquitted.

Ultimately, the scandal that ignited the outrage of several congresswomen was Lieutenant General Craig Franklin's decision to overturn Lieutenant Colonel James Wilkerson's court-martial conviction for sexual assault. To Franklin, it seemed incongruous that a man "who adored his wife and his 9-year-old son," a man who as a pilot had flown in the same unit as him, and a man who had been selected "for promotion to full colonel, a wing inspector general, a career officer" could be a sexual predator. So Franklin exercised the power granted him and other commanders under the Uniform Code of Military Justice (UCMJ) to reverse any verdict without explanation. Although this might have looked at the time like the decision of an out-of-touch commander from his lonely and lofty post, identifying more with the plight of

the accused than of the victim, emails related to the case revealed that generals of even higher rank than Franklin's supported his decision.

According to the Defense Department's own survey, 26,000 anonymous respondents claimed that they had been sexually assaulted in 2012, yet only 3,374 complaints were officially reported in that year. The incendiary mix of the skyrocketing rates of assault and the apparent indifference of some commanders to the plight of victims captured the attention of many women in Congress, and they demanded reform. These congresswomen, joined by some of their male colleagues, took aim at the heart of military culture, the sacrosanct military justice system, which can only be as impartial as the commander who oversees it. Senator Kristin Gillibrand (D-NY) proposed a two-part judicial system akin to those of many of our NATO Allies, a system that would take the most serious crimes like murder and sexual assault out of the chain of command and ensure that decisions to investigate, prosecute, and convict could not be arbitrarily reversed by a commander. In a statement issued December 20, 2013, Gillibrand said, "Nowhere in America do we allow a boss to decide if an employee was sexually assaulted or not, except in the United States military."

Senator Claire McCaskill (D-MO) fashioned a more moderate compromise that left the investigation and adjudication of crimes of sexual assault in the hands of commanders but that lifted the five-year statute of limitations on courts-martial for sex-related crimes, criminalized retaliation by commanders (but not by peers), provided counsel for victims, and did away with the "good soldier defense." The compromise carried the day, much to the chagrin of victims who regard the UCMJ as a system that often denies them justice.

For several years now the Department of Defense has required mandatory training intended to prevent sexual assault and sexual harassment, crafted public service announcements for broadcast on military TV stations, established hotlines for victims, and posted pleas in bathrooms on bases here and abroad for bystanders to step in when they see abuse taking place. Unfortunately, these costly efforts have failed to build trust in a military judicial system. Victims see these public campaigns as the military's efforts to protect the institution and not them. As long as the investigation and adjudication of sexual assault cases remain within such a command-centric judicial system, the partiality of a single individual can easily trump justice.

20

walking like a man?

kristen barber and kelsy kretschmer

spring 2013

Hundreds of people were gathered on the sidewalk outside of the Carbondale, Illinois, community theatre, carrying signs and banners. Women were dressed in tutus, glitter, fishnet stockings, and waving signs that read, "Honk if you <3 sluts," "My clothes aren't consent," and "I borrowed this outfit from your mom, do you still want to rape me?"

It was the town's first SlutWalk, organized to protest men's complicity in sexual assault. SlutWalk organizers challenge both the relative invisibility of male aggressors in sexual assault and the Madonna-whore dichotomy signified by the word "slut." This dichotomy divides women into virgins or sluts, and supports a double standard where men are encouraged to have multiple sexual partners while women are stigmatized for doing so.

While the turnout for the Carbondale walk was larger than expected, most striking was the sizable number of men who attended. Comprising about a fifth of the over 450 participants, men were some of the most enthusiastic and eye-catching participants, wearing kimonos, green jumpsuits, and cut-off shorts with midriff-baring shirts. They were there with friends, fraternity brothers, and resident halls, or came on their own to support the cause.

Since assault against women is historically seen as a "women's issue," feminist organizers often consider men to be ill-equipped to understand, let alone challenge, women's oppression. However, many scholars, activists, and organizers have come to see men's participation in feminist movements as important. Sociologist Mark Cohan suggests that men have multifaceted and sometimes counterintuitive reasons for participating in

feminist movements. Looking at men's identification with feminist causes, Cohan finds that while men may have an awareness of gender inequality, they can symbolically undermine gender politics at the same time they participate in such movements.

Men negotiate their relationship to gender politics and women's issues in both helpful and problematic ways, at times challenging sexism while also diverting attention from the central goals of the movement. With SlutWalk, these tensions emerge among a new generation of activists.

slutwalk and its critics

SlutWalk originated in 2011 after a Toronto police officer told a college audience that if women want to prevent becoming victims of sexual assault, they should "avoid dressing like sluts." The Toronto walk was followed by marches in New York City, Washington, D.C., Boston, Tallahassee, and a handful of smaller cities across the United States, and around the globe.

Many young women see the marches as a way to reclaim the word "slut" and avoid victim blaming. Siobhan Conners, an organizer of the 2011 Boston

SlutWalk, sees it as a way to "bring awareness to the shame and degradation women still face for expressing their sexuality." In a 2011 interview, writer Alice Walker praised the SlutWalk as a "spontaneous movement that has grown around reclaiming this word [slut]" that "speaks to women's resistance to having names turned into weapons used against them."

SlutWalk is not without its critics, however. Some feminists have objected to the movement's embrace of the pejorative term "slut." Women's studies professor Janell Hobson, writing in *Ms. Magazine* in 2011, suggests the term has a racial history that makes it easier for White women to reclaim than women of color, whose bodies "have inspired the dangerous rhetoric."

Others have criticized the fact that while some SlutWalks were more somber events—where some women wore the clothes they were assaulted in—SlutWalks can at times resemble parties, exuding a carnival-like atmosphere. In Carbondale, people were dressed in costume and came for a good time. Many women came provocatively dressed in fishnet stockings and bras or bustiers, suggesting that they should be able to dress as they please, free from sexual assault.

Whether men should be permitted to participate has also been a source of contention. While approximately one in four women experience sexual assault, men are almost always the perpetrators. On first glance, men's presence at the marches appears to be a sign of their growing concern about sexual assault. But when we consider the motivations of men who participate, as well as *how* they participate, a more complicated picture emerges.

real men don't rape

When men do participate in SlutWalk, they have varied reasons for doing so. In Carbondale, we encountered men who opposed traditional notions of masculinity, who wished to shake-up taken-for-granted ideas about what it means to be a "real" man. Several of them were dressed in black button-up shirts with big orange letters scrawled across the back that read, "Real Men Don't Rape."

A group of fraternity brothers marched together. "Fraternities get a bad rap," one marcher said. He beamed proudly as he told us that his fraternity was planning to organize an event the following month to promote awareness about domestic violence. The walk provided an opportunity for them to challenge the idea that male-only social fraternities are inherently hostile toward women. While these fraternity men did not necessarily identify as feminists, their attempts to redefine all-male spaces and challenge the meaning of manhood suggest they were acting as feminist allies.

"There's a perception that feminism is only for angry women who don't like men," said student Harpo Jaeger, who attended a Providence, Rhode Island SlutWalk. "But it should be possible for everyone to support women's rights." Yet, even when motivated by feminist concerns, men's participation can have unintended negative consequences. Although many of the women involved in SlutWalk were thrilled to have men participate in the event, some believed their presence diverted attention from women's experiences.

Gender studies scholar Hugo Schwyzer recognized this problem after helping to organize SlutWalk L.A. "I'd worried about going to SlutWalk as a man," he said. He was concerned that it would seem as though he was "cashing in on the excitement/activism/sexiness or trying to prove my feminist cred." He continued: "I won't even pretend that I didn't enjoy getting interviewed, but I was a bit worried that that too might be seen as stealing the stage." As he and others acknowledged, men's presence at SlutWalk can at times be helpful, and at other times can marginalize women.

In Boston, a group of men organized a "PimpWalk" that took place alongside the 2011 SlutWalk. These men dressed in colorful cowboy hats with feathers and held a boom box that played hip-hop and 1970s funk. Organizer Samuel Bilowski admitted it was a joke designed to "get some numbers" and to "talk to attractive women." SlutWalk marchers in Boston loudly criticized the PimpWalk organizers "for glorifying violence against women," since pimps promote and profit from the sale of women's bodies.

In Carbondale, we spoke with two men who marched in midriffs and cut-off shorts as a nod to the "slut" theme. One wore a t-shirt with the phrase "Respect Makes Me Horny" printed above a picture of a unicorn. He excitedly told us about how he and his friend had also participated in the Chicago SlutWalk a few weeks earlier. "Everyone got naked and jumped in a fountain!" he exclaimed. Other men contributed to the fun, party vibe by carrying signs that read, "Ruck Fape" or "Just because I have a nice butt doesn't mean I'm a slut." The march ended at a local bar, where of-age participants received bracelets upon entry and could continue the party.

The number of men who attended SlutWalk Carbondale was striking. Men were some of the most enthusiastic and eye-catching marchers.

While irony can be deployed in progressive ways, it can also be reactionary and antifeminist. The costumed men created a festive atmosphere, luring more people to the march, attracting media coverage, and making participation less intimidating. But when men pretended to be pimps, made jokes about naked women, and presented themselves as heterosexual voyeurs, it was off-putting. This form of participation undermined the point of the march—that women are often sexually assaulted and then blamed for their own victimization. These male marchers partied at the expense of the message.

victims and sympathizers

Many men participated in the SlutWalk because they wished to support a sister or a female friend who had been sexually assaulted. The SlutWalk provided them with an opportunity to march in solidarity with the women in their lives. When asked why he marched, one young man told us solemnly, "My sister was raped." At the SlutWalk in Storrs, Connecticut, fraternity president Bryant Dominguez said, "I have a lot of female friends who have been called names [like slut]. I wanted to be here in support." Another man who marched in Philadelphia while wearing a Superman costume said that he was "shocked" at how many of his female friends had experienced sexual assault.

By participating, these men demonstrated support for individual women. Some men came to learn how common sexual assault is, and how victims are often shamed after being raped. Some were exposed, too, to broader feminist ideas and values about gender equality.

Because men tend to see rape largely as an issue that does not affect them personally, they are often reluctant to engage in rape education programs, according to researchers Elizabeth Scheel, Eric Johnson, Michelle Schneider, and Betsy Smith, noting in 2001 that rape prevention education does not tend to be "well-received by men," who often become "defensive or indifferent" to "the movement to end rape." As a result, men are often unprepared to support the women in their lives who are victims of assault. Yet, many men, they argue, are "truly interested" in being "positive supporter[s]" and wish to "learn more about the 'correct' method of responding to a woman who has experienced rape." For men to become effective supporters of women, the researchers claim, they must learn how to stand by women.

For individual sympathizers who came to support a loved one at SlutWalk, marching alongside daughters, sisters, and friends who had been sexually assaulted was often a first step toward becoming feminist allies.

However, being a sympathizer does not necessarily make one a politically conscious participant. Most men we spoke with did not make the connection between the sexual assault of loved ones and cultural definitions of masculinity that valorize competition, aggression, and the sexual conquest of women. Indeed, many framed their participation in SlutWalk in traditionally masculine terms: the man in the Superman outfit, for example, saw himself as a chivalrous protector of women.

> *When men pretended to be pimps, made jokes about naked women, and presented themselves as heterosexual voyeurs, it was off-putting.*

As activist Jackson Katz noted in his 2006 book, *The Macho Paradox*, to move from the sympathizer role into the role of ally, men must recognize social structures that encourage victim blaming, and begin to acknowledge the role men play in perpetuating social problems such as sexual assault and violence. The "long-running American tragedy of sexual and domestic violence," he wrote, "is arguably more revealing about men than it is about women. Men, after all, are the ones committing the vast majority of the violence. Men are the ones doing most of the battering and almost all of the rape."

Still, some men used the SlutWalk as a vehicle for talking about their own victimization. In Tampa, Florida, a male college student came dressed in torn blue jeans, and told a reporter that they were the pants he was wearing when he was sexually assaulted years before. "Just because I'm dressed in torn-up jeans doesn't mean you can hurt me," he said. He went on to explain his motivation for coming to the event, making it clear that, "It does happen to men, too." Similarly, a man attending the 2011 Denver, Colorado SlutWalk carried a sign indicating what he had been wearing when he was sexually assaulted, "I was wearing khaki shorts."

> *For feminism to thrive, changing the hearts and minds of men is necessary—while keeping women's experiences at the center.*

Placing their own experiences at the center, they highlighted the fact that men, too, are victims of sexual assault—albeit at a lesser rate than women. While men who have been sexually assaulted are certainly invisible in discussions about sexual violence, when men use the SlutWalk to make claims about their own abuse, this dilutes the core message of the walk, according to some organizers. The march was organized to draw attention to how "slut" language is used to shame women who are sexually assaulted, and to control women's bodies; if men are assaulted too, it is probably not due to their choice of clothes. If men are seen as victims, the event becomes a more generalized protest against rape, drawing attention away from women's experiences.

men and feminist protest

Feminist activists struggle to involve men in social movements that work to improve the lives of us all. They agree that men's participation is vital, and that without serious cross-gender discussions of sexism we cannot effectively tackle issues such as sexual assault. As Jackson Katz suggests, getting men involved in feminist agendas means holding them responsible, and encouraging them to recognize the links between masculinity and sexism. If we exclude men from the conversation, they remain invisible in discussions of social problems in which they are centrally implicated.

But how, and under what conditions, can men become effective participants and feminist allies? Many of the women we spoke to at our local SlutWalk were greatly encouraged by men's attendance. Beyond the fact that they enlarged the crowd, activists hoped to change men's attitudes toward women and sexuality. And while some men suggested they are not part of the problem, many participated in these events, risking stigmatization and ostracism from others.

The ways men participate in SlutWalk illuminates dilemmas feminist organizers face in creating inclusive protests. How do you get men involved in helpful ways without alienating them? How do you make the movement fun and engaging, as well as serious, and sensitive to those who have been assaulted? How might you build an anti-rape movement that is inclusive of both female and male rape victims?

It is clear that many men wish to be involved in the conversation on sexual assault. Activists must figure out how to include men without diluting the core message of feminist protest: to make the world a better, safer place for women. For feminism to thrive, changing the hearts and minds of men is necessary—while keeping women's experiences at the center.

recommended resources

Bridges, Tristan S. 2010. "Men Just Weren't Made to Do This: Performances of Drag at 'Walk a Mile in Her Shoes' Marches," *Gender & Society 24*:5–30. An examination of men's involvement in feminist protest, and how performances of drag in protest often reproduce gender and sexual inequalities.

Cohan, Mark. 1997. "Political Identities and Political Landscapes: Men's Narrative Work in Relation to Women's Issues," *The Sociological Quarterly, 38*: 501–517. Examines how men explain their decisions to participate in feminist causes, as well as how these narratives connect to a larger political context.

Jardine, Alice, and Smith, Paul. 1987. *Men and Feminism*. London: Methuen. A collection of essays that addresses the consequences of men's participation in feminist movements.

Katz, Jackson. 2006. *The Macho Paradox: Why Some Men Hurt Women and How All Men Can Help*. Illinois: Sourcebooks. Discusses men's responsibility in preventing sexual assault and domestic violence against women.

Murphy, Michael J. 2009. "Can 'Men' Stop Rape?: Visualizing Gender in the 'My Strength is Not for Hurting' Rape Prevention Campaign," *Men and Masculinities 12*:113–130. Analyzes the "My Strength is Not for Hurting" rape prevention media campaign, and the contradictory messages wrapped up in this campaign.

Scheel, Elizabeth D, Johnson, Eric J, Schneider, Michelle, and Smith, Betsy. 2001. "Making Rape Education Meaningful for Men: The Case for Eliminating the Emphasis on Men as Perpetrators, Protectors, or Victims," *Sociological Practice 3*: 257–278. Considers men's experiences with and responses to anti-rape education, and presents ideas for increasing men's effectiveness as feminist allies.

carrying guns, contesting gender

jennifer dawn carlson

winter 2015

I remember looking at myself in the mirror that first morning, the familiar feminine ritual of checking my looks before heading out for the day disrupted by a new concern. I examined my hip for an unsightly bulge, hoping I had adequately concealed the handgun holstered on my right side. Deep into my research in Metro Detroit, I had decided to obtain a concealed pistol license from the state to better understand how people use guns to navigate social insecurity. The day the license arrived in the mail, I joined the roughly 11 million Americans who were licensed to carry a gun concealed.

I was nervous about adequately concealing my pistol that morning and carrying it into public space, but as a researcher, I was even more curious about what it was like to carry a gun on an everyday basis. Would it feel different to grab a cup of coffee knowing that I was armed with a 9 mm pistol—even if I was the only person who knew? How would my status as a licensed concealed carrier change how gun owners and carriers—disproportionately men—viewed me at the shooting range, in the firearm classroom, or at pro-gun events?

In many respects, gun culture is a man's world. As Scott Melzer argues in his book *Gun Crusaders: The NRA's Culture War*, the gun lobby's success since the 1970s can, at least in part, be tied to the way guns reinforce masculine identity in America. In legal gun use, the language of self-defense laws and doctrine suggest that guns are a man's prerogative: America's "No Duty to Retreat" doctrine has long been defended by the logic that "a man's house is his castle." And in their criminal uses, guns are sometimes wielded to enact gendered violence—especially domestic. According to a 2003 study by Jacquelyn Campbell and colleagues, an abuser's access to guns ranks (after previous abuse and employment

status) as one of the top predictors of a woman being killed by that abuser.

Others, however, highlight the protection guns can afford women. According to a series of papers published by Gary Kleck and colleagues that focus on women's victimization during street crime, acts of resistance against an attacker—including, but not limited to, brandishing or firing a gun—lessen the likelihood that an attack, such as sexual assault, is "completed." Indeed, many Americans argue women stand to gain as much as, if not more than, men from armed protection. From the NRA to the firearms industry to gun instructors, gun advocates are cozying up to the idea of women owning, learning about, and carrying guns.

Pundits and policymakers on both sides of the gun issue argue whether armed women represent collusion with the patriarchy or the dawn of armed feminism. But politically evocative as it may seem, this binary just doesn't capture the dynamic, contested, and at times pragmatic nature of women's participation in gun culture. At the shooting range, in the gun store, and walking through daily life with a holstered firearm, the women I met during my fieldwork defied a single, straightforward narrative. They engaged in an ever-changing set of *gendered negotiations* through which women's empowerment and masculine protectionism were meshed in sometimes familiar, sometimes surprising ways.

masculine terrains

I met Kathy at Gun Sports & More, a shop and shooting range nested deep in the suburbs of Detroit. I had heard about the store because they hold "ladies only" shooting nights and firearms classes for women. A blond, SUV-driving suburban mom who wore a smart polo shirt (the store uniform) and a holstered handgun, Kathy led Gun Sports' efforts with women: she oversaw many of the firearms courses and pressed range owners to open up dedicated range time for women.

In contrast to the male gun carriers I met, who couched their desire to carry in terms of crime and a desire to protect themselves and their families, Kathy offered a different narrative. Sure, she would be capable of willing to defend herself and her kids with a handgun if needed. But, given the low crime rates in the middle-class suburb where she lived, she thought that was unlikely. Kathy's decision to carry a gun was, instead, motivated by her involvement in gun culture as an enthusiast, an instructor, and a competitive shooter. As we chatted, I saw that Kathy simply enjoyed shooting firearms and loved excelling at a "men's" sport.

When she first started competitive shooting, Kathy experienced exclusion and ridicule based on her gender. Then she won a major championship. She was the only woman to compete that year, and she expected to be mocked and dismissed by the other competitors—especially if she placed in the top three. When her name was called for first place in a room full of men, "they all just clapped!"

Scholars like Michael Messner have talked about the gendering of space, arguing that certain arenas like sports and the military have long been "masculine terrain." These social spaces, predicated on women's exclusion, are where bonds among men are forged and links between masculinity and a variety of social attributes—strength, competitiveness, courage—are naturalized. Women who dare to cross the threshold have historically been rejected and ridiculed, told they can't cut it in a man's world. As women enter, these spaces become what Messner calls

From the NRA to the firearms industry to gun instructors, gun advocates are cozying up to the idea of women owning, learning about, and carrying guns.

"contested ideological terrain." The problem isn't their innate abilities, it's how women upset the male monopoly on certain social spaces and social practices.

Betty, who worked in the public sector, was one armed woman who crossed this threshold early in the 1960s, decades before Michigan's concealed carry law was changed. Back then, the law required demonstrating to licensing authorities that you had a legitimate need to carry a gun. Betty argued that her job made her vulnerable, particularly as a woman, and the gun board agreed. However, she recalled being bullied by her male co-workers: "'Look at you, why do you need a gun?' They were just jealous! They told me there's no way someone as small as me could even use a gun!"

Chris told a similar story: after her dad had been the victim of a kidnapping in Detroit's infamous Cass Corridor, she decided she wanted to learn how to use a gun for self-defense. When she called a couple of local gun stores to ask about an impromptu lesson, she "basically got laughed off the phone." She soon found out that in her county, women were being denied concealed pistol licenses because the men on the licensing boards couldn't wrap their heads around the idea of an armed woman capable of self-defense. Chris was angry: "Particularly for women who were in situations where they felt threatened by a former boyfriend, husband, any kind of stalking situation, being denied the ability to defend themselves is absolutely unacceptable."

Committed to teaching women how to shoot and use guns for self-defense, Chris eventually became politically active in the grassroots effort to pass Michigan's 2001 concealed carry law, which would remove the discretion of the licensing board to decide who was worthy of a concealed pistol license. As part of her activism, she was slated to speak at a men's-only hunting lodge. As she described it, she was one of the few women who "had ever crossed that doorway." In fact, it turned out that her invitation was a mistake: "[O]ne of the guys came over to me and said, 'I'm so sorry, Chris, we didn't realize, but with your name, we didn't know if you were a man or a woman, but we assumed you were a man.'" Instead of leaving, Chris decided she wouldn't "drop to that level" and lectured the men: "What about your wife? Your daughter? Your aunt? Your mother? Your grandmother? Your neighbor who doesn't have a husband or boyfriend? When you are not around to defend the homestead, what about them? Don't they deserve the right to take care of themselves and to do it with good training?"

Ten years later, when I started researching gun politics in 2010, I'd hear the same arguments—not just from women, but from pro-gun men, as well.

the great equalizer

Today, Chris's arguments about guns as gender equalizers—captured by slogans like "God Created Man and Woman, But Samuel Colt Made Them Equal"—have gained traction. Many of the men I met in Michigan during the course of my research insisted they liked the idea of armed women. And from the looks of shooting ranges, gun shops, and gun magazines, things are changing: at a local shooting range, you're likely to see pink handguns, pink rifles, and even ammunition labeled with a pink bow in support of breast cancer awareness.

Certain guns are feminized: small guns, pink guns, and revolvers have all become "women's guns," and there's now a whole cottage industry—from designer concealed carry bags to bra holsters—geared at making concealed handguns a fashionable, comfortable option for women. Gendering (and sexualizing) the "culture of fear"—to use Barry Glassner's term—gun advertisements often highlight women's vulnerability and promote guns as a "woman's best friend." Glock's "Wrong Girl" commercial depicts a young woman in a tank top and panties alone at home. She hears a disturbance and grabs her Glock. Before she can shoot, the would-be intruder passes out in shock. Was it the sight of the beautiful woman or the Glock? Either way, the threat is neutralized.

There's a good reason the firearms industry wants to make guns appealing to women: they represent a largely untapped consumer base in a market already swimming with 300 million guns. Women mean more gun sales, more NRA memberships. This embrace, as Chris intimated, also fits with dominant gender ideologies stipulating men as protectors: how can a man truly committed to protecting his family deny his wife and children a weapon of self-defense?

But old habits die hard. With this openness comes new narratives that negotiate women's presence in a "man's world." Today, Chris wouldn't be laughed off the phone or stage. Instead, she'd be encouraged: women are often assured that their gender makes them *great* shooters. Why? Male gun instructors told me women are more docile learners. And if they aren't quite the warriors that men are, they still have a natural, *maternal* instinct to protect. Their smaller fingers, which apparently make women "naturally" more dexterous, don't hurt either.

I seemed to be a prime example of just how wrong those generalizations were. It took a while for me to understand the feel of the gun at a tactile level, knowing just where the pad of my finger should sit on the trigger or how to roll with the recoil. Like other women I met, I became irritated that a gendered standard had already been set for me and my shooting abilities; it added another layer of stress to conducting fieldwork. And I found that while increasing my firearms proficiency and knowledge made me feel more comfortable and even, like Kathy, a bit "empowered" on the range, it didn't really change how men saw me and my gun. Most often, I was treated as a novice until the man saw how well I shot a .460 Rowland ("My wife would never shoot that!") or how detailed my knowledge of ammunition became ("You know what a 9mm Kurz round is? Most men don't even know that!")

>
> *At the shooting range, in the gun store, and walking through daily life with a holstered firearm, the women I met defied a single, straightforward narrative.*

Gender still matters on today's shooting range. There are men insisting that women carry uselessly small, but "gender appropriate," .380s or familiarize themselves with revolvers (semi-automatics might be too mechanically complicated). There are women "surprising" men with their full capability as shooters. But rather than a politics of exclusion, gender works more through a contradictory, contested politics that informally segregates everything from handguns to holsters into gender appropriate categories.

The shooting range is contested ideological terrain. Under new concealed carry laws, the gendering of guns and gun paraphernalia extends into public space, too.

public guns

Thanks to the passage of "shall-issue" laws in dozens of US states, guns can become part of everyday life. These laws require licensing authorities to issue a license to carry so long as the applicant meets a predetermined list of criteria. In contrast to Betty and Chris, who had to convince a gun board that they were fit to carry, in most states license applicants today can simply take a firearms course, fill out an application, pay a fee and—assuming their criminal record comes back clean—receive their license in a matter of weeks. In the US, there are roughly 11 million licensed gun carriers, and over 400,000 of them are in Michigan. Though there is no national database of concealed carriers, state-level data—such as Michigan's—suggests that about 1 in 5 of these licensees are women.

> *Carrying a gun—and the confidence that they can defend themselves—transforms how these women move through and experience space.*

For many women, the experience of carrying a gun—even if it is concealed—means experiencing public space differently. Angela, a woman in her 50s, became interested in guns during a camping trip "up north." She explained her first exposure in gendered terms: "You know how the story goes: the girls are talking about sewing, and the guys are talking about hunting. So I overheard one of the guys saying he wanted to go shooting. Nobody had any interest. So I said, 'I will!' " Angela's comfort on the range soon translated into a desire to learn more; she found herself in a concealed pistol licensing class. She didn't intend to ever carry her gun until she became friends with one of the instructors, who offered to go out with her on her first day as a gun carrier. No one could see her gun, of course, but she still felt nervous with it on her hip. What if someone saw? What if it somehow popped out of its holster? Angela told me stepping out of the car, going to the grocery store, or just walking around all felt different. But carrying her gun (eventually, two guns) gave her a degree of confidence: even if her concealed gun was her secret, she'd proved she was *capable* of carrying it.

Though she was acutely attentive to gender as she described her own turn to guns, Angela didn't use the term "feminist." In fact, only one woman gun carrier I met described herself in explicit feminist terms, jokingly calling herself a "feminazi." Nevertheless, Angela's story evokes Martha McCaughey's argument that self-defense is a form of "physical feminism": teaching one's body to "fight back" provides women with a skillset should they find themselves in a violent confrontation such as an attempted sexual assault. Carrying a gun, as well as the confidence that they can defend themselves, thus transforms how these women move through and experience space. It entails an *embodied* rejection of dependent femininity. Put differently, Angela's gun is a challenge to what Iris Marion Young calls masculine protectionism: the idea that men have an *exclusive duty* to protect women and children. With a gun at her hip, Angela feels confident she—and she alone—can protect herself.

But just as women's presence on the shooting range is contested ideological terrain, so too are women's holsters: men had a great deal to say about how, what, and when women carried. When I met Cheryl and Matthew, an older, White married couple, Cheryl linked the gun she carried to feelings of empowerment and fearlessness: "It's funny. When you got the gun, you aren't scared." She told me she felt freer in public spaces and less afraid of being victimized when working as a real estate agent, entering unknown spaces. Like Betty and other women, Cheryl's participation in the workforce was tied to her participation in gun culture.

But as I watched Cheryl and Matthew describe their gun carry habits and their politics, I soon realized that Matthew was the "gun nut" of the two. While Matthew emphasized politics, his disdain for the president, and his military service, Cheryl took a no-nonsense attitude—"He's the political one." Cheryl recognized the appeal of a gun, but she also asserted that she didn't need her gun *every* time she stepped outside. Matthew neither understood nor respected her logic. He insisted his wife *always* needed her gun, because "you never know." Motioning to her heavy purse, he argued, "If you can carry all that, you can carry a gun!" Matthew's words followed what I had observed among many other gun-toting men: they were vociferously in support of armed women, but on men's terms. By attempting to override Cheryl's capacity to discern whether and when she needed a gun, he strained to extend *his* duty to protect into *her* holster. Cheryl seemed unfazed by Matthew's finagling. More pragmatic than political, Cheryl laughed off her husband's insistence. Her embrace of situational self-protection was a subtle negotiation of masculine protectionism.

double-barreled

For all of my anticipation walking out the door that first day, carrying a firearm in itself did not transform—for better or for worse—my own gendered sense of self. No doubt, I felt the sense of confidence women had told me about. I also experienced strong encouragement—even pressure—from men who thought it was great that I was carrying a gun and who believed that, as a woman, I would be vulnerable to violent attack without one.

But, truth be told, that first experience of gun carry was anti-climatic. At the end of the day, the gun at my hip was just . . . a gun. It was gun *culture*—and the practices of gun-carrying men and women—that made my 9mm a gendered object.

In this regard, the proliferation of gun carry represents neither the dawn of a new feminism nor the resurgence of the patriarchy—at least not at the individual level of individual armed women, still largely outnumbered by men. Lying somewhere between the domain of "physical feminism" and "masculine protectionism," carrying guns serves—for the women I met—as a way to subtly and not-so-subtly negotiate gender norms around safety, security, and even caring for others. For some women, like Chris and Betty, the gendered world of guns transformed their weapons from tools of self-protection to symbols of women's empowerment. For other women, like Cheryl, guns simply balanced personal, pragmatic needs and men's desire to protect.

The visceral, lived experience of guns is contradictory and contested. A woman's gun can be a tool of embodied empowerment, but it can also be a vehicle of complicity with masculine protectionism. It might even be both, simultaneously. In a complicated, pro-gun country, the gendered meaning of the gun is double-barreled.

recommended resources

Browder, Laura. 2008. *Her Best Shot: Women and Guns in America.* Chapel Hill: University of North Carolina Press. Provocative and detailed, this book uses historical archives to chronicle women's participation in the world of firearms from the Civil War onwards.

Cook, Philip, and Goss, Kristin A. 2014. *The Gun Debate: What Everyone Needs to Know.* New York: Oxford University Press. An excellent primer on the current state of the gun debate in the U.S.

McCaughey, Martha. 1997. *Real Knockouts: The Physical Feminism of Self-Defense.* New York: NYU Press. An engaging ethnography of women's self-defense courses, including but not limited to gun training.

Melzer, Scott. 2009. *Gun Crusaders: The NRA's Culture War.* New York, NY: New York University Press. An ethnography and interview study of the National Rifle Association and its mobilization of gender politics to promote gun rights.

Messner, Michael. 2002. *Taking the Field: Women, Men and Sports.* Minneapolis: University of Minnesota Press. Examines how, despite women's entrance into sports (thanks in part to Title IX), sports continue to reproduce traditional expectations about gender, especially masculine identity.

22

stealing a bag of potato chips and other crimes of resistance

victor m. rios

winter 2012

Ronny was called in for a job interview at Carrows, a chain restaurant that served $9.99 sirloin steak and shrimp. He called me up, asking for help. I lent him a crisp white dress shirt, which I had purchased at a discount store when I worked as a server at a steak house during my undergraduate years. I convinced Ronny

to wear fitted khakis, rather than his customary baggy jeans. He agreed, on the condition that he would wear his white Nike Air Force Ones, a popular basketball shoe at the time. These shoes had been in and out of style in the urban setting since the early 1980s. By 2002, a famous rapper, Nelly, created a popular song named "Air Force Ones," and famous basketball players such as Kobe Bryant wore these shoes during games. Black and Latino youths in Oakland sometimes even wore them to more formal events such as high school proms, quinceañeras, and weddings. I asked Ronny why he insisted on wearing these shoes in a professional setting. He replied, "Because professionals wear them."

Many of the boys I worked with in my research believed they had a clear sense of what courteous, professional, and "good" behavior was. Despite their attempts to present themselves with good manners and good morals, their idea of professional behavior did not match mainstream ideas of professional behavior. This in turn created what I refer to as *misrecognition*. When the boys displayed a genuine interest in "going legit," getting a job, or doing well in school, adults often could not recognize their positive attempts and therefore criminalized them.

The boys had grown up in an environment which had deprived them of the social and cultural capital they needed to progress in school and the labor market. Therefore, they developed their own alternative social and cultural capital, which they used to survive poverty, persist in a violent and punitive social ecology, prevent violence, avoid incarceration, and attempt to fit into mainstream institutions. Education scholar Tara Yosso develops a framework for understanding and using the capital marginalized communities develop— what she calls *community cultural wealth*. She argues that marginalized communities have always generated community cultural wealth that's allowed them to survive and resist. Sociologist Martín Sánchez-Jankowski has recently discussed poor people's ability to organize their social world and maintain social order as "persistence." According to Sánchez-Jankowski, contrary to the popular academic belief that poor people live in a

> **Organic capital is the creative response the boys developed in the midst of blocked opportunity and criminalization.**

disorganized world where they have a limited capacity to generate "collective efficacy" (the ability of a community to solve its own social problems), the urban poor shape their behaviors around making sense of and creating social order within a marginal context. *Organic capital*, then, is the creative response the boys in this study developed in the midst of blocked opportunity and criminalization. Despite being well-intentioned, though, these efforts were often not well received by mainstream institutions.

Ronny's story is indicative of how many of the boys attempted to tap into mainstream institutions but failed. As they encountered rejection, they returned to the resilience and survival strategies that they had developed in their neighborhoods. I continued to prepare Ronny for his interview, helping him develop "acceptable" cultural capital. We prepared with mock questions: "Why do you want to work for us?" I asked him. He responded, "I am a hard worker." "That's a good start," I said. "How about expanding that and telling them that you're also a team player and that you enjoy the restaurant atmosphere?" Ronny nodded. The day of the interview, I walked into the restaurant separately from Ronny. To calm his nerves I told him, "You look great, man. This job is yours!" He looked sharp: a professionally dressed, athletically built, charismatic, tall, African American young man with a charming dimple every time he smiled. I was certain he would get the job. I sat down for lunch at a booth, in an attempt to observe Ronny being interviewed. I looked at the menu and, with a knot in my gut, nervous for Ronny, ordered what I knew would eventually give me a worse stomach ache: a Mile-High Chipotle Southwest Burger. I sat about twenty feet away from the table where Ronny sat with a manager.

Ronny tried to use his charisma to connect with the manager, but she kept her distance and did not look at Ronny, seemingly uninterested in what he had to say. At the end of the interview, Ronny stood abruptly and walked away from the manager, with no handshake or smile. He went outside. I ordered my burger to go, paid my bill, and met him in the parking lot. As I headed to the door, I turned to look in the manager's direction, and she was greeting a White male youth. She smiled, gave him her hand, and offered him a place to sit. Ronny's first contact with her was not this friendly. I walked outside to meet Ronny, who sat on the hood of my car.

I asked for a debriefing. He told me that he had a good feeling and that the manager had seemed to like him. I asked him to walk me through the interview. He had followed the plan flawlessly. I was proud of him. "You followed the plan. You did a great job," I told him. "Why didn't you shake her hand when you left?" I asked.

"'Cause," Ronny replied. "Why not?" I scolded. "Because it was a White lady. You not supposed to shake a White lady's hand. They be scared of a nigga. They think I'ma try to take their shit or fuck 'em. I just said thanks and walked out." Ronny did not get the job.

Ronny did all he could to land the job, but the limited resources at his disposal for showing respect may have kept him from getting the position. In this case, he believed that not shaking the manager's hand would show respect; instead, Ronny may have been perceived as a rude kid not able to hold employment in a restaurant environment. I asked Ronny to tell me how he learned about not shaking White women's hands. He told me that his White female teachers had asked him to keep his distance, White women on the street would clasp their purses when they saw him walking by, and White female store clerks would nervously watch him when he walked into an establishment. Ronny had been socialized from a young age to overcompensate around White women to show he was not attempting to harm or disrespect them. This behavior may have been a result of the stereotyped expectations of Black men as criminals and sexual aggressors, deeply rooted in American culture.

> *Feelings of exclusion from a network of positive credentials, education, and employment opportunities led to resistance identities.*

Ronny applied for multiple jobs. After about a dozen applications and three failed interviews, he became discouraged. He reported being asked by other managers about his "drug habits" and "criminal background." Ronny decided to abandon the job-search process and instead invested $20 in pirated DVDs; a few hours later, he'd made $50 from the illegally copied movies. He reinvested the $50 in a backpack full of pirated DVDs, and after a few weeks, Ronny had made enough to buy a few new pairs of glossy Air Force Ones. However, the six to ten hours he spent in front of the grocery store, waiting for customers for his DVDs, made him a measly $20 or $30 a day—certainly not worth the risk of getting arrested for a federal offense.

Still, Ronny, like many of the other boys, preferred to take on the risk of incarceration and the low wages that this underground entrepreneurship granted him in order to avoid the stigma, shame, and feeling of failure that the job-application process produced for him. Misrecognition of genuine attempts to do well in school, the labor market, or their probation program led to frustration—and to producing alternatives in which the boys' organic capital could be put to productive use.

resistance identities

In feeling excluded from a network of positive credentials, education, and employment opportunities, young people develop creative responses that provide them with the necessary tools to survive in an environment where they have been left behind and where they are consistently criminalized. *Resistance identities*, according to sociologist Manuel Castells, are those created by subordinated populations in response to oppression. These identities operate by "excluding the excluder." Some, like the boys I studied, develop practices that seem to embrace criminality as a means of contesting a system that sees them as criminals. Similarly, sociologist Richard Quinney argues that poor people engage in crimes such as theft as "acts of survival" in an economic system in which their well-being is not fulfilled by other collective means. He further argues that some poor and working-class people engage in "crimes of resistance," such as sabotaging workplace equipment and destroying public property, as a form of protest against their economic conditions.

> "
> **This self-defeating path led to trouble but also a sense of agency and dignity.**

The young men in this study constantly participated in everyday acts of resistance that baffled teachers, police officers, and community-center workers. From the perspective of the adults, these transgressions and small crimes were ridiculous: the risk of being caught was high and the benefit derived from the deviant act was minuscule. This frustration led adults to abandon empathy for the boys and to apply the toughest sanctions on them. "If they're going to act like idiots, I am going to have to give them the axe," explained one of the gang task-force officers.

Many of the adults I interviewed believed the boys' defiance was "stupid." Sarcastic remarks often followed when a youth purposely broke a simple rule, leading him to be ostracized, kicked out of class, or even arrested. Why would the boys break the simplest of rules knowing there would be grave consequences? For the boys, though, breaking the rules was resisting a system that seemed stacked against them. In many ways, criminality was one of the few resources the boys could use in response to criminalization.

the stolen bag of chips

One fall afternoon, I met with fifteen-year-old Flaco, a Latino gang-associated young man from east Oakland.

We joined three of his friends as they walked to their usual afterschool hang out, Walnut Park. They decided to make a stop at Sam's Liquor Store. I walked in with them, noticing a sign that read, "Only two kids allowed in store at one time." I realized they were breaking the store rule by entering in a group of four and pretended to walk in separately to see how the store clerk would respond to their transgression. I stood in the back of the store as Flaco walked up the candy-bar aisle—keeping a good distance between himself and the Snickers, Twix, and Skittles, to show the clerk, who was already staring him down, that he was not attempting to steal. He grabbed a candy bar, held it far away from his body, walked a few steps, and placed it on the counter. Many of the boys in this study often maintained their distance in the candy or soda aisles at stores to show they were not attempting to steal. Store clerks in the neighborhoods I studied were always apprehensive of customers: they watched people from the moment they walked in, had surveillance cameras set up, and one clerk had taped up pictures of himself holding an AK-47. The clerk at Sam's may have been concerned that too many kids in his store meant that he could not keep an eye on all of them.

A balding, middle-aged, Asian American male, the clerk pointed to the door and yelled, "Only two kids allowed in the store at a time!" The three youths in line to pay for their items looked at the clerk and at each other. Mike, closest to the entrance, responded, "We ain't doing shit." The clerk replied, "I am going to call the police!" Mike grabbed a twenty-five-cent bag of Fritos Flamin' Hot chips, lifted it up in front of the clerk's face, and said, "You see this? I was gonna pay for it, but now I ain't paying for shit, stupid mothafucka." He rushed out of the store with the bag of chips, as the clerk called the police. The rest of the youngsters dropped the snacks they were in line to purchase and ran out. I walked up to the store clerk and gave him a quarter for Mike, who had stolen the chips. Infuriated, the clerk said, "It's too late. The police are on their way to get the robbers."

I was not able to track down the boys until a few days later. When I ran into Flaco, he informed me that the police had arrested Mike that day for stealing the twenty-five-cent bag of chips. After interviewing the boys and observing the store clerk's interactions with them in the days and weeks after this event, I found that Mike's "irrational" behavior had actually changed the way the store clerk interacted with the boys. The boys believed the clerk had begun to treat them with more respect—he avoided provoking negative interactions with the boys, even if it meant allowing a few more youths into the store than policy allowed. While even Mike's peers believed that his actions were "crazy," they also acknowledged that something significant had changed. For example,

Flaco thought Mike had overreacted, but because of Mike, Flaco felt respected by the store clerk the next time he went in the store: "Mike fucked up. He was acting hyphy [crazy] that day. He should have paid the guy . . . But because of what he did, me and my dogs go into the sto', and the guy don't say shit. We all go in like five deep—like 'what?'—and dude don't say shit no more."

When I asked Mike why he had stolen the bag of chips, he responded, "That fool was trippin'. He should've come correct. I was gonna pay him. You saw, I had the money in my hand . . . . That fool knows not to fuck with us anymore. . . . I did get taken in for that, but it don't matter. They gave me probation and shit. I'll just keep it cool now since that fool will keep it cool now too." In Mike's worldview, fighting for dignity at the cost of giving up his freedom had paid off. Though Mike's actions resulted in his commitment to the criminal justice system, he was very aware of this risk when he stole the bag of chips. He had grown frustrated at the treatment he had received at school, by police, and then at the store. This frustration, and a deep desire to feel respected, led Mike to willfully expose himself to incarceration. In the end, Mike lost his freedom, coming under the supervision of the criminal justice system. Nonetheless, Mike gained a sense of dignity for himself and his peers.

I also asked Mike, "Why didn't you steal something more expensive?" He told me that he thought about it, but, in the moment, he didn't care what he took. He wanted to prove a point to the clerk: "Not to fuck with me." It wasn't about saving a quarter, accumulating the most valuable commodity he could get his hands on, or stealing because he was poor and wanted to eat a bag of chips. Although he may have had a desire for any or all of the above, he stole the chips to redeem himself for being shamed and feeling disrespected. In the end, despite facing further punishment, Mike and his friends felt that their actions were not in vain; they had won a small battle in a war they were so tired of losing. Authority figures expected the boys to follow their rules, and the boys expressed a deep desire "to be left alone" and remain free; one of the only resources they had to feel respected within the system was to actively engage in behaviors that defied the rules of the game. This, in turn, led to further misrecognition and criminalization.

defiance as resistance

Defiance constituted a temporary success to the boys. Watching interactions between the boys and authority figures was often like watching a life-sized game of chess, with a rook strategically moving in response to a queen's movement. A police officer would get out of his car, the boys would posture; an officer would grab a young man, his friends would prepare to run; an officer would humiliate one of the boys, and the boy would respond by not cooperating or by cursing back. As one side moved to repress, the other moved to resist. The boys were almost always captured and eliminated from the chess board, but not before they had encroached on the opponent's territory, changing, if even subtly, the game.

Mike and Ronny were searching for something beyond immediate gratification. They did not want to follow the rules to gain social rewards like a good grade, a legitimate bag of chips, completing a probation program, or becoming a "normal" citizen. Instead, the boys chose a road that at first seemed futile and ignorant, a self-defeating path that led them into more trouble but eventually provided them with a sense of agency and dignity against criminalization.

In mocking the system, these young people gained a sense of empowerment. However, these same strategies added fuel to the criminalization fire. Many realized that they were actively stoking that fire, but they believed it was worth the negative consequences. Maintaining a sense of dignity—feeling accepted and respected—was a central struggle. The boys consciously chose to fight for their dignity, even if it meant risking their freedom.

crimes of resistance

Many of the young men self-consciously "acted stupid" as a strategy to discredit the significance of a system which had excluded and punished them. These deviant politics garnered attention from the youth control complex, frustrating its agents: the police, school personnel, and others. This frustration led to more punishment, which led to a deeper crisis of control in the community. In the end, it was this crisis of control, when institutions were not able to provide a sufficient amount of social order, the young men consciously perceived to be a successful result of their defiance. As Flaco put it, "They trying to regulate me, right? So if they can't regulate me, then that means they not doing their job. So my job is to not-what's that word?-confirm [conform]."

The boys consistently chose to act "bad" in circumstances in which adults expected them to act "good." Almost all the acts that led to an arrest for violating probation were committed as conscious acts of resistance; in the boys' accounts, they knew they were facing severe consequences but decided to break the rules to make a point. This may have been their way of resisting what they perceived to be unfair treatment and punishment. These transgressions served as a resource for feeling empowered

> **Breaking the rules meant resisting a system; criminality was one of the few resources the boys could use in response to criminalization.**

and for gaining redress for the humiliation, stigma, and punishment they encountered even when they were being "good." Because they reported that they committed their transgressions as a way of "getting back at the system," as Ronny explained, I am calling these acts *deviant politics*, by which I mean the political actions—the resistance—that youth labeled by society as "deviant" use to respond to punishment that they ubiquitously encounter.

Boys who resisted often suffered real and drastic consequences. Sometimes, they did not even realize that they were resisting. Often, they were simply, as they called it, "getting stupid," meaning that they acted "bad" for the sake of being "bad." These kinds of practices had few long-term positive outcomes for any of the boys in the study.

In an environment in which there were few formal avenues for expressing dissent, which the boys believed to be extremely repressive, they developed forms of resistance they believed could change, even if only temporarily, the outcome of their treatment. The boys believed they had gained redress for the punitive social control they had encountered by adopting a subculture of resistance based on fooling the system. Their crimes of resistance, which made no sense to the system, were fully recognizable to those who had been misrecognized and criminalized.

when victims blame the victim
nicole bedera
summer 2015

According to the U.S. Department of Justice, 300,165 women were sexually assaulted in 2013. However, the Centers for Disease Control estimates that closer to 1.3 million women are raped every year. Both estimates come from surveys; the difference stems from methods. If a survey uses the word "rape" to gauge respondents' experiences, the rate is much lower than if when it uses the phrase "unwanted sex."

Why are so many victims of sexual violence seemingly reluctant to label their experiences "rape"?

Kaitiln Boyle and Ashleigh McKinzie explored that question in their recent study in *Social Psychology Quarterly*. They found that participants who did not label their unwanted sexual experiences as rape were typically protecting either their assailants or themselves. Protecting the assailant meant explaining away their partners' sexually aggressive or coercive behavior as a miscommunication or a social pressure that the assailant could not control. In blaming themselves, victims thought

they may have been teasing their assailants or they might simply not have a high enough sex drive. They defended their assailant's presumed good intentions. Protecting themselves came in the form of disparaging their younger selves, claiming to know better now how to avoid exploitive sexual situations. Often, they would come to call their unwanted sexual experiences with ex-boyfriends "rape" after the relationship ended, but they still blamed the rape on their own näievè.

Whether the crime was called rape or unwanted sex, the participants still described themselves and victims in simulations similar to their own as "powerless." And even if the participants did not report feeling traumatized after the encounter, feelings of powerlessness are known to have grave ramifications for maintaining healthy intimate relationships. Boyle and McKinzie's study exposes many of the subtle difficulties in fully recognizing and responding to sexual assault and its lasting effects.

23

changing men in south africa

shari l. dworkin and dean peacock

fall 2013

Dean Peacock is co-founder and Executive Director of the Sonke Gender Justice Network, a South African NGO working to promote gender transformation, human rights, and social justice across Africa. Dean's work and activism over the last 20 years have focused on issues related to gender equality, men and constructions of masculinities, HIV and AIDS, and social justice. He is a co-founder and co-chair of the Global MenEngage Alliance, a member of the United Nations Secretary General's Network of Men Leaders (formed to advise Ban Ki-Moon on gender-based violence prevention), and serves on the Nobel Women's Advisory Committee on ending sexual violence in conflict settings. An honorary senior lecturer at the University of Cape Town's School of Public Health and an Ashoka Fellow, Peacock's writing has been published in numerous books and peer-reviewed journals. He holds a BA in Development Studies from the University of California Berkeley and an MA in Social Welfare from San Francisco State University. Shari L. Dworkin, Vice Chair of the Department of Social and Behavioral Sciences at the University of California at San Francisco, talks to Peacock about his work and activism.

SHARI L. DWORKIN: Why did you go into work that attempts to reshape norms of masculinities to improve gender inequalities, violence, and HIV?

DEAN PEACOCK: My earliest engagement with issues of men, masculinities, and violence was through my connection with the End Conscription campaign when I was in my final year of high school in South

Africa. The campaign was focused on getting White men to challenge apartheid militarism by refusing to serve in the army. That was in 1985, the year that the state of emergency was imposed in South Africa and a lot of young White men like myself were finishing high school and then serving in the army (either in the covert war that was being fought against Cuban and Angolan troops in Angola, or in the townships in South Africa itself). I lived on the campus of the University of Cape Town, and I was introduced to activism there.

I began to think about the kind of deliberate targeting of men for a particular set of gendered roles. In that case, participation in militaries—a military that was overtly and explicitly oppressive, as most militaries, of course, are. So that was my very earliest exposure to the work. The other trajectory to this work was from the relationships I had with women who were feminist activists concerned about a range of different human rights and social justice and women's rights issues.

SD: So does the work resonate not just politically, but on a personal level?

DP: Yes, definitely. In my early 20s, my partner was working at a battered women's shelter as a volunteer, and she came back one day from a volunteer training that had been done by the then-director of an organization I hadn't yet heard of: Men Overcoming Violence (MOVE). She was visibly energized by the training at MOVE and urged me to check it out. When she talked about the work of men engaging men to end men's violence against women, I immediately thought, "Wow, that's something

101

that I actually do have a very direct connection to." I made a commitment to myself that I would learn more about that work and what I could do. So I checked out MOVE, and I had this incredible experience. I was invited to observe a group with perpetrators of domestic violence who were there either because they'd been arrested or because they identified violence as a problem they had to deal with. I listened in, and I was moved by the stories that I heard of men grappling with their own violence, trying to understand it, figure out how stop it, and deal with the aftermath of the destruction caused by violence in their relationships and in their families. I remember the facilitator asking a man how he felt, and he replied, "Well, I think that . . . " The facilitator stopped him immediately, and he said, "I'm not asking you what you think, I'm asking you how you feel." At that point in my life, I'd never made that distinction before. Just like the men in the group, I was being exposed to a whole new vocabulary and a set of experiences and insights that my male socialization and socialization of so many men had been deprived of.

SD: Sonke's work is not only focused on reducing men's violence against women and men, but also on reducing the spread and impact of HIV.

DP: Yes. It's critical to understand that intimate partner violence is common in South Africa, with studies showing that between 25 to 55 percent of women have experienced violence from a male partner. The rate of female homicide by male partners is six times higher than the global average. Studies also show that a large number of men admit to raping women and girls.

In terms of HIV, South Africa has the largest epidemic in the world. And young women's rate of HIV is far greater than young men's, though young men do face tremendous HIV vulnerabilities in South Africa—lots of pressure to drink, to have sex, and to not reveal any vulnerabilities or confusions about sex. Models of manhood in South Africa and across the world are a recipe for men acting in sexual ways that put themselves and their partners at significant risk.

Our work at Sonke goes "upstream." Our work is primary prevention of violence and HIV—to change national laws and policies, to change social norms at a societal level, and to engage men and boys. Our conversations with men help

them recognize the harm that contemporary models of masculinity do to everyone. We want them to become active in efforts to change that for their own good and for the health and human rights of women in their lives.

SD: Are these are difficult conversations to have with men?

DP: There are assumptions that men in South Africa (and men generally) would be very resistant to having conversations about masculinity and power and gender equality. But, it doesn't take much for men to say that they feel tremendous pressure about norms of masculinity and that many of those pressures are quite unbearable and certainly very unrealistic.

We use a number of different strategies to reach men, including media, community mobilization, and workshops. When we run workshops and do dynamic activities, it's not hard to get the men to feel a sense of outrage about human rights violations, women's rights, and violence in South Africa. Our task is to turn that outrage into action. We get men to reflect on the invisibility of patriarchy to men and the overt experience of patriarchy that women have all the time. Then we strategize with those men about what they're going to do to challenge men's violence.

SD: How has social science thinking influenced the work of Sonke Gender Justice?

DP: I think Raewyn Connell's work highlighting the plurality of masculinities and Judith Butler's work around the performativity of gender is very helpful in our work. Michael Messner's work around the costs to men of masculinity is a very useful entry point to talking with men in South Africa about what contemporary notions and norms around manhood mean for men and to help them understand their significant personal investment in challenging norms about manhood that come at such a high price for women—but also for them as men. This and other gender theory has helped us be more nuanced and more optimistic about what's possible.

For us, part of our theory of change is that it's not enough to simply run workshops and get men to reflect on their own process of socialization and consider making changes in their own relationship. With a problem as enormous as gender-based violence in South Africa, you then have to get men to think about what they're going to do at the community level. We help them to figure out how to engage their duty-bearers (local government, provincial government, national government) to make sure that elected representatives are properly implementing the law, whether that's the Sexual Offenses Act, the Domestic Violence Act, or any number of other laws

> *When my then-partner talked about the work of men engaging men to end men's violence against women, she was visibly energized, and I made a commitment to learn more about what I could do.*

that are related to ending domestic and sexual violence in South Africa.

SD: Part of what impresses me about the work of Sonke is that violence in the streets and violence in intimate relationships are intertwined, and working on masculinities is the point of intervention for both. Can you comment on why and how you intervene on these simultaneously?

DP: If a significant part of our strategy is to get men to recognize the costs that men pay for contemporary notions of manhood and for living in a patriarchal society, then of course we want men to reflect on their own experiences of violence at the hands of other men who adhere in particularly rigid ways to those social norms about manhood, right? So, in South Africa, the conversation with men about the costs to men of manhood and the pressures that men face to live up to those notions is an easy one.

This is because the relationship between HIV risk and contemporary ideas about manhood is so clear. If you grow up being told, "As a man, you're going to have lots of sexual partners, you shouldn't really be negotiating sex with people, you shouldn't be exhibiting any kind of fear that you might be exposed to risk," and you put together the mix of alcohol, ignorance, and pressures to have lots of sexual partners, it's easy to get men to recognize the ways in which manhood is set up for HIV infection and, subsequently, for not accessing critical health services (testing, treatment, support groups, and the like). The same applies to men's experiences of or fears of violence. In South Africa, men kill men at seven times the rate that men kill women. So it's not hard to get men to see these connections.

SD: As you're talking, I am reminded that you are not just talking about programs but are increasingly becoming active in the policy realm. Give me a sense of some policy work that you're most proud of at Sonke Gender Justice?

DP: One example of work we've done at a policy level was to stop the passage of the Traditional Courts Bill. It would have reinscribed patriarchal powers for traditional leaders in rural parts of South Africa and would have affected about 20 million people living mostly in areas that were formerly homelands. It would have essentially created two separate and unequal legal systems: a constitutional democracy, on the one hand, and, on the other hand, a traditional legal system, presided over by unelected traditional leaders, many of them apartheid-era leaders put in place by the apartheid government and

not "traditional" in any real sense (and, of course, I think anyone who claims things are "traditional" needs to be asked quite a few questions—"tradition" is so misused and manipulated in many postcolonial settings).

In existing traditional courts, women are usually not allowed to represent themselves or even to speak. Quite often, women are not allowed to be in traditional courts at all. And so we and many of our women's rights partners were very concerned

> *Intimate partner violence is common in South Africa, with studies showing that between 25 to 55 percent of women have experienced violence from a male partner.*

about what [legitimizing these courts at the national level] would mean for gender equality in South Africa. We saw it as a very dangerous potential erosion of women's rights as they are enshrined in the South African Constitution and as a reassertion of patriarchal power. We did a lot of work connecting to our partner organizations to educate men and women in rural communities about the bill and to get men and women to speak out against it together. (I think symbolically it was important that men and women be doing this work together—to speak out against the bill in their local communities.) Then, when provincial consultations were held to seek local input and opinion on the bills, we supported and mobilized and encouraged community members to attend those meetings and to speak up forcefully against the bill.

That's the piece of work I'm really excited about. It's one of those things that could easily go unremarked upon because we stopped a bill, rather than passed a law, but I think in some parts of the world, that's the most important work you can do—to resist the encroachment of conservatism and of patriarchal politics.

SD: Dean, you've done more work from your 20s to your 40s than most people do in a lifetime. What is your next set of aspirations at Sonke?

DP: At Sonke, we serve as the global co-chair of an alliance made up of organizations like ours that work with men and boys, and we're now active in 41 countries at last count. Forty-one countries are working to increase men's and boys support for gender equality!

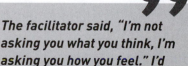

> *The facilitator said, "I'm not asking you what you think, I'm asking you how you feel." I'd never made that distinction before. I was being exposed to a whole new set of insights that my male socialization had been deprived of.*

This is an incredible accomplishment and something to really celebrate. Part of what we're now trying to figure out is how we use the power of a global network to advance shared policy positions.

And now, we're moving into an interesting period—the Millennium Development Goals have the target of 2015, so we're fast approaching 2015, and we're in the middle of the post-MGD deliberations at the moment as to what the next set of indicators should be to measure gender equality. We want to be involved in some of those global discussions—around the first MGDs—about the Beijing Platform for Action 20-Year Review that's happening in 2015 as well—the ICPD or Cairo Declaration deliberations—the Security Council Resolution 1325 plus 15 deliberations—and figure out how we get networks of organizations working with men and boys to support, in very real ways, the women's rights agenda in those global deliberative processes.

suicide's gender divide
lucia lykke
summer 2015

One of sociology's earliest contributions was Èmile Durkheim situating an apparently individual phenomenon—suicide—in social context. But early suicide research paid little attention to how gender inequalities at the macro-level might matter. In a recent article in *Journal of Health and Social Behavior*, Kathryn Nowotny, Rachel Peterson, and Jason Boardman examined how the gender system adolescents live in influences their likelihood of seriously considering suicide (suicidal ideation).

Using data gathered from adolescent boys and girls in the National Longitudinal Survey of Adolescent Health, the researchers constructed a unique measure of gender context. They used variables representing sex-typical traits (e.g., frequent crying, fighting, taking risks) and measured how much these traits differed by gender in each state.

The authors argue that the greater the gender differentiation on these traits, the greater the level of gender norm rigidity and regulation within that state. From there, they posited that higher levels of gender regulation by state are associated with a greater likelihood of suicidal ideation for individual adolescents—and that is what the results showed. The effect was stronger for girls, particularly girls who reported gender-typical personality traits, though high levels of gender regulation were harmful to boys' mental health as well.

This study brings Durkheim's model of fatalistic suicide up to date: whereas Durkheim considered fatalistic suicide caused by high levels of social regulation a marker of premodern societies, this research suggests gender regulation may be harmful to adolescents' mental health in the present day as well.

gendered institutions

overview

Gender lives not only in individuals but also in institutions. Schools, legal systems, families, states, among other institutions, perpetuate gender difference and inequalities.

Ann Mullen examines the gendering of the institution of higher education and the labor market ("The Not-So-Pink Ivory Tower"). While the numbers of women graduating college is surpassing that of men, women are disproportionately concentrated at less competitive schools and in non-STEM majors. They have had less success closing the gender gaps in the labor market than the gender gaps in higher education. In "What Gender Is Science," Maria Charles examines discrimination against women within STEM and the factors that prevent or discourage women and girls from pursuing STEM careers.

Orit Ashivai looks at women's role in religion, a primary site for gender inequality. In "Women of God," Ashivai explores how women adapt their religious practices to fit their lived reality and dominant gender ideologies. The way we structure bathrooms also enforces gender segregation. Kristin Schilt and Laurel Westbrook, in their article, "Bathroom Battlegrounds and Penis Panics" look at how the messages of bathroom laws move beyond discrimination against trans people to reinforce gendered norms and expectations more broadly.

Susan Sered's article, "Suffering in the Age of Personal Responsibility," considers what happens when institutions fail low-income women, and when the language of personal responsibility is the only one available with which they can understand their experiences.

Finally, feminist scholar Joan Acker (in an interview with Jennifer L. Pierce) discusses the intersections between feminism and economics, and Christine Williams offers advice to students who wish to create social change.

things to consider

- Where do you see gender in the institutions you are most intimately involved in (education, health care, criminal justice, government, religion, etc.)?
- Changing gender ideologies and practices in institutions can sometimes be more challenging than challenging individuals. Where are some places we can start? Think of your own university and where you might influence its ideology or policies.

24

the not-so-pink ivory tower

ann mullen

fall 2012

Since 1982, women in the United States have been graduating from college at higher rates than men; they currently earn 57 percent of all bachelor's degrees. Some view this trend as a triumphant indicator of gender egalitarianism, while others sound the alarm about the supposed "male crisis" in higher education and the problem of increasingly "feminized" universities.

Recently, the *New York Times* reported that when it comes to college, "women are leaving men in the dust," the Minneapolis *Star Tribune* announced that women's "takeover is complete," and the *Weekly Standard* described colleges as "where the boys aren't." Some have even predicted that sorority sisters will face increasing difficulty finding dates for formals, or eligible men to marry. Thomas Mortenson, a senior scholar at the Pell Institute for the Study of Opportunity in Higher Education, warned that if current trends continue, "the graduation line in 2068 will be all female."

But is higher education really feminizing? Have women's advances come at the cost of men? In 50 years, when they look around their classrooms, will undergraduate students be hard-pressed to see a male face? In other words, has the trend towards gender equality in higher education gone too far? To answer these questions, we need to look beyond the single statistic of the gender distribution of bachelor's degrees, and take a broader approach to understanding the contours of gender in higher education.

Women's increasing graduation rate isn't due to a decrease in the number of graduating male students, but to the fact that women's increases occurred faster than men's.

who's getting degrees

During the past 40 years, the gender distribution of bachelor's degrees reversed. In 1970, men earned 57 percent of all degrees; today, women do. This trend leads some to conclude that women are squeezing men out of higher education, and that women's success has led to men's decline. In fact, this zero-sum scenario is incorrect: the college-going rates for both men and women have increased substantially. Both genders are far more likely to graduate from college now than at any previous point in time. Women's increasing graduation rate isn't due to a decrease in the number of graduating male students, but to the fact that women's increases occurred faster than men's. Particularly between 1970 and 1990, as employment opportunities for women expanded, their college graduation rates grew more rapidly than did those of men.

The rates of growth for men and women have now equalized. Over the past decade, the number of degrees earned by both men and women actually increased by the identical rate of 38 percent. The U.S. Department of Education predicts that over the course of the next decade women's share of bachelor's degrees will rise by only one percentage point, to 58 percent of all degrees. In looking at these figures over time, we see that women's successes did not come at the expense of men, and that the gender gap is not growing uncontrollably. It has in fact stabilized, and has held steady for more than 10 years.

To fully assess the gender distribution of bachelor's degrees, we also need to look at what kinds of men and women graduate from college, and whether men and women of different racial, ethnic and class backgrounds have the same chances of graduating. Among 25- to 29-year-olds, across all racial and ethnic groups, more women than men hold bachelor's degrees. The gap is just over 7 percent among Whites and Hispanics, 6 percent among Blacks, and about 10 percent for Asians.

But in terms of race and ethnicity, the gaps in college completion far exceed that of gender: 56 percent of Asians between 25 and 29 years old hold bachelor's degrees, compared to only 39 percent of Whites, 20 percent of Blacks, and nearly 13 percent of Hispanics. Both White and Asian men are far more likely than Black or Hispanic students of either gender to earn a bachelor's degree. These racial gaps are actually larger now than they were in the 1960s: while students from all backgrounds are now more likely to graduate from college, the rates have increased more quickly for Whites and Asians.

Social class continues to be the strongest predictor of who will attend and graduate from college—one that far outweighs the effects of either gender, or race and ethnicity. Surveys by the U.S. Department of Education show that 70 percent of high school students from wealthy families will enter four-year colleges, compared to only 21 percent of their peers from low-income families. Gender differences also vary by social class background. According to education policy analyst Jackie King, for the wealthiest students, the gender gap actually favors men. (For families in the highest income quartile, men comprise 52 percent of college students, compared to 44 percent in the lowest income quartile, and 47 percent in the middle two quartiles). Age also plays a role: among adults 25 years and older, women are far more likely than men to return to college for a bachelor's degree. But among those 24 and under, women make up only 55 percent of all students, and the gender difference among enrollment rates for recent high school graduates is small (41 percent of men and 44 percent of women).

In other words, women's overall advantage in earning college degrees is not shared equally among all women. White women, Asian women, and wealthy women outpace women from other backgrounds. Gender differences are largest among students 25 years and up, Asians, and low-income students. But differences in relation to class, race and ethnicity greatly overshadow gender gaps in degree attainment.

not at caltech

In assessing gender equity in higher education, it's also necessary to take into account where men and women earn their degrees. While more women than men tend to graduate from college, women are disproportionately represented in less competitive institutions.

Sociologist Jayne Baker and I found that women earned more than 60 percent of degrees in the least selective institutions, but only slightly more than half in the most selective institutions. Women's gains have been greatest at institutions with lower standardized test scores and higher acceptance rates, while men and women are roughly on par with each other at elite institutions. Women are also underrepresented at the top science and engineering institutions, like Caltech and MIT. So, while women may be in the majority overall, their integration into higher education has been uneven, and they are more likely to attend lower status institutions.

> *Social class continues to be the strongest predictor of who will attend and graduate from college—one that far outweighs the effects of either gender, or race and ethnicity.*

Perhaps the most striking disparities are in the choice of college majors. In spite of their overall minority status, men still earn 83 percent of all degrees in engineering, 82 percent in computer and information sciences, 70 percent in philosophy, and 69 percent in economics. Women, on the other hand, continue to earn the lion's share of degrees in traditionally female-dominated fields: 77 percent in psychology, 80 percent in education, and 85 percent in nursing and other health professions. About a third of all men (or women) would have to change majors in order to achieve gender parity across majors today. This hasn't changed much in the last 25 years. (Through the 1970s and early 1980s, fields moved steadily toward becoming more integrated, but in the mid-1980s, this trend slowed and then stalled, shifting very little since then.)

Sociologists Paula England and Su Li found that most of the decrease in segregation came from the growth of gender-integrated fields, like business, and from the flow of women into previously male-dominated fields. Men are much less likely to move into female-dominated fields. They also found that women's entrance into predominantly male fields discourages later cohorts of men from choosing those fields. Women gain status and pay by entering predominantly male fields, while men lose out when they enter devalued, predominantly female fields of study.

Women and men are ostensibly free to select any field they wish, and they no longer face the blatant kinds of barriers to entry that have historically existed. But, other factors influence students' choices subtly, but powerfully. Sociologist Shelly Correll has done innovative experiments with undergraduate students that demonstrate how cultural beliefs about gender shape individuals' career aspirations. When exposed to the idea that men are better at certain tasks, male participants in the study rated their own abilities higher than the women, even though they were all given the same scores. These subjective assessments of their own competencies then influenced students' interest in related careers. Correll argues that widely shared cultural beliefs about gender and different kinds of competencies (like math and science) bias men's and women's perceptions of their own abilities, and their interest in pursuing these fields. She finds that men assess their own capabilities in math more generously than do women, which then encourages them to go into math and science fields.

Education researcher Maria Ong has studied the challenges young women of color majoring in physics face. Because their bodies do not conform to prevalent images of "ordinary" White, male scientists, their belonging and competence are questioned. To persevere in physics, these women confront the necessity of developing strategies for managing their physical appearance. In my own work, I found that students at an elite liberal arts institution choose majors in order to both carve out intellectual identities and settle on a career path. Students identify with the qualities of knowledge of different fields of study, which they often interpret in gendered ways. Men tend to reject female-dominated fields because of their perceived lack of rigor and objectivity.

Men and women also experience college differently. Education scholar Linda Sax uses 40 years of data about college freshmen, along with research from the 1990s that tracked individual students over time. She found some gender differences that have persisted over the past four decades, such as women's lower levels of academic self-confidence. Among first-year college students, according to Sax, women rate themselves lower than men on three out of four indicators of confidence, in spite of their significantly higher high school grades. In terms of overall intellectual self-confidence, only about half of women consider themselves above average or in the highest

> **Women earn more degrees than men, but men and women still diverge in the fields of study they choose, their experiences during college, and the kinds of jobs they get after graduating.**

10 percent compared to over two-thirds of men. This gender gap widens even further during the college years.

Because more women than men come from low-income families, women also come to college with greater concerns about financing their education. Women study harder than men during college, spend more time talking with their professors, and get better grades, while men are more likely to miss classes and not complete homework. By focusing only on the relative numbers of men and women at college, we overlook the ways their college experiences diverge, and the different obstacles and challenges they encounter along the way.

after college

Paradoxically, women's success in closing the gender gap in higher education has not closed the gender gaps in the labor market. Men and women still generally work in different kinds of jobs, and women still earn considerably less than men (even with the same levels of education). Occupational segregation remains high and the trend toward narrowing the gender gap in pay has slowed. Currently, young, college-educated, full time working women can expect to earn only 80 percent of the salaries of men ($40,000 annually compared to $49,800), a ratio identical to that of 1995. In fact, women with bachelor's degrees earn the same as men with associate degrees. Some of this pay gap can be attributed to students' undergraduate fields of study. Engineering graduates, for example, earn about $55,000 annually in their first year after graduation, while education majors bring home only $30,500. However, even after taking into account fields of study, women still earn less than men.

These pay disparities suggest an economic rationale for women's vigorous pursuit of higher education. Not only do women need to acquire more education in order to earn the same salaries as men, they also receive higher returns on their educational investments. Education scholar Laura Perna has found that even though women's salaries are lower than men's, women enjoy a greater payoff in graduating from college than men do. In the early years after graduating, a woman with a college degree will earn 55 percent more than a woman with a high school degree. For men, that difference is only 17 percent. What's more, men with only a high school education earn a third more than women do, and are more likely to find work in traditionally male blue-collar jobs that offer health care and other benefits—which are not available in the sales and service jobs typically held by women.

Though men with high school educations enjoy higher salaries and better benefits than do women, they are also more vulnerable to unemployment. In general, the rates of unemployment are twice as high for high school graduates as they are for college graduates. They are also slightly higher for men than for women at all educational levels below the bachelor's degree. According to data from a 2010 U.S. Census survey, the unemployment rate for high school graduates was 11.3 percent for men versus 9 percent for women (compared to 4.8 percent and 4.7 percent, respectively, for those with at least a bachelor's degree), due in part to the effects of the recent recession on the manufacturing sector.

In addition to offering access to better jobs, higher salaries, and less risk of unemployment, going to college offers a host of other advantages. College graduates live longer, healthier lives. They are less likely to smoke, drink too much, or suffer from anxiety, depression, obesity, and a variety of illnesses. They are more likely to vote, to volunteer, and to be civically engaged. Because of this broad array of social and economic benefits, we should be concerned about patterns of underrepresentation for any group.

incomplete integration

To some, the fact that women earn 57 percent of all degrees to men's 43 percent suggests the gender pendulum has swung too far. They claim that if the ratio still favored men, there would be widespread protest. But such claims fail to see the full picture: though women earn more degrees than men, the gender integration of higher education is far from complete. Men and women still diverge in the fields of study they choose, their experiences during college, and the kinds of jobs they get after graduating.

In the early 1970s, when men earned 57 percent of college degrees, women faced exclusion and discrimination in the labor market and earned less than two-thirds of what men earned. Many professions, and most positions of power and authority, were almost completely closed to women. While the ratio of college graduates now favors women, women are not benefiting from more education in ways that men did 40 years ago. In terms of the economic rewards of completing college, women are far from matching men, let alone outpacing them.

By paying exclusive attention to the gender ratio, we tend to overlook much more serious and enduring disparities of social class, race and ethnicity. This lessens our ability to understand how gender advantages vary across groups. If there is a crisis of access to higher education, it is not so much a gender crisis, as one of race and class. Young Black and Hispanic men and men from low-income families are among the most disadvantaged, but women from these groups also lag behind their White, Asian and middle-class counterparts. Addressing the formidable racial and economic gaps in college access will improve low-income and minority men's chances far more than closing the gender gap would.

The higher proportion of degrees earned by women does not mean that higher education is feminizing, or that men are getting crowded out. It seems that if women hold an advantage in any area, even a relatively slim one, we jump to the conclusion that it indicates a catastrophe for men. In the case of access to college degrees, that's simply not true.

recommended resources

England, Paula, and Li, Su. 2006. "Desegregation Stalled: The Changing Gender Composition of College Majors, 1971–2002," *Gender & Society* 20:657–677. Reviews trends in the gender segregation of fields of study and the reasons behind shifts towards integration as well as the stalling of desegregation.

Sax, Linda J. 2008. *The Gender Gap in College: Maximizing the Developmental Potential of Women and Men.* San Francisco, CA: Jossey-Bass. Examines the impact of college experiences, peer groups, and faculty on a comprehensive array of student outcomes.

U.S. Department of Education, National Center for Education Statistics, Institute of Education Sciences. (Washington DC, various years). *Digest of Education Statistics* and *The Condition of Education.* Comprehensive compendiums of education statistics, including a wide range of gender, race, ethnicity and class indicators.

what gender is science?

maria charles

spring 2011

Gender inequality crops up in surprising places. This is nowhere more evident than in science, technology, engineering, and mathematics (STEM) fields. The United States should be a world leader in the integration of prestigious male-dominated occupations and fields of study. After all, laws prohibiting discrimination on the basis of sex have been in place for more than half a century, and the idea that men and women should have equal rights and opportunities is practically uncontested (at least in public) in the U.S. today.

This egalitarian legal and cultural context has coincided with a longstanding shortage of STEMworkers that has spurred countless initiatives by government agencies, activists, and industry to attract women into these fields. But far from leading the world, American universities and firms lag considerably behind those in many other countries with respect to women among STEM students and workers. Moreover, the countries where women are best represented in these fields aren't those typically viewed as modern or "gender-progressive." Far from it.

Sex segregation describes the uneven distributions of women and men across occupations, industries, or fields of study. While other types of gender inequality have declined dramatically since the 1960s (for example, in legal rights, labor force participation rates, and educational attainment), some forms of sex segregation are remarkably resilient in the Industrial world.

In labor markets, one well-known cause of sex segregation is discrimination, which can occur openly and directly or through more subtle, systemic processes. Not so long ago, American employers' job advertisements and recruitment efforts were targeted explicitly toward either men or women depending on the job. Although these gender-specific ads were prohibited under Title VII of the 1964 Civil Rights Act, less blatant forms of discrimination persist. Even if employers base hiring and promotion solely on performance-based criteria, their taken-for-granted beliefs about average gender differences may bias their judgments of qualification and performance.

Sociologists and economists have documented this cognitive bias and "statistical discrimination" through diverse experiments. It turns out that people's beliefs about men's and women's different natures lead them to assess task performance accordingly, even in the absence of any actual performance differences. Such biased assessments reinforce existing patterns of sex segregation because many occupational tasks are regarded as quintessentially "masculine" or "feminine." For example, beliefs about women's capacity for nurturing and men's technical and mechanical skills might lead an employer to perceive gender-conforming applicants (say, male pilots and female nannies) to be better qualified.

But discrimination isn't the whole story. It's well-established that girls and young women often avoid mathematically-intensive fields in favor of pursuits regarded as more human-centered. Analyses of gender-differentiated choices are controversial among scholars

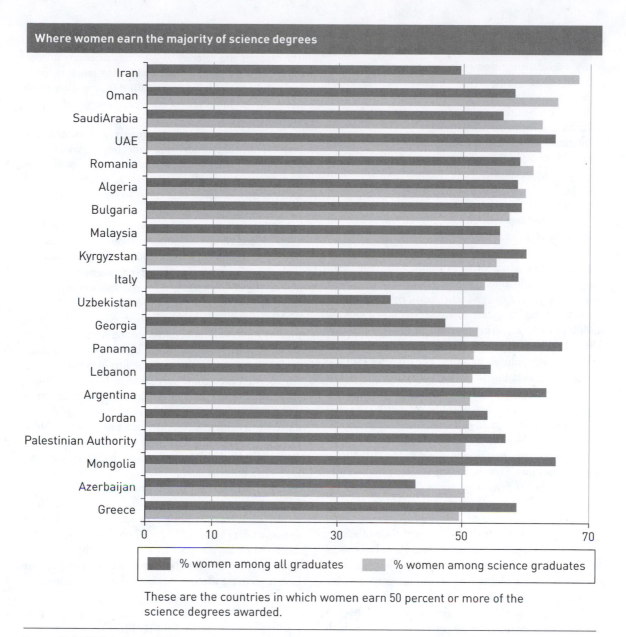

Where women earn the majority of science degrees

Legend: ■ % women among all graduates   ■ % women among science graduates

These are the countries in which women earn 50 percent or more of the science degrees awarded.

Source: UNESCO Data Center, 2010

because this line of inquiry seems to divert attention away from structural and cultural causes of inequalities in pay and status. Acknowledging gender-differentiated educational and career preferences, though, doesn't "blame the victim" unless preferences and choices are considered in isolation from the social contexts in which they emerge. A sociological analysis of sex segregation considers how the economic, social, and cultural environments influence preferences, choices, and outcomes. Among other things, we may ask what types of social context are associated with larger or smaller gender differences in aspirations. Viewed through this lens, preferences become much more than just individuals' intrinsic qualities.

An excellent way to assess contextual effects is by investigating how career aspirations and patterns of sex segregation vary across countries. Recent studies show international differences in the gender composition of STEM fields, in beliefs about the masculinity of STEM, and in girls' and women's reported affinity for STEM-related activities. These differences follow unexpected patterns.

STEM around the world

Many might assume women in more economically and culturally modern societies enjoy greater equality on all measures, since countries generally "evolve" in an egalitarian direction as they modernize. This isn't the case for scientific and technical fields, though.

Statistics on male and female college graduates and their fields of study are available from the United Nations Educational, Scientific, and Cultural Organization (UNESCO) for 84 countries covering the period between 2005 and 2008. Sixty-five of those countries have educational systems large enough to offer a full range of majors and programs (at least 10,000 graduates per year).

One way of ranking countries on the sex segregation of science education is to compare the (female-to-male) gender ratio among science graduates to the gender ratio among graduates in all other fields. By this measure, the rich and highly industrialized U.S. falls in about the middle of the distribution (in close proximity to Ecuador, Mongolia, Germany, and Ireland—a heterogeneous group on most conventional measures of "women's status"). Female representation in science programs is weakest in the Netherlands and strongest in Iran, Uzbekistan, Azerbaijan, Saudi Arabia, and Oman, where science is disproportionately female. Although the Netherlands has long been considered a gender-traditional society in the European context, most people would still be intrigued to learn that women's representation among science graduates is nearly 50 percentage points lower there than in many Muslim countries. As seen in the table on page 23, the most gender-integrated science programs are found in Malaysia, where women's 57-percent share of science degree recipients precisely matches their share of all college and university graduates.

"Science" is a big, heterogeneous category, and life science, physical science, mathematics, and computing are fields with very different gender compositions. For example, women made up 60 percent of American biology graduates, but only about 19 percent of computing graduates, in 2008, according to the National Center for Educational Statistics.

But even when fields are defined more precisely, countries differ in some unexpected ways. A case in point is computer science in Malaysia and the U.S. While American computer scientists are depicted as male hackers and geeks, computer science in Malaysia is deemed well-suited for women because it's seen as theoretical (not physical) and it takes place almost exclusively in offices (thought to be woman-friendly spaces). In interviews with sociologist Vivian Lagesen, female computer science students in Malaysia reported taking up computing because they like computers and because they and their parents think the field has good job prospects. The students also referenced government efforts to promote economic development by training workers, both male and female, for the expanding information technology field. About half of Malaysian computer science degrees go to women.

Engineering is the most strongly and consistently male-typed field of study worldwide, but its gender composition still varies widely across countries. Female representation is generally weaker in advanced industrial societies than in developing ones. In our 2009 article in the *American Journal of Sociology,* Karen Bradley and I found this pattern using international data from the mid-1990s; it was confirmed by more recent statistics assembled by UNESCO. Between 2005 and 2008, countries with the most male-dominated engineering programs include the world's leading industrial democracies (Japan, Switzerland, Germany, and the U.S.) along with some of the same oil-rich Middle Eastern countries in which women are so well-represented among science graduates (Saudi Arabia, Jordan, and the United Arab Emirates). Although women do not reach the fifty-percent mark in any country, they come very close in Indonesia, where 48 percent of engineering graduates are female (compared to a 49 percent share of all Indonesian college and university graduates). Women comprise about a third of recent engineering graduates in a diverse group of countries including Mongolia, Greece, Serbia, Panama, Denmark, Bulgaria, and Malaysia.

While engineering is uniformly male-typed in the West, Lagesen's interviews suggest Malaysians draw gender distinctions among engineering *subfields.* One female student reported, " . . . In chemical engineering, most of the time you work in labs . . . So I think it's quite suitable for females also. But for civil engineering . . . we have to go to the site and check out the constructions."

girl geeks in america

Women's relatively weak presence in STEM fields in the U.S. is partly attributable to some economic, institutional, and cultural features that are common to affluent Western democracies. One such feature is a great diversity of educational and occupational pathways. As school systems grew and democratized in the industrial West, educators, policymakers, and nongovernmental activists sought to accommodate women's purportedly "human-centered" nature by developing educational programs that were seen to align functionally and culturally with female domestic and social roles. Among other things, this involved expansion of liberal arts programs and development of vocationally-oriented programs in home economics, nursing, and early-childhood education. Subsequent efforts to incorporate women, *as women,* into higher education have contributed to expansion in humanities programs, and, more recently, the creation of new fields like women's studies and human development. These initiatives have been supported by a rapid expansion of service-sector jobs in these societies.

In countries with developing and transitional economies, though, policies have been driven more by concerns about advancing economic development than by interests in accommodating women's presumed affinities. Acute shortages of educated workers prompted early efforts by governments and development agencies to increase the supply of STEM workers. These efforts often commenced during these fields' initial growth periods—arguably before they had acquired strong masculine images in the local context.

Another reason for stronger sex segregation of STEM in affluent countries may be that more people (girls and women in particular) can afford to indulge tastes for less lucrative care and social service work in these contexts. Because personal economic security and national development are such central concerns to young people and their parents in developing societies, there is less latitude and support for the realization of gender-specific preferences.

Again, the argument that women's preferences and choices are partly responsible for sex segregation doesn't require that preferences are innate. Career aspirations are influenced by beliefs about ourselves (What am I good at and what will I enjoy doing?), beliefs about others (What will they think of me and how will they respond to my choices?), and beliefs about the purpose of educational and occupational activities (How do I decide what field to pursue?). And these beliefs are part of our cultural heritage. Sex segregation is an especially resilient form of inequality because people so ardently believe in, enact, and celebrate cultural stereotypes about gender difference.

Believing stereotypes. Relationship counselor John Gray has produced a wildly successful series of self-help products in which he depicts men and women as so fundamentally different that they might as well come from different planets. While the vast majority of Americans today believe women should have equal social and legal rights, they also believe men and women are very different, and they believe innate differences cause them to *freely choose* distinctly masculine or feminine life paths. For instance, women and men are expected to choose careers that allow them to utilize their hard-wired interests in working with people and things, respectively.

Believing in difference can actually produce difference. Recent sociological research provides strong

evidence that cultural stereotypes about gender difference shape individuals' beliefs about their own competencies ("self-assessments") and influence behavior in stereotype-consistent directions. Ubiquitous cultural depictions of STEM as intrinsically male reduce girls' interest in technical fields by defining related tasks as beyond most women's competency and as generally unenjoyable for them. STEM avoidance is a likely outcome.

Shelley Correll's social psychological experiment demonstrates the self-fulfilling effects of gender beliefs on self-assessments and career preferences. Correll administered questions purported to test "contrast sensitivity" to undergraduates. Although the test had no objectively right or wrong answers, all participants were given identical personal "scores" of approximately 60 percent correct. Before the test, subjects were exposed to one of two beliefs: that men on average do better, or that men and women perform equally well. In the first group, male students rated their performance more highly than did female students, and male students were more likely to report aspiring to work in a job that requires contrast sensitivity. No gender differences were observed among subjects in the second group. Correll's findings suggest that *beliefs about difference* can produce gender gaps in mathematical self-confidence even in the absence of actual differences in ability or performance. If these beliefs lead girls to avoid math courses, a stereotype-confirming performance deficit may emerge.

> *Sex segregation is especially resilient because people so ardently believe in, enact, and celebrate gender stereotypes.*

Concern about such self-fulfilling prophesies was one reason for the public furor that erupted when Lawrence Summers, then president of Harvard, opined in 2005 that innate biological differences might help explain women's underrepresentation in high-level math and science. Summers's critics, who included many members of the Harvard faculty, reacted angrily, suggesting that such speculation by a prominent educational leader can itself reduce girls' confidence and interest in STEM careers by reinforcing cultural stereotypes.

Enacting stereotypes. Whatever one believes about innate gender difference, it's difficult to deny that men and women often behave differently and make different choices. Partly, this reflects inculcation of gender-typed preferences and abilities during early childhood. This "gender socialization" occurs through direct observation of same-sex role models, through repeated positive or negative sanctioning of gender-conforming or nonconforming behavior, and through assimilation of diffuse cultural messages about what males and females like and are good at. During much of the 20th century, math was one thing that girls have purportedly not liked or been good at. Even Barbie said so. Feminists and educators have long voiced concerns about the potentially damaging effects of such messages on the minds of impressionable young girls.

But even girls who don't believe STEM activities are inherently masculine realize others do. It's likely to influence their everyday interactions and may affect their life choices. For example, some may seek to affirm their femininity by avoiding math and science classes or by avowing a dislike for related activities. Sociologists who study the operation of gender in social interactions have argued that people expect to be judged according to prevailing standards of masculinity or femininity. This expectation often leads them to engage in behavior that reproduces the gender order. This "doing gender" framework goes beyond socialization because it doesn't require that gender-conforming dispositions are internalized at an early age, just that people know others will likely hold them accountable to conventional beliefs about hard-wired gender differences.

The male-labeling of math and science in the industrial West means that girls and women may expect to incur social sanctions for pursuing these fields. Effects can be cumulative: taking fewer math classes will negatively affect achievement in math and attitudes toward math, creating a powerful positive feedback system.

Celebrating stereotypes. Aspirations are also influenced by general societal beliefs about the nature and purpose of educational and occupational pursuits. Modern education does more than bestow knowledge; it's seen as a vehicle for individual self-expression and self-realization. Parents and educators exhort young people, perhaps girls in particular, to "follow their passions" and realize their "true selves." Because gender is such a central axis

> **Ironically, freedom of choice seems to help construct and give agency to stereotypically gendered "selves."**

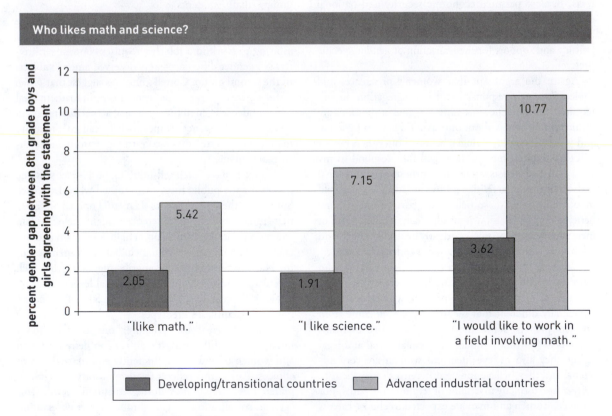

Who likes math and science?

percent gender gap between 8th grade boys and girls agreeing with the statement

- "I like math." — Developing/transitional countries: 2.05; Advanced industrial countries: 5.42
- "I like science." — Developing/transitional countries: 1.91; Advanced industrial countries: 7.15
- "I would like to work in a field involving math." — Developing/transitional countries: 3.62; Advanced industrial countries: 10.77

Developing/transitional countries   Advanced industrial countries

Values give male to female difference in percentage points, averaged across countries. Calculations of data from the Trends in International Math and Science Survey by Maria Charles and Karen Bradley, "Indulging our Gendered Selves? Sex Segregation by Field of Study in 44 Countries," *American Journal of Sociology* (2009), 114(4):924.

of individual identity, American girls who aim to "study what they love" are unlikely to consider male-labeled science, engineering, or technical fields, despite the material security provided by such degrees.

Although the so-called "postmaterialist" values of individualism and self-expression are spreading globally, they are most prominent in affluent late-modern societies. Curricular and career choices become more than practical economic decisions in these contexts; they also represent acts of identity construction and self-affirmation. Modern systems of higher education make the incursion of gender stereotypes even easier, by allowing wide latitude in course choices.

The ideological discordance between female gender identities and STEM pursuits may even generate attitudinal aversion among girls. Preferences can evolve to align with the gender composition of fields, rather than vice versa. Consistent with these arguments is new evidence showing that career-related aspirations are more gender-differentiated in advanced industrial than in developing and transitional societies. The gender gap in eighth-graders' affinity for math, confidence in math abilities, and interest in a math-related career is significantly smaller in less affluent countries than in rich ("postmaterialist") ones. Clearly, there is more going on than intrinsic male and female preferences.

questioning STEM's masculinity

Playing on stereotypes of science as the domain of socially awkward male geniuses, CBS's hit comedy "The Big Bang Theory" stars four nerdy male physicists and one sexy but academically challenged waitress. (Female physicists, when they do show up, are mostly caricatured as gender deviants: sexually unattractive and lacking basic competence in human interaction.) This depiction resonates with popular Western understandings of scientific and technical pursuits as intrinsically masculine.

But representations of scientific and technical fields as *by nature* masculine aren't well-supported by international data. They're also difficult to reconcile with historical evidence pointing to long-term historical shifts in the gender-labeling of some STEM fields. In *The Science Education of American Girls,* Kim Tolley reports that it was *girls* who were overrepresented among students of physics, astronomy, chemistry, and natural science in 19th century American schools. Middle-class boys dominated the higher-status classical humanities programs thought to require top rational powers and required for university admission. Science education was regarded as excellent preparation

for motherhood, social work, and teaching. Sociologist Katharine Donato tells a similar story about the dawn of American computer programming. Considered functionally analogous to clerical work, it was performed mostly by college-educated women with science or math backgrounds. This changed starting in the 1950s, when the occupation became attractive to men as a growing, intellectually demanding, and potentially lucrative field. The sex segregation of American STEM fields—especially engineering, computer science, and the physical sciences—has shown remarkable stability since about 1980.

The gender (and racial) composition of fields is strongly influenced by the economic and social circumstances that prevail at the time of their initial emergence or expansion. But subsequent transformative events, such as acute labor shortages, changing work conditions, and educational restructuring can effect significant shifts in fields' demographic profiles. Tolley, for example, links men's growing dominance of science education in the late 19th and early 20th century to changing university admissions requirements, the rapid growth and professionalization of science and technology occupations, and recurrent ideological backlashes against female employment.

A field's designation as either "male" or "female" is often naturalized through cultural accounts that reference selected gender-conforming aspects of the work. Just as sex segregation across engineering subfields is attributed to physical location in Malaysia (inside work for women, outside work for men), American women's overrepresentation among typists and sewers has been attributed to these occupations' "feminine" task profiles, specifically their requirements for manual dexterity and attention to detail. While the same skills might be construed as essential to the work of surgeons and electricians, explanations for men's dominance of these fields are easily generated with reference to other job requirements that are culturally masculine (technical and spatial skills, for example). Difference-based explanations for sex segregation are readily available because most jobs require diverse skills and aptitudes, some equated with masculinity, some with femininity.

looking forward

Should we be concerned about women's underrepresentation in STEM if this result follows from choices made in the absence of coercion or discrimination? I believe sex segregation should be of more than academic interest for at least three reasons. First, "separate but equal" principles often translate into "separate but unequal" outcomes, as is evident in the lower pay in female-than in male-dominated work. Second, sex segregation has feedback effects, reinforcing gender stereotypes and limiting perceived educational, family, and career options for subsequent generations. And third, women may represent an untapped labor pool in STEM fields where global shortages threaten to undermine national competiveness and economic development.

What then might be done to increase women's presence in STEM fields? One plausible strategy involves changes to the structure of secondary education. Some evidence suggests more girls and women complete degrees in math and science in educational systems where curricular choice is restricted or delayed; *all* students might take mathematics and science throughout their high-school years or the school might use performance-based tracking and course placement. Although such policies are at odds with Western ideals of individual choice and self-expression, they may weaken penetration of gender stereotypes during the impressionable adolescent years.

Of course, the most obvious means of achieving greater integration of STEM is to avoid reinforcing stereotypes about what girls and boys like and what they are good at. Cultural shifts of this sort occur only gradually, but some change can be seen on the horizon. The rise of "geek chic" may be one sign. Aiming to liberate teen-aged girls from the girls-can't-do-math and male-math-nerd stereotypes, television star and self-proclaimed math geek Danica McKellar has written three how-to math books, most recently *Hot X: Algebra Exposed,* presenting math as both feminine and fun. Even Barbie has been updated. In contrast to her math-fearing Teen Talk sister of the early 1990s, the new Computer Engineer Barbie, released in December 2010, comes decked out in a tight t-shirt printed in binary code and equipped with a smart phone and a pink laptop. Of course, one potential pitfall of this math-is-feminine strategy is that it risks swapping one set of stereotypes for another.

So, what gender is science? In short, it depends. When occupations or fields are segregated by sex, most people suspect it reflects fields' inherently masculine or feminine task content. But this presumption is belied by substantial cross-national variability in the gender composition of fields, STEM in particular. Moreover, this variability follows surprising patterns. Whereas most people would expect to find many more female engineers in the U.S. and Sweden than in Columbia and Bulgaria, new data suggest that precisely the opposite is true.

Ironically, the freedom of choice that's so celebrated in affluent Western democracies seems to help construct and give agency to stereotypically gendered "selves." Self-segregation of careers may occur because some believe they're naturally good at gender-conforming activities (attempting to build on their strengths), because they believe that certain fields will be seen as appropriate for people like them ("doing" gender), or because they believe they'll enjoy gender-conforming fields more than gender-nonconforming ones (realizing their "true selves"). It's just that, by encouraging individual self-expression in post-materialist societies, we may also effectively promote the development and expression of culturally gendered selves.

recommended resources

Correll, Shelly J. 2004. "Constraints into Preferences: Gender, Status, and Emerging Career Aspirations," *American Sociological Review* 69:93–113. Presents evidence from experiments on how beliefs about gender influence beliefs about our own competence and constrain career aspirations.

England, Paula. 2010. "The Gender Revolution: Uneven and Stalled." *Gender & Society* 24:149–166. Offers reasons for the persistence of some forms of gender inequality in the United States.

Faulkner, Wendy. 2000. "Dualisms, Hierarchies and Gender in Engineering." *Social Studies of Science* 30:759–792. Explores the cultural linkage of masculinity and technology within the engineering profession.

Fenstermaker, Sarah, and West, Candace. (eds.). 2002. *Doing Gender, Doing Difference: Inequality, Power, and Institutional Change.* London: Routledge. Explores how and why people reproduce gender (and race and class) stereotypes in everyday interactions.

Ridgeway, Cecilia L. 2011. *Framed by Gender: How Gender Inequality Persists in the Modern World.* London: Oxford University Press. Describes how cultural gender beliefs bias behavior and congnition in gendered directions and how this influence may vary by context.

Xie, Yu, and Shauman, Kimberlee A. 2003. *Women in Science: Career Processes and Outcomes.* Cambridge, MA: Harvard University Press. Uses data from middle school to mid-career to study the forces that lead fewer American women than men into science and engineering fields.

women of god

orit avishai

fall 2010

Is God bad for women? Media consumers in North America and Europe are probably familiar with this narrative: conservative and fundamentalist religions—those who take religion seriously and politicize religiosity—are on the rise, and that's bad for women. In France, wearing a the headscarf in public spaces is decried as an affront to French notions of citizenship and to women's personhood. In the United States, Afghan women's plight at the hands of the Taliban was used as a justification for American intervention. Since the emancipation of women and the diversification of family forms and sexualities are among the hallmarks of modernity and secularization, and since fundamentalist religious groups tend to hold traditional views on gender, sexuality, and the family, conservative religions are typically viewed as antithetical to women's interests (not to mention modern, democratic ideals of choice and the freedom to chart one's own destiny).

In a sense, conservative religions have *earned* this bad reputation; the historical record is full of instances in which girls and women have been restricted from access to health care, education, and employment in the name of God. Girls' and women's bodies and mobility are regulated, their chastity is "protected," and sometimes they are even maimed or killed as a marker of national or tribal pride, identity, unity, or boundaries. If this is the case, how can we explain women's willingness and motivation to participate in these religions? Some feel the Marxist explanation—religion is the opiate of the people—and its feminist incarnation—women's participation in conservative religions is a form of false consciousness—are sufficient. Others believe women involved in conservative religions are simply oppressed.

Sociologists, anthropologists, historians, and political scientists who study women's experiences in a range of religious traditions in diverse geographical locations have found that the "God is bad for women" formulation provides an impoverished picture of experiences with conservative religions. These studies show that women are simultaneously oppressed *and* empowered by their religion, that their compliance is as much a product of active strategizing as passive compliance, and that religion is as much a site of negotiating traditional gender norms as it is a site of reproducing patriarchal gender relationships. If that's true, it's certainly possible that conservative religions aren't inherently and universally antithetical to women's interests (at least not *all* of the time).

Some commentators make an even more provocative claim: the "God is bad for women" formulation rests on false assumptions about religion and liberal notions of freedom and choice. That is, these scholars argue that the trope ignores the similarities between women's complicity with religious regimes and their complicity with other gendered practices like Western beauty norms.

religion is bad for women

Religion is often viewed as a primary site for the articulation, reproduction, and institutionalization of gender inequality. The combination of male gods, institutions that encode gender inequality (think male-only clergy) and women's subordination (such as Evangelical teachings on male headship), ambivalence toward the female body (think the veil across the Muslim world and a Jewish man's daily prayer with a line that thanks God for not "having made me a woman"), and the belief that gender differences are natural and essential has produced a deep-seated suspicion toward conservative religions among the reform-minded. Elizabeth Cady Stanton captured this spirit in 1885 when she wrote, "History shows that the moral degradation of woman is due more to theological superstitions than to all other influences together." Such sentiments were echoed by many second wave American feminists who viewed religiously inspired ideas about women's work, reproduction, and bodies as detrimental to the women's movement's goals of gender equality and freedom.

Until the 1980s, the general view was that religion—as an ideology and as an institution—was nothing but a constraint on women's lives.

This view of religion poses a problem, though: women *are* involved with conservative religions. They join, and they stay. Are these women opposed to equality and freedom? Do they not recognize their complicity in a regime that requires submission? Until the 1980s, the general view was that religion—as an ideology and as an institution—was nothing but a constraint on women's lives, so women's active involvement with conservative religions was viewed as the product of oppression, lack of agency, or false consciousness.

Yet, when researchers turned to study women's *actual* experiences with religion (as opposed to ideologically driven assessments) in the late 1980s, their findings were startling: women—Protestant, Catholic, Jewish, Hindu, and others—are not necessarily oppressed and deprived of free choice by their religion.

multiple meanings

When scholars looked past religious dogma to lived experiences, they found discrepancies between ideologies and practices. Women, they saw, don't blindly submit to religious prescriptions; instead, they adapt their religious practices (if not iterations of belief) to the realities of their lives and to dominant gender ideologies. In the process, they sometimes (consciously or unconsciously) subvert and resist official teachings without much fanfare and without explicitly resisting religious gender norms.

This subtlety, though, serves to perpetuate the myth that women are uniformly oppressed by religion. For example, when sociologists Sally Gallagher and Christian Smith interviewed Evangelical men and women in the U.S. about their family lives, their respondents professed an unwavering support for ideologies such as male headship and women's submission while rejecting egalitarian gender ideologies. Nevertheless, their *real-life* choices about work, family, and child rearing exhibited a de-facto egalitarianism that belied their ideological stance: most of the Evangelical women in their study worked outside the home and routinely participated in domestic decision making. Gallagher and Smith labeled this disjuncture "symbolic traditionalism and pragmatic egalitarianism."

In other cases, researchers have found that what looks like oppression is often a set of strategic choices made to help women navigate gender relations. In a now-classic study, sociologist Lynn Davidman explored why educated American women might embrace highly patriarchal and conservative strands of Orthodox Judaism. Rather than being duped into an anachronistic religion, these women said that they consciously turned to Orthodox Judaism as a response to problems generated by modern American culture, including its emphasis on careerism, individualism, and gender equality. Caroline Chen, a sociologist who studied the experiences of Taiwanese women who converted to conservative strands of Buddhism and Christianity after immigrating to the U.S., found women used religion to negotiate with patriarchal family structures and to carve out a space of independence and authority. Their newfound religion allowed women to undermine oppressive traditional Taiwanese practices that left them without much power within the family. Gallagher also saw similar dynamics in her study of low-income Syrian women, who use religious and cultural rationales to improve their access to income and employment while avoiding unattractive employment opportunities. The Syrian women consciously enlist religion to expand their autonomy while simultaneously maintaining a semblance of deference. Defining their economic activities as "not work," for example, means they can contribute to the family economy (sometimes earning up to 40 percent of the family's income) in a society that emphasizes women's primary responsibilities as domestic. The point is: some women achieve progressive ends using traditional, but subversive, means.

So, women aren't oppressed dupes. On the contrary, women like these use religion to make choices and improve their lives; they are strategic actors who appropriate religious traditions and practices to meet the demands of contemporary life, often to further extra-religious ends such as economic opportunities, domestic relations, political ideologies, and cultural affiliation.

Other studies show how seemingly oppressive practices can serve empowering and liberating functions. This is the case with regard to the issue that best symbolizes conservative religion's purported oppression of women: the veil.

In the 1980s, when political scientist Arlene MacLeod and Turkish sociologist Nulifer Gole studied the emergent phenomenon of Muslim women's embrace of veiling in Egypt and Turkey, respectively, each found that context matters. In the Egyptian case, women's embrace of the veil came at a time when economic conditions compelled women to find gainful employment outside the home. Their movement into the workplace was at odds with traditional Egyptian notions of modesty and domesticity. These ideas had discouraged women from venturing into public spaces unaccompanied by men and frowned upon close contact between unrelated men and women. Veiling provided a solution, as it preserved women's modesty and affirmed their domesticity while also providing the mobility to work outside the home. As it opened unprecedented opportunities for women to venture beyond the domestic, the veil became liberating. Macleod terms the veil's liberating potential as "accommodating protest."

In Turkey, Gole found that, to the generation of young, educated, women who embraced the veil on college campuses, veiling symbolized resistance to Western values. Veiling, Gole argues, wasn't imposed on these women, so the act of veiling reveals them to be empowered and strategic political actors. Research on Latin American Pentecostal women reports similar dynamics of women's empowerment through the embrace of religion.

These studies notwithstanding, not all commentators are equally impressed by religion's liberating potential. In her award-winning study of South Korean Evangelical women, sociologist Kelly Chong writes that conversion to Evangelical Christianity helps some women navigate the forces of modernity while also reinforcing highly patriarchal and non-egalitarian gender dynamics. Further, Chong asserts that religion is *also* a site where the rules of gender relations are constantly being rewritten.

The aggregate message of these studies is that conservative religions are not necessarily oppressive, nor is religion thoroughly anti-modern. Context is extremely important but often lost in popular depictions of conservative religions and their symbols—the veil, men's headship, male-only clergy—as uniformly oppressive. In some instances, the forces of modernity increase the appeal of conservative religion. In others, the embrace of religion helps women cope with and sometimes even challenge preexisting oppressive gender norms and social structures.

> This view of religion poses a problem, though: women are involved with conservative religions. They join, and they stay.

Yet, it seems that each study begins with the notion that women's involvement with conservative religions is paradoxical—only to find, time and time again, that this formula provides only a very narrow perspective on the religious experience. More recent research takes issue with the notion that women's complicity and submission are paradoxical, investigating, instead, the assumptions on which this perspective is based.

past the paradox

Experts' bewilderment over women's embrace of conservative religions is symptomatic of the broader assumptions about religiosity and modern personhood that have shaped discussions of religion since the Enlightenment. One set of assumptions concerns the incompatibility of religion and modernity. Throughout much of the 20th century, everyone expected the significance of religion would progressively decline. Known as the "secularization thesis," the theory was that modernization and secularization (and, implicitly, westernization) are intrinsically related and that progress—including the emancipation of women from the hold of oppressive religions—follows a uniform and linear (western) trajectory. Religion, in this conception, is incompatible with rational, complex, and individualistic modern societies. When empirical reality proved this theory wrong (conservative and fundamentalist religious movements, for instance, have been on the rise around the world since the 1980s, as evidenced by the 1979 Iranian revolution, the rise of Pentecostalism in Latin America, the increased visibility of Evangelicals in American political life, and the fervor of Orthodox Jewish nationalists), the secularization thesis was replaced by explanations that recognized that *some* aspects of religion were compatible with modernity.

However, a second set of assumptions about the incompatibility of religion with liberal notions of agency, freedom, and choice persists. It is in this set of assumptions that the paradox approach is rooted. The liberal notion of freedom assumes that individuals should strive to be free of commitment and submission to a higher power—thereby precluding many forms of religious devotion. This is why explanations of women's involvement with conservative religion that revolve around strategic choice, the liberatory potential of religion, or passive resistance have been so attractive: women who realize their own economic, political, or intimate interests against the weight of custom and tradition are *redeemed*.

> **Women don't blindly submit to religiousprescriptions; instead, they adapt their religious practices to the realities of their lives.**

Yet, such explanations ultimately provide binary explanations of religion: either it's a site where women are oppressed and gender inequality is reproduced, or it's a site of empowerment, resistance, strategic planning and negotiation of gender. What's missing is the possibility that women embrace religious practices such as veiling and male headship in pursuit of religious goals—namely, the cultivation of oneself as a pious *religious* subject.

This is the account that anthropologist Saba Mahmood provides in her study of Islamic revival and piety among women in Cairo. Starting in the 1990s, many Egyptian women began to attend mosques to teach each other Islamic doctrine. This trend, facilitated by women's increased mobility and education, has subversive potential since scholarly and theological materials had previously been the sole purview of learned men. Yet, these Muslim women were *not* seeking to undermine existing power structures or to resist the secular state, which discouraged their kind of learning and religious piety. Rather, their main motivation was to learn, attain, and uphold Islamic virtues of modesty and docility and reintegrate Islamic knowledge and practices (including those that organize gender relationships) into every-day Egyptian life. For Westerners, it seems impossibly paradoxical: the nature of piety that these women promote depends on subordina-

> **It's not God, but man, who's detrimental to or affirming of women's interests.**

tion to Islamic virtues of femininity that includes modesty and docility and is achieved by teaching the body "modest disciplines" through practices such as veiling and the cultivation of shyness.

It's easy to dismiss something like the cultivation of shyness as oppressive, functional, or a symbol of resistance

to the forces of modernity. However, Mahmood presents a different explanation: this practice provides a pathway to achieve piety and to make meaning in the world. Mahmood likens the achievement of piety through submission to the lengthy and painful regime of learning to which musicians or dancers subject themselves as they seek mastery in their field. Like a dancer or musician, the religious woman submits herself to a lifelong regime of ongoing discipline; she becomes a masterful religious woman through daily practice. But, like the dancer or the musician, the religious woman is not oppressed by her regime; rather, her very personhood and agency are predicated upon the ability to be instructed and transformed by submission to her practices.

Mahmood came under fire for positing that the embrace of docility doesn't necessarily amount to oppression and that "freedom" and "choice" aren't universal terms; most discussions of religion, it seems, still spring from the "God is bad for women" formulation. Yet, the most important point that Mahmood makes is that the assumptions that shape discussions of women's experiences with conservative religions are flawed. A shift in perspective opens up new avenues for thinking about religion as a site of identity making. Other commentators approach this question of assumptions from a different perspective by noting the irony of anti-religious fervor among Westerners and citing the similarities between patriarchal regulations emanating from religious dogma and those hailing from cultural norms and standards like the Western beauty ideal.

church of god, church of beauty

Bring up conservative religion and its symbols on any American college campus, and students will immediately point out paradoxes of complicity. With astonishing predictability, they associate compliance with conservative religions with lack of agency, choice, or freedom. Students are usually willing to concede that complicity sometimes masks strategic choices or latent resistance, but arguments such as Mahmood's—that women find meaning through docility—are a hard sell. Students like to point out—triumphantly—that *their* lives in a modern democracy that values women are free of the constraints that characterize the lives of veiled women.

Fatima Mernissi, a Moroccan sociologist who has written extensively about gender and religion in the Middle East, puts these self-satisfied indictments in perspective. In the late 1990s, Mernissi lectured extensively in Europe and the U.S. about her memoir. In it, she recounts her childhood in a typical Moroccan household: a harem.

This multi-generational living arrangement housed siblings, families, and parents. The harem limited women's spatial mobility, but was also a site of ongoing power struggles. In the course of her book tour, Mernissi was inundated by questions that exposed the depth of Westerners' ignorance about gender relations in Muslim societies. Westerners, she learned, assumed that Muslims were women-haters and that Muslim women were oppressed, dependent, sex starved, and powerless.

Intrigued by the dissonance between Western perceptions and her own experiences, Mernissi set out on a complementary mission (and wrote a complementary book) to uncover how Westerns represent Muslim gender relations. In the process, Mernissi stumbled upon a revelation: Westerners, too, have their own harem, one that she titles "size 6." Mernissi criticizes Western commentators for feigning ignorance in light of the similarities between the oppressive nature of the Church of God and the oppressive nature of the church of beauty. Recounting her experience in an American department store, where she was deemed "too big" for its elegant selection, Mernissi revealed parallels between the violence of the veil that restricts women's movement and the violence of Western beauty norms that compel women to follow strict diet regimes and undergo dangerous surgeries.

Mernissi's rhetoric is simplistic, but the simplicity helps drive home a more sophisticated claim: the "God is bad for women" formulation is not the truism many believe. Instead, it's a myth that hinges on assumptions about the nature of religion, personhood, freedom, and choice.

Overall, then, *is* God bad for women? Research over the past twenty years has shattered conventional views of conservative religions as monolithic sources of oppression. Social scientists have demonstrated that women can be empowered by their religion, that compliance is often strategic, that religion is a site where gender rules are constantly being rewritten, and that religiosity is produced through acts of devotion. More than anything, these studies show that asking "Is God bad for women?" is misguided, based on ideological assumptions rather than on sound empirical evidence. Ultimately, like most questions about culture and society, the answer can only be "it depends."

Context—social, cultural, historical—is paramount, and it's impossible to assess the implications of women's involvement with religion without taking into account the diverse circumstances in which women encounter conservative religions. It's not God, but man, who's detrimental to or affirming of women's interests, both in the practices and behaviors we condemn and condone.

recommended resources

Bush, Evelyn. 2010, September. "Explaining Religious Market Failure: A Gendered Critique of the Religious Economies Model." *Sociological Theory 28*(3). Argues that although women constitute the majority of religious participants, religious messages continue to favor men's interests.

Chong, Kelly H. 2009. *Deliverance and Submission: Evangelical Women and the Negotiation of Patriarchy in South Korea.* Cambridge, MA: Harvard University Press. Explores how women's religious participation constitutes part of their effort to negotiate the dilemmas of contemporary family and gender relations.

Davidman, Lynn. 1991. *Tradition in a Rootless World: Women Turn to Orthodox Judaism.* Oakland, CA: University of California Press. A now-classic look at women's embrace of a conservative religion.

Gallagher, Sally K. 2003. *Evangelical Identity and Gendered Family Life.* New Brunswick: Rutgers University Press. A balanced study of Evangelicals' perspectives on gender, family life, and faith.

Mahmood, Saba. 2005. *Politics of Piety: The Islamic Revival and the Feminist Subject.* Chicago: University of Chicago Press. A study of Islamic revival in Egypt that challenges key assumptions within feminist theory about religious practices.

Mernissi, Fatima. 2001. *Scheherazade Goes West: Different Cultures, Different Harems.* New York: Washington Square Press. Probes representations of Muslim women in Western culture and juxtaposes the relations between men and women in Europe with those in the Muslim world.

bathroom battlegrounds
and penis panics

kristen schilt and laurel westbrook

spring 2015

In January 2008, the city commission in Gainesville, Florida, passed an ordinance prohibiting discrimination on the basis of "gender identity and gender expression" in employment and public accommodations (such as public restrooms and locker rooms). Advocates argued that the legislation was a key step toward addressing discrimination against transgender and gender variant people. However, 14 months later voters were considering a ballot initiative to overturn the law.

Even though there had been no reported problems, those that were pushing for the repeal of the new ordinance suggested that such protections had unanticipated, dangerous consequences for women and children. Citizens for Good Public Policy ran a TV ad that featured a young, White girl on a playground. She jumps off a merry-go-round, and, alone, enters a doorway clearly marked "Women's Restroom." A moment later, a White man with a scraggly beard, dark sunglasses, and baseball cap slung low on his forehead approaches the door, looks around furtively, and enters. As the door swings shut, the ad cuts to black and the message appears: "Your City Commission made this legal. Is this what you want for Gainesville?"

The question at the heart of the ballot initiative—the place of transgender people in society—has never been a more visible issue than it is today. Advocates for

> *In none of the media accounts we analyzed have opponents been able to cite an actual case of bathroom sexual assault after the passage of transgender-supportive policies.*

transgender rights have effectively demonstrated that transgender and gender variant people face large-scale discrimination in areas such as employment, housing, and education. Yet, while city and state policies to address such discrimination are rapidly expanding, each new transgender-supportive law or policy typically results in an outbreak of protest.

As sociologists of gender, we were interested in accounting for the opposition to transgender rights in the face of greater societal acceptance of transgender people, as it presents a puzzling aspect of gender: why are transgender people accepted in some spaces and not others? We did a content analysis of media articles about transgender-inclusive legislation from 2006–2010, and discovered that the Gainesville ad was not an anomaly. Opponents of transgender recognition often brought up the specter of sexual predators in sex-segregated spaces as an argument against the passage of transgender rights legislation. Interestingly, such fears centered exclusively on women's spaces, particularly restrooms.

What do sexual predators have to do with transgender rights? Moreover, why is the concern only about women's spaces? In our research, we find that opponents are making an argument against any bodies perceived as male having a legal right to enter a woman-only space because they imagine such bodies to present a sexual danger to women and children. Under this logic, they often conflate "sexual predators" (imagined to be deviant men) and transgender women (imagined to be always male). This exclusive focus on "males" suggests that it is genitals—not gender identity and expression—that are driving what we term "gender panics"—moments where people react to a challenge to the gender binary by frantically asserting its naturalness. Because most people are assumed by others to be heterosexual, sex-segregated bathrooms are imagined by many people to be "sexuality-free" zones. Opponents' focus on bathrooms centers on fears of sexual impropriety that could be introduced by allowing the "wrong bodies"—or, to be more precise, penises—into spaces deemed as "for women only." Gender panics, thus, could easily be relabeled "penis panics." The shift from gender panics to penis panics as a point of analysis accounts for critics' sole focus on the women's restroom—a location that, opponents argue, should be "penis-free."

While such arguments are not always politically effective—Gainesville, for instance, did not repeal its ordinance—they reinforce gender inequality in a number of ways. Opponents disseminate ideas that women are weak and in need of protection—what one of us (Laurel Westbrook) frames as creating a "vulnerable subjecthood"—and that men are inherent rapists. At the same time, they generate fear and misunderstanding around transgender people along with the suggestion that transgender people are less deserving of protection than cisgender women and children (cisgender people are those whose gender identity conforms to their biological sex). As such, the battle over transgender people's access to sex-segregated spaces is both about transgender rights and about either reproducing or challenging damaging beliefs about what it is to be a man and what it is to be a woman.

transgender rights legislation to "bathroom bills"

The public response to transgender-supportive policies has varied across different social contexts. Within gender-integrated settings, such as college campuses and workplaces, the trend toward transgender-inclusive health care coverage and non-discrimination policies in terms of hiring and promotion has become widely accepted as an important dimension of diversity. Yet, transgender inclusion in sex-segregated settings has proven to be more controversial. In particular, the part of inclusive policies that allows transgender people to use a bathroom that aligns with their gender identity and expression—rather than with their chromosomes or genital configurations—has generated a great deal of opposition.

Supportive politicians and advocates frame transgender rights policies as a way to alleviate discrimination against transgender and gender variant people. Opponents, in contrast, reframe the debate as being about bathroom access. This concerted effort to focus on bathrooms was evident in the media accounts we analyzed. Critics did not discuss "transgender rights legislation," but rather "bathroom bills." Reporters picked up on this aspect of the debate, creating pithy, attention-grabbing headlines such as "Critics: Flush Bathroom Bill" (*Boston Herald*) and "Bathroom Bill Goes Down the Drain" (*New Hampshire Business Review*).

Opponents repeatedly expressed their belief that public restrooms have to be segregated on the basis of gender and that people's genitals, not their gender identities, should determine bathroom access. Kris Mineau of the conservative Massachusetts Family Institute, quoted in *The Republican*, worried about the potential outcome of the proposed state transgender rights bill. "This is a far-reaching piece of legislation that will disrupt the privacy of bathrooms, showers, and exercise facilities including those in public schools. . . . This bill opens the barn door to everybody. There is no way to know who of the opposite biological sex is using the facility for the right purpose." Evelyn Reilly, a spokesperson for the same institute, told *The Berkshire Eagle*, "Men and women bathrooms [sic] have been separated for ages for a reason. . . . Women need to feel private and safe when they're using those facilities."

In actuality, the segregation of public bathrooms on the basis of gender is a relatively recent phenomenon in the United States. Prior to the Victorian era, men and women used the same privies and outhouses. With the invention of indoor plumbing came water closets and later bathrooms, which were not segregated until Victorian ideals of feminine modesty—and the mixing of men and women in factory work—established a new precedent. By the 1920s, laws requiring segregated public facilities were de rigueur across the country. As sociologist Erving Goffman has pointed out, men and women share bathrooms in their homes. In public restrooms, by contrast, the sense that men and women are opposite is exacerbated by the placement of open urinals in men's rooms and the private stalls found in women's rooms. Such separation, then, is not biologically necessary but rather socially mandated. Highlighting this point, bathroom segregation is not universal, as some European countries, such as France, often have gender-integrated public restrooms.

Transgender-supportive policies present a sharp challenge to this bathroom segregation logic. Opponents struggle with the sense that their belief in a static gender binary determined by chromosomes and genitals is being undermined by institutional and governmental support for transgender people. The outcome of the resulting gender panics is often a call to socially reinforce what opponents position as a natural division of men and women. In a "Letter to the Editor" in *The Bangor Daily News*, a concerned author contests transgender bathroom access, arguing, "What makes an individual able to claim gender? As I always understood it growing up—and I know I am not alone in this—your anatomy dictates your sex." A follow-up response on *The Bangor Daily News* "ClickBack" page read, "The policy should be boys use the men's room and girls use the lady's room. Identification does not change physical plumbing."

These ideological collisions between those advocating transgender rights and those who insist on sex at birth determining gender, and the ensuing panics, put into high relief the often-invisible social criteria for "who counts" as a woman and a man in our society. Yet, in our study, such gender panics focused exclusively on the threat that transgender-supportive bills present to cisgender women and children. Highlighting this point, opponents to trans-inclusive policies proposed in Massachusetts and New Hampshire in 2009 and 2010 repeatedly discussed that these policies would, as *The Associated Press* reported, "put women and children at risk." It was in these fears of "risk" that the image of the sexual predator emerged.

enter the sexual predator

The conception of the "sexual predator" is deeply gendered. People often assume that they can establish whether someone is a potential sexual threat by simply determining if they are male (possible threat) or female (not a likely threat). Critics charge that transgender rights laws will make such determination difficult and, will, like "sheep's clothing" on a wolf, give predators open access to those seen as vulnerable. Evelyn Reilly,

Explicit bodily criteria for access to sex-segregated spaces can quell gender panics, but these criteria force transgender people into restrictive, normative forms of gendered embodiment that perpetuate the belief that genitals and gender must be linked.

a spokesperson for the Massachusetts Family Institute, argued that a proposed state-level law protecting gender identity and gender expression would allow "a sexual predator using the guise of gender confusion to enter the restrooms." In Colorado, Bruce Hausknecht, a policy analyst for the evangelical organization Focus on the Family Action, fought against a proposed transgender rights bill in 2009, stating: "The fear . . . is that a sexual predator would attempt to enter the women's facilities, and the public accommodation owner would feel they had no ability to challenge that." In Nevada in 2009, conservative activist Tony Dane told *The Las Vegas Review-Journal* that transgender-rights policies would allow men to legally enter women's restrooms "in drag," which would "make it easier for them to attack women and evade capture."

from gender panics to penis panics

Transgender people, along with gay men and lesbian women, have a long history of being conflated with pedophiles and other sexual predators. Within the articles we analyzed, opponents worried about what transgender women, who they assume have penises, might do if they were allowed access to women-only spaces. Demonstrating such concern, reporters frequently highlighted critics' fears about "male anatomies" or "male genitalia" in women's spaces. Transgender women in these narratives are always anchored to their imagined "male anatomies," and thus become categorized as potential sexual threats to those vested with vulnerable subjecthood, namely cisgender women and children.

In contrast, transgender men—assumed by critics to be "really women" because they do not possess a "natural" penis—are relatively invisible in these debates. Transgender men are mentioned directly by opponents only *once* in all of the articles we analyzed. After conservative opponent Tony Dane expressed his concern that the proposed Nevada policy would make women "uncomfortable" in the bathroom because they might have to see a transgender woman, a reporter for *The Las Vegas Review-Journal* asked about his position on transgender men. He stated, "they should use the women's bathroom, regardless of whom it makes uncomfortable, because that's where they're supposed to go." Transgender men are never referenced as potential sexual threat to women, men, or children. Instead, they are put into a category that sociologist Mimi Schippers labels "pariah femininities." They are not dangerous to cisgender women and children, but they also do not warrant protection and rights because they fall outside of gender and sexual normativity.

As our research reveals, policies that would allow transgender people to access sex-segregated spaces and do not have specific requirements for genital surgeries generate a great deal of panic. These panics matter, as they frequently result in a reshaping of the language of such policies to require extensive bodily changes before transgender people have access to particular rights and locations. Such changes place severe limitations on transgender people who may not want or cannot afford genital surgeries. Further, while explicit bodily criteria for access to sex-segregated spaces can quell gender panics, these criteria force transgender people into restrictive and normative forms of gendered embodiment that perpetuate the belief that genitals and gender must be linked.

transgender rights and the struggle for gender equality

In 2011, the National Center for Transgender Equality and the National Gay and Lesbian Task Force published "Injustice at Every Turn," a report that highlights the findings of the largest ever survey of the experiences of transgender and gender variant people. The report documents wide-ranging experiences of discrimination. For instance, respondents had double the rate of unemployment compared to the general population and 90% reported experiencing workplace discrimination, including being unable to access a bathroom at work that matched their gender identity.

Anti-discrimination legislation that offers protections for a person's gender identity and gender expression is an important strategy for addressing inequality in hiring and promotion. Additionally, these policies allow transgender people to use public accommodations, such as bathrooms, in line with their gender identity. In other words, a transgender man with a beard would not be legally required to use the women's restroom simply because he had been assigned female at birth. While the adoption of transgender-supportive policies has grown rapidly at the state, city, and corporate level in the last ten years, in 2015 there are limited federal protections— a situation that would be addressed by the passage of the Employment Non-Discrimination Act (also known as ENDA). The regional variation in protection for gender identity and gender expression—and the widespread violence and discrimination aimed at transgender people— makes this a key political issue for gender equality.

unmasking the real debate

Gender panics gain legitimacy in the realm of debate because many people believe that women and young children are inherently vulnerable and in need of protection from men. In dominant U.S. culture, men—or more specifically, people assumed to have penises—are both conceived of as the potential protectors of vulnerable people they have relational ties to, such as wives, sisters, daughters, and mothers, and a potential source of sexual threat to others. This idea emerges from a belief that men constantly seek out sexual interactions and will resort to violence to achieve these desires. As transgender women are placed into the category of persons with penises—making them, for many opponents, "really men"—they become an imagined source of threat to cisgender women and children. And, as there are no protective men present in women's restrooms, opponents to transgender rights imagine women (and often children, who are likely to accompany women to the restroom) as uniquely imperiled by these non-discrimination policies.

Proponents of transgender-inclusive laws and policies can make strong arguments about the need for protections. The increasingly large body of empirical data on transgender people in the United States emphasizes that transgender people are much more likely to face violence in the restroom rather than to perpetrate such violence. In fact, in none of the media accounts we analyzed have opponents been able to cite an actual case of bathroom sexual assault after the passage of transgender-supportive policies. But deep-rooted cultural fears about the vulnerability of women and children are hard to counter.

> *Raising the specter of the sexual predator in debates around transgender rights should be unmasked for the multiple ways it can perpetuate gender inequality.*

It is not to be suggested that sexual assault is not a serious and troubling real issue; rather, such assaults rarely occur in public restrooms and no cities or states that have passed transgender rights legislation have witnessed increases in sexual assaults in public restrooms after the laws have gone into effect. Raising the specter of the sexual predator in debates around transgender rights should be unmasked for the multiple ways it can perpetuate gender inequality. Under the guise of "protecting" women, critics reproduce ideas about their weakness; depict males as assailants, and work to deny rights to transgender people. Moreover, they suggest that there should be a hierarchy of rights in which cisgender women and children are more deserving of protections than transgender people.

Beliefs about gender difference form the scaffolding of structural gender inequality, as those that are "opposite" cannot be equal. Thus, bathroom sex-segregation must be reconsidered if we want to push gender equality forward. Many college campuses are moving toward gender-integrated bathrooms and widespread availability of gender-neutral bathrooms. And, in California, bill AB1266, passed in 2013, authorizes high school students to use bathrooms that fit their gender identity and gender expression. These examples demonstrate that the social order of the bathroom can change. While such changes may spark gender panics, these examples suggest that the battles fought over bathroom access can be won in favor of gender equality.

recommended resources

Cavanagh, Sheila. 2010. *Queering Bathrooms: Gender, Sexuality, and the Hygienic Imagination.* Toronto, ON: University of Toronto Press. An instructive and exhaustive look at the cultural construction of bathrooms, including how they maintain binary understandings of gender and disadvantage queer and transgender people.

Goffman, Erving. 1977. "The Arrangement Between the Sexes," *Theory and Society* 4(3):301–331. This classic article theorizes the social construction of gender by exploring several venues, including bathrooms, which are designed to support the deeply held view that males are opposite and superior to females.

Grant, Jaime M, Mottet, Lisa A, Tanis, Justin, Harrison, Jack, Herman, Jody L, and Keisling, Mara. 2011. *Injustice at Every Turn: A Report of the National Transgender Discrimination Survey.* Washington, D.C.: National Center for Transgender Equality and the National Gay and Lesbian Task Force. Summarizes the findings of the largest ever survey of transgender and gender variant people, including experiences of unemployment, discrimination, and violence.

Molotch, Harvey, and Noren, Laura (eds). 2010. *Toilet: Public Restrooms and the Politics of Sharing.* New York: New York University Press. An interdisciplinary set of essays examining the history and implication of public restrooms.

suffering in an age of personal responsibility

susan sered

spring 2014

I was sitting on a stoop with Gloria, an African American woman in her early 50s, when a man came by who had been stalking her, and making threatening and suggestive gestures. I had heard him call out the window to her with an aggressive demand for sex. This was not a one-time event: Gloria has been violently assaulted, raped, homeless, broke, and incarcerated throughout much of her adult life.

Her comments to me that afternoon were surprising.

"People helped me realize [that] I went up into my head too much." The issues were "all up in my head," and "I have stopped going there."

Why, I wondered, was Gloria saying that her "issues" had to do with her own mental state rather than with the actions of the stalker—and the many other men who have abused her?

Gloria is like many women who have been victimized by sexual and physical assaults, and seen the blame turned back on them either for making "bad choices" to put themselves in "dangerous situations" or for failing to "get over the trauma" in a timely fashion.

I first encountered Gloria in 2008 when she agreed to participate in a five-year project designed to understand the life experiences of women in Massachusetts who have been incarcerated. At first we interacted primarily at a halfway house for women on parole and at a drop-in center where homeless women could put down their bags and relax in easy chairs. Our relationship grew gradually as I visited Gloria and several dozen other women in prisons, hospitals and shelters; joined them for coffee and

participated in family events; and frequently picked them up curbside when they were kicked out by a boyfriend, evicted from housing, released from jails or hospitals or simply could not bear another night on the street.

vicious cycles

Like Gloria, more than three-quarters of incarcerated women have been targets of sexual abuse. Nearly all are poor and living with chronic pain and illness. A vicious cycle shapes their lives: they may initially run away from abusive homes, partners, and husbands only to find that they are struggling to survive on streets without support for themselves and their children. Shoplifting or other petty crimes often become the only way to scrape by, and illicit drug use may be increasingly attractive in order to "self medicate" (Gloria's words) in the wake of fear, pain, and violence. Addiction exacerbates the struggle to maintain health and stability, arrest and incarceration add more layers of misery, and on it goes. Among women in my project, nearly two-thirds left home by the age of seventeen, only 30 percent graduated high school, less than half have ever held a full-time job, nearly all lack stable housing, all live with chronic physical and mental illnesses, and all but one were arrested for drug-related offenses.

Gloria has spent a great deal of her adult life traveling through various institutions that serve the poor and afflicted, from jails and prisons, to hospitals and rehabilitation programs, social worker and welfare offices, and homeless shelters. While the mandates of each institution vary—punishment, protection, helping, curing—each promotes, albeit in different words, the notion that individuals can choose their health, employment and social status, and that we are responsible for our own misfortune. In line with the American narrative of individualism, the penal-welfare-healthcare circuit drills women like Gloria in an ideological script that attributes suffering to private trauma, personal flaws, female gender attributes, and their own poor choices.

> **The suffering of individuals is attributed to private trauma, personal flaws, and their own poor choices.**

Despite abundant good will on the part of nearly all caseworkers, nurses, doctors, therapists—and even many correctional officers—this institutional circuit repeatedly has failed to help Gloria gain health, security, or financial self-sufficiency. Ignoring the real social, racial, gender and economic inequalities and violence that thrust her and kept her stuck in miserable circumstances, the institutional script attributes her suffering to her own flaws to explain why she suffers.

Highly gender specific, this script typically casts women as "co-dependent," "stuck in a victim mentality," or "lacking self-esteem." Echoing ideas that resonate throughout American culture, this script holds enormous power for women like Gloria. Adhering to it may bring rewards, including custody of children, appropriate medical care, and reinstatement of welfare eligibility. Individuals who choose not to play their assigned role, by failing to "own up" to their own role and blaming others or the "system" for their situation, may find that they do not "earn" early release from prison, favorable evaluations from caseworkers, or other benefits. Despite the harshness of their lives, the homeless, impoverished, abused, and criminalized women whom I have come to know do not describe the world as a place of relentless suffering. Rather, they depict themselves as anomalous in that they suffer so much in a world in which other people are able to have "normal" (their word) families, jobs, houses, and health. Most believe (or at least hope) that someday they will have the kinds of homes and families they see on television.

gloria's "choices"

The daughter of blue- and pink-collar workers, Gloria grew up in a working-class African-American family in one of Boston's racially segregated neighborhoods. Shortly after graduating high school Gloria gave birth to her first child. Unable to rely on the baby's father, Gloria continued living with her mother who helped her take care of the baby. Shifts "dancing" (stripping) at a local bar were not her first choice of employment, but they helped pay the bills. At about that time Gloria met a man who gave her one hit of a crack pipe. A year later Gloria fell in love with a man who tried to pimp her. Shortly afterwards, her mother died and she became homeless. And, when it looked like bad couldn't get worse, Gloria suffered an assault that changed her life. Attacked in a drug deal gone bad, she suffered a traumatic head injury causing chronic memory loss. After two years in the hospital and a rehabilitation facility receiving treatment for a brain injury and PTSD, she was released to the streets, homeless, with an expectation that she would get by on her disability payment (Social Security Income) of less than $700 each month. For the next 10 years Gloria moved in and out of homeless shelters, the apartments of male acquaintances (in return for sex), crack houses and occasionally spent nights at her son's grandmother's apartment. She relies on an impressive array of pharmaceuticals to get by—anti-anxiety, anti-depressant, and sundry pain medications. She has become one of millions of Americans who, according to recent studies over the past four decades, take psychiatric medication to cope with day-to-day pressures.

beating herself up

Gloria's greatest concern has been housing. Without a stable place to live she is dependent on men, vulnerable to assaults on the streets, and visible to police who stop her for loitering, soliciting or simply "walking while Black."

Shortly after I first met her, she was placed into an SRO (single resident occupancy) building by an agency that helps the homeless. She enjoyed coming and going as she pleased. She liked the local caseworker who visited. But, without her own bathroom or access to a kitchen or extra bedroom for guests and her children, the downsides of her rooming house are clear. To make matters worse, because she is officially housed, she has been removed from the priority list for subsidized apartments. "They are giving them first to homeless people and I [already] have a place," Gloria says wistfully.

Gloria witnesses the byzantine nature of bureaucracies, but her explanations for her plight focus on herself as the source of her problems. She blames herself for not finding an agency that could place her in an apartment instead of an SRO (although the waiting list for an apartment is years as opposed to months for an SRO). She legitimates her self-blame, pointing out that, "even my caseworker says I need to work on myself first, before I can work on better housing." If housing is Gloria's biggest worry, men are a close second. For two years, she has been stalked at the SRO by a man who lives directly above her, and she is harassed by a different male neighbor. Though she reports these problems, the SRO building manager takes little action. All the while, Gloria reiterates the language of therapeutic culture by framing her suffering as the result of her own "paranoia" or inability to "be alone and stand up for myself."

Making matters worse, her boyfriend John was released from prison and insisted on staying with her. Gloria could be evicted for hosting an overnight guest and she pleaded for John to leave, but he ignored or mocked her cries. (In his defense, he was released from prison with no money, no job, no chance of finding a job with his criminal record, and, due to his record, no eligibility for public housing.)

Within days of moving in with her, John resumed his drug use and began helping himself to Gloria's money and possessions. Soon, he began to wage a campaign of physical abuse. She didn't call the police because, like many women, she was afraid to make her abuser even angrier.

Like so many other women, she struggles to come to terms with his behavior. "He is the best man I've ever been with," she says. "He makes me feel loved. He hugs me on the street." And, when we speak, she blames herself, saying, "my problem is that I need a man, I don't want to be on my own" and then her own "paranoia" as the cause of her fear of John. Gloria's focus on her own deficiencies is part of a widespread tendency in America to blame victims for their lot in life. In her book *The Cult of True Victimhood: From the War on Welfare to the War on Terror*, scholar Alyson Cole argues that in American culture blaming others for one's misfortunes is often seen as "an expression of weakness, moral or psychological, and a dangerous abdication of personal responsibility," and that victimhood has come to be associated with weakness, dependence, effeminacy, being manipulative, and even criminality. Sentiments of this sort were infamously proclaimed in 2012 presidential candidate Mitt Romney's comment that there are "47 percent of Americans who will automatically vote for Obama . . . [These are people] who are dependent upon government, who believe that they are victims, who believe the government has a responsibility to care for them, who believe that they are entitled to health care,

to food, to housing, to you-name-it . . . These are people who pay no income tax."

Although Romney did not win the election, his remarks resonate with the personal responsibility script that Gloria and other women learn throughout the social service and correctional circuit. Not only has this script failed to help Gloria stay out of danger or out of jail, it has compounded her misery by telling her that her problems are her own fault.

> *Institutions too often fail to help Gloria and others gain health, security or financial self-sufficiency. Instead, they give them simple—and simplistic—language to explain why they suffer.*

admitting powerlessness

A year or so after John moved in with her, Gloria's drug use escalated and her family responded. Her adult sons and sisters kept her with family, and then eventually registered her at a drug rehab program for women. While there is a spectrum of rehabilitation facilities, ranging from the elite Betty Ford clinic to programs associated with prisons or homeless shelters, the core ideologies tend to be similar. Understanding drug use as a symptom of an individual being out of control, these programs tend to be highly structured and routinized. At Gloria's facility, residents cannot leave to see their children and they have limited phone privileges.

The program is modeled on the Twelve Step principles made famous by Alcoholics Anonymous. Staff members encourage women to "work on themselves" in terms of dealing with resentment, disappointment, frustration, anger and sadness, and supports "spiritual growth."

Group leaders—some of whom are psychotherapists and some of whom are simply AA/NA (Alcoholics Anonymous/Narcotics Anonymous) "veterans"—preach that the individual is responsible for his or her failings, that blaming others for one's suffering is actually a symptom of the disease of addiction ("denial"), and that it is either hubris or pathology to try to change the world. Women are urged to admit "powerlessness" over the incurable disease of addiction, turn their lives over to a Higher Power, and carry out an audit of their "defects of character." Over the past decades Gloria has participated in countless Twelve Step groups.

> *By assigning individual rather than collective responsibility for human suffering, we absolve governments and corporate leaders from responsibility.*

Judges mandate AA/NA attendance for individuals accused or convicted of drunk driving or illegal drug use; drug courts routinely include AA/NA meetings as part of the program; and AA/NA attendance is often required by a judge as a condition for contact with children or for parole. While AA/NA participation is not obligatory in Massachusetts prisons, obtaining a certificate attesting one's attendance at meetings can prove to caseworkers that one is "doing the right thing" and earn early release from jail or satisfy the demands of a parole or probation officer. As a consequence of repeated contact with AA/NA, Gloria is a pro at reciting AA/NA slogans such as "Let Go and Let God."

Gloria's program also provided individual and group therapy sessions on topics such as "how to lose the victim mentality." Requirements to attend therapy are common for women on probation or parole and for women who are involved with child welfare services as a condition to see or keep their children. Many have been treated in in-patient hospital settings and have seen therapists while in prison. And virtually all of the women spend large amounts of time, especially while in prison and in programs, watching television shows such as *Jerry Springer* and *Oprah* that implicitly and explicitly rehearse psycho-therapeutically informed scripts that mock women for masochistically choosing to stay with cheating men (Jerry) or encourage women to develop the self-esteem to leave abusive men (Oprah).

Repeatedly, in virtually all settings within the rehabilitation program, Gloria was coached in the iconic American script for individuals down on their luck: they should "work harder," "pull themselves together" and "get over it."

self-blaming

A few days after leaving rehab, Gloria stopped by my office to share her excitement about the progress she had made in the program. I asked why this most recent program was so helpful while the many other similar programs she had done in the past had not led to changes in her life circumstances. After a bit of thought she explained that, "this time I was ready to hear it," and she shared this example: "In one group [therapy session] they asked about bad things that happened in our childhoods. I said I couldn't think of anything. The counselor told me that I am blocking something. But I didn't remember any bad things. Then I heard a voice in the room say 'abandonment' and I thought 'yes, that is it!' God was showing me [through this voice] that is thing I am blocking—abandonment."

Gloria had never before mentioned that she had been abandoned as a child; quite the contrary, she often described growing up as the beloved baby sister in a large close-knit family. On more than one occasion she had told me that her mother and father "were the best parents ever—they stuck it out 'til death do us part.'" Later on, after we went our separate ways, I mused on cruelty in the encouragement Gloria was given to "discover" that the true cause of her current misery lay in her own experiences and family—when, in fact, her family has been the sole source of physical and emotional support for her over decades in which she has struggled with poverty, homelessness, racism and violence. In this way, the script of personal responsibility for suffering pours salt on the wounds of sufferers. At the same time, by assigning individual rather than collective responsibility for human suffering, we divert attention from the misery caused by economic, racial and gender inequalities and absolve governments and corporate leadership from public responsibilities for the wellbeing of citizens.

When I first met Gloria, the United States had the highest incarceration rate in the world, and those rates were steadily going up. Six years later, incarceration rates are declining (more so for men than for women) and the White House has outlined a new drug policy that shifts the focus from punishment to treatment for drug abuse. While treatment aimed at helping the individual is certainly more benign than prison, both place the onus of responsibility on the personal flaws of individuals rather than on the broader social inequalities, including sexual violence, that shape the life worlds of women like Gloria. As I have learned in Massachusetts, even with the best of intentions—and virtually all of the rehab staff, therapists, doctors, nurses, social workers, caseworkers and even correctional officers I have met are indeed well-intentioned—individualized treatment cannot cure structural inequalities.

recommended resources

Chesney-Lind, Meda. 2012. *The Female Offender: Girls, Women, and Crime* (now in its third edition). Thousand Oaks, CA: Sage. A well-researched, non-voyeuristic book covering a variety of aspects of women and criminalization.

Cole, Alyson M. 2007. *The Cult of True Victimhood: From the War on Welfare to the War on Terror.* California: Stanford University Press. Deconstructs the gendered and political meanings of "victimhood" in American culture.

Haney, Lynne. 2010. *Offending Women: Power, Punishment, and the Regulation of Desire.* Oakland, CA: University of California Press. Describes community-based prison alternative programs for women. In these programs, the emphasis is on women's personal pathologies.

McCorkel, Jill. 2013. *Breaking Women: Gender, Race, and the New Politics of Imprisonment.* New York: New York University Press. Analyzes the shift from rehabilitation to "habilitation" in women's prisons.

Richie, Beth E. 2012. *Arrested Justice: Black Women, Violence, and America's Prison Nation.* New York: New York University Press. Provides a thoughtful analysis of how cultural attitudes and social policies damage the health, freedom and well-being of Black women.

Whitaker, Robert. 2010. *Anatomy of an Epidemic: Magic Bullets, Psychiatric Drugs, and the Astonishing Rise of Mental Illness in America.* New York: Broadway Paperbacks. A highly accessible introduction to questions regarding the use of psychiatric medication.

egalitarian preferences, gendered realities
lucia lykke
spring 2015

Sociologists have been studying the gender revolution's stalled progress for the several decades. Data reveal a slowdown of women's entry into the workforce and stagnation in the trend toward more liberal gender attitudes. So which gendered practices in key social and economic institutions might discourage women from achieving equality at work and at home: lack of parental leave, inflexible work hours, employer expectations? For researchers, the question is how do you isolate the effects of institutional policies and practices from individuals' gendered selves and preferences?

David Pedulla and Sarah Thebaud took a stab at this causal conundrum in the *American Sociological Review.* They presented young, unmarried, childless adults with several hypothetical relationship forms, including an egalitarian partnership, a neotraditional (male breadwinner/female homemaker) relationship, a self-reliant model (preferring financial independence and a career over having a partner), or a reverse-traditional relationship. Using an experimental survey design, the researchers manipulated the degree of institutional constraint respondents faced in three conditions: a high-constraint condition (respondents were not given the option of being in an egalitarian relationship at all), a medium-constraint option (respondents could select that they wanted an egalitarian relationship but were not given information about workplace policies), and a low-constraint option (supportive work-family policies were mentioned).

Overwhelmingly, men and women, regardless of education level, preferred egalitarian relationships when given the option. However, when egalitarian relationships were not an option, class and gender differences emerged. Higher educated men and women, as well as working-class men, when faced with institutional constraints, preferred a neotraditional arrangement, while working-class women preferred self-reliance. The authors' finding is clear: workplace practices and policies are crucial for shaping ongoing gender inequality at work and at home.

29

a feminist's work is never done

jennifer l. pierce and joan acker

spring 2012

For more than 35 years, Joan Acker's work has been at the cutting edge of feminist scholarship, providing incisive analyses of gender and social stratification, comparable worth, workplace organizations, welfare reform, and capitalism. In 1973, in the pages of the *American Journal of Sociology*, she took scholars of social stratification to task for "intellectual sexism." Her most recent book, *Stretched Thin*, investigates the consequences of neoliberal restructuring for welfare workers, administrators, and recipients. A past recipient of the American Sociological Association's Jesse Bernard Award, Acker is professor emeritus at the University of Oregon. Jennifer L. Pierce, Professor of American Studies at the University of Minnesota, talked with her in January.

JENNIFER L. PIERCE: In your 2006 book, *Class Questions, Feminist Answers*, you take up concerns that have long been central to your scholarship: gender and social class in workplace organizations. Can you talk about what influenced you to write that book?

JOAN ACKER: My early theoretical training, as an undergraduate at Hunter College in the 1940s, was in Marxism. However, my earliest feminist influence, beginning in 1972, came through the work of Dorothy Smith, and later, that of political scientist Carole Pateman. They were very important to me in developing an understanding of the basic flaws in most sociological theory, particularly, the ways in which our main theoretical works wrote out, conceptually, half of human activity. My overall theorizing has changed over time, greatly expanded, and become more complex through work on intersectionality—that is,

approaches that analyze the intersections of gender, class, and race. Here I am thinking of the work of Patricia Hill Collins, Elizabeth Higginbotham, Bonnie Thornton Dill, and Lyn Weber. This work greatly influenced my thinking in *Class Questions*.

JP: Most of your influences are feminist theorists. Can you say more about that?

JA: I resist saying I am a Weberian, a Marxist, or even a Smithian . . . [laughs] Dorothy Smith would hate that . . . It implies a lack of thought. It's a barrier to real thinking to say that I am a Marxist and that tells you everything that I think. I have never accepted any one system of thought. All systems of thought close out other ways of thinking. I had training in Marxism as an undergraduate in the years before McCarthy. Then in graduate school in the early 1960s, I ran into structural functionalism. We couldn't even mention C. Wright Mills or Marx in graduate school. Soon after I got my degree in 1968, feminist theory was beginning to develop. But, I actually first read *The Second Sex* in 1956. I knew it was there and it was a mediating factor in the kind of social theory I taught. I have never had reverence—if this is irreverence—for any of the social theorists who had their moment in the spotlight as great thinkers.

Still I always liked being a sociologist. We ask interesting and important questions. We don't always have the best answers, but the attempt to find answers is stimulating and interesting. So, I would never begin asking a question within a theoretical frame. Instead, I would ask: why is this happening? And, is it really happening? And, how can I find out? Interviews? Statistics? My approach to building theory and using theory is to start from what is "problematic in everyday life"—which happens to be a good title of a book by Dorothy Smith.

JP: Your most recent book, *Stretched Thin: Poor Families, Welfare Work, and Welfare Reform*, written with Sandra Morgen and Jill Weigt, examines the relations between social workers and welfare recipients in the transition from welfare to workfare. One of the central arguments in the book is about how neoliberal reforms, such as the Personal Responsibility and Work Opportunity Reconciliation Act, have created devastating consequences for poor women. Could you say more about what you think neoliberalism is, and what is wrong with it?

JA: For me, neoliberalism is the stripped down version of the basic idea of capitalism we have today. In other words everyone, including women, are expected to survive on their own. To survive, they have to get out and earn a living. Individual enterprise and determination are deemed essential. The feminist critique is that neoliberalism turns women into the "abstract worker," removing the context and specificity of women's material reality as mothers of children, caretakers of the elderly, and other family members. Neoliberalism, as an ideology, does not take into account these kinds of responsibilities; it is still assumed that women will do these things. Of course, this ideology also assumes the myth of the male breadwinner, that is, that there is a man in the family earning a sufficient income to support everyone—kids, spouses, the elderly, etc.—with women at home caring for everyone else. Only a minority of families in the United States today can actually meet that ideal. In most families, both parents work because they have to support their families. And, there are a huge number of single parent families. They are the ones who are most vulnerable to neoliberal policies.

JP: What kind of policy recommendations do you and your co-authors make in *Stretched Thin*?

JA: The social policies we recommended are extraordinarily important, achievable, but also highly unlikely to take place in our current political climate. Still, I believe that we could have policies in place like those in Scandinavian countries. These would include things such as universal medical care, and cracking down on the exorbitant pricing of drug companies. Eliminating insurance companies. Creating living wages and universal child care allowances—every other Western nation has universal child care! Reducing the cost of higher education. I would like to see Temporary Assistance for Needy Families reformed. We also need a better safety net and

emergency help. We need an income support program that is open to anybody who needs it with fairly elastic eligibility rules. People get into tough situations and can't meet federal regulations for assistance if they own a house, but have no money coming in. So, they don't qualify. We should have programs that meet the needs of all. What we need is total reform and a "social safety net" economy to insure that no one suffers. I am sure the good ol' neoliberals will say "lots of luck" with that.

JP: Still, with the Great Recession, there have been challenges to neoliberal policies. Here, I am thinking of the people involved in the Occupy Wall Street movement. What do you think we can do?

JA: We need to defeat Republicans at the polls and get politically active. I have done canvassing in neighborhoods and will do it for the next election too. We need to think about what is good for society. Though some sociologists don't think you can do good research with politics, I disagree. Political action is going to be extraordinarily important in this next presidential election, but it's going to be much harder this time. It's not Obama so much as it is Congress. Can we defeat the Tea Partiers?

JP: In the 1980s, Judith Stacey and Barrie Thorne first published an article entitled the "Missing Feminist Revolution in Sociology." Is the "feminist revolution" still missing today? And, where do you see your own work moving in the future?

JA: It's a different problem for feminist scholars in sociology today than it used to be. Feminist sociology is a strong discipline today and it is accepted as such with some standing in the profession. What I find disturbing is that our original goal was to reform sociology— theoretically and empirically—with gender as an integral part of the discipline. That hasn't happened. Still, I'm obsessed with the notion of building a sociology that is fully integrates gender. In some ways I try to do that in *Class Questions*.

Using the concepts of gendered institutions, gendered processes, and gendered organizations is one approach. This involves taking sociological concepts and reinterpreting them through a "gender lens." I continue to be interested in questions about gender and class. Mainstream economics does not show how dependent our economy is on the *unpaid* work of women. Conventional economists still act as if the economy is organized solely by capitalism, finance, and production. I think it is important to retrieve earlier feminist scholarship on women and unpaid household labor to challenge these mainstream economic models. Much of social policy is informed by these models and assumptions. And, it has had a devastating impact on the poor. Now is a good time to challenge this kind of thinking. There is now a huge body of research theorizing "caring labor," but it seems to constitute a subfield that "general theory" ignores.

Another area that I have been very interested in is football as an economic and symbolic group of activities that perpetuate gender inequalities, as well as a kind of masculinity that is dangerous. Actually, I have an informal campaign to eliminate football. So far, I have not been able to recruit more than two or three people [laughs]! But, seriously, for kids, football creates serious problems. Think about all the research on concussions for kids. At the collegiate level, there is major money for universities that focus on football rather than academics. At the University of Oregon, one of our alumni, Phil Knight, the co-founder of Nike Corporation, gives millions to the University, mostly for athletics and football, and buildings related to football. His excessive influence became most visible when students organized and joined with the campaign against products produced through slave labor.

But, the greatest issue about football, and the reason that I want it to be abolished, is that it glorifies and legitimates a certain form of male violence. Vast crowds spend considerable money to watch young men injure each other. Yes, they also throw and catch balls and run for the goal, but those activities do not mitigate the main message that violence in pursuit of winning is okay. This is also how capitalism operates, as well as the U.S. military, which is always ready to send its troops wherever. As for the future, I would like to see research on the role of masculinity in generating the global crisis.

Joan Acker died in 2016.

30

got power?

christine williams

spring 2012

Part of the job of being a professor is offering career advice to undergraduates. For years I have used Max Weber's "Science as a Vocation" as my guide. Find your passion. Only you can decide what career will be meaningful to you. *Blah blah blah.* I no longer say that. My message to my students is now clear and unambiguous: I don't care what you do, as long as you have power. Go work for Wal-mart, the CIA, Exxon-Mobil, whatever. It doesn't matter. The only thing that matters is that you end up calling the shots.

I had this epiphany at a recent showing of "Misrepresentation" on my campus, a film about pervasive sexism in the media. The audience of 300+ stayed behind to discuss the film and brainstorm about possible solutions. As an invited discussant, I found myself becoming increasingly agitated as one student after another stood up and passionately spoke of the need to "educate" others about sexism, especially children. I ended up haranguing them: Why would you want to teach children about this? Children have no power! They can't change anything. And it's useless to try and change the opinions of people who do have power. They are the ones promoting these sexist images! Only YOU can change society! So let's cut out the middleman and get down to business. How are YOU going to get power so YOU can change these dastardly media images NOW?

Let me back up. The people who come to me for career advice are not a cross-section of the population. They've taken my courses in gender, sexuality, or labor and labor movements. Most are women, with a few feminist men sprinkled in. I've taught them about discrimination and inequality, and now they want to do something about it.

These are the people who need to be in charge.

If I encourage them to follow their "vocation," a lot of these folks will end up supporting, educating, and helping other people. They tell me that they want to help the less fortunate, teach girls, and empower women. Their gender socialization is reflected in these choices, and the labor force is structured to provide opportunities in these roles, as teachers and social workers and nurses. Don't get me wrong, I don't discourage them from pursuing these noble professions. But if they ask for my advice, I tell them they must aspire to become superintendent of schools or head of the hospital. Otherwise, nothing will ever change.

Looking back over my 30-year career studying gender and organizations, it's a surprise to me that this basic insight was so long in coming. Chalk it up to my own gender socialization and to too much Weber (or not enough Foucault). Now I can't shut up about it. I'm currently studying women scientists in the oil and gas industry. I interviewed a senior woman geophysicist at a major multinational corporation who is the "executive assistant" to a man who is her intellectual equal, and prior to his latest promotion, her organizational equal. I asked her: Why didn't he become your assistant? This time I'll quote her directly: "His personality type is very much to be a leader. On the other hand, my personality type is more to be a supporter. I spent years supporting VPs

> **I don't care what you do, as long as you have power.**

and got asked by VP after VP after VP to either come and do special projects, or to be their assistant. Because I'm so good at supporting them, they can take it easy while I'm there. And I really like to be somebody who supports a person that I believe in." Reader, please forgive my indiscretion, but I just had to intervene. This woman is an environmentalist and a feminist. I told her that she should be the CEO of the oil and gas company. Unfortunately, she wasn't interested in my advice. She didn't want that cutthroat political job, she told me; she would rather "help people." Clearly, this gendered discourse provides a ready-made survival strategy in her male-dominated world—a world that is intent on forever casting her in the role of the assistant, never the leader.

Unlike oil and gas industry executives, my sociology students are interested in my advice. As a mentor to young women and feminist men, I think it's my responsibility to tell them to get power. Quit helping people—and start changing the world.

women: agents of change
moriah willow
spring 2016

Women have made a lot of progress toward gender parity in professional and managerial jobs, though gender inequality in upper management and government remains high. Currently, there are only 20 women (4%) who hold CEO positions at S&P 500 companies. In the U.S. House of Representatives, women hold just 19% of seats. And even when women do rise to the top, many still question whether they help other women up the ladder. That is, women in power may be more "cogs in the machine" than "agents of change." We know that occupational gender segregation—that is, the concentration of men and women in different jobs—contributes to the gender wage gap. In their *Gender and Society* article, Kevin Stainback, Sibyl Kleiner, and Sheryl Skaggs analyze individual Fortune 1000 workplaces to see whether they have women at the top—on boards of directors, in corporate executive positions, and in workplace-level managerial positions. Then they ask whether having women at the top reduces the companies' gender segregation. The results show that a greater proportion of women in managerial jobs, on corporate boards, and in executive positions is associated with lower levels of gender segregation in the workplaces they lead. Women in leadership positions apparently act as change agents, bringing benefits to women at all levels of the organizational hierarchy.

SEXUALITY

introduction
navigating sexuality

jodi o'brien

I have a fantasy of little sex-ed-book-and-videomobiles parked near schools, health clinics, libraries, malls, and laundromats, offering a cafeteria of information about sexuality to citizens of all ages. We have to enable people to get information about sexuality that doesn't come from the pharmaceutical industry, Hollywood, or Madison Avenue. There's no turning back the clock on sexuality, and realistic and positive sexual lives require new models and new policy initiatives.

—Leonore Tiefer

What is sexuality? Where is located? The common belief is that sexuality is an aspect of our bodies and unconscious psyches—a set of urges or desires that are triggered in response to attraction. Sex is just natural, some people might say. And attraction is just chemistry. In her book *Sex Is Not a Natural Act* sexologist Leonore Tiefer suggests that, far from being a set of natural practices, sexuality is a social behavior that is culturally learned. This doesn't mean that sexuality isn't physiological. Through our bodies we experience sexual desires and arousal and our attractions do reflect preferences that likely include biological aspects. But as with gender, this isn't an either/or nature/nurture process. Our bodies, desires, and minds are tightly interconnected and our *ideas* about sexuality have a large influence on our sexual feelings and expressions. As with gender, we get our ideas about sexuality from our culture. Specifically, we learn *sexual scripts*. These scripts tell us what good and bad sex is, how we're supposed to do it and feel about it, and what we can do and with whom.

food and sex

Consider a comparison with food. What are some of your favorite foods? Do you eat them all the time at the exclusion of everything else? How did you come to like these foods? Are there foods and drinks that you had to develop a liking for—acquired tastes? Although we think of food preferences as individually based tastes, what we eat is deeply cultural and also contextual. We are introduced not only to specific food items based on our culture, but we learn cultural rules for when to eat certain types of meals. Different foods are associated with different times of day and with various significant events and celebrations. The idea of "breakfast for dinner" implies that sometimes our craving of the moment doesn't quite fit the customary food grouping, so we accommodate the craving but still maintain the quotidian delineations (breakfast food is still breakfast food, but what counts as breakfast in one part of the world varies considerably in another). We also have rules for what we can eat with whom. For instance, holidays such as Thanksgiving or a Passover Seder consist of ritual feasts that we share with specific people. Close friends and family are likely to feel slighted if you don't include them on such occasions. You're not so accountable if "grab lunch or a beer" with a casual acquaintance, but a "romantic dinner" holds completely different expectations for the food, setting, and companionship.

Food is one of the most significant markers of cultures and religious groups. Abstaining from certain foods (e.g., the Mormon abstention from alcohol and caffeine or Seventh-Day Adventist vegetarianism) and ritual fasting such as during the Muslim month of Ramadan, serves to connect individuals to their beliefs and their groups. Notice that those engaged in these practices do not typically have an identity around the behavior (e.g., I'm a "faster"), rather the eating behavior is an aspect of cultural or religious identity (Jewish, Mormon, Muslim). A variation is food-based identities that mark deviation from prevalent cultural eating practices, such as vegetarianism in a meat-based culture. In this regard, people do make identity-based claims such as "I'm vegan," but this is typically a choice about eating practices that is based in a combination of philosophy (health, environmental) and preferences. For the most part, people are aware that they have a wide range of food preferences and that these preferences are culturally informed and contextually practiced. Eating is a natural act, but what, how, and with whom we eat is culturally constructed and practiced.

If we know this about food, why is it so difficult to understand the similar interconnections between culture, preferences, and behaviors around sexuality? As Tiefer points out, one of the most enduring cultural beliefs about sexuality is that it is a natural act. Presumably, under the right circumstances with the right person our bodies will simply know what to do. In comparison with our understanding of cultural learning around food, this idea should seem preposterous. Yet it persists, even among health professionals.

In a course I teach on sexual politics I ask students to recall their first awareness of sex (not their own sexuality, simply the idea of sex). Most of them have memories of this (which is noteworthy in itself in terms of cultural significance—people are less inclined to have first memories of an awareness of death, god, etc.) and the experiences tend to be in the age range of 6-9 years old. These recollections typically include incidents in which the child was banned from viewing something on TV; told they weren't old enough to receive answers to questions about sex and reproduction; or told that a particular behavior (such as genital touching) was bad or nasty or not ok in public. One student shared a story of her otherwise mild-mannered father rushing into the yard and turning the hose on two dogs as she and her sister watched. Her father's panicked "Stop that you nasty dogs!" terrified and confused the girls. To them, the dogs were just playing, but her father saw otherwise and his reaction shaped the earliest imprinting his daughter has of sex.

Most people have similar recollections of a hazy awareness that "something" was up around this sex thing and that it was a very big deal, but that the adults around them tended to clam up and seem uncomfortable about it. The first typical cultural imprinting around sexuality in contemporary U.S. culture is that sex is very significant, yet it's marked with silence and shame. Imagine how confusing this is for young children. The confusion is confounded as children move into adolescence in a society saturated with sexual imagery and unspoken assumptions and expectations everywhere they turn. When I ask my students how, in our society, we unlearn these initial impressions and gain a useful set of mature, realistic guidelines for our sexuality they eventually realize

that we don't. We have no formal, systematic method for bringing young people into a healthy understanding of sexuality. Even the most comprehensive sex education curriculum is rarely more than what many educators refer to as the "plumbing model" with an emphasis on gender differences in reproductive physiology and cautions about sexually transmitted infections. Young people are unlikely to learn much about relational sexuality in school programs, yet nearly every aspect of social media portrays sexual behavior as constant and highly significant. What maps are we using to sort this out? Perhaps one of the most profound truths about contemporary sexuality is that most of us are operating from the same hazy, shame- and silenced-based scripts we were first exposed to.

In a society infused with sexual images and references, many would object that this is not true—we are sexually liberated. But, it's difficult to be liberated if you aren't fully aware of the cultural rules and scripts guiding your expectations. The proliferation of sexuality scripts through media further perpetuate notions that sexuality is natural, that it defines our happiness (or more likely unhappiness) and that it is ongoing—everyone is doing it all the time, except perhaps you. Tiefer writes that it's like being in a society in which gin rummy is a really big deal and you're a nobody if you're not in a game all the time. But, and here's the rub, no one will tell you how to play because it's supposedly just natural. If you have to ask you're not fit to be in the game.

The sociology of sexuality focuses on cultural sexual scripts. These studies expose and explore the (usually hidden) patterns that proliferate through contemporary media, religions, education, law, and other social institutions. As with gender, an examination of these patterns reveals some prevalent beliefs that aren't necessarily true: sex is natural, we have relatively fixed tastes and preferences, and some sexual expressions are naturally bad or good. The scripts aren't always straightforward. It's possible that sexual scripts are some of the most convoluted that we encounter. Learning to recognize the underlying patterns and the ways in which we unwittingly self-define and judge ourselves and others is the basis of a more genuine sexual liberation.

sexual scripting and biological determinism

Sociologists John Gagnon and William Simon developed the idea of "sexual scripts" to explain the social constructionist theory that social processes shape sexuality. This was a radical idea when they introduced it. At the time, scholarly (mostly medical-psychological) and popular notions of sexuality were that it consisted of inborn drives and urges that were then repressed by society. This was consistent with Freudian theories that society *civilized* the animal instincts in humans. Depending on your point of view, this repression of basic human urges by society was either a good thing or a bad thing. On the one hand, without society's civilizing influence, we would be asocial beasts. On the other, it was believed that too much civilization represses our creative, expressive nature. Religions have long been criticized for having an overly repressive influence on sexuality. Much early sexology (think Kinsey or Masters and Johnson) was an attempt to define a supposed "normal" range of sexuality that we could then endorse and aspire to as a society.

In opposition to these views of sexuality as either a beast in need of taming or a range of biological expressions (some of which might fall out of normal range and need containment), Gagnon and Simon were not simply arguing that nurture trumped nature in the shaping of sexual expression, they rejected the entire model of sex as unconscious urges repressed by society. In place of an unconscious psyche they posited the "intrapsychic" or "socially based form of mental life" by which the social self becomes aware of and understands and evaluates its own feelings and behaviors through social interaction and social scripts.

Sociologist Stevi Jackson extends these ideas to the construction of the sexual self in late modernity. For her, sexuality is part of an everyday process whereby, "sexual conduct and sexual self are fully social, embedded in wider patterns of sociality" (p. 5). Similar to other feelings and expressions (such as eating behaviors) our sense of our sexual self is ongoing and develops contextually and interactionally in concert with the zeitgeist of the times. For instance, it's only been since late modernity that sexuality has achieved such high acclaim as a pivotal element in the pursuit of individual happiness. The idea of high-intensity sex drives (especially for men) is also recent. In this case, men are influenced by culturally created sexual scripts that lead them to think they should desire to be sexually engaged as often as possible. Products such as Viagra feed this cultural notion of men as sexual power tools. Note here that cultural expectations are driving the development of products that shape physiological capacity (biology), rather than the other way around.

Jackson and Gagnon and Simon are not claiming that there is nothing biological about sexuality. As with gender, this is a complex mind-emotion-body interplay. Their emphasis is that we are reflective sexual selves trying to figure who we can be and what we can do in a social context, and we get our scripts for this from our culture. As we noted in the gender discussion, nature doesn't determine, it hints. Sexual scripting suggests an interplay between possible feelings and expressions, and the wider cultural development of new ways of sexual conduct. For instance, throughout recent history the cultural understanding of homosexuality has shifted from sin to sickness to identity and lifestyle. In the first case, the script for same-gender attraction was dictated largely through religion and people made sense of their own or others feelings through the idea of sin (which was accompanied by shame and exclusion). With the rise of medical-psychiatric paradigms as forms of cultural authority and legitimacy for "normality" the sin-based script gave way to the supposedly more humane version of "afflicted" or "sick"—homosexuality fell outside the range of scientifically defined normal sexual development. According to this script, homosexuality is still abnormal, but it's an expression of psychological and/or physiological pathology rather than evil. This script entreated others to treat the homosexual with compassion.

More recent scripts disrupt taken-for-granted assumptions about a gender binary and posit a kind of gender/sexuality smorgasbord in which preferences reflect a range of possibilities for attraction and intimacy. The sin/sick scripts are still present and continue to carry significant social authority in some cultural contexts (for example as the rationale for gay conversion therapies), but many young people now come into their sense of sexuality with expectations of same-gender attraction as part of a normal range of sexual feeling.

Young people today have countless examples (scripts) available that depict not only loving family acceptance for some forms of sexual difference, but also acceptance from many religious communities. And as with the food example, the proliferation of diverse genders and sexualities expands scripts and may lead some people to acknowledge that their own desires, tastes, and preferences might be wider than previous cultural experience (based on a gender and sexual binary) suggested.

sexual identities, significant others, and reference groups

Sexual identity is a modern construction. The idea that our sexuality is a central aspect of who we are is indicated in the notion of sexual identities (gay, lesbian, bi, queer, straight, etc.). Contrast this with our eating behaviors and consider why it is that people form sexual identities. It's worth pondering why these "identities" are typically based on the gender of the supposed object of attraction (i.e., straight or gay) rather than specific tastes or preferences (e.g., foot fetishes; cuddling). Sexual identities reflect the sociohistorical context and, like other significant aspects of self-definition, they are shaped by those who have influence in our lives (significant others) and by the groups (real or imagined) whose perspectives shape our views and attitudes (reference groups).

Consider the expression, "losing my virginity." Most people use this expression to refer to the first experience of becoming sexually active. Virginity/non-virginity is one of the most taken-for-granted sexual identities. What acts "count" as "losing virginity"? What is the cultural-historical meaning of "virginity" and its "loss." Is this a gendered identity? Why do we continue to use this phrase rather than something like "coming into my sexuality"? Brainstorm about all the underlying cultural expectations and ideas reflected in the concept of "virginity" as identity and then think about its varying significance across different reference groups (e.g., your religious congregation if you have one versus your sports team) and significant others (parents, best friends, etc.). Sexual scripts reflect the attitudes and expectations of varying reference groups and shape how we conduct ourselves with different significant others and in particular contexts. This includes how we think and talk about sexuality as well as what we do. Because of this, sexual expression is variable, even among those who supposedly have a strong sense of a particular sexual identity.

Sex researchers have long known that people's behavior differs markedly from their sexual identities. Sexual identities are situational. Most straight or gay identifying people have had sexual experience with (or attractions to) those who are not the gender preference their identity would suggest. Although the range of my sexual experience includes multiple genders, I identify as lesbian or queer, in part because it most accurately describes my everyday life and relationships and also because of the political implications. As a senior faculty member in a Jesuit Catholic educational environment, it's important to me to claim this identity openly. Conversely, I have colleagues who consider themselves exclusively gay or lesbian but who do not identify publically as such because they do not feel it's safe for them to do so in this environment.

sexual social organization

Some people find the social constructionist approach to sexuality problematic because they think it implies a sexual lifestyle that can be easily changed. This is a real concern in a society that continues to see sexuality primarily in terms of a (natural) gender binary. From the perspective of many religious and political groups, if sexuality is fluid then people should give up their nonconforming sexual lifestyles and focus on fitting in. Defining same gender attraction as a natural (biological) aberration

provides a rationale for some LGBTQ groups to combat these beliefs and the corresponding attempts to "make gay people straight again." The sociological response to this is to take a step back and note, again, the complex interplay between culture and biology. Rather than trying to fit sexual expression into boxes (either nature or identities or both), the pertinent questions for the sociologist of sexuality is, What is the *social organization* of sexuality? Within specific cultural-historical contexts how significant is sexuality? How is it defined? What are the prevailing rules and attitudes about sexual activities and relationships and how do these reflect other aspects of social organization (sexuality is organized very differently in capitalist economies that promote nuclear family models than in extended family models prevalent in some agrarian/communitarian societies).

These questions move us away from identity-based nature/nurture debates and back to the social realm wherein we see that historically, most cultural rules emphasized social class, race, and kinship (see Intimacy section). In many modern societies, people of wealth and influence were allowed to express their sexuality in ways that would be considered quite deviant by some of our current standards. This "libertas quirkus" or freedom to be quirky, reflects social privilege. The resulting sexual scripts were based in types of acts (fetishes and kinks) rather than identities. The significance of sexuality itself as well as what's considered normal and desirable differs across time and cultures. The social organization of sexuality includes scripts for good or proper behavior and deviant behavior. When these behaviors or expressions take on additional significance, they become identities and these identities often imply bad or good sexual citizenship within the scripted social boundaries (e.g., virgin, prostitute, adulterer).

Until the late 1800s, same-gender sexual engagement was simply a form of sexual expression, especially among the wealthy. This began to change when Victorian courts, seeking to establish the middle-class family as a foundational basis for virtue and capitalism, started to spotlight and prosecute homosexual behavior. The well-known trials of the writer Oscar Wilde (beginning in 1895) portrayed homosexuality as an act of licentious indulgence that detracted people (especially men) from settling into proper married life. At the time, it was a punishable behavior, but as married heterosexuality became more prevalent as a form of social engineering, those who refused to participate became deviant subjects—they themselves were now deviant rather than just their sexual behavior. In cultural-historical terms, a particular form of sexual expression such as same gender-intimacy becomes an identity only when it is juxtaposed with a heightened emphasis on married heterosexuality as a form of social organization.

Anthropologist Tom Boellstorff's ethnographic work in Indonesia illustrates the shifting forms of sexual identification that occur through changes to broader systems of marriage and family. As Boellstorff traces it, for many years the predominant marriage system in Indonesia has been organized around economic and political needs. Within this system, homosexuality is a behavioral expression that exists outside of, and not necessarily as a threat to, marriage. Significantly, the behavior is not associated with identity. However, the proliferation of "love-centered" marriages in recent years has been accompanied by an increase in gay and lesbian *identities*. Boellstorff attributes this to a cultural shift that implies that marriage is now the site for ful-filling sexual and romantic desires as well as familial obligations. This shifting cultural system singles out and marks as deviant a lack of interest in heterosexual love and romance; in other words, if you're not interested in this, it's now much more evident and desires that once could be directed outside of marriage with little concern must now be accounted for. According to Boellstorff, this sociocultural environment is one in which Western notions of "sexual identity" find fertile ground as people begin to adopt gay and lesbian as a rationale for opting out of love-based marriages. This example illustrates the ways in which multiple, varying, tastes and preferences are channeled into available forms of social expression depending on the larger social organization. As social organization around marriage, family, and the meaning of gender and sexuality changes, some sexual behaviors may become the basis for a sexual identity.

Recently, "celibacy" has become a more marked sexual identity for many people. How can we understand this in terms of current sexual organization and scripting? Certainly people are not sexually engaged at all times, just as they are not eating all the time. The identity implies a set of cultural assumptions (especially for young people) that *you should be* interested in seeking sex all the time. One way to understand celibacy as identity (rather than a typical state of existence for most people) is as a reflection of and reaction to contemporary cultural assumptions that sexuality is one of the most important things about us.

gendering sexuality

Despite the increase in media portrayals of gender and sexual variation, sexuality remains firmly organized around a gender binary. Central formulations of sexual-ity in religion, law, and education as well as in health sciences assume that the primary function of human sexuality is reproduction. Based on this assumption, it is further assumed that the most natural form of sexuality is male–female vaginal–penile intercourse with the possi-bility of reproduction. Reproductive sexuality is the refer-ence point or measuring stick for all other forms of sexual expression. For instance, many people who are sexually active in other ways consider themselves "virgins" if they have not had intercourse. Anthropologists and biologists have provided countless examples of other bases for sex-ual intimacy beyond reproduction (bonding and alliance for instance), but the expectation of reproductive sexual-ity as the normal baseline remains culturally entrenched.

This belief structure supports ideas of a gender binary wherein men and women are presumed to have different (biologically based) orientations to sexuality: men have a natural urge to pursue and conquer as many women as possible ("to spread their seed") and women have a pro-pensity toward mating and nurturing. These gender beliefs are tightly woven throughout the entire fabric of our cul-ture. In terms of sexuality, they surface as very different standards and expectations for sexuality between boys and girls. Historically, women are represented as objects of beauty, virtue, and family; these characteristics are idol-ized through virginity, which must be protected (from marauding bands of seed-spreading men). Accordingly, women do not *have* sexuality, they *are* sexuality. They are not sexual agents but rather sexual objects. In this same story, men are sexual beasts in need of taming (by the lure of the beautiful wife and family). It is in their nature to pursue women and women are held responsible for help-ing men to resist promiscuous temptation and for leading them instead into monogamous family life. In this same story, men achieve status through expressing their mascu-linity (as a virile, athletic, good provider, assertive, etc.) and women achieve status through landing a man.

Many people resist this characterization as old-fashioned, but a closer examination of contemporary sex-ual scripts reveals that it is still very much in play—with some disturbing implications. In the 1990s several stud-ies revealed that adolescent girls suffered notable drops in self-esteem while boys of the same age seemed to expe-rience higher self-esteem. Curious about this, journalist Peggy Orenstein attended middle school for a year. In her subsequent book, *School Girls,* Orenstein chronicles the emotional downslide girls experience as their bodies mature and they are thrown into the wrenching world of teenage social negotiation. One of the most profound shifts for girls is the dawning realization that they are no longer kids whose lives revolve around the activities they enjoy (playing with friends, school, sports, etc); rather their status is now tied to being able to attract boys. According to Orenstein, the drop in self-esteem comes from an awareness that this is not something most girls can control directly. Popularity becomes contingent on factors such as the right body (leading many young girls to feel deeply betrayed by their bodies) and, especially, the capacity to strike the right balance between encouraging boys' sexual attraction, but not being a slut. Orenstein finds that this dance between the "fear of falling" or being a slut and gaining popularity through attention from boys is the central struggle for most teen-age girls. The tragedy is that girls have very little agency in this scenario.

Tandem to this research, psychologist Deborah Tolman studies sexual desire in teenage girls. Her central finding is that girls have no idea what they're feeling sexually. They have been socialized to attend carefully to cues about what boys want. In the quest for popularity they set aside their own intuitions in order to please boys. Developmentally, one implication is that girls are often unable to identify their own desires and to practice communication and limit setting. Girls are socially rewarded for successfully gaining the attention of boys. When a girl does follow an instinct to keep a boy at bay, especially if he is popular, she is chastised. Tolman notes that, psychologically, this leaves girls confused and increasingly less able to trust their own feelings. This same dynamic extends to sexual engagement whereby girls have minimal expectations of personal sexual enjoyment; their focus is on making the boys happy.

In contrast, boys are socialized to *think that they should* pursue sex aggressively—rather than fear of being sluts, they should strive to be studs. It's in their nature. Sociologist Mark Cohan studies how teenage boys talk about sex. He finds that when they are alone most adolescent boys express some shyness and reticence about sexuality. They are aware that, as boys, they are expected to be sexually motivated, but they don't necessarily feel this way. However, in one another's company, boys readily engage in sexual talk and the talk tends to be scripted in terms of a "hunt" or "conquest." As Cohan points out, even boys who have no immediate personal interest in girls or sex quickly adapt to the peer script of aggressive sex talk in the company of other boys. Sociologists who study masculinities note that this conquest-oriented, sex-obsessed talk is the cultural capital of boys and men looking to express their masculinity. Regardless of how they feel privately, boys learn early on that participating in this kind of "locker room" banter is the path to inclusion in the very competitive arena of masculinity. Sex-talk and the related preparations for "hunting girls" is a form of homosocial bonding for men. In a study of fraternity men preparing to go out for an evening on the prowl, sociologist David Grazian describes the myriad ways in which these rituals connect men and give them a collective sense of power.

Despite media saturated with teen sexuality and notions of contemporary hooking-up culture, the upshot is that boys and girls continue to be sexually socialized very differently: boys are taught that they should have a constant desire and that sexual achievement is a form of conquest, girls learn to displace their own feelings and dissociate from their desire in order to please boys. Contemporary sexual scripts reflect age-old myths that hypersexualize men and center women's sexuality around relationships. For example, current studies on "hooking-up" behavior among college students (see reading 33) indicate that far from being a more liberatory experience for girls, it sets up expectations to "have to have more bad sex." The time-old strategy of telling a boy that she just "wants to be friends" has now become a verb, "friendzoning." Guys now tell their friends, "She friendzoned me." Implicit in this seemingly innocuous phrase is the long-standing expectation that if a boy shows a girl sexual attention, he is entitled to the response he wants. In a culture that casts girls as achieving status only through connections to men, boys quickly, if not always consciously, pick up the expectations that girls are supposed to pay attention to them. And if a girl doesn't respond as he would like, he is entitled to feel angry. This propensity exits as evidence that our cultural scripts still do not encourage and respect girls' articulations of their own desires on their own terms.

sexual violence

Masculinities expert Michael Messner focuses on cultural scripts that teach boys that a successful manifestation of masculinity is sexually conquering girls. He explores the ways in which these scripts play out in male-dominated spaces such as sports and fraternities. In his assessment, masculinity expectations are unattainable for most boys, yet culturally we continue to hold them to impossible standards and they respond by collectively egging one another on in attempts to jostle for position on the masculinities hierarchy. The homosocial prowling that results in extreme violence, including campus rape, and gang beatings of queer and trans folks perceived as "other" is a direct result of this socialization.

Campus sexual violence is a subject of national concern and university officials are scrambling to respond. Research in this area has focused on individual-level theories (the "one bad apple") or collective-level theories in the form "rape culture" (society supports male entitlement and violence toward women as a aspect of "boys will be boys" logic). Sociologists have suggested that these theories need to include organizational-level analyses that explore how institutional policies and practices (e.g., in universities, workplaces, and sports) provide opportunities for sexual assault. For instance, sociologist Elizabeth Armstrong and her colleagues identify several features of university fraternity life that give control to groups of young men explicitly looking to get women drunk. Policies such as no campus drinking make fraternity-based parties attractive, but these spaces enhance the homosocial sexual conquest orientation among men and put women attendees (who are often early in their college careers and inexperienced) in vulnerable situations. Other policies give the appearance that the institution is in *compliance* with federal laws that grant women equal education and a nondiscriminatory environment. But in practice they further disempower women by removing their agency about how to respond to sexual assault.

Given the extreme gender differences in sexual socialization, it's a wonder people are able to develop healthy sexual intimacies at all. The continued focus on relationship status and denial of female desire disempowers women to make strong, active choices and the relentless press for men to prove masculinity, especially through homosocial expressions of sexual interest and conquest, provide a foundation for sexual violence. British scholars Melissa Burkett and Karine Hamilton capture the poignancy of this cultural moment in a study of college women who feel even less safe in the "just say no" environment of today's supposedly liberated sexual culture. They interview women who report feeling even more pressure to have sex in this supposedly sexually freer time for women. All of a sudden they are supposedly sexual agents who can just say no, but the problem is that very little else has changed: men still feel entitled to sex just because they desire a woman. However, given the scant emphasis on women's sexual desire, she may be ambivalent, but there is no room for ambivalence in this new equation. If she was in the situation in the first place and unable to confidently say no and repel her suitor, she is guilty of leading him on. In short, the script of "just say no" insufficiently captures a very long history of women's inexperience with and ambivalence around sexual desire.

conclusions

Keep in mind that this discussion is about sexual scripts. Many individuals do not personally resonate with these cultural scripts. However, the prevalence of these scripts throughout media and other social institutions leaves many people wondering if their own feelings and desires are out of whack: Should I want more sex? Should I have a more fixed sexual identity? Is it okay to be sexually attracted to both genders? At what age should I start exploring my sexuality? Did my parents talk to me about sex or did they expect my health class at school to feed me sexual education? Because sex is supposedly such a big deal in this culture, many people struggle to understand their own sexuality. The persistence of sexual scripts

rooted in shame and silence, leaves many people, especially young people, feeling out of place and alone. If sex were a natural act we wouldn't have to think so much about it, let alone be plagued with so much concern, confusion, and guilt. The fact that it occupies so much of our private and cultural lives indicates the extent to which it is a social construction and one that, for our current culture, could use some improvement in terms of communication and relational engagement, especially across traditional gender divides. The sociology of sexuality provides a blueprint for navigating this confusion. Exploring sexual expectations, feelings, and expressions within specific cultural contexts and in accordance with sexual scripts liberates us from the notion that sex is just something natural and empowers us to make conscious thoughtful choices.

recommended resources

Armstrong, Elizabeth, Hamilton, Laura, and Sweeney, Brian. 2006. "Sexual Assault on Campus," *Social Problems* 53:483–499.

Boellstorff, Tom. 2005. *The Gay Archipelago: Sexuality and Nation in Indonesia.* Princeton: Princeton University Press.

Burkett, Melissa, and Hamilton, Karine. 2012. "Postfeminist Sexual Agency: Young Women's Negotiations of Consent." *Sexualities* 15:815–833.

Cohan, Mark. 2009. "Adolescent Heterosexual Males Talk about the Role of Male Peer Groups in their Sexual Decision-Making," *Society & Culture* 13:152–177.

Grazian, David. 2007. "The Girl Hunt: Urban Nightlife and the Performance of Masculinity as Collective Activity," *Symbolic Interaction* 30:221–243.

Jackson, Stevi. 2007. "The Sexual Self in Late Modernity." In M. Kimmel (ed.), *The Sexual Self: The Construction of Sexual Scripts.* Nashville, TN: Vanderbilt University Press.

Gagnon, John, and Simon, William. 1974. *Sexual Conduct: The Social Sources of Human Sexuality.* London: Hutchinson.

Messner, Michael. 2014. "Can Locker Room Rape Culture Be Prevented?" *Contexts* 14(2):22–23.

Orenstein, Peggy. 1995. *School Girls: Young Women, Self-Esteem, and the Confidence Gap.* New York: Anchor Books.

Tiefer, Leonore. 2004. *Sex is Not a Natural Act.* Boulder, CO: Westview Press.

Tolman, Deborah. 2002. *Dilemmas of Desire: Teenage Girls Talk About Sexuality.* Cambridge, MA: Harvard University Press.

slut-shaming romance writers

nicole bedera

fall 2015

Romance is the most widely read fiction genre, but stigma means few own up to that readership. Instead, groups of giggling girls claim to pick up *Fifty Shades of Grey* as a joke and romance readers hide their books in public. If the love of romance is complicated for readers, what about its writers? In a new *Gender and Society* article, Jennifer Lois and Joanna Gregson report findings from a four-year ethnographic study of the romance novel industry and its authors.

Lois and Gregson find that outsiders to the romance writing subculture contributed to "slut-shaming" authors through sneering or leering. In sneering, female writers are shamed for having and publicly displaying sexual desire. (The few male writers in the study's sample were not shamed in the same way.) In leering, outsiders direct sexual gestures or comments toward writers. In most cases, a male outsider leered at a female romance writer in order to pursue sex; however, leering between female outsiders and female writers also happened when outsiders would over-share personal sexual experiences or opinions about sex work without regard for the writer's comfort.

While sneering and leering appear to be opposites—leering is ostensibly an act of approval, whereas sneering reflects disapproval—Lois and Gregson argue that both reactions are forms of slut-shaming. Central to both reactions is the assumption that romance novels are not rightly considered fiction, but instead are the writers' actual fantasies and sexual experiences. Whether sneering or leering, outsiders labeled romance writers as sexual deviants and welcomed themselves into conversation about the writers' private sex lives. Despite the widespread popularity of the romance genre, romance writers face intense public shame for their exposure of women's sexual desire.

navigating sexuality

overview

Sexuality encompasses behaviors, attractions, and identities, and dovetails with gendered ideologies and practices. As individuals navigate intimate relationship they enter into discussions about cultural beliefs and sexual politics. Such discussions often begin as they start puberty and young adulthood.

Stefanie Mollborn examines this critical phase in her article "Mixed Messages about Teen Sex," which looks at how different communities approach the topic of teen sex and pregnancy and how parents talk about sex outside of marriage. Such talk differs across nations, as Amy Schalet ("Love, Sex, and Autonomy in the Teenage Sleepover") shows. American parents tend to embrace a restrictive view of teenage sexuality whereas Dutch parents see teen sex as normal.

As young adults begin to explore their sexuality many young women are confronted with double standards. In their article "Is Hooking Up Bad for Young Women?" Elizabeth Armstrong, Laura Hamilton and Paula England look at the gendered effects of casual sex among young adults. Leila J. Rupp and Verta Taylor's article "Straight Girls Kissing" investigates the reasons college-age women choose to experiment sexually with other women.

Surveying young adults, Traci Luff, Kristi Hoffman, and Marit Bernston explore the widespread cultural belief that young adults are opting out of dating and mainly engaging in hookups. In "Hooking Up and Dating Are Two Sides of the Same Coin," they suggest that dating is still common.

Navigating the tricky road of sexuality doesn't end in late middle and old age. As Linda J. Waite explores in her article "Sexuality Has No Expiration Date," people over the age of 59 who continue to be sexually active are faced with new roadblocks, such as declining sexual function and an increased rate of health issues which complicate sexual expression.

things to consider

- The majority of these readings focus on the messages (moral, ethical, and social) young adults receive when they begin to explore their sexuality. Often these messages are contradictory, inviting experimentation while promoting shame. If you were to create a sexual education course for high school freshmen, what five topics would you cover? How might you combat the pervasive negativity surrounding sexual expression, while acknowledging the risks that such expression may introduce?

- Having read "Is Hooking Up Bad for Young Women?" and "Hooking Up and Dating Are Two Sides to the Same Coin" consider the experience and effects of hookup culture on adolescent men. Do men and women confront similar set of issues surrounding casual sex or sexual expression?

mixed messages about teen sex

stefanie mollborn

winter 2015

Patton grew up in a mostly White, wealthy, liberal town. He thinks about half of the kids in his high school, mostly the "cool" ones, were having sex. Mostly, they practiced safe sex, and few ended up pregnant. Parents, he said, "turned their head because they didn't want to know what their kid was doing." This made teen sex and pregnancy a taboo topic. Parents gave their teenage children a clear message about "being careful"—avoiding sex or using contraception consistently—to avoid getting pregnant. Patton says, "As a whole, it was more kids practicing safe sex rather than being a focus on being abstinent." Teens who messed up paid a social price, and pregnant girls were shunned. Someone from the same town said, "A pregnancy is just like a physical marker that you are a slut."

Patton's story contrasts sharply with Annika's experiences in a conservative, White, lower-income mining town with deep Evangelical roots. There, the message was "don't have sex before marriage." But most teens were having sex anyway, and hiding it from parents. Annika thinks because most teens were with someone they eventually expected to marry, they weren't as motivated to "be careful" with contraception. Many of the kids in her high school were pregnant. The school didn't try to hide them as Patton's school did—on the contrary, the senior class president was eight months pregnant at graduation. Annika links this openness to teen pregnancy to the fact that people in her town were very anti-abortion; some teens even wore "abortion is homicide" shirts to school. Pregnant teens who chose not to have abortions were sometimes praised by older people, whom Annika said thought, "it was a gift from God."

It may seem like Annika and Patton come from different worlds when it comes to messages about teen sex and pregnancy, but their hometowns are in the same U.S. state. It's striking that Patton's "very liberal" town accepted that teen sex may happen but ostracized pregnant teens, while Annika's "very conservative" town grudgingly accepted pregnant teens. Both of these communities are communicating messages to teens that work to reproduce their cultural values in the next generation. But as we will see, mixed messages may be less than effective.

The vast majority of American adults today have had sex outside of marriage, but most adults think teenagers shouldn't have sex. Even so, researchers at the Guttmacher Institute have found that most young people become sexually active in their teens: Just 16% have had sex by age 15, over 60% by 18, and 71% by 19. And about one in four teen girls ends up pregnant. (This article focuses on self-identified heterosexual teens—additional research would be helpful for understanding the experiences of teens who identify in other ways.) Research collaborators and I interviewed 57 college students and 76 teen moms and dads about the messages they heard about sex, contraception, and pregnancy in high school. The college students all attended a large public university in the West but came from all regions of the United States. Most teen parents were non-White and living in or near poverty in an urban area.

Even though their backgrounds are so different, there are important experiences these young people have in common. Most teens they know eventually have sex, most adults seem clueless that it's happening, and most adults disapprove. Teens themselves are petrified that their parents and other adults might find out they're having sex. But there are also tremendous differences in the messages teens hear about sexual behavior in different communities. Here, I examine these messages—which tend to be inconsistent and confusing—and the ways teens react to them.

practical concerns, moral messages

In the *New Yorker* article "Red Sex, Blue Sex," Margaret Talbot argues that teens' experiences of sex and pregnancy differ in fundamental ways between liberal, secular "blue" areas like Patton's and conservative, highly religious "red" areas like Annika's. I conclude that people in Patton's town are communicating a *practical* message, one that is focused mostly on careful contraception if teens decide to have sex. They talk about things like maturity, responsibility, and being smart about your future. In high-poverty, secular urban communities regardless of race, the messages about responsibility and protecting your future sound much the same as in wealthier ones—but they feel different because teens and those around them realize that their futures are precarious.

In contrast, Annika's highly religious community takes a two-pronged approach of teaching abstinence until marriage, and if that fails, strongly discouraging abortion. As Bryce sums up the message in his Catholic-dominated community, "we were taught that premarital sex and pregnancy outside of wedlock is against God, and therefore wrong." This *moral* message is in line with conservative Christian religious teachings but—as evaluations of abstinence-only sex education and virginity pledges have shown—it is not as useful for reducing teen pregnancy. Teens from wealthier religious communities may resolve an unwanted pregnancy through a secret abortion. But teens from lower-income communities like Annika's have less to gain by aborting a pregnancy in violation of their community's message.

Sociologists call these messages social norms, rules about how people should behave that result in punishment if they aren't followed. The moral and practical communities are not just teaching teens how to behave—they're trying to pass on their cultural values that represent different sides in what has been called a "culture war." Both Annika's and Patton's communities aren't just sending messages to teens about what they should or should not do—they're communicating expectations about how to treat someone who has violated a norm against pregnancy, sex, contraception, or abortion. Metanorms (norms about how to enforce norms) ensure that teens who violate age norms against sexual behaviors are punished by family, friends, and community members. Metanorms often tell us to punish people differently depending not only on their gender, but also by their race and social class. For instance, teens who are seen as part of the "social problem" of teen parenthood (usually non-White girls from lower-income families or areas) are held accountable for their sexual behavior and socially punished. But as the people we interviewed said repeatedly, teens who are not identified with this "social problem" are often excused for "making a mistake" if they have sex or use contraception inconsistently. Boys hear the same messages as girls and face some of the same social punishment for violating norms, but it tends to be weaker.

how messages are mixed

Teens hear messages about sex that are mixed in several ways. Both the moral and practical messages are internally inconsistent. They start out with a similar norm discouraging teen sex but combine it with different norms in ways that can seem contradictory to teens. People communicating a practical message say, "Don't have sex, but use contraception." Inconsistent metanorms tell people to support teen parents in the community but view teen mothers as sluts who should be shunned. The moral message is equally inconsistent. People communicating this message say, "Don't have sex, but carry your pregnancy to term." Isaac summarizes the mixed messages communicated to teens in his lower-income, rural town as: "Don't get pregnant, I don't care how you do it, I'm not gonna give you condoms, you're not supposed to get pregnant when you're 17." The moral message's metanorms confusingly encourage people to condemn teens who have had premarital sex but praise teen mothers because they refused to have abortions.

This means that even in towns like Patton's or Annika's that have a fairly cohesive culture, teens hear mixed messages about sexual behavior from adults. But in other communities, the presence of both practical and moral messages sends teens mixed messages about sex. Teens who hear a practical message from their communities often hear a moral one from grandparents or other older people. In higher-income conservative communities where teens have a lot to lose, some parents and teachers privately give teens a practical message about contraception and abortion, which is different from what teens are hearing from other adults. School administrators and community organizations like health clinics or churches are often strong defenders of the community's practical or moral message.

But friends, siblings, and schoolmates often communicate a third message that is neither moral nor practical, intensifying the experience of mixed messages. By late in high school, either quietly among close friends or publicly around school, most teens are talking about how sex is "normal" or something to do when you're "ready." Close friends help each other be sexually active away from the judging eyes of adults. Especially for girls, even revealing sexual activity to schoolmates who aren't good friends is a potential danger because they may consider at least some types of female sexual activity "slutty" and tell adults. In Helena's liberal school, she says most teens were having casual sex, but they still worked hard to avoid people finding out. "Because it was such a small school, they just didn't want to talk about it all with people, as things go around really quickly. So, yeah, they would just keep their mouths shut."

Both the practical and moral messages conflict with certain trends in broader U.S. society, making them feel even more inconsistent to teens. Some watch shows like MTV's *16 and Pregnant* or *Teen Mom* and see real girls enjoying success because they had babies, which conflicts with the practical and moral messages. Teens who hear a moral message learn to carry a pregnancy to term because abortion is evil, but teen pregnancy has been constructed so visibly as a "social problem" and linked to failure that they know some people in every community will treat them badly if they become mothers. Our society goes back and forth about teen sexuality, alternatively glamorizing and demonizing it in ways that make the messages teens hear even more mixed.

battles

The fight for control of the sexuality messages communicated to teens is a fight over which value systems adults want the next generation to reproduce. The "abstinence-only" programs favored by former president Bush's administration communicate a moral message about teen sexuality. The Obama administration, while still funding some abstinence-only programs, has shifted its focus towards "comprehensive" or "abstinence-plus" programs that teach teens about using contraception.

Schools and outside organizations work to influence teens. I have found that schools often work with organizations that conform to the community's predominant message and that target the "right kind" of teen.

> **Our society goes back and forth about teen sexuality, alternatively glamorizing and demonizing it.**

Larena's school in a low-income urban community let a nurse distribute birth control pills onsite with parental consent. These were considered the "right kind" of teens to be put on long-term contraception. But in Madelyn's wealthy conservative suburb, a pro-abstinence Christian youth group located next door to her high school held daily meetings, and the school allowed students to go for free periods. These were seen as the "right kind" of teens to absorb moral messages.

As teens' legal guardians, parents have even more control over them, and many go to great lengths to constrain teens' sexuality. Dylan says, "Parents' talks were like, 'You don't do this [have sex]. This is wrong, religiously, morally.'" They paired this moral message with threats: "If you [got pregnant], it would completely destroy our family." Physical control is also important, with many rules about how to behave when an opposite-sex friend visits and threats of being grounded if these rules are broken. A surprisingly common strategy in which parents and teens implicitly cooperate is for girls to start taking birth control pills for apparent reasons other than sexual activity. Kara said, "I was on birth control for different medical reasons, and so I think that put my parents at ease, because they knew that I was on birth control, even though it wasn't for sex initially. So I think that kind of took some pressure off." Noelle thought girls themselves took some initiative: "A lot of the girls were on the pill. People would start early for cramps or to clear their face, so they didn't have to have the conversation with their parents if they're already on the pill." Even if the "medical reasons" are valid, this strategy allows both parents and teens to protect a daughter from pregnancy (though not sexually transmitted infections) without acknowledging sexual activity.

teens' reactions

The pressure brought to bear on teens by the people in their social worlds can be hard to withstand, and for most of adolescence most teens don't even want to withstand it. When younger, teens have internalized community norms saying teen sex is inappropriate and don't feel "ready." Yet most Americans end up having sex in their late teens when many people still disapprove. So at some point, teens start finding ways to resist attempts to regulate their sexuality.

Because different people send different normative messages and those messages are themselves inconsistent, teens have some "wiggle room" to negotiate normative pressures. If a teen wants to have sex, he might disregard the part of his community's normative message that discourages teen sex and focus instead on conforming to the part that encourages consistent contraception. Or he might become more peer-oriented, choosing sexually active friends who support his behavior and "tuning out" adult influences as much as possible. As Kaitlyn says, "Once their friends have sex and start experimenting it starts to be okay. . . . You start to think, 'Everyone is doing it, so why am I not doing it?'" But there are limits to teens' behavioral options. Our participants are too dependent on adults for resources, and on friends for social interaction, to risk openly going against the messages they hear.

Teens start finding ways to resist attempts to regulate their sexuality.

Although U.S. teens start having sex at about the same age as in many other places, they don't use contraception as consistently, so sexually transmitted infections and teen pregnancies, abortions, and births are more widespread than in many other countries. Could this have to do with the normative pressures on teens coming from mixed messages? The practical message tells teens sex is risky, and the moral message says it is wrong. Moral, practical, peer, and media messages may vie for teens' attention, but they all tell teens that sex will screw up their lives. This negative message about teen sex is one overarching piece of the message that *isn't* mixed. The sex-negative cultural frame in the U.S. is a stark contrast to some other countries, as Amy Schalet shows in the Netherlands. That sex-positive frame views teen sex—when done right, which means in a loving relationship, when the teen feels ready, and with consistent contraception—as a positive aspect of adolescent development. Ironically, this sex-positive frame results in less risky sex because sex often happens at home with the protection of more effective long-acting contraceptives.

The sex-negative cultural frame and the mixed messages about teen sex put our society in a double bind. It's hard to communicate a strong message discouraging teen sex when you're simultaneously giving advice about contraception and abortion. And it's hard to convincingly teach young people to support teen parents when you're also socially punishing them for having violated community messages. Open communication about sexuality becomes difficult when the messages are mixed, and it's also hard for teens to absorb the messages. Faced with this challenge, many adults become ineffective supports for teens struggling with responsible sexuality. So which is more important for our society, eliminating teen sexual activity or minimizing its negative consequences? This is what battles over sex education are largely about—the moral message says the first is more important, and the practical message says the second. Acknowledging the mixed messages teens are hearing and breaking the silence around their sexuality may be a good first step towards communicating more effectively.

recommended resources

Bearman, Peter S, and Brückner, Hannah. 2001. "Promising the Future: Virginity Pledges and First Intercourse," *American Journal of Sociology 106*: 859–912. This influential article's findings on the effects of virginity pledges have been used by both sides in cultural debates about teen sexual behavior.

Elliot, Sinikka. 2012. *Not My Kid: What Parents Believe About the Sex Lives of Their Teenagers.* New York: New York University Press. Articulates the complex ways in which parents think about their teenagers' sex lives and how they communicate with teens.

Fields, Jessica. 2008. *Risky Lessons: Sex Education and Social Inequality.* New Brunswick: Rutgers University Press. Documents community debates around sex education and the role of social inequalities.

Mollborn, Stefanie, and Jacobs, Janet. 2012. "'We'll Figure a Way': Teenage Mothers' Experiences in Shifting Social and Economic Contexts," *Qualitative Sociology 35*:23–46. Investigates how cultural and structural changes over time have shaped the consequences of teen parenthood.

Schalet, Amy T. 2011. *Not Under My Roof: Parents, Teens, and the Culture of Sex.* Chicago, IL: University of Chicago Press. By comparing middle-class messages about sexual behaviors in the United States and the Netherlands, this book sheds light on our takenfor-granted cultural understandings.

sex, love, and autonomy in the teenage sleepover

amy schalet

summer 2010

Karel Doorman, a soft-spoken civil servant in the Netherlands, keeps tabs on his teenage children's computer use and their jobs to make sure neither interferes with school performance or family time. But Karel wouldn't object if his daughter Heidi were to have a sexual relationship.

"No," he explains. "She is sixteen, almost seventeen. I think she knows very well what matters, what can happen. If she is ready [for sex], I would let her be ready." Karel would also let his daughter spend the night with a steady boyfriend in her room, if the boyfriend had come over to the house regularly before-hand and did not show up "out of the blue." That said, Karel suspects his daughter might prefer a partner of her own sex. If so, Karel would accept her orientation, he says, though "the adjustment process" might take a little longer.

Karel's approach stands in sharp contrast to that of Rhonda Fursman, a northern California homemaker and former social worker. Rhonda tells her kids that premarital sex "at this point is really dumb." It's on the list with shoplifting, she explains, "sort of like the Ten Commandments: don't do any of those because if you do, you know, you're going to be in a world of hurt." Rhonda responds viscerally when asked whether she would let her fifteen-year-old son spend the night with a girlfriend. "No way, Jose!" She elaborates: "That kind of recreation . . . is just not something I would feel comfortable with him doing here." She might change her mind "if they are engaged or about to be married."

Karel and Rhonda illustrate a puzzle: the vast majority of American parents oppose a sleepover for high-school-aged teenagers, while Dutch teenagers who have steady boyfriends or girlfriends are typically allowed to spend the night with them in their rooms. This contrast is all the more striking when we consider the trends toward a liberalization of sexual behavior and attitudes that have taken place throughout Europe and the United States since the 1960s. In similar environments, both parents and kids are experiencing adolescent sex, gender, and relationships very differently. A sociological exploration of these contrasts reveals as much about the cultural differences between these two countries as it does about views on adolescent sexuality and child rearing.

adolescent sexuality in contemporary america

Today, most adolescents in the U.S., like their peers across the industrialized world, engage in intercourse—either opposite or same-sex—before leaving their teens

> *American adolescent sexuality has been dramatized rather than normalized.*

(usually around seventeen). Initiating sex and exploring romantic relationships, often with several successive partners before settling into long-term cohabitation or marriage, are now normative parts of adolescence and young adulthood in the developed world. But in the U.S., teenage sex has been fraught with cultural ambivalences, heated political struggles, and poor health outcomes, generating concern among the public, policy makers, scholars, and parents. American adolescent sexuality has been dramatized rather than normalized.

In some respects, the problems associated with adolescent sexuality in America are surprising. Certainly, age at first intercourse has dropped in the U.S. since the sexual revolution, but not as steeply as often assumed. In a recent survey of the adult American population, sociologist Edward Laumann and colleagues found that even in the 1950s and '60s, only a quarter of men and less than half of women were virgins at age nineteen. The majority of young men had multiple sexual partners by age 20. And while women especially were supposed to enter marriage as virgins, demographer Lawrence Finer has shown that women who came of age in the late 1950s and early '60s almost never held to that norm. Still, a 1969 Gallup poll found that two thirds of Americans said it was wrong for "a man and women to have sex relations before marriage."

But by 1985, Gallup found that a slim majority of Americans no longer believed such relations were wrong.

> *Dutch parents downplay the dangerous and difficult sides of teenage sexuality, tending to normalize it.*

Analyzing shifts in public opinion following the sexual revolution, sociologists Larry Petersen and Gregory Donnenwerth showed that among Americans with a religious affiliation, only conservative Protestants who attended church frequently remained unchanged. Among all other religious groups, acceptance of premarital sex actually grew, although Laumann and colleagues reported a majority of the Americans continued to believe sex among *teenagers* was always wrong. Even youth agreed: six in ten fifteen to nineteen-year-olds surveyed in the 2002 National Survey for Family Growth said sixteen-year-olds with strong feelings for one another shouldn't have sex.

Part of the opposition to adolescent sexuality is its association with unintended consequences such as pregnancy and sexually transmitted diseases. In the U.S., the rate of unintended pregnancies among teenagers rose during the 1970s and '80s, dropping only in the early '90s. However, despite almost a decade and a half of impressive decreases in pregnancy and birth rates, the teen birth rate remains many times higher in the U.S. than it is in most European countries. In 2007, births to American teens (aged fifteen to nineteen) were eight times as high as in the Netherlands.

One would imagine the predominant public policy approach would be to improve education about, and access to, contraception. But "abstinence-only-until-marriage" programs, initiated in the early 1980s, have received generous federal funding over the past fifteen years, and were even written into the recent U.S. health reform law (which also supports comprehensive sex education). For years, schools funded under the federal "abstinence-only" policy were prohibited from educating teens about condoms and contraception and required to teach that sex outside of heterosexual marriage was damaging. A 2004 survey by NPR, the Kaiser Family Foundation, and Harvard University found that most parents actually thought that contraception and condom education should be included, but two thirds still agreed sex education should teach that abstinence outside of marriage is "the accepted standard for school-aged children." And for most parents, abstinence means no oral sex or intimate touching.

While American parents of the post-Sexual Revolution era have wanted minors to abstain, few teens have complied. Many American teenagers have had positive and enriching sexual experiences; however, researchers have also documented intense struggles. Comparing teenage boys and girls, for example, University of Michigan sociologist Karin Martin found that puberty and first sex empowered boys but decreased self-esteem among girls. Psychologist Deborah Tolman found the girls she interviewed confronted dilemmas of desire because of a double standard that denies or stigmatizes their sexual desires, making girls fear being labeled "sluts." Analyzing the National Longitudinal Survey of Adolescent Health, researchers Kara Joyner and Richard Udry found that even without sex, first romance brings girls "down" because their relationship with their parents deteriorates.

Nor are American girls of the post-Sexual Revolution era the only ones who must navigate gender dilemmas. Sociologist Laura Carpenter found that many of the young men she interviewed in the 1990s viewed their virginity as a stigma which they sought to cast off as rapidly as possible. And in her ethnography, *Dude, You're a Fag,* C.J. Pascoe found boys are pressured by other boys to treat girls as sex objects and sometimes derided for showing affection for their girlfriends. But despite public pressures, privately boys are as emotionally invested in relationships as girls, found Peggy Giordano and her associates in a recent national study out of Toledo, Ohio. Within those relationships, however, boys are less confident.

In the 1990s, the National Longitudinal Study for Adolescent Health found that steady romantic relationships are common among American teenagers. Girls and boys typically have their first intercourse with people they are dating. But the Toledo group found that once they are sexually experienced, the majority of boys and girls also have sex in non-dating relationships, often with a friend or acquaintance. And even when they have sex in dating relationships, a quarter of American girls and almost half of boys say they are "seeing other people" (which may or may not include sexual intercourse).

teen sexuality in the netherlands

In a late 1980s qualitative study with 120 parents and older teenagers, Dutch sociologist Janita Ravesloot concluded that in most families, parents accepted that sexuality "from the first kiss to the first coitus" was part of the youth phase. In middle class families, teenagers reported that parents accepted their sexual autonomy, but didn't engage in elaborate conversations with them because of lingering feelings of shame. Working-class parents were more likely to use their authority to impose norms, including that sex belonged only in steady relationships. In a few strongly religious families—Christian or Islamic—parents categorically opposed sex before marriage: here there were "no overnights with steady boy- or girlfriends at home."[1] But such families remain a minority. A 2003 survey by *Statistics Netherlands* found that two thirds of Dutch fifteen to seventeen-year-olds with steady boy- or girlfriends are allowed to spend the night with them in their bedrooms, and that boys and girls are equally likely to get permission for a sleepover.

This could hardly have been predicted in the 1950s. Then, women *and* men typically initiated intercourse in their early twenties, usually in a serious relationship (if not engagement or marriage). In the late '60s, a national survey conducted by sociologist G.A. Kooy found most respondents still rejected premarital sex when a couple was not married or planning to do so very shortly. But by the early 1980s, the same survey found that six out of ten respondents no longer objected to a girl having intercourse with a boy as long as she was in love with him. Noting the shift in attitudes since the 1950s, Kooy spoke of a "moral landslide." His colleague, sociologist Evert Ketting, even went as far as to speak of a "moral revolution."

What changed was not just a greater acceptance of sex outside of the context of heterosexual marriage. There was also serious new deliberation among the general public, health professionals, and the media about the need to adjust the moral rules governing sexual life to real behavior. As researchers for the Guttmacher Institute later noted, "One might say the entire society has experienced a course in sex education." The new moral rules cast sexuality as a part of life that should be governed by self-determination, mutual respect, frank conversation, and the prevention of unintended consequences. Notably, these new rules were applied to minors and institutionalized in Dutch health care policies that removed financial and emotional barriers to accessing contraceptives—including the requirements for a pelvic examination and parental consent.

Indeed, even as the age of first sexual intercourse was decreasing, the rate of births among Dutch teenagers dropped steeply between 1970 and 1996 to one of the lowest in the world. What distinguished the very low Dutch teenage birth rate from, for instance, that of their Swedish counterparts, was that it was accompanied by a very low teen abortion rate. Despite the AIDS crisis, by the mid1990s, funding agencies were so confident that, in the words of demographer Joop Garssen, youth were doing "wonderfully well," they decided further study of adolescent sexual attitudes and behavior wasn't warranted.

Sex education has played a key role. Sociologists Jane Lewis and Trudie Knijn find that Dutch sex education curricula are more likely than programs elsewhere to openly discuss female sexual pleasure, masturbation, and homosexuality. The Dutch curricula also emphasize the importance of self-reliance and mutual respect in negotiating enjoyable and healthy sexual relationships during adolescence.

A 2005 survey of Dutch youth, ages twelve to twenty-five, found the majority described their first sexual experiences—broadly defined—as well-timed, within their control, and fun. About first intercourse, 86 percent of women and 93 percent of men said, "We both were equally eager to have it." This doesn't mean that gender doesn't matter. Researcher Janita Ravelsoot found that more girls than boys reported that their parents expected them to only have intercourse in relationships. Girls were also aware that they might be called sluts for having sex too soon or with too many successive partners. And although most of the 2005 respondents said they were (very) satisfied with the pleasure and contact they felt with their partner during sex, men were much more likely to usually or always orgasm during sex and less likely to report having experienced pain.

It also appears that having sex outside of the context of monogamous romantic relationships isn't as common among Dutch adolescents, especially older ones, as among their American counterparts. Again in the 2005 survey, two thirds of male youth and 81 percent of Dutch females had their last sex in a monogamous steady relationship, usually with a partner with whom they were "very much in love." Certainly, Dutch adolescents have "non-relational" sex—indeed, one in three males and one in five females had their last vaginal or anal sex outside of a monogamous romantic relationship. That said, relational sex seems to remain the norm, especially as young people age: two thirds of fifteen to seventeen-year-olds, and three quarters of those eighteen to twenty, had their last intercourse in a monogamous relationship. Among the oldest group—nineteen to twenty-four-year-olds—almost half of gay men surveyed, six in ten straight men and lesbians, and nearly three quarters of straight women were in long-term relationships.

explaining the differences

So why do parents in two countries with similar levels of development and reproductive technologies have such different attitudes toward the sexual experiences of teenagers? Two factors immediately spring to mind. The first is religion. As the Laumann team found, Americans who do not view religion as a central force in their decision-making are much less likely to categorically condemn teenage sex. And devout Christians and Muslims in the Netherlands are more likely to exhibit attitudes towards sexuality and marriage that are similar to those of their American counterparts. That Americans are far more likely to be religiously devout than the Dutch, many of whom left their houses of worship in the 1960s and '70s, explains part of the difference between the two countries.

A second factor is economic security. Like most European countries, the Dutch government provides a range of what sociologists call "social" and what reproductive health advocates call "human" rights: the right to housing, healthcare, and a minimum income. Not only do such rights ensure access, if need be, to free contraceptive and abortion services, government supports make coming of age less perilous for both teenagers and parents. This might make the prospect of sex derailing a child's life less haunting. Ironically, the very lack of such rights and high rates of childhood poverty in the U.S. contributes to high rates of births among teenagers. Without adequate support systems or educational and job opportunities, young people are simply more likely to start parenthood early in life.

While they no doubt contribute, neither religion nor economics can solve the whole puzzle. Even Dutch and American families matched on these dimensions still have radically divergent views of teenage sexuality and the sleepover. After interviewing 130 White middleclass Dutch and American teenagers (mostly 10th graders) and parents, I became convinced that a fuller solution is to look at the different cultures of independence and control that characterize these two middle classes.

In responding to adolescent sexuality, American parents emphasize its dangerous and conflicted elements, describing it in terms of "raging hormones" that are difficult for young people to control and in terms of antagonistic relationships between the sexes (girls and boys pursue love and sex respectively, and girls are often the losers of the battle). Moreover, American parents see it as their obligation to encourage adolescents' separation from home before accepting their sexual activity. Viewing sex as part of a larger tug of war between separation and control, the response to the question of the sleepover, even among many otherwise socially liberal parents is, "Not under my roof!"

Dutch parents, by contrast, downplay the dangerous and difficult sides of teenage sexuality, tending to normalize it. They speak of readiness (*er aan toe zijn*), a process of becoming physically and emotionally ready for sex that they believe young people can self-regulate, provided they've been encouraged to pace themselves and prepare adequately. Rather than emphasizing gender battles, Dutch parents talk about sexuality as emerging from relationships and are strikingly silent about gender conflicts. And unlike Americans who are often skeptical about teenagers' capacities to fall in love, they assume that even those in their early teens fall in love. They permit sleepovers, even if that requires an "adjustment" period to overcome their feelings of discomfort, because they feel obliged to stay connected and accepting as sex becomes part of their children's lives.

These different approaches to adolescent sexuality are part of the different cultures of independence and control. American middleclass culture conceptualizes the self and (adult) society as inherently oppositional during adolescence. Breaking away from the family is necessary for autonomy, as is the occasional use of parental control (for instance, in the arena of sexuality), until teenagers are full adults. Dutch middleclass culture, in contrast, conceptualizes the self and society as interdependent. Based upon the assumption that young people develop autonomy in the context of ongoing relationships of interdependence, Dutch parents don't see teenage sexuality in the household as a threat to their children's autonomy or to their own authority. To the contrary, allowing teenage sexuality in the home—"domesticating" it, as it were—allows Dutch parents to exert more informal social control.

what it means for kids

The acceptance of adolescent sexuality in the family creates the opportunity for Dutch girls to integrate their sexual selves with their roles as family members, even if they may be subject to a greater level of surveillance. Karel's daughter, Heidi, for example, told me she knows that her parents would permit a boyfriend to spend the night, but they wouldn't be happy unless they knew the boy and felt comfortable with him. By contrast, many American girls must physically and psychically bifurcate their sexual selves and their roles as daughters. Caroline's mother loves her boyfriend. Still, Caroline, who is seventeen, says her parents would "kill" her if she asked for a sleepover. They know she has sex, but "it's really overwhelming for them to know that their little girl is in their house having sex with a guy. That is just scary to them."

American boys receive messages ranging from blanket prohibition to open encouragement. One key message is that sex is a symbol and a threat—in the event of pregnancy—to their adult autonomy. Jesse has a mother who is against premarital sex and a father who believes boys just want to get laid. But like Caroline, Jesse knows there will be no sleepovers: "They have to wait for me to break off from them, to be doing my own thing, before they can just handle the fact that I would be staying with my girlfriend like that," he says. By contrast, Dutch boys are, or anticipate being, allowed a sleepover. And like their female counterparts, they say permission comes with a social control that encourages a relational sexuality and girlfriends their parents like. Before Frank's parents would permit a sleepover, they would first have "to know someone well." Gert-Jan says his parents are lenient, but "my father is always judging, 'That's not a type for you'."

These different templates for adolescent sex, gender, and autonomy also affect boys' and girls' own navigation of the dilemmas of gender. The category "slut" appears much more salient in the interviews with American girls than Dutch girls. One reason may be that the cultural assumption that teenagers can and do fall in love lends credence to Dutch girls' claims to being in love, while the cultural skepticism about whether they can sustain the feelings and form the attachments that legitimate sexual activity put American girls on the defensive. Kimberley, an American, had her first sex with a boy she loves, but she knows that people around her might discount such claims, saying "You're young, you can't fall in love." By contrast, in the Netherlands, Natalie found her emotions and relationship validated: her mother was happy to hear about her first intercourse because "she knows how serious we are."

In both countries, boys confront the belief and sometimes the reality that they are interested in sex but not relationships. But there is evidence in both countries that boys are often emotionally invested. The American boys I have interviewed tend to view themselves as unique for their romantic aspirations and describe themselves, as Jesse does, as "romantic rebels." "The most important thing to me is maintaining love between me and my girlfriend," while "most guys are pretty much in it for the sex," he says. The Dutch boys I interviewed did not perceive themselves as unusual for falling in love (or for wanting to) before having sex. Sam, for instance, believes that "everyone wants [a relationship]." He explains why: "Someone you can talk to about your feelings and such, a feeling of safety, I think that everyone, the largest percentage of people wants a relationship."

culture's cost

How sexuality, love, and autonomy are perceived and negotiated in parent-child relationships and among teenagers depends on the cultural templates people have available. Normalization and dramatization each have "costs" and "benefits." On balance, however, the dramatization of adolescent sexuality makes it more difficult for parents to communicate with teenagers about sex and relationships, and more challenging for girls and boys to integrate their sexual and relational selves. The normalization of adolescent sexuality does not eradicate the tensions between parents and teenagers or the gender constructs that confine both girls and boys. But it does provide a more favorable cultural climate in which to address them.

recommended resources

Bozon, Michel, and Kontula, Osmo. 1998. "Sexual Initiation and Gender in Europe: A Cross-Cultural Analysis of Trends in the Twentieth Century." In M. Hubert, N. Bajos, and T. Sandfort (eds.), *Sexual Behaviour and HIV/AIDS in Europe: Comparisons of National Surveys*. London: University College London. Documents historical trends in sexual initiation in Europe during the last half of the 20th century.

Ketting, Evert, and Visser, Adriaan P. 1994. "Contraception in the Netherlands: The Low Abortion Rate Explained." *Patient Education and Counseling* 23:161–171. Describes various factors, including healthcare delivery and media education, which have contributed to the low teenage pregnancy rate in the Netherlands.

Lewis, Jane, and Knijn, Trudie. 2003. "Sex Education Materials in The Netherlands and in England and Wales: A Comparison of Content, Use and Teaching

Practice," *Oxford Review of Education* 29(1):113–132. Provides an analysis of the politics and content analysis of Dutch sex education as compared to programs in the U.K.

Pascoe, C.J. 2007. *Dude You're a Fag: Masculinity and Sexuality in High School.* Oakland, CA: University of California Press. An ethnographic study of a racially diverse working-class high school that shows American boys' pressures to "perform" masculinity.

Tolman, Deborah L. 2002. *Dilemmas of Desire: Teenage Girls Talk about Sexuality.* Cambridge, MA: Harvard

University Press. Illuminates how American girls grapple with the experience and articulation of their sexual desires in face of social and cultural pressures.

note

1 Note, this quote and subsequent quotes from Dutch sources are the author's translations. Names have been changed to protect anonymity.

online dating choices, constrained
fall 2015
joanna pepin

Single people have an ever-expanding array of choices for romantic partners. Arranged marriages are no longer prevalent, and norms and laws have expanded the range of acceptable partners. *Loving v. Virginia*, for example, invalidated U.S. prohibitions on interracial marriages in 1967, and this year's *Obergefell v. Hodges* decision held that states can no longer ban same-sex marriages. The Internet has further expanded the pool of potential partners (as explored by comedian Aziz Ansari and sociologist Eric Klinenberg in their new book *Modern Romance*).

> **With more tools and fewer legal restrictions on who and how to date, there's just one big holdup: our own biases still constrain our perceptions of available mates.**

With more tools and fewer legal restrictions, there's just one big holdup: our own biases still constrain our perceptions of available mates. For example, Gert Stulp and colleagues showed in 2013 that men are taller than their female mates in more couples than would be expected by chance alone. And a recent *Marriage and Family Review* article confirms that around the world, on average men in heterosexual married partnerships are a few years older than their female partners.

Preferences and biases shape our notion of how big our dating pool might be.

As it happens, interracial marriage is still relatively rare, but it's more common in lesbian and gay relationships than among straight couples. What we haven't known is whether this is due to more limited dating markets or more open racial preferences. Jennifer Lundquist and Ken-Hou Lin took on the question, examining the dating behavior of White people who identified as straight, lesbian, or gay on a major dating website. Their findings, published in *Social Forces*, show that White daters correspond most frequently with other White people. However, straight White men and White lesbians are more likely than other Whites to contact or respond to non-White potential dates. Among Whites, straight women were the least likely to contact or respond to prospective partners who were non-White. Overall, minority men, straight or gay, were the least desired partners among these White daters. The researchers conclude that higher rates of interracial cohabitation for gay men reflect constrained dating markets, whereas the prevalence of interracial lesbian coupledom demonstrates more open racial preferences.

In other words, laws, norms, and technology can expand the sea of potential partners, but social biases still shape how many "fish" we think are out there.

is hooking up bad for young women?

elizabeth a. armstrong, laura hamilton, and paula england

summer 2010

"Girls can't be guys in matters of the heart, even though they think they can," says Laura Sessions Stepp, author of *Unhooked: How Young Women Pursue Sex, Delay Love, and Lose at Both*, published in 2007. In her view, "hooking up"—casual sexual activity ranging from kissing to intercourse—places women at risk of "low self-esteem, depression, alcoholism, and eating disorders." Stepp is only one of half a dozen journalists currently engaged in the business of detailing the dangers of casual sex.

On the other side, pop culture feminists such as Jessica Valenti, author of *The Purity Myth: How America's Obsession with Virginity is Hurting Young Women* (2010), argue that the problem isn't casual sex, but a "moral panic" over casual sex. And still a third set of writers like Ariel Levy, author of *Female Chauvinist Pigs: Women and the Rise of Raunch Culture* (2005), questions whether it's empowering for young women to show up at parties dressed to imitate porn stars or to strip in "Girls Gone Wild" fashion. Levy's concern isn't necessarily moral, but rather that these young women seem less focused on their own sexual pleasure and more worried about being seen as "hot" by men.

Following on the heels of the mass media obsession, sociologists and psychologists have begun to investigate adolescent and young adult hookups more systematically. In this essay, we draw on systematic data and studies of youth sexual practices over time to counter claims that hooking up represents a sudden and alarming change in youth sexual culture. The research shows that there is some truth to popular claims that hookups

are bad for women. However, it also demonstrates that women's hookup experiences are quite varied and far from uniformly negative and that monogamous, long-term relationships are not an ideal alternative. Scholarship suggests that pop culture feminists have correctly zeroed in on sexual double standards as a key source of gender inequality in sexuality.

the rise of limited liability hedonism

Before examining the consequences of hooking up for girls and young women, we need to look more carefully at the facts. *Unhooked* author Stepp describes girls "stripping in the student center in front of dozens of boys they didn't know." She asserts that "young people have virtually abandoned dating" and that "relationships have been replaced by the casual sexual encounters known as hookups." Her sensationalist tone suggests that young people are having more sex at earlier ages in more casual contexts than their Baby Boomer parents.

This characterization is simply not true. Young people today are not having more sex at younger ages than their parents. The sexual practices of American youth changed in the 20th century, but the big change came with the Baby Boom cohort who came of age more than 40 years ago. The National Health and Social Life Survey—the gold standard of American sexual practice surveys—found that those born after 1942 were more sexually active at younger ages than those born from 1933–42. However, the trend toward greater sexual activity among young people appears to halt or reverse among the youngest cohort in the NHSLS, those born from 1963–72. Examining the National Survey of Family Growth, Lawrence B. Finer, Director of Domestic Research for the Guttmacher Institute, found that the percent of women who have had premarital sex by age 20 (65-76 percent) is roughly the same for all cohorts born after 1948. He also found that the women in the youngest cohort in this survey—those born from 1979–1984—were less likely to have premarital sex by age 20 than those born before them. The Centers for Disease Control, reporting on the results of the National Youth Risk Behavior Survey, report that rates of sexual intercourse among 9th12th graders decreased from 1991–2007, as did numbers of partners. Reports of condom use increased. So what are young people doing to cause such angst among Boomers?

The pervasiveness of *casual* sexual activity among today's youth may be at the heart of Boomers' concerns. England surveyed more than 14,000 students from 19 universities and colleges about their hookup, dating, and relationship experiences. Seventy-two percent of both men and women participating in the survey reported at least one hookup by their senior year in college. What the Boomer panic may gloss over, however, is the fact that college students don't, on average, hook up that much. By senior year, roughly 40 percent of those who ever hooked up had engaged in three or fewer hookups, 40 percent between four and nine hookups, and only 20 percent in ten or more hookups. About 80 percent of students hook up, on average, less than once per semester over the course of college.

In addition, the sexual activity in hookups is often relatively light. Only about one third engaged in intercourse in their most recent hookup. Another third had engaged in oral sex or manual stimulation of the genitals. The other third of hookups only involved kissing and non-genital touching. A full 20 percent

of survey respondents in their fourth year of college had never had vaginal intercourse. In addition, hookups between total strangers are relatively uncommon, while hooking up with the same person multiple times is common. Ongoing sexual relationships without commitment are labeled as "repeat," "regular," or "continuing" hookups, and sometimes as "friends with benefits." Often there is friendship or socializing both before and after the hookup.

Hooking up hasn't replaced committed relationships. Students often participate in both at different times during college. By their senior year, 69 percent of heterosexual students had been in a college relationship of at least six months. Hookups sometimes became committed relationships and vice versa; generally the distinction revolved around the agreed upon level of exclusivity and the willingness to refer to each other as "girlfriend/boyfriend."

And, finally, hooking up isn't radically new. As suggested above, the big change in adolescent and young adult sexual behavior occurred with the Baby Boomers. This makes sense, as the forces giving rise to casual sexual activity among the young—the availability of birth control pill, the women's and sexual liberation movements, and the decline of *in loco parentis* on college campuses—took hold in the 1960s. But changes in youth sexual culture did not stop with the major behavioral changes wrought by the Sexual Revolution.

Contemporary hookup culture among adolescents and young adults may rework aspects of the Sexual Revolution to get some of its pleasures while reducing its physical and emotional risks. Young people today—particularly young Whites from affluent families—are expected to delay the commitments of adulthood while they invest in careers. They get the message that sex is okay, as long as it doesn't jeopardize their futures; STDs and early pregnancies are to be avoided. This generates a sort of limited liability hedonism. For instance, friendship is prioritized a bit more than romance, and oral sex appeals because of its relative safety. Hookups may be the most explicit example of a calculating approach to sexual exploration. They make it possible to be sexually active while avoiding behaviors with the highest physical and emotional risks (e.g., intercourse, intense relationships). Media panic over hooking up may be at least in part a result of adult confusion about youth sexual culture—that is, not understanding that oral sex and sexual experimentation with friends are actually some young people's ways of balancing fun and risk.

Even though hooking up in college isn't the rampant hedonistic free-for-all portrayed by the media, it does involve the movement of sexual activity outside of relationships. When *Contexts* addressed youth sex in 2002, Barbara Risman and Pepper Schwartz speculated that the

> **Hooking up isn't the rampant, hedonistic free-for-all portrayed by the media.**

slowdown in youth sexual activity in the 1990s might be a result of "girls' increasing control over the conditions of sexual intercourse," marked by the restriction of sex to relationships. They expressed optimism about gender equality in sexuality on the grounds that girls are more empowered in relationship sex than casual sex. It appears now that these scholars were overly optimistic about the progress of the gender revolution in sex. Not only is casual sex common, it seems that romantic relationships themselves are riddled with gender inequality.

hookup problems, relationship pleasures

Hookups are problematic for girls and young women for several related reasons. As many observers of American youth sexual culture have found, a sexual double standard continues to be pervasive. As one woman Hamilton interviewed explained, "Guys can have sex with all the girls and it makes them more of a man, but if a girl does then all of a sudden she's a 'ho' and she's not as quality of a person." Sexual labeling among adolescents and young adults may only loosely relate to actual sexual behavior; for example, one woman complained in her interview that she was a virgin the first time she was called a "slut." The lack of clear rules about what is "slutty" and what is not contribute to women's fears of stigma.

On college campuses, this sexual double standard often finds its most vociferous expression in the Greek scene. Fraternities are often the only venues where large groups of underage students can readily access alcohol. Consequently, one of the easiest places to find hookup partners is in a male-dominated party context. As a variety of scholars have observed, fraternity men often use their control of the situation to undermine women's ability to freely consent to sex (e.g., by pushing women to drink too heavily, barring their exit from private rooms, or refusing them rides home). Women report varying degrees of sexual disrespect in the fraternity culture, and the dynamics of this scene predictably produce some amount of sexual assault.

The most commonly encountered disadvantage of hookups, though, is that sex in relationships is far better for women. England's survey revealed that women orgasm more often and report higher levels of sexual satisfaction in relationship sex than in hookup sex. This is in part because sex in relationships is more likely to include sexual activities conducive to women's orgasm. In hookups, men are much more likely to receive fellatio than women are to receive cunnilingus. In relationships, oral sex is more likely to be reciprocal. In interviews conducted by

England's research team, men report more concern with the sexual pleasure of girlfriends than hookup partners, while women seem equally invested in pleasing hookup partners and boyfriends.

The continuing salience of the sexual double standard mars women's hookup experiences. In contrast, relationships provide a context in which sex is viewed as acceptable for women, protecting them from stigma and establishing sexual reciprocity as a basic expectation. In addition, relationships offer love and companionship.

> **The most commonly encountered disadvantage of hookups is that sex in relationships is far better for women.**

relationship problems, hookup pleasures

Relationships are good for sex but, unfortunately, they have a dark side as well. Relationships are "greedy," getting in the way of other things that young women want to be doing as adolescents and young adults, and they are often characterized by gender inequality—sometimes even violence.

Talking to young people, two of us (Hamilton and Armstrong) found that committed relationships detracted from what women saw as main tasks of college. The women we interviewed complained, for example, that relationships made it difficult to meet people. As a woman who had just ended a relationship explained:

Women also complained that committed relationships competed with schoolwork. One woman remarked, "[My boyfriend] doesn't understand why I can't pick up and go see him all the time. But I have school . . . I just want to be a college kid." Another told one of us (Hamilton) that her major was not compatible with the demands of a boyfriend. She said, "I wouldn't mind having a boyfriend again, but it's a lot of work. Right now with [my major] and everything . . . I wouldn't have time even to see him." Women feared that they would be devoured by relationships and sometimes struggled to keep their self-development projects going when they did get involved.

> **I'm happy that I'm able to go out and meet new people . . . I feel like I'm doing what a college student should be doing. I don't need to be tied down to my high school boyfriend for two years when this is the time to be meeting people.**

Subjects told us that relationships were not only time-consuming, but also marked by power inequalities and abuse. Women reported that boyfriends tried to control their social lives, the time they spent with friends, and even what they wore. One woman described her boyfriend, saying, "He is a very controlling person . . . He's like, 'What are you wearing tonight?' . . . It's like a joke but serious at the same time." Women also became jealous. Coping with jealousy was painful and emotionally absorbing. One woman noted that she would "do anything to make this relationship work." She elaborated, "I was so nervous being with Dan because I knew he had cheated on his [prior] girlfriend . . . [but] I'm getting over it. When I go [to visit him] now . . . I let him go to the bar, whatever. I stayed in his apartment because there was nothing else to do." Other women changed the way they dressed, their friends, and where they went in the hope of keeping boyfriends.

When women attempted to end relationships, they often reported that men's efforts to control them escalated. In the course of interviewing 46 respondents, two of us (Hamilton and Armstrong) heard ten accounts of men using abuse to keep women in relationships. One woman spent months dealing with a boyfriend who accused her of cheating on him. When she tried to break up, he cut his wrist in her apartment. Another woman tried to end a relationship, but was forced to flee the state when her car windows were broken and her safety was threatened. And a third woman reported that her ex-boyfriend stalked her for months—even showing up at her workplace, showering her with flowers and gifts, and blocking her entry into her workplace until the police arrived. For most women, the costs of bad hookups tended to be less than costs of bad relationships. Bad hookups were isolated events, while bad relationships wreaked havoc with whole lives. Abusive relationships led to lost semesters, wrecked friendships, damaged property, aborted pregnancies, depression, and time-consuming involvement with police and courts.

The abuse that women reported to us is not unusual. Intimate partner violence among adolescents and young adults is common. In a survey of 15,000 adolescents conducted in 2007, the Centers for Disease Control found that 10 perecent of students had been "hit, slapped, or physically hurt on purpose by their boyfriend or girlfriend" in the last 12 months.

If relationships threaten academic achievement, get in the way of friendship, and can involve jealousy,

> **The costs of bad hookups tend to be less than the costs of bad relationships: bad hookups are isolated events, but bad relationships wreak havoc with whole lives.**

manipulation, stalking, and abuse, it is no wonder that young women sometimes opt for casual sex. Being open to hooking up means being able to go out and fit into the social scene, get attention from young men, and learn about sexuality. Women we interviewed gushed about parties they attended and attention they received from boys. As one noted, "Everyone was so excited. It was a big fun party." They reported turning on their "make out radar," explaining that "it's fun to know that a guy's attracted to you and is willing to kiss you." Women reported enjoying hookups, and few reported regretting their last hookup. Over half the time women participating in England's survey reported no relational interest before or after their hookup, although more women than men showed interest in a relationship both before and after hookups. The gender gap in relationship interest is slightly larger after the hookup, with 48 percent of women and 36 percent of men reporting interest in a relationship.

toward gender equality in sex

Like others, Stepp, the author of *Unhooked,* suggests that restricting sex to relationships is the way to challenge gender inequality in youth sex. Certainly, sex in relationships is better for women than hookup sex. However, research suggests two reasons why Stepp's strategy won't work: first, relationships are also plagued by inequality. Second, valorizing relationships as the ideal context for women's sexual activity reinforces the notion that women shouldn't want sex outside of relationships and stigmatizes women who do. A better approach would challenge gender inequality in both relationships and hookups. It is critical to attack the tenacious sexual double standard that leads men to disrespect their hookup partners. Ironically, this could improve relationships because women would be less likely to tolerate "greedy" or abusive relationships if they were treated better in hookups. Fostering relationships among young adults should go hand-in-hand with efforts to decrease intimate partner violence and to build egalitarian relationships that allow more space for other aspects of life—such as school, work, and friendship.

recommended resources

Bogle, Kathleen A. 2008. *Hooking Up: Sex, Dating, and Relationships on Campus.* New York: New York University Press. A provocative investigation of college hookups based on 76 interviews.

England, Paula, Shafer, Emily F., and Fogarty, Alison C. K. 2008. "Hooking Up and Forming Romantic Relationships on Today's College Campuses." In M. Kimmel and A. Aronson (eds.), *The Gendered Society Reader,* 3rd edition. Oxford: Oxford University Press. Overview of the role of gender in the college hookup scene.

Glenn, Norval, and Marquardt, Elizabeth. 2001. *Hooking Up, Hanging Out, and Hoping for Mr. Right: College Women on Mating and Dating Today.* New York: Institute for American Values. One of the first empirical investigations of college hookups.

Hamilton, Laura, and Armstrong, Elizabeth A. 2009. "Double Binds and Flawed Options: Gendered Sexuality in Early Adulthood," *Gender & Sexuality 23*:589–616. Provides methodological details of Hamilton and Armstrong's interview study and elaborates on costs and benefits of hookups and relationships for young women.

Kreager, Derek A, and Staff, Jeremy 2009. "The Sexual Double Standard and Adolescent Peer Acceptance," *Social Psychology Quarterly 72*:143–164. New empirical research confirming the continued existence of sexual double standards.

Manning, Wendy D, Giordano, Peggy C, and Longmore, Monica A. 2006. "Hooking Up: The Relationship Contexts of 'Nonrelationship' Sex," *Journal of Adolescent Research 21*:459–483. Part of a series on sexual activity among younger adolescents.

straight girls kissing

leila j. rupp and verta taylor

summer 2010

The phenomenon of presumably straight girls kissing and making out with other girls at college parties and at bars is everywhere in contemporary popular culture, from Katy Perry's hit song, "I Kissed a Girl," to a Tyra Banks online poll on attitudes toward girls who kiss girls in bars, to AskMen.com's "Top 10: Chick Kissing Scenes." Why *do* girls who aren't lesbians kiss girls?

Some think it's just another example of "girls gone wild," seeking to attract the boys who watch. Others, such as psychologist Lisa Diamond, point to women's "sexual fluidity," suggesting that the behavior could be part of how women shape their sexual identities, even using a heterosexual social scene as a way to transition to a bisexual or lesbian identity.

These speculations touch on a number of issues in the sociology of sexuality. The fact that young women on college campuses are engaging in new kinds of sexual behaviors brings home the fundamental concept of the social construction of sexuality—that whom we desire, what kinds of sexual acts we engage in, and how we identify sexually is profoundly shaped by the societies in which we live. Furthermore, boys enjoying the sight of girls making out recalls the feminist notion of the "male gaze," calling attention to the power embodied in men as viewers and women as the viewed. The sexual fluidity that is potentially embodied in women's intimate interactions in public reminds us that sexuality is gendered and that sexual desire, sexual behavior, and sexual identity do not always match. That is, men do not, at least in contemporary American culture, experience the same kind of fluidity. Although they may identify as straight *and* have sex with other men,

they certainly don't make out at parties for the pleasure of women.

The hookup culture on college campuses, as depicted in another article in this issue, facilitates casual sexual interactions (ranging from kissing and making out to oral sex and intercourse) between students who meet at parties or bars. Our campus is no exception. The University of California, Santa Barbara, has a longstanding reputation as a party school (much to the administration's relief, it's declining in those rankings). In a student population of twenty thousand, more than half of the students are female and slightly under half are students of color, primarily Chicano/Latino and Asian American. About a third are first-generation college students. Out of over two thousand female UC Santa Barbara students who responded to sociologist Paula England's online College and Social Life Survey on hooking-up practices on campus, just under one percent identified as homosexual, three percent as bisexual, and nearly two percent as "not sure."

National data on same-sex sexuality shows that far fewer people identify as lesbian or gay than are sexually attracted to the same sex or have engaged in same-sex sexual behavior. Sociologist Edward Laumann and his colleagues, in the National Health and Social Life Survey, found that less than two percent of women identified as lesbian or bisexual, but over eight percent had experienced same-sex desire or engaged in lesbian sex. The opposite is true for men, who are more likely to have had sex with a man than to report finding men attractive. Across time and cultures (and, as sociologist Jane Ward has pointed out, even in the present among White straight-identified men), sex with other men, as long as a man plays the insertive role in a sexual encounter, can bolster, rather than undermine, heterosexuality. Does the same work for women?

The reigning assumption about girls kissing girls in the party scene is that they do it to attract the attention of men. But the concept of sexual fluidity and the lack of fit among desire, behavior, and identity suggest that there may be more going on than meets the male gaze. A series of formal and informal interviews with diverse female college students at our university, conducted by undergraduates as part of a class assignment, supports the sociological scholarship on the complexity of women's sexuality.

the college party scene

What is most distinctive about UC Santa Barbara is the adjacent community of Isla Vista, a densely populated area made up of two-thirds students and one-third primarily poor and working-class Mexican American families. House parties, fraternity and sorority parties, dance parties (often with, as one woman student put it, "some sort of slutty theme to them"), and random parties open to anyone who stops by flourish on the weekends. Women students describe Isla Vista as "unrealistic to the rest of the world . . . It's a little wild," "very promiscuous, a lot of experimenting and going crazy," and "like a sovereign nation . . . a space where people feel really comfortable to let down their guards and to kind of let loose." Alcohol flows freely, drugs are available, women sport skimpy clothing, and students engage in a lot of hooking up. One sorority member described parties as featuring "a lot of, you know, sexual dance. And some people, you know, like pretty much are fucking on the dance floor even though they're really not. I feel like they just take it above and beyond." Another student thinks "women have a little bit more freedom here." But despite the unreality of life in Isla Vista, there's no reason to think life here is fundamentally different than on other large campuses.

At Isla Vista parties, the practice of presumably heterosexual women kissing and making out with other women is widespread. As one student reported, "It's just normal for most people now, friends make out with each other." The student newspaper sex columnist began her column in October 2008, "I kissed a girl and liked it," recommending "if you're a girl who hasn't quite warmed up to a little experimentation with one of your own, then I suggest you grab a gal and get to it." She posed the "burning question on every male spectator's mind . . . Is it real or is it for show?" As it turns out, students offered three different explanations of why students do this: to get attention from men, to experiment with same-sex activity, and out of same-sex desire.

> *The reigning assumption about girls kissing girls in the party scene is that they do it to attract the attention of men, but there may be more going on than meets the male gaze.*

getting attention

Girls kissing other girls can be a turn-on for men in our culture, as the girls who engage in it well know. A student told us, "It's usually for display for guys who are usually surrounding them and like cheering them on. And it seems to be done in order to like, you know, for the guys, not like for their own pleasure or desire, but to like, I don't know, entertain the guys."

Alcohol is usually involved: "It's usually brought on by, I don't know, like shots or drinking, or people kind of saying something to like cheer it on or whatever. And it's usually done in order to turn guys on or to seek male attention in some way." One student who admits to giving her friend what she calls "love pecks" and engaging in some "booby grabbing" says "I think it's mainly for attention definitely. It's usually girls that are super drunk that are trying to get attention from guys or are just really just having fun like when my roommate and I did it at our date party . . . It is alcohol and for show. Not experimentation at all." Another student, who has had her friends kiss her, insists that "they do that for attention . . . kind of like a circle forms around them . . . egging them on or taking pictures." One woman admitted that she puckered up for the attention, but when asked if it had anything to do with experimentation, added "maybe with some people. I think for me it was a little bit, yeah."

experimentation

Other women agree that experimentation is part of the story. One student who identifies as straight says "I have kissed girls on multiple occasions." One night she and a friend were "hammered, walking down the street, and we're getting really friendly and just started making out and taking pictures," which they then posted on Facebook. "And then the last time, this is a little bit more personal, but was when I actually had a threesome. Which was at a party and obviously didn't happen during the party." She mentions "bisexual tendencies" as an explanation, in addition to getting attention: "I would actually call it maybe more like experimentation." Another student, who calls herself straight but "bi-curious," says girls do it for attention, but also, "It's a good time for them, something they may not have the courage to express themselves otherwise, if they're in a room alone, it makes them more comfortable with it because other people are receiving pleasure from them." She told us about being drunk at a theme party ("Alice in Fuck-land"): "And me and 'Maria' just started going at it in the kitchen. And this dude, he whispers in my ear, 'Everyone's watching. People can see you.' But me and 'Maria' just like to kiss. I don't think it was like really a spectacle thing, like we weren't teasing anybody. We just like to make out. So we might be an exception to the rule," she giggled.

In another interview, a student described a friend as liking "boys and girls when she's drunk . . . But when she's sober she's starting to like girls." And another student who called herself "technically" bisexual explained that she hates that term because in Isla Vista "it basically means that you make out with girls at parties." Before her first relationship with a woman, she never thought about bisexuality: "The closest I ever came to thinking that was, hey, I'd probably make out with a girl if I was drinking." These stories make clear that experimentation in the heterosexual context of the hookup culture and college party scene provides a safe space for some women to explore non-heterosexual possibilities.

same-sex desire

Some women go beyond just liking to make out and admit to same-sex desire as the motivating factor. One student who defined her sexuality as liking sex with men but feeling "attracted more towards girls than guys" described her coming out process as realizing, "I really like girls and I really like kissing girls." Said another student, "I've always considered myself straight, but since I've been living here I've had several sexual experiences with women. So I guess I would consider myself, like, bisexual at this point." She at first identified as "one of those girls" who makes out at parties, but then admitted that she also had sexual experiences with women in private. At this point she shifted her identification to bisexual: "I may have fallen into that trap of like kissing a girl to impress a guy, but I can't really recollect doing that on purpose. It was more of just my

own desire to be with, like to try that with a woman." Another bisexual woman who sometimes makes out with one of her girlfriends in public thinks other women might "only do it in a public setting because they're afraid of that side of their sexuality, because they were told to be heterosexual you know . . . So if they make out, it's only for the show of it, even though they may like it they can't admit that they do."

The ability to kiss and make out with girls in public without having to declare a lesbian or bisexual identity makes it possible for women with same-sex desires to be part of the regular college party scene, and the act of making out in public has the potential to lead to more extensive sexual activity in private. One student described falling in love with her best friend in middle school, but being "too chicken shit to make the first move" because "I never know if they are queer or not." Her first sexual relationship with a bisexual woman included the woman's boyfriend as well. In this way, the fact that some women have their first same-sex sexual encounter in a threesome with a man is an extension of the safe heterosexual space for exploring same-sex desire.

heteroflexibility

Obviously, in at least some cases, more is going on here than drunken women making out for the pleasure of men. Sexual fluidity is certainly relevant; in Lisa Diamond's ten-year study of young women who originally identified as lesbian or bisexual, she found a great deal of movement in sexual desire, intimate relationships, and sexual identities. The women moved in all directions, from lesbian to bisexual and heterosexual, bisexual to lesbian and heterosexual, and, notably, from all identities to "unlabeled." From a psychological perspective, Diamond argues for the importance of both biology and culture in shaping women as sexually fluid, with a greater capacity for attractions to both female and male partners than men. Certainly the women who identify as heterosexual but into kissing other women fit her notion of sexual fluidity. Said one straight-identified student, "It's not like they're way different from anyone else. They're just making out."

Mostly, though, students didn't think that making out had any impact on one's identity as heterosexual: "And yeah, I imagine a lot of the girls that you know just casually make out with their girlfriends would consider themselves straight. I consider myself straight." Said another, "I would still think they're straight girls. Unless I saw some, like level of like emotional and like attraction there." A bisexual student, though, thought "they're definitely bi-curious at the least . . . I think that a woman who actually does it for enjoyment and like knows that she likes that and that she desires it again, I would say would be more leaning towards bisexual."

everybody but lesbians

So, although girls who kiss girls are not "different from anyone else," if they have an emotional reaction or really enjoy it or want to do it again, then they've apparently crossed the line of heterosexuality. Diamond found that lesbians in her study who had been exclusively attracted to and involved with other women were the only group that didn't report changes in their sexual identities. Sociologist Arlene Stein, in her study of lesbian feminist communities in the 1980s, also painted a picture of boundary struggles around the identity "lesbian." Women who developed relationships with men but continued to identify as lesbians were called "ex-lesbians" or "fakers" by those who considered themselves "real lesbians." And while straight college students today can make out with women and call themselves "bi-curious" without challenge to their heterosexual identity, the same kind of flexibility does not extend to lesbians. A straight, bi-curious woman explained that she didn't think "the lesbian community would accept me right off because I like guys too much, you know." And she didn't think she had "enough sexual experience with the women to be considered bisexual." Another student, who described herself as "a free flowing spirit" and has had multiple relationships with straight-identified women, rejected the label "lesbian" because "I like girls" but "guys are still totally attractive to me." She stated that "to be a lesbian meant . . . you'd have to commit yourself to it one hundred percent. Like you'd have to be in it sexually, you'd have to be in it emotionally. And I think if you were you wouldn't have that attraction for men . . . if you were a lesbian."

In contrast to "heteroflexibility," a term much in use by young women, students hold a much more rigid, if unarticulated, notion of lesbian identity. "It's just like it's okay because we're both drunk and we're friends. It's not like we identify as lesbian in any way. . . ." One woman who has kissed her roommate is sure that she can tell the difference between straight women and lesbians: "I haven't ever seen like an actual like lesbian couple enjoying them selves." Another commented, "I mean, it's one thing if you are, if you do identify as gay and that you're expressing something." A bisexual woman is less sure, at first stating that eighty percent of the making out at parties is for men, then hesitating because "that totally excludes the queer community and my own viewing of like women who absolutely love other women, and they show that openly so, I think that it could be either context." At that point she changed the percentage to fifty percent: "Cause I guess I never know if a woman is like preferably into women or if it's more of a social game." A bisexual woman described kissing her girlfriend at a party "and some guy came up and poured beer on us and said something like 'stop kissing her you bitch,'" suggesting that any sign that women are kissing for their own pleasure puts them over the line. She went on to add that "we've gotten plenty of guys staring at us though, when we kiss or whatever, [and] they think that we're doing it for them, or we want them to join or whatever. It gets pretty old."

> **Straight women can be "barsexual" or "bi-curious" or "mostly straight," but too much physical attraction or emotional investment crosses over the line of heterosexuality.**

So there is a lot of leeway for women's same-sex behavior with a straight identity. But it is different than for straight men, who experience their same-sex interactions in a more private space, away from the gaze of women. Straight women can be "bar-sexual" or "bi-curious" or "mostly straight," but too much physical attraction or emotional investment crosses over the line of heterosexuality. What this suggests is that heterosexual women's options for physical intimacy are expanding, although such activity has little salience for identity, partner choice, or political allegiances. But the line between lesbian and non-lesbian, whether bisexual or straight, remains firmly intact.

recommended resources:

Diamond, Lisa M. 2009. *Sexual Fluidity: Understanding Women's Love and Desire.* Cambridge, MA: Harvard University Press. A longitudinal study of women's shifting sexual behaviors and identities in the contemporary United States.

Hamilton, Laura. 2007. "Trading on Heterosexuality: College Women's Gender Strategies and Homophobia," *Gender & Society 21*:145–172. Looks at the sexual constructions adopted by college-aged women.

Stein, Arlene. 1997. *Sex and Sensibility: Stories of a Lesbian Generation.* Oakland, CA: University of California Press. A sociological study of American lesbian feminist communities in the 1980s.

Thompson, Elisabeth M, and Morgan, Elizabeth M. 2008. "'Mostly Straight' Young Women: Variations in Sexual Behavior and Identity Development," *Developmental Psychology* 44(1):15–21. A psychological study of U.S. college students' shifting sexual behaviors and identities.

Ward, Jane. 2008. "Dude-Sex: White Masculinities and 'Authentic' Heterosexuality Among Dudes Who Have Sex With Dudes," *Sexualities 11*: 414–434. A sociological study that complicates the concept of "men who have sex with men."

abstinence and masculinity
nicole bedera
winter 2016

For most young males, a central part of becoming a man is having sex—and a lot of it with a lot of women. But what happens to masculinity if you opt out of promiscuity?

In a recent *Gender & Society* article, Sarah Diefendorf explores how Evangelical men who refused premarital sex negotiated their masculine identities both before and after marriage. Diefendorf conducted participant observation, focus groups, and interviews with men in a program called The River, which supported bachelors in maintaining sexual abstinence. She focused on language surrounding the "beastly" and the "sacred"—referring to premarital sex and sex within marriage, respectively—and how each discourse related to participants' displays of masculinity.

When they were bachelors, the men overwhelmingly categorized their sexual desires and practices as beastly—but also inevitable. Their difficulty remaining abstinent highlighted their virility while the use of a support group provided a space to endorse a hybrid masculinity that did not express virility through promiscuity.

Surprisingly, the participants seemed to struggle most with their masculine identities after becoming sexually active. Some married men in the sample expressed frustration with their inability to control other beastly desires or have the pleasurable, sacred sex lives they had been promised by their church. In short, sexual desire became *both* beastly and sacred, so the expression of masculinity through sex became more complicated. They began to use their wives' emphasized femininity to express their masculinity in other aspects of married life, rendering sex less important to their presentations of self than when they were virgins.

35

hooking up and dating are two sides of a coin

tracy luff, kristi hoffman, and marit berntson

winter 2016

Dating, especially among college students, has been declared dead many times in the last half century. In 2014, student writer Chloe Finch lamented in *The Galleon*, "We've forgotten how to date; there are just no 'rules' for how it should work anymore." Social science research tells a much different story.

Although college students often participate in hookups, they still go out on dates and frequently form committed relationships. According to our research with more than 600 students on two college campuses, 41% had a sexual intercourse hookup in the last semester and 73% reported going on a date (not including dates with boyfriends or girlfriends). Over half of the students (56%) were or had been in a committed relationship. Other researchers document similar findings. Psychologist Jessica Siebenbruner, for instance, found that 47% of the college students in her study had a sexual intercourse hookup and 71% had dated.

Contemporary media emphasize concern about the promiscuity of college students, but sociologists Martin Monto and Anna Carey maintain that concerns about an increase in hooking up and casual sex on campus have been greatly exaggerated. Their research compared the sexual behavior and attitudes of 18- to 25-year-old adults who had completed at least one year of college during two time periods: 1988–1996 and 2002–2010. They found no significant differences between the two cohorts in the number of sex partners, frequency of sex, or the permissiveness of sexual attitudes. They did find that the young adults in the 21st century were more likely to engage in sexual behavior outside of a committed relationship, whether with a friend, casual date, or an acquaintance. Hookup culture, then, has not led to college students having more sex, but to a shift in the social conditions under which uncommitted sex takes place. Further, Monto and Carey argue that the function of dating may be changing. Students may not rely on dating to get to know a potential long-term partner, but dating has not disappeared. Today's college students seem to simply experience less pressure to maintain the pretense of a committed relationship within which to enjoy a sexual partner.

> *Hooking up privileges sexual intimacy, while dating privileges emotional intimacy.*

hookup or date

Rather than two endpoints on a continuum, dating and hooking up may be better viewed as two sides of the same coin. Whether it's a hookup or a date, our study revealed few differences in how students met their partners (see below). In addition, the majority of hookup and dating partners were not strangers. Most students described both dates and hookup partners as friends (42%) or someone

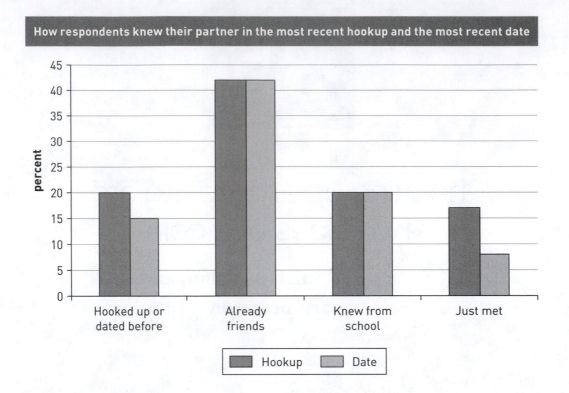

How respondents knew their partner in the most recent hookup and the most recent date

Legend: ☐ Hookup ☐ Date

they knew from school (20%). Hookups (17%) were more likely than dates (8%) to involve a partner the student had just met. Arielle Kuperberg and Joseph Padgett's review of more than 25,000 dates and hookups among students from 22 colleges similarly revealed few differences in how they met their hookup and dating partners. Still, an examination of the range of sexual behaviors that take place in hookups and dates yields some interesting parallels.

The sensationalism associated with hooking up in popular culture is due, in part, to a lack of understanding about the ambiguous term "hookup." A hookup might end in oral sex or sexual intercourse, but often it involves just kissing and making out. As a result, most social science researchers carefully distinguish between different types of hookups. In our study, 65% of students reported hookups in which they "just made out," compared to those who had sexual intercourse (45%) or oral sex (44%) hookups.

Sexual intercourse is more likely to occur during a hookup (54%) than on a date (13%), where sexual behavior is more likely to be limited to kissing (38%) or fondling (14%) (see below left). About one-third of dates involve no sexual behavior at all. The large sample examined by Kuperberg and Padgett found that hookups were twice as likely as dates to include sexual intercourse. There is less sexual activity in hookups than commonly assumed, yet they generally still involve some intimacy. Both hooking

up and dating provide opportunities for sexual experimentation, but hookups emphasize sexual activity.

Not surprisingly, sexual attraction was reported most often as the reason for both hookups and dates, but it was far more common for hookups: 63% versus 39% (see below right). Students also sought emotional intimacy in both hookups and dates. However, they were more likely to report wanting a relationship as a motive for dates (33%) than for hookups (18%). Being intoxicated was the second most common reason given for hooking up (34%), but it did not apply to dates. This reflects the important role of alcohol and drugs in hookup culture. Students were also more likely to hook up with someone more than once (30%) than to date someone with whom they had previously hooked up (11%). Thus, hooking up and dating allow students to explore and engage in different forms of intimacy; hooking up privileges sexual intimacy while dating privileges emotional intimacy.

why both?

So, two patterns coexist on college campuses. Young adults may choose to hook up at some times and date at other times. In fact, Siebenbruner's study of female undergraduates reveals that women who hooked up reported *more* dates and romantic relationships than

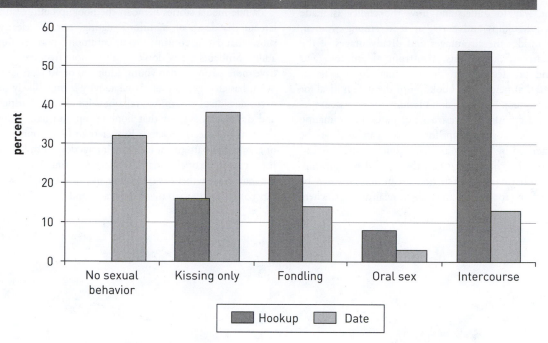

Sexual behaviors occurring on most recent hookup and most recent date

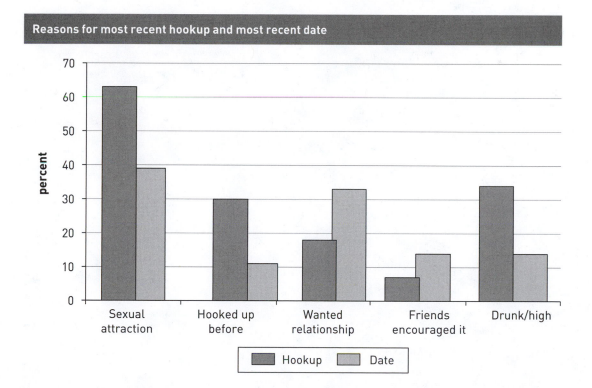

Reasons for most recent hookup and most recent date

women who had never hooked up. In our sample, this finding was stronger for males than females.

One way to understand how the choice is made between hookups and dates, at least among women, is to consider the advantages and disadvantages of the two patterns. Sociologists Armstrong, Hamilton, and England pointed out in the Summer 2010 issue of *Contexts* that neither the hookup nor the date is ideal for college women. Hookups don't require the time commitment and emotional investment of dates and romantic relationships. Relationships for women can, at times, be characterized by jealousy and emotional turmoil. A bad hookup is much easier to end than a bad relationship. On the other hand, they suggest sex in hookups may be less satisfying for women than sex in relationships, where sexual and emotional reciprocity are expected and more often received.

While media stories bemoan the hookup culture and lament the death of traditional dating, research clearly shows that dating continues to be common among young adults. Students today don't have sex more frequently or have more partners than young adults 20 or 30 years ago. What has changed is that sexual activity is more likely to occur outside of committed relationships. The similarities and differences suggest that hooking up and dating are distinct, but clearly related. Rather than being opposite or competing patterns of intimate interaction, with hooking up eclipsing or eliminating collegiate dating, it is more accurate to view them as coexisting and even complementary patterns with their own advantages and disadvantages.

sexuality has no expiration date

linda j. waite

summer 2010

To the casual observer of television, movies, or popular magazines, sexuality would seem like the province of the young. And the first major national study of sex in the U.S., done in the early 1990s, stopped at age 59, as if sexuality did too.

Of course, as any Baby Boomer can now tell you, this isn't the case. The aging of this cohort, combined with the development of medications to treat sexual problems common among older men, has brought the sexual interests of mature adults into public discourse. Several recent surveys of sexuality at older ages allow researchers to paint a detailed picture of sex at older ages—including attitudes toward sex, motivation to find a partner, sexual behavior, and sexual functioning. Although sexual activity declines and some sexual problems can arise with age, many older adults remain sexually active and satisfied into their 80s.

Two key factors set the course of sexuality over the second half of life: availability of a partner and health. Older men are more likely than older women to *have partners* and more likely to *repartner* should they lose one. Women tend to be younger than their partner and tend to live longer. So by ages 75–85, about twice as many men as women have a partner with whom they might have sex (clearly, that partner has to function at some minimal level or sex isn't in the cards). Those in poor health face much worse prospects for an active sex life; diabetes, cancer, arthritis, obesity all make sex more difficult and less rewarding. Recent studies suggest that these challenges of

poor health take a bigger toll on the sex lives of men than of women, perhaps because of men's traditionally more active role in initiating sex and in intercourse itself.

So the chances of having a partner drop with age, and the chances of having sex (given that one has a partner) also decline. Adults in their 50s and early 60s who have partners are virtually all sexually active, regardless of their health. But by their early- to mid-80s, the picture changes, and trajectories of sexual behavior diverge for men and women, with health playing a bigger role. More than half of older partnered men in good health are sexually active, compared to about a quarter of those in fair to poor health. Four in ten older partnered women in the best health are sexually active in their 80s, but among those in fair to poor health, only one in six is. Despite these caveats, many older adults remain sexually active, and, for those who do, sex is generally more than a once-in-a-long-while activity; more than half of sexually active older adults in their mid-70s to early-80s have sex several times a month and about a quarter have sex at least several times a week.

Sexual attitudes and practices show a generational divide of sorts. Those who came of age in the 1960s or later are more liberal in their attitudes, more likely to masturbate, and more likely to include oral sex in their repertoire than those who grew up in an earlier and more conservative time. Older men are more interested in sex than are older women (paralleling the gender difference at younger ages), and interest in sex declines with age for both men and women. Older unpartnered men are much more likely to have had sex with *someone* in the past year—about a quarter said they did—than are older women, who almost never report this behavior.

And about half of older men and older women report at least one problem with sex that bothers them. Women are most likely to say that they lacked interest in sex,

failed to lubricate, or had difficulty reaching climax. Men are most likely to report problems achieving or maintaining an erection, a lack of interest in sex, or climaxing too quickly. Those in poor health are more likely to have poor sexual function, some of which could result from the consequences of disease.

Careful consideration shows that sex among older adults seems like much else in life: functioning declines with age, but fairly slowly, and many people function well even at advanced ages. Further, despite our tendency to pretend otherwise, sexuality exists in a dynamic relationship, intimately connected with other aspects of good health over the entire adult life.

sexual knowledge

overview

What do we know about sexuality and how do we learn it? Sociologists explore sexuality in ways that range from ethnographies of marginal groups to formal surveys. One interesting finding is that diversity of sexual experience and expression is connected to available knowledge about sexuality—the more we study it, the more we expand the contexts through which to express it. Conversely, sociologist and sex researcher Janice Irvine contends that contemporary practices by university human subjects review boards reflect a moral panic that gets in the way of researchers who study human sexuality and limits the flow of useful knowledge. Gender scholars Verta Taylor and Leila Rupp discovered that the local drag queens in Key West, Florida, challenged much of what they thought they already knew about gender performance. In a second piece in this section, Irvine asks why it is that we're so fascinated with the sex lives of sex researchers and what we hope to learn from our voyeurism into their private lives.

As cultural scripts for the acceptability of queer and transgender people expand, how do straight people respond. James Dean explores this question in his study of straight men and how they negotiate their masculinity in a "post-closeted" social environment. Social researchers Tina Fetner and Lucia Lykke provide contrasting views on LGBT acceptance in the U.S. Are attitudes generally more favorable or are people just increasingly less comfortable expressing overt prejudice?

things to consider

- Where do most people get their knowledge of sexuality from? What general themes are reflected in these sources?
- In the U.S. it is relatively easy to find explicit sexual content in various media. Does this make the U.S. an "open society"? If so, why do people seem to experience so much shame and silence in talking about sexuality?
- Consider your own sexual education. How much of it focused on relationships and the negotiation of desire and sexuality?
- Can we simultaneously be a repressed sexual society and an open one?

37

can't ask, can't tell

how institutional review boards
keep sex in the closet

janice m. irvine

spring 2012

Sexuality research has a history of controversy that long predates the more recent institutionalization of human subjects review. In the early 20th century, for example, obscenity disputes arose over sexuality studies, such as those by British sexologist Havelock Ellis. As sexual science emerged in the United States during the 1950s, the work of researchers such as Alfred C. Kinsey also triggered volatile conflicts. In 1987, *The Chronicle of Higher Education* featured an article on sexuality researchers entitled, "Out of the Closet Now but Misunderstood." As the headline suggests, social scientists and historians described careers marked by marginalization and discrimination. Many had been humiliated by colleagues at public academic events because of their research topics. Some kept their research a secret from family members; others spoke of institutional bias in promotion and funding.

More recently, new subfields within the social sciences and humanities, as well as the emergence of interdisciplinary fields such as sexuality studies and queer studies, have expanded academic inquiry into sexuality. Sexuality researchers may be "out of the closet now"—but not necessarily their work. Institutional Review Boards (IRBs)—federally-mandated but decentralized bureaucracies for ethical regulation of research—play a significant but largely unnoticed role in the marginalization of sexuality research. In the sense that we understand "the closet" as hidden, stigmatized sexuality, IRBs keep sex in the closet. But while "the closet" refers to structures of oppression applying to sexual minorities, the IRB closet obstructs a broad production of sexual knowledge—not simply about identities and communities, but also about a range of sexual acts, desires, and attitudes.

Despite myriad critiques of IRBs among social scientists over the last decades, there is little discussion of the impact IRBs have had on specific fields of research such as sexuality studies. Sexuality has been a "special case" in the history of IRB expansion over the social sciences, falling among a few topics automatically deemed "sensitive" and therefore generally subject to enhanced scrutiny in IRB deliberations. Consequently, IRBs operate as bureaucracies of sexuality simultaneously constraining sexual knowledge while reinforcing sexual stigma.

bureaucracies of sexuality

Ethical review has proceeded unevenly in the decades since Nazi experimentation triggered concern about protection of human subjects. Biomedical abuses, such as the Tuskegee Syphilis Study (made public in 1972), led to Congressional passage of the National Research Act in 1974, and the establishment of the National Commission for the Protection of Human Subjects of Biomedical and Behavior Research. By 1979, the Commission published *The Belmont Report: Ethical Principles and Guidelines for the Protection of Human Subjects of Research.* Belmont's three so-called pillars—respect for persons, beneficence, and justice—are the principles that guide IRB reviews. Through the 1980s and mid-'90s, however, IRB oversight of the social sciences and humanities was less sweeping than it would later become.

The late '90s marked what historian Zachary Schrag calls "the crackdown" on the social sciences, when power over research moved from researchers themselves to federal ethics regulators. The shift was striking, as qualitative researchers in particular had been largely oblivious to IRBs. For example, sociologist Julia Ericksen noted that when she began research on sex surveys in the early 1990s, "There was no sense that I had to go through something called an IRB. So I just contacted people, did my interviews and kept the data thereafter." All that changed a few years later. Since 2000, the Department of Health & Human Services Office of Human Subjects Research (OHRP) has enforced *Belmont's* principles through The Criteria for Institutional Review Board Approval of Research Involving Human Subjects. As Schrag notes, *Belmont* now has "quasi-legal force." Researchers must submit even unfunded proposed work to an IRB for approval. Thousands of decentralized bureaucracies across the country now weigh the potential harm that might be inflicted by online surveys, interviews, ethnographies, oral history projects, or focus groups.

We know little about how often IRBs block social research, or how often IRBs demand that researchers substantially modify their proposals. Sociologist Jack Katz, who is documenting cases of what he calls "IRB censorship" at U.S. universities, suggests that it may be impossible, based on anecdotal cases, to determine "the iceberg of suppressed research plans from the tips." IRB horror stories circulate among sexuality researchers but, until recently, there has been no systematic evidence on the experiences of sociologists in this subfield.

To address this question, in the summer of 2011, I conducted a survey with members of the American Sociological Association Section on Sexualities. Using 80 questions, I inquired about aspects of their academic careers, such as graduate training, access to funding, promotion decisions, IRB experiences, and potential controversies. The section is fairly young, founded in 1997, with approximately 450 members at the time of my survey. With a response rate approaching 40 percent, it is the only survey of its kind to examine the career experiences of sociologists who study sexuality. The comments in this article derive from this survey and from a number of follow-up interviews.

> **IRBs exert a chilling effect on sexuality research.**

Survey responses suggest ongoing dilemmas of stigma and marginalization, with the questions about IRBs prompting some of the most impassioned responses. Of 155 respondents who reported conducting research, 119 had submitted sexuality-related projects to an Institutional Review Board. Of these, 52 sociologists—approximately 45 percent—report that they had experienced difficulty getting IRB approval. IRB practices, according to these researchers, had either slowed down or discouraged their research. Moreover, 41 percent report that other sexuality researchers at their university had also had IRB difficulties.

a chilling effect

Many responses suggest that IRBs may exert a chilling effect on sexuality research. Some researchers simply give up. As one sociologist noted, "I am less likely to do research on alternative sexualities." Twenty-six percent of faculty in my survey reported that their students had experienced trouble getting IRB approval for sexuality projects. One said, "A student who wanted to use letters written by queer prisoners had a difficult time getting approval. After the third try, he changed topics." Some professors warned students away entirely. As one noted, "I have tended to discourage students from trying to investigate topics of youth sexuality, generally telling them that it will be hard to get past IRB." In some cases students censor themselves. One professor said, "I think that what happens is that graduate students have a sense of what the IRB will and won't approve. So they don't even try to do certain kinds of research because they assume that it won't be approved."

Restrictive IRB practices may disadvantage faculty for promotion or other career moves. One junior scholar noted: "It's made [my research] actually very difficult. I'm facing tenure review right now and needing to explain, for example, why my book's not published yet. Well, I spent a year and a half getting IRB [approval].

It's definitely hindered my ability to do the actual research and then write up the results, spending so much time trying to get the approval, and then all of the torturous hurdles they put in front of me as well makes it more difficult." Another said, "By and large, the IRB is the most difficult process and institution I encounter in my sexuality research. The word "sex" sets off a set of red flags that can double or triple the amount of red tape I have to go through to get approval for my research." IRBs can shape a field of knowledge and discourage researchers, simply through following their bureaucratic procedures.

sex & sensitivity

Cultural anxieties about sex may disadvantage research projects that pertain to sexuality. IRB history reveals early fears about the danger that sexuality allegedly posed in research. For example, James Shannon, director of the National Institutes for Health in the 1960s, told an interviewer in 1971, "It's not the scientist who puts a needle in the bloodstream who causes the trouble. It's the behavioral scientist who probes into the sex life of an insecure person who really raises hell." Shannon was probably referring to the research scandal after the publication of sociologist Laud Humphreys's 1970 book about sex between men in public places, *Tearoom Trade*. The book was referenced regularly in deliberations by the National Commission during 1977–78 as they began developing their formal recommendations for the protection of human subjects. Zachary Schrag told me, "It became a kind of shorthand for the perils of interview research, rather than something that was investigated in any depth, the way that the Commission did, say, go out to prisons to talk with prisoners about their participation in medical experimentation."

Humphreys was never invited to a Commission meeting to discuss his research methods, nor did the Commissioners specify which of his methods they considered unethical. Although other social researchers at that time had used deception, for example posing as patients at hospitals or attending Alcoholics Anonymous meetings, no studies other than *Tearoom Trade* were discussed by the Commission. Of course, none of these studies had generated the controversy that Tearoom Trade did, a development likely not unrelated to his research topic. As sociologist Earl Babbie notes, "Only adding the sacrifice of Christian babies could have made this more inflammatory for the great majority of Americans in 1970."

In later regulatory deliberations, sexuality was typically clustered with "deviance": criminal behavior, substance use, and mental illness. In the late seventies, as health officials debated the level of risk posed by surveys and observation, a federal official proposed that all survey research be excluded from regulation if it did "not deal with sensitive topics, such as sexual behavior, drug or alcohol abuse, illegal conduct, or family planning." Regulations in 1981 specified that social research be exempted from IRB review unless it "deals with sensitive aspects of the subject's own behavior, such as illegal conduct, drug use, sexual behavior, or use of alcohol." So while earlier regulators were willing to exempt most social science research, sexuality fell outside these boundaries. My survey responses suggest that many IRBs still assume that sexuality research is "sensitive."

Additionally, IRBs may treat the researchers themselves as suspect because of their interest in sexuality. Sociologist Laura Stark found that one key aspect of IRB decision-making was the members' assessment of the researcher. They read proposals "like tea leaves for signs of good character." This strategy, unfortunately, disadvantages sexuality researchers, who have historically been vulnerable to mischaracterizations such as "pervert," "pedophile," and "sex-crazed." Many respondents in my survey reported such stigmatizing experiences. One said, "No one at my university will even talk about the work. They seem to think it's shameful." Another said, "I've been called 'obsessed with sex' in a derogatory and judgmental manner." As Stark notes, group process in IRB meetings can elicit both the strengths as well as "the most unsavory biases" of individual members. It would not be surprising, given broader cultural suspicion about sex, if some board members gazed with mistrust upon sexuality researchers.

risk and vulnerability

Two ambiguous but powerful concepts routinely trouble contemporary IRB deliberations on sexuality research: risk and vulnerability. Both connote danger. Regulations require that "risks to subjects are minimized." "Risk," however, is not defined beyond "harm or discomfort." Likewise, the term "vulnerable populations" is defined only through examples: "The IRB must be particularly attentive to the special problems that may arise when research involves vulnerable populations, such as children, pregnant women, prisoners, mentally disabled persons, or economically or educationally disadvantaged persons." Such safeguards, which make sense for biomedicine, are easily misapplied in social science research, where IRB members may be influenced by cultural anxieties or personal bias when interpreting vague terms like "risk."

Belmont's "respect for persons" principle has two prongs: individuals should be treated as autonomous agents; and individuals of diminished autonomy should be protected. Many of the decisions reported by respondents to my survey equate vulnerability to social discrimination with diminished autonomy. Under the guise of protection, IRBs exclude sexual minorities from research and deny them a voice which, as my respondents note, actually reinforces hierarchies: "The process reproduces inequality, for example: it's not okay to ask someone about their sexuality if they are presumed to be LGBTQ, but it is okay if they are presumed to identify as heterosexual." Also while many IRBs automatically view sexuality research as risky, they differ in where they locate it.

Often, it is the sexual subjects themselves whom IRBs consider too vulnerable to speak. Some of these cases involve children or adolescents, an explicitly protected category in IRB regulations. For this reason, sexuality researchers tend to avoid such projects ("In general, my students are leery of studying sexuality because of perceived problems with IRB, especially studying child and youth sexuality"). In an alarming twist, however, my respondents reported that IRBs routinely blocked research on adult sexual minorities, particularly LGBTQ communities, because of their alleged vulnerability. For instance, one respondent noted, "Demographic surveys could not include any identifying information. I was told that because the information I was collecting was "sensitive" (life histories of Black gay men), this would prevent the unanticipated "outing" of participants. Somehow the sexual identity of my participants was construed as clandestine and shameful."

Another respondent reports, "They made me change the reporting of names to be completely anonymous even though almost all of my subjects WANTED to be identified in the study—it was a Pride organization whose entire goal was about being out and proud!!" My own student, Shawn, became the only researcher in our department to have his proposal rejected by the university IRB. His proposed study was to explore the impact of the military policy, Don't Ask, Don't Tell (DADT) on the day-to-day lives of gay servicemen. The IRB wrote that because DADT prohibits military personnel from disclosing their homosexuality, "the Committee considered the risks to subjects too great and could not grant approval of the study." Denied sexual citizenship by federal military policy and thereby made "vulnerable," lesbian and gay soldiers were then denied opportunity by the IRB to exercise political agency and speak out, even anonymously.

Sometimes IRBs view projects as too risky because they consider the researcher to be vulnerable. In these cases, the research subjects are deemed dangerous, typically because of non-normative identities or behaviors.

For example, sociologist Elisabeth Scheff of Georgia State University proposed a study of people who identify as kinky. IRB approval "took just a hideously long time. They said that I couldn't go to respondents' homes to interview them. That it wasn't safe. These people, who knew what they would do, if they were going to engage in kinky sex, maybe they would kidnap and torture me. And I was like, 'it doesn't really work that way.' I had to agree to meet people in my office, a public library, cafés." She found that the prohibition to go to her respondents' homes interfered with her ability to recruit subjects and conduct private interviews. In some cases when IRBs see the sexual subject as the source of risk, their decisions seem designed to protect the university: "My student was doing interviews with sex workers. The IRB expressed concern that this population was dangerous. They seemed scared that putting the university name on the flier would invite sex workers to campus."

> **IRBs turn us all into "outlaws" and "low-level cheaters."**

a dangerous method?

Critics have observed IRB "mission creep," as a new industry of IRB professionals, often having little or no research experience themselves, review proposals. One outcome has been requirements for design modifications. For example, many survey respondents reported that IRBs required them to incorporate therapeutic provisions in the event that participants became overwrought while talking about sexuality. As one professor notes, "My student was told that GLBTQ people are mentally vulnerable and that he would need to provide counseling if one of them caved in sharing his or her coming out story." Another reports, "This was about fear [by the IRB] that teenagers would be upset in a focus group interview, and requiring a counselor be 'on hand' in case they were. The school chose not to participate under this condition."

IRBs may also require researchers to change their theoretical framework or methodological strategies. My respondents reported demands that certain questions be expunged from surveys and interview schedules, or protocol requirements that impeded the project. Reports such as the following were typical, "The IRB would not allow me to conduct traditional snowball sampling of women who are consultants for at-home sex toy parties, despite the fact that my participants run successful businesses selling sex toys/sexual aids and they often advertise their businesses in public places." Or, "They objected to asking questions about sex life. Basically the IRB wanted nothing to do with an ethnographic investigation of gender and sexuality among high school students. [My proposal was held] to a higher standard, initially arguing that I would need to get permission from every parent in the high school to conduct an ethnography, not just the principal's permission (which was suitable for all the other projects, apparently)."

IRB reviews may even object to the commonly used language. One respondent reports, "One of the significant changes I had to make to my IRB application was removing the word 'queer' from my title and all recruiting materials. The IRB felt that it would be potentially offensive. This seriously hinders my ability to recruit queer-identified women, many of whom specifically don't identify as lesbians." In the end, these IRB practices may turn sexuality researchers into "outlaws" and "low-level cheaters," as they bargain, omit information, and, finally, ignore impossible demands.

Another pernicious IRB requirement is that researchers must destroy their data. This practice prevents longitudinal research, historical comparisons, and the vital accumulation of knowledge. My respondents report requirements to either destroy or never collect identifying information on their interviewees, under the guise of protecting confidentiality. Scheff, for example, submitted a proposal on polyamory as a graduate student: "They were very nervous about me studying adult polyamorists." The IRB approved her study as long as she instructed her respondents to sign consent forms using pseudonyms ("Mary," for example) and did not collect identifying names with pseudonyms. Later Scheff found that longitudinal follow-up was impossible. "Naively, I thought, 'Oh well, I'll just remember.' Well, fifteen years later, I can't remember who 'Mary' was." The IRB made her destroy her interview tapes. She has the transcripts but "that doesn't help me find people for longitudinal research. Really, if you're going to resample the original sample, you need to know who the initial sample was." Because of these IRB requirements, Scheff could not locate members of her original sample.

Regarding her research on breast cancer, Julia Ericksen notes that her IRB was concerned that "it was about breasts and about sex." They required that she destroy all of her data—tapes and transcripts of 98 interviews. Ericksen said, "I had marvelous data in them. Even though people will again interview women who had breast cancer, they won't interview women at that particular moment in time." IRB requirements for data destruction not only make longitudinal work impossible, but prevent archiving interviews for future scholars. "It would have been very interesting for somebody 50 years from now, to go back and say, hypothetically, 'Now we know how to cure breast cancer, and we have this historical material from people from when they didn't know.'"

Cumulatively, these findings suggest that boards may apply tropes of danger and risk to projects involving sexuality. But is talking about sex to a researcher harmful, and if so, how harmful? IRB regulations allow expedited or exempt review for research estimated as "minimal risk," defined as not exceeding harm normally encountered in daily life. Anecdotal evidence, dating back to Kinsey's respondents, suggests that many interviewees may even enjoy participating in sexuality research. As Julia Ericksen noted, "IRB members assume people don't want to talk about these things and that was not my experience." Not surprisingly, we have little empirical data. In 1977, two years before *Belmont's* publication, psychologist Paul Abramson conducted an impact experiment on 80 undergraduates. His procedure—designed to replicate protocols of that era—involved deception, soft pornography in a waiting room, and tests to measure sexual orientation. He found that subjects enjoyed the research and reported no negative aftereffects. More recently, health researcher Brian Mustanski found that 90 percent of adolescent participants in an LGBT health study reported that they were "very comfortable" or "comfortable" answering questions about sexuality, and he urged researchers not to let IRBs discourage them from sexuality research with adolescents. Ironically, IRBs might well block further research of this type that could inform their deliberations.

Ironies abound in IRB regulation of sexuality research. IRBs keep sex in the closet while themselves operating in what Katz calls a "miasma of discretion," with virtually no public oversight or transparency to the researchers they regulate. IRBs that assume sexuality is "sensitive" prohibit the very research that might demonstrate that, for many, it is not. IRBs that presume sexuality is "risky," prohibit the production of sexual knowledge and silence the voices of diverse sexualities—knowledge which might itself challenge cultural fears about sex. IRB practices that disadvantage sexuality research have the effect of wresting sex out of politics and history and denying the possibility of social change. Timeless and taboo, sex remains outside of what is knowable.

recommended resources

Childress, James, Meslin, Eric, and Shapiro, Harold (eds). 2005. *Belmont Revisited: Ethical Principles for Research with Human Subjects*. Washington, DC:

Georgetown University Press. Examines the findings of the original Belmont Report, with insider perspectives as well as critiques.

Schrag, Zachary. 2010. *Ethical Imperialism: Institutional Review Boards and the Social Sciences, 1965–2009.* Baltimore, MD: Johns Hopkins Press. Documents the emergence and expansion of federal regulation over social science and humanities research.

Stark, Laura. 2012. *Behind Closed Doors: IRBs and the Making of Ethical Research.* Chicago, IL: University of Chicago Press. Draws on firsthand observation and historical material to explain how IRBs make decisions.

limits to same-sex acceptance
lucia lykke
spring 2015

In President Obama's 2015 State of the Union address, he heralded progress for same-sex couples as a "story of freedom," pointing out that seven in ten Americans live today in a state where gay marriage is legal. But do legal and institutional changes match up with this greater social acceptance?

In the *American Sociological Review*, Long Doan, Annalise Loehr, and Lisa Miller investigated two facets of attitudes toward gays and lesbians: 1) formal rights, operationalized as support for partnership benefits (e.g., family leave and insurance benefits), and 2) informal privileges, operationalized as acceptability of the couple's public displays of affection (e.g., kissing and holding hands in public). The authors also examined support for the couples' right to be legally married. The researchers used an experimental vignette design to capture attitudes about three types of couples: cohabiting (unmarried) gay, lesbian, and heterosexual couples.

The researchers found that heterosexual respondents did not favor heterosexual couples when it came to formal rights, but they were less likely to approve of informal privileges (public displays of affection) for homosexual couples. This pattern applied for gay/lesbian respondents, who were also less approving of same-sex public affection than heterosexual PDA—possibly evidence of internalized stigma. Finally, the authors found that hetero- versus homosexual respondents view marriage differently: heterosexuals are more likely to view marriage as an informal privilege, homosexuals are more likely to view marriage as a formal right.

Although the U.S. has made quick and major strides when it comes to the legal rights of gays and lesbians, social acceptance is not complete. Prejudice persists in subtle, multidimensional ways.

38

learning from drag queens

verta taylor and leila j. rupp

fall 2006

drag queens can teach us a lot about sexual desire—especially our own

In American society, people tend to think of males and females and heterosexuals and homosexuals as distinct and opposite categories. Drag performances challenge the biological basis of gender and the fixed nature of sexual identity. As a place where for an hour or two gay is normal and straight is other, drag shows use entertainment to educate straight people about gay, lesbian, bisexual, and transgendered lives.

 They announce from the start that they are gay men, they talk in men's voices, they make jokes about their large clitorises and "manginas" and complain that they are having "testical difficulties" when the music does not work.

Milia, one of the drag queens who performed at the 801 Cabaret, the Key West club we studied for our book *Drag Queens at the 801 Cabaret*, once proclaimed, with both exuberance and self-mockery, "We're going to be in class-rooms all around the world! . . . No more George Washington, no more Albert Einstein, you'll be learning from us!" All the drag queens in the troupe laughed, but in fact, as we came to realize, they do teach their audience members complex lessons about the porous boundaries of gender and sexuality. Drag shows may be entertaining, and diverse people may flock to

them to have a good time, but that does not belie the impact that a night of fun can have. The drag queens are, we think, more than entertainers. As Sushi, the house queen, insisted in a newspaper interview, "We're not just lip-synching up here, we're changing lives by showing people what we're all about." In the process of showing people what they are all about, they bring together diverse individuals, illustrating the official Key West philosophy that we are "One Human Family." How exactly do they do that? And do people take away the lessons they teach?

These were some of the questions we explored by studying the 801 Girls, a troupe of gay men who perform as drag queens every night of the year for mixed crowds of tourists and local residents, women and men, heterosexual, gay, lesbian, bisexual, and transgender people. The performers are economically marginal men who make barely enough to support themselves in a town where property is expensive and affordable housing is in short supply, as Barbara Ehrenreich conveyed so vividly in her depiction of Key West in *Nickel and Dimed: On (Not) Getting By in America*. We interviewed in all sorts of contexts and spent time with eight drag queens to find out why they do what they do and what their performances and interactions with audience members mean to them. We spent night after night at the shows, taping their banter and the songs they lip-synch and talking to audience members. And we recruited diverse people to come back the next day and talk to us about the shows in a focus-group setting. That is how we learned that there is more to drag shows than meets the eye.

drag shows

Drag shows have a long history as central institutions in gay communities and as places where, at least in tourist towns, straight people come in contact with gay life. From the drag balls in cities such as New York and Chicago in the 1920s to the famous Finocchio's in San Francisco in the 1940s and the popularity of RuPaul and Lady Chablis in the 1990s, men dressed in women's clothing have served as a visible segment of the gay community and have also enthralled straight audiences. The 801 Girls are no exception. On a one-by-four-mile island closer to Cuba than to Miami, populated by diverse communities—Cuban, Bahamian, gay and lesbian, hippie, and increasingly Central American and Eastern European—drag queens are central to the mix. They are everywhere: on stage, on the streets, at benefits. As the local paper put it, "You know you're from Key West when . . . your Mary Kay rep is a guy in drag."

The shows at the 801 Cabaret are an institution in Key West, described by visitors as "the best show in town." Every night at quarter after ten, four or five of the girls take to the sidewalk outside the bar, hand out flyers for the show, and banter with passersby. That is how they recruit an audience. Some tourists avert their eyes or cross the street, but most are intrigued, stop to chat, and many decide to come to the show. Upstairs over a gay bar, the cabaret has small tables up front where unsuspecting tourists serve as props for the girls, a bar in the center, and mostly standing-room-only space around the bar. Gay men congregate and cruise at the back, behind the bar.

A typical show consists of 15 to 20 numbers, some performed individually and some in groups. There is a lot of interaction with the audience, which sets the show apart from similar ones performed at gay bars across the country. But in terms of the repertoire of songs, the comedy, and the dialogue, what happens at the 801 is typical of a style of drag that emerged in conjunction with the gay and lesbian movement, a style of drag that goes beyond female impersonation.

For these drag queens, although they dress in women's clothing and can be as beautiful as biological women, there is no pretending. They announce from the start that they are gay men, they talk in men's voices, they make jokes about their large clitorises and "manginas" and complain that they are having "testical difficulties" when the music does not work. Some do not even shave their legs or underarms or tuck their genitals. Inga, a statuesque blond from Sweden, would be introduced as "Inga with a pinga," and Milla, often mistaken for African American, sometimes appeared with a dildo gripped in her crotch, calling attention to the real item

hidden away. Sushi occasionally pulls down her dress and bra to reveal her male chest, provoking the same kind of wild audience response a real female stripper might, even though the sight of male nipples is nothing new in a tropical town where men do not need to wear shirts walking down the street. Sushi also performs "Crazy World" from *Victor/Victoria,* a song about a world "full of crazy contradictions." Behind a sheer white curtain, she strips down to nothing but keeps her genitals tucked between her legs as she backs off stage, revealing what transgender activists would call a "gender-queer" body.

For the final number of the weekend shows, R.V. Beaumont, who perfected drag while working at Disney World and learned to do Bette Midler numbers from watching Bette Midler impersonators, used to change out of drag on stage to the Charles Aznevour ballad, "What Makes a Man a Man?," transforming himself from woman to man. And a regular feature of the Saturday night "Girlie Show" is Kylie, Sushi's best friend from high school, who does a mean California valley girl, stripping entirely to "Queen of the Night," leaving the audience with the contrast between her blond wig, makeup, high heels, and well-hung body. These are the ways they educate their audiences about the performativity of gender and the slip-periness of sexual desire.

> *Verta Taylor and Leila J. Rupp* coauthored **Drag Queens at the 801 Cabaret.**

"troubling" gender

The drag queens at the 801, at least some of them, have slipped back and forth between genders. Milla, who grew up in a working-class family in St. Petersburg, Florida, with an alcoholic and abusive father, "decided that I wanted to be a woman." She (the drag queens tend to use their drag names and female pronouns, although they also switch back and forth with some ease) got hormones from a counselor she was seeing for her adolescent drug problems by telling him that she would get them anyway from the drag queens on the street. She grew breasts and went out dressed as a woman and had "the men fall over, all over me, and with no clue, no clue." She loved it and seriously considered sex-reassignment surgery. But then "I started to love myself. I pulled away from that whole effeminate side . . . and I became a man." Milla continues to attract men and women of all sexual desires and pronounces herself "omnisexual."

Gugi, born to a Puerto Rican family in Chicago, also passed for a woman for a time. "What I've always wanted was to be a woman," Gugi said, although she added, "I don't know if it is because I wanted to be a woman or because I was attracted to men that I preferred to be a woman." She also took hormones for a time and grew breasts, but she stopped because "it wasn't the right time. . . . I did it to get away from my dad's death" and a painful breakup with a lover.

The one who is in charge of the shows and makes everything happen is Sushi, who never looks like a man even out of drag. Sushi, whose Japanese mother married an American G.I., describes herself as "some place in between" a woman and a man. She began to dress in drag in high school and for a time was a street prostitute in Los Angeles. At first, she thought that wanting to wear women's clothing meant that she wanted to be a woman, but then she came to realize that it just meant that she was a drag queen. "I know I'm a drag queen; I finally realized that I'm a gay man who puts on women's clothing and looks good." Yet she still worries that she is really a closeted transgendered person. One night we asked her the difference between being a drag queen and being transgendered and she replied, "A drag queen is someone like Kylie who has never ever thought about cutting her dick off."

What it means about the social basis of gender that men can look like beautiful women is not lost on audience members. A local straight woman described thinking of them as women during the show. A straight male tourist agreed, saying of Milla, "She was a woman." His wife agreed: "Uh-huh, she was a woman. It never even entered my mind. She was a beautiful woman." A young straight woman, at her first drag show, explained that she thought of them as both. "Back and forth, I think. Yeah, I was confused and went back about twelve times." A gay man, as if echoing what at least some of the girls might say about themselves, said, "I don't think of them as really any of it. feel like they're their own thing. I feel like a drag queen is something completely different. . . . It's way more than being a woman and it's definitely not being a man."

As that last comment suggests, there is more going on here than just mimicking traditional female beauty. Even the girls who are the most beautiful in drag—Sushi, Milla, Inga, and Gugi—do not really look like women, because they are too tall or have muscled arms or men's waists and buttocks. They are beautiful as drag queens. And they perform alongside other girls who are old or overweight or do not shave their chests and who perform numbers that criticize traditional feminine ideals of beauty. Scabola Feces, whose very name belies any hint of impersonating beautiful women, performs "Wedding Bell Blues" in a ripped-up wedding dress, Coke-bottle glasses, and a mouthful of fake rotten buck teeth, and

R.V. appears in hair curlers as a hooker or madam in such songs as "The Oldest Profession" and "When You're Good to Mama."

Their performances force audience members to think differently about what it means to be a man, what it means to be a woman. A local gay man described "older married couples" watching R.V. perform "What Makes a Man a Man?" "with their jaws hitting the floor. Especially when the eyelashes come off and the wig and the makeup disappears like that. . . . And they're like, I think they're still shocked when they leave that way like, 'Oh my god, I don't believe it.' They want to believe that they're women and it's hard for them to accept that they're not." This is what feminist scholars mean when they talk of "troubling" gender, causing people to think outside the binary of male/female. The 801 girls are very good teachers.

arousing new sexual desires

The drag queens also have an impact by arousing sexual desires in audience members not congruent with their sexual identities. A central part of the show involves bringing audience members on stage to represent different sexual identity categories. The drag queens call for a straight man, a gay man, a straight woman, and a lesbian, sometimes a bisexual or transsexual. While this seems to affirm the boundaries of sexual desire, the intent of the drag queens is quite the opposite. First of all, they allow a great deal of latitude in who represents what categories, and audience members are creative, so that gay men might call out that they are lesbians and straight women might play lesbian for a night. And then, once on stage, during the time that we studied the shows, the girls arranged the couples in positions simulating sex acts, the two women as the drag queens say "bumping pussy" and the gay man on his back with the straight man crouched over his pelvis Each participant got a shot of liquor poured into his or her mouth with a lot of teasing about fellatio.

Usually the people on stage really get into the act. One night the straight woman seemed eager to have the lesbian touch her and said she was "willing to try pussy-licking." Another time one of our research assistants volunteered as the lesbian, and a woman there with her husband came up to her and said, "I'm totally straight, but that just turned me on" and kissed her on the mouth. A young straight woman described feeling sorry for a young straight man brought up on stage. "I thought for him it had to be confusing because the drag queen that was coming on to him was, to me, the prettiest, and I kept thinking, 'God, that's a guy, that's a guy' . . . And he's probably thinking, 'God, she's hot.' Forgetting that she's a he. And I think that when she got on top of him, he was probably embarrassed because he was turned on." Sometimes audience members take the initiative. One night a very thin young woman in skimpy clothes came onstage to dance with Desiray, a new member of the troupe who became a drag queen because he fell in love with the show as a tourist. The woman stripped down to a thong and eventually grabbed Desiray to mime having anal sex with her.

For the drag queens, a central part of the show is the arousal of straight men. They love to move through the crowd and touch and fondle them. One night a straight couple got in a fight because the man got an erection when Sushi grabbed his penis. A straight woman tourist, on the other hand, loved when the girls fondled her husband. "It's like here's this man touching my husband, it's like really cool. And he's standing there letting him." She found this the "sexiest" part of the show, "there was something crackling the most . . . The line was crossed the most at that moment. . . . And I liked it." Her husband described his own response: "I'm sitting there and there's a little bit of me saying, 'This is sexually exciting' and there's another part of me saying, 'Wait a minute, don't do this. You're not supposed to be sexually excited, this is a man." At one show, a very macho young man there with his girlfriend took one look at Sushi and confided in us, "I could do her."

And it is not just straight men who experience sexual desires outside their identities. A lesbian described feeling very attracted to Milla: "She was so sexy," and a straight woman agreed, commenting that "I was very drawn to her sexually. I felt like kissing her. And I'm not gay at all." Yet she described being attracted because Milla "was a woman. She was a beautiful woman." Another straight woman "started falling in love with" Milla and announced, "I want to make love with her." When Sushi and Milla, or Sushi and Gugi, perform the lesbian duet "Take Me or Leave Me" from *Rent,* it has a powerful erotic impact on all sorts of audience members. More than once, during the shows, straight women started kissing their women friends. One night two Mormon women on vacation without their husbands started talking with us. By the end of the show, one confided that, if she were going to be with a woman, she would choose her friend.

As a result of these kinds of interactions and responses, many people at the shows conclude that the labels of "gay" and "straight," like "man" and "woman," just do not fit. For one gay man, "You leave them at the door." Said another, the drag queens are "challenging the whole idea of gender and so forth and they're breaking that down." A straight male tourist put it this way: "I think that one of the beauties of attending a show like this is

that you do realize that you . . . shouldn't walk out and say, 'I only like men,' and you shouldn't say 'I only like women,' and it all kind of blends together a lot more so than maybe what we want to live in our normal daily lives." Because the drag shows have the potential to arouse powerful desires that people perceive as contrary to their sexual identities, they have a real impact on people's thinking about the boundaries of heterosexuality.

> **Because the drag shows have the potential to arouse powerful desires that people perceive as contrary to their sexual identities, they have a real impact on people's thinking about the boundaries of heterosexuality.**

drag queens creating change

And this is just what the drag queens intend, as Milla's and Sushi's opening comments suggest. Kylie announces, "I intend to challenge people." Sushi explains that "I'm not just doing a number. . . . I'm trying to make more of an experience, a learning thing. . . . And I have a platform now to teach the world. . . . Even less than five minutes of talking to somebody, just that little moment I share with somebody from New Zealand or Africa or your college professor or whoever, they go back to their hometown. They remember that five-minute conversation, they realize, 'I'm not gonna call this person a fag,' you know what I mean?" Says Mi Ma, "We are attractive to everybody. We have taken gender and thrown it out of the way, and we've crossed a bridge here. And when we are all up there, there is no gay/straight or anything."

One of the remarkable things about the drag shows is the way they bring people together across all kinds of boundaries, not just differences in gender and sexual identities. Inga described the audiences as ranging "from the worst faggot to the butchiest lesbian to the happily married couple with the kids, the honeymoon people, the people who hate gays but maybe thought it was something interesting." A gay male tourist thought the shows had a "really big mass appeal to a cross section of everyone," and in fact we have met Mormons, brides out on the town the night before their weddings, transsexuals, grandmothers and grandfathers, female strippers, bikers, and everyone in between. Although the shows express and affirm pride in gay or lesbian or bisexual or transgender identities, they also emphasize what we all have in common.

Milla, putting a negative spin on it, confessed once, "What I love the most is that all these people come to our shows—professors, doctors, lawyers, rich people—and they're as fucked up as we are." Margo, a sixty-something New Yorker who also wrote a column for the local gay newspaper, introduced the classic gay anthem "I Am What Am" in a more positive way: "The next song I'm going to do for you will explain to everyone who, what, and why we are. We are not taxi drivers or hotel clerks or refrigerator repair people. We are drag queens and we are proud of what we do. Whether you are gay or straight, lesbian, bisexual, trisexual, transgender, asexual, or whatever in between, be proud of who you are." Sushi, too, preaches a message of pride and love. One night she raised her glass to toast to gay love and then corrected herself, "Oh no, here's to love. To love, baby, all across the world." Another time, more vulgarly, she introduced her best friend Kylie and announced, "This is the person that . . . told me that was special and that every single one of you is special no matter if you suck a cock or lick a pussy." Using words that typically describe same-sex sex acts to divide people into new categories, the drag queens bring together gay men and straight women, lesbians and straight men.

The audience takes in the lessons. A gay New Yorker put it this way, "The message really comes across that it doesn't matter who you are." Another gay man commented that, at the 801, "Everybody is equally fabulous." A local straight woman realtor who had seen the shows many times commented to us, "They bring a gay guy up, then a straight woman, and a straight man, and a lesbian. By the end, you just think, 'What's the difference?'" Summing up the hopes and dreams of the drag queens, a young gay man with theatrical ambitions explained that the show "signifies for me . . . that we have these differences but here we are all together within this small space Communing, interacting, being entertained, having a good time and everything is going well. . . . and I think the idea being to make some sort of, like, Utopia or this is the way it could be. Once we all leave this bar, if we can all see four different people that are different and commune together, or at least respect each other, then when we leave this bar, wouldn't the world be a little bit better place?"

The drag queens do indeed work to make the world a better place. As one of the few ways that straight people encounter gay culture—where, in fact, straight people live for an hour or two in an environment where gay people are the majority—drag shows, especially in a tourist town like Key West, have the potential to bring people together and to create new gender and sexual possibilities. Precisely because drag shows are entertaining, they attract people who might never otherwise be exposed to gay politics. As one female audience member put it, they "take something difficult and make it light." Because the

shows arouse visceral emotions, even sexual desires that fall outside people's usual sexual identities, they have the potential to make a real impact. Through a complex process of separating people into gender and sexual identity categories, then blurring and playing with those boundaries, and then bringing people all together again, the drag queens at the 801 succeed, as the comments of audience members attest, in "freeing people's minds," "removing their blinders," "opening their minds," sometimes even "changing their lives." The diverse individuals who flock to the 801 come away with an experience that makes it a little less possible to think in a simple way about gender and sexuality or to ignore the experiences of gay, lesbian, bisexual, and transgendered people in American society.

recommended resources

Gagné, Patricia, and Tewskbury, Richard (eds). 2002. *Gendered Sexualities: Advances in Gender Research*, Volume 6. JAI. A collection of articles that explore the intersection of gender and sexuality.

Newton, Esther. 1972. *Mother Camp: Female Impersonators in America.* Chicago, IL: University of Chicago Press. The classic account of drag queens in the late 1960s, just before the emergence of the gay liberation movement.

Rupp, Leila J, and Taylor, Verta. 2003. *Drag Queens at the 801 Cabaret.* Chicago, IL: University of Chicago Press. A full analysis of the drag queens, their shows, and their impact on audiences.

Schacht, Steven P, and Underwood, Lisa (eds.). 2004. *The Drag Queen Anthology.* New York: Harrington Park Press. An interdisciplinary collection of articles about drag queens in different parts of the world.

photo by Jim Smith

Verta Taylor and Leila Taylor (seated, right) with the queens of the 801 Cabaret.

the sex lives of sex researchers

janice m. irvine

fall 2014

With the recent Showtime series *Masters of Sex*, sexuality research assumed its 15 minutes in the spotlight. The docudrama about sexologists William Masters and Virginia Johnson and their mid-twentieth century sexuality laboratory normalizes sex research while relying on its exoticism for the show's buzz. It delighted reviewers, one of whom enthused, "*Masters of Sex* is a contemporary show about retro attitudes that we can look back on now from the safety of more enlightened times."

In recent years, we have seen the emergence of a new genre: life stories about sex researchers. Recent biographies feature Alfred Kinsey, Michel Foucault, Richard von Krafft-Ebing, Magnus Hirschfeld, and Jeannette Foster Howard, the first librarian at the Kinsey Institute. And there is the 2004 Oscar-nominated film, *Kinsey*, in addition to Thomas Maier's biography of Masters and Johnson that inspired the Showtime series.

These stories purport to shed light on the motivations of sexuality scholars, the quality of the work, and the status of sex research itself—a field that has long struggled to achieve academic legitimacy. While this visibility is welcome, these stories suggest a troubling pattern: they tend to focus on researchers' alleged sexual proclivities, spinning them as deviant motivations which compromise the research.

For example, James Miller's biography of Michel Foucault links Foucault's work to unconventional sexual activities like sadomasochism. Thomas Maier begins his biography with Virginia Johnson losing her virginity, portrays her as a sexually conniving secretary, and delights in exposing complicated aspects of the researchers' sex life together. And historian James Jones depicts Kinsey as deeply twisted.

The problem is not simply that sexuality research remains stigmatized. It is that, in many circumstances, sex itself remains stubbornly discrediting. Sexuality's cultural meanings are paradoxical—it is simultaneously repulsive and attractive, taboo yet vital to our happiness. It is difficult to write sexual stories without reproducing what Michael Warner calls "the ordinary power of sexual shame." Moreover, stories that examine sex research through the prism of the researcher's sex life rely on the simplistic notion that there is a specific connection between one's sexual experiences and research.

My two recent projects unexpectedly converged around the problem of how researching sex can discredit the researcher. In a study on biographies of sex researchers, I explored archives and interviewed authors, looking at how these stories are told against the cultural backdrop of stigma. I also conducted a survey of current sociologists of sexuality, who reported experiences of sexualization and marginalization because of the topics they researched. Both projects complicate the notion that we live in enlightened times.

My investigations began where most tales of modern sex research commence: with Alfred C. Kinsey, the pioneering sex researcher, and his circle.

the kinsey archive

The Kinsey report, released in 1948, was the first scientific sexuality study in the United States to become a runaway bestseller. Based on extensive sex histories of 5,300 White men, the report suggested that the sex lives of American men were far more robust and unconventional than popularly imagined in the mid-twentieth century. Kinsey criticized the harsh sex laws and restrictive social norms of his day, insisting that behaviors like homosexuality and masturbation were natural artifacts of "our mammalian origins."

> **Researching sex can discredit the researcher since the focus often turns to sex researchers' personal lives.**

At the height of public clamor over the study, a newsmagazine quoted Kinsey's wife as saying, "I hardly see him anymore since he's taken up sex." The quote went viral, as we would say now, repeated so often that its original source became elusive. In one sentence it seemed to condense multiple stories, the most irresistible one being the paradox by which the sex researcher's fanatical devotion to the work of sex seemingly produced a sexless marriage. When Laura Linney, playing Mac (as Clara Kinsey was known) in the 2004 film, *Kinsey*, delivered the line in earnest, she revived it for a new generation.

Today, however, there is little ambiguity about the Kinseys' sex life. Two major biographies of Alfred Kinsey were published in the mid-1990s, one by historian James Jones (*Alfred C. Kinsey*, 1997), and a year later, *Sex the Measure of All Things*, by British author Jonathan Gathorne-Hardy. Both biographers worked in the same archive, combed the same documents, and interviewed the same informants. But biographers select life events and decide how to interpret them, and choose, as American author Joyce Carole Oates points out, "slant, emphasis, tone." A study in contrasts, these biographies illustrate how differently the same story about a sexuality researcher can be told, depending on the narrative framing.

> **A biography of Kinsey concludes that Kinsey's research was driven by "inner demons" including homosexuality, masochism, voyeurism, exhibitionism.**

Aptly subtitled *A Public/Private Life*, James Jones's book was the first to publicly expose details of the Kinseys' private sex life, relating activities among the Kinsey research team and their wives, including the fact that Alfred enjoyed sex with men, Mac had other lovers, and sex among members of the research team and their wives was not uncommon. The researchers filmed sexual activities (in the so-called "attic films"), including one in which Mac was allegedly shown masturbating.

The Jones biography illustrates how sex as a framing device tilts toward stigma: he concluded that Kinsey's research was driven by "inner demons" including homosexuality, masochism, voyeurism, exhibitionism. Kinsey, he asserted, regularly engaged in "bizarre behavior," such as inserting objects into his urethra. Jones cast Kinsey, as he gardened without a shirt, or shaved nude in the bathroom, in the most unflattering light. The biography strikes a tone of disgust, and offers a cascade of judgments, describing its subject as "grotesque," "twisted," and "compulsive," and suggests that Kinsey's suspicious sexual motivations undermined the validity of his studies.

Having long studied sexuality scholars, the stigmatizing strategies of the Jones biography are familiar ones to me. I have seen how opponents discredit sexuality researchers, depicting them as deviants (the early twentieth century), communists (the 1960s), or pedophiles (the culture wars of the 1990s).

But a second Kinsey biography explicitly repudiated a stigmatizing frame. Written by Jonathan Gathorne-Hardy, this biography offers not only a radically different reading of an archive, but a biographical narrative that refuses easy appeals to sexual sensationalism. Just when it seemed that there'd be nothing left to say about the Kinseys, it turned out there were more stories and different ways to tell them.

resisting sensationalism

I spent a day in England talking with Gathorne-Hardy, who is known as Jonny. After a white-knuckle drive navigating the "other" side of roads and roundabouts through rural England, I sat in his attic study in the tiny village of Binham, and we discussed the Kinseys and the ethics of narrating their stories.

Jonny was in the later stages of his own Kinsey biography when the Jones book was published. Every scholar's nightmare, he had not known that someone else was also working on this topic. Having kept a journal for his entire life, Jonny regularly plucked yellowing notebooks from a towering pile and read from sections he had penned during his work on the biography. In one excerpt, he had just received the Jones biography and was "by turns appalled, astonished, exhausted, depressed," he wrote. "I have to go to America again. Oh God!"

When Jonny returned to the Kinsey Institute at Indiana University, a key source told him that the Jones book was riddled with exaggerations and misreadings.

Principal interviewees disputed Jones's interpretations, and in some cases even the facts he reported. (In my own reading of Jones' oral histories at the Institute archive, I found he consistently put a negative spin on questions, attempting to lead interviewees to disparage Kinsey's leadership style, personality, and even his "spartan" furniture.) In his book's Introduction, Gathorne-Hardy challenged the framing of Jones's biography as "an unrelenting stream, pejorative page after pejorative page" in which "there emerges a portrait of someone so unpleasant as to be actually grotesque."

Because it resisted rather than reinforced the cultural frame of stigma, Jonny's narrative of Kinsey was a more difficult story to tell. I asked him why he decided to challenge Jones so directly. "I was angry," he said, "and it seemed the only thing to do, particularly as I went into it in detail, just how wrong [the book] was. I felt I couldn't let it stand."

Sex was, of course, an important part of Jonny's story of the Kinseys, too. But rather than demonizing them, he narrates them as a sexually vibrant, experimental couple, though admittedly outside the norms of their 1940s Midwestern community. Jones suggested that Kinsey coerced Mac into sexual activity with others; Jonny's version, in contrast, features her agency and pleasure. Jones viewed the attic films as evidence of Kinsey's voyeurism; Jonny saw them as scientific. "If you are to study some field scientifically," he told me, "you must know as much of it as possible. Nothing can be evaded—and Kinsey didn't evade. He not only filmed every variant of sexual behavior that he could, he observed where he couldn't film."

routinizing sex

Biographers weave a story about the connections between life and work, teasing out what anthropologist Ruth Behar calls the "emotional motivations" of their subjects. To Jones, Kinsey's "inner demons"—his alleged perversions motivated a career in sexuality research. Gathorne-Hardy, in contrast, contextualized the sexual lives of the research team within the intense dynamics of their pioneering research project. He told a sociological story, where history, context, and situation matter in interpreting the sex lives of sex researchers.

Once we see their stories sociologically, we can appreciate how the Kinseys' (and Masters and Johnson's), scientific aspirations prompted them to abandon certain notions of sexual conformity, fostering a deep ease with the topic. In a case of art imitating life, Lizzy Caplan—the actor playing Virginia Johnson in the television series *Masters of Sex*—described this normalizing dynamic

during the filming: "I was driving home one day and it dawned on me, like, 'Oh yeah, I measured a girl's nipple today.' And I forgot about it. Because it just happens now all the time." As sociologist John Gagnon frequently notes about sex, the situation is the motive.

Alluding to the disclosure that some of Kinsey's interviewers had sex with one another, Gathorne-Hardy said he could never have worked for Kinsey: "Whether I could have allowed the team to bugger me or not, I sort of doubt it." I suggested his reluctance might have diminished had he been part of the team over the years. "Quite," he conceded, "And obviously all of them who stayed there, lost all inhibitions." For Gathorne-Hardy, it was obvious that Kinsey was "dead set on sex, condemning moralism and embracing sexual variation." He was interested in "all sorts of sex," and that's why "he tried to have some homosexual experiences." According to Gathorne-Hardy, "To get a proper sex history Kinsey thought you should have experienced as much as you can of sexual practices. And I have no doubt he was right."

Rather than focusing on how the researcher is motivated by sex, one could say, then, that the sexual situation shapes the researcher. "Clearly this was true of Kinsey and I imagine it was true of Mac," according to Galthorne-Hardy. "The conventions gradually sort of evaporate really, through habituation. And Kinsey was convinced that an open and free sex life was very, very important and they should both have it. And I think Mac agreed."

privacy and politics

The Kinseys and their colleagues went to great length to keep their sexual activities private, and in the 1940s, the days before our present media-saturated culture, they had no reason to think their activities would ever be exposed. But as Irish writer Oscar Wilde once wrote, "biography lends to death a new terror." Biographies, memoirs, and works of social science are fraught with dilemmas about how to frame stories, which stories to tell and which to hold back to protect those we observe.

Death, in other words, does not protect subjects. Rather, it raises ethical questions about narrating secrets and exposing private details when subjects are no longer able to reframe their own stories. The potential impact of such stigmatizing stories also extends beyond the subject, to family and friends. Galthorne-Hardy worried about how the Kinsey daughters might respond to his own work.

He read me an excerpt from his journal from 1997, written after he had read the Jones biography: "For the first time, that criticism some reviewers make about how distasteful all this prying into the private lives of the dead is, which I've always dismissed as prudish and absurd, I now feel. As for poor Joan Reid and Anne Call, I don't see how they will survive. Their lives will be ruined."

Before Jonny left Bloomington, Kinsey's daughter Joan phoned him. The Jones book had just come out, and she wanted to know: "is it true?" Jonny told her: "Yes it is, a lot of it anyway," including "your father's sexual experiments." Her father was not homosexual, he told her. He was, however, "an extremely courageous man."

Jonny was reframing the story, but not simply to soothe Kinseys' descendants. He imagined if he himself were in their position. "If I had discovered at age 72 that my father and mother had done what Kinsey and Mac had done, I would be surprised. But not horrified. And certainly wouldn't desperately deny it," he wrote in his journal. "But for Joan and Anne, it is far more as if a murder had been committed. As if Kinsey and Mac had turned out to be these two murderers Ian Brady and Myra Hindley, who killed about eight little children."

Director Bill Condon had long wanted to make a film about Kinsey, Jonny told me, but then, "they read the Jones book and thought 'we can't make the film.'" After Jonny's book came out, Condon based the film largely on that story, although tell-tale scenes from the Jones book, depicting Kinsey as repressed and tortured, crept into the film.

Recently, while doing research at the Kinsey Institute, I spent two social occasions with Kinsey and Mac's daughter, Anne Kinsey Call, then in her mid-80s, and their granddaughter Wendy Kinsey Corning. At dinner in Bloomington, Wendy told me that when Kinsey was released in 2004, Indiana University held a special screening for researchers and associates of the Kinsey Institute. Paul Gebhard, a surviving member of the original Kinsey team, stood up at the end and in the silent theater loudly proclaimed, "Well, at least we didn't harm any animals," and then walked out. His reaction spoke of how the film stumbles in its depiction of the team's passionate attachments to research, as well as to each other.

Today, the judgments, and stories, about the Kinseys and their team continue to travel internationally, producing new forms of cultural and political knowledge about sex. For example, religious conservatives, who have long blamed Kinsey for launching the sexual revolution, immediately adopted the Jones biography as ammunition in their culture wars over sex. So did British journalist Timothy Tate, director of a 1998 documentary *Secret History: Kinsey's Paedophiles*. The film draws heavily on the James Jones biography, which repeated long-discredited allegations that Kinsey was a pedophile.

In 2013, American conservative religious activist Judith Reisman spoke out at Parliament against Croatia's new sexuality education program, accompanied by Tate's film. Croatia's Constitutional Court subsequently suspended the public school program, and a headline read: "Croatian court quashes Kinsey-based national sex-ed."

vulnerable researchers

Passions drive our research in ways that may have little to do with our personal lives. Yet choosing a career in sexuality studies often elicits curiosity and judgment, and leads others to make assumptions about one's sexual proclivities.

In 1987, *The Chronicle of Higher Education* featured an article on sexuality researchers entitled, "Out of the Closet Now but Misunderstood." Social scientists and historians described careers fraught with stigma and bias because of their research on sexuality. Some kept their research a secret from family members; others spoke of discrimination in promotion and funding. One woman noted, "If you are researching adultery, people automatically assume that you're into it. There is also the attitude that nice girls don't study sex, so you find yourself excluded from some groups."

In the book *Vulnerable Subjects*, G. Thomas Couser looks at biographical writing about people whose stories are easily distorted and exploitable, such as those—like mental illness or physical challenges—where the subject has a "disadvantaging or stigmatizing" condition. Couser warns of the risk of over-writing the story, by which he means imposing an "alien shape" on it. His caveat also applies to those who research particular subjects as well, such as sexuality.

Sociology has long been vexed by the relationship between our biographical experiences and our research. At times we value participant-observation, as well-received ethnographies of musicians and boxers attest. But in marginalized areas of social life, identification can be read as lack of objectivity. Many assume that a stigmatized topic would only be studied by someone who her/himself occupies that stigmatized status. For example, sociologist Abigail Saguy noted that after writing a book about the cultural framing of obesity, audiences expected her to be overweight herself—and a fat advocate. (And yet they never considered her thinness to be a standpoint or bias.)

Sex is culturally "sticky." Its complicated cultural meanings attach to sexuality scholars, leaving them vulnerable to those who would discredit their motivations

> *Despite decades of cultural liberalization, we still frame sexuality researchers in relation to the topics they study, making up stories about how they live.*

and research. As pioneering sexuality researcher Martin Weinberg, who has studied topics such as nudism, homosexuality, and bestiality since the 1960s, recently told me, "Every study I've done, people assume it's about behavior I engage in myself. The allegations are always there."

Despite decades of cultural liberalization, we still frame sexuality researchers in relation to the topics they study, making up stories about how they live. For example, when I surveyed members the American Sociological Association's Section on Sexualities recently, I found that three quarters of its members reported that others made assumptions about their sexual identities, and almost half said others made assumptions about their sexual practices. "I constantly hear how people make assumptions about my sexual orientation based on my research," one said. Another noted, "I have been at times reluctant to see myself as a 'sexualities scholar' because many of my colleagues leap to conclusions about my sexual identity and then treat me differently."

Some women mentioned that others interpreted their research as implying their own sexual availability. As one put it, "I avoided dating people who thought my research meant I'd do anything with anyone." In more extreme cases, women scholars reported that their research on sexuality made them a target of harassment. One said, "I received emails from male stalkers around the world from the U.S. to Asia." Some sociologists said that leaving the field of sexuality studies was the only way they could see escaping the persistent stigma attached to it.

After Indiana University held its special screening of *Kinsey*, Kinsey's granddaughter Wendy lamented, "As a film, it is beautifully made, amazingly well acted and directed. But as a story of my family, there are certainly some parts of it that I think should remain private." As a sexuality researcher myself, I understand her feelings. Still, I would suggest that the problem is less about the fact that certain sexual details were revealed, but rather how they were framed.

Instead of secrecy, we need more and better stories, ones that normalize and contextualize rather than demonize sex, difference, and non-conformity. We need stories that refuse and reframe the well-worn and highly marketable frame of sexual stigma, stories which help produce alternative meanings—not just about sexuality research—but about sexuality more broadly. That is how culture changes.

recommended resources

Behar, Ruth. 1997. *The Vulnerable Observer: Anthropology That Breaks Your Heart.* Boston, MA: Beacon Press. Challenges social researchers to acknowledge and incorporate their emotional involvement in their work.

Couser, G. Thomas. 2004. *Vulnerable Subjects.* Ithaca, NY: Cornell University Press. Considers ethical dilemmas in writing life stories.

Gathorne-Hardy, Jonathan. 1998. *Sex the Measure of All Things: A Life of Alfred C. Kinsey.* Bloomington, IN: Indiana University Press. Challenges the stigmatizing frames of the Jones biography.

Jones, James. 1997. *Alfred C. Kinsey: A Public/Private Life.* New York: W.W. Norton & Company. Based on interviews and archival research, this biography prompted broad critical reaction for over-reaching interpretations.

40

being straight in a post-closeted culture

james joseph dean

summer 2015

Crossing the street, I eavesdropped on a conversation between two teenage boys. They were making fun of two other men we had just walked past. The boys thought these two men's excitement over taking a bicycle "for a spin" was tinged with a homosexual overtone. One of the boys remarked, "That guy should have said, 'Take it for a spin—No homo.'"

Phrases like "no homo" demonstrate the anxiety of being straight today. Although the boy may not have intended it as a homophobic insult, he clearly wanted his straight/no homo status to be projected to others. Phrases like "that's so gay" are signs of anxious straight identities as American society has increasingly become a "post-closeted culture."

By a post-closeted culture, I don't mean a society in which homophobia has been eradicated. Rather, it's a society with visible and openly gay and lesbian people and an array of lesbian, gay, bisexual, transgender, and queer (LGBTQ) representations across a range of cultural institutions.

Many journalists and scholars have focused on how LGBTQ people are affected by this new cultural dynamic, but it's worth considering how straight Americans react as well. Based on my research interviewing straight Americans in recent years, I found that many straight people are now more conscious, reflective, and defensive about establishing their sexual identity status in everyday life.

> **Phrases like "no homo" demonstrate the anxiety of being straight today.**

the post-closeted culture

The normalization of homosexuality and Americans' liberalization toward homosexuals are relatively recent social and historical developments. Two periods stand out in the rise of a post-closeted dynamic as a national formation. First, the Stonewall riots of 1969 signaled the rise of the politics of coming out of the closet and the development of large, visible gay and lesbian communities and institutions throughout the country. In chronicling gay and lesbian movements in the United States at this time, historians and social movement scholars have found a rapid proliferation of gay organizations, such as newspapers, crisis hotlines, and social clubs, which increased from just 50 in 1969 to more than a thousand in 1973. These developments, made possible by the growth of lesbian and gay subcultures, made coming out to straight society its political centerpiece.

The mid-1990s opened a second important period of coming out, marked by increased visibility in mass media. The unprecedented popularity of sitcoms like *Will & Grace*, which featured openly gay lead characters, came alongside the inclusion of same-sex commitment and wedding ceremonies in the *New York Times*' Sunday Styles section. At the same time, gays and lesbians continued to achieve significant social and political gains, from the development and spread of domestic partner benefits and antidiscrimination laws to significant attitudinal shifts among Americans.

Polls over the last decades confirm the increase in liberal attitudes regarding gays and lesbians. For instance, as shown at right, when Americans were asked whether lesbians' and gay men's marriages "should or should not be recognized by the law as valid," 27% of Americans supported same-sex marital rights in 1996. Today, 60% of Americans embrace the recognition of gay marital rights. This historic high in polling data along with the recent Supreme Court decision in *Obergefell v. Hodges*, which made same-sex marriage the law of the land, show the growing support behind same-sex marriages and relationships.

Still, many media depictions of gays and lesbians are often stereotypical, and many members of the LGBTQ community still face daily discrimination. A vocal minority of Americans opposes the extension of LGBTQ rights. Yet, with Americans increasingly supportive of lesbians' and gays' legal rights and more normalized media portrayals of same-sex couples, we have seen the emergence of a post-closeted culture.

straight identities

In my research, I interviewed a diverse group of straight men and women living in the northeastern U.S. about their heterosexuality and the kinds of interactions they had with lesbian and gay men. Not only has a post-closeted culture been liberating for gays and lesbians, it has also given straight men new freedom in expressing their masculinity in non-homophobic ways.

For many of the straight men I talked to, homophobia used to be the tried and true way to establish straightness. Now, many aim to avoid being seen as homophobic. Straight men who might have used words like "fag" or "queer" in the past now exclude the slurs from their everyday vocabulary.

Today, many straight people have developed an anti-homophobic stance. Being *anti-homophobic* ranges from countering prejudice and discrimination against gays and lesbians to renouncing one's straight status and privilege. This development makes sense as a post-closeted culture has created a climate where homophobia is stigmatized as wrong and mean-spirited in many contexts, although this is uneven across different settings and groups.

In gay-friendly contexts, anti-homophobic straight men and women earn a kind of honor or prestige by being gay-friendly and supporting LGBTQ rights. For example, Nick, a single White male in his early 20s, expressed an anti-homophobic sentiment by noting that the line between who is and isn't gay is often blurred today: "I have guys and girls come on to me. So I know for a fact that I don't protrude a straight, exact heterosexual or homosexual identity. I realized that the lines are so blurred these days that you really can't tell who's gay and straight."

For Nick, being viewed as potentially non-straight is not an affront to his masculinity and it doesn't trigger a homophobic defensiveness that might prompt him to try to reclaim a clear straight status. Nick explained that many of his gay male friends are "conventionally

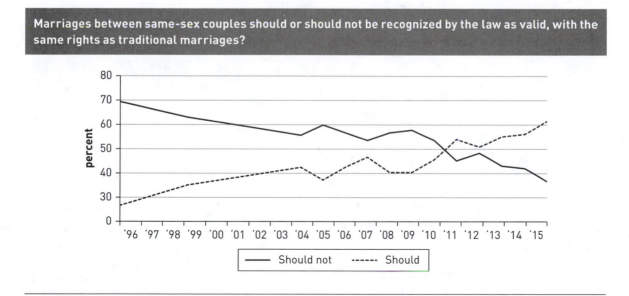

Marriages between same-sex couples should or should not be recognized by the law as valid, with the same rights as traditional marriages?

Note: Trend shown for polls in which same-sex marriage question followed questions on gay/lesbian rights and relations. 1996–2005 wording: "Do you think marriages between homosexuals . . . "

masculine," and so he doesn't view his heterosexuality or his gay friends' homosexuality as connected to being masculine. This decoupling of masculinity from heterosexuality in part explains Nick's anti-homophobic stance that allows him to be comfortable in being viewed as possibly gay in some contexts.

These changes are even more salient among straight women. The straight women I interviewed expressed their solidarity with LGBTQ friends and communities in ways that their straight male counterparts didn't. The most anti-homophobic straight women described their sexualities as socially constructed, malleable, and fluid.

In her book *Sexual Fluidity*, psychologist Lisa Diamond defines sexual fluidity as "situation-dependent flexibility in women's sexual responsiveness" to both women and men as objects of desire, fantasy, and sexual partnership. But she applied the concept only to non-heterosexual or lesbian and bisexual women. The anti-homophobic straight women I talked to identified themselves as straight, but had strong political identifications with their LGBTQ friends. For them, same-sex feelings, fantasies, and experiences attested to their solidarity with LGBTQ people. That is, straight women shared their same-sex sexual encounters with me as proof of the lack of shame in homosexual sex acts and as a badge of being a strong political ally. Queer culture is now part of some straight women's lives, not just expanding the boundaries of femininity, but also breaking down the sexual line that privileges straightness over gayness.

Of all the straight people I interviewed, the anti-homophobic straight women were the ones who augur the possibility of a truly post-closeted era in which the line between straightness and gayness isn't a form of social hierarchy and denigration, the minority group doesn't feel the need to come out to show their pride, and the majority group doesn't take for granted *their* sexual status as normal, natural, or rightly ideal.

Commenting on a same-sex encounter, Erica, a single Black female in her early 20s, said, "I consider myself heterosexual. Just the same way, like I said before, politically, I consider myself Black. But I'm more than that in terms of my ethnic makeup. Just as in sexuality, I'm more than just a straight female. I'm attracted to different things. I don't make myself any promises that I'll never change. I believe that a lot of things are based on the individual person. Give me a woman who does everything right for me and we'll see. This particular woman did not."

While anti-homophobic attitudes seem to be on the rise among straight Americans and allies like Erica embrace experiences of sexual fluidity, American society is still divided by a sexual hierarchy that privileges heterosexuality over homosexuality. In other words, neither has the closet disappeared nor have all straight people become allies to LGBTQ communities. But with homophobia on the decline and post-closeted culture on the rise, straight Americans have started to rethink what it means to be straight and their place in America in the twenty-first century.

U.S. attitudes toward lesbian and gay people are better than ever

tina fetner

spring 2016

The year was 1955. Police routinely raided lesbian and gay bars, arresting patrons and publishing their names and addresses in the paper. Sex between two women or two men was illegal, and homosexuality was understood by psychiatrists to be a mental illness. In many places it was illegal for women to dance with women, or men with men. In response to these oppressive conditions, a group of eight women formed the Daughters of Bilitis, the first lesbian activist organization founded in the United States. Phyllis Lyon and Del Martin, a lesbian couple, were two of the founders. Like their gay male counterparts in the Mattachine Society, these brave women took on the fight for civil rights against all odds.

In 2008, Phyllis and Del were married by San Francisco Mayor Gavin Newsom. Celebrating the newly established right of same-sex marriage, they were the first lesbian couple to marry in San Francisco. Together for 56 years, the legal status of their marriage was settled just this year by the U.S. Supreme Court, when it ruled that the right to marry is guaranteed to same-sex couples by the Constitution. In a country that has been reticent to guarantee equal rights to lesbian and gay people, this marks an important step forward in the slow, hard-fought battle for full citizenship. In light of these political changes, it is worth asking how Americans feel about lesbian and gay people, and how these attitudes have changed over time. Below, I provide an overview of the social science data on attitudes toward lesbian and gay people and recount how sociologists understand the social forces behind changing attitudes.

In the last sixty years, much more has changed for lesbian, gay, bisexual and transgender people than just same-sex marriage. Laws prohibiting discrimination on the basis of sexual orientation are in place in 21 states; 18 of these also prohibit discrimination against transgender people. In addition, it is against the law to discriminate against lesbian and gay people in numerous cities and counties, as well as among employees and contractors with the federal U.S. government. This year, the U.S. Equal Employment Opportunity Commission ruled that federal employment discrimination laws should be interpreted to apply to lesbian and gay workers. If that ruling holds up in court, this will extend anti-discrimination laws to most workplaces across the country.

These policy shifts are happening rapidly and come from many sources: the courts, bureaucratic agencies, and state legislative bodies. They are the direct result of the long-term efforts of the LGBT movement, which has been fighting for decades for equal treatment, public recognition, and full citizenship for lesbian, gay, bisexual and transgender people. Throughout much of this time, this movement fought an uphill battle

> **With the majority of Americans now favoring equal rights, it will increasingly become difficult to pass legislation that marginalizes LGBT people.**

> **This large-scale increase in support is an unprecedented change in social attitudes, more sudden and more dramatic than we've seen on other issues like racial animosity or attitudes toward immigrants.**

in a social setting that made them invisible: government officials who refused to meet with them, newspapers that would not print news of their protests, and a mental health system that diagnosed them as diseased but would not listen to their views.

Over much of this history, little ground was gained. For decades, anti-discrimination bills were proposed and defeated or held up in committees. Battles to decriminalize consensual homosexual sex were met with great opposition. Even when some early ground was gained—the American Psychological Association eliminated homosexuality as a mental illness in 1973, a few cities passed ordinances banning discrimination against lesbian and gay people in the 1970s—opponents formed a countermovement to roll back these small victories. In the 1980s, the HIV crisis decimated the gay community and took the lives of numerous activists.

Still, the movement fought on, now against a powerful opposing movement that we came to know as the religious right: organizations like the Moral Majority, Concerned Women for America, and the Christian Coalition. Despite their anti-gay activism, the LGBT movement began to realize some gains. Neighborhoods that had started as safe spaces become celebratory hubs of LGBT culture, building communities and strengthening collective identities. Annual pride parades spread across the country into big cities and small towns alike, making LGBT lives visible to wide audiences. Lesbian and gay lives began to appear on television shows, in movies, and in the news. Just over a decade ago, consensual same-sex sexual activity was decriminalized throughout the country. More and more cities and states began to make it illegal to discriminate on the basis of sexual orientation and gender identity. Most recently, same-sex marriage was given equal legal status throughout the United States.

we've got a new attitude

It is not only policies that are changing. Our attitudes toward lesbian and gay people are undergoing rapid change over time as well. The U.S. General Social Survey began asking Americans about their attitudes toward lesbian and gay people in the early 1970s. Throughout the 1970s and 1980s, U.S. attitudes toward homosexuality were consistently negative. A large majority of Americans judged sexual relations between two adults of the same sex very harshly, with about 85% of survey respondents indicating that this

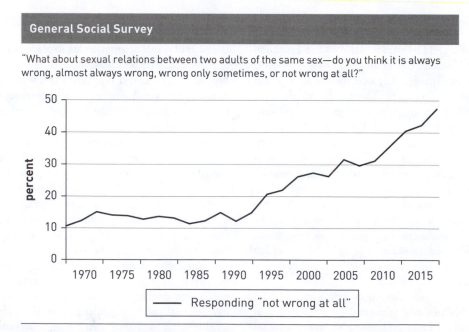

General Social Survey

"What about sexual relations between two adults of the same sex—do you think it is always wrong, almost always wrong, wrong only sometimes, or not wrong at all?"

Responding "not wrong at all"

Source: http://www.electionstudies.org/

Gallup: In general, do you think homosexuals should or should not have equal rights in terms of job opportunities?

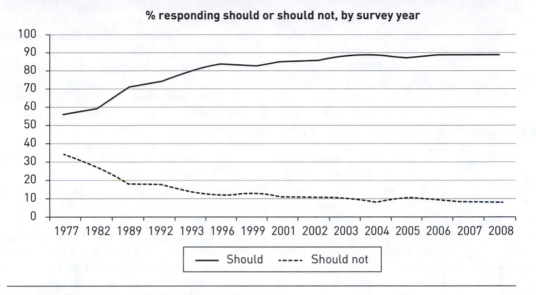

% responding should or should not, by survey year

Source: http://www.gallup.com/poll/1651/Gay-Lesbian-Rights

Gallup: Do you think marriages between same-sex couples should or should not be recognized by the law as valid, with the same rights as traditional marriages?

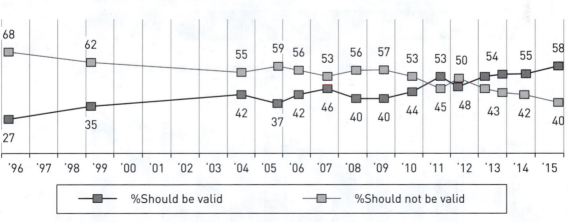

% responding yes or no to same-sex marriage, by year

Note: Trend shown for polls in which same-sex marriage question followed questions on gay/lesbian rights and relations. 1996–2005 wording: "Do you think marriages between homosexuals . . ."

Source: http://www.gallup.com/poll/1651/Gay-Lesbian-Rights.aspx

was morally wrong, at least sometimes. As recently as 1990, the General Social Survey tells us that fewer than one in ten people said that same-sex sexual relations were "not wrong at all."

Since 1990, however, U.S. attitudes have shifted dramatically. By 2014, about half of all respondents tell us that same-sex relations are not wrong at all. Using these and other measures, we can see that there has been a large shift in the last twenty-five years toward moral approval of lesbian and gay sexual relations, greater support for lesbian and gay rights, and friendlier feelings toward lesbian and gay people. This large-scale increase in support is an unprecedented change in social attitudes, more sudden and more dramatic than other issues like racial animosity or attitudes toward immigrants.

> **Americans are more positive about lesbian and gay people than about the moral question of homosexuality, more positive still about equal rights for lesbian and gay people.**

Let's take a closer look at the specific lesbian and gay issues about which Americans have been asked their opinions. As you will see, in each case, attitudes are changing rapidly and becoming more positive in the last decade or two. The question that the General Social Survey has been asking the longest is a question about morality: whether same-sex relations are considered wrong or right. Those considering same-sex relations "not wrong at all" were a small minority for twenty years, growing

steadily for the next twenty-five years to reach about half of the U.S. population.

Other surveys have asked how Americans feel toward lesbian and gay people as a group, and the trends over time are similar. For example, the American National Election Study asks respondents how they feel about lesbian and gay people on a "feelings thermometer" scale of 1–100, with low scores reflecting colder feelings and high scores being warmer, more friendly feelings. You can see in the chart below that Americans' feelings toward lesbian and gay people have been steadily warming over the years. 2012 was the first year that the mean response was above 50.

When we ask for opinions about lesbian and gay rights, the responses are even more positive. We can approve of granting rights to groups even if we consider their actions immoral, and this is the pattern that the surveys have shown. Americans are more positive about lesbian and gay people than about the moral question of homosexuality, more positive still about equal rights for lesbian and gay people. Even on this last question, however, responses have grown more positive over time.

Nowhere is this shift more dramatic than when measuring support for one type of equal right in particular: the right to same-sex marriage. This issue was not among the lesbian and gay movement's demands until recently, precisely because the public opinion was so strongly against extending marriage to same-sex couples. Gallup polls, which have been asking since 1996, show that support for same-sex marriage has doubled since then.

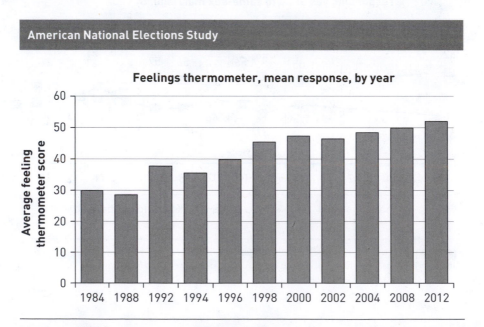

American National Elections Study

Feelings thermometer, mean response, by year

Source: https://gssdataexplorer.norc.org/variables/634/vshow

American National Elections Study
Respondents asked to rate their feelings about "gay men and lesbians" in American society.

Feeling thermometer ratings from 50–100 indicate favorable, warm feelings toward the group; ratings of 50 indicate no real opinion; and ratings from 0–50 indicate unfavorable, cool feelings toward the group.

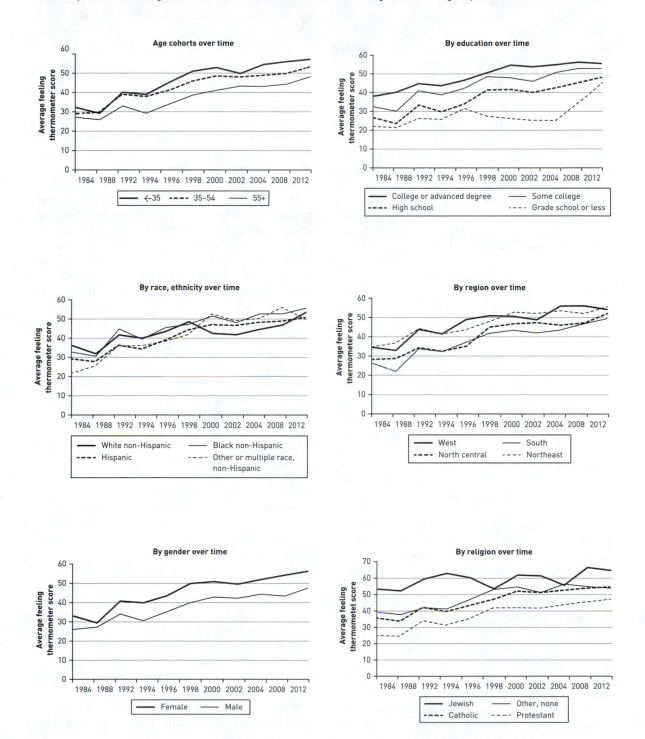

Now, a majority of Americans approve of marriage equality for lesbians and gay men.

As someone who has studied the LGBT movement's activism for some time, I have been surprised by this major shift in support for same-sex marriage. Since the 1990s, I have observed the powerful organizations of the religious right use the issue of same-sex marriage to fight against lesbian and gay rights. Until very recently, they had been very successful at securing policy changes that would exclude same-sex couples from marriage at the federal level, as well as in many states. Following passage by a Republican congress, President Clinton, who has since disavowed his actions, signed the Defense of Marriage Act into law in 1996, limiting federally recognized marriages to those between one man and one woman—excluding lesbian and gay couples. At this time, only 27% of Americans thought that same-sex marriage should be legal. It seemed like a slam-dunk win for those interested in restricting lesbian and gay rights. Thirty-five states passed laws restricting marriage to straight couples.

A few years later, the tide began to turn. The lesbian and gay movement mobilized in full force to fight for marriage equality. They brought lawsuits to courts all across the country. They pressured elected officials to support their cause and introduced marriage equality legislation in several states. In states where same-sex marriage was not legally recognized, protests included county clerks issuing marriage licenses and officials holding same-sex weddings. In 2004 in San Francisco, Phyllis and Del were at the front of the long line of same-sex couples who participated in wedding ceremonies that were later deemed invalid. Local and national television and print news media gave broad coverage to the spectacle of these protest weddings, drawing the attention of the nation to this issue. Supporters from all across the country sent flowers to the happy couples waiting to be married.

Sociologists who studied these protest weddings argue that they were an innovative social movement tactic that used our culture's warm feelings toward weddings, love, and family to draw attention to the injustice of excluding same-sex couples from marriage. These weddings sparked a statewide marriage equality movement as they captured the hearts of a broad audience. As courts issued the expected decisions to render the protest weddings invalid, Americans witnessed the state taking away marriages from these same-sex couples. To many, this seemed particularly unfair.

Movement success followed quickly on the heels of this activism. Massachusetts legalized same-sex marriage in 2004, and several other states followed suit. Some courts began to rule against the recently passed laws excluding same-sex couples from marriage. All this time, public support for same-sex marriage climbed and climbed. Some key figures in the religious right stopped fighting against marriage equality, and in 2013, dozens of high-level Republican Party insiders submitted an amicus brief to the U.S. Supreme Court in support of same-sex marriage. This year's Supreme Court decision settled the matter legally, and now more than half of Americans agree that marriage equality should be the law of the land.

why so much change, so quickly?

We rarely see such rapid changes in social attitudes. Usually, opinions change at a glacial pace. This is because people mostly form their opinions as young adults and then remain steadfast in them throughout their lifetimes. Most change in attitude comes from the passage of time, as older generations pass away, replaced by younger generations with different attitudes. We see this effect with attitudes toward lesbian and gay people as well; younger people have more positive attitudes than older people. However, on this topic, some people of all ages have changed their minds about lesbian and gay people. The graph below reveals this trend; people under the age of 35 have the most positive attitudes, and those over 55 have the most negative. Yet, all three age groups are growing more positive over time, at about the same rate.

The growing approval of lesbian and gay rights has been surprisingly widespread. Gender, race and education level mark social divisions in Americans' attitudes toward lesbians and gay people, and yet we see improvements over time among men and women, among people of all races, and among people with all levels of education. Like age groups, these show people in all of these social groups changing their minds.

The fight over lesbian and gay rights has been particularly heated in some parts of the country, and among some religious groups. Attitudes have been more negative in the South than the rest of the country. Jewish people and people with no religion have had more positive attitudes than Catholics and Protestants. Once again, however, we see that people in all parts of the country, belonging to all religious groups, are becoming more positive over time.

These trends show that the United States is undergoing a large cultural shift toward greater acceptance of lesbian and gay people, as well as for equal rights for this group. While more positive portrayals of lesbian and gay people on television, in films and in music may be responsible for some of this change, another important factor is closer to home. One of the strongest predictors of positive attitudes is having personal connections with lesbian and gay people. Those who know lesbian and gay people in their families, at work, or in their neighborhoods, have much more positive attitudes toward them in general than those who do not know any. That LGBT people are in families, schools and churches in every neighborhood, in all regions of the country, among every race and religion, is one of the main reasons why these social changes are so consistent throughout all these diverse groups of people.

Looking into the future, there is reason to believe that attitudes will continue improving. People who live in states with laws that prohibit discrimination against lesbian and gay people have more positive attitudes than people in states where it is legal to discriminate. As schools, government agencies, and workplaces put in place policies against discrimination, their policy changes send messages to all their students, customers, and employees that equality for lesbian and gay people is valued. Policies and attitudes are mutually reinforcing. The personal connections between straight people and LGBT people are also likely to grow as laws protecting lesbian and gay people from discrimination become institutionalized in workplaces across the country, and more people will feel comfortable being out of the closet.

Of course, it is not all good news. A recent study found that people are much more positive toward formal rights than they are toward informal privileges, such as public displays of affection. Americans' discomfort with same-sex affection reveals that acceptance of lesbian and gay sexuality is incomplete. This study reminds us that, though attitudes are improving quickly, we still see sizable minorities of Americans who hold negative opinions. There are still anti-gay activists working to marginalize LGBT people, such as in the recent repeal of Houston's anti-discrimination ordinance. Recent legislative battles in North Carolina and elsewhere have focused on keeping transgender people out of public restrooms (see the recent *Contexts* article by Kristen Schilt and Lauren Westbrook). Some scholars see these developments and argue that it is dark times for LGBT people. However, I disagree. With the majority of Americans now favoring equal rights, it will increasingly become difficult to pass legislation that marginalizes LGBT people.

For decades, the LGBT movement in the United States has worked tirelessly to secure equal rights and to increase social acceptance. From the early days of the Daughters of Bilitis, when activists fought against police raids on gay bars, to the recent fights for same-sex marriage, LGBT activism has produced slow, uneven gains as well as some losses. It is too soon to tell whether the recent policy victories of the LGBT movement will carry over into new areas where inequalities for LGBT people still exist, such as housing discrimination and violence against transgender people. However, the LGBT movement has seen much change since those early days of the Daughters of Bilitis, both in policy and in culture. Americans' attitudes toward lesbian and gay people are better than ever, and it looks like this will continue to improve into the future.

recommended resources

Andersen, Robert, and Fetner, Tina. 2008. "Cohort Differences in Tolerance of Homosexuality: Attitudinal Change in Canada and the United States, 1981–2000," *Public Opinion Quarterly* 72:311–30. Shows change over time in attitudes by age group in two countries.

Doan, Long, Loehr, Annalise, and Miller, Lisa R. 2014. "Formal Rights and Informal Privileges for Same-Sex Couples: Evidence from a National Survey Experiment," *American Sociological Review* 79:1172–95. Examines nuances in attitudes with the most up-to-date statistics.

Taylor, Verta, Kimport, Katrina, Van Dyke, Nella, and Andersen, Ellen. 2009. "Culture and Mobilization: Tactical Repertoires, Same-Sex Weddings, and the Impact on Gay Activism," *American Sociological Review* 74:865–890. Studies protest weddings in San Francisco as an innovative social movement tactic.

Ghaziani, Amin. 2014. *There Goes the Gayborhood?* Princeton, NJ: Princeton University Press. Examines the exodus of gay populations from urban neighborhoods that have historically been cultural safe havens.

sexual orientation versus behavior—different for men and women?

eliza brown and paula england

february 2016

If you know which sexual orientation people identify with, how much does that tell you about whether they have sex with women, men, or both? How similar or different are the links between identity and behavior for women and men? Building on our post from last June, "Women's sexual orientation and sexual behavior: How well do they match?" we update the analysis of women to include more recent data and add an analysis of data on men.

We're using data from the 2002, 2006–2010, and 2011–2013 National Survey of Family Growth for men and women 15 to 44 years of age. Detailed tables, along with how we generated our measures, are in the Appendix at the end of this post. Here we focus on a few specific questions:

how common is it for heterosexual men and women to have sex with same-sex sexual partners?

Unsurprisingly, almost none of the men identifying as heterosexual have had only male sexual partners and only 2% say they have had even one male sexual partner (Table 1). For women, like men, almost none of those who identify as heterosexual have had only female partners, but 10% say they have had at least one same-sex partner, five-times the rate reported by men. (We'll only mention differences between men and women if they are statistically significant at the .05 level.) In sum, it is more common for heterosexual women than men to have had sex with members of their same sex.

We can get a little closer to assessing how common inconsistency between identity and behavior is by comparing men and women's current identity with whether they've had same-sex sexual partners *in the last year*. Here we get a much smaller figure—only .4% of men and 2% of women who called themselves heterosexual on the survey report that they had sex with a same-sex partner in the last year (Table 2). Thus, behavior usually aligns with identity in any short (one year) time range. But here too the percent of heterosexuals having same-sex partners is larger for women than men. The graph below shows the percent of each gender that identify as heterosexual but report having had a same-sex partner ever, and in the last year.

How should we interpret the finding that some men and women who identify as heterosexual have had sex with other-sex partners? It may mean that they had sex that doesn't match their stated sexual orientation at the time, perhaps because of the stigma associated with same-sex partnerships in some quarters. Another possibility is that, although they see themselves as straight now, they identified as gay/lesbian or bisexual

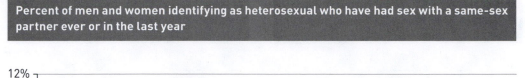

Percent of men and women identifying as heterosexual who have had sex with a same-sex partner ever or in the last year

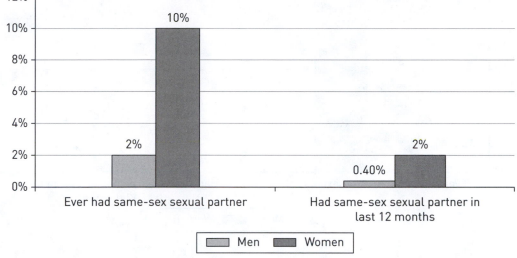

at the time they had same-sex partners, so there was no inconsistency between identity and behavior. This is especially plausible regarding with whom one has had sex "ever." If that is the explanation, then women's higher rate may mean that they are more likely than men to change the sexual orientation they identify with. But we are speculating; we would need panel data following the same people over time and repeatedly asking about orientation and recent behavior to distinguish (a) changing sexual orientation where behavior and identity are almost always consistent from (b) inconsistency between current identity and current behavior. It is also possible that the way people see their own orientations don't fit neatly into the three categories provided in the survey in most years, so some respondents choose the best fit of not-well-fitting categories.

how common is it for gay men and lesbians to have sex with other-sex sexual partners?

As the graph below (drawing from Tables 1 and 2) shows, 39% (37% + 2%) of gay men have had a female sexual partner sometime in their lives, whereas a much higher 59% (5% + 54%) of lesbians have had a male

sexual partner sometime. The proportion of either gay men or lesbians who have ever had sex with other-sex sexual partners is much larger than the proportion of heterosexual men and women who have had sex with same-sex sexual partners. And it is much larger than the proportion of gays/lesbians who have had sex with an other-sex partner in the last year, 5% (3% + 2%) for men and 18% (5% + 13%) for women.

As for how things differ by gender, it is clear that lesbians are more likely than gay men to have ever had sex with an other-sex sexual partner, whether in the last year (5% for men and 18% for women) or ever (39% for men and 59% for women). The larger share of lesbians than gay man who had other-sex partners in the past year comes both from lesbian being more likely than gay men to have partners of both sexes (13% of lesbians), as well as being more likely to have had sex with only other-sex partners (5% of lesbians).

Why would this be, that lesbians have sex with men more than gay men have sex with women? One explanation is that women's sexual attractions don't fit the three categories allowed by the survey as well, or that women are more likely than men to change the sexual orientation with which they identify. Either can be seen as more fluidity in women's sexuality than men's, a topic taken up by Lisa Diamond and Leila Rupp and her coauthors. Another possibility is that either evolution or cultural conditioning make guys the initiators in sex. So it is probably a less likely scenario that a young man who thinks

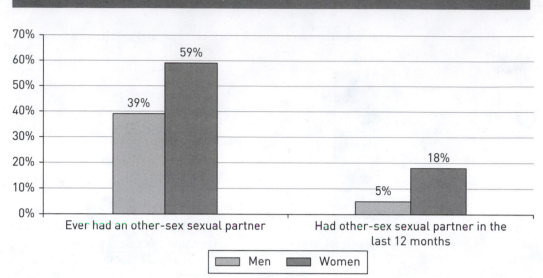

Percent of men and women identifying as gay or lesbian who have had sex with an other-sex partner ever or in the last year

that he may be gay is approached by a woman for sex and acquiesces despite not wanting it, compared to an analogous scenario in which a young queer woman has sex with a man she doesn't want. Indeed, both lesbians and gay men are likely to have men as their first sexual partners, according to research conducted by Karin Martin and Ritch C. Savin-Williams. In some cases these early partners may have raped them, as indicated by research on the prevalence of sexual assault among gay, lesbian, and bisexual individuals by Emily Rothman and her coauthors. We suspect, however, that greater sexual fluidity among women and the frequency of male initiation contribute more to the gender differences in partnership patterns than sexual assault.

how does the behavior of bisexual men and women differ from that of gay and heterosexual men and women?

Given that the common-sense meaning of the term "bisexual" is an interest in having sex and romantic relationships with men and women, we would expect more bisexual than heterosexual or lesbian/gay individuals to

have had sex with both men and women. Indeed, we find that 62% of bisexualmen and 73% of bisexual women have (ever) had sex with both sexes, higher than the analogous figures for gay men and lesbians, and drastically higher than the figures for heterosexual men and heterosexual women.

Who have bisexual men and women had sex with *in the last year*? As the graph below shows, drawing from Table 2, the percent that have had sex with both women and men in the last year is 33% for bisexual men, 27% for bisexual women; 2% for gay men, 13% for lesbians; and 0.4% for heterosexual men, and 2% for heterosexual women. Thus, as we would expect, bisexuals are much more likely than either gays/lesbians or straight men or women to have had sex with both sexes. They are also more likely to have had sex only with other-sex partners in the last year than are gay men or lesbians, but are less likely to have done so than are heterosexuals.

All this suggests a tendency for behavior to conform to identity in any short time range, and that bisexual women and men in some respects are a middle point between straights and gays.

What about gender differences between bisexual men and bisexual women? The two groups have a similarly low percent who have ever had sex only with the other sex (14% for men and 12% for women), but it is much more likely for bisexual women than men to have had sex only with the other sex in the last year—34% for men but 53% for women (Table 2).

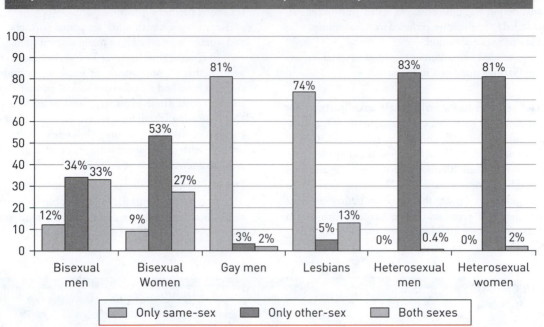

Percent of bisexual, gay and heterosexual men and women who have had only other-sex, only same-sex, and both male and female sexual partners last year

Legend: Only same-sex | Only other-sex | Both sexes

Bisexual men: 12%, 34%, 33%
Bisexual Women: 9%, 53%, 27%
Gay men: 81%, 3%, 2%
Lesbians: 74%, 5%, 13%
Heterosexual men: 0%, 83%, 0.4%
Heterosexual women: 0%, 81%, 2%

conclusion

We have shown that identity—the sexual orientation one identifies with—is strongly, but by no means perfectly, associated with whether men and women have had sex with women, men, or both. Heterosexual men and women are the most likely to have had sex only with other-sex partners, bisexual men and women are the most likely to have had sex with both women and men, and gay men and lesbians are the most likely to have had sex only with same-sex partners. In this sense, behavior is roughly consistent with sexual orientation. Unsurprisingly, this consistency between current identity and behavior is much stronger when the behavior being asked about is in the last year rather than over the whole lifetime.

However, the patterns differ between men and women. Women, both lesbian and straight, are more flexible with either their identities or behavior than men. Thus, they are more likely than men to have what could be seen as mismatches between identity and behavior. As an example of this, looking at behavior in the last year, heterosexual women are more likely than heterosexual men to have had sex with women, and lesbians are more likely than gay men to have had sex with an other-sex partner.

As part of women's "flexibility," women are more likely to have partners of both sexes than men are.

Taking people of all sexual orientations combined, 14% of women, but only 4% of men have ever had both male and female sexual partners, as Table 1 shows. Similarly, in the past year, 3% of all women had both male and female sexual partners, compared with less than 1% of men. This is partly because more women than men identify as bisexual, but is also influenced by the higher proportion of women than men among those who identify as either heterosexual or gay having had *both* male and female sexual partners.

technical appendix

Our analysis uses data from the 2002, 2006–2010, and 2011–2013 National Survey of Family Growth (NSFG) on men and women 15 to 44 years of age.

To explore the relationship between sexual orientation and behavior, we began with the measure of sexual orientation in the survey. Men and women were asked whether they "think of themselves as" "heterosexual or straight," "bisexual," or "homosexual, gay, or lesbian." Actually, the wording of these options changed slightly between waves. In 2002 the "gay" option for both men and women was "homosexual," whereas in 2006 and later, it was "homosexual, gay, or lesbian" for women and "homosexual or gay" for men. Also, in some years of the survey (2002 to mid-2008), respondents were also given the option of calling their sexual orientation "something else." Because this response option was not consistent across years of the survey included in analysis, we excluded men and women who selected this response option.

We generated two different measures of sexual behavior from various questions in the survey.

1. Have you ever had a male/female sexual partner? For this measure, we relied on two questions. One question asked men and women the number of male (if male) or female (if female) sexual partners they have had during their lifetime, but did not specify what sexual behavior was meant for "sexual partners." Men were asked to answer this question if they reported that they had ever had oral or anal sex with a man and women were asked to answer the question if they

reported that they had ever had a sexual experience with a woman. If men and women said they had had one or more, we considered them to have had a same-sex sexual partner for this measure.

Regarding sex with other-sex sexual partners, men and women were asked how many women (if male) or men (if female) they had ever had vaginal intercourse with; if this number was 1 or more we considered them to have had an other-sex sexual partner during their lifetime. These items were used to create a variable indicating whether each man had had no sexual partners of either sex, sex only with one or more men, sex only with one or more women, or sex with one or more women and one or more men.

2. Did you have a male/female sexual partner last year? This is constructed just like 2) above, but using questions about the number of female and male sexual partners one has had in the last 12 months.

TABLE 1. Percent of men and women of each sexual orientation who have ever had only other sex partners, only same sex partners, both female and mak partners, or no sexual partners

	Sex with Only Other-Sex Partners	Sex with Only Same-Sex Partners	Sex with Both Women and Men	Sex with Neither Women Nor Men	% of Sample in Identity Category
Heterosexual					
Men	83%*	0%*	2%*	14%*	97%*
Women	77%*	.3%*	10%*	1.2%*	94%*
Gay					
Men	2%	55%*	37%*	6%	2%*
Women	5%	37%*	54%*	5%	1%*
Bisexual					
Men	14%	9%*	62%*	15%*	2%*
Women	16%	5%*	73%*	7%*	5%*
Total					
Men	81%*	1%	4%*	14%*	100%
Women	73%*	.9%	14%*	12%*	100%

Note: Men are asked their number of male sex partners if they report ever having had oral or anal sex with a man, and are asked their number of female sex partners if they have ever had intercourse with a woman. Women are asked their number of female partners if they report they have ever had a sexual experience with a woman, and are asked their number of male sex partners if they have ever had intercourse with a man. N=14,732 men, weighted. N=17,140 women, weighted. The asterisks indicate that men and women's sexual activity are significantly different from one another, at p←0.05, two-tailed test.

One might worry that respondents would not be honest about same-sex sex or non-heterosexual identities, given the social bias against them. To try to avoid respondents saying what they thought the interviewer wanted to hear rather than the truth, the questions on sexual identity and sex with same-sex partners were asked through an Audio Computer-Assisted Self-Interview (ACASI) system in survey waves prior to 2011. The interviewer handed the respondent a computer and earphones and stepped away to provide privacy while the respondent keyed answers into the computer. This ACASI approach was used for questions on sexual orientation, as well as the questions on number of same-sex partners, and what specific sexual behaviors respondents had done with a man and with a woman. In the survey wave from 2011-2013, these questions were moved to the main male respondent questionnaire.

One might also be concerned that there seems to have been a higher bar to saying a man than a woman had sex with a same-sex partner, since men were only asked the question of how many same-sex partners they had had if they reported they had ever had oral or anal sex with a man, whereas women were asked the question if they reported they had ever had any sexual experience with a woman. (Only in 2002, when an oral sex screener question was used, would women have had to have oral sex to be counted as having had a same-sex partner.) However, we have ascertained that over 90% of those who report having had a female sexual partner (whether or not they have had any male partners) also report having had oral sex with a woman sometime. This convinces us that most women we are counting as having had female partners are not referring to experiences such as public kissing, but to sexual activity involving genitals.

TABLE 2. Percent of men and women of each sexual orientation who, in the last 12 months, have only other-sex, only same-sex, both female and male, or no sexual partners					
	Sex with Only Other-Sex Partners	Sex with Only Same-Sex Partners	Sex with Both Women and Men	Sex with Neither Women Nor Men	% of Sample in Identity Category
Heterosexual					
Men	8.3%*	0%	.4%	17%	97%*
Women	81%*	0%	2%*	17%	94%*
Gay					
Men	3%	81%	2%*	13%	2%*
Women	5%	74%	13%*	8%	1%*
Bisexual					
Men	34%*	12%	33%	21%*	2%*
Women	53%*	9%	27%	12%*	5%*
Total					
Men	81%*	2%	.9%*	17%	100%
Women	79%*	1%	3%*	16%	100%

Note: Men are asked if they have had male sex partners in the past 12 months if they have ever had oral or anal sex with a man, and are asked if they have had female sex partners in the past 12 months if they have ever had vaginal, oral or anal intercourse with a woman. Women are asked if they have had female sex partners in the past 12 months if they report they have ever had a sexual experience with a female and are asked if they have had male sex partners in the past 12 months if they have ever had vaginal, oral or anal sex with a male. N=14,732 men, weighted. N=17,140 women, weighted. The asterisks indicate that men and women's sexual activity are significantly different from one another, at p←0.05, two-tailed test.

mapping sexual commerce and politics

overview

How does sexuality operate in the public sphere? Beyond individual experience, sexuality studies serve as a prism through which to view the complex interplay of religion, politics, education, and economics. Battles continue to be waged over sexuality as something that can be bought, sold, traded, regulated, policed, and protected. The politcs of sexual commerce and regulation are deeply intertwined with contemporary global dynamics that include rural/urban shifts, changing labor markets, and immigration patterns.

Travis Kong explores the lives of China's "Money Boys," young, often rural, sex workers who transact with men in urban areas. These boys trade sexuality for money and the opportunity to live an urban lifestyle with what they hope is the promise of greated social acceptance and mobility.

Kimberly Kay Hoang delves into the fascinating phenomenon of "gender vertigo" in transnational marriages between women from developing countries such as Vietnam and men from Western countries such as the United States, Canada, or Australia. Hoang describes the experiences of young, poor, women in Vietnam who engage in sex work specifically with Western men in hopes of exchanging sexual and emotional labor for economic mobility and the chance for a new life. But what happens if they do marry these men and move away?

Catherine Connell examines the politics of sexuality in her article, "Pride and Prejudice and Professionalism," in which she describes how teachers deliberate about whether or not to come out in their workplace and to their students.

What are the implications of gays and lesbians clustering in specific neighborhoods? In his articles, "Lesbian Geographies" and "There Goes the Gayborhood," Amin Ghaziani maps the politics of LGBTQ geographies.

things to consider

- Sexual scripts have a regulatory effect on acceptable sexual expression and sexual relationships. How does this manifest in your own response to Kong's and Hoang's articles?.
- Map the different dynamics—immigration, local economies, etc.—that give rise to the experiences that Kong and Hoang describe.
- How are these dynamics reflected in U.S. neighborhood geographies and politics?
- Does it matter if elementary school teachers are open about their sexual partnerships with their colleagues and the children they teach? Think of some other social statuses that are not immediately relevant that may have an impact on students and teachers.

sex entrepreneurs in the new china

travis s.k. kong

summer 2012

Liu Liu was born in a small village. "My family was very poor," he told me. "When I was young I did not do well in education and knew that I would not be able to go to university. Even if I could, my family would not have enough money to afford my study. I decided to go out to work." He desperately wanted to move away from his rural home, hoping for a brighter life in the city. "I swore that I would never stay in a small village for the rest of my life. I swore I would live in a big city!"

After a string of low-wage, demanding jobs, Liu Liu soon realized that urban life could be as hard as rural life. He went to work in a restaurant in Xi'an when he was 16 years old. The wage was about 60 yuan, about 8 dollars per month, plus meals and accommodation. "I stayed there for about half a year, I then went back home," he said. He went to Shanghai to work in a factory, where the pay was somewhat higher, and sold pirate DVDs for a while.

Liu Liu shared the dream of many rural-to-urban migrants: he wanted to become an entrepreneur by starting a small business or opening a small shop such as a restaurant, grocery store, or boutique. These aspirations were never realized. So, rather than moving back to his village, he grasped an opportunity to earn some quick money, and became a sex worker. In 2006, through some friends he made chatting on the Internet, he began to work in a bar and to earn money from sex work.

In China, male sex workers who predominantly serve men are called "money boys," or *zai* ("son," "boy"), while those who serve women are called *yazi* ("duck") or *nan gongguan* ("male public relation"). Money boys comprise the largest group of male sex workers. The actual size of this population is unknown, and estimates vary widely. Of the 2 million to 20 million men who have sex with other men in China, 5 to 24 percent of them are money boys.

For gay money boys, migration represents a way to escape from the rural homophobic environment and avoid familial pressures to get married. In Shenzhen, perhaps the most liberal city in China, Liu Liu says, "I can make love with men, lots of men!" Like other rural migrants, he was drawn into sex work when he became disillusioned with the hardships of both agricultural and industrial work. He wanted the freedom offered by an urban lifestyle. "I thought I would earn some money, and yes indeed, I have earned quite a lot of money," he says. "And my clients helped me buy a flat! I can tell people that I live much

> *Transience characterizes the lives of money boys, self-reliance is their motif of survival, and urban entrepreneurship is their dream.*

happier than any one of my relatives who still live in my home village."

Since 2004, I have conducted ethnographic research on the male sex work industry in three major Chinese cities that have large concentrations of money boys: Beijing, Shanghai, and Shenzhen. I have interviewed more than 60 money boys, and participated in non-government organization outreach teams, visiting venues frequented by money boys and gay men, such as parks, bars, saunas, massage parlors, and nightclubs.

Most Chinese people see money boys as powerless young men who suffer personality deficits, childhood traumas, and family dysfunction, or as rural-to-urban migrants with little or no education, who are unaware of the illegality of prostitution. Attracted to the quick money that can be earned through sex work, these innocent young men, they believe, are lured by pimps, who then lock them up in brothels and force them to have sex with clients. Such experiences lead to severe depression, substance abuse, and high-risk sex for money boys, who become vectors of sexual diseases and victims of exploitative capitalism.

Contrary to this widespread view, what I've found is that money boys are rural-to-urban migrants who have made a rational choice to engage in sex work in order to become successful urban citizens and entrepreneurs. The experiences of men like Liu Liu must be understood within the context of China's quest for urbanization, modernization, and globalization. The reconfiguration of the "capitalist" market and the "socialist" party-state in reform China has generated new forms of possibility and control on both the societal and the individual level, opening up a labor market that has led to massive rural-to-urban migration. This, and the state's diminished control over private life, has led to a growing informal sex labor market, as well as the emergence of gay and lesbian identities and communities.

The growing emphasis on capitalist ideals in China means that individuals are being encouraged to pursue their fortunes, prompting many to move from the countryside to the city. Sex work provides financial and other rewards at a time when China is undergoing rapid change and modernization. It enables some to escape the constraints of their daily lives, but also leads to dislocation and displacement.

becoming a money boy

In China, the state's increasing promotion of the market economy has led to a massive "floating population" of rural-to-urban migrants. The adverse working lives of these migrants have been well documented: from the increasing numbers of protests and strikes by rural migrant workers in recent years, to the recent suicide cases at Foxconn, where Apple iPhones and other products are manufactured.

Money boys move to cities with the same goals as other rural-to-urban migrants: they want to earn money, experience a new world, and become successful urban citizens. Primarily ethnic Han Chinese (the dominant group), they tend to be from rural or semi-rural villages, and sometimes second-tier towns. Most self-identify as homosexual or bisexual, while a few identify as heterosexual. The majority are single, having been raised in conventional families and possessing similar levels of education as other rural migrants. Few report having suffered from sexual abuse, or being forced to enter the sex industry against their will.

Like other migrants, money boys are governed by the system of *hukou* ("household registration"), through which a registration number is designated to an individual based on his or her locality and family background. Since 1958, the *hukou* has controlled the flow of internal migration, especially rural-to-urban, governing people's lives and providing the government with a mega-database on the populace.

If you are born in a rural village, you acquire a rural *hukou*, and are eligible for lesser housing, healthcare, and education benefits than those with an urban *hukou*. Consequently, rural-to-urban migrants end up in the temporary, menial jobs in the construction, retailing, or catering industries that most urban citizens are unwilling to take, or they simply drift from place to place.

While the Chinese state claimed that it had successfully eradicated prostitution in the Mao period, it "resurfaced" in the late 1970s, coinciding with China's move to a market-based economy, and has since become a highly lucrative business. Prostitution offers a relatively attractive alternative to other menial jobs, not just in terms of monetary rewards, but also in terms of the potential for self-management, flexibility, social mobility, self esteem, and sexual pleasure. There are many types of sex workers: independent workers like hustlers at parks, bars, and on the Internet; brothel workers, who labor under a manager (or a pimp), who are often required to stay at the brothel; and houseboys, who are kept by a man.

Compared to female prostitution, the organizational structure of male sex work is relatively loose, and workers can move quite freely from one type of work to another. Street prostitution is also not as stigmatized for men as it is for women. While prostitution provides career opportunities, it's also a risky business. China operates a "prohibition" model in which all prostitution activities are illegal, and sex workers and clients are subject to detention and possible fines if they are caught. Third-party prostitution is considered to be a serious criminal offense punishable by years of imprisonment. Because they fear being caught, money boys find it difficult to move up the ladder to become managers, or pimps. There is also the constant risk of physical violence, and robbery, rape, sexual disease, and stress.

As Ah Jun, a 20-year-old man who worked full time at a brothel for three years, told me, "Some [clients] took you out and you had to drink with them and take pills with them, they wanted to get 'high' and then brought you home and had sex with you . . . they could then do it many times . . . day and night . . . I think I kind of abandoned myself. I don't want to learn anything. If I have clients, I work; if not, I just watch television, play cards. Every single day I am idle, I don't know how a day is spent . . . time just passes . . . I can't think about the future, I don't know what it will be . . . I just hang in there."

There are also the stresses of a short-lived career. Internal competition among money boys is fierce; the sex industry is constantly looking for "fresh meat." The longer one is in the business, the less one is paid. As a result, money boys are a highly mobile class of migrants, shifting continuously from one occupational setting to another—between street hustling, brothel/massage parlors, freelance, and houseboy varieties—in China, Hong Kong, Macau, or other South East Asian countries like Singapore, Malaysia, and Thailand. This transnational "circuit of desire" is the lifeblood of sex tourism in Asia.

Because prostitution is traditionally defined as a feminine activity, the masculinity of money boys is often suspect, and they are not considered "real men." Their same-sex activities are also stigmatized. Since 2000, lesbians and gay men in China have been transformed from pathological, deviant subjects to responsible, respectable consumer citizens. This emerging homosexual subject—urban, cosmopolitan, civilized, consumerist, and middle-class—is the new homosexual norm. In this context, money boys are often seen as "failed" gay citizens: "bad" gays that mix sex with money, corrupting the image of middle-class gay men.

migrants "on the wing"

While the *hukou* system certainly contributes to their political, economic, and social exclusion, most money boys do not view *hukou* as a structural problem. Rather, they see it as something they must learn to bear. Very few have managed to raise the amount of money they would need to buy an urban *hukou*, so they tend to remain suspended within the rural-urban chasm, often moving between their home village and the city.

Xiao Hao, a 35-year-old gay man who was born in a small village in Chongqing and spent six years as a money boy, suffered a lot at the hands of the *hukou* system. "I hate the *hukou* system very much . . . wherever I go, I need to apply for a temporary resident permit," he said. "If I stay here [he now resides in Shenzhen], I should be able to live here without hassle, right? Since you are not from here, you cannot enjoy the insurance, medical care, etc. Why should one family treat its members so differently?" He has no medical care if he gets sick, and needs to go home. If he goes abroad, he must provide certificates from his hometown. "If I am married and have babies, it will cost more for them to study," he says. "It is very troublesome."

Given these common experiences, it is no wonder many migrants seize the opportunity to become transient city wanderers. Xiao Qing, a 25-year-old gay man who has freelanced for the past eight years, mainly meets men through the Internet. He chats with clients online and they send him travel money. He moves around and stays with any client that wants to "buy" him for a few hours, a few months, or a few years, watching for opportunities he can seize "on the wing." It is precisely through this transient, temporary way of operating that Xiao can maximize his profits from different clients. Soliciting on the Internet is also less dangerous than soliciting in public, or working in a brothel that may be raided by the police at any moment. Without a physical entity, the Internet serves as a *hukou*-less world, which allows him to erase rural-urban boundaries and perhaps even escape the criminalizing gaze of the state.

> One man told me, "I live much happier than any of my relatives who are still in my home village. I can make love with men, lots of men!"

Many money boys don't see selling sex for money as work. Instead, they adopt the attitude that "this is not a job, it's just a tool to earn money"—words I heard time and again. They stress that it is simply a way to meet "friends" and have fun, downplaying the exchange of their body for financial rewards. This is particularly true for the gay money boys, who view sex work as a way to find a boyfriend, someone to love, who might help them get out of the industry. This leads to a blurring of the boundaries between love and money, friend and client, and sex and work.

This weak work identity, which leads them to reject the professionalization of sex work, has made the fight for rights in a collective sense difficult. Under constant threat of violence from clients and triad members (Chinese criminal underground organizations which control illegal gambling, human trafficking, and prostitution), and sanctions from police and government officials, money boys have no legitimate channel for protest.

Due to social stigma, few money boys come out to their families and friends; they are doubly closeted. They cannot hide their money boy identity in the gay community as gay men are their potential clients. Due to the prevalent anti-money boy atmosphere, most choose to keep their distance from the gay community, carefully choosing friends whom they can come out to. "People from society look down upon us," says Xiao Hao. "The gay circle is the same . . . they discriminate against us. They don't think we are proper. I think people should make their own choice, live their own lifestyles."

> *Money boys challenge middle-class gay sensibilities and the logic of cosmopolitan consumerism they embody.*

urban dreams—and risks

Contrary to conventional understandings that may construct them as innocent, as naïve, or as sociopaths, money boys are in many respects like other rural-to-urban migrants. Tired of the dead end of menial labor, with its long hours and shamefully poor wages, they chose an alternative route. The men I spoke with are well aware of the hardships sex work may entail, but are determined to take responsibility for their own lives and rely on themselves rather than on a state that has failed to accommodate them. Transience characterizes the lives of money boys, self-reliance is their motif of survival, and becoming an urban citizen and an entrepreneur is their dream.

Money boys illustrate many of the contradictions within China's rapid transformation towards urbanization, modernization, and globalization. The state's capitalist labor market strategies produce massive job opportunities in the cities, while the *hukou* system deprives rural-to-urban migrants of rights and benefits, leaving many in hopeless job situations. Prostitution offers rural migrants an opportunity to escape these situations, and fulfill their dreams of becoming urban citizens and entrepreneurs. Although money boys enjoy job satisfactions such as financial rewards, control, and freedom, they are also exposed to physical, sexual, social, and psychological risks.

The burgeoning informal sex labor market of the past few decades coexists with the state's prohibitionist stance on prostitution, which in turn contributes to the stigma surrounding the occupation. The state's decreasing control over private life has led to the emergence of gay and lesbian identities and communities which have

long been suppressed (especially in rural areas), and adds to the growing demands for sex workers. But money boys pose dilemmas for the gay community; their "provincial," "bad," and "disrespectable" image challenges newly established middle-class gay sensibilities, which operate according to the logic of consumerism and cosmopolitanism.

Money boys' engagement with sex work can be seen as a form of resistance to an adverse formal labor market. But the stigmatized nature of the work means that they are not keen to organize to improve their migrant status, labor benefits, or sexual rights. They are shunned by urban citizens as migrants, stigmatized for sexually servicing other men, and rejected by the gay community.

Like many other participants in China's bid for modernization, they search for independence and empowerment but endure displacement and dislocation.

recommended resources

Pun, Ngai, and Lu, Huilin. 2010. "Unfinished Proletrarianization: Self, Anger, and Class Action among the Second Generation of Peasant-Workers in Present-Day China," *Modern China* 36(5):493–519. Analyzes recent protests and actions taken by rural-to-urban migrants in response to adverse working conditions in the cities.

Richard, Parker. 1999. *Beneath the Equator: Cultures of Desire, Male Homosexuality, and Emerging Gay Communities in Brazil.* London: Routledge. Chapter Six examines Brazilian male prostitutes who find sex, love, and work through sexual migration within and outside the continent of South America.

Rofel, Lisa. 2010. "The Traffic in Money Boys," *Positions: East Asia Cultures Critique* 18(2):425–58. Locates money boys in the context of neoliberalism in China, and argues that money boys pose a dilemma for the Chinese urban gay man's search for "proper" desires and cultural citizenship.

Dorothy, Solinger. 1999. *Contesting Citizenship in Urban China: Peasant, Migrants, the State, and the Logic of the Market.* Oakland, CA: University of California Press. Documents the work experiences of migrant workers in cities in terms of reform China's increasing promotion of the market economy and declining government benefits.

Tiantian, Zheng. 2009. *Red Lights: The Lives of Sex Workers in Postsocialist China.* Minneapolis, MN: University of Minnesota Press. Examines the lives of young rural women trying to become modern and independent subjects by becoming "karaoke hostesses" (female sex workers) in the northeastern China seaport of Dalian.

transnational gender vertigo

kimberly kay hoang

spring 2013

I first met Tram in 2006 in a tiny bar on Pham Ngu Lao Street in Ho Chi Minh City (formerly Saigon), in a neighborhood frequented by backpackers from abroad. Tram and other sex workers in the bar, disguised as bartenders, catered to Western budget travelers seeking brief encounters or longer relationships-for-hire. They were the bar's key attraction, but the women received no wages from the owner; they were independent entrepreneurs in a niche of the sex trade.

Tram, 27 years old and adorned with bracelet, rings, and a diamond necklace, was a model of success and economic mobility. She lived in a brand-new luxury condo with two servants, a full-time housecleaner and a cook who prepared Western foods for her new American husband. Tram had come from a poor village, she told me, where the only jobs were in the rice fields. In Ho Chi Minh City, she worked first as a maid and then in a clothing factory. But after two years of earning no more than the equivalent of US$70 a month, Tram had saved no money, could barely cover food and rent, and saw no hope for improvement. "Life in the city is so expensive," she said. She saw sex work as her best route out of poverty.

Tram met William, 70, as a client, and quickly began to develop a more intimate relationship with him, hoping that her emotional labor might lead to ongoing economic support—in a remittance relationship, or marriage. Many Western men come to Vietnam seeking wives, or they become attached to women they hired once there, sympathizing with their plight, and wanting to take them out of the sex trade and care for them. Six months after they met, William asked Tram to marry him and move to North America. They were married in 2007.

In 2009, I reconnected with Tram, along with William and their three children at an airport outside of Montreal, Canada. As we drove the three hours to their home, passing lumber farms, acres of undeveloped land, and pastures sprinkled with sheep, I commented on its beauty and tranquility. But Tram expressed no such sentiments. She had never intended to escape small town Vietnam, she said, only to end up in another small town in rural Canada. She had hoped to move to the United States, and had dreamed of living in Los Angeles or New York, "a big city, like the movies."

Instead, she found herself isolated, in a cold climate and working long hours. Williams' savings had dwindled, thanks to the expense of immigration, and they had arrived in North America smack in the middle of a global recession. For a year and a half, she worked nights and weekends for her brother in-law's lumber company. She did see progress: By June of the year I came to visit, she had saved over US$20,000 and, with her sister in-law, opened a small shop selling local produce. But she was now

She had dreamed of living in Los Angeles or New York, "a big city, like the movies."

the primary breadwinner, while William, retired but without much of his savings, stayed home with the children. "This is not what I thought my life would be like," she lamented.

The story of Tram and William, like that of other couples in my study, suggests a reversal of the usual trajectory of marital journeys. Ethnographers Denise Brennan and Amalia Cabezas have shown that sex workers often feign love as a strategy to obtain visas to migrate abroad. In Vietnam, the opening to the West in recent decades has inspired some women, usually between the ages of 17 and 32, to seek strategic marriages with Western men through sex work. Of the 71 sex workers I interviewed, 30 got married, and of the 30 just 12 women were able to obtain visas and emigrate. While 12 may not represent a large sample, I followed them for three to six years, spending as much as a week at their homes after they landed in the United States, Australia, France and Canada. While women who traveled from Vietnam to Western countries to be with their husbands did not intend to seek out employment, two-thirds of the women in my study ended up becoming their family's primary breadwinner—reversing typical expectations.

> **Two-thirds of the women ended up becoming their family's primary breadwinner— reversing typical expectations.**

William, like most men in my study, had come to Vietnam deliberately seeking a wife, while others discovered these opportunities once they arrived on visits. Either way, they were eager to find women who would enter a marriage with traditional gender roles that were fast disappearing at home. Their expectations were simple; the men would provide the economic support and the women would provide care, housekeeping and emotional labor.

What happened instead was a classic case of "gender vertigo." Sociologist Barbara Risman used this term to describe the dizzying effect on people who adopt, or find themselves having to embrace, a radical and unfamiliar social role that upends their ideas of how family structures and society work. Dating back to the 1970s at least, this vertigo hit couples engaging in egalitarian role sharing, where husband and wife occupy both roles— breadwinner and nurturer. But in recent years, especially since the Great Recession that began in 2007, this model has shifted 180 degrees. In my study, most of the women had expected to end their working days once they reached their destination. Instead, most of them quickly ended up finding jobs, looking for income to supplement their husbands' and hoping to send some home to family in Vietnam, and 8 of the 12 women quickly became the main breadwinner, often working double shifts, with husbands working less lucrative jobs or at home doing childcare.

In Tram's case, she was able to move beyond the daily grind to open her own business. Others struggled more—and longer.

from sex worker to wife

Thy, then 28, had met her future husband, Mitchell, in 2007. "When I first met him I did not really love him," she explains. But "life in Vietnam was hard, and I was looking for a way to get out. Even after we married I had other boyfriends because I did not think that he would get me out [of Vietnam]." But after two years of visits back and forth, and paying fees to immigration lawyers both in Vietnam and Australia, Thy was finally able to migrate.

In the mid 2000s, stung by marriage scandals, and wary of enabling sex trafficking, more visas were denied by the United States, and the emigration process became increasingly long and arduous, taking an average of two years after a couple married. Most of the men in my study depleted their savings on attorney fees, on the cost of flights back and forth, and by sending money from the United States to support wives or fiancés waiting in Vietnam. The uncertainty in turn could complicate the marriage dynamic; many women hesitate to make the commitment unless it came with some kind of assurance that they would be supported; nor did they want to drop out of the sex business if they weren't assured support.

Thy landed in Melbourne in 2010. Using Skype, she walked me through her and Mitchell's modest apartment, joking about how her standard of living in Australia was much lower than the one that she had in Vietnam. "The first time I went to the grocery store was a shock," she remembered. "Eggs were $4 (Australian dollars) and a whole chicken was $15. Mitchell just kept filling the cart. The bill was $150. It was so expensive." Soon both spouses were working just to cover the necessities.

"I feel like a machine," Thy said, tears welling in her eyes. Everyday we wake up at 6:30 to make breakfast and pack lunch. He leaves, and then around 8:00, I walk to his mom's house," where she works as a maid for neighbors. Mitchell's mother had introduced Thy, and spent three weeks working alongside her to instruct her on how to meet each homeowner's personal expectations. "I work [all day] in empty houses when everyone goes to work, and when I come home, Mitchell is all I have," said Thy. She has come to love Mitchell and to be grateful for all he sacrificed to bring her to Australia and in his work there. "Everyone in his family is very nice to me," says Thy "His mom buys me clothes in the winter, and she always tries to make me feel welcome. But it is very lonely."

None of the 12 women thought of returning to sex work. Most held typical working-class jobs, although one told me in confidence that she worked in a local massage parlor that offered a number of erotic services (but not sexual intercourse). Her husband didn't know this about the spa. She agreed to perform some of these services in order to earn more money, but she drew clear boundaries for herself around the kinds of sexual practices she would perform. What she did like about the job was that she didn't have to struggle to speak English to colleagues or customers. "I don't have to talk to anyone. It is mostly body language."

For their part, many of the men in these relationships felt great anxiety and guilt that they couldn't provide for their wives as they had promised. Most of the couples had arrived in the men's countries in the middle of the worldwide financial crisis, and many found that they had lost their savings or retirement funds in the faltering markets. If they wanted to keep working, or to come out of retirement, they had trouble finding jobs, especially the older men.

Lawrence, in his 60s, living with his wife Nhi in Florida, told me that she "didn't know much about life in the United States—except that I promised I would take care of her and provide her with a better life than the one she had in Vietnam. She wants so many things, and it's hard to say no when she asks for things." Brian, who spends idle days in Vermont, just says he's afraid to turn on the TV to hear more news about how bad the economy is doing. His 401(k) fund is nearly gone and his $1200 a month Social Security payments are "barely enough for us to just get by."

Younger husbands too had been through futile and humiliating job searches; 3 of the 12 were unemployed. Even for couples lucky enough to have two jobs, money was tight. Jeremie, a French man in his early 40s, had traveled to Vietnam as a tourist, and found that he and his lover, Quyen "could live it up." Food was cheap, housing was cheap, and labor was cheap. Western men also had more opportunity; they could take up jobs as English teachers or as editors or translators for local Vietnamese companies. Back in the West, the exchange rate and status they had enjoyed in Vietnam evaporated.

But it didn't help many of the couples to seek out other Vietnamese immigrants abroad. Some of the women found jobs in the Vietnamese ethnic enclaves, in nail salons, restaurants, or coffee shops. But when the details of their marriages were revealed, they suffered new isolation. The stigma associated with being a young Vietnamese woman married to a Western man made it difficult to establish trust or social bonds with them.

Hoai told me, "When the [Vietnamese] owners [of a nail salon] found out that I was married to an older White man, they started to trust me less with the money. They look at me like I might steal something from them because I was a bar girl in Vietnam. The female boss always watches me around her husband."

between love and money

As I heard more stories of struggle and isolation, I began to wonder—and ask—why some of the women didn't leave their husbands, either to live on their own, in different locations or communities in their new countries, or to return to Vietnam. Most of the women in fact, believed that they could easily escape their marriages but remain in their new countries if they claimed that their husbands were abusing them; authorities would believe they were victims of human trafficking. But none wanted to do this, and none wanted to return home.

One reason was pride. Like many immigrants who boldly leave home, full of grand expectations, some of the women hid the truths of their new lives from family at home. Thanh Ha, age 26, was painfully reluctant to reveal what she was doing to earn a living in the United States. She told me at first that she had found work in a tortilla chip factory. I spent nearly four days with the family in their cramped apartment before she finally revealed what she

> *The couples had arrived in the men's countries in the middle of the worldwide financial crisis. Many lost their savings or retirement funds in the faltering markets.*

was doing. "I work in a chip factory," she said, haltingly. "But I don't work on the line." She hesitated. "My job is to collect garbage."

Struck by her emotion, I tried to reassure her that this kind of job could be a stepping-stone to better things. Shaking her head, she said, "When I was in Vietnam, my first job [in a wood factory] was a step-up from my village; the bar was another step up. I was making more money. Picking up trash in America is both a step up and a step down."

When Jeremie suggested returning to Vietnam to live, his wife Quyen was unwilling. She couldn't imagine returning without enough money or Western luxuries to display. One of the reasons the women wanted to send money home, in fact, was to maintain the veneer of upward mobility.

But perhaps the bigger surprise in these developments is the way the women and men began to acclimate to their vertiginous situations. One pleasure for the women was how supportive their husbands were about their earning money—even when they out-earned the men. Thu was surprised by her husband Roger's approach to the money she earned. "He never tells me how to spend it. If I was married to a Vietnamese man, it would probably be hard for him to accept. But Roger is proud; he calls me superwoman."

"I'm lucky because Thomas lets me work," says Xuan, 26, "and he never asks me how I spend the money I earn." Xuan's Vietnamese co-workers who are married to Vietnamese men "always have to ask their husbands if they can send money to Vietnam." These immigrants may "look down on me for my past life in Vietnam, but I have more freedoms, and I live a more carefree life than they do."

Not only were many of the men supportive, they were comforted to know that their wives would be self-sufficient without them. Stanley, a man in his late 70s, said, "She is young, and I want her to be able to take care of herself when I pass away. I had my whole life to work and build my career. She should get to do that too." The women, meanwhile, seemed to have developed affection, even love for their husbands, and certainly a sense of loyalty, a belief that they owed their husbands a great deal. "When I married Jeremie he took care of me and paid for everything," said his Quyen. "When you marry an older man you will have to pay back your debt to him and take care of him too."

Several of the women were still optimistic about their economic prospects, and they maintained the pragmatism that had made them marry these men in the first place. Van explained to me, "We are saving money to open a small shop together. He knows English and can handle the paperwork, and I can run the shop."

Seeking economic security and a pathway out of Vietnam, the women in my study found themselves, thousands of miles away, in marriages where they became the breadwinner. Although they wanted women whom they could support financially who would offer them emotional security, the men found themselves in non-traditional relationships they had not bargained for. This experience of transnational gender vertigo reframes our understandings of sex work, migration, and gendered relationships across transnational spaces.

These couples stayed married, for better or for worse, as the transformation of marriage, migration, and love gave rise to new and different dreams for the future. As Van said, "Do Tinh Den Bac," a phrase that means when you have luck with love or romance, your economic luck may decline. While she and the other women I studied embarked on migration journeys believing that they were sacrificing love for economic fortune, many ended up struggling economically—and some found love along the way.

recommended resources

Brennan, Denise. 2004. *What's Love Got to do with it? Transnational Desires and Sex Tourism in the Dominican Republic.* Durham, North Carolina: Duke University Press. An ethnographic exploration of how sex workers strategize to get married and migrate.

Cabezas, Amalia. 2009. *Economies of Desire: Sex and Tourism in Cuba and the Dominican Republic.* Philadelphia: Temple University Press. This book examines the emotional labors that sex workers perform in their relations with Western tourists.

Cheng, Sealing. 2010. *On the Move for Love: Migrant Entertainers and the U.S. Military in South Korea.* Philadelphia: University of Pennsylvania Press. This book examines Filipina migrant sex workers relations with American GIs in South Korea.

Kempadoo, Kamala. 2004. *Sexing the Caribbean: Gender, Race and Sexual Labor.* London: Routledge. This ethnography examines the racialized and gendered relations in the Caribbean's sex tourism industry.

Schaeffer, Felicity. 2012. *Love and Empire: Cybermarriage and Citizenship across the Americas.* New York: New York University Press. This book looks at the commercialization of intimacy in marriage tourism between the United States and Latin America.

45

pride and prejudice and professionalism

catherine connell

fall 2015

"Out of the closet and into the streets!" has been the guiding principle of lesbian, gay, bisexual, and transgender (LGBT) activism in the U.S. since the 1960s. From the riots at Stonewall and Compton's Cafeteria to the 21st century marriage equality movement, coming out has been the lynchpin in the politics of gay pride. Even the ubiquitous phrase "out and proud" explicitly links coming out and having pride as a package deal. The result is a sometimes subtle, yet pervasive message that coming out is tantamount to a sacred duty for contemporary LGBTs. But is there a drawback to that imperative? What happens when gay pride comes into direct conflict with professionalism?

This question is especially relevant in the lives and careers of gay and lesbian public schoolteachers, for whom professionalism demands an ostensibly sexually neutral presentation of self. On its face, this ethic of sexual neutrality includes teachers both gay and straight, all of whom are expected to uphold strict standards of desexualized dress, talk, and biographical detail with their students. For heterosexual teachers, though, there's a range of indicators of sexuality that are deemed within the bounds of professionalism— pictures of, talking about, and visits from their spouses in the classroom are considered benign displays of sexuality that don't undermine their professionalism (and are often encouraged). Yet the idea that gay and lesbian teachers might do the same remains taboo in all but the most progressive and gay-friendly of schools. How, then, do gay teachers balance the demands of pride and professionalism?

In interviews with 45 gay and lesbian public school teachers in California and Texas, I found that most feel caught in a no-win situation, where coming out in the classroom feels like a fulfillment of their responsibilities to gay pride and a failure of their responsibilities as teaching professionals. This catch-22 is further complicated by the fact that the majority of gay and lesbian teachers (and LGBT workers more generally) can't rely on nondiscrimination protections to mitigate the riskiness of coming out. To date, only 21 states prohibit workplace discrimination on the basis of sexual identity, while even fewer (18 states, plus Washington, D.C.) have nondiscrimination protections for transgender and gender nonconforming workers.

> *Mauricio: "I still believe my job here should be to be your science teacher, not your gay science teacher."*

the pride/professionalism dilemma

When we spoke in 2008, Mauricio, a 20-year veteran of middle school teaching in Texas, still felt passionate and excited about going to work every day. Mauricio was not out to his students, because, in his words, "I literally am just their teacher, their science teacher. I see my sexuality as a gay man as being this much [holds up fingers to indicate inches] of my being. It's a small, small part of who I am. I think the majority of my life is being a science teacher." While Mauricio was initially adamant that his sexuality had no bearing on his work as an educator, he later articulated a sense of guilt about shirking another duty: to be out and proud in school. When I asked how schools could do better by LGBT students and teachers, Mauricio replied, "This is going to say a lot about me, but I wish there were more openly gay men and lesbians in the field. I'm not one of them, obviously, not to my current students, anyway. Because we have to be role models. We definitely have to be role models. . . . Again, I'm not going to run out and out myself because I still believe my job here should be to be your science teacher, not your gay science teacher. But, no, that's important though. Wow, listen to myself."

> Amy: "We help our students by being visible. . . . If they don't see adults feeling comfortable in their own sexuality, what's it saying to them?"

Mauricio's reply demonstrates how even teachers who don't want to and don't choose to be out at school feel the tug of the role modeling demands at the heart of contemporary gay pride discourse. At the end of our interview, he asked anxiously, "I'm not the only one who doesn't come out, am I? There have to be others like me, right?"

I also spoke with Hugh, a Texas high school teacher who was not out to students, and he echoed Mauricio's ambivalence: "You know, I'm kind of a hypocrite because—teachers coming out . . . It would definitely give [LGBT students] a positive role model." Amy, a California high school teacher, articulated the predominant rationale of gay pride's role modeling demand: "We help our students by being visible . . . If they don't see adults feeling comfortable in their own sexuality, what's it saying to them? How does it affect them? If you're coy about it or secretive or whatever."

> "I think, first and foremost, I see myself as a teacher. I don't mix my sexual orientation with my career. You know, it's my career first."

According to this rationale, teachers who are not out to students are being "coy" and "secretive" about their sexuality and in the process are modeling not pride, but shame. It's no surprise, then, that the majority of my interviewees referenced the importance of role modeling gay pride in schools, regardless of their own decisions about coming out.

Part of what made many reluctant to fulfill this role modeling expectation was their acute awareness of how professionalism, in the context of teaching, is infused with heteronormativity. Teaching, as a profession, has a uniquely moral character, one that has been historically sex negative and anti-gay. Teaching contracts often include "moral turpitude" clauses, which allow a school district to fire any teacher who doesn't comply with (vaguely and broadly defined) community standards of moral behavior. While the U.S. is, in many ways, becoming a gay-friendlier place, the idea that children should be protected from the supposedly confusing and even corrupting knowledge of LGBT issues has been very slow to change.

As a result, the prevailing advice about professional comportment that is disseminated through teacher education programs, professional associations, mentors, and administrators discourages even the mildest expressions of non-heterosexuality. Gay and lesbian teachers often feel this injustice keenly. California middle school teacher Rufus explained, "[Heterosexuality in schools gets to be] a range of experience, a way of being. [Straight teachers] talk about their husbands, wives, their straight lives in a way that has an impact on their students and their ideas," while gay and lesbian teachers are rarely afforded the same kind of nuance and candor about their personal lives. In fact, many gay and lesbian teachers felt that the heteronormative strictures of teaching professionalism rendered them virtually invisible—as Mauricio put it, "We're here, we're among you. And I think about it in my own classroom, we're sitting amongst you and you don't even know it."

As a result, gay and lesbian identity comes to be defined as at best, irrelevant to teaching, and at worst, unprofessional and inappropriate—even by gay and lesbian teachers themselves. Cheryl, a California elementary school teacher, explained, "No, [I'm not out at school] because I think, first and foremost, I see myself as a teacher. I don't mix my sexual orientation with my career. You know, it's my career first. I've never even thought about it." Texas elementary school teacher Phillip took it a step further, arguing, "I just don't think it's appropriate for them to know about me at seven or eight years old." Although Phillip referenced the young age of his students as a rationale, Hugh used nearly the same words when talking about high school students: "Children are impressionable . . . . I just don't think it's appropriate to bring up."

Again and again, teachers referenced the idea that identifying oneself as gay or lesbian was unprofessional, inappropriate, or overly personal, even as they readily identified ways that heterosexual teachers reference their straight identities in the classroom. Between the pressures of teaching professionalism, which ask gay and lesbian teachers to leave their sexual identity at home, and the pressures of gay pride's role modeling expectations, many teachers feel stuck.

splitting, knitting, and quitting

Teachers generally take one of three paths for managing this dilemma—they *split* off their professional selves from their sexual selves, they try to *knit* the two together, or they may decide to *quit* by moving into administration or out of the career entirely. Splitters tried to maintain a strict division between the identities of teacher and gay/lesbian. They felt that their sexual identity, like an overcoat or a hat, could be taken off at the schoolhouse doors and re-claimed at the end of the workday. Cheryl, quoted above, demonstrates this line of thinking when she insists that she doesn't "mix" her sexual orientation and her career. Mauricio, too, wanted to be seen as just the science teacher, not the "gay science teacher," despite the pressures of gay pride. He explained, "As a gay man, I should be proud to be out and stuff, and I am. But I'm here at work to do work." Still, he said, he *would* be out in the classroom if he didn't have to worry about administrators and parents penalizing him for it. Splitters came to their decisions with varying degrees of comfort and different kinds of motivations, but they were united by sense that the dictates of teaching professionalism required them to keep their workplace and sexual selves separate.

Knitters tried to resolve the pride/professionalism duality by carefully integrating their gay and lesbian identities into their teaching performance. Chelsea, a California high school teacher, offered a common explanation: "For me, to not be open would be just defeating the purpose of going to work. So I, on the first day of school . . . I actually said, 'And I'm a lesbian' in my introduction . . . . I just think it's really important, that teachers need to be out and open in order to support their kids." Knitters chose to integrate their sexual and professional selves as both a gay rights strategy and as a way of feeling more authentic or whole. Rufus offered, "Just from my own personal experience, I think it has really benefited my teaching experience, by being out. And I see and hear from my students, just them knowing that, it makes them more comfortable with gay people." Chelsea

concurred, "I think the purpose of being a teacher is to connect with other human beings and guide them. And you can't do that without being an honest person. And you're not being honest if you're not being yourself."

While knitting may seem like the ideal solution to the pride/professionalism dilemma, it was a virtually impossible one for teachers who weren't legally protected from employment discrimination, who didn't have supportive colleagues and administrators, and who weren't economically secure enough to risk possible fallout from their openness. Even for teachers who did have all this, the risks were steep—Rufus routinely faced harassment from students, including defamatory graffiti on his classroom door and taunts in the hallway. Knitters deeply internalized the out-and-proud dictates of gay pride and it shaped their on-the-job choices at a significant cost.

> John: *"I was just so tired of lying to them and lying to myself. . . . like, almost eight hours a day, I had to hide who I was."*

For many, splitting and knitting were unsatisfactory or unrealistic. For some, quitting became the only viable solution. John, a California middle school science teacher, started out his career by splitting, only to find it unbearable: "I was just so tired of lying to them and lying to myself . . . like, almost eight hours a day, I had to hide who I was." He resolved to try knitting: "I wanted to just be honest with them, you know, this is who I am. And I'm still your teacher, I'm still the same person, and you know, accept me or not accept me." Unfortunately for John, several students and coworkers chose the latter. He struggled through a year of harassment and isolation before deciding to quit and pursue a new career where he would not have to make these difficult choices. While quitting allowed teachers to escape the no-win choice between splitting and knitting, it did so only through opting out of classroom instruction entirely.

> Chelsea: *"I think the purpose of being a teacher is to connect with other human beings and guide them. And you can't do that without being an honest person. And you're not being honest if you're not being yourself."*

beyond pride or professionalism

The fact that gay and lesbian teachers, regardless of geographic context, evinced a shared frustration with the incompatibilities of gay pride and teaching professionalism demonstrates a fundamental problem with the overreliance on coming out as a political strategy. It suggests that nondiscrimination legislation alone is not enough to improve LGBT working conditions. Instead of putting the onus on individuals to come out, we need to consider how institutions like schools are embedded in (and reproductive of) heteronormativity and homophobia.

Schools and workplaces are structured into what feminist sociologist Joan Acker calls "inequality regimes." Acker argues that heterosexuality (alongside Whiteness, maleness, and middle-class status) is an obscured, but essential component of the day-to-day rules, practices, policies, and interactional norms of most organizations. By virtue of their distance from it, gay and lesbian teachers' experiences show us how heterosexuality is embedded in the very fundamentals of teaching as a profession.

To ease the fundamental tensions between gay pride and teaching professionalism that make working in education so challenging for so many, a stronger and more expansive network of nondiscrimination protections for all LGBT workers is certainly important. Comprehensive employment rights are a necessary precondition for dismantling the heteronormativity built into the professional standards and expectations of teaching. But, as I demonstrated above, it's not enough—even teachers who currently have those protections feel pressured to keep their sexuality out of the classroom. Once nondiscrimination policies are in place across the U.S., the norms of teaching professionalism will still need to change. Some educational advocates have begun the crucial work of developing "queer pedagogy," a philosophy of education that challenges the sexually neutral ethic of teaching professionalism. A queer pedagogical approach not only breaks down normative assumptions about sexuality and gender through the everyday practices of education, it also encourages students to challenge intersecting inequalities, including racism, classism, ableism, and others. Queer pedagogy could help dismantle institutionalized inequality regimes. While this perspective is slowly gaining some traction within the field, it's been slow and difficult going, as highlighted in a recent article of the journal *Education and Urban Society*. Increased support for and integration of queer pedagogical insight into the curriculum and policy of schools will go far to ease some of the burden gay and lesbian teachers face.

The responsibility for change, of course, does not lie entirely with schools. The one-size-fits-all model of gay pride that demands coming out at any cost is far too individualistic and exclusionary a rights tactic. The coming out mandate ignores the fact that some people are more vulnerable to negative outcomes than others. It asks all LGBT-identified people to foreground their sexual identities above all others. It also leaves organizational heteronormativity more or less unchecked.

Rather than rely on coming out as the key strategy for combating sexual and gender inequalities, more focus should be placed on the ways that sexual normativity and oppression are woven into the daily fabric of our lives and sacred institutions.

recommended resources

Beigel, Stuart. 2010. *The Right To Be Out: Sexual Orientation and Gender Identity in America's Public Schools*. Minneapolis: University of Minnesota Press. Traces the legal and policy history of LGBT identification in schools; Chapter Three is especially useful for understanding the partial and tenuous legal protections available to LGBT teachers.

The Beyond Bullying Project. beyondbullyingproject.com. Gathers stories of LGBTQ sexuality in schools with the intention of moving the discussion beyond the limiting frameworks of bullying, mental health, and risk.

GLSEN (Gay, Lesbian, and Straight Education Network). glsen.org. An advocacy organization committed to improving the school experience for LGBTQ students; their biennial National School Climate Survey has been influential in shaping educational policy and research.

Fredman, Amy J, Schultz, Nicole J, and Hoffman, Mary F. 2015. "'You're Moving a Frickin' Big Ship': The Challenges of Addressing LGBTQ Topics in Public Schools," *Education and Urban Society* 47(1):56–85. Addresses educators' efforts to implement queer pedagogy in their classrooms.

Harbeck, Karen. 1997. *Gay and Lesbian Educators: Personal Freedoms, Public Constraints*. Malden, MA: Amethyst Press and Productions. A groundbreaking history of gay and lesbian public schoolteachers in the U.S. that provides an excellent overview of why and how heteronormativity became embedded in the very nature of teaching.

lesbian geographies

amin ghaziani

winter 2015

When we think about gay neighborhoods, many of us are not immediately imagining lesbians. But like gay men, lesbians also have certain cities, neighborhoods, and small towns in which they are more likely to live. Back in 1992, for example, the *National Enquirer* cheekily declared the small town of Northampton, Mass. "Lesbianville, USA." *Newsweek* piggybacked on the reference a year later and sealed the area's Sapphic reputation: "If you're looking for lesbians, they're everywhere," said Diane Morgan, who used to codirect an annual summer festival that drew thousands of women. "After living here for a couple years, you begin to forget what it's like in the real world." The bucolic town—"where the coffee is strong and so are the women"—had a lesbian mayor, Mary Clare Higgins, who held a near-record tenure of political office—six consecutive two-year terms.

If Northampton is the Lesbianville of the Northeast, then Portland, Ore. and Oakland, Calif. are the ladyloving capitals of the West, while Atlanta, Ga. and St. Petersburg, Fla. remain hot in the Southern imagination. And let us not forget about Park Slope in Brooklyn: "Being a dyke and living in the Slope is like being a gay man and living in the Village," one resident remarked to geographer Tamar Rothenberg. In recent years, New York City has also seen an influx of lesbians in Kensington, Red Hook, and Harlem.

There is an astonishing diversity of queer spaces for men and women alike, as Census data on zip codes shows us.

Sometimes lesbians live in the same areas as gay men, like Provincetown, Mass., Rehoboth Beach, Del., and the Castro in San Francisco, Calif. But lesbian geographies are also quite distinct. Coupled women tend to live in less urban areas, while men opt for bigger cities (regrettably, the Census only asks about same-sex partner households, and so we cannot track single gays and lesbians). We do not have a good grasp on why this happens, but cultural cues regarding masculinity and femininity play a part. One rural, gay Midwesterner confided to sociologist Emily Kazyak: "If you're a flaming gay queen, they're like, 'Oh, you're a freak, I'm scared of you.' But if you're a really butch woman and you're working at a factory, I think it's a little easier." Lesbians who perform masculinity in rural environments (by working hard labor or acting tough, for example) are not as stigmatized as effeminate gay men. This makes rural contexts safer and more inviting for women.

Concerns about family formation and childrearing come into play as well. According to an analysis by the Williams Institute, a think tank at UCLA, more than 111,000 same-sex couples are raising 170,000 biological, step, or adopted children. There are some striking gender differences within this group. For instance, among those individuals who are younger than 50 and living alone or with a partner, nearly half of LGBT women (48%) and a fifth of LGBT men (20%) are raising a child under the age of 18. Among couple households, specifically, 27% of female and 11% of male couples are raising children. Finally, among lesbian, gay, and bisexual adults who report ever having given birth to or fathered a child, 80% are female. All these numbers tell us the same thing: lesbians are more likely than gay men to have and raise children.

Higher rates of parenting by lesbians create different housing needs for them. Traditional gay neighborhoods

Highest Concentrations of Gay and Lesbian Households

Same-Sex Male Couples				Same-Sex Female Couples			
zip code	location	% of all households	median price per sq. foot	zip code	location	% of all households	median price per sq. foot
94114	Castro, San Francisco, CA	14.2%	671	02657	Provincetown, Cape Cod, MA	5.1%	532
92264	Palm Springs, CA	12.4%	146	01062	Northampton, MA	3.3%	187
02657	Provincetown, Cape Cod, MA	11.5%	532	01060	Northampton, MA	2.6%	189
92262	Palm Springs, CA	11.3%	136	02130	Jamaica Plain, Boston, MA	2.4%	304
33305	Wilton Manors, Fort Lauderdale, FL	10.6%	206	19971	Rehoboth Beach, DE	2.4%	187
90069	West Hollywood, Los Angeles, CA	8.9%	481	95446	Guerneville, north of San Francisco, CA	2.2%	197
94131	Noe Valley/ Glen Park/ Diamond Heights, San Francisco, CA	7.4%	564	02667	Wellfleet, Cape Cod, MA	2.2%	340
75219	Oak Lawn, Dallas, TX	7.1%	160	94619	Redwood Heights/ Skyline, Oakland, CA	2.1%	230
19971	Rehoboth Beach, DE	7.0%	187	30002	Avondale Estates, suburban Atlanta, GA	1.9%	97
48069	Pleasant Ridge, suburban Detroit, MI	6.8%	107	94114	Castro, San Francisco, CA	1.9%	671

Source: 2010 U.S. Census, analyzed by Jed Kolko, Trulia Trends

are more likely to offer single-occupancy apartments at relatively high rents, but lesbian households with children seek the reverse: lower-rent, more family-oriented units. This steers women either to different neighborhoods in the same city (Andersonville or Rogers Park rather than Boystown in Chicago for example, or Oakland instead of the Castro in San Francisco), or to non-urban areas, as we can see in the earlier table and graphics below.

Same-sex female couples per 1,000 households by county (adjusted)

Alaska

Hawaii

0 - 1.8
1.9 - 2.9
3.0 - 3.4
3.5 - 16.4

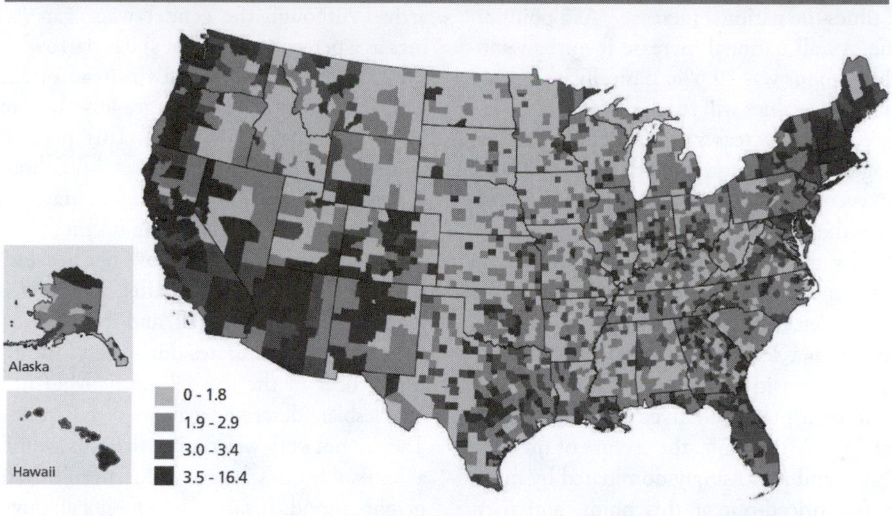

Same-sex male couples per 1,000 households by county (adjusted)

Alaska

Hawaii

0
0.1 - 2.7
2.8 - 3.7
3.8 - 24.8

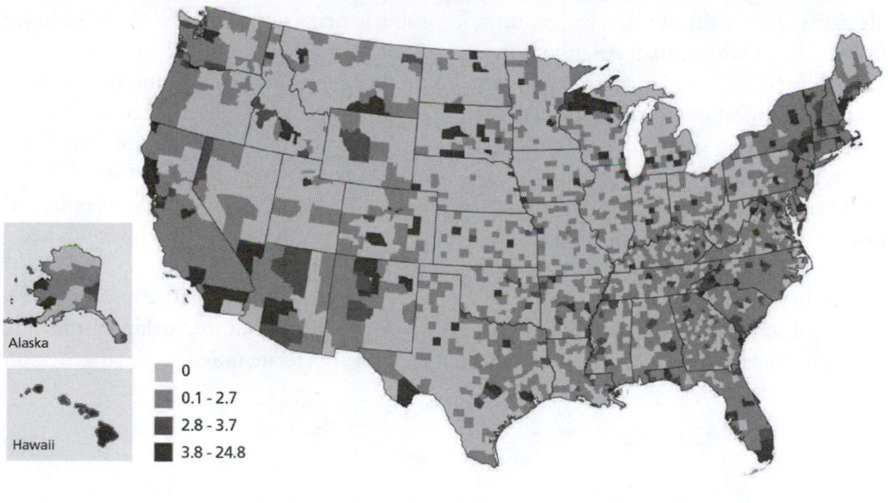

Source: 2010 U.S. Census, analyzed by Gary J. Gates and Abigail M. Cooke, The Williams Institute

Back in the city, lesbians exert a surprising influence on cycles of gentrification. The idea that gay people initiate renewal efforts is widely known but imprecise. Lesbians actually predate the arrival of gay men in developing areas. A 2010 *New York Observer* article put it this way: "[L]esbians are handy urban pioneers, dragging organic groceries and prenatal yoga to the 'frontier' neighborhoods they make hospitable for the rest of us. In three to five years." Lesbians move in first—they are "canaries in the urban coal mine"—and try to create a space for themselves. Gay men arrive next as they are priced out of previous enclaves. According to a 2013 Trulia report, "Neighborhoods where same-sex male couples account for more than one percent of all households (that's three times the national average) had price increases, on average, of 13.8%. In neighborhoods where same-sex female couples account for more than one percent of all households, prices increased by 16.5%—more than one-and-a-half times the national increase." As a point of comparison, the overall national increase for urban and suburban neighborhoods was 10.5%. Basically, the gayer the block, the faster its values will rise. Lesbian neighborhoods experience greater increases probably because they are in earlier stages of gentrification, further from a ceiling where prices eventually plateau, and because they had lower values from the start.

Gay men follow the trailblazing lesbians (awareness of where the women are circulates by word of mouth). As the numbers of men increase, the identity of the area gradually shifts from a lesbian enclave to a "gayborhood." During this transition, the composition of the district where the men previously lived becomes demographically straighter. Meanwhile, the texture of the new area becomes gayer and increasingly dominated by men. Many lesbians feel priced-out at this point, and they migrate elsewhere, initiating another round of renewal.

Subcultural differences also help explain why it is harder to find lesbian lands. Gay men are more influenced by sexual transactions and building commercial institutions like bars, big night clubs, saunas, and trendy restaurants, while gay women are motivated by feminism and countercultures. This is why lesbian neighborhoods often consist of a cluster of homes near progressive, though not as flashy, organizations and businesses that were already based in the area—think artsy theaters and performance spaces, alternative or secondhand bookstores, cafes, community centers, bike shops, and organic or cooperative grocery stores. This gives lesbian districts a quasi-underground character, making them seem hidden for those who are not in the know.

But this begs us to ask another question: why, after gay men arrive, do some lesbians leave? One reason pertains to women's relative lack of economic power. Real estate values and rents continue to increase as more gay men arrive. Although the gender wage gap (women's earnings as a percentage of men's) has narrowed, according to the US Labor Department's Bureau of Labor Statistics, women still earn, on average, less than men—81% of what men earned in 2012. This persistent economic inequality explains why lesbian households are located in lower-income areas, and unfortunately, such material threats are always encroaching on them.

Finally, some lesbians move out because they perceive the area as unwelcoming after the male invasion. Gay men are still men, after all, and they are not exempt from the sexism that saturates our society. In reflecting on her experiences in the gay village of Manchester, England, one lesbian described gay men as "quite intimidating. They're not very welcoming towards women." Similarly, a lesbian from Chicago told me: "Boystown is a gay neighborhood. It's *boys'* town—it's all guys. Boystown is super, super male. Andersonville is definitely more lesbian . . . It's very female-oriented. It's lesbian." Indeed, some women refer to Andersonville as "Girlstown," "the lesbian ghetto," or "Dykeville." Although gay men and straight newcomers often arrive at about the same time, some lesbians feel especially resentful toward the former. Another woman from Chicago vented, "The straight couples are guests in our community. The gay men are coming to pillage. Imperialism is coming up from Boystown."

What does all of this mean? Jim Owles of the New York Gay Activist Alliance said in 1971 that "one of society's favorite myths about gay people is that we are all alike." More than forty years have passed, but the myth is still hard to shake. Our ideas about a gay neighborhood rely on a fairly unimaginative and singular understanding of queer life and culture, making it much harder for us to see and appreciate unique lesbian geographies.

there goes the gayborhood?

amin ghaziani

fall 2010

Lesbian and gay residential patterns are shifting today. A recent flurry of media reports captures popular anxieties that urban enclaves long considered "gay neighborhoods"—places with a visible clustering of gay residents and tourists; gay and gay-friendly commercial establishments; and gay community symbols such as the rainbow flag—are disappearing as more straights move in and fewer gays express interest in residing in or relocating to them. The *Chicago Tribune* measured the pulse of these changes in two 2007 features, "Culture Clash Boystown Shifting as More Families Move In" and "Gay Neighborhoods Worry About Losing Their Distinct Identity."

And in an eye-catching companion piece, one of Chicago's free daily papers, the *RedEye,* ran a cover story playfully titled "There Goes the Gayborhood." A provocative photograph of one of the rainbow-colored pylons that adorn North Halsted Street and designate it as the city's main gay artery accompanied the piece—but the colors were fading and bleeding. The story reported, "With more families moving in and longtime residents moving out, some say Boys-town [the informal moniker of Chicago's gayborhood] is losing its gay flavor . . . Some residents and activists welcome the gay migration, saying it's a sign of greater equality, while others say Boys-town is losing its identity."

The social forces contributing to this gay outmigration (and replacement by straights) stretch beyond the Windy City San Diego's Hillcrest, Houston's Montrose, Atlanta's Midtown, Miami's South Beach, D.C.'s Dupont Circle, Boston's South End—each is an example of a traditional American gay neighborhood, and each seems to be on a list of endangered urban species.

It's quixotic to think that gay neighborhoods have always been around and will never change. Neighborhoods and the cities that surround them are organic, continuously evolving places But neither should we sing a requiem for the death and life of great gay villages, as some media reports presage. Thinking within this binary box isn't sociologically productive. We might instead ask why gay neighborhoods initially formed, and what factors explain the changes we're witnessing now. With these questions as our guide, we can use media attention to understand the relationship between sexuality, residential choice, and urban forms.

World War II was pivotal in the formation of gay territories. Many men and women were dishonorably discharged from the military for their homosexuality, and rather than return home disgraced, they remained in port cities such as San Francisco. According to the U.S. Census, from 1950 to 1960 the number of single-person households in San Francisco doubled and accounted for 38 percent of the city's total residential units During this time, bars helped create dense gay networks that made gays more visible and, over time, inspired them to assert a right to gather in pubic places.

> *Like the cities around them, gay neighborhoods are organic, continuously evolving places.*

A lot has changed since then. Gay life in the U.S. is now so open that it may be moving "beyond the closet," says sociologist Steven Seidman, despite a persistent privileging of heterosexuality by the state, societal institutions, and popular culture. This mere possibility prompted British journalist Paul Burston to coin the term "post-gay" in 1994 as an observation and critique of gay culture and politics. The term found an American audience four years later when *Out* magazine editor James Collard argued in the *New York Times,* "We should no longer define ourselves solely in terms of our sexuality—even if our opponents do Post-gay isn't 'un-gay.' It's about taking a critical look at gay life and no longer thinking solely in terms of struggle." In a separate *Newsweek* feature, Collard elaborated: "First for protection and later with understandable pride, gays have come to colonize whole neighborhoods, like West Hollywood in L.A. and Chelsea in New York City. It seems to me that the new Jerusalem gay people have been striving for all these years

won't be found in a gay-only ghetto, but in a world where we are free, equal, and safe to live our lives."

The way Americans understand sexuality affects people's location patterns (why they choose to live where they do) and urban forms (why neighborhoods look and feel the way they do). The closet era (think pre-World War II) gave rise to discrete locales where individuals with same-sex desires could find each other. The coming out era (World War II to 1997, but especially after the 1969 Stonewall riots in New York), in contrast, witnessed the development of forma urban gay enclaves like the Castro. And finally, the post-gay era (1998 to today) impacts these gay neighborhoods by potentially unraveling them and rendering them "passé," as the *New York Times* characterized them in October 2007. The *Advocate* remarked that same year, "As the country opens its arms to openly gay and lesbian people, the places we call home have grown beyond urban gay ghettos. The *Advocate* welcomes you to this

Gay and lesbian couples in the U.S.

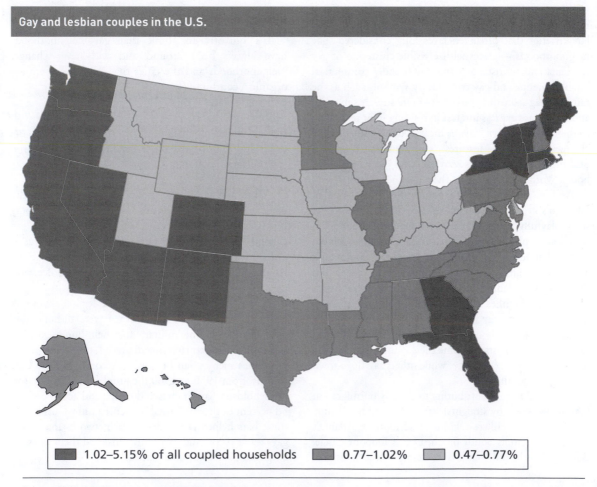

| ■ 1.02–5.15% of all coupled households | ■ 0.77–1.02% | □ 0.47–0.77% |

Source: 2000 U.S. Census data analyzed by Gary Gates.

new American landscape." When the magazine polled its readers, asking if they'd "prefer to live in an integrated neighborhood rather than a distinct gay ghetto," 69 percent said yes.

One year later in an *Advocate* article titled "Where the Gays Are," UCLA demographer Gary J. Gates reported that, according to the 2000 U.S. Census, "Same-sex couples live virtually everywhere in the country," and their numbers are "increasing in some of the most conservative parts of the country." Gates's research shows that "same-sex unmarried partners"—the only category the Census included in 2000 to count lesbians and gay men and one that clearly ignores single people—were present in 99.3 percent of all U.S. counties. Why do post-gay gays tend to think outside the gayborhood box?

We have to look at the factors driving the transition to today's putatively post-gay era, notably the role of assimilation, or the social process of absorbing people (in this case, lesbian, gay, bisexual, and transgender people) into mainstream society. The assimilation of American gays has generated feelings of acceptance, integration, and safety, which is reversing an earlier propensity of lesbians and gay men to concentrate in discrete urban enclaves. This new socio-psychological profile works in two ways. First, assimilation contributes to an overextension of the gay residential imagination. As Don Romesburg, co-chairman of the GLBT Historical Society of Northern California, told the *Washington Post* in 2007, "What I've heard from some people is, 'We don't need the Castro anymore because essentially San Francisco is our Castro.'" The pattern persists in smaller cities, too. Consider Northampton, Massachusetts: "There are gay enclaves, but there's no place know where the gay population is so integrated into the community," said Julie Pokela, a local business owner and former head of the Chamber of Commerce. Some people have dubbed her entire city "Lesbianville, USA."

Although very different, San Francisco and Northampton both show how assimilation has broadened the spatial positioning of homosexuality from the specific streets of a gay enclave to an entire city itself. But here we encounter a contradiction: if an entire city is a gay village, then no particular neighborhood is uniquely so. San Francisco-as-our-Castro looks and feels different from the Castro as a discrete gay urban entity. Thus, assimilation may expand a gay person's horizon of residential possibilities, but it also shrinks the situating of homosexuality in urban space.

Second, assimilation motivates some gays to think of their sexuality as indistinguishable from straights, and this compels them to select residences outside of traditional gay villages. As an example, a 2004 *New York Times* story interviewed a lesbian couple that had

relocated to a New Jersey suburb. Neither woman considered herself "any sort of activist," and both wanted "a suburban family life that is almost boringly normal." But why not relocate to a place like Asbury Park with its visible concentration of gay residents? "We're specifically not moving into gay neighborhoods here. Within the state of New Jersey, we feel comfortable living anywhere," said one woman. Her partner added, "Here, we're just part of a neighborhood. We weren't the gay girls next door; we were just neighbors. We were able to blend in, which is what you want to do, rather than have the scarlet letter on our heads." It seems that post-gay residential choice comes with a desire to deemphasize the differences between gay and straight. "There is a portion of our community that wants to be separatist, to have a queer culture, but most of us want to be treated like everyone is," Dick Dadey, executive director of Empire State Pride Agenda told the *Times* in 1994. "We want to be the neighbors next door, not the lesbian or gay couple next door."

Straights are on board, too. A 2010 Gallup poll found that, for the first time in history, the percentage of Americans who find gay and lesbian relations morally acceptable crossed the symbolic fifty-percent threshold. In fact, many straight women who live in gayborhoods say they feel safer in them. But why would straight men move there? Sociologist Michael Kimmel told *New York Times* columnist Charles M. Blow that "men have gotten increasingly comfortable with the presence of, and relative equality of, 'the other.'" If they respond to gay identity disclosure today with "Gay? Whatever, Dude" (as Blow titled his piece), then a gay neighborhood is hardly out-of-bounds. Crossing the symbolic moral threshold, along with the preference structure of many single straight women, has resulted in a ratio of single heterosexual women to men that makes gayborhoods especially attractive to the latter—minus all the baggage that comes with homophobia.

So, what should we make of media cries like "There goes the gayborhood"? The transition to a post-gay era is generating a particular attitude and corresponding behavior: gays are deselecting traditional gay neighborhoods and straights are selecting them as a place of residence. Assimilation is expanding the gay urban imagination and residential repertoire at the same time that it's erasing the identifiable location of gays in place. This post-gay effect manifests in big cities and small towns alike. Gays in both places seek neighborhoods that are

> *There's no reason to believe the uneven and incomplete post-gay trend signals the end of American gayborhoods.*

demographically diverse and where their sexual orientation adds to an already lively mix. But recall that 31 percent of *Advocate* readers still preferred to live in "a distinct gay ghetto." The post-gay trend, in other words, is uneven and incomplete—and there is no compelling reason to believe that it signals the definitive end of American gayborhoods, as some media reports predict. A sociological approach shows that it's not a zero-sum game.

did baby boomers opt out or lean in?
virginia little
spring 2016

Women in the labor force face challenges juggling work and family, which may mean temporarily putting careers on hold to marry and have children. In his new *Demography* article "Opting Out and Leaning In," Javier Garcia-Manglano investigates the paths U.S. Baby Boom women followed into and out of jobs and careers.

Using national data from more than 5,000 surveys of women born between 1944 and 1954, Garcia-Manglano found that women's workforce trajectories can be classified into four groups: women who stayed steadily employed in middle age; women who worked most in young adulthood then decreased working time as they aged; women who gradually increased work time as they aged; and women who opted out of the labor force entirely. He identified specific factors affecting women's career timing and duration, including spousal support or workplace discrimination. Declining health also contributed to women decreasing work time or stopping working altogether, while the need for income was a major factor keeping women in the job market.

Despite challenges to women's labor force participation, Garcia-Manglano found that 40% of his sample (the largest single group he identified) stayed steadily employed through middle age. This means that, among Boomers, a great number *were not* forced to opt out of working due to family or health constraints. His findings also point to policy and culture changes that could support women's employment throughout the life course. Yet another road paved by the Baby Boomer women who sought employment and wage equality and opened opportunities for future generations of women.

INTIMACY

introduction
mapping intimacy

jodi o'brien

For thousands of years, love, passion and marriage were considered a rare and undesirable combination. Almost no one believed that falling in love was a great and glorious thing that should lead to marriage, or that marriage was a place to achieve sexual fulfillment. In fact, Christian veneration of married love is hard to discern in the first 1,500 years of church history. As one 12th-century authority wrote, no one "disapproves" when "a gentle and honest sentiment" softens the bonds of a marriage, but "it is not the role of marriage to inspire such a feeling." Similarly, it was not the role of such tender feelings to inspire marriage.

—Stephanie Coontz

In a study of nineteenth-century American diaries, family historian Stephanie Coontz observes that both men and women write in great detail about intimate friendships, but say very little about their spouses or those they are courting. In these diaries, people give elaborate descriptions of outings and conversations with dear friends but say little about supposedly major events such as having gotten engaged to be married. For most people during this historical period, marriage did not include love and romance. It was a practical affair intended to produce children and fulfill social and economic functions of the larger group.

Companionate marriage is a relatively recent occurrence. Historically, marriage practices and laws served as a form of social engineering: political alliances between households, tribes, or countries; a basis for the transfer of property from one kinship group to another; or a way to ensure the transmission of specific genetic traits. In Western agrarian cultures, laws of marriage (and divorce) emerged to protect the property and inheritance interests of the wealthy. People with no property did not need to be married because there was nothing to pass on.

These historically sociopolitical collaborations are far from the contemporary image of marriage as a union between two loving partners who seek recognition from the state and, often, formal blessings from their respective religious organization. As Coontz points out, even this modern view was not predicated on expectations of companionate love until quite recently. Even when this love-based form became to take hold, laws about who could marry whom persisted as a means to preserve racial

and class-based divisions. Anti-miscegenation laws—laws forbidding interracial marriage (or even interracial sexual intimacy)—were especially severe and extended not only to Black/White relationships, but to many other ethnic immigrant groups deemed "other." For example, Chinese railroad workers in the late 1800s were prohibited from marrying White women as a means of discouraging reproduction among a group considered to be a social threat. These racist social engineering practices continued in many states until 1967. It took a long time and an act of the U.S. Supreme Court to declare love across racial lines socially legal. Even so, there is considerable stigma attached to interracial love and marriage.

The modern model of marriage, especially as conveyed in popular cultural programs such as *Ozzie and Harriet* or *Leave It to Beaver*, emphasized a tranquil gendered division of labor (male provider, female homemaker) wherein the mostly White, mostly suburban couple produced and socialized children, and fed, clothed, educated, and nurtured them to become the next generation of good citizens. If the couple felt strong love and attraction to one another, that was a bonus. In recent decades, that bonus love has become the central defining characteristic of a marriage. Couples are now expected not only to fulfill all the functions above, but to do so as one another's best friends and lovers. That's a lot to accomplish for two people who, especially in the current economy, may be struggling just to provide food and housing.

Sociological studies of marriage and family explore the ways in which marriage is a form of cultural, economic, and political belonging in contemporary society. In its current form, the *conjugal nuclear family* serves as the basic unit of U.S. economics and politics. It's also the supposed basis for intimacy. From a sociological perspective, without significant social support systems (economic and social), these expectations are out of reach for the average family, but current social policies and cultural practices tend to punish couples and individuals who are unable to provide full economic and social resources for their families *and* maintain love and intimacy. Couples themselves tend to feel something is wrong with them if can't manage children and household affairs and maintain high intensity intimacy.

Marriage is one of those taken-for-granted social practices that we rarely question. But from a sociological perspective the structure of conjugal nuclear marriage, with its excessive demands on small family units, raises many questions. Sociologist Anthony Giddens has observed that the transformation of intimacy in marriage and the resulting individual choice and emphasis on love makes for a fragile foundation on which to build sustainable social units. Yet, culturally, love-based marriage has become the *sin qua non* of belonging in contemporary society. Marriage confers social status, rights, benefits, even citizenship. It is believed to be the most natural and normal thing that people do. These beliefs are supported by ideals of love and romance and family values—if the love is there and you have the right attitude, you can do it.

Sociologists are not against marriage, but we do invite critical examination of the many unquestioned assumptions and myths that underlie the presumed naturalness of contemporary conjugal nuclear families. This examination helps us to see how some people are unfairly left out of the full benefits of society based on their family structures. Critical sociological studies of marriage and intimacy also look at the ways individuals are blamed for a failure to live up to the ideals of contemporary marriage. Many people feel disconsolate or inadequate because they can't afford to live the kind of "family values" life portrayed in media and other popular notions of marriage. And what about people who simply don't want to participate? How are they viewed? A related sociological approach looks at varying models of kinship, child-rearing, and support and points out the disconnect in the U.S. between how many families actually function and the myth of the conjugal nuclear family as the most prevalent and ideal form.

heteronormativity and citizenship

Heteronormativity is not just a form of sexuality, it is a term for the ideals of the conjugal nuclear family pervade

our society. This form of family life is considered normal and expected. Any deviation must be accounted for. At a certain age, friends and relatives tend to start asking young people when they plan to marry (and start a family). Acceptable excuses for not actively pursuing this life include a calling to a celibate ministry (nun or priest), or perhaps delaying for a time to finish school and earn more money. Now that we have marriage equality, being gay or lesbian is no longer an excuse for not marrying. Minimally, a desire to pursue coupled intimacy with the possibility of children or at least conjugal care-taking is an expected aspect of adult life. If you have no intention of pursuing romantic, couple-based intimacy, you have to explain yourself. Sociologist Shelly Budgeon has written on the culture of "coupleness." She notes that people feel entitled to ask single people why they are not dating or married but that no one interrogates married people about their decision to couple. She writes, somewhat tongue-in-cheek, that when people ask her why she is single she retorts, "Why are you married?" And they usually stare blankly at her. Her point is that there are many forms of intimacy and nurturing, but we tend to assume that anything other than marriage or cohabitating romance-based relationships are less than or wanting.

Budgeon is part of a team of British sociologists who were commissioned by the government to study care-taking and nurturing in Britain's aging population. Demographically, there appear to be many people growing old and living alone. The government is interested in this population because of the impact on social welfare systems when these people make claims for assistance for care-taking. What this team found is that elderly people are engaged in many creative ways of mutual support and care-taking, but because the government only recognizes traditional marriage in its census counts, these alternative care-taking relationships are unseen. Legal-economic policies are centered around the conjugal nuclear family and impede other forms of relational sharing and care-taking. For instance, elderly widows who want to combine households as a way of sharing resources, companionship, and care-taking are often prohibited from doing so because of marriage-based inheritance laws that make it difficult for one or the other to dissolve her properties without huge penalty fees. These studies demonstrate the gap between the innovative ways in which people seek companionship, support and nurturing and legal-economic policies that recognize only one type of family model. People are stymied in their attempts to care for one another because of these policies, which, ironically, puts more burden on state resources.

Additional examples of non-romantic or heteronormative models of care-giving and companionship include the legions of extended family households that exist in the U.S. Because they do not fit the normative model, these families face obstacles in caring for one another. In the case of grandparents and other relatives raising young children, the state requires that birth parents relinquish parental rights in order for the relative to receive recognition and state assistance. This can be a wrenching decision for a parent who may intend one day to return to the child (e.g., an incarcerated parent), and it further burdens relatives who are then unable to care for the child as fully as they would like. There are also many aging people in the U.S. whose adult children live in other countries and who would like to come and care for their parents, but current immigration policies make this nearly impossible in most cases. Likewise, the unquestioned practice of providing benefits such as insurance only to spouses and legally dependent children prohibits people from extending these benefits to elderly parents or disabled siblings who may be dependents, but who are not recognized as such under family-based laws.

Researchers at the U.S. Census Bureau are particularly aware of the inadequacy of the nuclear family model for capturing the range of interdependent caregiving arrangements across the country. They point out that the unquestioned status of the nuclear family as the basic legal, political, and economic unit in U.S. society is at odds with reality and makes it difficult for them to do their job. The rationale for a census is accurate charting of the citizens that make up a country and their rights to the benefits of that citizenship. For Census researchers, the heteronormative construct that guides U.S. policy does not reflect the full range of family configurations that exists; it excludes many viable family forms and makes it difficult for people who want to engage in care-taking beyond the narrow definition of family to do so.

learning from marriage equality

It surprises some people to learn that there is considerable dissent among LGBTQ groups and individuals regarding marriage equality. For many feminist scholars and activists, marriage is a coercive, patriarchal institution that perpetuates gender inequality and confers cultural and legal status and belonging to some while excluding others. Giddens describes the conjugal nuclear family as a "jealous institution" that turns people's interests away from society and civic responsibility inward to care only about protecting the well-being of their small family unit. Queer activism in the 1970s and '80s focused on advancing alternative expressions

of love and intimacy—not just same gender sexuality, but alternatives to the nuclear family as a basis for cultural, social, and economic organization. Relatively higher rates of poverty, family abandonment, illness, and related effects of discrimination motivated queer people to strive for models that centered interdependency and care-giving rather than conjugal intimacy as the basis for social, legal, and economic recognition. These activist groups were robustly critical of traditional marriage as the primary basis of social organization, benefit distribution, and cultural and legal belonging and pointed to all those who were systematically included from this system.

There were some early gains in this struggle for recognition of a wider range of relationships such as the passing of domestic partnership acts and city and state-based legislation that allowed government employees to name *any adult* as a "legally domiciled adult" who could share their health and related employment benefits. The person did not have to be a spousal equivalent. The aim was to divorce state-based benefits from marriage; to recognize individuals rather than conjugal unions as a basic unit for political and economic rights related to connection and care-giving. Much of this focus has been eclipsed in the fight for marriage equality and the early gains in expanding models of domestic sharing have slipped away as a result of its success.

Some of the first advocates of same-gender marriage were self-described politically conservative gay men who sought to elevate gay relationships above stereotypes of promiscuity and instability. In 1996 two legislative acts were passed that further entrenched the traditional family as the basis of a healthy society. The logic behind the Marriage Promotion Act as well as the Defense of Marriage Act (DOMA) was that the country had been in its prime in the 1950s when traditional families were strong and virtuous (and a gender division of labor was in place). In her book, *The Way We Never Were,* Coontz deftly illustrates that this myth of family bliss never was a reality due, in part to economic and gender limits. In the few pockets of the country were traditional families did thrive it was due largely to accumulated wealth and support from government programs such as the Federal Housing Act and other benefits. She notes however, that by the 1980s there was a nostalgia for these seemingly better times. Rather than blame the draconian economic and social policies that had thrust even more people into debt and social instability, the finger was pointed at gays and single-mothers. Scapegoats in the form of lesbians, gay men, and unmarried women with children living in poverty were vilified and the new legislative acts implied a link between the decline of the so-called utopia of traditional family life and selfish sexual choices.

Seeking to distance gay men from this dystopian stew of bad sexual citizens, gay marriage advocates highlighted all the ways in which gays and lesbians were just like everyone else: desirous of loving, monogamous family relationships and the opportunity to contribute to society. As the movement gained traction, family members and religious communities, as well as many civic and corporate organizations, extended a welcoming hand and climbed onto the marriage equality bandwagon. For many observers and supporters, marriage equality enshrines love and romance in the form of conjugal intimacy as the highest social achievement and the bedrock foundation of society. Historian Lisa Duggan coined the term "homonormativity" to describe the ways in which contemporary gay and lesbian experiences mirror and reinforce traditional nuclear family models and values. The early HIV-AIDS activist taunt, "we're here, we're queer, get used to it" has given way to the more demure, "We're here, we're queer, let's go to Pottery Barn."

Queer activists who remain critical of marriage equality are quick to acknowledge that it is indeed a major gain in a society in which cultural inclusion and belonging, as well as many significant rights and benefits, are organized around marriage. Not being able to be make decisions for a dying partner, or share their benefits, or be included in significant everyday events are painful and destabilizing experiences that many lesbians and gay men feel will be lessened through marriage. At the same time, critical activists remind us that although marriage equality is truly radical in terms of shifting the relationship between gender and the traditional family, nothing else has changed regarding the primacy of the conjugal nuclear model as the basic unit of social organization. Given this, we must ask: Who is left out and what are the consequences for those who can't or don't want to participate in this hetero/homonormativity?

These concerns are articulated in a 2006 brief authored by a group of LGBTQ activists under the title, "Beyond Same-Sex Marriage: A New Strategic Vision for all Our Families and Relationships." The authors write:

> To have our government define as "legitimate families" only those households with couples in conjugal relationships does a tremendous disservice to the many other ways in which people actually construct their families, kinship networks, households, and relationships. For example, who among us seriously will argue that the following kinds of households are less socially, economically, and spiritually worthy?

- Senior citizens living together, serving as each other's caregivers, partners, and/or constructed families
- Adult children living with and caring for their parents
- Grandparents and other family members raising their children's (and/or a relative's) children
- Committed, loving households in which there is more than one conjugal partner
- Blended families
- Single parent households
- Extended families (especially in particular immigrant populations) living under one roof, whose members care for one another
- Queer couples who decide to jointly create and raise a child with another queer person or couple, in two households
- Close friends and siblings who live together in long-term, committed, non-conjugal relationships, serving as each other's primary support and caregivers
- Care-giving and partnership relationships that have been developed to provide support systems to those living with HIV/AIDS.
- Marriage is not the only worthy form of family or relationship, and it should not be legally and economically privileged above all others. While we honor those for whom marriage is the most meaningful personal—for some, also a deeply spiritual—choice, we believe that many other kinds of kinship relationship, households, and families must also be accorded recognition.

For these activists, queer experiences should be in the vanguard toward forging and gaining social and political recognition of models of intimacy, interdependency, and care-taking that reflect the larger realities of how many people are living and loving and supporting one another.

conclusions

Most people long for community and connectedness. Critical sociologists and groups such as *#beyondmarriage* are inviting us to take a more engaged, realistic look at what counts as intimacy, family, and support in our society. These studies suggest that the modern conjugal nuclear family is both an ideology and institution. It is often considered the moral and emotional center of society. Current government policies expect families to fulfill the functions of raising and educating children and caring for the elderly mostly on their own. The policies emphasize personal responsibility and diminish the role of shared economic and community support in sustaining the modern family. These policies are buttressed by public scape-goating of family forms that don't fit this ideal type. Traditional marriage is not likely to fade away anytime soon, but it's worth paying attention to alternative forms of connection and care-giving and asking hard questions about who is included or excluded based on their family choices and circumstances. How do we judge ourselves and others based on our expectations of the "right kind" of love and intimacy? How realistic are these expectations and what can we learn from alternative practices? How is the traditional family model linked to increasing privatization of social services and what are the consequences of this neoliberalism? What would an alternative caring civil society look like?

recommended resources

www.beyondmarriage.org

Budgeon, Shelly. 2008. "Couple Culture and Negotiating Singleness." *Sexualities 3*:301–325.

Coontz, Stephanie. 2000. *The Way We Never Were: Americans and the Nostalgia Trap.* New York: Basic Books.

——. 2005. *Marriage: A History.*

——. 2005. "Historically Incorrect Canoodling." *New York Times.* February.

Giddens, Anthony. 1992. *The Transformation of Intimacy: Sexuality, Love, and Eroticism in Modern Societies.* Palo Alto, CA: Stanford University Press.

Nagle, Joane. 2003. *Race, Ethnicity, Sexuality: Intimate Intersections, Forbidden Frontiers.* Cambridge, MA: Oxford University Press.

an unexpected box of love research

michelle janning

winter 2015

Two years ago, in a rare spare moment of household organization spurred by procrastination, I stumbled upon a box of letters I had saved from 1990–1994, my college years. For several hours, I read through the pile of intricately folded spiral notebook paper letters—the communication form most used by me and my friends and boyfriends when we left our rural Minnesota town for our respective academic pursuits. These letters kept us together across time and geography. They made it seem as if no time had passed when we reunited. My high school friends and I wrote during class when our professors thought we were taking notes. My college boyfriends and I wrote during breaks, when our distance seemed more painful than a deep paper cut.

Sitting in this pile of paper, I started to wonder whether *where* I stored this memento box mattered in how much it meant to me. After all, I had forgotten about it. The letters were not only folded, they were in a bag in a box in a closet in a dark corner of our basement storage room.

My husband, the boyfriend who emerged in graduate school (he's a sociologist, too), noticed me sitting in the letter pile in our living room. He looked at me funny—maybe because some of the letters were from past boyfriends or maybe because he figured he'd be vacuuming all of the paper shreds after my little nostalgia party was done. Then he paused and noted that he had a much smaller pile of saved letters, but had no idea where it was. He also said that when we entered college there was no widespread Internet or e-mail use; by the time we left, we were all using e-mail. Surely, he claimed, we must represent the last generation of paper letter writers.

A few weeks later, I had two lunches with two different female friends from two different generations. Our conversations tended toward a discussion of love letters. My older friend reminisced about her box of saved love letters from her husband. My younger friend talked about an e-mail folder she had created on her phone: "Messages from Cute Boys."

Inspired by these interactions, I began a new line of research. I've set out to see whether gender and generation affect the meaning people attach to love letters, and whether the form of a love letter—digital or paper—matters in that meaning.

In line with my short attention span and well rounded liberal arts education, this research question sent me down numerous cross-disciplinary paths: from geography to human-computer interaction studies; from the psychology of nostalgia to British material culture studies; from consumer studies to gender and communication studies. As a sociologist, I had published on married co-workers' work-family boundary permeability as shown through briefcases and home offices, young adults' assessment of their bedrooms and parent relations post-divorce, and gender and the preservation of digital family photos. The sociology of love letters fit nicely as the next step in my sociological inquiry of objects and spaces.

I conducted an online survey that asked people about one love letter from a past romantic relationship. I thought that, rather than just asking whether this letter is meaningful, I'd inquire about its form, its storage location, and how often it was revisited. Because our values and memories and definitions of self may be represented by what we have and how we interact with it, I was really trying to learn about the rituals associated with the love letter's possession and curation. Because the storage location of a memento and its likelihood to be revisited say something about its meaning, I also included interesting notions of what some consumer studies scholars call "heated" and "cooled" locations. Heated locations are accessible and central to activities in the home. Cooled locations are harder to reach. All of these concepts joined together in my survey to creatively measure how social actors singularize objects—give them personal meaning.

Some interesting findings are already emerging. First, people tend to save paper letters more than digital ones, regardless of gender and generation. Second, women save more relationship mementos, including love letters, than men. And third, men look at the letters they've saved more often than women, and they are more likely to store them in places that are "heated."

These findings could suggest that men are more sentimental than women, or perhaps that men are conforming to masculine ideals of displaying "trophies" of their ability to secure romantic relationships. Or the findings could suggest that women are more likely to spend time organizing and storing objects that symbolize relationships. This is what I'm wrestling with as I finish the manuscript. Maybe if I clean another closet or re-organize my e-mail folders, I'll stumble upon the correct interpretation.

locating intimacy

overview

All cultures have rules and expectations for love and kinship. For instance, contemporary U.S. cultural practice emphasizes monogamous marriage as a central way of organizing are two people who, "in love." This cultural form is supported by legal and religious mandates and encouraged in myriad ways in popular media. Many people live contentedly within this cultural script, while many others find themselves outside the boundaries set up through gender, race, and class expectations, as well as expectations about how to feel and be. Each of the articles in this section illustrate the complexities of the taken-for-granted family model of intimacy.

Until the 1970s, marriage across racial lines was still illegal in many U.S. states. Amy Steinbugler shares the stories of couples who are navigating that divide today. Katie Acosta disrupts some of the general ideas about lesbian couples and identities by placing these within the context of the family among gender and sexually nonconforming Latinas.

Are you a real family if you don't have children? What about people who have children but aren't married? This is the question that Kathryn Edin and Maria Kefalas take up in "Unmarried with Children." And what happens to your sense of love and intimacy, as well as your family social status when you lose a spouse? Deborah Carr explores this and other questions in *Good Grief: Bouncing Back from a Spouse's Death in Later Life.* From the personal to the bird's-eye view, United States Census Bureau researchers Nancy Bates and Theresa J. Demaio describe the challenges in trying to count same-sex relationships in a society that, until recently, does not formally acknowledge their existence.

things to consider

- What is your idea of a family? What is intimacy and does it have to include sexuality? Where did you get these family ideas or intimacy scripts?
- Consider where you draw the line between "close friends" and "family"—what rules do you use to make this distinction?
- Name some popular television shows that have "alternative" family models. What lines are they crossing?
- What are some reasons why people don't participate in the expected family/intimacy forms? Are some reasons more culturally acceptable than others (i.e., a nun or priest)?
- Families and couples who follow the general cultural practices receive more social acceptance. Do you think this outside acceptance has an impact on the success and happiness of the relationship?

loving across racial divides

amy steinbugler

spring 2014

"I think that people in interracial relationships give up something, you know, give up an ease about living, in some ways," said Leslie Cobbs, a 30-something White woman, surrounded by novels, textbooks, and old photographs, in the Brooklyn apartment she shares with her Black partner Sylvia Chabot.

Leslie acknowledges that African Americans have to "think about race all the time," but insists that there are unique racial issues that stem from being in an interracial relationship.

Sylvia and Leslie face challenges that are usually less overt than those Black/White couples would have confronted 50 years ago. There is little chance that they might lose their jobs, get kicked out of their church, or be denied housing simply because one of them is Black and the other is White. While injustices like these still occur, when they do they are noteworthy. Undisguised discrimination against interracial couples is no longer typical. Nor do relationships like theirs inspire the raw disbelief that Sidney Poitier and Katharine Houghton famously elicited when they portrayed a young couple in the 1967 film, *Guess Who's Coming to Dinner.*

Still, Sylvia says, "We're always looking for spaces where we can be together as a couple, [be] validated, feel comfortable." Compared to straight interracial pairs, same-sex partners like Sylvia and Leslie can count on far fewer legal protections, and also are vulnerable to homophobia from coworkers, family members, and strangers on the street.

Interracial couples in the United States have always attracted public scrutiny. Until the mid-twentieth century, this attention was almost entirely negative. Legal sanctions prevented people of African, Asian and, sometimes, Native American descent from marrying Whites. Black/White relationships, especially those between White women and Black men, drew the harshest condemnation. Black communities treated such couples as disreputable; White communities often threatened, physically harmed, or ostracized them.

In recent years, interracial couples are more likely to encounter hope than censure, at least in terms of public discourse. Some observers liken current legal prohibitions against same-sex marriage to anti-miscegenation laws before the 1967 Supreme Court ruling in *Loving v. The State of Virginia*. Social commentators paint contemporary interracial marriage as a victory for equality and freedom. A 2001 *Time* magazine article celebrated interracial unions as representing an intimate "vanguard" who "work on narrowing the divisions between groups in America, one couple at a time."

More recently, a Pew Research Center report released in 2012 suggests a positive shift in public attitudes towards intermarriage. Forty-three percent of Americans now view the trend for more people of different races to marry each other as a change for the better. About two-thirds say it would be fine with them if a family member "married out" of their racial or ethnic group. Even Black/White relationships, which have long elicited the fiercest disapproval and the strongest legal sanctions, are becoming more acceptable.

Despite the supposed acceptance of dating and marrying across racial lines, only a small percentage of people in the United States—according to the 2010 Census, less than 7 percent of all heterosexual married couples—actually do so. Among gay and lesbian couples, approximately 14 percent are interracial—about the same proportion as among heterosexual unmarried partners.

Low intermarriage rates notwithstanding, many people embrace the popular notion that Americans have truly become "colorblind." But racism is more than just a matter of prejudice; liberalizing racial attitudes coexist with the stubborn persistence of racism. For the past 12 years, I have studied couples who love across racial difference in Philadelphia, New York, and Washington, D.C. What I've found is that while hostility toward interracial pairs, like racism itself, has become more subtle, race continues to powerfully impact everyday life for Sylvia, Leslie, and the other 39 interracial couples I interviewed. Racism, manifested in neighborhood segregation and racial self-understandings, shapes everyday life, creeping up in the most ordinary circumstances, like walking through their neighborhood, or deciding where to get a drink.

raced spaces

Mary Chambers, a heterosexual woman of Afro-Caribbean descent, knew that her husband Neil was sometimes uncomfortable in their middle-class, majority-Black neighborhood. The neighborhood, which includes many sprawling, three-story, Tudor houses, feels suburban, though it is located in a small city less than 30 miles from Manhattan. Mary thinks that Neil "would prefer to live in a community where he's more comfortable with the people, in a community where he can look around and see his own race. [One] with more White people." She finds this discouraging. "I wish that I could change his perspective on it and really make him see that the community we live in is valuable."

In the years Neil spent in this neighborhood, he became very aware of his own Whiteness. It was impossible for him not to think about race in everyday social interactions. It was typical, he says, to go into the grocery store or the post office and be "the only White guy there." He continues, "It's not a bad thing, you know. It's not like I feel like I'm going to get mugged or, um, I'm going to get hurt. But you have to understand, it's kind of like when you deal with White people, they have their prejudice—they have what they're used to. And then when you deal with Black people, it's really the same thing, you know?"

The residential racial segregation of Blacks and Whites has been slowly declining nationwide. But in northeastern cities like New York and Philadelphia, highly segregated neighborhoods remain the norm. (In New York, the racial composition of neighborhoods is so lopsided that 79 percent of Blacks would have to move in order to achieve a balanced distribution—in which the percentage of Blacks in every neighborhood mirrors their share of the city's total population.)

> *Hostility toward interracial couples, like racism itself, has become more subtle.*

Neighborhoods that are Black or White often pose problems for interracial couples because they set the stage for situations in which one partner feels uncomfortable or conspicuous. "No matter where we live," one White woman lamented, "one of us is not going to be in the right neighborhood." A Black partner agreed, "As diverse as [New York] city is, to me it's still pretty segregated." This sense of belonging or not belonging is something interracial partners often brought up as we talked.

Neighborhood divisions are stressful when one partner feels conspicuous and has to look out for racial undercurrents in everyday social interactions. Such divisions create racial fatigue, though they affect Black and White partners differently. For Neil Chambers and other Whites in my study, being in the racial minority feels awkward because it happens so rarely. Noticing one's own Whiteness is a new experience that can prompt an unsettled feeling. One of the taken-for-granted privileges of being White is the tendency to think of yourself not as a *White* person—*just* as a person. I asked one White woman who is married to a Black man how often she thinks of herself as White. "I don't," she said. "Well, maybe if I were in an all-Black environment, and I'm the only White person there. That's the only time."

Black interracial partners also noticed when they were among only a handful of Blacks in a neighborhood or social gathering. But for these middle-class Americans, that experience was not uncommon. Many worked or had gone to school in majority-White environments. Compared to the Whites in my study, Black partners tended to be much more accustomed to being in the numerical minority. In contrast to the unease of White partners, who sometimes felt intimidated in Black neighborhoods, the discomfort of Black partners was linked to a history of violence against their

> *Neighborhood divisions are stressful when one partner feels conspicuous and has to look out for racial undercurrents in everyday social interactions.*

racial group. It was one of many instances in which Black and White partners perceived race very differently.

racial orientations

Tamara is White, and Scott is Black. When this 30-something unmarried straight couple decided to move in together, they needed to transport countless boxes of books and clothes from Tamara's place in Philadelphia to a nearby city. Tamara wanted Scott to drive the SUV she had borrowed from a friend. But like many other Black men in the United States, Scott was concerned about racial profiling. He didn't want to get pulled over driving a borrowed car, especially given that his cell phone wasn't working properly.

Scott recalls telling Tamara, "'I'd really rather you drive . . . because when—if [I] get pulled over . . . I can't dial [the woman who owns the car]. Now it's just me and some cop and he's probably going to treat you better than he's going to treat me.'" For Scott, this was a routine calculation. For Tamara, it didn't seem like a big deal. This reflects a broader disjuncture in how—and how often—each of them thinks about race. Scott, continuing the story of the move, tells me, "It's my job to consider that, whereas . . . I don't think [me getting pulled over] is automatically something that she considers—and you know what? It doesn't bother me that it isn't, because how could it be? Someone [who is] Black can really, really think, like could have their mind go to that."

For Scott, anticipating everyday acts of prejudice and discrimination is second nature, ever since his grandmother told him about the lynching of Emmett Till. But Tamara, whose Whiteness has shielded her from being the target of racial animus, is only now learning to consider how the accumulation of a lifetime of racial experiences informs even small decisions, like who will drive an SUV full of books and clothes 30 minutes away.

Daniel, who is Black, and Shawn, who is White, thought their racial orientations were very similar until they became the adoptive parents of two Black boys. When Daniel and Shawn began to talk about their sons' future schooling, they soon discovered that they conceptualize racism differently. "We both share the same basic political views," Shawn explained. But Daniel, he believed, "subscribes to a kind of conspiracy theory that White America has banded together to exclude Black America." Shawn sees the racism, he says, but "I don't see it as being organized in

> **The prejudice interracial couples encounter from strangers is only one small part of how race shapes their everyday lives.**

the same way. Because I'm White and nobody ever came to me and said, 'Hey, lets get together and do this thing to the Black people.' So that's a difference of philosophy." Daniel sees "[racism] as institutionalized and I see it just as kind of widespread."

Daniel and Shawn's perspectives lead to important differences in dealing with racism. While Shawn has no intention of letting his sons get hurt, he is more comfortable taking a wait-and-see approach. Daniel feels more strongly about the need to be pro-active about racial discrimination at school. "I'm not looking for trouble," says Daniel. It's just that "I don't want to be asleep when that stuff happens."

For Daniel, there are limits to what a White person can understand about discrimination. Shawn, he says, "doesn't expect that kind of behavior and it's hard [for him] to believe that in fact that can happen." He "just doesn't believe that a teacher would look at an eight-year-old and actually treat one eight-year-old differently from another simply because of the color of their skin." While both men are deeply invested in protecting their sons from racism, their conflicting racial orientations to the subject remain unresolved.

Shawn's strategies for parenting Black sons and Tamara's skepticism about racial profiling reflect the attitudes of many White Americans who question the scope and severity of contemporary racism. Surprisingly, White partners' intimacy with Black people did not substantially challenge their racial perspectives, casting doubt on the notion that interracial partners represent an enlightened, "post-racial" vanguard.

stereotypes—and exceptions

Gary, 54 and his wife Soonja, 58, met in Korea. They have been married for 20 years. Gary chose to marry a Korean woman because, he said, a "good" wife should be loyal and subservient, and to him, Soonja's race signifies these traits. Soonja, too, believes that her choice of husband may reflect upon the kind of person she is. She chafes at being associated with what Koreans regard as stereotypical "international marriages," temporary sexual relationships between local, uneducated Korean women and American military men.

Gary's Whiteness and American citizenship did not hold any special appeal for Soonja or her family. But over time, part of what has made their marriage work is that Soonja believes there are distinct cultural differences that make American husbands better partners than Korean husbands. "I'm glad that I didn't marry a Korean, who ignores his wife, drinks a lot, and comes home late." Gary confides that many of his friends "actually say that they envy me because they understand that Asian women are very good wives and . . . good mothers."

Sociologist Kumiko Nemoto has researched marriages between Whites and Asians in the United States. White men, according to Nemoto, commonly associate Asian and Asian American women with family and domesticity. Younger Asian women in interracial relationships, she found, are more likely to define themselves as egalitarian, ambitious, and aesthetically (as opposed to domestically) feminine, challenging these stereotypes.

Vivian, 25, who grew up in a Chinese family is attracted to Peter, 27, in part because she sees them as equals. He is intelligent, got good grades in college, and is economically mobile. "We have a mental connection," she says. Peter's professional ambitions and work ethic help Vivian think of herself as a modern Asian American woman. Peter, for his part, is proud to appreciate beauty that falls outside of normative White femininity: "[I'm] more attracted to ideas and people who are more exotic . . . I think Asian features are prettier than White features." He likes "darker-skinned women" and the "shapes of Asian eyes."

In the U.S. racial order, particular Asian groups (such as Japanese and Chinese) are positioned much closer to Whites than Blacks. Asian Americans certainly experience racial discrimination and the false presumptions embedded within the idea of the "model minority." Even so, some Asian groups are increasingly seen as what sociologist Eduardo Bonilla-Silva calls "honorary Whites." As the 2010 Census shows, intermarriages between Asian Americans and Whites are far more common than those between Blacks and Whites.

Couples in my study also used racial-gender stereotypes about their partners to describe themselves. Still, some Whites were careful to portray their partner as exceptional, rather than a typical example of their racial group. As Neil said of Mary, who is of African American descent: "She's not someone who would curse or, you know, say anything that's inappropriate or off color. Not that she's a saint but—she has a certain background—she's not offensive to you. She's very pleasant."

What this and other examples suggest is that the prejudice interracial couples encounter from strangers is only one small part of how race shapes their everyday lives. Race is a social system that shapes neighborhoods, orientations, and identities, and plays a critical role in intimate relationships. Despite the gains of the Civil Rights movement and the historic election of the first Black president, the racial categories we are assigned to at birth have tremendous material consequences for how our lives unfold. Racial inequalities affect the wealth which we have access to, the neighborhoods we live in, the type and amount of the healthcare we are able to get, and the quality of our children's schools. Even in this supposed post-racial moment, our position in the racial system shapes the way we see the world.

recommended resources

Dunning, Stefanie K. 2009. *Queer in Black and White: Interraciality, Same Sex Desire, and Contemporary African American Culture.* Bloomington, IN: Indiana University Press. A critical account of how interracial sexuality intersects with notions of racial authenticity and nationalism in Black film, music, and literature.

Nagel, Joane. 2003. *Race, Ethnicity, and Sexuality: Intimate Intersections, Forbidden Frontiers.* Cambridge, MA: Oxford University Press. An excellent analysis of how race, ethnicity, and sexuality have been co-constituted in colonial projects and on "ethnosexual" frontiers.

Nemoto, Kumiko. 2009. *Racing Romance: Love, Power, and Desire Among Asian American/White Couples.* New Brunswick, NJ: Rutgers University Press. A qualitative study of interracial intimacy between Asians/Asian Americans and Whites that pays special attention to how race and gender shape couples' identities and interactions.

Pascoe, Peggy. 2010. *What Comes Naturally: Miscegenation Law and the Making of Race in America.* New York: Oxford University Press. A sophisticated history of miscegenation laws that prohibited sexual relationships and marriage between Whites and Asians, African Americans, and Native Americans.

Wang, Wendy. 2012. *The Rise of Intermarriage: Rates, Characteristics Vary by Race and Gender.* Washington, DC: Pew Research Center. A recent study that examines the frequency of intermarriage and changing public opinion towards these unions.

we are family

katie l. acosta

winter 2014

Jasmin, a 22-year-old Puerto Rican woman and recent college graduate lives with her partner Mariela in a large U.S. city with a growing Latina/o population. The couple occasionally attends church with Jasmin's parents, Seventh-Day Adventists who accept their daughter's relationship with Mariela, despite their conservative religious values.

"They're really good to Mariela and at Christmas my mom bought her a present. Valentine's Day, my mom got her a present. I'm graduating soon and my mom already talked to her about what they're going to do, and graduation plans," Jasmin said. However, Mariela paints a slightly different picture. Jasmin's mother, she says, is deeply conflicted about their relationship, blaming her for her daughter's sexual nonconformity.

"Her mom started questioning me," Mariela said. "She was like 'you know, I love you as a person but I hate the fact that you're with my daughter. I know this isn't the lifestyle for my daughter. My daughter is just on the wrong side. She just needs to find God and then this will all change' . . . It was a very uncomfortable situation for me. I didn't know what to reply to her mom. I was like 'I'm sorry you feel that way.' And that was all I said."

This conflict reflects the tensions and contradictions that arise in the couple's efforts to integrate their families. Jasmin plays the role of mediator, asking Mariela to be patient while trying to make her own mother feel more comfortable with their same-sex relationship. Jasmin takes on this role because among sexually nonconforming Latinas, parents' acceptance of partners—and maintaining closeness with one's family of origin—is critically important.

In *Same Sex Intimacies: Families of Choice and other Life Experiments*, Jeffrey Weeks, Brian Heaphy, and Catherine Donovan use the term "families of choice" to describe the families adult LGBTQ individuals create. In their view, when they create families, queer men and women refuse to privilege biological ties. My own work, which draws upon over 40 in-depth interviews with sexually nonconforming Latinas, suggests that these women see family as an integrated support system that draws on both biological and social ties.

Sexually nonconforming Latinas go to extraordinary lengths to integrate their parents, siblings, partners, friends, children and community members into one kin network. Like Jasmin and Mariela, they believe it is more important to negotiate acceptance from their parents and cultivate a social support system that is vibrant and harmonious than to distance themselves from unsupportive families of origin.

The stories of Jasmin and Mariela and other couples, illuminate the centrality of family for these Latinas and the conflicts they face in integrating their support networks. Sexually nonconforming Latinas embrace multiple marginalized identities, and seek to integrate these different identity networks. Regardless of whether their parents accept them, they work to integrate and expand their familial networks, mediating among these different networks in order to enhance the visibility of their same-sex relationships.

tacit subjects, integrated families

Much of the day-to-day work involved in doing family and negotiating acceptance remains unspoken. Even if they have never formally disclosed their sexualities to their parents, sexually nonconforming Latinas find ways to include their partners in family events as amigas or friends—thereby enabling their partners to form their own relationships with their families of origin.

In *Tacit Subjects: Belonging and Same-Sex Desire Among Dominican Immigrant Men*, scholar Carlos Decena notes that homosexuality is one of many "tacit subjects"— matters of common knowledge which are not openly discussed. Some of the Latinas I interviewed allowed their relationships with other women to remain tacit within their families of origin. However, despite the silence, these women, like Jasmin and Mariela, strive to preserve a support system which includes their partners, friends and parents.

When I first met Minerva she was grieving the loss of two very important people in her life—both her mother and her partner Daniela died in close succession of one another. Minerva and Daniela had been in a committed relationship for over 15 years before Daniela's untimely death. The two purchased a home together and had several nieces and nephews. Daniela always accompanied Minerva on visits to her mother's house and with Minerva's siblings, the two enjoyed holidays and a variety of special occasions together. Minerva describes Daniela and her mother as having a very special bond filled with love and mutual respect.

For more than 15 years, there was never any formal acknowledgement that these women were more than friends. And, yet, despite her mother's lack of verbal validation of her lesbianism, Minerva felt self-affirmed in the caring relationship they all shared.

Minerva, like many other women I interviewed, was raised to see her family of origin as a stabilizing force. She was taught to rely upon her parents and siblings for advice, support and community. As she describes, "The message was you're part of this family, you're here to be devoted to your family and that's it, you know. Do well in school and be devoted to your family . . . " Minerva carries these values with her into adulthood, and even after coming to a lesbian existence in college, she chooses to allow this topic to remain tacit so as not to disrupt her stabilizing unit.

She never verbally asks her parents or siblings to support her same-sex relationship, nor has she ever felt this is necessary. Daniela was Minerva's "amiga." In the role of a friend, Daniela enjoyed a strong relationship with Minerva's family of origin. While Minerva's family understood that the same-sex relationship existed, they chose not to discuss the romantic aspect of the relationship. However, some sexually nonconforming Latinas who maintain tacit relationships find subtle ways to gain greater visibility for their partnerships.

speaking without words

Manuela, a 27-year-old Guatemalan woman, lives with her partner Rosali in a city in the northeastern United States. Manuela's parents live in Guatemala. Like Minerva, Manuela integrated Rosali into her family of origin as a friend. While her relationship with Rosali has remained a tacit subject, Manuela believes her parents understand that the two women are lovers.

When I asked Manuela to explain how this tacit subject arises in the context of her family of origin, she recounted the time she took Rosali to meet her aunt and uncle, who live in another city. "My aunt kept telling me, 'Oh you should move to Chicago. You should move to Chicago,'" she recalled. "Finally, I said, 'No. I don't want to move to Chicago. Besides, what about Rosali?' She [Manuela's aunt] thought about it and she was quiet and didn't say anything for a while. And then, when they met her they were very nice to her . . . at least they made the effort."

> **Even if they have never formally disclosed their sexualities to their parents, sexually nonconforming Latinas find ways to include their partners in family events as amigas or friends.**

When Manuela and Rosali visited her aunt and uncle, they gave them one bed to sleep in. "That was big," Manuela said, interpreting it as a sign that they understand and that they are making an effort to be accepting. Even though there is no explicit validation, Manuela believes this gesture affirms their relationship.

Regardless of their family's level of acceptance of their sexual nonconformity, the Latinas I interviewed learned to negotiate visibility and invisibility within their families of origin. If they knew their mothers struggled with their daughters' sexuality, they used gender-neutral language when referring to their partners so as not to draw attention to the perceived transgression.

Alexis is a college student who is in her first relationship with another woman, Sara. Since coming out as bisexual, Alexis's relationship with her mother has deteriorated, and yet Alexis struggles to preserve this connection: "We were very, very close—not as mother and daughter—but as friends. She is the only person that I feel has my best interest. Ever since I came out to her, I haven't been able to talk to her because she's like 'I need to go, or I don't want to talk about this.'"

Alexis stopped using gender pronouns when talking about her same-sex relationships. "I talk about 'this person said this to me (*esta persona me dijo esto*).' I no longer say, 'he told me this.'" Her mother, she said, "has a hunch that I'm dating someone and I've let her ask questions that might lead to her solidifying her suspicions, but for the most part, we haven't addressed it at all. And when we get close to it, I'm like, 'mom I'd appreciate it if you'd give me advice as if it was a person.'"

Alexis wants her mother to continue to play the role of confidant and friend even though she disapproves of her bisexuality. They straddle lines of visibility and invisibility. Alexis talks to her mother about her relationship issues but deflects from focusing on the gender of her partner, fluctuating in and out of visibility in order to defuse any tensions that might emerge.

going public

In her book *Invisible Families: Gay Identities, Relationships, and Motherhood among Black Women*, Mignon Moore finds that families of origin are more concerned about the public aspects of their kin's sexual nonconformity than they are about their same-sex intimacies. Similarly, the Latinas I interviewed experienced the most tension with their families of origin when trying to achieve public visibility for their relationships.

Luisa is a 30-year-old bisexual woman of Ecuadorian descent. She and her partner Courtney are busy planning their wedding; they are also planning to have a baby. But they have experienced disapproval and a lack of support from Luisa's devout Catholic parents, which has been devastating for them.

"It was horrible," said Luisa, referring to visiting her parents. "Whenever we'd go [Courtney would] spend the four hour drive back crying the whole way. She felt like here are these people who don't like her just because of who she is. They weren't getting to know her. They treated her like an outsider. She could tell that more than anything else my mom was disgusted by us. And that's really different than having a moral opposition."

Over time, Luisa's parents grew more tolerant. However, the couple's wedding plans reignited Luisa's parents' reservations about publicly displaying their relationship. Luisa explains, "I started to tell people in my family [about the engagement] and what I found out is that even the people who were pretending to be polite, when they realized I wasn't kidding, that I was engaged . . . very quickly this elation turned from that to, oh my God, these people who are my blood relatives, who would otherwise lie in the street for me, not only will they not come, I'm not welcome in their house, she's not welcome in their house. They're not going to tell their kids because they think this is immoral and unnatural."

Her father told Luisa she was "breaking his heart" and that "this was the worst thing that I could possibly do." Her mom said "my brother isn't coming. He's too young. Who wants to have a party that nobody is going to go to and the people who are going to come are grossed out by being there? Who wants to have that party?"

Disheartened, Luisa pushed her wedding date back several years. By delaying their wedding, she gains time to play the role of mediator. She troubleshoots her parents' discomfort, resists their claims that her relationship is unnatural, and guides them towards growing acceptance. This delay also gives Courtney more time to overcome the hurt she feels from the rejection from Luisa's family and gives Luisa's family of origin more time to get to know Courtney as a person.

More than anything, Luisa wants to marry her partner and expand their family. However, despite all of the hurt and rejection they have endured, Luisa feels these momentous events are incomplete without the support of her parents and extended family of origin. Since parental support is so important to her, Luisa continues to search for ways to integrate her family of origin with the one she is building with her partner.

maintaining family ties

While some of the couples I interviewed have been able to take advantage of the right to legally marry, for many of them, the decision to marry isn't just about gaining access to legal protection, as dominant discourse would suggest. They are just as concerned with gaining familial recognition. Marriage, for those who desire it, is not just about legal rights: it is also about visibility in their families.

For Luisa, who is in a financially stable relationship and holds a professional job, the benefit of being able to marry is about bringing her origin family to a heightened level of acceptance and understanding of the commitment she shares with Courtney. For them and for others in this study, the acceptance of families of origin, and the visibility that comes with this acceptance is of utmost importance.

What this suggests, then, is that lesbian, bisexual and queer Latinas enjoy varying degrees of acceptance and visibility from their families of origin. They work to achieve integration of their families at times by maintaining tacit relationships and other times by making their relationships public.

Regardless of the level of acceptance and support they receive, these women mediate between their families of origin and their intimate relationships. In attempting to incorporate their partners into their families of origin, they move in and out of visibility. While integrating their family units can put grave strains on their same-sex partnerships, they refuse to consider minimizing their connection with their families of origin. Instead, they do whatever possible to avoid distancing themselves from any of the members of their support network.

In addition to being racial or ethnic minorities, these women are immigrants, or the daughters of immigrants. Some are undocumented, and struggle for financial independence. By looking at this population we gain new insight into how diverse sexually nonconforming women create family: they build integrated familial support networks which require compromise, sacrifice and hard work.

recommended resources

Bernstein, Mary, and Renate Reimann. 2001. *Queer Families Queer Politics: Challenging Culture and the State.* New York: Columbia University Press. This edited volume is a compilation of articles on LGBTQ families and the role of activism and policy in shaping their lives.

Decena, Carlos U. 2011. *Tacit Subjects: Belonging and Same-Sex Desire Among Dominican Immigrant Men.* Durham, NC: Duke University Press. This book provides an account of transnationalism among Dominican gay men with an emphasis on the body, language and contested relationships.

Moore, Mignon R. 2011. *Invisible Families: Gay Identities, Relationships, and Motherhood Among Black Women.* Berkeley, CA: University of California Press. This book explores family formation among Black gay women and how this process is influenced by race, class and gender.

Weeks, Jeffrey, Heaphy, Brian, and Donovan, Catherine. 2001. *Same Sex Intimacies: Families of Choice and Other Life Experiments.* London: Routledge. This book provides an account of families of choice among lesbian, gay and bisexual men and women in Britain.

Weston, Kath. 1991. *Families We Choose: Lesbians, Gays Kinship.* New York: Columbia University Press. This book sets out to look at gay kinship and the relationship between families of origin and families of choice.

unmarried with children

kathryn edin and maria kefalas

spring 2005

Have poor, unmarried mothers given up on marriage, as middle-class observers often conclude? To the contrary, most of the time they are simply waiting for the right partner and situation to make it work.

Jen Burke, a White tenth-grade dropout who is 17 years old, lives with her stepmother, her sister, and her 16-month-old son in a cramped but tidy row home in Philadelphia's beleaguered Kensington neighborhood. She is broke, on welfare, and struggling to complete her GED. Wouldn't she and her son have been better off if she had finished high school, found a job, and married her son's father first?

In 1950, when Jen's grandmother came of age, only 1 in 20 American children was born to an unmarried mother. Today, that rate is 1 in 3—and they are usually born to those least likely to be able to support a child on their own. In our book, *Promises I Can Keep: Why Poor Women Put Motherhood Before Marriage*, we discuss the lives of 162 White, African American, and Puerto Rican low-income single mothers living in eight destitute neighborhoods across Philadelphia and its poorest industrial suburb, Camden. We spent five years chatting over kitchen tables and on front stoops, giving mothers like Jen the opportunity to speak to the question so many affluent Americans ask about them: Why do they have children while still young and unmarried when they will face such an uphill struggle to support them?

> **More than seven in ten women who had a child outside of marriage will eventually wed someone.**

romance at lightning speed

Jen started having sex with her 20-year-old boyfriend Rick just before her 15th birthday. A month and a half later, she was pregnant. "I didn't want to get pregnant," she claims. "*He* wanted me to get pregnant." "As soon as he met me, he wanted to have a kid with me," she explains. Though Jen's college-bound suburban peers would be appalled by such a declaration, on the streets of Jen's neighborhood, it is something of a badge of honor. "All those other girls he was with, he didn't want to have a baby with any of them," Jen boasts. "I asked him, 'Why did you choose me to have a kid when you could have a kid with any one of them?' He was like, 'I want to have a kid with *you*.'" Looking back, Jen says she now believes that the reason "he wanted me to have a kid that early is so that I didn't leave him."

In inner-city neighborhoods like Kensington, where childbearing within marriage has become rare, romantic relationships like Jen and Rick's proceed at lightning speed. A young man's avowal, "I want to have a baby by you," is often part of the courtship ritual from the beginning. This is more than idle talk, as their first child is typically conceived within a year from the time a couple begins "kicking it." Yet while poor couples' pillow talk often revolves around dreams of shared children, the news of a pregnancy—the first indelible sign of the

244

huge changes to come—puts these still-new relationships into overdrive. Suddenly, the would-be mother begins to scrutinize her mate as never before, wondering whether he can "get himself together"—find a job, settle down, and become a family man—in time.

Jen began pestering Rick to get a real job instead of picking up day-labor jobs at nearby construction sites. She also wanted him to stop hanging out with his ne'er-do-well friends, who had been getting him into serious trouble for more than a decade. Most of all, she wanted Rick to shed what she calls his "kiddie mentality"—his habit of spending money on alcohol and drugs rather than recognizing his growing financial obligations at home.

Rick did not try to deny paternity, as many would-be fathers do. Nor did he abandon or mistreat Jen, at least intentionally. But Rick, who had been in and out of juvenile detention since he was 8 years old for everything from stealing cars to selling drugs, proved unable to stay away from his unsavory friends. At the beginning of her seventh month of pregnancy, an escapade that began as a drunken lark landed Rick in jail on a carjacking charge. Jen moved back home with her stepmother, applied for welfare, and spent the last two-and-a-half months of her pregnancy without Rick.

Rick sent penitent letters from jail. "I thought he changed by the letters he wrote me. I thought he changed a lot," she says. "He used to tell me that he loved me when he was in jail. . . . It was always gonna be me and him and the baby when he got out." Thus, when Rick's alleged victim failed to appear to testify and he was released just days before Colin's birth, the couple's reunion was a happy one. Often, the magic moment of childbirth calms the troubled waters of such relationships. New parents typically make amends and resolve to stay together for the sake of their child. When surveyed just after a child's birth, eight in ten unmarried parents say they are still together, and most plan to stay together and raise the child.

Promoting marriage among the poor has become the new war on poverty, Bush style. And it is true that the correlation between marital status and child poverty is strong. But poor single mothers already believe in marriage. Jen insists that she will walk down the aisle one day, though she admits it might not be with Rick. And demographers still project that more than seven in ten women who had a child outside of marriage will eventually wed someone. First, though, Jen wants to get a good job, finish school, and get her son out of Kensington.

Most poor, unmarried mothers and fathers readily admit that bearing children while poor and unmarried is not the ideal way to do things. Jen believes the best time to become a mother is "after you're out of school and you got a job, at least, when you're like 21. . . . When you're ready to have kids, you should have everything ready, have your house, have a job, so when that baby comes, the baby can have its own room." Yet given their already limited economic prospects, the poor have little motivation to time their births as precisely as their middle-class counterparts do. The dreams of young people like Jen and Rick center on children at a time of life when their more affluent peers plan for college and careers. Poor girls coming of age in the inner city value children highly, anticipate them eagerly, and believe strongly that they are up to the job of mothering—even in difficult circumstances. Jen, for example, tells us, "People outside the neighborhood, they're like, 'You're 15! You're pregnant?' I'm like, it's not none of their business. I'm gonna be able to take care of my kid. They have nothing to worry about." Jen says she has concluded that "some people . . . are better at having kids at a younger age. . . . I think it's better for some people to have kids younger."

when i became a mom

When we asked mothers like Jen what their lives would be like if they had not had children, we expected them to express regret over foregone opportunities for school and careers. Instead, most believe their children "saved" them. They describe their lives as spinning out of control before becoming pregnant—struggles with parents and peers, "wild," risky behavior, depression, and school failure. Jen speaks to this poignantly. "I was just real bad. I hung with a real bad crowd. I was doing pills. I was really depressed. . . . I was drinking. That was before I was pregnant." "I think," she reflects, "if I never had a baby or anything, . . . I would still be doing the things I was doing. I would probably still be doing drugs. I'd probably still be drinking." Jen admits that when she first became pregnant, she was angry that she "couldn't be out no more. Couldn't be out with my friends. Couldn't do nothing." Now, though, she says, "I'm glad I have a son . . . because I would still be doing all that stuff."

Children offer poor youth like Jen a compelling sense of purpose. Jen paints a before-and-after picture of her life that was common among the mothers we interviewed. "Before, I didn't have nobody to take care of. I didn't have nothing left to go home for. . . . Now I have my son to take care of. I have him to go home for. . . . I don't have to go buy weed or drugs with my money. I could buy my son stuff with my money! . . . I have something to look up to now." Children also are a crucial source of relational intimacy, a self-made community of care. After a nasty fight with Rick, Jen recalls, "I was crying. My son came in the room. He was hugging me. He's 16 months and he was hugging me with his little arms.

He was really cute and happy, so I got happy. That's one of the good things. When you're sad, the baby's always gonna be there for you no matter what." Lately she has been thinking a lot about what her life was like back then, before the baby. "I thought about the stuff before I became a mom, what my life was like back then. I used to see pictures of me, and I would hide in every picture. This baby did so much for me. My son did a lot for me. He helped me a lot. I'm thankful that I had my baby."

Around the time of the birth, most unmarried parents claim they plan to get married eventually. Rick did not propose marriage when Jen's first child was born, but when she conceived a second time, at 17, Rick informed his dad, "It's time for me to get married. It's time for me to straighten up. This is the one I wanna be with. I had a baby with her, I'm gonna have another baby with her." Yet despite their intentions, few of these couples actually marry. Indeed, most break up well before their child enters preschool.

i'd like to get married, but…

The sharp decline in marriage in impoverished urban areas has led some to charge that the poor have abandoned the marriage norm. Yet we found few who had given up on the idea of marriage. But like their elite counterparts, disadvantaged women set a high financial bar for marriage. For the poor, marriage has become an elusive goal—one they feel ought to be reserved for those who can support a "white picket fence" lifestyle: a mortgage on a modest row home, a car and some furniture, some savings in the bank, and enough money left over to pay for a "decent" wedding. Jen's views on marriage provide a perfect case in point. "If I was gonna get married, I would want to be married like my Aunt Nancy and my Uncle Pat. They live in the mountains. She has a job. My Uncle Pat is a state trooper; he has lots of money. They live in the [Poconos]. It's real nice out there. Her kids go to Catholic school. . . . That's the kind of life I would want to have. If I get married, I would have a life like [theirs]." She adds, "And I would wanna have a big wedding, a real nice wedding."

Unlike the women of their mothers' and grandmothers' generations, young women like Jen are not merely content to rely on a man's earnings. Instead, they insist on being economically "set" in their own right before taking marriage vows. This is partly because they want a partnership of equals, and they believe money buys say-so in a relationship. Jen explains, "I'm not gonna just get into marrying him and not have my own house! Not have a job! I still wanna do a lot of things before I get married. He [already] tells me I can't do nothing. I can't

go out. What's gonna happen when I marry him? He's gonna say he owns me!"

Economic independence is also insurance against a marriage gone bad. Jen explains, "I want to have everything ready, in case something goes wrong. . . . If we got a divorce, that would be my house. I bought that house, he can't kick me out or he can't take my kids from me." "That's what I want in case that ever happens. I know a lot of people that happened to. I don't want it to happen to me." These statements reveal that despite her desire to marry, Rick's role in the family's future is provisional at best. "We get along, but we fight a lot. If he's there, he's there, but if he's not, that's why I want a job . . . a job with computers . . . so I could afford my kids, could afford the house. . . . I don't want to be living off him. I want my kids to be living off me."

Why is Jen, who describes Rick as "the love of my life," so insistent on planning an exit strategy before she is willing to take the vows she firmly believes ought to last "forever?" If love is so sure, why does mistrust seem so palpable and strong? In relationships among poor couples like Jen and Rick, mistrust is often spawned by chronic violence and infidelity, drug and alcohol abuse, criminal activity, and the threat of imprisonment. In these tarnished corners of urban America, the stigma of a failed marriage is far worse than an out-of-wedlock birth. New mothers like Jen feel they must test the relationship over three, four, even five years' time. This is the only way, they believe, to insure that their marriages will last.

Trust has been an enormous issue in Jen's relationship with Rick. "My son was born December 23rd, and [Rick] started cheating on me again . . . in March. He started cheating on me with some girl—Amanda. . . . Then it was another girl, another girl, another girl after. I didn't wanna believe it. My friends would come up to me and be like, 'Oh yeah, your boyfriend's cheating on you with this person.' I wouldn't believe it. . . . I would see him with them. He used to have hickies. He used to make up some excuse that he was drunk—that was always his excuse for everything." Things finally came to a head when Rick got another girl pregnant. "For a while, I forgave him for everything. Now, I don't forgive him for nothing." Now we begin to understand the source of Jen's hesitancy. "He wants me to marry him, [but] I'm not really sure. . . . If I can't trust him, I can't marry him, 'cause we would get a divorce. If you're gonna get married, you're supposed to be faithful!" she insists. To Jen and her peers, the worst thing that could happen is "to get married just to get divorced."

Given the economic challenges and often perilously low quality of the romantic relationships among unmarried parents, poor women may be right to be cautious about marriage. Five years after we first spoke with her, we met with Jen again. We learned that Jen's second pregnancy ended in a miscarriage. We also learned that Rick was out of the picture— apparently for good. "You know that bar [down the street?] It happened in that bar. . . . They were in the bar, and this guy was like badmouthing [Rick's friend] Mikey, talking stuff to him or whatever. So Rick had to go get involved in it and start with this guy. . . . Then he goes outside and fights the guy [and] the guy dies of head trauma. They were all on drugs, they were all drinking, and things just got out of control, and that's what happened. He got fourteen to thirty years."

these are cards
i dealt myself

Jen stuck with Rick for the first two and a half years of his prison sentence, but when another girl's name replaced her own on the visitors' list, Jen decided she was finished with him once and for all. Readers might be asking what Jen ever saw in a man like Rick. But Jen and Rick operate in a partner market where the better-off men go to the better-off women. The only way for someone like Jen to forge a satisfying relationship with a man is to find a diamond in the rough or improve her own economic position so that she can realistically compete for more upwardly mobile partners, which is what Jen is trying to do now. "There's this kid, Donny, he works at my job. He works on C shift. He's a supervisor! He's funny, three years older, and he's not a geek or anything, but he's not a real preppy good boy either. But he's not [a player like Rick] and them. He has a job, you know, so that's good. He doesn't do drugs or anything. And he asked my dad if he could take me out!"

These days, there is a new air of determination, even pride, about Jen. The aimless high school dropout pulls ten-hour shifts entering data at a warehouse distribution center Monday through Thursday. She has held the job for three years, and her aptitude and hard work have earned her a series of raises. Her current salary is higher than anyone in her household commands—$10.25 per hour, and she now gets two weeks of paid vacation, four personal days, 60 hours of sick time, and medical benefits. She has saved up the necessary $400 in tuition for a high school completion program that offers evening and weekend classes. Now all that stands between her and a diploma is a passing grade in mathematics, her least favorite subject. "My plan is to start college in January. [This month] I take my math test . . . so I can get my diploma," she confides.

Jen clearly sees how her life has improved since Rick's dramatic exit from the scene. "That's when I really started [to get better] because I didn't have to worry about what *he* was doing, didn't have to worry about him cheating on me, all this stuff. [It was] then I realized that I had to do what I had to do to take care of my son. . . . When he was there, I think that my whole life revolved around him, you know, so I always messed up somehow because I was so busy worrying about what *he* was doing. Like I would leave the [GED] programs I was in just to go home and see what he was doing. My mind was never concentrating." Now, she says, "a lot of people in my family look up to me now, because all my sisters dropped out from school, you know, nobody went back to school. I went back to school, you know? . . . I went back to school, and I plan to go to college, and a lot of people look up to me for that, you know? So that makes me happy . . . because five years ago nobody looked up to me. I was just like everybody else."

Children, far from being liabilities, provide crucial social-psychological resources—a strong sense of purpose and a profound source of intimacy.

Yet the journey has not been easy. "Being a young mom, being 15, it's hard, hard, hard, you know." She says, "I have no life. . . . I work from 6:30 in the morning until 5:00 at night. I leave here at 5:30 in the morning. I don't get home until about 6:00 at night." Yet she measures her worth as a mother by the fact that she has managed to provide for her son largely on her own. "I don't depend on nobody. I might live with my dad and them, but I don't depend on them, you know." She continues, "There [used to] be days when I'd be so stressed out, like, 'I can't do this!' And I would just cry and cry

Given the economic challenges and often perilously low quality of the romantic relationships among unmarried parents, poor women may be right to be cautious about marriage.

and cry. . . . Then I look at Colin, and he'll be sleeping, and I'll just look at him and think I don't have no [reason to feel sorry for myself]. The cards I have I've dealt myself so I have to deal with it now. I'm older. I can't change anything. He's my responsibility—he's nobody else's but mine—so I have to deal with that."

Becoming a mother transformed Jen's point of view on just about everything. She says, "I thought hanging on the corner drinking, getting high—I thought that was a good life, and I thought I could live that way for eternity, like sitting out with my friends. But it's not as fun once you have your own kid. . . . I think it changes [you]. I think, 'Would I want Colin to do that? Would I want my son to be like that . . . ?' It was fun to me but it's not fun anymore. Half the people I hung with are either . . . Some have died from drug overdoses, some are in jail, and some people are just out there living the same life that they always lived, and they don't look really good. They look really bad." In the end, Jen believes, Colin's birth has brought far more good into her life than bad. "I know I could have waited [to have a child], but in a way I think Colin's the best thing that could have happened to me. . . . So I think I had my son for a purpose because I think Colin changed my life. He *saved* my life, really. My whole life revolves around Colin!"

promises i can keep

There are unique themes in Jen's story—most fathers are only one or two, not five years older than the mothers of their children, and few fathers have as many glaring problems as Rick—but we heard most of these themes repeatedly in the stories of the 161 other poor, single mothers we came to know. Notably, poor women do not reject marriage; they revere it. Indeed, it is the conviction that marriage is forever that makes them think that divorce is worse than having a baby outside of marriage. Their children, far from being liabilities, provide crucial social-psychological resources—a strong sense of purpose and a profound source of intimacy. Jen and the other mothers we came to know are coming of age in an America that is profoundly unequal—where the gap between rich and poor continues to grow. This economic reality has convinced them that they have little to lose and, perhaps, something to gain by a seemingly "ill-timed" birth.

The lesson one draws from stories like Jen's is quite simple: Until poor young women have more access to jobs that lead to financial independence—until there is reason to hope for the rewarding life pathways that their privileged peers pursue—the poor will continue to have children far sooner than most Americans think they should, while still deferring marriage. Marital standards have risen for all Americans, and the poor want the same things that everyone now wants out of marriage. The poor want to marry too, but they insist on marrying well. This, in their view, is the only way to avoid an almost certain divorce. Like Jen, they are simply not willing to make promises they are not sure they can keep.

Maria Kefalas is an ethnographer who writes about social class, community, and culture. She teaches at Saint Joseph's University in Philadelphia. As part of this project, Kathryn Edin and her family moved into one of the eight poor communities, East Camden, for two and a half years, detailed in Promises I Can Keep. She lives in Philadelphia and teaches at the University of Pennsylvania.

recommended resources

Edin, Kathryn, and Kefalas, Maria. 2005. *Promises I Can Keep: Why Poor Women Put Motherhood Before Marriage* Berkeley, CA: University of California Press. An account of how low-income women make sense of their choices about marriage and motherhood.

Gibson, Christina, Edin, Kathryn, and McLanahan, Sara. 2004. "High Hopes but Even Higher Expectations: A Qualitative and Quantitative Analysis of the Marriage Plans of Unmarried Couples Who Are New Parents." Working Paper 03-06-FF, Center for Research on Child Wellbeing, Princeton, NJ: Princeton University. Online at http://crcw.princeton.edu/workingpapers/WP03-06-FF-Gibson.pdf. The authors examine the rising expectations for marriage among unmarried parents.

Hays, Sharon. 2003. *Flat Broke with Children: Women in the Age of Welfare Reform.* London: Oxford University Press. How welfare reform has affected the lives of poor moms.

Lareau, Annette. 2003. *Unequal Childhoods: Class, Race, and Family Life.* Berkeley, CA: University of California Press. A fascinating discussion of different childrearing strategies among low-income, working-class, and middle-class parents.

Nelson, Timothy J, Clampet-Lundquist, Susan, and Edin, Kathryn. 2002. "Fragile Fatherhood: How Low-Income, Non-Custodial Fathers in Philadelphia Talk About Their Families." In C. Tamis-LeMonda and N. Cabrera (eds.), *The Handbook of Father Involvement: Multidisciplinary Perspectives*. Mahwah, NJ: Lawrence Earlbaum Associates. What poor, single men think about fatherhood.

good grief

bouncing back from a spouse's death in later life

deborah carr

fall 2006

Why are some older adults devastated when their partners die, while others enjoy improved psychological health and social relations? The experience of loss differs for men and women, and also depends on how one's spouse died and how the couple related during their marriage.

On the night before New Year's Eve 2003—one month before his 40th wedding anniversary—John Gregory Dunne sat down to eat dinner with his wife and writing partner Joan Didion. Moments later, he suffered a heart attack and died instantly. When Dunne, 71, was pronounced dead at the hospital later that evening, Didion kept her emotions in check—a hospital staffer called her "a cool customer." Didion, 69, chronicled the year following her husband's death in her 2005 book *The Year of Magical Thinking*. While critics hailed her work as a "masterpiece" and a "taut, clear-eyed memoir of grief," many readers disagreed. In book groups and online chat rooms, readers—many of them newly bereaved themselves—raged against Didion's "cool" memoir. Where was the emotion, the devastation, the proof of her love for her late husband? Grieving spouses are supposed to be visibly distraught; something must be wrong with Didion.

Sociologists have documented the importance of "feeling rules": the cultural guidelines that shape appropriate emotional responses to life events and experiences. Those who violate the rules—such as a widow who grieves her husband's death too calmly, for too short a time, or not at all—are maligned as "insensitive" at best and "pathological" at worst. Yet recent research reveals that many older men and women—those 65 and over— survive such losses with only a brief spell of depressive symptoms, while many report no depressive symptoms at all. Still others, released from stressful caregiving responsibilities, an unhappy marriage, or from watching their loved one suffer an incurable, protracted illness, enjoy improved psychological well-being. These survivors are neither "pathological" nor "cool." Rather, they reveal that there is no single, universal way to grieve. The ways that older widows and widowers grieve reflect how the couples related during marriage, how their spouses died, the strains experienced during the final weeks and months, and their other roles and relationships that might protect against (or exacerbate) the pain of losing a loved one.

the universality of grief

Early psychological writings on spousal bereavement claimed that profound sadness is a universal response to loss, so that "virtually everyone whose spouse dies exhibits some signs and symptoms of depression." In fact, depression is assumed to be such a normal, natural, and expected reaction to loss that the *Diagnostic and Statistical Manual* (DSM) of the American Psychiatric Association exempts depressed bereaved persons from a diagnosis of "depression." Stress researchers, too, view spousal loss as potentially devastating; survey instruments used to assess life stress, such as the Social Readjustment Rating Scale (SRRS), regard the death of a spouse as the life event that requires the most intense adjustment.

Early clinical studies concluded that widows and widowers who did not grieve (who experience what is referred to as "absent" or "inhibited" grief) were suffering from denial, inhibition, narcissism, immaturity, or an inability to maintain meaningful relationships with a loved one. Moreover, these symptom-free survivors were considered to be trapped in a state of denial that would later erupt in the form of an intense "delayed grief." The way to regain emotional equilibrium was to "work through" the loss. As Freud described this process, the bereaved person reviews "each single one of the memories and hopes which bound the libido" to the deceased. Therapeutic interventions followed suit, encouraging widows and widowers to think about their late spouses, confronting rather than avoiding reminders of the deceased and expressing their feelings through writing, talking, or facial expressions. Therapists assumed that those who did not display overt distress were avoiding the critical task of "working through" their loss.

Early studies of bereavement also identified risk factors for severe grief. For instance, adherents of psychoanalytic and attachment theories proposed that losing a spouse was most painful for those whose marriages were conflicted or ambivalent. Freud observed that these people struggled with feelings that oscillated between anger toward and strong attachment to their late spouses. These conflicting feelings made it hard for survivors to let go of their loved ones, yet they felt angry at the deceased for abandoning them. As a result, Freud—and psychoanalytically trained therapists—maintained that the unhappily married would have the greatest difficulty in adjusting emotionally to their loss.

Deborah Carr studies spousal loss, dying, and how families prepare for the end of life.

Other research showed that spouses were most grief-stricken when their loved ones died unexpectedly. Studies in the 1940s found that the wives of men serving in World War II experienced sadness and anxiety before their spouses died, but they disengaged emotionally and fared reasonably well after the event. In contrast, the relatives of young adults who were killed suddenly and unexpectedly in the infamous 1942 Coconut Grove nightclub fire suffered severe grief. Researchers and clinicians concluded that those who anticipate the death of a spouse can prepare for it psychologically, while those who lose their loved ones suddenly are unprepared, shocked, and psychologically devastated.

older bereaved spouses

Mounting evidence questions whether depression is universal among the bereaved, whether "absent grief" is pathological, and whether "working through" a loss is necessary for recovery. Moreover, recent empirical studies show that sudden deaths are not necessarily more distressing than expected ones, and that bereaved people who had strained marriages actually feel less grief than those who had close and loving ones. Certainly, some widows and widowers experience profound depression in the months and even years following their loss. Many find comfort in confronting and working through their loss. Yet for the majority of older bereaved spouses, death is simply a part of life (albeit a sad part), and recovery and resilience are the rule rather than the exception.

Studies of older widows and widowers concur that only 15–25 percent experience clinical levels of depressive symptoms in the months immediately following the death, while 25–45 percent report mild symptoms, and anywhere from 30–50 percent report no depressive symptoms. Depressive symptoms typically are measured as the number of times in the past week that a person felt sad, blue, lonely, and lacking energy or motivation. (See "The Epidemic in Mental Illness: Clinical Fact or Survey Artifact" in the Winter 2006 issue of *Contexts* for a discussion of the measurement and diagnosis of depression.) Research tracking people who have lost a spouse over longer time periods further reveals that even those who are distressed initially manage to bounce back reasonably quickly after their loss.

One analysis based on the Changing Lives of Older Couples (CLOC), a multiwave study of bereavement among spouses age 65 and older, found that nearly half (46 percent) of older widows and widowers were "resilient," showing no or few depressive symptoms at both 6 and 18 months after their loss. Rather than showing signs of denial, emotional inhibition, or delayed grief, these relatively symptom-free older adults believed that death was a part of life, and they took great comfort in memories of their deceased spouses. One in ten showed what the authors called the "common grief" pattern, experiencing strong depressive symptoms six months after their loss, but improving considerably over the following year. Another 10 percent (whom the authors dubbed "depressed-improved") had significant depressive symptoms prior to the loss, but then improved considerably after it occurred. Just 16 percent reported "chronic grief," or strong depressive symptoms for more than 18 months following the loss. Eight percent experienced "chronic depression," which encompasses high, constant levels of depressive symptoms both before and after the loss.

What accounts for the glaring discrepancy between early clinical writings and recent empirical research based on large samples of older adults? And why are some bereaved spouses physically and emotionally incapacitated by their loss, while others show little if any decline in their well-being? In large part, the difference reflects the samples and research methods used. Many early studies were based on clinical observations of widows and widowers who had sought medical or psychiatric help. Studies based on help-seeking populations tend to overstate the problematic consequences of loss because they include only the most troubled. Other early studies used cross-sectional data, or snapshots at a single point

in time of bereaved people. Most of these studies did not track these people over time, nor did they ascertain their characteristics before the death. Because bereaved people often have poorer physical health and economic well-being than their married peers even before the loss, studies that fail to consider preloss characteristics may also overstate the harmful consequences of a spouse's death.

Perhaps most important, classic theories and studies often failed to consider three of the most important influences on spousal bereavement: the age of the husband and wife, how the spouse died, and what the couple's life was like prior to the death. Most early studies focused on age-diverse samples and did not explicitly consider the unique case of older widows and widowers, who not only account for the vast majority of spousal losses each year, but also have distinctive personal resources (and risk factors) that make their bereavement different than it is for younger adults.

spousal loss late in life

Televised images of distraught widows and widowers often focus on the young—the teenage brides of fallen soldiers in the Iraq war or the junior executives who lost their wives on September 11th. But today the loss of a spouse is a transition overwhelmingly experienced by older adults. Of the 900,000 Americans who lose a mate each year, nearly three-quarters are 65 or older. Patterns of spousal loss mirror mortality patterns overall. The death rate, or the number of people who die in a given year per 100,000 in the population, increases sharply beyond age 65. Losing a spouse is simply inevitable for most older married couples. As sociologist Helena Lopata has observed, the only way to avoid such a loss is to avoid marriage.

Yet these patterns also suggest that older bereaved spouses have an important coping resource that is seldom available to younger widows and widowers: friends, peers, and siblings who also are adjusting to such a loss. Older adults often "rehearse" for losing a spouse by watching their peers go through the same experience; they can turn to one another for wisdom, practical support, and camaraderie.

The meaning of life and death also differs for older and younger

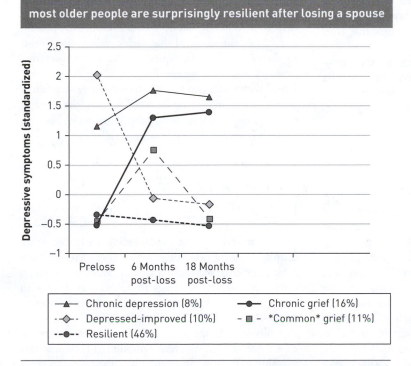

most older people are surprisingly resilient after losing a spouse

Legend:
- ▲ Chronic depression (8%)
- ◆ Depressed-improved (10%)
- ● Resilient (46%)
- ● Chronic grief (16%)
- ■ *Common* grief (11%)

Source: *Bonanno et al.,* Journal of Personality and Social Psychology *(2002)*

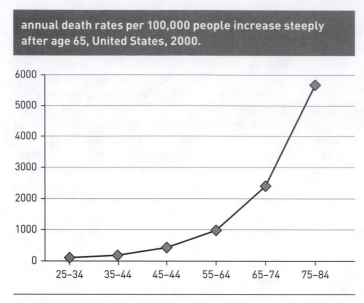

annual death rates per 100,000 people increase steeply after age 65, United States, 2000.

Source: *U.S. Census Bureau*

persons. Death may be viewed as the natural conclusion to an elderly spouse's long and meaningful life, rather than the interruption of a life yet to be lived. Most older persons experience such losses after decades of marriage. They have raised their children, celebrated the births of their grandchildren, and enjoyed at least a few years of relaxation together after retiring. Few feel they are being robbed of a long future together. Older adults also differ from their younger counterparts in how they respond emotionally to stress. Psychologists document that older adults have lower levels of "emotional reactivity." This means that they are better able to regulate their emotions, and they report less extreme emotional responses than do younger people. Their grief reactions tend to be shorter-lived and less intense than those of younger widows and widowers.

(stroke), chronic lower respiratory disease, influenza or pneumonia, and diabetes mellitus. Consequently, most older adults find that the final weeks (or even months and years) with their spouses are filled with difficult and emotionally wrenching caregiving chores. Although advances in medical technology have increased the life span of ailing adults, they also increase the burden on spouses to manage complex care and medication regimes. Many life-threatening illnesses are now treated in the home, so spouses must manage everything from insulin shots to morphine use and spinal injections.

Even those caring for a relatively healthy yet frail spouse often find that caregiving is so time-consuming as to tax their emotional resources and prevent them from paying attention to their own health symptoms. Older caregivers report high levels of strain and depressive symptoms when their spouses are still alive, yet many bounce back shortly after their spouses die. One recent study found that by seven months after spousal loss, bereaved caregivers reported depressive symptom scores that were no higher than either bereaved noncaregivers or married older adults. Another study of caregivers for dementia patients showed that they had high levels of depressive symptoms while caring for their spouses, yet showed a dramatic decrease in symptoms after their spouses had died. More than 90 percent felt that death was a relief to the patient, and 72 percent admitted that the death was also a relief to them. These studies question the assumption that expected deaths are necessarily "better" for the survivor; rather, they reveal that losing a spouse is a process rather than an event. For many bereaved spouses, the event of the loss is not as painful as the long "death watch" period, which is often filled with drawn-out suffering.

cause of death

Age is not the only factor that shapes the experience of losing a spouse; the cause of death is also important. Most older spouses die of a chronic illness, or a long-term illness that causes physical pain or disability and often requires intensive care. The leading causes of death today among those age 65 and older are heart disease, cancer, cere-brovascular disease

> *Caregiving is so time-consuming as to tax their emotional resources and prevent them from paying attention to their own health symptoms.*

the experience of loss reflects the marriage

Another reason that some older people are spared severe distress is that the death of a spouse may be a release from a marriage that was stifling or unrewarding. Although early psychoanalytic writings suggested that those with troubled marriages had the most difficulty in coming to terms with their losses, data from the CLOC study reveal that people with the most close-knit, loving marriages experience the most severe symptoms of sadness and yearning in the first six months after their loss. Yet these symptoms fade as time elapses, and the survivors eventually come to enjoy memories of their beloved spouses without experiencing pangs of grief.

The CLOC study also shows that widows and widowers who had the most problematic marriages show better psychological health following their loss than do their married peers who remain in such troubled relationships. Married women who are most emotionally dependent on their husbands report lower self-esteem than do widows who had been highly dependent on their husbands. Widows experience a boost to their self-esteem when they are freed from a marriage that had been stifling. Moreover, both widows and widowers who had been highly dependent on their spouses for practical matters, like homemaking or home maintenance, offer the strongest endorsement for statements such as "I am a stronger person as a result of dealing with the loss of my spouse," and "As a result of having to manage without my spouse, I have become more self-confident." Such people may receive psychological rewards from realizing that they have withstood and survived an event that had earlier seemed insurmountable.

"his" and "her" loss?

Men and women experience marriage in very different ways, so they also experience the loss of a spouse differently. These differences include not only psychological responses but also practical readjustments to daily life. In the early 1970s, Jesse Bernard wrote about "his" and "hers" marriage. "His" marriage brought men good health, power, and satisfaction, while "her" marriage subjected women to stress, self-sacrifice, and depression. While numerous studies conducted since the 1970s show that marriage benefits both men and women, most sociologists recognize that marriage carries different rewards (and costs) for men and women. Among today's older adults, husbands were typically the "breadwinners" in their marriages and often took responsibility for "masculine" tasks such as making home repairs, paying bills, and managing finances. Their wives usually had sporadic (if any) paid work experience and were responsible for homemaking activities, including meal preparation, child care, and housework.

This traditional division of labor means that widows and widowers face different challenges. For women, widowhood often means a sharp dip in economic resources. Because men earn more than women during their working lives, they receive higher Social Security benefits upon retirement or disability. When the husband dies, these monthly checks are reduced. Economists estimate that a widow's cost of living is about 80 percent of what the couple's was, but the monthly Social Security payments decline to just two-thirds of their previous level. Economists also have documented that married couples often underestimate how many years a widow will outlive her husband, so that they often do not save enough money to cover a widow's future needs. Widows are consequently more likely than widowers to experience distress and anxiety about money.

Men are more likely than women to experience sickness, disability, and death after their wives die. While popular lore and a handful of early studies claim that these men may "die of a broken heart," the loss of a helpmate and caretaker is the real culprit. Wives typically monitor their husbands' diets, encourage them to exercise, remind them to take their medications, and urge them to give up vices like smoking and drinking. When their wives die, these reminders cease as well. Not surprisingly, recently widowed men are more likely than married men to die of accidents, alcohol-related deaths, lung cancer, and chronic ischemic heart disease—but not from other causes that are less closely linked to health behaviors.

Even worse for men, though, is that their wives are often their primary (if not only) source of social support and integration. Social support is essential for physical and emotional health, especially in later life. Today's older men, often raised to be

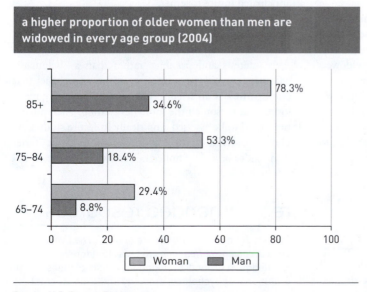

a higher proportion of older women than men are widowed in every age group (2004)

85+: 78.3% / 34.6%
75–84: 53.3% / 18.4%
65–74: 29.4% / 8.8%

Woman   Man

Source: U.S. Census Bureau

strong and silent, have few close friends with whom they can share their private concerns. Wives often are the family "kinkeepers"—the ones who send birthday cards to the kids, arrange dinner parties with friends, and organize outings with the grandchildren; when a man loses his wife, he also loses his social networks.

Women tend to have more extensive social networks. For many women, supportive relationships with friends, children, and other relatives, as well as participation in community activities, partially fill the emotional void created by the death of their husbands. Widows report much higher levels of both practical and emotional support from their children than do widowers, reflecting long-established patterns of reciprocity. Because women usually are more involved in raising and nurturing their children than men, these strong relationships offer a unique source of strength to older women when their spouses die.

For these reasons, widowers are much more motivated than widows to seek new romantic partners soon after their loss. According to the U.S. Census Bureau, just 2 percent of older widows but 20 percent of older widowers eventually remarry. For widowers, remarriage and dating are ways to bounce back from the loneliness and sadness of loss. Older men who have remarried show levels of mental health that are just as good as—if not better than—those of their peers who are in long-term marriages. Data from the CLOC study show that six months after losing a spouse, one-third of older widowers but just 16 percent of widows say they would like to remarry some day.

Not only do men have a greater motivation to remarry—they have more opportunities to find new partners. The sex ratio in the United States today is 1.5 women for every man age 65 and older, and 3 women for every man 85 and older. This gender gap reflects gender differences in late-life mortality. Women are more likely than men to outlive their spouses; life expectancy at birth today is 74 for men and 80 for women. Older women also are more likely to remain widowed, given widowers' greater propensity to remarry younger women. Among persons ages 65 to 74, 29 percent of women but just 9 percent of men are widowed. These proportions jump to 78 percent of women and 35 percent of men ages 85 and older. Taken together, these numbers suggest that for older widows, remarriage is seldom an option.

with more than 75 million babies born between 1946 and 1964, tens of millions of older Americans will lose their spouses in the coming decades. Social gerontologists debate whether adjusting to a spouse's death will be more or less difficult for boomers, compared to their parents' generation. Baby boomers are expected to adapt well to the necessary "practical" or daily life readjustments, although they may find emotional adjustment particularly challenging.

Female boomers have more education, more work experience, and higher personal earnings than past cohorts of older women. They may depend less on their husbands for income or assistance with chores such as home repair or financial management. Likewise, each cohort of men is more likely than their fathers' generation to take on homemaking and childrearing tasks. As the boundaries separating traditional gender roles in marriage blur, widows and widowers will likely face fewer challenges (and less anxiety) as they manage homemaking, home maintenance, and finances after their spouses die.

Adjusting emotionally to spousal loss may become even more difficult for future cohorts, however. While past generations of older adults often stayed in difficult marriages because of cultural or religious prohibitions against divorce, baby boomers can freely divorce if their marriages are unsatisfying. If the men and women of the baby boom dissolve troubled marriages, those who remain married until late in life may have particularly warm and close relationships, and may be the most grief-stricken upon their loss. Moreover, increasing numbers of divorced boomers remarry in their 50s and older. For these mature newlyweds, the death of a spouse—even a spouse in his or her 60s—may rob them of a much-anticipated future together.

Some family sociologists argue further that the marital relationship has been idealized in recent decades. Young men and women today seek a "soul mate" who shares their interests and passions, rather than a "helpmate" who pays the bills or washes the dishes. The belief that one's partner is an irreplaceable "soul mate" may make losing that person all the more devastating. Such projections need to be assessed empirically in future studies. As Didion observed in *The Year of Magical Thinking*: "Grief turns out to be a place none of us know until we reach it."

how will baby boomers grieve?

In the coming decades, the number of older adults who become widowed each year will increase dramatically. Given the sheer size of the baby-boom cohort,

recommended resources

Archer, John. 1999. *The Nature of Grief: The Evolution and Psychology of Reactions to Loss*. London: Routledge. A ground-breaking synthesis of ideas from evolutionary psychology, ethology and experimental psychology on the process of grief. Archer argues that grief is a natural reaction to loss, rather than an illness to be cured or a psychiatric disorder.

Bonanno, George A, Wortman, Camille B, Lehman, Darrin R. Tweed, Roger G, Haring, Michelle, Sonnega, John, Carr, Deborah, and Nesse, Randolph M. 2002. "Resilience to Loss and Chronic Grief: A Prospective Study from Preloss to 18-Months Postloss," *Journal of Personality and Social Psychology 83*: 1150–164. A rigorous and innovative analysis of a diverse range of psychological reactions to spousal loss.

Carr, Deborah, Nesse, Randolph, and Wortman, Camille B. (eds.). 2006. *Spousal Bereavement in Late Life*. New York: Springer Publishing. Wide-ranging theoretical, empirical, and practice-related essays from social scientists studying the social and psychological consequences of late-life widowhood.

Hansson, Robert O, and Stroebe, Margaret S. 2006. *Bereavement in Late Life: Coping, Adaptation and Developmental Influences*. Washington, DC: American Psychological Association. An in-depth account of the ways older adults cope with loss, authored by leading scholars of gerontology and bereavement, respectively.

Lopata, Helena Z. 1973. *Widowhood in an American City*. Cambridge, MA: Schenkman. A classic study of older widowed women in the greater Chicago area.

Wortman, Camille B, and Silver, Roxanne. 2001. "The Myths of Coping with Loss Revisited." In *Handbook of Bereavement Research: Consequences, Coping, and Care*. Washibgton, DC: American Psychological Association. Among the most widely cited works in bereavement research, this article uses compelling data and theory to dispel common myths about coping with loss.

gender and status matching
angela o'brien
winter 2015

Research shows, women do not trade beauty for status when selecting male mates. A lot of previous research only examined attractiveness for women and status for men. Writing in *American Sociological Review*, however, Elizabeth Aura McClintock examined the role of exchange and matching in romance. When you consider both attractiveness and education traits for both partners, it turns out most people are matching on both. To collect her data, McClintock's team used a personal attractiveness index to examine how equally matched a particular couple was, considering physical attractiveness, grooming, and personality. The researchers found that across 1,507 couples, romantic partners tended to be equally attractive, regardless of socioeconomic status.

Meanwhile, researchers David McClendon, Janet Chen-Lan Kuo, and Kelly Raley, in the journal *Demography*, studied why men and women tend to select equally educated partners. Rather than finding a simple story of advantaged people choosing advantaged partners, they found evidence that the labor market is facilitating graduate-to-graduate matches: more couples meet at work now that most women are employed. Since educational level strongly correlates with occupation, individuals are generally exposed to potential partners at the same educational level. The authors also found that women in occupations with more college graduates are more likely to marry and more likely to marry instead of cohabiting than those women in occupations with few degree holders. The pattern doesn't hold for men.

These studies suggest women are wielding their own power—and standards—in the making of marriage.

measuring same-sex relationships

nancy bates and theresa j. demaio

spring 2013

When social scientists need information about demographic trends, they immediately turn to the U.S. Census Bureau, the most highly regarded collector of data on Americans' rapidly changing lives. However, even the Census Bureau faces challenges in measuring certain trends. At the national level, Census Bureau scientists must ask their questions within the confines of federal restrictions. At the individual level, Census Bureau researchers must frame their questions in ways their respondents will comprehend, even as terms commonly ascribed to some populations are rapidly changing. The measurement of same-sex relationships challenges Census Bureau experts on all of these fronts.

measuring family ties

The measurement of family relationships, living arrangements, and marital status has a long history at the U.S. Census Bureau. Over time, the census categories have changed to reflect changes in U.S. society and laws that define the institution of marriage and other legal and non-legal relationship statuses. In fact, how the census measures marital status has evolved for more than a century. In 1880, the categories consisted only of single, married and

> *42 percent of the U.S. population now live in areas where some form of same-sex couple recognition is legal.*

widowed/divorced. By 1890, widowed and divorced each became its own category and in 1950, the category of separated was added. For the relationship item, instructions for enumerating roommates, boarders, and lodgers go back to the nineteenth century. In 1980, the form added a combined partner/roommate category, and in the 1990 Census, the category of unmarried partner was included for the first time.

Recently, challenges in accurately measuring relationships have involved the growing recognition of same-sex couples. Unlike other countries such as Britain and Canada, U.S. laws recognizing same-sex couples vary. At the federal level, there is no legal recognition while state laws range from no legal recognition to full marriage equality. Passage of the Defense of Marriage Act (DOMA) in 1996 had ramifications for how federal statistical agencies count same-sex couples. DOMA requires the federal government to define marriage as a legal union exclusively between one man and one woman. Partly in response to DOMA, for Census 2000, an edit procedure was introduced whereby same-sex couples who checked husband or wife were automatically reallocated as unmarried partners.

When the Census Bureau announced in 2008 that the same edit procedure would be used in the 2010 Census, gay advocacy groups took notice. A coalition of many different lesbian, gay, bisexual and transgender (LGBT) groups formed a census advocacy campaign known as Our Families Count. Groups lobbied for the Census Bureau to tabulate same-sex couples as they had originally reported on their census forms. In 2009, the Census Bureau announced that, while the Census 2010 tabulations would still reflect the unmarried partner re-edit classification, the agency would produce state-by-state counts of same-sex couples who identified themselves as spouses.

Because the laws governing same-sex marriage are fragmented and constantly evolving, the federal statistical system faces an enormous challenge to accurately reflect today's increasingly complex relationship configurations. Given that approximately 42 percent of the U.S. population now resides in an area where some form of same-sex couple recognition is legal, statistical agencies must find a way to adapt their current measures.

asking questions about the questions

To understand how gay and lesbian couples think about and report their relationships on official forms, the Census Bureau sponsored a two-part qualitative research project as part of a federal interagency task force. Using focus groups, we first explored the nomenclature of the current relationship and marital status questions—how do gay couples interpret them, what terms are used by this subpopulation, and under what circumstances? This enabled us to develop alternative questions that were then evaluated during one-on-one "think-aloud" interviews. This is how the Census Bureau "cognitively tests" the understanding of questions.

Between January and March 2010, investigators conducted a total of 18 focus groups across seven geographically diverse locations ranging from cities like Boston to rural areas in Georgia. Fourteen groups consisted of individuals in same-sex relationships with members recruited according to relationship status (legally married, in a domestic partnership or civil union, or had no legally recognized status). In addition, four groups consisted of persons in opposite-sex relationships who were not legally married. Members of all groups were cohabiting with their partners.

We first asked participants to describe how they usually introduced their "better halves." This was followed by a request to complete a form containing the 2010 American Community Survey items of name, relationship to householder, gender, age, and date of birth followed by the marital status question (see questionnaire on next page). Moderators then led a discussion of how participants answered the questions and why. Moderators focused on whether answers were predicated on current legal relationship status, existing laws in their states of residence, whether participants interpreted the questions to be asking about a legal status or something else, and what alternative terms or categories they expected to see on the forms.

listening to people think

Following the focus groups, we crafted two new versions of the relationship and marital status items. We tested these items using "think-aloud" interview techniques where respondents read questions aloud and verbalize their thought processes as they formulate answers. Forty interviews were conducted in four different cities between March and April 2011. Locales ranged from Washington, D.C. to Charlotte, North Carolina and represented a variety of state laws regarding same-sex partner recognition. Participants were all from cohabiting couples—15 were straight and the other 25 were gay and lesbian. As in the focus groups, we recruited participants with a wide range of legal statuses ranging from married same-sex couples, same (and opposite-sex) domestic partners, to couples with no legal recognition.

The questionnaire on page 69 illustrates the two versions randomly assigned to participants. After completing the randomly-assigned version, participants completed the alternative version followed by a debriefing that also determined which, if any, version they preferred.

We found that gay and straight participants often use the same terms upon introduction. Most often among these were: wife, husband, partner, boyfriend and girlfriend. The term partner was more often ascribed to gay and lesbian relationships (especially by opposite-sex couple groups). We also found that, particularly for gays and lesbians, participants' use of terms was not static but was conditional upon assessment of the setting. For examples, a gay male from rural Georgia responded, "How would I introduce my partner? It depends on the setting. If it's this setting, I would say 'my partner [name].' If it's outside, 'my good friend [name] or 'uncle.'" So, a "wife" among friends is a "roommate" when the cable repairman comes to the house. Likewise "single" on a flex insurance health plan becomes "married" on a census form.

However, upon probing we found that most participants viewed the census questions through a legal prism, believing it to be measuring state-sanctioned legally recognized relationships. Consequently, most answers aligned with legal couple statuses. Persons in same-sex couples without legal recognition residing in areas that did not recognize gay marriage indicated willingness to select "unmarried partner" because it was both legally accurate and the word "partner" was viewed as an adequate descriptor for their relationship. We also found that a legal marriage trumped local laws, at least for participants who had a legal marriage performed somewhere (inside or outside the United States). A lesbian from rural Georgia stated, "Oh, I would check off [wife], absolutely. I don't care if it would make everybody pissed off, and I really don't care if it wouldn't be recognized where I'm at."

2010 American Community Survey Relationship Question

How is this person related to Person 1? Mark (X) ONE box.

- ☐ Husband or wife
- ☐ Biological son or daughter
- ☐ Adopted son or daughter
- ☐ Stepson or stepdaughter
- ☐ Brother or sister
- ☐ Father or mother
- ☐ Grandchild
- ☐ Parent-in-law

- ☐ Son-in-law or daughter-in-law
- ☐ Other relative
- ☐ Roomer or boarder
- ☐ Housemate or roommate
- ☐ Unmarried partner
- ☐ Foster child
- ☐ Other nonrelative

2010 American Community Survey Marital Status Question

What is this person's marital status?

- ☐ Now married
- ☐ Widowed
- ☐ Divorced

- ☐ Separated
- ☐ Never married

Version 1 of revised relationship and marital status questions

How is this person related to Person 1? Mark ONE box.

- ☐ Husband/wife/spouse
- ☐ Unmarried partner
- ☐ Biological son or daughter
- ☐ Adopted son or daughter
- ☐ Stepson or stepdaughter
- ☐ Brother or sister
- ☐ Father or mother
- ☐ Grandchild

- ☐ Parent-in-law
- ☐ Son-in-law or daughter-in-law
- ☐ Other relative
- ☐ Roomer or boarder
- ☐ Housemate or roommate
- ☐ Foster child
- ☐ Other nonrelative

What is this person's current marital status? Mark (X) ONE box.

- ☐ Now married—skip to question X.
- ☐ Widowed
- ☐ Divorced

- ☐ Separated
- ☐ Never married

Is this person currently living in a registered domestic partnership or civil union?

- ☐ Yes
- ☐ No

Version 2 of revised relationship and marital status questions

How is this person related to Person 1? Mark (X) ONE box.

- ☐ Opposite-sex husband/wife/spouse
- ☐ Same-sex husband/wife/spouse
- ☐ Opposite-sex unmarried partner
- ☐ Same-sex unmarried partner
- ☐ Biological son or daughter
- ☐ Adopted son or daughter
- ☐ Stepson or stepdaughter
- ☐ Brother or sister
- ☐ Father or mother

- ☐ Grandchild
- ☐ Parent–in-law
- ☐ Son-in-law or daughter-in-law
- ☐ Other relative
- ☐ Roomer or boarder
- ☐ Housemate or roommate
- ☐ Foster child
- ☐ Other nonrelative

What is this person's current marital status? Mark (X) ONE box.

- ☐ Now married
- ☐ In a registered domestic partnership or civil union
- ☐ Widowed

- ☐ Divorced
- ☐ Separated
- ☐ Never married

I don't care if I was in Antarctica, I would say wife, absolutely." And a gay male from Ft. Lauderdale commented, "I would still check husband or wife. As far as I'm concerned, I'm legally married, I don't care what the federal government thinks."

encountering resistance and confusion

This is not to suggest that all same-sex couples were perfectly happy with the current options, particularly marital status. Participants from same-sex couples who lived in areas where marriage was not allowed and had no legal partnership status viewed the options as "marriage-centric" and without categories to describe their situations. Most marked "never married" and a few marked "divorced." Gay and lesbian participants who had been divorced from a previous heterosexual marriage felt frustrated that their marital status would be defined by a long-ago relationship unimportant compared to their current relationship.

Likewise, same-sex couples in registered domestic partnerships and civil unions expressed an undercurrent of dissatisfaction because the current options do not allow them to acknowledge the legally recognized component of their union. Overall, many did not feel any of the options adequately reflected their current lives, and felt personally discounted as expressed by comments such as this one, "I can't answer . . . this would be blank. I couldn't answer it because 'now married' would be false in every sense . . . And 'never married' is utterly false to my heart. So I consider this unanswerable. This is one of those forms where no appropriate answer is provided." Or this one, "If you want accurate information then give me the choice to give you that information. If you're failing to get that information then the census is not going to be correct to begin with, it's going to be skewed."

When presented with the revised questions, respondents were pleased to see the changes that attempted to accommodate their situations: moving unmarried partner to the second response category and disaggregating same-sex and opposite-sex couples. But, we had a concern as to whether there would be sensitivity issues among respondents in opposite-sex couples with the question that disaggregated response categories for same-sex and opposite-sex couples. In particular, we took notice of interviews conducted in Charlotte, North Carolina to gauge this reaction.

One straight White female expressed this view: "This [version] actually might, would offend me a little bit, because I think it's . . . I feel like we're kind of just lowering the standards . . . [as in] 'Okay we've got to conform to everyone, we want to be politically correct.' And that just really gets on my nerves, honestly . . . you know in a different part of the country, you might not be hearing this, but, that's how I feel about it." Another straight female stated, "[That version] tries too hard . . . it's making a point. [That version means] 'we're gonna put it out there . . . that we're including **everybody'** (emphasis added). But I get that . . . it's fine . . . we're in America." However, when pressed directly, neither indicated this opinion would lead them to discard the survey or otherwise not participate. Or, as one put it, "I wouldn't write my Congressman. I wouldn't go on Facebook about it . . . it's not that deep." Of course, this is a hypothetical judgment given in the context of a think-aloud interview, so we can only surmise their actual behavior.

> *Persons in same-sex couples without legal recognition were willing to select "unmarried partner."*

The inclusion of the category "In a registered domestic partnership or civil union" in the marital status question revealed a general lack of understanding about the concept among both gay and straight respondents and regardless of legal status. Only a few people said they were unfamiliar with either domestic partnerships or civil unions, but confusion abounded about what they were. One common misunderstanding was equating this concept to gay marriage. "In California you can do a domestic partnership, which is a same-sex marriage." Another misunderstanding equated it to common-law marriage as in this comment: "It seems like domestic partnership may be you've been living together for awhile. I think, legally after five years in North Carolina it's considered . . . I can't think of the term." Or this one, a civil union is "two people that have lived together for at least seven years." For these reasons, we recommend a separate question as a means of measuring domestic partnerships/civil unions.

catching up to the future

The social and legal landscape for same-sex couples has changed dramatically since Massachusetts first recognized same-sex marriage. Since then, other states have passed similar legislation as well as civil unions and domestic partnerships for gay and lesbian couples. In this respect, federal agencies have not kept up with the times, and new measures must be constructed to reflect recognition that, in some cases, is intended to confer the same rights and responsibilities as marriage.

In reality, designing a one-size-fits-all federal form when the legal reality of same-sex partner recognition is fragmented poses a challenge for questionnaire designers. However, accurately counting gay and lesbian couples is paramount since legislative bodies, courts, and voters are making decisions that affect the day-to-day lives of this population. Will they receive partner health insurance, Social Security, or pension benefits like their straight couple counterparts? Will they be allowed to adopt children or visit their partners in the hospital?

With the qualitative testing complete, federal agencies should follow best practices and quantitatively test the new questions in an environment that closely resembles a large-scale production survey. Only then can we be certain the data are valid and reliable. Ultimately, the Census Bureau and other statistical agencies must be responsive to social changes so our vital statistics accurately mirror and help support America's diverse population.

online friends affect relationship status
joanna pepin
summer 2014

Complain about your job on Facebook? Your children? What about your marriage?

Hannah Seligson, author and *New York Times* contributor, contends that unhappy marriages are Facebook's last taboo. Seligson argues that complaining about one's spouse in public violates the marital code of silence. So, as people attempt to manage and influence how others perceive their relationships, social networks also affect couples' views of their own relationships. Approval from friends and family can positively affect the stability and quality of romantic relationships, while social disapproval may be a negative, sometimes relationship-ending force.

In a 2010 article, Richard Slatcher found that friendships with other couples, particularly meaningful connections, increased feelings of closeness in one's own relationship. It also turns out that perceptions of others' opinions are more predictive of relationship stability than the actual views of network members. Thus social network approval has a positive influence on the partnership, including increased feelings of love and commitment.

As for the doubters, a new article in *Social Psychology Quarterly* by Colleen Sinclair and colleagues investigates how different personality types (different ways of handling emotions stemming from perceptions of limited freedom) moderate social network disapproval of romantic partners. In addition to following network pressure, people who perceive a threat to their ability to choose a romantic partner could react by doing the opposite of that encouraged by their network; others resist social influence and instead pursue self-determination. This team used survey data, a vignette design, and a laboratory-based dating game experiment to examine sensitivity to social network opinions. They report that relationship approval does have consistent positive effects on feelings of love and commitment. But when it comes to disapproval, people differ. Those with independent personalities were most able to ignore social network disapproval and continue loving their romantic partner. But contrary to expectations, defiant personalities did not magnify their commitment to their partner when confronted with network opposition. Although others' approval of a couple's relationship may reinforce relationship stability, reactions to social disapproval depends on one's personality.

If Seligson is right that people don't like to share negative marriage news on social networks, maybe that's protective. Feelings toward a romantic partner seem to benefit from social approval, but if social networks negatively view their relationship, it doesn't necessarily spell doom for the partnership, at least for people with independent personalities.

marriage

overview

Marriage isn't just a personal relationship, it's an institution. The traditional form of monogamous heterosexual marriage sanctioned by the state (and ideally blessed by the church) is a cornerstone of modern social organization and the primary way of organizing sexuality and kinship. In recent years the institution of marriage has undergone significant shifts. The articles in this section chronicle some of these changes.

In "The Changing Landscape of Love and Marriage," Kathleen E. Hull, Ann Meier, and Timothy Ortyl look at the shift in recent years away from marriage as a means of traditional and economic family ties to marriage as compulsory and taken-for-granted arrangement. What explains this shift? The authors present two prominent theories about the changes in marriage; Anthony Giddon's "confluent love," a new way of understanding intimacy, and Andrew Cherlin's "deinstitutionalization of marriage," resulting in seemingly more freedom for whether and how individuals participate in marriage. At the same time, arguing that the reality is a combination of both. more freedom in whether and how individuals participate in marriage, while arguing that the reality is a combination of both.

Individual participation in marriage may be changing, but the social expectations for marriage as a economic foundation loom large, especially in the politics of low-income families and single mothers. In "Marriage Goes to School," Orit Avishai, Melanie Heath, and Jennifer Randles explore the world of federally funded marriage education. These programs are often a requirement for Temporary Assistance to Needy Families (TANF) and tend to promote the idea that marriage is a solution to poverty.

Within marriage, social and economic differences are significant in the dynamics of a couple. In "Marrying Across Class Lines," Jessi Streib describes the tensions that arise in class differentiated marriages regarding management of money, distribution of household chores, and child-rearing.

Does gay marriage strengthen or challenge the traditional institution of marriage? In "For Better—and—For Worse," Verta Taylor and Leila J. Rupp argue that marriage equality has the potential to queer marriage rather than straighten out queer people. In contrast, Suzanna Walters contends that the persistent "tolerance" discourse around marriage equality perpetuates a sense of moral superiority for straight allies.

In South Korea, recent marriage trends have forced the nation to become more multicultural. In "Korean Multiculturalism and Marriage," Sangyoub Park discusses the reasons for and outcome of the current imbalance between numbers of marriageable men and marriageable women. Since the number of marriageable men significantly outweigh the number of marriageable women, Korean men are looking to neighboring countries for wives and thus creating more international marriages and children—a new phenomenon for the homogenous South Korea.

South Korea's skewed sex ratios at birth has also resulted in a rise in single person households and remarriages, specifically between divorced women and never married men. In "A Silent Revolution in the Korean Family," Sangyoub Park investigates the social context that creates the "silent revolution" and the results of this on the Korean familial and social structures.

things to consider

- What are some scripts you have received about marriage? How have those scripts changed in comparison to the messages you parents or grandparents received?
- Consider television shows like *Modern Family*. What's different about the expected marriage scripts in these shows and what's the same.?
- Discuss the implications of marriage equality for making gay people more straight or straight marriages less traditional.
- Consider how factors such as age and gender demographics influence marriage patterns. Think of examples in addition to South Korea.

53

the changing landscape of love and marriage

kathleen e. hull, ann meier, and timothy ortyl

spring 2010

Celebrities breaking up, making up, and having kids out of wedlock. Politicians confessing to extramarital affairs and visits to prostitutes. Same-sex couples pushing for, and sometimes getting, legal recognition for their committed relationships. Today's news provides a steady stream of stories that seem to suggest that lifelong love and (heterosexual) marriage are about as dated as a horse and carriage. Social conservatives continue sounding the alarm about the consequences of the decline of marriage and the rise of unwed parenting for children and for society at large. Are we really leaving behind the old model of intimacy, or are these changes significant but not radical? And what are the driving forces behind the changes?

In the United States, marriage historically has been an important and esteemed social institution. Historian Nancy Cottargues that, since colonial times, Americans have viewed marriage as the bedrock of healthy families and communities, vital to the functioning of democracy itself. But today, nearly half of all marriages end in divorce. People are getting married later than they used to; the median age at first marriage is now 28 for men and 26 for women, compared to 23 and 20 in 1960. The proportion of adults who never marry remains low but is climbing; in 2006, 19% of men and 13% of women aged 4044 had never married. Roughly one-third of all births are to unmarried parents, and unmarried cohabitation has gone from a socially stigmatized practice to a normal stage in the adult life course (more than half of all American marriages now begin as cohabitations). Many of the same patterns are seen in Europe, although divorce is lower there.

These demographic trends raise two seemingly undeniable conclusions: marriage has lost its taken-for-granted, nearly compulsory status as a feature of adult life, and, as a result, both adults and children are experiencing more change and upheaval in their personal lives than in the past. Sociologists have entered the fray to try to make sense of these trends, both by offering causal explanations and by predicting the depth and future direction of changes in intimacy.

rethinking commitment

Prominent sociologists offer two different but related theories about what is happening to intimacy in modern Western nations today. The British theorist Anthony

Giddens argues that we are witnessing a "transformation of intimacy," while the American family scholar Andrew Cherlin suggests that we are witnessing the "deinstitutionalization" of marriage.

In his 1992 book *The Transformation of Intimacy*, Giddens observes that intimacy is undergoing radical change in contemporary Western societies. The romantic love model, which emphasizes relationship permanence ("till death do us part") and complementary gender roles, is being displaced by what Giddens calls "confluent love." The confluent love model features the ideal of the "pure relationship," one that's entered into for its own sake and maintained only as long as both partners get enough satisfaction from it to stick around. Partners in a pure relationship establish trust through intense communication, yet the possibility of breakup always looms. Giddens sees the rise of confluent love resulting from modernization and globalization. As family and religious traditions lose influence, people craft their own biographies through highly individualized choices, including choice of intimate partners, with the overarching goal of continuous self-development. Giddens argues that pure relationships are more egalitarian than traditional romantic relationships, produce greater happiness for partners, and foster a greater sense of autonomy. At the same time, the contingent nature of the relationship commitment breeds psychological insecurity, which manifests in higher levels of anxiety and addiction.

Cherlin's deinstitutionalization argument focuses more specifically on marriage now and in the future. The social norms that define and guide people's behavior within the institution of marriage are weakening, he writes. There's

greater freedom to choose how to be married and when and whether to marry at all. The deinstitutionalization of marriage can be traced to factors like the rise of unmarried childbearing, the changing division of labor in the home, the growth of unmarried cohabitation, and the emergence of same-sex marriage. These large-scale trends create a context in which people actively question the link between marriage and parenting, the idea of complementary gender roles, and even the connection between marriage and heterosexuality. Under such conditions, Cherlin argues, people feel freer to marry later, to end unhappy marriages, and to forego marriage altogether, although marriage stills holds powerful symbolic significance for many people, partly as a marker of achievement and prestige. The future of marriage is hard to predict, but Cherlin argues it is unlikely to regain its former status; rather, it will either persist as an important but no longer dominant relationship form or it will fade into the background as just one of many relationship options.

> *Americans still place a high value on traditional, romantic love ideals like lifelong marriage. Yet, all evidence suggests that many of us do not follow through.*

marriage's persistent pull

Recent empirical studies suggest that the transformation of intimacy predicted by Giddens is far from complete, and the deinstitutionalization of marriage described by Cherlin faces some powerful countervailing forces, at least in the U.S. In her interview study of middleclass Americans, sociologist Ann Swidler found that people talking about love and relationships oscillated between two seemingly contradictory visions of intimacy. They often spoke about love and relationships as being hard work, and they acknowledged that relationship permanence is never a given, even in strong marriages. This way of talking about intimacy reflects the confluent love Giddens describes. But the same people who articulated pragmatic and realistic visions of intimacy also sometimes invoked elements of romantic love ideology, such as the idea that true love lasts forever and can overcome any obstacles.

Swidler speculates that people go back and forth between these two contradictory visions of love because the pragmatic vision matches their everyday experience but the

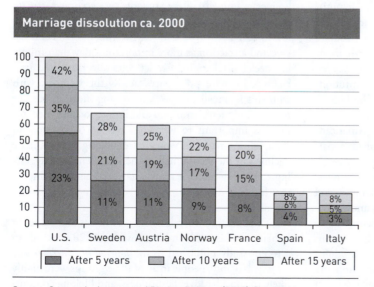

Marriage dissolution ca. 2000

Legend: After 5 years | After 10 years | After 15 years

Country	After 5 years	After 10 years	After 15 years
U.S.	23%	35%	42%
Sweden	11%	21%	28%
Austria	11%	19%	25%
Norway	9%	17%	22%
France	8%	15%	20%
Spain	4%	6%	8%
Italy	3%	5%	8%

Source: Gunnar Andersson and Dimiter Philipov (2002), "Life-Table Representations of Family Dynamics in Sweden, Hungary, & 14 Other FFS Countries," Demographic Research 7:67-145

romantic love myth corresponds to important elements in the institution of marriage. In other words, the ongoing influence of marriage as a social institution keeps the romantic model of intimacy culturally relevant, despite the emergence of a newer model of intimacy that sees love very differently. Swidler's findings at least partially contradict the idea of a wholesale transformation of intimacy, as well as the idea that marriage has lost much of its influence as a cultural model for intimate relationships.

Other studies have also challenged Giddens's ideas about the nature and extent of change occurring in intimate relationships. A 2002 study by Neil Gross and Solon Simmons used data from a national survey of American adults to test Giddens's predictions about the effects of "pure relationships" on their participants. They found support for some of the positive effects described by Giddens: people in pure relationships appear to have a greater sense of autonomy and higher relationship satisfaction. But the survey results did not support the idea that pure relationships lead to higher levels of anxiety and addiction. A 2004 British interview study of members of transnational families (that is, people with one or more close family members living in another country) found that people often strike a balance between individualistic approaches to marriage and attention to the marriage values of their home countries, families and religions. Study authors Carol Smart and Beccy Shipman conclude that Giddens's theory of a radical transformation of intimacy overlooks the rich diversity of cultural values and practices that exists even in highly modernized Western nations. And sociologist Lynn Jamieson has critiqued Giddens's theory for ignoring the vast body of feminist research that documents ongoing gender inequalities, such as in housework, even among heterosexual couples who consider their relationships to be highly egalitarian.

In his recent book *The Marriage-Go-Round,* even Cherlin acknowledges the fact that the deinstitutionalization of marriage has not gone as far in the U.S. as in many other Western countries. Americans have established a pattern of high marriage and remarriage rates, frequent divorce and separation, and more short-lived cohabitations, relative to other comparable countries. The end result is what Cherlin calls a "carousel of intimate partnerships," leading American adults, and any children they have, to face more transition and upheaval in their personal lives. Cherlin concludes that this unique American pattern results from the embrace of two contradictory cultural ideals: marriage and individualism.

> **Americans value the security of a lifelong partner, but we also want the option of an exit.**

The differing importance placed on marriage is obvious in the realm of electoral politics, for example. The current leaders of France and Italy, President Nicolas Sarkozy and Prime Minister Silvio Berlusconi, have weathered divorces and allegations of extramarital affairs without any discernible effect on their political viability. In the U.S., by contrast, the revelations of extramarital dalliances by South Carolina governor Mark Sanford and former North Carolina senator John Edwards were widely viewed as destroying their prospects as future presidential candidates.

broader horizons

Mainstream media paints a picture of different generations holding substantially different attitudes toward intimacy. In some ways, young people's attitudes toward relationships today are quite similar to the attitudes of their parents. A 2001 study by sociologist Arland Thornton and survey researcher Linda Young-DeMarco compares the attitudes of high school students from the late 1970s to the late 1990s. They find strong support for marriage among all students across the two-decade period. The percentage of female students who rated "having a good marriage and family life" extremely important was roughly 80% throughout this time period, while for males, it hovered around 70%.

Some studies track changes in young people's specific expectations regarding intimate partnerships. For example, a study by psychologist David Buss and colleagues examined college students' preferences for mate characteristics over a period of several decades. They found that both male and female students rank mutual love and attraction as more important today than in earlier decades. Changing gender roles also translated into changes in mate preferences across the decades, with women's financial prospects becoming more important to men and men's ambition and industriousness becoming less important to women. Over all, differences in the qualities men and women are looking for in a mate declined in the second half of the 20th century, suggesting that being male or remale has become a less important factor in determining what young people look for in intimate partnerships.

We compared the relationship attitudes and values of lesbian/gay, bisexual, and heterosexual 1828 year olds in a recent study published in the *Journal of Marriage and Family*. Notably, people in all of these groups were highly likely to consider love, faithfulness, and lifelong commitment as extremely important values in an intimate relationship. Romantic love seems to be widely embraced by most young adults, regardless of sexual orientation, which contests stereotypes and contrary reports that sexual minorities have radically different aspirations for intimacy. Yet, we also found modest differences that indicate that straight women are especially enthusiastic about these relationship attributes. They are more likely to rate faithfulness and lifelong commitment as extremely important compared to straight men and sexual minorities. Our findings are similar to other studies that consistently show that while both men and women highly value love, affection, and lifelong marriage, women assign greater value to these attributes than men.

Sociologist Michael Rosenfeld argues in *The Age of Independence* that both same sex relationships and interracial relationships have become more common and visible in the last few decades in large part because of the same social phenomenon: young people today are less constrained by the watchful eyes and wishes of their parents. Unmarried young adults are much less likely to be living with their parents than in generations past, giving them more freedom to make less traditional life choices. And making unconventional choices along one dimension may make people more willing to make unconventional choices along other dimensions. Thus, while people's aspirations for romantic love may not be changing substantially, partner choice may be changing over time as taboos surrounding a broader range of relationships erode. In our study, we find that sexual-minority young adults report being more willing to date someone of a different race or enter into less financially secure relationships than heterosexual young adults, lending support to Rosenfeld's claim.

weighing our options

If the ideas of today's young adults are any indication, Americans still place a high value on traditional, romantic love ideals for their relationships, including the ideal of lifelong marriage. Yet, all evidence suggests that many of us do not follow through.

In 2004, sociologist Paul Amato outlined the typical positions on whether that shift matters. The *marital decline position* argues that changes in intimacy are a significant cause for concern. From this perspective, the current decline in lifelong marriage and the corresponding increase in single-parent and disrupted families are a key culprit in other social ills like poverty, delinquency, and poor academic performance among children. This is because stable marriages promote a culture in which people accept responsibility for others, and families watch over their own to protect against falling prey to social ills. In short, marriage helps keep our societal house in order.

The *marital resilience perspective*, in contrast, contends that changes in family life have actually strengthened the quality of intimate relationships, including marriages. From this perspective, in the past many people stayed in bad marriages because of strong social norms and legal obstacles to exit. Today, however, no-fault divorce provides an opportunity to correct past mistakes and try again at happiness with new partners. This is a triumph for individual freedom of choice and opportunities for equality within intimate relationships.

Perhaps today's intimacy norms dictate more individualism and a corresponding reduction in the responsibility we take for those we love or loved. Maybe we are better for it because we have more freedom of choice—after all, freedom is one of America's most cherished values. Americans in general seem willing to live with mixed feelings on the new norms for intimacy. Most of us value the commitment and security of a lifelong partner, but we also want the option of exit (tellingly, almost half of people who marry use this option).

> Sociologist Andrew Cherlin concludes that a "carousel of intimate partnerships" results from the embrace of two contradictory American ideals: marriage and individualism.

Some evidence does suggest, though, that the "carousel of intimate relationships" may be taking its toll. Sociologists Mary Elizabeth Hughes and Linda Waite recently compared the health of middle-aged Americans who were married once and still with their partner to those who were never married, those who were married then divorced and remarried, and those who were married, divorced, and not remarried. They found that those who experienced divorce reported more chronic conditions, mobility limitations, and depression years later, and remarriage boosted health some (particularly mental health), but not to the level of those who never divorced in the first place. Those who divorced and did not remarry had the worst health, even after accounting for many factors that may make one more likely both to have poor health and to divorce. Having loved and lost appears to have lasting consequences.

Academic and policy debates, as well as conversations among friends and neighbors, often hinge not on adults, but on what's best for children. A fair amount of research suggests that kids are more likely to avoid most social ills and develop into competent, successful adults if they are raised by two happily and continuously married parents. But marital *happiness* is key. A number of studies have found that frequently quarrelling parents who stay married aren't doing their kids many favors. Children of these types of marriages have an elevated

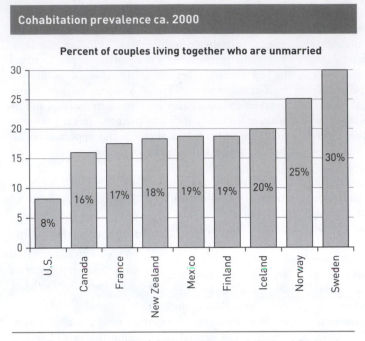

Cohabitation prevalence ca. 2000

Percent of couples living together who are unmarried

U.S. 8%
Canada 16%
France 17%
New Zealand 18%
Mexico 19%
Finland 19%
Iceland 20%
Norway 25%
Sweden 30%

Source: Statistics Canada (2002), "2001 Census Analysis Series: A Profile of Canadian Families and Households"

risk of emotional and behavioral problems. But with the notable exception of parents in highconflict marriages, most children who are raised by caring parents—one or two of them, married or not—end up just fine. Further, if our social policies provided greater support to all varieties of families, not just those characterized by lifelong heterosexual marriage, we might erase the association between growing up with happily married parents and children's wellbeing. More family supports, such as childcare subsidies, might translate into happily-ever-after for most kids regardless of family form.

Finally, the new rules of relationships have societal implications that go well beyond family life. If social order is substantially buttressed by traditional marriage, and a new model of intimacy is weakening the norm of lifelong, heterosexual marriage, logic suggests that we're eroding social cohesion and stability. If we think this is a threat, it seems a few policy adjustments could help to promote social order. For example, if marriage has the benefits of status, institutional support, and legitimacy, granting the right to marry to same-sex couples should bolster their relationships, making them more stable and long-lasting. Therefore, same-sex marriage would bring some Americans into the marital fold, benefiting the adults and children in these families and society more generally.

> **Perhaps we're in the midst of a transition to a brave new world of intimacy.**

In the meantime, there'd still be legions of those who already have access to the rights and protections of marriage, and either chose to divorce or never marry at all. Without reinforcing marriage as the ideal family form, some question whether healthy, well-functioning societies can be maintained. Evidence from other Western nations does suggest that different models of intimacy are compatible with societal wellbeing, but they also show that social policy must be aligned with the types of relationships that individuals choose to form. Many comparable countries have lower marriage rates and higher cohabitation rates than the U.S.

Those that extend significant legal protection and recognition to nonmarital relationships seem to do as well as, or sometimes better than, the U.S. on key measures of social and familial wellbeing. For example, Swedish children who live with only one parent do better, on average, than American children in the same circumstance, possibly because of Sweden's pro-family policies including long periods of paid maternity and sick leave and government-subsidized, high-quality childcare. Since all Swedes are eligible for these family supports, the differences in care received by children across family types are minimized.

In the end, current research suggests a paradox. Most people, including young adults, say things to researchers that suggest they hold fast to the ideal of an exclusive, lifelong intimate partnership, most commonly a marriage. Yet often people behave in ways more aligned with the "pure relationship" Giddens argues is the ascendant model of intimacy. Perhaps it's harder than ever for people to live out their aspirations in the area of intimacy. Or perhaps we are indeed in the midst of a transition to a brave new world of intimacy, and people's willingness or ability to articulate new relationship values has not yet caught up with their behavior.

recommended resources

Cherlin, Andrew J. 2009. *The Marriage-Go-Round: The State of Marriage and the Family in America Today.* New York: Alfred A. Knopf. Describes how Americans' simultaneous embrace of of marital commitment and individual freedom has resulted in a "carousel of intimate partnerships."

Coontz, Stephanie. 2005. *Marriage, a History: From Obedience to Intimacy or How Love Conquered Marriage.*

New York: Viking. Offers a historical look at the linking of marriage and romantic intimacy.

Giddens, Anthony. 1992. *The Transformation of Intimacy: Sexuality, Love and Eroticism in Modern Societies.* Stanford, CA: Stanford University Press. Argues that romantic love is being replaced by the ideal of the "pure relationship."

Stacey, Judith. 1996. *In the Name of the Family: Rethinking Family Values in the Postmodern Age*

Boston, MA: Beacon Press. Examines the fluid and contested nature of the "postmodern family condition," arguing that most contemporary social problems are not the result of innovations in family form.

Swidler, Ann. 2001. *Talk of Love: How Culture Matters.* Chicago, IL: University of Chicago Press. Uses interviews with middle-class Americans to show that people oscillate between a romantic love ideology and a more pragmatic, contingent vision.

54

marriage goes to school

orit avishai, melanie heath, and jennifer randles

summer 2012

Mikalea, a 27-year-old White woman, and David, 28, an African American man, had been together five years, and were raising a daughter from Mikalea's previous marriage. They were expecting a son when they enrolled in a federally funded relationship skills class for low-income couples in California. They were living paycheck-to-paycheck, trying to finish college, and constantly fighting about money, especially since David had become unemployed and Mikalea discovered she was pregnant.

Though the baby was unexpected, they were both excited about it. They both felt their relationship was emotionally and financially tenuous but were determined to make it work.

The relationship skills classes didn't change their views of marriage, which they believed was at least 10 years off—a milestone they anticipated after their economic situation improved, and the tension in their relationship was reduced. Yet the classes taught them to empathize with one another and communicate better, and helped them understand that much of what they fought about was common to couples trying to raise a family under similar socioeconomic circumstances. Mikalea enjoyed the classes so much and found them so helpful that she planned to become an instructor herself. Reflecting on what she most appreciated about them, she said: "It shows people they're not on their own."

While Mikalea and David were learning how to be a better couple in California, in Oklahoma, Kathy, a 35-year-old African American mother of three, attended a relationship skills workshop as part of her training to receive Temporary Assistance to Needy Families

(TANF)—welfare benefits. A high-school dropout, she had worked at dozens of low-end jobs and possessed few skills to obtain a job that would allow her to make ends meet. Still, she was happy to be single; in her experience, a man can get in the way of moving forward because, she says, "most men are just dogs!" While at first she was wary of the workshop, and thought the class was just about marriage, she was pleasantly surprised to learn that the skills could be used to build better relationships with "your kids or your grandparents or anybody."

The classes Mikalea, David, and Kathy attended were part of a nationwide, government-funded marriage promotion and education program, an anti-poverty policy that emerged in the 1990s. Based on the philosophy that single parenthood is a cause of poverty, its proponents argue that strengthening marriage, along with work requirements, reduces poverty. These policies are a product of the 1996 welfare reform bill—the Personal Responsibility and Work Opportunity Reconciliation Act—which promoted job preparation, work, and marriage as a way of ending dependence on government benefits.

Federal marriage promotion programs gained prominence as social policy under the George W. Bush Administration. The federal Healthy Marriage Initiative (HMI) created a patchwork of funding that added up to about $200 million, and the 2005 welfare legislation included $500 million earmarked for marriage programs over five years. In 2011, Congress approved $75 million of President Obama's proposed Fatherhood, Marriage, and Family Innovation Fund. Some states have also used portions of their TANF grants for marriage promotion activities.

But marriage promotion policy is controversial. Advocates argue that marriage is a social good that leads to lower poverty rates for married adults and their children, and superior social, economic, academic, and health outcomes for children who grow up with their biological, married parents—compared with the children of unwed or divorced couples. Skeptics contend that marriage promotion obscures the structural causes of poverty—lack of education and stable, decent-paying jobs—and diverts funds from programs that directly benefit poor families, such as cash assistance or work supports.

Mikalea and David were targeted by marriage promotion policies because they are a "fragile family," defined as a low-income, unmarried couple with one or more children. As such, they face a greater risk of family instability and economic insecurity than couples who have children after marriage. While fragile families, as well as single women like Kathy who rely on welfare, are the primary constituents of marriage education programs, existing research offers little support for the claim that such programs can effectively address poverty.

Nine years ago, sociologist Andrew Cherlin, writing in these pages, predicted as much, arguing that marriage education is driven by ideology rather than by social science. The recent recommitment of funds at the state and federal levels means that marriage and relationship education has become entrenched public policy.

But what does marriage education actually mean for people like Mikalea, David, and Kathy?

relationship science

Marriage education is founded on the belief that relationship success is rooted in individual skills and couple dynamics, and that couples can learn specific skills to help them stay together. These ideas are informed by a burgeoning science of relationships in psychology, sociology, and communication studies.

As evidence mounted in the field of relationship science in the 1990s that marriage failure or success hinges on predictable patterns of interpersonal interactions, relationship experts began to translate this knowledge into teachable skills. Some skills, such as not rolling one's eyes during an argument, are relatively easy to learn; others, such as achieving what relationship guru John Gottman calls the 5 to 1 ratio between positive and negative behaviors during arguments, are more difficult to master.

In Oklahoma City, Angel and Emily, who have been married seven years and have a toddler, arrived at a class sponsored by the state's marriage initiative. For two consecutive Saturdays, they and another couple learned rules for handling conflict and communication techniques. They watched videos of couples fighting over issues like whether to add laundry detergent before or after the dirty clothes, and they practiced communication skills to resolve such disputes.

> **Marriage promotion is controversial. Advocates argue it leads to lower poverty rates. Skeptics contend that it obscures the structural causes of poverty.**

Exercises such as these are based on a deceptively simple premise: that having a healthy marriage is something one can *learn*; and that people who receive the information, practice the skills, and develop the attributes known to be linked to healthy marriages will be able to achieve marital bliss, regardless of social and economic constraints. That is, relationship education is based on the logic that it is not *what* a couple fights about that matters, but rather *how* they fight.

Theresa and Sandy who led the workshop in Oklahoma City offered examples of problems with communication, such as when men want to fix things and women just want to be heard. Sandy told us that when she lost a spreadsheet on her computer at work, her husband advised her to get a better computer. This wasn't what she wanted to hear; she just wanted sympathy. Emily, a lawyer, could relate. She disclosed how she would call Angel from work to complain about a client, and he would not offer very useful advice. She wanted him to listen to her frustrations rather than offer solutions—a typical relationship dynamic that many relationship classes address by teaching participants active listening techniques.

Low-income parents like Mikalea, David, and Kathy were taught the same types of communication and problem solving skills as Angel and Emily. Yet, their economic and social circumstances couldn't be more different. Angel and Emily are White, middle class, college-educated, and had their child after they married—all factors associated with marital success—while Mikalea and David, an interracial "fragile" family, and Kathy, an African American single parent, have experienced persistent economic and family instability over their lifetimes.

While marriage education can help *some* couples enjoy better marriages, there is little evidence that promoting better marriages can alleviate poverty. Our research points to two key reasons why marriage education is failing as welfare policy: it does not address the structural and economic foundations of poverty, and does not always serve low-income individuals, who are less likely to marry.

money management for the poor

Since getting people like Mikalea and David in the door of marriage education classes is not an easy task, a significant portion of the program's money is used to encourage participation. Low-income couples receive free childcare, a $10 per class transportation stipend, and catered hot meals. They also receive a $100 "graduation stipend" after attending 14 hours of classes. Though this worked out to less than four dollars per hour per person, the money was significant for Mikalea and David, and for other participants who are unemployed and in debt. Programs that target low-income couples report that they spend around $500 per couple in direct costs.

Advocates of marriage education argue that it is money well spent; marriage education is less expensive than the social costs of family dissolution. Yet there is little evidence that such programs alleviate poverty. In fact, studies of marriage education efficacy have never attempted to evaluate the causal relationship between marriage education and poverty rates, focusing instead on evaluating communication and couple satisfaction—ignoring the structural and economic foundations of poverty, and the demographics of marriage and divorce.

The program Mikalea and David participated in, which we call "Thriving Families," focused on the teaching of two main types of skills: communication and money management. The communication skills units taught them how to become active and empathic communicators and conflict resolvers. The financial skills unit focused on how couples could manage their money more effectively by budgeting, cutting expenses, and aligning their spending habits with their values.

This mismatch between the philosophy of marriage education as an anti-poverty measure and the lived

> **"**
> *The financial tips couples received were minimally helpful because they had little money to manage.*

experience of poverty was reflected in interviews with Thriving Families couples. Participants said while they appreciated the information they received, the financial tips were minimally helpful because they had little money to manage.

As Josh, an 18-year-old White participant said, the information about "money would have been much more helpful if we had any." The problem for Josh and his fiancée, Sarah, 17-years-old and White—a view echoed by many Thriving Families couples—was that the little money they had could only be stretched so far. Josh's frustration points to a significant flaw in the logic of using skills-based approaches to address poverty: it presumes that unmarried parents' economic challenges are largely behavioral, and ignores the socio-structural underpinnings of those challenges.

Recent research from the Pew Foundation, an independent research institute, has recently shown that educated, middle-class women and men like Emily and Angel are more likely to get and stay (happily) married than poor and low-income Americans like Mikaela and David. The most important predictors of marriage and divorce are not whether an individual has mastered good communication skills, but whether he or she has a stable job and a college degree.

In other words, conflicts over who does the laundry are very different from conflicts over how to stretch a welfare check. Yet such distinctions do not often figure into marriage education—at least not in the version conceived by the Bush Administration.

middle-class problems

In April 2004, thirty couples attended the Sweethearts Weekend in Oklahoma to learn how to strengthen their marriages. The couples were relatively privileged: they had their own transportation, childcare, and the time to attend the free workshop.

Larry and Nancy, the facilitators, used the PREP (Prevention and Relationship Enhancement Program) curriculum, one of the most popular and profitable programs, developed in the 1980s by Denver University psychologists. The curriculum is peppered with examples of couples negotiating middle-class concerns. Larry tells them, "if you have kids, you've always got sports going on," and describes the conflicts he and his wife had over who would chauffeur the kids to their games.

Audience members shared their experiences of the ways these commitments place stress on middle-class families. Working class and poor families' stressors, which are largely rooted in economic instability, were never mentioned. (In 2006, the creators of PREP designed a new version of the curriculum, intended to better address the needs of low-income couples).

In Florida, Sam and Janet, a middle class African American couple who led a weekend relationship retreat for distressed couples, demonstrated to the class a communication skill. "The daily temperature reading," a tool developed by psychologist Virginia Satir, encourages couples to touch base daily by going through a structured monologue during which spouses take turns sharing appreciations, wishes, hopes, and dreams, new information, puzzles, complaints, and requests for change. The listener is not allowed to interrupt while the other is speaking. Janet's complaint to her husband was about his habit of cleaning out her car—a late model SUV—every time he borrowed it. When his turn came, Sam said that he only borrows the car when he goes golfing with his buddies, and the mess embarrasses him.

As these examples suggest, marriage education fails to achieve its intended goals because it largely draws and caters to middle-class audiences. By focusing on disputes over laundry and eye-rolling, it fails to address the challenges facing disadvantaged couples, and the toll financial strain takes on their daily lives. Many programs funded through the 2005 welfare legislation have not followed the original intention to serve needy populations. Our analysis of federal grantees suggests that the *majority* of funded programs fail to target low-income and poor couples. Many programs use their grants to fund a range of activities, including heavily subsidized or free workshops, or couples retreats in luxurious locations, which often include catered meals and free tours.

In emphasizing the goal of strengthening marriage, such programs tend to serve relatively privileged couples like Angel and Emily, redistributing welfare money away from those who need it most.

a better strategy

Though it may be well-intentioned, marriage promotion and education programs do not alleviate poverty. Rather than targeting poor Americans, most programs serve the "general public." But even when they target the poor, by focusing on skills, such programs ignore the roots of the problem. Social and economic advantages matter more for marriage success than knowing how to de-escalate a heated argument.

Nevertheless, the low-income couples and individuals we interviewed found relationship skills classes helpful. Even though they rarely influenced their views about marriage, they had a positive impact on participants' relationships, they believed.

Attending the classes taught David and Mikalea to solve problems cooperatively, they said. Others spoke of learning skills that would help them to better communicate with significant people in their lives. Kathy, the single African American mother of three, said the skills "can help you with a lot of things. Not just with relationships with your partner, your friend, your teacher, but with the outside world—period."

Even as they emphasized personal solutions, the classes offered participants a structural context for interpreting their seemingly personal problems. They helped David, in his words, "understand that we're not the only ones going through these problems . . . almost everyone in the class had the exact same problems, especially with money."

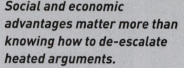

Social and economic advantages matter more than knowing how to de-escalate heated arguments.

They helped parents understand that many struggles were not the products of personal shortcomings, but were often the direct result of trying to keep a family together while in poverty.

As sociologists Paula England and Kathy Edin have argued, low-income couples face many economic and social barriers to creating and maintaining stable marriages. Challenges with co-parenting, higher emotional standards for marriage, and low relationship quality, combined with struggles over employment, low earnings, and the stress of economic deprivation, impede marriage and marital instability among low-income couples. But relationship classes alone are insufficient interventions. The Obama administration has recognized that family and economic stability are linked; recent grants emphasize healthy *relationships* rather than *marriage*, and they view relationship skills in relation to a broader range of services, including employment assistance. This indicates a new, more positive direction in marriage promotion policy.

Scholars and policymakers across the political spectrum tend to agree that anti-poverty policy should support family-formation goals, and encourage parents to create secure families for children. Relationship skills education can support this goal by recognizing the connection between family and economic security. This is especially important for low-income parents under financial stress who have limited access to counseling services. Time will tell if the policy direction taken by the Obama administration is a step in this direction.

recommended resources

Cahill, Sean. 2005. "Welfare Moms and the Two Grooms: The Concurrent Promotion and Restriction of Marriage in US Public Policy," *Sexualities*, 8:169–187. Analyzes the contradictory approaches in American public policy and law concerning poor, unmarried mothers and same-sex couples.

Cherlin, Andrew. 2003. "Should the Government Promote Marriage?," *Contexts*, *2*(4):22–29. An early assessment of marriage promotion programs which argues that these programs are premised on ideological agendas rather than solid social science evidence.

England, Paula, and Edin, Kathryn (eds.). 2007. *Unmarried Couples with Children.* New York: Russell Sage Foundation. A collection of empirical essays investigating relationship and family dynamics among low-income, unmarried couples with children.

Heath, Melanie. 2012. *One Marriage under God: The Campaign to Promote Marriage in America.* New York: New York University Press. The first ethnography to assess the discriminatory consequences of marriage promotion policies as they are practiced on the ground.

Pope-Parker, Tara. 2010. *For Better: The Science of a Good Marriage*. New York: Dutton Adult. A highly accessible book that summarizes the science of healthy relationships and translates it into practical advice.

marriage blurring racial boundaries
lucia lykke
spring 2016

In 2012, the number of non-White births in the U.S. exceeded the number of White births for the first time, driven largely by growing numbers of Asians, Latinos, and multiracial Americans. However, the U.S.'s "melting pot" history tells us that over time, some non-White groups may "become" White, as Italian, Irish, and Jewish people have. In his new article "Expanding Boundaries of Whiteness?" Michael Miyawaki investigates marriage between Whites and multiracial people who are Black/White, Asian/White, and Native American/White to ask whether the boundaries of American Whiteness are expanding yet again.

Miyawaki uses Census data to compare the likelihood that part-White multiracials marry Whites compared to other racial groups. Multiracials are more likely to marry Whites than any other group: 54% of Black/White multiracials, 72% of American Indian/White multiracials, and 69% of Asian/White individuals are married to White people. This tendency is significantly greater for Asian/Whites and American Indian/Whites than for Black/Whites (and the relationship holds after controlling for factors such as education level and the size of a racial group in a particular state). Gender matters too: Asian/White women and Black/White men are more likely than their respective male and female counterparts to marry Whites.

Miyawaki argues that boundary shifting is taking place, particularly for Asian and American Indian multiracials in the U.S. Indeed, the high marriage rate of Black/White multiracials with Whites could be an indicator that even the boundaries between multiracial Blacks and Whites are more porous than prior research has suggested.

55

marrying across class lines

jessi streib

spring 2015

Christie, a cheerful social worker in her mid-40s, told me about the first time she met her husband, Mike. It was over thirty years ago, when they were in junior high school. She used to watch Mike as he wiped off the tables before the next round of students entered the school cafeteria. She thought he was cute and smart. And she was not fooled by his job—she knew that it was people like her who usually cleaned tables, not people like Mike. In fact, her father worked on the maintenance crew at their school.

Mike's father, by contrast, was a productive professor who authored famous books and traveled the world attending conferences and giving lectures. As Christie knew, Mike washed tables in exchange for being allowed to go to the front of the line to collect his food, not because he needed the money.

When the couple began dating, their class differences became obvious. Her parents rarely bought new items; their cars were used and the ping pong table they gave her for Christmas was put together with items they found. Pop Tarts were her favorite food, but one that they could rarely afford. Mike's family bought expensive new cars, went on annual vacations, had cable TV, and had enough money left over to tuck a good amount away in Mike's trust fund. But while they had grown up with different amounts of resources, by the time we talked, Christie did not feel that their differences mattered. Over 25 years of marriage, they shared a house, a bank account, a level of educational attainment, and, later, three children. Their lives had merged, and so had their resources. To Christie, their class differences were part of their pasts, and, in any case, never mattered much: "I don't think that it was the actual economic part that made the tension for Mike and I. It was personality style more than class or money."

Christie was one of the 64 adults in 32 couples I interviewed about their marriages, their current families, and their pasts. In order to focus on how class background matters in a small sample, all respondents were White college-educated adults in heterosexual marriages. Half were like Christie—they had grown up in the working-class. The other half were like Mike—they had grown up in the middle-class. All were married to a partner whose class origin was different than their own. My goal was to discern how what most respondents, like Christie, did not think mattered—their class background—was related to their ways of attending to their own lives and to their marriages. Although respondents tended to think their class differences were behind them, irrelevant to their current lives, instead they left a deep imprint that their marriage, their shared resources, and their thousands of days together did not erase.

social class and family life

It is common knowledge that families located in different social classes develop different ways of going about daily life. Such differences were made famous in the 1970s by sociologist and psychologist Lillian Rubin in her classic book, *Worlds of Pain*. Rubin interviewed couples and demonstrated that the texture of family life, as well as ideas of what it means to be a good parent, child, and spouse, are all shaped by the resources and jobs available to families. Later, sociologist Annette Lareau offered another in-depth look, observing that the daily interactions between parents and children, and, to some degree, between adult members of the family, differed by social class. Middle-class parents, she found, tended to manage their children's lives, while working-class parents more often let their children grow. French sociologist Pierre Bourdieu also observed wide class differences. He theorized that class not only shapes family life, but also individuals' ideas and instincts about how to use resources, spend time, and interact with others. Sociologists do not see each family as wholly unique, but shaped by the resources available to them in their class position.

Such work suggests that people like Christie and Mike, who grew up in different social classes, were likely to have different experiences of family and develop different ideas about a "good life." However, when scholars of social class and family life conduct research, they usually focus on the divide between college-educated couples and everyone else. This divide is critical for understanding inequality, but it is problematic to simply call couples like Christie and Mike a college-educated, middle-class couple. The label erases that Christie and Mike spent two decades in a class apart, and that upwardly mobile people like Christie may carry their ideas of family and a good life with them into their marriage and the middle-class.

Indeed, simply referring to Christie and Mike as a college-educated, middle-class couple ignores that Christie knew what it was like to grow up with limited savings, watch a parent go to a job that was consistently framed as a means to an end, and grow up in a family that expressed their emotions immediately and intensely. It ignores that Mike knew of none of these things. He knew, instead, of family safety nets, jobs that were enjoyed beyond their financial ends, and emotions that were rationalized and guarded.

When social scientists ignore these background differences, they present only differences between college-educated and high-school educated couples, overlooking differences within college-educated couples. And when married couples ignore these differences, they ignore that the class of each partner's past organizes and shapes the contours of their marriage.

> **Although respondents tended to think their class differences were behind them, they left a deep imprint that their marriage, shared resources, and thousands of days together did not erase.**

the organization of difference

Christie believed that her differences from Mike were driven by their personalities. She wasn't wrong. What she did not realize, however, was that what she called their personalities were, in turn, related to their class trajectory. People like Christie—born into the working-class but now college-educated—tended to prefer taking what I call a *laissez-faire* approach to their daily lives. They preferred to go with the flow, enjoy the moment, and live free from self-imposed constraints. They assumed things would work out without their intervention. People like Mike—those born into the middle class—instead tended to prefer to take what I call a *managerial* approach to their daily lives. They preferred to plan, monitor, organize, and oversee. They assumed that things would not work out without their active intervention.

The people I interviewed did not just apply laissez-faire and managerial tendencies to one aspect of their lives, but seven. When it came to how to attend to their money, paid work, housework, time, leisure, parenting, and emotions, middle-class-origin respondents tended to want to plan, organize, and oversee. Working-class-origin respondents more often preferred to let things take their own course without as much intervention.

Take, for example, how Christie and Mike thought about money. When I met them, they had shared a bank account for over two decades, but they did not share ideas of how to use the money in it. Referring to money, Christie repeatedly told Mike: "Live for the day!" Growing up, saving for long-range plans was not possible. Christie's family had to spend what they had to pay their bills today. A small amount in savings was also normal to her as a child, and continued to be normal to her as a college-educated adult. Christie said that she learned from her parents' experience that worrying about money was unnecessary: even without much money, things would work out. Now that she and Mike were both college-educated professionals who earned much more than her parents, this seemed especially true. Free from concerns over necessities, she now made a point to be free from worrying about money.

Mike, however, grew up in a family with more money and more options. His family could pay for their daily needs, then choose how to save for college tuition, retirement, rainy days, and leisure. For him, thinking about how to manage money was normal and he learned that management could make a difference. As an adult, Mike budgeted, monitored their current expenditures, forecasted their future expenses, and worried about whether he was earning enough. When Christie told him to "live for the day" and worry less, he reported responding: "I see that. But at the same time, we had three kids in college, and we're in our mid-forties. We have a lot of expenses." He felt that Christie's laissez-faire philosophy was reasonable, but he felt more comfortable with a managerial one.

Their differences also extended to work. Christie grew up observing her father work in a job as a maintenance worker at her public school while her mother did unpaid labor at home. There was no career ladder for her father to climb. Hours were circumscribed by a time clock and putting in more hours would not lead to more status or opportunities. Mike also saw his mother doing unpaid home labor, but observed his father, a professor, on a career ladder—from graduate student, to assistant, associate, and then full professor. More hours could lead to more books published, more prestige, and more opportunities to share his ideas.

Such differences likely shaped Christie and Mike's ideas of work. Mike felt he had to prod Christie, a social worker, to not be "status quo"—to work longer hours and think about how moving to a new place might give them opportunities to get ahead. Christie, for her part, admired Mike's dedication to work, but did not understand it. Mike owned his own business. He worked long hours (despite not being paid by the hour) and he constantly felt pressure to achieve more. Christie asked him to work fewer hours and have more faith that his business would do fine without his planning, strategizing, and long hours. So, just as Mike asked Christie to take a more managerial approach to work—one where she organized and planned her career trajectory—Christie asked Mike to take a more laissez-faire approach—one where he put in less time, did less planning, and assumed his career would be okay. Though each understood the other's perspective, neither adopted it. Christie maintained her hands-off approach to work. Mike maintained his hands-on one.

This hands-on/hands-off, or managerial/laissez-faire divide organized many other aspects of their lives. Mike wanted to manage the division of housework by putting "more structure in the whole idea of who is going to do what" around the house. Christie wanted each to do the household tasks as they got around to them. Mike preferred to manage his feelings—to slowly process and weigh how to express them. Christie felt it was more genuine to express emotions as they were felt and in the way they were felt. Christie summarized their differences when she described Mike as Type A, driven, and organized—all things that she felt she was not.

Some of the differences that Christie and Mike expressed might sound like gender differences. Gender certainly shapes *how much* time each spouse spends on each task and *how much* power they have over decisions in different spheres. But with the exception of the highly gendered spheres of housework and parenting in which it was mainly women who followed the managerial/laissez-faire divide, class origin alone shaped how each partner wanted to tackle each task and use each resource. Take, for example, Leslie and Tom. They proudly proclaim that they are nerds: they met at a science-fiction convention, continued their courtship though singing together in a science-fiction themed choir, and, as a married couple, engage in role-playing games together. Their shared interests and college degrees, however, could not mask the lingering ways their class backgrounds shaped their lives and their marriage.

> *Just as taking the person out of the class did not take the class out of the person, a marriage was not a new beginning that removed the imprints of each partner's class past.*

Leslie, a fit forty-year-old with short brown hair and glasses, was raised by a graduate-school-educated middle-manager and a college-educated homemaker. She attended private school with the sons and daughters of celebrities, judges, and politicians—where, she said, "famous and rich were people were the norm." Her husband, Tom, a shy, dark-haired forty-eight-year-old grew up as the son of a high-school-educated security guard and a nurse. He attended public school. While their childhood class differences certainly could have been wider, they still mapped onto ways of organizing their lives. Leslie, like Mike, preferred a managerial approach to her life—scheduling, planning, organizing, and monitoring. Tom, like Christie, felt that a hands-off approach was a better way to live.

> *Class origin shaped how each partner wanted to tackle each task and use each resource.*

The differences that Leslie and Tom described about money mirrored those that Mike and Christie expressed. Leslie stated simply: "I'm the saver and he's the spender." But it was not just how much Tom spent that bothered Leslie, it was also that Tom did not actively think about managing their money. Leslie complained: "I do the lion's share of work. Beyond the lion's share of the work . . . Balancing stuff, actually paying the bills, keeping track of things, saying we need to have some goals. Both big picture and small picture stuff." She said that Tom did not manage money; he spent without thinking.

Tom knew of Leslie's concern: "She worries a lot more about money than I do. About how we're doing . . . I think she would like it if I paid more attention to what our expenses are and how the money is going out." They had been having these debates for the past 20 years, but their differences had not gone away. Leslie said she still couldn't get Tom to set financial goals or think about how each expense fit in with their overall plan. Their compromise was that Tom checked with Leslie before making big purchases. But this was not an optimal solution for Leslie, who called herself the "superego"—the one who still had to make the decisions about how to manage their money, about what they really needed and what they could forego. Tom still assumed it would all work out, that a hands-off approach would do just fine.

Leslie also noted that she took a managerial approach to work, whereas Tom took a laissez-faire one. At the time of the interview, Leslie was college-educated, part-time secretary at her children's school. Tom was a college-educated computer programmer. Though Leslie's job was less prestigious, she found much more satisfaction in it, talking about the sense of accomplishment she had at work, the meaning of doing good work, and her goals for the future. She was not sure what her next career move would be, but she knew one thing: "I want to get somewhere." Tom didn't want to get anywhere with work. Leslie cried as she explained: "He's been at the same job for quite awhile and only moves when forced to."

Leslie clarified that her concern was not about how much Tom earned, but about his approach to his career: "I can totally understand being content. It's more that sometimes I just don't know what he wants and I'm not sure he knows. And this may sound dumb, but the actual goals, what they are, worry me less than not having any." To Leslie, careers were to be managed. Goals were to be created and worked toward. Tom did not have the same sense.

Their differences also extended past what is directly related to class—money and work—to other parts of their lives. Like Mike, Leslie wanted to structure housework more than Tom did, so she delegated tasks and monitored his work. Tom, like Christie, figured the housework could be done when he got to it, without as much of a schedule. Leslie and Mike liked to plan and organize in general. However, while Mike appreciated that Christie got him to pause his planning and "stop to smell the roses," Leslie was upset that Tom did not plan. She expressed it as a deficiency: "If you plan, if you're a planner, you do that mental projecting all the time. You're thinking ahead, saying, 'What's going to happen if I do this?' I really don't think he does that. I don't know if it's because he doesn't want to, it's too hard,

he doesn't have the capacity, I don't know. But he just doesn't do that." Tom defended his approach: "She definitely wants more structure in things we do, more planning. I'm more of a 'Let's just do it' [person] and it will get done the best way we can get it done."

Leslie also insisted that their children's time be structured by adults, guided by routines, and directed at learning-related outcomes. But Tom, again, questioned this approach: "Leslie thinks they need more structure than they really do." As such, when he was in charge of parenting, he did not ask their daughters to have a regular reading time or strict bedtime. He did not view each of the kids' behaviors as in need of monitoring, assessing, or guiding. As sociologist Annette Lareau observed of people currently in the working-class, Tom, who was born into the working-class but no longer a member, felt that the kids would be fine without parents' constant management.

navigating difference

The laissez-faire/managerial differences that couples like Christie and Mike and Leslie and Tom navigated were common to the couples I interviewed—college-educated couples in which each partner grew up in a different class. The systematic differences that these couples faced meant that class infused their marriages, usually without their knowledge. These differences, however, were not experienced in a uniform way.

Most of the people I interviewed appreciated their spouse's differences, or at least found them understandable and valid. A minority of couples, however, found their differences to be more divisive. In these couples, middle-class-origin respondents disdained their spouse's attitudes and asked their spouse to change.

Christie and Mike were one of the couples who dealt with their differences with respect and even admiration. Mike did not always agree with Christie's laissez-faire approach, but he appreciated her sense that he sometimes needed to manage less and live in the moment more. Christie sometimes found Mike's managerial style frustrating, but she also admired how organized he was. She appreciated how well Mike had done in his career and respected that he needed more planning, organization, and monitoring to feel secure. They preferred different approaches, but they saw the benefits of the other's way and tried to accommodate their partner's differences.

Leslie and Tom did not navigate their differences with such ease. Leslie defined Tom's hands-off approach as deeply flawed. As such, her strategy was to get him to change—to get him to do things in a more managerial way. But her strategy left them both unhappy.

Tom resented being asked to change; Leslie fumed that Tom would say he would change, but did not. She explained: "Mostly what happens is he says, 'You're right. That would be better.' But the implementation is just not always there." Leslie remained frustrated with what she saw as the inadequacy of Tom's style, and Tom remained frustrated that Leslie did not see the benefits of living a life that was less structured, scheduled, and planned. Asking for assimilation was a failed strategy, both in that it did not work and in that respondents said that it left them disappointed and dissatisfied.

Regardless of how they navigated their differences—with respect or demands for change—couples like Mike and Christie and Leslie and Tom had to navigate the subtle ways that the class of their pasts still shaped their lives and their marriages. The decades that each couple was together, their shared college degrees, and their shared resources did not erase the fact that the middle-class-origin partners preferred to take a managerial approach to their lives while working-class-origin partners favored a laissez-faire one. Just as taking the person out of the class did not take the class out of the person, a marriage was not a new beginning that removed the imprints of each partner's class past.

recommended resources

Bourdieu, Pierre. 1984. *Distinction*. Cambridge, MA: Harvard University Press. Offers a theoretically sophisticated examination of how social class is related to tastes, worldviews, and dispositions.

Carlson, Marcia, and England, Paula (eds.). 2011. *Social Class and Changing Families in an Unequal America*. Palo Alto, CA: Stanford University Press. Charts demographic changes that have occurred between families in different social classes.

Lareau, Annette. 2003. *Unequal Childhoods*. Berkeley, CA: University of California Press. Explains how parenting styles differ by social class.

Rubin, Lillian. 1976. *Worlds of Pain*. New York: Basic Books. Provides a detailed account of how marriage, parenting, and work are related to social class, especially for the working-class.

for better—and—for worse

veta taylor, leila j. rupp, and suzanna danuta walters

spring 2014

[Editor Jodi O'Brien's Introductory Comments] Last spring, after we'd worked our way through the critical sociological compendium on marriage, one of the students in my "sexual politics" seminar exclaimed, "are we even for gay marriage?" His fellow students nodded in befuddlement. My home state, Washington, had recently passed a ballot initiative in support of marriage equality and the students at the Jesuit university where I teach like to think they're on the most progressive side of current social issues. Their puzzlement began early in the term when they realized that I (their openly queer professor) was not an unabashed supporter of same-sex marriage.

Marriage equality has become a front and center social issue and the terrain is changing rapidly in this recent post-DOMA era. Currently 17 states have legalized same-sex marriage through either legislation or ballot measures (or in some cases, both). At a glance, this is reason for celebration. But as the students in my seminar quickly came to realize, the issue is complex. Like most engaging sociology, the movement for marriage equality is rooted in considerations of underlying status and privilege; it abounds with questions of who really benefits and what status quo is being unsettled or reaffirmed. At the end of the seminar several students remarked that the class discussions had enabled them to "take the debate up a notch," or "shift the paradigm" on the issue.

Toward that end, we invited commentary from three high-profile scholars who each identify as lesbian feminists, but who have different perspectives on the marriage equality movement. We hope that everyone reading these essays, especially students, will recognize that those most closely aligned with social issues—those who occupy marginal positions—may agree that justice is needed, but they don't necessarily share the same ideas about the path to social reform. It's complicated and worthy of deeper consideration and debate.

are we still queer even though we're married?

by verta taylor and leila j. rupp

We got married for our 30th anniversary, although not on the actual day. How queer people determine their anniversaries is an interesting question in its own right, so let's just say that ours does not date back to a commitment ceremony. Ours is also a floating anniversary, like Thanksgiving: it's the Saturday before the start of the academic year. This remains our anniversary, despite the signing of our marriage license in the summer of 2008 when it was briefly legal in California, before Proposition 8 shut down the marriages. We like to say we waited to make sure we were really compatible.

In reality, despite our feminist reservations about the institution of marriage, we did it for political reasons, as an act of resistance to those who loudly and publicly asserted, especially in the Prop 8 campaign, that same-sex couples did not deserve the right to marry because we would corrupt children and destroy the institution of marriage. About the latter, all we can say is, good for all of us. We are certainly not the only couple to express ambivalence about marriage. We recently received an invitation to the wedding of two gay men who have been together for 30 years. On the back was a *New Yorker* cartoon of a man reading a newspaper while his wife watches television. The caption reads, "Gays and lesbians getting married—haven't they suffered enough?"

Don't get us wrong: we did not need the state to validate our relationship. We did want access to the rights that came along with marriage, even though we wholeheartedly agree with the queer argument that those rights should be distributed in some other fashion. Our nuptials were a quickie at the famous Santa Barbara courthouse. In California, we found out, the only thing we had to say is that we wanted to marry, so we wrote a thirty-second ceremony declaring that we'd already been through richer and poorer and sickness and health and didn't need anyone to tell us about the nature of love, but we did want to be married. That was it. We married during what came to be known as the "summer of love," when over 18,000 same-sex couples tied the knot in California as part of the collective effort to halt the Religious Right's well-financed campaign to overturn marriage equality in California.

So we got married. Does that make us less queer?

advancing justice [or] the shifting terrain of justice

We are getting tired of the conflict over marriage within the queer community. Verta's and Mary Bernstein's book *The Marrying Kind?* lays out the variety of queer arguments against marriage. For instance, there's no reason that so many material rights should be attached to marriage. And sure, there are more important issues than marriage: without passage of the Employment Non-Discrimination Act (ENDA), in 29 states, people can still be fired for being gay or lesbian.

Yet in a study of ordinary LGBTQ people's attitudes toward same-sex marriage, sociologists Kathleen Hull and Timothy Ortyl find that a majority support the movement's emphasis on marriage and family issues. Despite hesitations among many queers, the strength and virulence of anti-gay opposition mobilized the marriage equality movement. Since 1974, the Religious Right has sponsored over 150 ballot measures challenging LGBTQ rights at the state and municipal levels. At least a third of these ballot measures, as sociologist Amy Stone points out in *Gay Rights at the Ballot Box*, were bans on same-sex marriage and other forms of relationship recognition for same-sex couples. This was a wake-up call to action, even for queers opposed to the idea of marriage in general.

The reality is that the state-by-state and country-by-country granting of the right to marry is a major, if imperfect, advance in what we hope is the march toward equality and social justice. In the United States, 17 states and the District of Columbia currently allow same-sex marriage, and it is legal in 8 tribal nations and 15 other countries. State-level Defense of Marriage Acts have been falling like dominos since the Supreme Court invalidated the federal Defense of Marriage Act (DOMA), which restricted marriage to "one man and one woman." Even the recent Supreme Court decision to halt same-sex marriage in Utah has to be balanced

so we got married. does that make us less queer?

against the fact that, for 17 days, a U.S. District Court ruling allowed same-sex marriages to take place in a state where Mormons dominate legal and political circles.

The year 2013 will likely be remembered as a watershed for same-sex marriage. The Court's decision on DOMA extended the federal benefits of marriage to all legally married same-sex couples, regardless of their state of residence, opening the door for legal challenges to state-level DOMAs by same-sex couples across the United States. A recent survey of Fortune 500 companies by the Human Rights Campaign finds that corporate support for gay and transgender workers is also increasing in new regions of the country since the Supreme Court struck down the Defense of Marriage Act, with more than 90 percent of large employers offering health insurance and other spousal benefits to same-sex domestic partners.

Change in public opinion on the issue of same-sex marriage has been astoundingly rapid, with support, according to a 2013 Gallup Poll, climbing from 40 percent to 54 percent in four short years. Most commentators attribute the shift in public opinion to the more favorable attitudes of younger cohorts, as well as contact with increasingly open queer family members, friends, and coworkers. A more recent Washington Post-ABC News poll puts support for same-sex marriage at 58 percent overall, with 81 percent of those between 18 and 29 in favor. As one activist who participated in the 2004 same-sex wedding protest in San Francisco proclaimed, "This is the civil rights fight of our generation." This sea change bodes well for other important advances.

What is missing from much of the discussion about changing public opinion is the impact of the LGBTQ movement. After Proposition 8 passed in California, the movement for marriage equality countered by building strength through national organizations with close ties to local and state LGBTQ groups and progressive allies across the country, even in red states. As scholar Sidney Tarrow observes in his book *The Language of Contention*, what has been most striking about the recent campaign for same-sex marriage is that not only LGBTQ activists, but also politicians courting public opinion, have increasingly come to use the language of love to justify the right to wed. After the defeat in California, proponents of same-sex marriage realized that the movement's emphasis on "rights" failed to resonate with the ideals of love and commitment, which is how most Americans think about marriage.

The movement also adopted a number of tactical innovations that emphasized the emotional aspects of marriage and identity deployment to make LGBTQ people more visible to the general public. In California, Freedom to Marry launched an innovative campaign in which gay couples were shown alongside straight couples to emphasize similarities between their families and the problems they face. Across the country, National Freedom to Marry Day featured groups of same-sex couples dressed in wedding gowns and tuxedos strolling down city streets, and same-sex couples continued to engage in protest by demanding marriage licenses at county clerk's offices in states with bans on same-sex marriage. Through a statewide "Get Engaged Campaign," Marriage Equality Florida is targeting public opinion to put on the ballot a constitutional amendment guaranteeing the right to marry.

> *It's possible that same-sex marriage will queer marriage rather than straighten out queer people.*

Celebrities in institutional sectors such as sports, the military, politics, television, and the film industry, where the closet doors had been firmly closed for decades, have used coming out as a tactic to educate the public and promote same-sex marriage. Families, even in Republican circles and the Mormon Church, bastions of anti-gay opposition, began to confront LGBTQ people in their midst and were forced, in some cases, to embrace their LGBTQ daughters and sons despite prior public opposition to same-sex marriage. Witness the bitter spat between former Vice President Dick Cheney's married lesbian daughter Mary and her sister, Liz, who was running for a Senate seat in Wyoming as an opponent of same-sex marriage but withdrew for family reasons.

homonormativity?

Despite the marriage equality movement's strategic emphasis on the claim that "we're just like you," the reality is also that marriage has not necessarily turned out to be the beginning of an inexorable slide into hetero- or homonormativity, as queer theorists predict. The Right is right about one thing: our marriages have the potential to undermine marriage as we now know it. Consider, first of all, the way that a younger generation of queer people is wielding and transforming the terms "wife" and "husband." We have some disagreement about this from a personal perspective, Verta kind of liking to refer to Leila as her wife as the ultimate affront to maintainers of the status quo and Leila retaining a feminist shudder at the word because of the inequity that has resulted from the maligned legacy associated with the "husband/wife" pairing. Yet we both appreciate the in-your-face nature of same-sex couples who feel comfortable claiming the terms. It is not unheard of for a stranger to assume a woman who refers to her wife has misspoken and to correct her, saying "you mean your husband." That's in-your-face. Is it possible to imagine that marriages between two men or two women, not to mention transgender or genderqueer people, will transform the meaning of the words "husband" and "wife"? For the better?

It's possible that same-sex marriage will queer marriage rather than straighten out queer people. *In Queering Marriage*, sociologist Katrina Kimport finds that the majority of the over 4,000 gay and lesbian couples who married in San Francisco's "Winter of Love" characterized their weddings as an opportunity to challenge heterosexual privilege. Lesbians, who outnumbered gay men at the altar, in part because they are more likely to have children, often expressed ambivalence about the institution of marriage, emphasizing its history of exacerbating gender inequality. But, at the same time, they strongly believed that same-sex marriage could remake the institution.

Sociologist Judith Stacey has pointed to the creative ways that gay men have organized their relationships outside the norms of monogamy, suggesting that they might serve as useful models for a more flexible heterosexuality (along the lines of the polyamorous community). Sociologist Adam Isaiah Green, in his research on same-sex marriages in Canada, discovered that most couples negotiated a domestic division of labor and rejected the need for marital fidelity. When we told some of the drag queens we wrote about in *Drag Queens at the 801 Cabaret* that at least some male couples found that marriage allowed them the security to pursue sex outside the relationship, they responded, "But of course!" Getting married is a public pronouncement of love and commitment to a partner of the same-sex, but for many queer couples, a committed relationship includes interrogating traditional monogamy and supporting one's partner in sexual freedom. This is hardly a model of homonormativity.

And consider the fact that marriage, across blue states in the United States and a number of other countries, is becoming something that heterosexuals enter into later or not at all. Or that they enter into it but exit out of it with increasing frequency. That should reassure us that younger queer people will not necessarily be pressured into marriage just because it is a possibility. For those to whom it means a lot—because it is an important personal expression of love and commitment, because it brings recognition from family and friends, because it provides health insurance or immigration rights or needed tax benefits or inheritance rights or parental rights or the right to make life and death decisions—it may be an option. For those to whom it means or brings nothing, it can be an option not taken. And if queer people, like straight people, more and more eschew marriage, then perhaps the rights that we all deserve will no longer be tied to a marriage license.

So just as we reject the notion that getting married magically bestows endless happiness and a lifelong commitment on anyone who ties the knot, we reject the notion that it severs us from the queer community. When strangers ask us if we are sisters, or even twins, as they are increasingly wont to do, and if we say in response, "No, we're married," we can assure you that they don't then think of us as just like them. They still look at us as if we are, well, queer.

the trouble with tolerance

by suzanna danuta walters

I've been thinking about marriage a lot lately. Mostly, how to avoid it. Sometimes how to convince others to do a dramatic about face and, like Julia Roberts in *Runaway Bride*, run screaming from the altar. Or maybe Katherine Ross in *The Graduate* is a better role model; although she runs into the arms of another man (boring) she doesn't run into a different marriage, or at least not in the life span of the film.

But, post-Supreme Court gay-marriage bonanza, it's getting harder and harder to live the "alternative" in alternative lifestyle. One by one, non-marrying friends are dropping like flies. Queer Nation types who once marched down the streets proclaiming, "we're here, we're queer, get used to it" are now saying "I do" at alarming rates. And we're talking here about card-carrying feminists; die-hard dykes with dutifully unshaven legs and righteous rage against the patriarchy. When those sisters tie the knot you begin to realize that resistance is futile. Even Lily Tomlin is thinking of getting married to her partner of 40+ years, Jane Wagner, although she assures us—in an interview with E!—that there will be "no rings, no bridal dresses," and instead that, "maybe we'll be dressed like chickens."

First there were the friends who weren't much of a surprise, kinda traditional gals and guys whose commitments to anything alternative were more akin to liking alt-rock radio than embracing queer family values. I may have cringed when they talked of "proposals" and "engagement parties" but their desire to wear the white and join the married masses was no real surprise to me, although I was a bit perturbed that some have given up their own names, a fine patriarchal tradition if ever there was one! Then there were those whose weddings I only found out about on Facebook. These friends knew my political persuasions (which I thought they shared!) and wanted to avoid my snide remarks and vitriolic mockery. How rude of them!

To add insult to injury, I now see a bumper crop of marriage lemmings emerging. These new converts were—not so long ago—part of the small but hardy band of queers critical of the overweening focus on marriage, for reasons ranging from resource allocation (what happens to those queer youth centers if all our money goes to marriage initiatives?) to the more philosophical (why should social benefits come only through commitments to one particular form of intimacy? And what about the sexist and racist history of the institution of marriage?). Many of those critics have jumped ship too, like one high-profile lesbian couple I know who simply felt, after decades of devotion to each other, that it was "time," or the gay dudes—longtime radical activists—who apologetically invited me to their wedding, with a mumbled claim that "our parents just wanted this sooo much." But when my best friend Annie—valiant midwife, she of the unshaven bravado and unshakeable feminist faith—murmured that she too might be marrying her partner of 25 years, I was stunned. "You have," I declared, "put a knife through my feminist heart." To which she responded (after the obligatory eye roll), "Please. I am disgusted with myself. I so don't want to do this!" So why do it?

> *As a topic for mass popular consumption, same-sex marriage couldn't be sexier and safer at the same time; it mixes up religion, the state, kids, and romance in a way that links love and legitimacy.*

benefits for all

Annie has one word for me: money. The lure of pension benefits and Social Security and joint tax returns has flipped even the most resolutely nonmarital and made it hard to just say no. For years, Annie's partner has been on her health plan and she's been taxed on it, an amount in the thousands. Add to that all the other aforementioned monetary perks and the reality of marriage as a financial and governmental institution is quickly revealed. One couple, about 10 years older than me and seemingly just as unlikely to jump on the marriage bandwagon, shook their heads and said, "We did the math. Fifty grand more just in retirement benefits and much more down the pike." Surely many embrace the romantic storyline of love and marriage that permeates our media culture, but one of the things same-sex marriage reveals is the monetized core hiding in plain sight. As we sociologists are wont to repeat (endlessly and pedantically), a phenomenon is no less experienced or lived or felt if it is socially constructed. The heart wants what it wants, even as we recognize that wanting marriage per se is less a product of the heart than of a culture that has consistently sold and marketed it as sign of maturity, a marker of commitment, and a testament to the values of family, faith, and country.

The time is past to laboriously review the objections to the marriage mania, at least to a smart academic audience who should support the civil right, but be critical of both the normative familialism (see, we look just like those regular families!) and the hierarchical framing (marriage as the route to acceptance and as that form of socially and legally benefited public intimacy) that underlie the seemingly benign equality impetus. Feminists and queer scholars and activists have been writing about this—eloquently—for years. If you still think that marriage rights are an unalloyed mitzvah you need to wake up and smell the acrid stink of heteronormativity.

But as a topic for mass popular consumption, same-sex marriage couldn't be sexier and safer at the same time; it mixes up religion, the state, kids, and romance in a way that links love and legitimacy. More to the point, same-sex marriage is easy for liberal straight allies (who yearn to be "accepting") to glom on to; supporting gay marriage proves how über-tolerant one is but cannily avoids getting caught up in the messiness of queer difference, queer sex, queer liberation. The gauzily iconic image of the wedding can replace the debased image of the (take your pick) gay bar/drag ball/dykes on bikes and is a win-win: gays get their marriage, and straights get their feel-good pat on the back. Same-sex marriage can be easily analogized to the repeal of miscegenation laws and can be framed in the language of love. It is, therefore, a media-friendly issue tailor-made for straight support. Let's face it: liberals love same-sex marriage. As blogger George Berkin puts it, "supporting gay marriage is fashionable."

> **We don't speak of tolerating a good book or a sunshine-filled day.**

the tolerance trap

But marriage rights are the bait that lures us into the tolerance trap. Support for same-sex marriage is a popular and safe demonstration of heterosexual goodwill and alliance; in this formula, rights are equated with access to marriage and the tolerant society grants it in exchange for quiescence on more troublesome exclusions.

And what, you may ask, is wrong with tolerance as our goal? Really, who doesn't applaud tolerance? What individual doesn't want to be seen as tolerant? It seems to herald openness to difference and a generally broad-minded disposition. Indeed, one of the primary definitions of "tolerance" concerns sympathy or indulgence for beliefs or practices differing from or conflicting with one's own. But it is a word and a practice with a more complicated history and with real limitations. The late Middle English origins of the word indicate the ability to bear pain and hardship. In fact, some of the first uses of the word can be found in medieval pharmacology and toxicology, dealing with how much poison a body can "tolerate" before it succumbs to a foreign, poisonous substance.

In more contemporary times, we speak of a tolerance to something as the capacity to endure continued subjection to it (a plant, a drug, a minority group) without adverse reactions. We speak of people who have a high tolerance for pain or worry about a generation developing a tolerance for a certain type of antibiotic because of overuse. In more scientific usages, it refers to the allowable amount of variation of a specified quantity—the amount "let in" before the thing itself alters so fundamentally that it becomes something else and the experiment fails. So tolerance almost always implies or assumes something negative or undesired or even a variation contained and circumscribed.

To tolerate something indicates that we think that it's wrong in some way. To say you "tolerate" homosexuality is to imply that homosexuality is bad or immoral or even just benignly icky. You are willing to put up with (to tolerate) this nastiness, but the toleration proves the thing (the person, the sexuality, the food) to be irredeemably nasty to begin with. Alternatively, if there is nothing problematic about something (say, homosexuality), then there is really nothing to "tolerate." We don't speak of tolerating a good book or a sunshine-filled day. We do, however, take pains to let others know how brave we are when we tolerate the discomfort of a bad back or a nasty cold. We tolerate the agony of a frustratingly banal movie that our partner insisted on watching and get points for our endurance. We tolerate, in other words, that which we would rather avoid. Tolerance is not an embrace but a resigned shrug or, worse, that air kiss of faux familiarity that barely covers up the shiver of disgust.

One of the central arguments of straight supporters of gay marriage reveals this tolerance motif at work. "How," they ask with righteous moral authority, "does Jim marrying Bob in any way challenge or undermine my wedded bliss with my wife?" And here's the conundrum: if it doesn't challenge your life, it's not very radical, and if it does challenge your life, we won't get it. Politically, gay rights advocates argue that this is a cut-and-dried (albeit difficult to achieve) civil rights issue, analogous to ending miscegenation laws years earlier. But they typically amend the civil rights push with a more personal insistence that gay marriage won't hurt or change or alter "your" marriage a bit. Worse, gay-marriage advocates can't seem to avoid the language of "just like you."

Activist leaders claim that we are just as capable of making committed relationships as "you" are and that our marriages are no different. The upshot of all this tolerance and sameness?: we ask nothing of you. There's the catch. Marriage as a right is a trap, at the heart of the misguided tolerance project. As sociologist Joe Rollins remarks, "Proponents minimize the imagined differences between gay and straight couples, opponents are striving to render an image of same-sex marriage as a cultural and political monstrosity, and the critically inclined worry that we are making a Faustian bargain."

As long as marriage rights are framed as the pinnacle of gay liberation and, simultaneously, pose no challenge to hetero business as usual, then the jaws of the tolerance trap will have snapped shut, keeping out the more transformative possibilities. The overweening emphasis on this—not just as an obvious civil right, but as *the* sign of gay inclusion—is a contraction of the expansive potential of sexual freedom imagined by earlier activists. The shift to a rhetoric of "marriage equality," rather than "same-sex" or "gay" marriage, indicates a desire to take the messiness of sex out of the picture, to remove the specter of homosex from the hominess of marriage. Just as the main pro-gay-marriage organization has the bland name "Human Rights Campaign," effectively nullifying the specificity of queerness in the very title, so too does "marriage equality" implicitly de-queer our inclusion in that institution, making heterosexual unions the default point of comparison.

We must dethrone the reigning image of gay marriage as *the* civil rights achievement that will signal the death knell of homophobia and discrimination. For no other minority group do we imagine this: do we think misogyny has been vanquished now that legal gender discrimination is a thing of the past? Do we think anti-Semitism is gone because Jews no longer must wear the yellow star? Has the integration of women into the labor force eradicated sexism? Has the election of a Black president and the end of legal segregation slain the scourge of racism?

> *Advocating for a tolerant society is like marrying your best friend: comforting but just not sexy.*

An expansive and robust future of sexual and gender freedom can't be imagined when tolerance is the objective, marriage is the pinnacle, and sameness is the road most traveled. And that future is most assuredly further out of reach when we foolishly buy into the progress narrative that claims a "post-gay" homo friendliness that just isn't there. The dominant frameworks we are working with today—acceptance, tolerance, sameness—may get us some traction but inevitably fall short or even actively undermine the potential for deeper challenges. Advocating for a tolerant society is like marrying your best friend: comforting but just not sexy. Let's hold out for the sexy.

korean multiculturalism and the marriage squeeze

sangyoub park

summer 2011

South Korea (hereafter, Korea) is a culturally and racially homogenous country, which projects an image of a single unified Korean identity to the world. This sense of shared identity is based on common ethnic, cultural, and linguistic heritage, but it may be eroding. Some experts say that rising numbers of Korean men, facing a shortage of prospective Korean brides, are marrying women from other nations and cultures. They are unintentionally forging the nation's transition to a more diverse society.

This "marriage squeeze"—the imbalance between the number of marriageable men and women—is a consequence of Korea's history of an imbalanced sex ratio,

especially during the 1970s and 1980s, when baby boys profoundly outnumbered baby girls. The typical sex ratio at birth in any nation is roughly 105 male babies per 100 female babies born. This ratio quickly reaches a balance, since baby boys have a higher rate of infant mortality; within the first month of life the number of boys and girls evens out.

In Korea, by contrast, the sex ratio is highly skewed, peaking at 116 boys born for every 100 girls in 1990. This stark gender imbalance can be traced to Korean parents' historic preference for sons and the widespread practice of sex-selective abortion in the 1970s and 1980s. Although abortion was banned in 1987, the law did not succeed in curbing the practice of sex-selective abortion.

This "missing girls" phenomenon is not unique to Korea; it's been observed in China and other surrounding nations in East Asia. The desire for boys is strongly linked to males' advantaged social and economic roles in Korean families. Sons are expected to carry on the family name and be

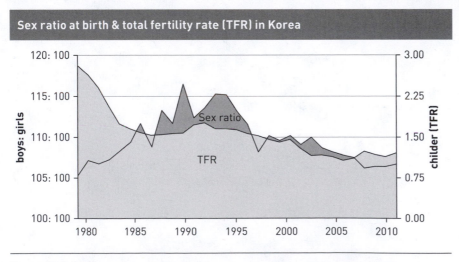

Sex ratio at birth & total fertility rate (TFR) in Korea

boys: girls

childer (TFR)

Sex ratio

TFR

Source: Statistics Korea

284

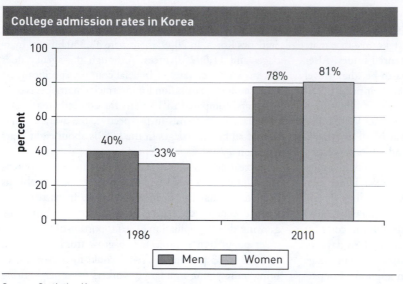

College admission rates in Korea

Source: Statistics Korea

financial support from children in their post-retirement life and prefer daughters as caregivers.

Although son preference has all but eroded, Korea still pays the price for the son preference that prevailed in earlier decades. The disproportionately large cohort of baby boys born in the 1970s and 1980s—now in their 30s and 40s—has created a stark imbalance in young adults' marriage market prospects. Prospective grooms face a shortage of "marriageable females." This marriage squeeze is most pronounced among males who lack higher education (and are thus seen as undesirable husbands) and males in rural areas.

The bride shortage is exacerbated by another demographic trend: women's rising levels of educational attainment. Korean women outpaced men in college admission rates in 2010; 80.5 percent versus 77.6 percent respectively (see next page). In contrast, a slightly higher proportion of men than women (40 versus 33 percent) entered college in 1986, according to Statistics Korea. Today's small cohorts of highly educated young women can afford to be "choosy" when it comes to selecting a mate, and many will choose not to "marry down" with a less accomplished or less educated male.

The shortage of potential wives has forced Korean men to "import" young women from neighboring countries, especially from poor countries. Interracial marriage is encouraged to alleviate the excess of marriageable grooms. (The term interracial indicates international in Korea. Koreans also use the terms biracial or multicultural to describe interracial couples and families.) In 2010, 10 percent of married couples were interracial, an increase from four percent in 2000, according to Statistics Korea. The prevalence of interracial couples is dramatically higher in rural areas. About 40 percent of married couples in Korean rural areas are interracial couples; it is projected that biracial children will represent about 50 percent of rural children in 2020.

financially responsible for their aging parents. Families without sons often continue having children until they have a son.

Data from Statistics Korea vividly illustrate these patterns. The graph above reveals a simultaneous decline in both the sex ratio (106:100 in 2010) and the total fertility rate (1.2 in 2010), defined as the average number of children born per woman over her childbearing years (usually considered to be ages 15 to 49). Both very low fertility rates and the typical sex ratio at birth indicate that Korean parents no longer have a strong son preference, and anecdotal evidence further suggests that Korean couples prefer girls over boys today. This tectonic change may be attributed to the fact that parents now expect no

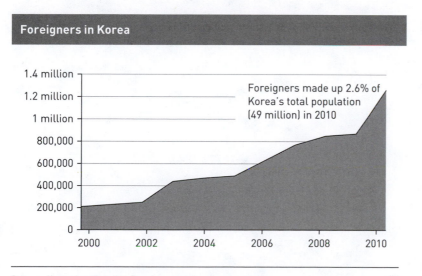

Foreigners in Korea

Foreigners made up 2.6% of Korea's total population (49 million) in 2010

Source: Korea Immigration Service

A 2007 *New York Times* report by Norimitsu Onishi described the marriage tour of Korean grooms. The article described how Korean men take five-day marriage tours to Vietnam to meet potential brides. After the initial meeting with their brides-to-be, they travel to the brides' home province to meet their parents and in-laws and to register for their marriages. They then marry in Vietnam and return to Korea. Vietnamese women account for about 22 percent of all interracial couples in Korea, lagging only behind Chinese women (34 percent) as the most popular international brides in 2009. The description from the Korean Times provides a vivid picture of the process of finding a mate through matchmaking companies: "[A single man has] spent an average 13 million won [$10,600] in costs for interracial marriages. It takes an average 88 days, or about three months, to complete an interracial marriage through agencies—from the Korean applicant's departure to interview with his or her prospective spouse and their entry here."

Although private marriage companies are flourishing in Korea (about 1,800 companies operated in 2010), many of the matchmaking companies are unlicensed and have scammed prospective grooms. The government has had to implement tighter measures to regulate these companies. More importantly, large numbers of immigrant brides arrive in Korea unprepared for life in their new homeland. Social problems such as domestic abuse, the abandonment of biracial children, and high school dropout rates among interracial children have spread rapidly. These problems are exacerbated by language and cultural barriers.

This may explain higher rates of martial dissolution among interracial couples. According to data from Statistics Korea, in 2009, there were 33,330 biracial marriages and 11,692 divorces. Although the agency does not track divorce rates of biracial couples, specifically, it finds the average duration for interracial marriages is only 3.5 years, compared to 13 years for domestic marriages. (To place these trends in perspective, the average duration of all first marriages in the U.S. is about eight years based on a 2011 Census report.)

Increasing the immigrant population is a potential solution to a wide range of demographic problems beyond the marriage squeeze in Korea. In particular, a sharp decline in the nation's fertility rate and a rapidly growing elderly population (The proportion of the 65 and older population is projected to grow from 11 percent in 2010 to 33 percent in 2040.) could force Koreans to bring more young immigrant workers from neighboring countries mainly due to their own shrinking labor pool. Experts project that foreigners will account for five percent of the Korean population in 2020. This explains why the government has begun relaxing current immigration laws, lowering the cash requirement for investors to obtain permanent residency, and implementing new public policies like mandatory education on the cultures of potential brides' countries. Most of all, Korea should be prepared to embrace foreigners as full members of Korean society and to accept multiple identities in lieu of emphasizing "homogeneity identity." When Korea becomes a more tolerant society, the descriptors multicultural and diverse will become a reality, not just rhetoric.

a silent revolution in the korean family

sangyoub park

spring 2015

One of the most significant changes in American family structure is a growing number of cohabiting couples. By contrast, the structure and composition of the Korean family is undergoing dramatic changes due to a rising number of singles, remarried couples, and the elderly widowed. Without much fanfare, demographic, social, cultural, and economic shifts have radically transformed the structure and composition of the Korean family in just the past decade. What caused this silent revolution and what does it mean to Korean society?

A driving force behind the silent revolution is the growing share of single-person households. While one-person households represented only 9% of total households in 1990, they accounted for nearly 26% in 2013, according to Statistics Korea. In other words, one in every four households consists of only one person, and these households are projected to steadily increase to 34.3% in 2035. Two different demographic trends help explain the surge: the growing gray population and the rising never-married population.

About 26% of one-person households were Koreans ages 65 and over in 2012. The fast-aging population in Korea stems from prolonged life spans. In 2013, life expectancy for Koreans was 81.9 years (85.1 for women and 78.5 for men). This means that the number of elderly Koreans living alone is projected to increase by 45% in 2035, according to Statistics Korea (see right).

The other trend contributing to the rise in one-person households is the uptick in young single Korean adults, a trend that is strongly associated with a retreat from marriage. Traditionally, Korea has a pro-marriage culture; marriage is viewed as a social obligation. According to Confucian values, marriage signals young people's transition to adulthood, which leads to having their own children and caring for their elderly parents.

While Korean lives have traditionally centered on the family, the growing influence of individualistic attitudes and Western values have meant young Koreans today delay marriage or abandon marriage for their careers. The average age of first marriage was 29.6 for women and 32.2 for men in 2013, compared to 24.8 for women and 27.8 for men in 1990, according to Statistics Korea. Financial uncertainty among young Koreans is also likely exacerbating negative attitudes toward marriage. Statistics Korea found that four out of 10 Koreans in their 20s and 30s seemed to quit dating in 2014, mainly due to financial hardship.

These Koreans, in fact, are called the *sam-po* generation, combining the word for three (*sam*) and the word for giving up (*po*). The sam-po generation refers to young Korean adults who abandon dating, marriage, and having children because of growing economic uncertainty. In the United States, many members of the so-called "boomerang generation" have moved back into their parents' homes. Young Korean adults may continue to stay at the

Without much fanfare, demographic, social, cultural, and economic shifts have radically transformed the Korean family in just a decade.

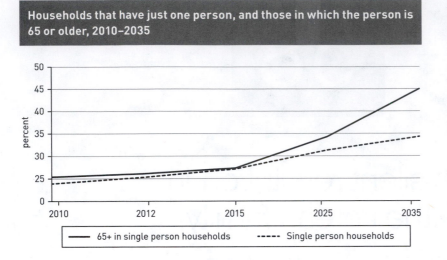

Households that have just one person, and those in which the person is 65 or older, 2010–2035

65+ in single person households — Single person households

---

parental homes and becoming a long-term "kangaroo generation" (as opposed to a boomerang generation), and many have moved away from the strong sense of responsibility to support their parents financially that was held by earlier generations. To them, marriage is simply one option. It is a personal choice rather than an obligation to others.

remarriage

The other driving force of this quiet revolution in family structure is an increasing number of remarriages. Divorce was strongly discouraged in traditional Korea, especially for women. In a Confucian patriarchal family, a wife belonged to her husband's family. As a consequence, the remarriage of women was deeply frowned upon. As a practical matter, few women were financially independent and they lacked the means to divorce. As marriage has become a more individual choice and divorce rises, attitudes toward remarriage have relaxed. Marriage is becoming more individualized: the satisfaction of individual needs, personal fulfillment and growth, and emotional intimacy are all cited as important in a good marriage. In particular, more tolerant attitudes toward remarriage may reflect this new meaning of marriage.

In 2013, 25% of new marriages included at least one partner who had been married before, compared to only 10% in 1990. Remarriage has increased particularly rapidly among women due to their improving economic status and autonomy within Korean society. Statistics Korea reports that women's remarriages now outnumber men's by 10%. The number of women's remarriages jumped by 228% between 1982 and 2012, compared with an increase of 94% for men.

More interestingly, much of the growth in remarriages is not from recent divorcees finding each other or from older men finding younger wives. Remarriages between divorced women and never-married men nearly doubled to 26.9% of total remarriages in 2012 from 15.1% in 1982, compared to a striking *drop* in remarriages between formerly-married men and never-married women (from 44.6% in 1982 to 13.5% in 2012). These previously-married women are called *dol-sing-nyu*, literally meaning returned-single-women (or, second-timer-women). Dol-sing-nyu who are well educated and financially stable seek out mates to pursue happiness and self-fulfillment. In remarriages between second-timer women and first marrying men, the wife tends to be older. While such couples were once uncommon and even considered deviant, the older-woman-younger-man relationship (yun-sang-yun-ha in Korean) has become the new norm.

Along with improvements in women's economic status, the gender imbalance in the marriage market helps account for these couples. There is a surplus of marriageable males as a consequence of Korea's history of skewed sex ratios at birth. Additionally, lopsided numbers of marriageable males and females are exacerbated by men's propensity to marry younger women. These "maritally squeezed" men must now seek out mates among older Korean women. At the same time, the mass media, especially television dramas such as *Witch's Romance* and *Cunning Dol-sing-nyu*, and celebrities in older woman-younger man relationships have helped people rethink age differences. They've created an image of age-mismatched couples as "cute husbands and responsible/mature wives." By contrast, as Korean men's economic prospects dim, dol-sing-nam (second-timer-men) are less desirable on the marriage market.

With delayed marriage, an aging population, and greater acceptance of divorce, it is no surprise that remarriage among Koreans ages 50 and over has been on the rise for decades. Men in their 50s represented about 10% of the total men's remarriages in 1982, and their share

> **Blended families with older female matriarchs are challenging long-standing hierarchies.**

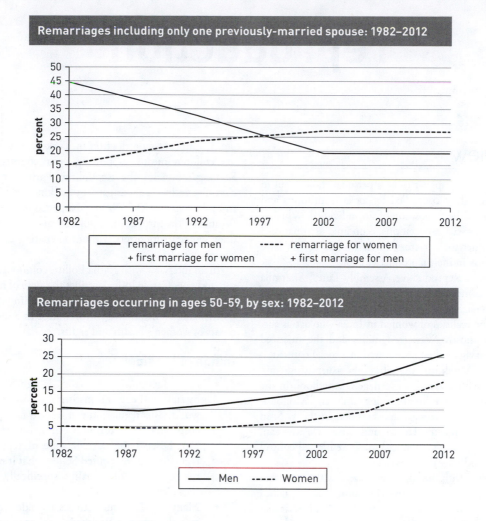

Remarriages including only one previously-married spouse: 1982–2012

Legend:
— remarriage for men + first marriage for women
- - - - remarriage for women + first marriage for men

Remarriages occurring in ages 50-59, by sex: 1982–2012

Legend:
— Men
- - - - Women

increased to about 26% in 2012. Women in their 50s accounted for 18% of total women's remarriages in 2012, a dramatic increase from 5% 30 years earlier. These gray remarrying folks seem to believe that they have a second chance to make more fulfilling marriages and enjoy them throughout their long life expectancies. The rising rate of divorce and ever-longer life expectancies will continue to expand the pool of Koreans who are eligible to tie the knot again.

The silent revolution in the Korean family has many implications for Korean society. Eric Klinenberg's *Going Solo: The Extraordinary Rise and Surprising Appeal of Living Alone* explored how the growing number of Americans who live alone are redesigning single life; the same holds true in Korea. The Korean government, for example, has promised to construct more small houses for the growing singles demographic. Television networks are producing popular shows about singles (e.g., *Roommates, What Are You Eating Today?*) and remarriage (e.g., *With You Together*) in Korea. Dating websites like

Sunwoo or Only You treat second-timers as their main customers, not just clients for a niche market. These businesses are all a part of what Klinenberg dubs the "solo economy." Singles, especially young singles, have gained new cultural and economic clout.

With so many remarriages, there are also an increasing number of blended families or stepfamilies. Traditionally, Korea has been a patriarchal society. But blended families with older female matriarchs are challenging longstanding hierarchies and creating new social scripts within and surrounding families. While the growing individualism surrounding marriage and the higher degree of gender equity in divorce and remarriage resemble patterns in the U.S., the relative lack of cohabitation and the status of dol-sing-nyu as compared to divorced men are quite different. Sparked by shifting values, especially in the status of women, this silent revolution has already brought about significant new developments in Korean culture and social structure.

reproduction

overview

Reproduction can appear to be a personal choice, but in reality, it is tightly controlled by social institutions and factors beyond the disposition of the individual. Whether through law, social expectations, economic or situational access, or other social factors, many women do not have full autonomy in their reproductive choices.

In "India's Reproductive Assembly Line," Sharmila Rudrappa complicates the prevalent understanding of reproductive labor as inherently exploitative. Rudrappa describes the realities of women in India who act as surrogates for mostly Western families and the nuanced ways they navigate their choice within a social context.

Stefanie Mollborn describes the surprising and stereotype-defying trends of teenage motherhood in the United States in, "Children Having Children." Mollborn paints a picture of teenage motherhood in the U.S. in which young, mostly Latina and African American, women of low socioeconomic status have limited control over when and how they have children.

Contrasted with the stigma associated with unmarried motherhood as described by Mollborn, Sarah Hayford and Karen Guzzo describe the myth of the "Single Mother by Choice." Popularized in current media, this single mother is an affluent woman who decides to stop waiting for a man and have a baby on her own. But is this a reality?

For some, motherhood is not about individual desire but about the social pressures of nationalism. In "Reproducing the Nation," Özlem Altiok describes the politicization of reproduction in Turkey, in which having children means supporting your country. Deana Rohlinger explains the Republican Party's attempt to close the voting "gender gap" by backing the birth control pill in her article, "What Happened to the War on Women?" The birth control pill becomes a useful tool to draw women supporters without alienating the socially conservative base.

In an interview with Katha Pollitt, columnist, professor, and poet Carole Joffe describes the state of reproductive rights in the U.S. She emphasizes the importance of normalizing abortion and birth control as essential elements of women's health and rights.

things to consider

- Reproduction, like sexuality, is tightly regulated by state and cultural institutions throughout the world. This regulation can lead to new gendered employment opportunities or a rise in nationalism. Discuss the current state of reproduction regulation in the United States, what it means for the regulation of sexuality, specifically women's sexuality.

- Many scholars and activists consider the surrogacy described in Rudrappa's article to be exploitative. Within the context of these women, can it be both empowering and exploitative?

- What do the articles on teen pregnancy and single mothers indicate about common scripts or expectations for reproduction in our society?

59

india's reproductive assembly line

sharmila rudrappa

summer 2012

"If you asked me two years ago whether I'd have a baby and give it away for money, I wouldn't just laugh at you, I would be so insulted I might hit you in the face," said Indirani, a 30-year-old garment worker and gestational surrogate mother. "Yet here I am today. I carried those twin babies for nine months and gave them up." Living in the southern Indian city of Bangalore, married at 18, and with two young children of her own, she had delivered twins a month earlier for a Tamil couple in the United States.

I met Indirani when she was still pregnant and living in a dormitory run by Creative Options Trust for Women, Bangalore's only surrogacy agency at the time. COTW works with infertility specialists who rely on the Trust to recruit, house, care for, and monitor surrogate mothers for their clients. Straight and gay couples arrive from all over India and throughout the world to avail themselves of Bangalore's expertise in building biological families. Indirani and other mothers introduced me to 70 other surrogates they had gotten to know through their line of work. Some of them, including Indirani herself, double as recruiting agents, bringing new laborers into Bangalore's reproductive assembly line.

India is emerging as a key site for transnational surrogacy, with industry profits projected to reach $6 billion in the next few years, according to the Indian Council for Medical Research. In 2007, the *Oprah* show featured Dr. Nayna Patel in the central Indian town of Anand, Gujarat, who was harnessing the bodies of rural Gujarati women to produce babies for American couples. Subsequent newspaper articles and TV shows, as well as blogs by users of surrogacy, popularized the nation as a surrogacy destination for couples from the United States, England, Israel, Australia and to a lesser extent Italy, Germany, and Japan.

The cities of Anand, Mumbai, Delhi, Hyderabad, and Bangalore have become central hubs for surrogacy due to the availability of good medical services, inexpensive pharmaceuticals, and, most importantly, cheap and compliant labor. The cost of surrogacy in India is about $35,000–40,000 per baby, compared to the United States, where it can run as high as $80,000, which makes it particularly appealing to prospective parents. It is working class women who make India's reproductive industry viable. In Bangalore, the garment production assembly line is the main conduit to the reproduction assembly line, as women move from garment factories, to selling their eggs, to surrogacy.

Indirani's life typifies that of other women in Bangalore's garment factories. Paid low wages, she works intermittently in one of the city's many garment factories. She quit when she became pregnant, and joined the line again when her two children attended school, taking time away when she was sick, or to care for sick family members. Bangalore's reproduction industry affords women like her the possibility of extracting greater value from their bodies once they have been deemed unproductive workers in garment factories. Because of its life affirming character, Indiriani and others see surrogacy, however exploitative, as a more meaningful and creative option than factory work.

disposable workers

The popular understanding is that women who have large debt burdens and are destitute opt to become surrogate mothers. But while they are in debt, the 70 mothers I met were not among the poorest in Bangalore. Many were part of dual or multiple income households, and tended to be garment workers who earn more than the average working woman in the city.

Former surrogate mothers, who also work as recruiting agents, have extensive networks among women in prime reproductive age in their own extended families, and among neighbors and friends who work as maids, cooks, street sweepers, or construction workers. Because cuts in food, education, and medical subsidies due to state divestment, along with volatile markets and global financial crises, lead to unsteady factory work and low wages, their greatest recruiting success is among garment workers.

> *In Bangalore, the garment production assembly line is the main conduit to the reproduction assembly line.*

Like garment workers in sweatshops across the world, women in Bangalore are underpaid and overworked. In order to meet short production cycles set by global market demands, they work at an inhumanely fast pace, with few or no breaks. They frequently suffer from headaches, chest pain, ear and eye pain, urinary tract infections, and other health problems. Sexual harassment and abuse are rampant on the production line. The supervisors, almost all men, castigate women in sexually derogatory terms when they do not meet production quotas, and often grope the women as they instruct them on how to work better. "Sometimes," says Indirani, "I wouldn't take a lunch break when pieces piled up. I didn't want to be shamed in front of everyone. I would go to any length to avoid calling the supervisor's attention to me."

Indirani earned $100 to $110 monthly, depending upon her attendance, punctuality, and overtime hours. Frequently, she and her co-workers were unable to meet the inordinately high production targets and were required by supervisors to stay past regular working hours to meet their quotas. "Playing" catch-up, however, did not necessarily result in overtime pay. Indirani's husband became suspicious if her paycheck did not reflect her overtime hours. He wondered whether she was really at the factory, or whether she was cavorting with another man. Indirani, like many of the women I interviewed, reported that she felt debased at work and at home.

Prior research on Bangalore's female garment workers suggests that they work an average of 16 hours a day in the factory and at home doing laundry, cooking, taking care of children, and commuting to work. Working in the factory all day, and then returning home to complete household tasks was absolutely exhausting. Indirani's friend Suhasini, who was also a surrogate mother, avoided garment work altogether. Her mother, sister, and other women family members had worked the line, and she knew it was not what she wanted for her life. "But I need money," she told me. "For us," she says, "surrogacy is a boon." She describes Mr. Shetty who started COTW, as "a god to us." When I met her again in December 2011, Suhasini was receiving hormonal injections so that she could be a surrogate mother for a second time.

For much of her working life Indirani has been intermittently employed in one of Bangalore's many garment factories. She quit when pregnant, and joined the line again when her two children attended school. She also stopped factory work when she was sick, or had to care for sick family members. From the perspective of the garment factories, when Indirani is healthy she is a valuable worker for the firm. But during her pregnancies and illnesses, or when she has to attend to her family's needs, she loses her value as a worker, and the company replaces her. She is, as anthropologist Melissa Wright calls it, a "disposable worker." Upon recovering her health, or managing family chores efficiently, Indirani cycles back into the garment factory again, this time miraculously having regained her value for the production process. Over her working life, Indirani has shifted from being valuable, to becoming an undesirable worker who must seek other forms of employment to help support her family.

making babies

Indirani and her auto-rickshaw worker husband have struggled for much of their married life to make ends meet, and to support their small children. Indirani's husband did not earn much money. He rented his vehicle from an acquaintance, and the daily rental and gasoline costs cut significantly into the household income. So Indirani and he decided to borrow money from her cousin to purchase an auto-rickshaw of their own. Their troubles worsened when they were unable to pay back the loan, and the cousin would often arrive at their door, demanding his money and screaming expletives at them. He would come to the factory on payday and take Indirani's entire paycheck. She said, "I'd work hard, facing all sorts of abuse. And at the end of it I wouldn't even see any money. I felt so bad I contemplated suicide." When a friend at work suggested that she sell her eggs to an agency called COTW for approximately $500, Indirani jumped at what she perceived as a wonderful opportunity. After "donating" her eggs, Indirani decided to try surrogacy; she became pregnant with twins on her first attempt.

When I asked Indirani whether the hormonal injections to prepare her for ova extraction, and subsequently for embryo implantation, were painful or scary, she avoided answering directly. *"Aiyo akka,"* she said. "When you're poor you can't afford the luxury of thinking about discomfort." When I told her about the potential long-term effects of hyperovulation, she shrugged. Her first priority was getting out of poverty; any negative health threats posed by ova extraction or surrogacy were secondary.

Indirani did not find surrogacy to be debasing work. She earned more money as a reproduction worker than she did as a garment worker, and found the process much more enjoyable. She was exhausted physically and emotionally working as a tailor in the factory and then cleaning, cooking, and taking care of her family. Upon getting pregnant, however, Indirani lived in the COTW dormitory. At first she missed her family, often wondering what her children were doing. Was her mother-in-law taking care of them? "I was in a different place surrounded by strangers," she recalled. But soon she began to like the dormitory. She didn't have to wake up by 5 am to prepare meals for the family, pack lunches for everyone, drop the children off at the bus stop so they could get to school, and then hop onto the bus herself to get to the garment factory. Instead, she slept in, and was served breakfast. She had no household obligations and no one made demands on her time and emotions. Surrogacy afforded her the luxury of being served by others. She did not remember a time in her life when she felt so liberated from all responsibilities.

surveillance and sisterhood

As she got to know the other women in the COTW dormitory, Indirani began to feel as though she was on vacation. For Indirani and many of the surrogate mothers I interviewed, it was easier to talk with the friends they made in COTW than with childhood friends and relatives; they felt they had more common with one another. Through the surrogacy process, many women told me, they lost a baby but gained sisters for life.

Indirani's husband brought the children over to visit on some weekday evenings, and her daughter stayed overnight with her on weekends. Her older sister Prabha, also a garment worker who was similarly strapped for cash, joined her at COTW two months after Indirani arrived, becoming a gestational surrogate for a straight, White couple. Like most surrogates, she had no idea where they were from, or where her contract baby would live.

Noting the closed circuit cameras that monitored the mothers' every move in the dormitory, I asked how they felt about them. Indirani said they didn't bother her; in fact, most of the mothers did not register the cameras' presence. While this initially surprised me, I soon realized that they were accustomed to surveillance in their everyday lives. Living under the gaze of relatives and inquisitive neighbors, and housed in one-two room homes

> **Many women spoke of losing a baby but gaining sisters for life.**

where it was common for six to eight households to share a bathroom, notions of privacy were quite foreign. Surveillance at the dormitory was benign in comparison to the surveillance and punishment meted out for supposed infractions on the garment shop floor, where long conversations with teammates, taking a few minutes of rest, or going on breaks were all curtailed. In comparison, surveillance at COTW, designed to check on whether the women were having sex with their men folk who visited the facilities, seemed relatively banal.

The surrogate mothers delivered their babies through caesarian surgeries between the 36th and 37th week of gestation in order to conform to the scheduling needs of potential parents. Indirani was initially fearful of going under the knife, but she saw many mothers survive caesarians and was

> **They derived more meaning from surrogacy than working under the stern labor regimes of the garment factory.**

no longer anxious. In the end, she found the caesarian method of delivering the twins she had carried easier than the vaginal births of her own two children.

The $4000 Indirani earned was far less than the $7000 the surrogacy agency charged for the children.

While she was legally entitled to a larger amount because she carried twins, Indirani made no more money than those mothers pregnant with singletons. Her take-home pay actually ended up being less than $4000 after she paid the recruiting agent $200 and bought small, obligatory gifts for the COTW staff who cared for her during her pregnancy. Indirani had the option of staying on in the dormitory for up to two months after delivering her twins, but like all the mothers I interviewed, she chose not to do so because COTW charged for post-natal care, and for food and board. She could not afford to lose her hard-earned money on what she perceived as a luxury, so she returned home within days of delivery to all the household work that waited. Within a week of returning home, her remaining earnings went directly to her cousin, the moneylender. Still, knowing her debts were paid off gave her peace of mind.

Indirani claimed she does not feel any attachment to the twins she carried. "They were under contract. I couldn't bring myself to feel anything for them," she told me. "They were never mine to begin with, and I entered into this knowing they were someone else's babies." It is hard enough for her to take care of her own two children, she said. "Why do you think I'm going through all this now? What would I do with two more? They are burdens I cannot afford." On the other hand, some mothers professed deep attachments to the babies they had given up. Roopa, a divorced mother who gave birth to a baby girl three years ago, always celebrated her contract baby's birthday. "June 21st *akka*," she said, "I cook a special meal. My daughter doesn't know why we have a feast, but it's my way of remembering my second child. I still cry for that little girl I gave away. I think about her often. I could never do this again."

life out of waste

Regardless of how they felt about the babies they had given up, the women almost all said they derived far more meaning from surrogacy than they did working under the stern labor regimes of the garment factory. In our conversations, time and again, women described the many ways they are deemed worthless in the garment factory. Their labor powers exhausted, their sexual discipline suspect, their personal character under question, they are converted to waste on the shop floor—until they are eventually discarded. On the other hand, Bangalore's reproduction industry, they said, gave them the opportunity to be highly productive and creative workers once more.

Indirani contrasted the labor processes in producing garments and producing a baby: the latter was a better option, she said. "Garments? You wear your shirt a few months and you throw it away. But I make you a baby? You keep that for life. I have made something so much bigger than anything I could ever make in the factory." Indirani observed that while the people who wore the garments she'd worked on would most probably never think about her, she was etched forever in the minds of the intended parents who took the twins she bore.

Indirani and the other mothers I met did not necessarily see selling eggs or surrogacy as benign processes. Nor did they misread their exploitation. However, given their employment options and their relative dispossession, they believed that Bangalore's reproduction industry afforded them greater control over their emotional, financial, and sexual lives. In comparison to garment work, surrogacy was easy.

Surrogacy was also more meaningful for the women than other forms of paid employment. Because babies are life-affirming in ways garments are obviously not, surrogacy allowed women to assert their moral worth. In garment work their sexual morality was constantly in question at the factory and at home. At the dormitory, in contrast, they were in a women-only space, abstaining from sex, and leading pure, virtuous lives.

Through surrogacy, Indirani said, she had built a nuclear family unit and fulfilled one infertile woman's desire to be a mother. In the process, she had attempted to secure the future of her own family and her own happiness. As a garment worker Indirani felt she was being slowly destroyed, but as a surrogate mother she said she was creating a new world. She was ready to go through surrogacy once again to earn money for her children's private schooling. The last time we met in December 2011, Indirani asked me, "If anyone you know wants a surrogate mother, will you think of me? I want to do this again."

recommended resources

Haimowitz, Rebecca, and Sinha, Vaishali. 2010. *Made in India*. San Antonio, TX. This is a feature length documentary film on surrogacy in India, which explains the organization of the industry through the journey of one American couple to an Indian surrogate.

Pande, Amrita. 2010. "Commercial Surrogacy in India: Manufacturing a Perfect Mother-Worker," *Signs 35*: 969–992. This is an account of surrogate mothers living in dormitories in Anand, India.

Teman, Elly. 2010. *Birthing a Mother: The Surrogate Body and the Pregnant Self*. Berkeley, CA: University of California Press. The book documents the relationships between straight women and their surrogates in Israel, where assisted reproductive technologies are subsidized for heterosexual couples.

Wright, Melissa. 2006. *Disposable Women and Other Myths of Global Capitalism*. London: Routledge. An anthropological description of how women inthe global south are seen as bad workers, and yet their work is crucial to multinational companies' profits.

"children" having children

stefanie mollborn

winter 2011

adriana's story

Meet Adriana. She's 17, lives with her parents, and, like about 1 in 6 teen girls in the U.S., she has a child. My research team got to know Adriana and 75 other teen parents through in-depth interviews in the Denver area in 2008–2009. A Latina high school student who looks and acts older than her age, Adriana has a two-year-old son, Marlon. Like the overwhelming majority of teen mothers, Adriana didn't intend to get pregnant: "I would always play with my little baby dolls and stuff, but I wasn't really thinking about, 'Oh, when am I gonna be a mom?' I didn't really care about that stuff. And then actually, to tell you the truth, when I got pregnant, I wasn't really thinking about being a mom yet, either. It just kind of happened."

Similarly, Adriana's boyfriend Michael was like many other young dads: "happy," even "over-excited," about becoming a father. But Adriana said, "Once I found out I was pregnant, I didn't want him to be my boyfriend." Still, he moved in with her family. Later, they lived with Michael's family. In contrast to stereotypes about uninvolved young fathers, it's very common for teen births to occur in the context of a long-term romantic relationship and for the child's father to live with the mom. However, these teen relationships frequently dissolve. Michael and Adriana were together for three years: "...after I had my son . . . I told him it was either my own place or I was leaving him. So he got me my own place.

> In America, teen parenthood is commonplace but polarized—and polarizing.

We lived there for about a year and a half, and then, like, we would fight all the time. . . . We just realized that we were unhappy together. And last year we just broke up. It's been kind of hard on the baby." She says the breakup is "also a reason, kind of, why I feel awkward about getting pregnant so young, because I didn't really know what love was. I think it would be better if my son had his mom and his dad there together in a relationship, growing up with both parents involved daily. And I think that if I would have waited longer, I would have knew a little more, been a little wiser about who to have a baby with." Marlon saw his father infrequently right after the breakup, but now it's just on weekends at Michael's mother's house.

Marlon now lives with Adriana, her father and stepmother, grandmother, and several siblings. Adriana's father (a fast food worker) and grandmother pay for housing and other bills. Michael provides limited help, but as is typical for teen moms who don't live with their child's father, Adriana is responsible for keeping track of her son's needs and asking Michael for support. Michael's mother helps by providing child care. Medicaid pays Adriana's medical bills, and the WIC program helped her with buying formula. This reliance on a network of extended family members for considerable support, supplemented by health care and nutritional support from the government (but not by welfare payments), is common. Despite this assistance, Adriana is still in a precarious financial situation. She doesn't often have spending money, because "as long as I don't need something really bad, I don't want to ask for it." Adriana worries about straining her family's resources.

While Adriana's story is certainly personal, it is far from unique. About 1 in 3 girls in the U.S. becomes pregnant before turning 20. About a third of these pregnancies end in abortion, but the majority of the rest become parents. (American girls ages 15–19 are about 3 times as likely as their Canadian peers to have a child, 7 times as likely as Swedes, and almost 9 times as likely as Japanese teens.) Adriana's experience exemplifies many of the larger social realities shaping teen parenthood today. These include historical changes in the typical American life course, shifting attitudes about the "problem" of teen pregnancy, social inequality and the polarized experience of teen parenthood in the U.S., and the many social consequences teen parents face for being "kids having kids."

who are the kids who have kids?

Parenting is not evenly distributed among American teenagers. In fact, we might say that teen parenthood is an extremely polarized experience—common in some segments of the population and rare in others.

Teen mothers and fathers overwhelmingly come from lower-income families and neighborhoods, and they are often struggling in school even before the pregnancy. A national study of babies born in 2001 revealed that about half of teen mothers' children live in poverty, and more than half of all children living in poverty have a mother who was once a teenage parent. Teen parenting

also varies by race and ethnicity, with Latinos, African Americans, and Native Americans having the highest rates. On the other hand, teen parenthood is relatively rare in high socioeconomic status, Asian American, and White families and neighborhoods.

There's little doubt that contraception (or lack thereof) is an important part of this package. While American teenagers start having sex at similar ages to their peers in many other Western countries, they are much more likely to get pregnant and have children, even though the vast majority of teen pregnancies are unintended. Many researchers attribute this difference to American teens' less consistent contraception patterns. Geography is another intriguing dimension of variation in teen parenthood. White teens in parts of the Southeast are more likely to get pregnant than elsewhere, as are Latina and African American teens in this region. Perhaps counterintuitively, states with high levels of conservative religious affiliations have some of the highest teen birthrates (see map below), and many Evangelical young people are at risk of becoming teen parents.

My recent interviews with college students showed that particularly in low socioeconomic status, conservative religious communities, a negative view of teen parenting is balanced against a "pro-life" social norm that encourages teens not to have an abortion. Teens are told that having the child is the "lesser of two evils." This echoes the Palin family's reaction to daughter Bristol's unwed teen pregnancy, and some of our

Teen birth rates (per 1,000 ages 15–19) by state, 2008

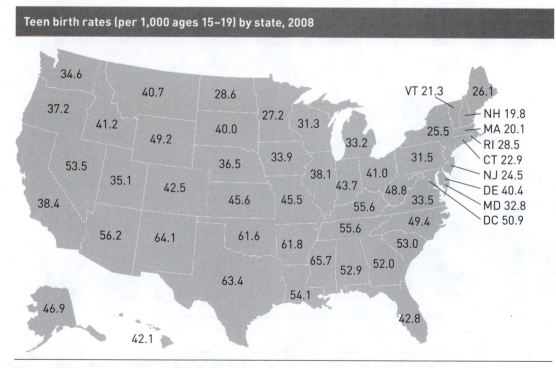

Source: http://www.cdc.gov/nchs/data/databriefs/db46.pdf

participants told us it was a recent opinion shift in their communities. In most of the study's higher socioeconomic status, less religious communities, there's no cautiously positive take on teen parenting. Parents actively encourage their children to delay sex, but believe that if they do have sex, they should contracept consistently. Teens who "mess up" by getting themselves or a partner pregnant are not judged as immoral, but as "stupid."

problematic perceptions

For many, teen parenthood symbolizes "what's wrong" with America today. Media outlets breathlessly report the details of celebrity pregnancies and create reality shows about teen mothers, then air call-in sessions about the irresponsibility of young people. This simultaneous attention and condemnation is shared by the general public. In a 2004 opinion poll, teen pregnancy was rated by 42 percent as a "very serious problem" in our society, and another 37 percent considered it to be an "important problem."

Why is such a commonplace event viewed so negatively? The fact that teenage pregnancy disproportionately impacts racial minorities and low-income communities is key. Such patterns play into mainstream fears about social disorder and excessive reliance on social services and the welfare state. There is a persistent, racialized public stereotype of the Black or Latina "welfare queen" (even though the vast majority of teenage mothers do not receive welfare benefits).

This interpretation is somewhat confirmed by the fact that the general public's attitudes about teen childbearing are divided along racial lines, too. In a 2005 survey of American adults, for example, I asked people how embarrassed they would be by a hypothetical unwed teen pregnancy in their household. African Americans reported less embarrassment than other racial groups, and people who had attended college reported more embarrassment than those with less education.

Some historical perspective is important here as well. The U.S. has a long history of teen childbearing. Looking at the teen birthrate since the start of the Second World War, the high point for teen births was in the mid-1950s. Yet teen parenthood did not fully emerge as an important "social problem" until the 1970s. The explanation probably lies in the marital context of teen births.

Back in the 1950s, it was common and socially acceptable for people to get married and immediately become parents in their late teens or early twenties. Technically, this made lots of young people teen parents, but it wasn't considered a problem because they were engaging in a "normal" life course. In contrast, nonmarital births were rare and stigmatized.

Since then, the experience of early adulthood has changed. Many young people now enjoy a longer period of independence before settling into to adult roles, and most

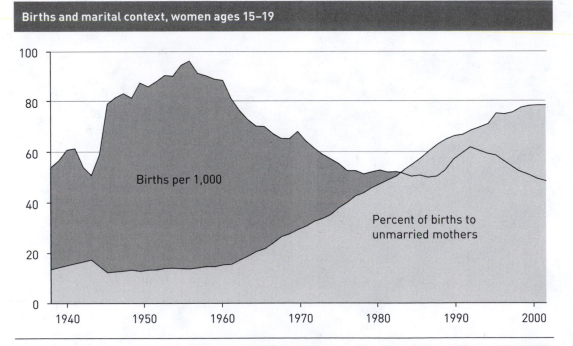

Births and marital context, women ages 15–19

Births per 1,000

Percent of births to unmarried mothers

Source: Stephanie Ventura (2001). "Births to Teenagers in the United States." Nonmarital birth data before 1951 not available every year; interpolated by author.

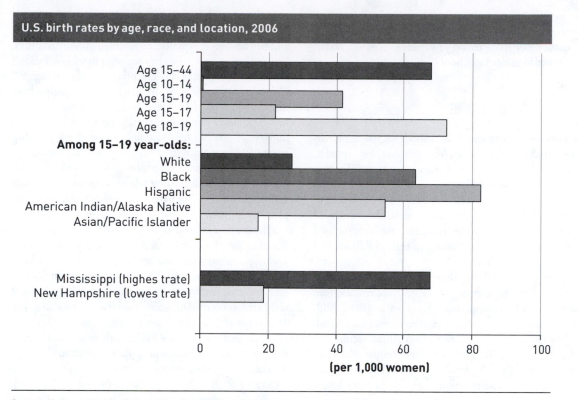

U.S. birth rates by age, race, and location, 2006

(per 1,000 women)

Age 15–44
Age 10–14
Age 15–19
Age 15–17
Age 18–19

Among 15–19 year-olds:
White
Black
Hispanic
American Indian/Alaska Native
Asian/Pacific Islander

Mississippi (highes trate)
New Hampshire (lowes trate)

Source: National Vital Statistics Report Vol. 57, No. 7 (2009).

Americans delay marriage until at least their mid-twenties. At the same time, most have sex before their twentieth birthday, putting them at risk for unintended pregnancy. As it has for all births (4 in 10 births in the U.S. are now nonmarital, compared to 4 in 100 in 1950), the proportion of teen births that are nonmarital has risen dramatically over time: 87 percent of teen births were nonmarital in 2008. Sociologist Frank Furstenberg has pointed out that, as nonmarital teen births increased, so did the visibility of teen parenting as a social problem.

These social attitudes and community norms clearly impact young people. In my analysis of a national survey of teenagers in 1995, most teens said they would feel embarrassed if they got (or for boys, got a girl) pregnant. This contradicts the popular idea that teens today think pregnancy is "cool."

Adriana's story illustrates how family and community reactions can shape teen parents' lives. Some of her family members reacted fairly well to her pregnancy, but others did not. Adriana's intelligence and morality were questioned. "My mom was just like, she didn't get mad. She just kind of said that my boyfriend has to take responsibility, 'cause he's the one who got me pregnant. So she kind of was like, 'Oh, well, I guess you're moving in tomorrow and you're gonna pay this bill and this bill and this bill . . . You're not

taking my daughter out of the house.'" Adriana's brother called her "stupid" and wanted "to beat my boyfriend up." But "the only one who really made me feel bad was my grandma," who told her that it was "wrong" for her to get pregnant so young. Adriana said, "I was really close to her. So I took it kind of hard. . . . We really don't talk any more. She talks to my son more than to me."

Adriana also feels socially ostracized. She says, "I really don't have lots of friends." This social isolation is typical and differs sharply from the common stereotype of teen girls encouraging their friends to get pregnant or forming "pregnancy pacts." Out in public, she attracts negative attention: "Sometimes I would be on the bus and people would just stare at me . . . [At] prenatal appointments, people were like, 'How old are you? What are you gonna do with a kid this young?' Stuff like that . . . It looks kind of bad to see a really young girl pregnant, but also, they don't know me, what I do." She's learning to cope, she says. "Now when I look at people, I'm like, 'Whatever. You don't even know me.' . . . I'm like, 'I still go to school.' I can throw that in their face . . . I have something that would possibly hold me back, and I still do it."

Media outlets' simultaneous attention to and condemnation of teen pregnancies are shared by the public.

Like many other teen moms, Adriana has been forced to learn coping skills to negotiate public stigma. Proving skeptical people wrong is one reason why many teen parents told us they wanted to succeed in school.

consequences

The consequences of teen parenthood, for young parents and their children alike, are complicated. For decades, researchers have documented negative outcomes for teen mothers in terms of education, income, mental health, marriage, and more. Teen fathers have lower levels of education and employment than their peers, and, compared to other kids, children of teen parents have compromised development and health starting in early childhood and continuing into adolescence.

In research explaining these consequences, two surprising findings have emerged. First, by comparing teen mothers to natural comparison groups such as their childless twins and sisters and pregnant teens who miscarried, scholars like public health researcher Arline Geronimus and economist V. Joseph Hotz have shown that most of the negative "consequences" of teen childbearing are actually due to experiences in teens' lives from before they got pregnant, such as socioeconomic background and educational achievement. In other words, the experience of teen childbearing itself only moderately worsens these teens' life outcomes.

Second, the negative consequences of teen parenthood are more severe in the short term. In the long term, many teen parents end up with better outcomes than it looked like they would have when they were teens. For example, developmental psychologist Julie Lounds Taylor found in a predominantly White, socioeconomically advantaged sample of 1957 Wisconsin high school graduates that at midlife, former teenage mothers and fathers lagged behind peers with similar characteristics in terms of education, occupational status, marital stability, and physical health. On the other hand, their work involvement, income levels, satisfaction with work and marriage, mental health, and social support were similar. Using more recent data from a national longitudinal study of eighth graders from 1988, I found that 75 percent of teen mothers and 62 percent of fathers finished a high school degree or GED by age 26. However, compared to the typical American, their out-comes were still problematic: both teen moms and dads ended up with two years less education than average by age 26.

Adriana's story is again illustrative. She wasn't on a traditional path to academic success before she got pregnant. As a Latina from a family with low socioeconomic status, she already belonged to a high-risk group, and her academic experiences reflected it. Adriana says, "Before I was a mom, I didn't really go to school. I didn't like school." But once she got pregnant, she thought, " 'What am I gonna give my son?' . . . He's gonna have the same life that I had, and then he can follow in my footsteps, and I don't want that. I want him to do some things . . . " She started attending a school for pregnant teen girls. "Ever since then . . . I've passed all my classes, and now I graduate in December." There are supportive teachers and understanding fellow students. Infant care and other forms of support are available. Adriana now plans to enroll in postsecondary education.

The support context of teen parenthood varies widely. For example, there are racial and ethnic differences in the key people helping teen mothers. My analysis of a national sample of babies born in 2001 found that about 60 percent of Latina and White teen moms were living with their child's father nine months after the birth, compared to just 16 percent of Black teen moms. Instead, nearly 60 percent of Black teen moms were living with other adults, such as a parent. It's not clear which of these situations is most beneficial for teen moms and their children: although as a society we often wish for fathers to be more involved, teen relationships often break up, and instability in mothers' relationships can compromise children's development.

effective social supports

American teen parenthood is commonplace but polarizing. As our societal safety net shrinks, low-income families' prospects worsen, and education becomes increasingly important for financial success, teen parents face increasingly long odds. Adriana's story helps show how many teen parents are motivated to work hard and make a better life for themselves and their children. Our country has made an important commitment to reducing levels of teen pregnancy, but we also need to find better ways to support teens who are already parents so their families can have a better future.

The federal government has now committed substantial funding for both prevention of teen pregnancies and support for teens who are already parents. Supporting parenting teens is a smart societal investment. First, because most mothers of children living in poverty today were teen moms, targeting these families for intervention would be an effective way to help some of the most marginalized members of our society. This is true regardless of whether the negative outcomes were caused by teen parenthood itself or by factors related to the teen's situation before the pregnancy.

Second, with less financial support available from the government, especially since welfare reform was passed

Supporting parenting teens is a smart societal investment.

in 1996, teen parents and their children are more dependent on their families for survival. Many low-income families have less money and time than they did in the past, making it harder for them to support teen parents and their children. Research finds that families still provide substantial support, but it often severely strains their budgets and their relationships with the young parents, and many teens' and children's basic needs such as for food and warm clothing are not being met. The current economic crisis has exacerbated this situation.

Finally, as many service providers have long known, the time after a teen birth is a magic moment when societal investments can help nudge young families onto a successful trajectory. Unlike many older parents who can take time out from the labor force and still have attractive options when they re-enter, teens are in a life stage when it is critical for them to invest in education and work. And almost all the teen parents we interviewed were willing to sacrifice to meet their goals. A strong motivation to achieve for their children's sake was common.

Without support from social programs, though, this motivation may not be enough. For example, though Adriana is fully committed to her education and has her family behind her, she has to surmount massive obstacles like transportation and childcare to stay in school. Talking to teen parents like her, it's easy to see how much some short-term support would pay off for her, her son, and our society in the long term.

recommended resources

Burton, Linda M. 1990. "Teenage Childbearing as an Alternative Life-Course Strategy in Multigeneration Black Families," *Human Nature 1*: 123–143. Argues, provocatively, that teen motherhood is a rational strategy for girls in very disadvantaged contexts.

Edin, Kathryn, and Kefalas, Maria. 2005. *Promises I Can Keep: Why Poor Women Put Motherhood before Marriage*. Berkeley, CA: University of California Press. An influential ethnographic exploration of why a majority of women in some low-income communities have children outside marriage.

Furstenberg, Frank F. Jr. 2003. "Teenage Childbearing as a Public Issue and Private Concern," *Annual Review of Sociology 29*: 23–29. An authoritative overview of teen parenthood in the past several decades.

Kaplan, Elaine B. 1997. *Not Our Kind of Girl: Unraveling the Myths of Black Teenage Motherhood*. Berkeley, CA: University of California Press. Shows the complex and often negative reactions to teen parenting through interviews with African American teen mothers and their families.

Luker, Kristin. 1996. *Dubious Conceptions: The Politics of Teenage Pregnancy*. Cambridge, MA: Harvard University Press. Tackles the "social problem" of teen pregnancy and makes the case that it is often a consequence, rather than a cause, of poverty and social disadvantage.

Turley, Ruth N. L. 2003. "Are Children of Young Mothers Disadvantaged because of their Mother's Age or Family Background?" *Child Development 74*(2): 465–474. An exemplary article showing how teen mothers' family backgrounds matter more for understanding their life outcomes (and those of their children) than the fact that they gave births as teens.

Names and identifying characteristics have been changed to protect anonymity.

the single mother by choice myth

sarah r. hayford and karen benjamin guzzo

fall 2015

You've probably already been introduced to the new mom in town, the "single mother by choice" (SMC for short). Perhaps you met her in 2010, when *The Switch* featuring Jennifer Aniston, and *The Back-Up Plan*, featuring Jennifer Lopez, came out in theaters. Or maybe you learned about her from a profile in a magazine or followed a link to her parenting blog. You can picture her: she's in her mid-to-late 30s, smart and professionally successful, but she just never met the right guy at the right time, and her biological clock is ticking. She's the epitome of the modern independent woman who wants to have it all, career *and* family—taking her future into her hands, acting decisively, and doing what it takes to achieve her goal of motherhood, with no need for a man. The SMC represents a new phenomenon, appealing to some and worrisome to others. But does she really exist? Has there been a dramatic rise in well-educated single women choosing to have children on their own, or is this new approach to motherhood more common in the media than in reality?

> **She's the epitome of the modern independent woman.**

growing visibility

The term "single mother by choice" first emerged in 1981, when New York City psychotherapist Jane Mattes (herself an SMC) founded an organization to provide support and resources to such moms (singlemothersbychoice.org). But it wasn't until 2005 that the concept really entered the mainstream with Mikki Morrissette's popular book, *Choosing Single Motherhood: The Thinking Woman's Guide*, and her organization (choicemoms.org). Attention snowballed from there.

Sociologist Rosanna Hertz's book, *Single by Chance, Mothers by Choice*, a qualitative study of single mothers, came out in 2006, and four documentaries on SMCs were released between 2007 and 2013. Movies and TV shows often feature SMCs either prominently or as secondary characters, and there are reality shows in the works—one to follow women through the journey of becoming an SMC and another seeking single moms who all used the same sperm donor.

The rising visibility dovetails with the growing ease in becoming an SMC, thanks to the proliferation of sperm banks and fertility clinics since the 1970s. Although initially many sperm banks would not serve unmarried women, the clientele has shifted over time. Some sperm banks, like California Cryobank, report nearly 30% of their clients are SMCs. And changes in the population mean that there are plenty of women eligible to become SMCs. The proportion of employed women with college degrees or more has more than tripled since 1970, accompanied by increases in the proportion of women in highly-paid professions, such as law, medicine, and engineering. A substantial minority (about 20%) of college-educated women never marry, and many more are single after a divorce. Put together, these medical, social, and demographic trends support the notion that SMCs have grown over time.

Articles on SMCs frequently cite the growing proportion of births that take place to unmarried women (41% in 2013) and the rising age of unmarried mothers (23% of nonmarital births are to women 35 and older). But it is not clear that these trends indicate an increase in the affluent single mothers typically described by the SMC label. We know, for instance, that the growth in nonmarital childbearing is primarily due to increases in births to cohabiting women (who are technically unmarried, of course, but aren't single). In fact, there is a notable lack of concrete statistics on the characteristics of SMCs or their overall prevalence. The Choice Mom and Single Mothers by Choice websites, respectively, note that "sadly, there is no comprehensive survey of who [SMCs] are" and describe SMCs vaguely as "career women" in their 30s or 40s with a college degree or higher. One thing, however, is quite clear from both the media and organizations—SMCs emphasize the role of "taking initiative" and "deciding to have a child," distancing themselves from mothers who became single after a break-up or with unplanned pregnancies. The intentionality of motherhood for these women contrasts with what social scientists know about unmarried mothers and nonmarital births. By and large, most pregnancies that occur outside of a coresidential relationship are unintended, and women having births outside of marriage tend to be relatively disadvantaged.

is the smc real?

In fact, the choice mom remains a relatively rare phenomenon. We analyzed the 1988, 1995, 2002, and 2006–2010 National Surveys of Family Growth, which surveyed women aged 15–44 to provide nationally representative data on families and childbearing. This allows us to show trends in first births to SMCs and the proportion of women who follow this model. We define SMC by the context of the first birth: The mother is neither cohabiting nor married and the conception is intended. We separate out mothers who are age 35 or older with at least a bachelor's degree in some figures. Unfortunately, we are unable to identify mothers who adopt children or mothers who are age 45 or over.

We are also unable to account for women's responses to an unintended pregnancy. Surveys typically measure intendedness by asking women how they felt at the time

---

Nonmarital First Births, 1988–2006–10

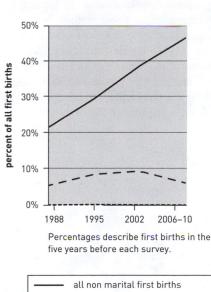

by intendedness, and age of mother

Percentages describe first births in the five years before each survey.

- ——— all non marital first births
- – – – intended births
- ------- intended births, age 35+ with a BA

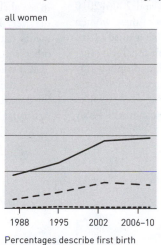

women aged 40-44, not cohabiting, by intendedness of birth and age

all women

Percentages describe first birth experiences of women recalled at age 40-44 in each survey.

- ——— all first births
- – – – intended first births
- ------- intended births, age 35+

women with a bachelor's degree or higher

Percentages describe first birth experiences of women recalled at age 40-44 in each survey.

- ——— all first births
- – – – intended first births
- ------- intended births, age 35+

Source: National Surveys of Family Growth, 1988, 1995, 2002, 2006–10.

of conception. But of course, even women who didn't plan to get pregnant may feel happy about the birth of the child, and women may make a deliberate decision to carry an unintended pregnancy to term. (The 1990s TV character Murphy Brown, for instance, an early version of the fictional single mother by choice, became pregnant by accident, but decided to have the baby as a single mother.) Women who carry an unintended pregnancy to term have, in some sense, chosen single motherhood. But they don't fit the SMC image of taking the initiative and deliberately planning to become a single mother.

As shown above, the proportion of first births that take place outside of marriage increased dramatically between the 1980s and the 2000s—from 21.9% of births to 46.8% of births. If we look only at first births to women who aren't married or cohabiting, and who intended the pregnancy, both the proportion of births and the increase is much smaller. In the five years before 1988, 5.5% of first births were intended births to unpartnered mothers; in the early 2000s, the corresponding figure was 6.2%, although levels were slightly higher in the 1990s. And if we further restrict to women who match the characteristics of the SMC archetype—women age 35 and older with a college degree—the numbers drop to almost zero.

What if we consider the experiences of women rather than the distribution of births? Looking at the lifetime experience of women who were aged 40–44 in each survey, we can see (above right) that the proportion single at the time of their first birth—not married or cohabiting—more than doubled between the 1988 and 2006–2010 surveys, from 9.2% to 19.7%. But few of these women were single mothers by choice. Less than a third of the women who reported a nonmarital, non-cohabiting first birth said that the birth was intended, and only a tiny fraction of unpartnered women with intended first births had these births at age 35 or over. Among women with a college degree, many fewer became single mothers—only

6% by the most recent survey. Although about half of births to these women were intended, it's still the case that less than 3% of college-educated women became single mothers by choice in the early 2000s. (This proportion was slightly larger, around 4.7%, in the 2002 survey.) Over the past few decades, then, remarkably few college-educated women became single mothers by choice at age 35 or older.

the meaning of the myth

By any definition, there are few "single mothers by choice," and there are even fewer women who match the age and educational profile proposed by media portrayals and SMC support organizations. Why, then, is the image of the SMC so persistent? One possibility is that SMC are much more common in the social networks of journalists and media professionals, who tend to be well-educated and often delay family formation as they establish careers, than in the population overall, and these individuals are making the mistake of generalizing from their own lives and experiences. Perhaps more concerning are the implications of this portrayal. The SMC archetype is implicitly contrasted with other stereotypes of unmarried mothers—reckless teens with unplanned pregnancies and "welfare mothers" who have children without being able to provide for them. Each of these portrayals frames childbearing as an individual decision (and an individual responsibility) rather than a reaction to social change or economic constraints. By focusing on the (very few) affluent, older single mothers by choice, media narratives at best ignore and at worst disparage other single parents. Most importantly, the focus on SMCs takes attention away from the high levels of single motherhood, often *not* by choice, that have existed for decades among the disadvantaged and are linked to structural social and economic conditions.

reproducing the nation

özlem altiok

spring 2013

My grandmother gave birth to nine children starting at age 16. My mother delivered the first of her three babies at 27. I gave birth to my only child when I was 32. Prime Minister Erdoğan believes I am not doing my duty as a Turkish citizen.

"Have at least three children," Erdoğan regularly exhorts audiences. "It is easier these days since the economy is doing well." But, today, at a time of high unemployment rates, stagnant real wages, job insecurity, and soaring school expenses, most Turks find it difficult to raise three children.

Erdoğan boasts that his wife washed their four children's diapers by hand. It is women's job to raise children, he implies. He argues that raising children is "easy these days." On a recent visit to Kazakhstan, looking at that country's vast land base, he advised each family to have five children.

Speaking at a population conference, he declared that abortion is murder.

Many doctors are highly critical of such claims, and of the prime minister's politicization of reproductive health and rights. So are feminists. Maternal mortality rates will go up, they counter, if abortion is criminalized. The state should reduce the number of unwanted pregnancies, they say, instead of instituting bans. But Erdoğan is unmoved.

"We are preparing the abortion legislation, and we will pass it," he declared recently. Erdoğan drew a troubling analogy, too, between abortion and the Turkish Army's December 2011 killing of 34 Turkish Kurds—all civilians, half of them children—in Uludere, on the Iraqi border. He said, "There is no difference between killing a child in her mother's womb, and killing him outside."

Erdoğan has also politicized Caesarean births, arguing that Turkey has more Caesarians than similar countries, and that the procedure lowers the nation's population growth rate. Curtailing the use of unnecessary Caesarians can promote women's (and babies') well-being—thus the relatively small outcry against his comments on Caesarians—but Erdoğan's argument against the procedure rests on the mistaken notion that multiple C-sections render a woman incapable of further births.

Claiming that current trends will push Turkey's population into decline by 2037, Erdoğan suggests that Caesarian births and abortions are part of a "conspiracy to wipe this nation from the world stage." But people *want* fewer children (than the current average of 2.7 per rural, and 2 per urban, household). It is this trend that most concerns him.

lie back and think of turkey

No demonstrable increase in the numbers of abortions occurred to spark this novel politicization of abortion in Turkey. Abortion rates increased in the decade following the legalization of elective abortions in 1983, but began a steady decline in the mid-1990s due to increased access to healthcare, and affordable contraceptives.

Birth control methods used in Turkey (1993–2008)

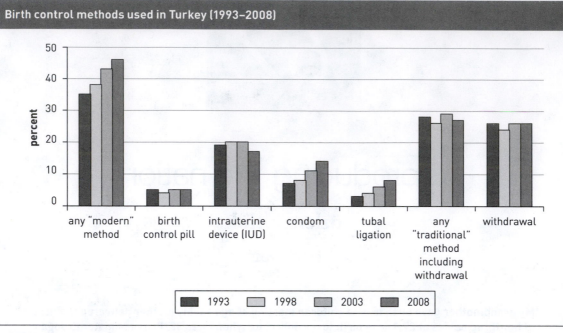

Source: Turkish Demographic and Health Survey, 2008

The move to ban abortion in Turkey is part of an effort to manage the population by disciplining women's fertility. It is indicative of a new "reproductive governmentality" that works across borders to limit reproductive choice—a "choice" that is always constrained by economic and cultural realities. It highlights the vulnerability of women's reproductive rights and well-being even in the formally democratic and relatively progressive Turkey. To the extent that Erdoğan and his conservative government are considered a model for the transitioning Arab countries, their discourse and policies do not bode well for the future of women's reproductive health and rights in the region.

Throughout the world, women's bodies and fertility have long been a matter of public policy. In the United States and Europe women's reproductive rights have been defended in relation to the right to privacy, respect for religious diversity, and a woman's right to choose.

In Turkey, by contrast, the debate over abortion has historically been framed as a population issue. Modern contraceptives were made available in 1965 and elective abortions in 1983, following the diffusion of population control models as a means to industrial development in the Third World.

> **The move to ban abortion in Turkey is part of an effort to manage the population by disciplining women's fertility.**

From the 1920s until the 1960s, Turkey encouraged childbearing in the service of nation-building and agricultural development. Pro-natalist policies tried to reverse population decline following a decade of war. The 1936 Turkish Criminal Code classified abortion as a "crime against the unity and health of the race," illustrating the subjugation of women's reproductive choice to the nationalist project in this period.

Representations of ideal motherhood were selectively incorporated into nationalist discourses, as the tragic story of "Sister Serife" illustrates. As national myth has it, a young Turkish woman, from a small Black Sea village, helped the war effort by transporting ammunition. Placing her baby girl in an ox-drawn ammunition cart, and covering both with the only blanket she had, Serife froze to death after an all-night journey on foot.

Turkish officers found the crying baby under her mother's dead body the next morning. It is said that the officers handed the orphaned baby to a woman nearby who nursed and raised her. In other versions of the story, a military commander's wife adopted her. It is also possible that the baby—like her mother, and like many children in war zones today—died.

After sacrificing their lives and babies to carry ammunition to the front during the Turkish War of Liberation of 1919–22, in the subsequent phase of nation-building women were expected to replenish the population. Pro-natalism, arose out of the need for labor power in this largely agricultural society, and included a ban on importing contraceptives, free obstetrical care, tax policies favoring larger families, and lower legal age of marriage. Even more telling perhaps, is the fact that certificates and medals were awarded to women who had given birth to six children.

Turkey's pro-natalist policies, together with improvements in agricultural production, health, education, and life expectancy, led to population growth just as "population control" was emerging as a hegemonic idea on the world stage.

from pro-natalism to population control

In the 1950s and 60s, fearing that population growth might destabilize economically "underdeveloped" countries and create a "breeding ground" for communism, powerful states, international organizations and state agencies began to promote anti-natalist state policies around the world. Social scientists and health professionals busily surveyed fertility rates and family planning practices, promoting population control technologies to Third World governments and state agencies. Curtailing women's fertility, they believed, would facilitate industrial development.

As U.S. aid agencies and the U.N. Population Fund—half of whose initial funding came from the United States—promoted population control as a national development strategy in the 1960s, Turkey turned away from pro-natalist policies, lifting the ban on imports of contraceptives, and promoting family planning nationally.

The dominance of the ideal of modernization, which promoted industrialization and Westernization, meant that anti-natalist policies became uncontroversial. Islam, too, had long permitted birth control. A series of Islamic conferences in the 1960s condoned the use of birth control, facilitating the adoption of population control policies in several Muslim-majority countries.

In 1983, when elective abortions within ten weeks of pregnancy were legalized, Turkey joined a number of countries that formally embraced population control as a strategy of industrial development. The law also permitted, for the first time, voluntary sterilization for men and women. Enacted in the last months of military rule, it defined "population planning"—a curious coinage that fuses "population control" and "family planning"—as "individuals having as many children as they want and when they want."

Notably, there were no women at the National Security Council meeting where elective abortions and voluntary sterilizations were debated and legalized. For married women, the law required the husband's consent. Though feminists today protest Erdoğan's suggestion of a ban on abortion, saying that rights that were "won" will not be subject to negotiation, reproductive choice was not in fact "won." Nor was it conceived of as a "woman's right."

internationalizing family values

Erdoğan himself positions himself with conservative forces elsewhere when he says: "In many Western societies there are laws about abortion. And now we are studying these. This has its place within our own values. Abortion cannot be allowed. God forbid, a threat to [the mother's] life and such, those are separate issues."

Framing women's reproductive health and choices as a matter of population and morality, Erdoğan criticizes "the West" for its effort to limit population in Muslim-majority countries, and praises it for upholding a religiously based morality that criminalizes abortion. Dovetailing with a "right to life" discourse during the past two decades, the current Turkish prime minister's anti-abortion stance ignores the gendered nature of bearing and rearing children.

As Doris Buss and Didi Herman show in their book *Globalizing Family Values*, a conservative network championing what it sees as "traditional family" values—against individualism, extramarital sexual relations, homosexuality, and abortion—has been organizing at international conferences on population and women's rights to limit women's right to choose.

In advance of the 1994 U.N. Population Conference in Cairo, the Vatican reportedly reached out to Iran and Libya in search of a joint Catholic-Muslim stance against population control and abortion. As Iranian foreign minister Mohammad Rafsanjani publicly stated, "The future war is between the religious and the materialists.

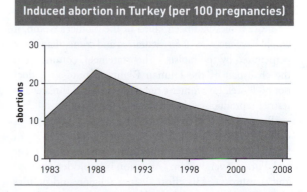

Induced abortion in Turkey (per 100 pregnancies)

Source: Turkish Demographic and Health Survey, 2008

Collaboration between religious governments to outlaw abortion is a fine beginning for the conception of collaboration in other fields."

While theocratic states have at times made appeals on the basis of a universal morality in order to limit abortion, religious traditions have differing views on contraception and abortion. Islam permits contraception; to medieval churchmen, this was one of its sexual "horrors." Similarly, classical Islamic doctrine, while not condoning abortion, is less rigid on the issue.

> *In order to restrict reproductive choice, conservatives will claim that religious-cultural values are expressions of universal moral laws.*

In contrast to the Vatican's flat condemnation of abortion under any circumstances, for Muslims, saving the mother's life has always been a valid reason for abortion. Several Muslim-majority countries also permit abortions in the early stages of the pregnancy in cases of rape and fetal development problems. In Turkey and Tunisia, women may have abortions in the first trimester without having to provide a reason.

Iran, Saudi Arabia, and the Vatican are committed to limiting women's access to reproductive rights. It is unlikely that Turkey, a pioneer in expanding women's political, economic and civil rights in the region, will ban abortion by reference to Islamic law. It is possible, however, that conservatives there will claim that religious-cultural values are expressions of universal moral laws in order to restrict reproductive choice.

denying choice

Today, religious conservatives suggest that universal morality trumps the rights and well-being of individual women. When asked whether women who have been raped must carry a resulting pregnancy to term, Sefer Üstün, a prominent member of Erdoğan's party responded, "of course." Discussing women raped in Bosnia in the 1990s, he said: "If those babies had been killed in the mother's womb, it would have made for a *bigger* drama, and crime, than those perpetrated by the rapists." This statement, coming from the chairman of the Human Rights Commission, does not bode well for women's rights in Turkey. It threatens to restrict reproductive choice on religious grounds.

But what exactly Islam says about abortion is debated. Mehmet Görmez of the Presidency of Religious Affairs (PRA), a peculiar institution in "secular" Turkey, weighed in: "Abortion is forbidden (*haram*) and is murder." His effort to fuse religion and politics glossed over disagreements between the main Islamic schools of thought over exactly when the fetus gains a soul ("ensoulment")—ranging from 40 to 120 days from conception.

Interestingly, recent arguments for stricter interpretations of the Koran have drawn upon science as well as religious doctrine. According to Görmez, "as long as men of science, genetics experts, tell us, based on certain scientific data, that the fertilized egg cell has a heart separate from that of the mother's, that both have separate blood circulation systems, and [the fertilized egg] is connected to the mother only through nutrition, not only [the PRA] but all religions, legal systems, see that abortion is an assault on human life."

Turkey's new reproductive governmentality seeks to discipline women via political institutions and religious traditions dominated by men. In exceptional cases, the director of the PRA has declared, abortion may be permitted by religious scholars, psychiatrists, and forensic doctors. The women whose bodies are subject to expert decision-making have been conspicuous by their absence.

It is unlikely that many people in Turkey will heed Erdoğan's advice to have more children. At the time of this writing, Turkey's government has passed legislation stipulating that Caesarians should be used only in cases of "medical necessity;" in the face of intense protest, it has not legislated further restrictions on abortion.

As feminists protest efforts to ban abortion in Turkey, they do so in a nation where reproductive choice has never really been seen as a woman's right. This most recent reproductive governmentality, which is likely to lead to tens of thousands of unwanted pregnancies, does not bode well for women. By limiting reproductive choice, it compromises women's health and rights.

recommended resources

Boli, John, and Thomas, George M. (eds.). 1999. *Constructing World Culture: International Nongovernmental Organizations since 1875*. Stanford, CA: Stanford University Press. Presents a variety of case studies of the impact of international non-governmental organizations. Includes a chapter by D. Barrett and D. J. Frank that discusses how population control discourse was brought to the Third World in the 1960s.

Buss, Doris, and Hermann, Didi. 2003. *Globalizing Family Values: The Christian Right in International Politics*. Minneapolis: University of Minnesota Press. Documents Christian Right activism at the United Nations, and includes a chapter on its gender agenda and the institutional leadership role of the Vatican.

Hessini, Leila. 2007. "Abortion and Islam: Policies and Practice in the Middle East and North Africa," *Reproductive Health Matters 15*: 75–84. Provides an overview of abortion policy and practice in 21 Muslim-majority countries.

Kürtaj Yasaklanamaz. 2006. "Ethical Evaluation of the Legal Dimension of Abortion in Turkey and the World" by Muhtar Çokar. Provides historical background on abortion policies in Turkey (in Turkish). Kurtaj Yasaklanamaz is a website created in summer of 2012 by feminist activists in response to Erdoğan'scomments. kurtajyasaklanamaz.com/kategori/kaynaklar. Some of its content is available in English at saynoabortionban.com/.

Maguire, C. Daniel (ed.). 2001. *Sacred Choices: The Case for Contraception and Abortion in Ten World Religions*. London: Oxford University Press. Discusses traditions of reproductive choice within major religions. Includes a chapter by Sa'diyya Shaikh on contraception and abortion in Islam.

The Population Studies Institute at Hacettepe University. The 2008 report of the Turkish Demographic and Health Study (TDHS), part of the worldwide DHS Project, is available on the Institute's website hips.hacettepe.edu.tr/yayin.shtml The Institute's mission is to train qualified demographers and contribute to population policymaking and implementation.

birth control, religion, and the social construction of whiteness
nicole bedera
winter 2015

Most people think of access to birth control as a women's issue, but its history is a lot more complicated. Melissa Wilde and Sabrina Danielsen describe the birth control movement's tangled web of race, class, and religious dynamics in the *American Journal of Sociology*. They argue that women's rights were not the central concern in the religious debate over birth control—instead, religious leaders focused on the preservation of Whiteness.

In "Fewer and Better Children: Race, Class, Religion, and Birth Control Reform in America," Wilde and Danielsen categorize the pervasive religious groups of the early 1900s by their attitudes toward contraception and "race suicide"— the eugenicist belief that White Anglo-Saxon Protestants were being outbred by southern and eastern European immigrants. Based on religious articles and sermons, they find a surprising amount of overlap between the two topics. In fact, the American Eugenics Society recruited many religious groups to the cause of legal birth control.

The central debate between outspoken birth control advocates and opponents often came down to whether people in the second-wave European immigrants (specifically Catholics) were considered White. All religious groups seemed to agree that widespread use of birth control would most strongly impact birth rates among the poor, but Christian sects in the North supported birth control to minimize Catholic growth and preserve traditional Whiteness and Protestant dominance. Christian sects in the South opposed birth control in hopes that the immigrant Catholic community would expand and become recognized as White to counteract the growing Black population.

Both sides of the debate left little room for any discussion of women's rights. If anything, the authors find, religious leaders assumed that White members of their own congregations would avoid using contraception in order to reproduce more than ever. Ultimately, the historical religious birth control debate boiled down to an argument over which kind of White supremacy would suit the United States best.

what happened to the "war on women"?

deana a. rohlinger

winter 2015

In 2013, Texas senator Wendy Davis slipped on a pair of pink sneakers and filibustered a bill regulating abortion clinics for 11 hours straight. The bill, which passed amid protests after Davis was removed from the Senate floor, prohibits abortions after 20 weeks, requires abortion providers to have admitting privileges at a local hospital, and regulates abortion clinics as ambulatory surgical centers.

Davis's efforts drew praise and criticism across the country. Supporters of safe and legal abortion cheered her stand and continue to use the Twitter hashtags #SupportWendyDavis and #StandWithWendy to discuss the "war on women" in Texas and elsewhere. Davis's opponents have called her an extremist and, playing on Davis's good looks and blonde hair, labeled her "Abortion Barbie."

In a surprising move, Davis distanced herself from the abortion issue in her recent gubernatorial run. Her website listed education—not battling the "war on women"—as the top issue. And she wasn't the only Democrat who avoided the once-galvanizing phrase in the midterm election cycle. Why? Did the "war on women" end? Not exactly.

2012 was a bad year for the Republican Party in terms of its relationship with women voters. Several Republican candidates made politically unfortunate comments about rape and abortion. Todd Akin (R-MO) infamously explained that women rarely become pregnant from rape because "The female body has ways to try and shut that whole thing down." Richard Mourdock, a Republican U.S. Senate candidate, opined, "I think even

if life begins in that horrible situation of rape, that it is something God intended to happen."

These comments put abortion on the political map. The table on the following page summarizes voters' responses to the survey question, "Do you think the issue of abortion is a critical issue facing the country, one among many important issues, or not that important compared to other issues?" Voter concern over legal abortion spiked during the 2012 election cycle.

Republicans' poor relationship with women voters was evident in the 2012 election outcomes as well. The "gender gap," which refers to the differences in how men and women vote, reached a new high. According to Gallup, President Obama won women's votes by 12 percentage points while Mitt Romney won men's votes by eight. This 20-point gender gap is the largest Gallup has measured since it began tracking presidential voting behavior by subgroup in 1952.

Not surprisingly, the Republican Party made attracting women voters a 2014 priority. Republican strategists recognized that winning women was unlikely, but believed they could narrow the gender gap. The efforts to woo women changed quickly. Republicans launched a campaign to refute the existence of a "war on women" in the developed world. This effort to show women that the GOP cared was combined with a campaign to highlight instances in which the actions of Democrats did not match their "pro-women" rhetoric.

Soon, however, the Republican Party realized there was a popular issue they could use to combat the "war on

"Do you think the issue of abortion is a critical issue facing the country, one among many important issues, or not that important compared to other issues?"

	2009	2011	2012	2013
A critical issue facing the country	15%	30%	31%	18%
One among many important issues	33%	28%	33%	27%
Not that important compared to other issues	48%	39%	35%	53%
Don't know/Refused	3%	3%	2%	2%

From the Pew Research Center for the People & the Press/Pew Forum on Religion & Public Life Religion & Public Life Survey

"Do you support or oppose a recent federal requirement that private health insurance plans cover the full cost of birth control for their female patients?"

	2011	2012	2014
Support	66%	66%	61%
Oppose	24%	26%	32%
Don't Know/Refused	10%	8%	7%

Pew Research Center for the People & the Press/Pew Forum on Religion & Public Life

women" rhetoric directly: birth control. Page 71 summarizes voters' responses to the survey question, "Do you support or oppose a recent federal requirement that private health insurance plans cover the full cost of birth control for their female patients?"

Unlike abortion, birth control is consistently a winning political issue—and one that voters typically associate with the Democratic Party. Republicans aim to change this association. Since July 2014, Republican candidates from Colorado, North Carolina, Minnesota, and Louisiana have all rolled out plans to make oral contraception available over-the-counter.

Beating the drum for over-the-counter birth control has another political purpose, of course. Republicans needed to attract women without alienating their socially conservative base, which opposes abortion and some kinds of birth control, such as intrauterine devices (IUDs). Easy access to the pill, Republicans maintain, balances religious freedom and women's rights because it makes the pill available to women whose employers who do not want to offer contraceptives on religious grounds.

This political rationale satisfied Republican candidates. Even staunch anti-abortion supporters advocated publicly for the pill's availability. In his advertisement,

Colorado Senate candidate Cory Gardner, an uncompromising opponent of legal abortion, said he believed, "The pill ought to be available over the counter, round the clock, without a prescription." Gardner ousted the Democratic incumbent, Mark Udell in November.

Democrats and women's organizations were furious with the Republican Party's rhetorical turn, calling it a cynical ploy to get votes. Cecile Richards, president of Planned Parenthood Federation of America, told NPR, "It really is quite ironic that suddenly now the Republican Party and candidates, after voting repeatedly to take away birth control access for women, are trying to kind of do this before the November elections."

Proponents of women's rights, including advocacy groups like MoveOn.org, have pointed out that making the pill available over-the-counter does not actually resolve the tension between women's rights and religious freedom. IUDs, for instance, are eligible for coverage under the Affordable Care Act. Since some religious denominations argue that life begins at fertilization, they believe that IUDs, which prevent egg implantation, end innocent lives—an argument with which users of IUDs disagree. Progressives also note that making the pill available over-the-counter may actually cost women: most birth control is available with no co-pay under the Affordable Care Act, but would *cost* an individual upwards of $600 a year if purchased outside the insurance system.

Republicans dismiss these claims. They argue Democrats are just angry because they were caught off guard by successful efforts to "defang" the "war on women" rhetoric that had kept female voters leaning Democrat. Kelly Anne Conway, a Republican pollster, told NPR Democrats "think that they've got a monopoly on talking to women from the waist down. Anything that has to do with reproduction and birth control and abortion—they call it, quote, 'women's health' and they call it women's issues."

Thus, the "war on women" became the "war for women voters." A war that Republicans looked poised to win in the November election.

Why? Because Conway's assessment of the Democratic Party is correct. Democrats have depended on "women's issues," and the abortion issue in particular, to mobilize women on election day. Republican candidates made that job a lot easier in 2012. Absent Republican candidates making outlandish claims opposing legal abortion or the existence of rape, the "war on women" rhetoric lost its luster and mobilization potential.

Arguably, the "war on women" line became a political liability for another reason. The mantra, which assumes that women have the right to control their reproductive decisions, was pitted against the ability of individuals (as corporate owners) to exercise their religious freedom by refusing to allow their employer-paid insurance to cover birth control in the Supreme Court's decision *Burwell v. Hobby Lobby*. Choosing what or whose rights take precedence meant that the Democratic Party might alienate some subset of voters and corporate contributors—a losing prospect, electorally speaking.

This new political terrain explains why Democratic candidates like Wendy Davis quietly distanced themselves from the "war on women" rhetoric in the midterm election cycle. Now that the dust from the election has settled, it is clear that Republican Party faces an uphill battle to woo women. Though they lost many seats, Democrats held onto the majority of women voters in 2014. The Pew Research Center reported that the gender gap remained wide in November.

The new Republican strategy could be a winning one in the end. If nothing else, progressives found themselves battling Republicans for the hearts and minds of women voters on what they once considered strictly left-leaning political terrain. The war for women's votes has just begun.

race and contraception
melissa brown
fall 2015

As this summer's American Sociological Association presidential address by Paula England showed, sex, pregnancy, and contraception present a thorny set of problems for sociologists as well as policy makers.

U.S. pregnancy rates among adolescent females ages 15–19 have been declining for more than two decades. Despite this shift, the disparity in pregnancy rates, abortion rates, and unintended pregnancies between Black and White teens remains pronounced: young Black women are more likely to get pregnant, and especially to have unplanned pregnancies. In their recent *Demography* article, sociologists Jennifer Barber, Jennifer Yarger, and Heather Gatny use the new Relationship Dynamics and Social Life study to investigate this disparity. Using a sample of 18- and 19-year-old Black and White women, they analyze pregnancy desires and related attitudes to see why the disparity in unintended pregnancies emerges during the transition to adulthood. Participants completed a survey rating their agreement with statements on expectations and willingness regarding sex, contraception, and pregnancy.

Results show that both groups have very similar levels of desire to become pregnant or prevent a pregnancy. Beyond that, important differences emerged. Black women had more negative attitudes toward sex than Whites (largely associated with their more religious upbringing) but also were less willing to refuse a partner who wants sex. Black women expressed less difficulty accessing birth control than their White peers, but associated it with several negative consequences, including sending distrust signals to their partners. Black women also felt less negatively than White women about the potential impact of pregnancy on their lives, in part because they were more likely to have been raised by single mothers.

As a result of these differences, the authors conclude that Black teens may be less motivated to take the steps necessary to prevent unplanned pregnancies.

the poetry of politics

carole joffe and katha pollitt

spring 2013

In 2011, Katha Pollitt, the longtime columnist at The Nation, *received the American Sociological Association's award for Excellence in the Reporting of Social Issues. One of the country's leading political commentators, Pollitt is the author of seven books, including two volumes of poetry. She is currently writing a book about the abortion conflict in the United States. Carole Joffe is a professor at the Bixby Center for Global Reproductive Health at the University of California, San Francisco and the author of* Dispatches from the Abortion Wars: The Costs of Fanaticism to Doctors, Patients and the Rest of Us. *She regularly blogs on reproductive politics at RHRealitycheck.org,* Huffington Post, *and elsewhere.*

CAROLE JOFFE: Tell us about the pathway that led you to *The Nation*, where you are, as the American Sociological Association (ASA) award statement put it, "a serious gadfly on the social consciousness of the public!"

KATHA POLLITT: Sometimes I feel my career began in the Middle Ages. The other night I was at a book event for about 20 feminist journalists, where I was only one of two people over 40. I was the only one whose career began in paper media and basically stayed there. I started writing book reviews for the *New York Times Book Review* and elsewhere soon after I graduated from college, and, along with my poetry publications, that led me to *The Nation*, where I was the literary editor in the early 1980s. I've stayed there ever since. Before I began my column, I was an associate editor for the front section.

The Nation is a great home for a columnist. I have a great deal of freedom to write whatever I want, to develop my own voice and style, to have fun. At *The Nation* we assume that readers are intelligent and knowledgeable, writers don't have to spell everything out every time they write, as if the reader had just awoken from a coma. I have had fantastic editors who make my column better than it would otherwise be. I should always take their suggestions! The balancing of poetry and political prose is a struggle for me. Poetry tends to lose out.

CJ: Speak about your relationship to sociology and the social sciences in general. In your writings, you make periodic use of social science research that you find relevant—but at the same time, you do not hesitate to criticize academic writing you find irrelevant or inaccessible to the general reader. In particular, what is your overall assessment of academic feminism and how useful this field has been to women in the "real world"?

KP: Academic writing is often turgid and jargon-ridden. Sociology is far from the worst offender! At least sociology, like anthropology, is often about real people the author has often actually spent time with. A great ethnographic work is like a wonderful novel: what is it like to be these people and live under those conditions? How does the world look to them? What has made them what they are? What are the concrete effects of social policy? At the ASA, a man came up to me after my little talk where I had praised sociology and said, "The kind of sociology you like has very little status in the profession. These days it's all about numbers."

All the social sciences seem to have economics envy these days, don't they? Feminist scholarship has revolutionized every field: history, literary studies, biography, psychology, medicine, law, biology, theology, philosophy and sociology too. Of course, not every male scholar realizes that! A lot of them trundle along as if nothing has changed.

Academic feminism has had practical effects. Think of the way Susan Bordo's *Unbearable Weight*, to choose just one example, has shaped the discourse around body image, gender, eating disorders and obesity, or the way Dorothy Roberts' *Killing the Black Body* has complicated discussions of foster care and adoption. Feminist theory—or "theory" as it is often called—seems less illuminating to me, partly because it is divorced from other disciplines and from empirical research. For example, can you really understand why we invaded Iraq by studying the masculinist metaphors used to describe it: penetration, domination, dropping bombs being like playing a video game, etc.? Domestic U.S. politics, the economics of oil, and the foreign policy objectives of the Bush Administration strike me as getting us closer to understanding what went on.

CJ: A consistent theme in your writing is the status of the feminist movement, both in the United States and elsewhere. What is your sense of contemporary feminism and its ability to address the longstanding generational and racial tensions?

KP: I actually think the feminist movement is coming back from the doldrums. Thanks to the Internet, young feminists are finding each other: there are dozens of websites, like Feministing, Feministe, and Jezebel. There's quite a bit of activism, too, especially around sexual violence, reproductive rights, body issues and misogyny in pop culture. Today's young feminism has an edgy, sexy, sarcastic vibe—think of Slutwalk [covered in this issue of *Contexts*]. That tone puts off some older women, and some younger women too, but it also draws in women who thought of feminism as dowdy and pleasure-denying. Of course the Republicans have helped a lot here. When candidates talk about legitimate rape and pregnancy from rape as part of God's plan, when Rush Limbaugh and his ditto heads call women sluts for using birth control, that gets women's attention.

CJ: Another major focus of your writing is abortion, and you have written (brilliantly, in my view) about the abortion rights movement, the anti-abortion movement and the predicament of abortion providers and patients alike. What have you tried to accomplish in your new book on the topic?

KP: I think the pro-choice movement has been much too defensive for too long. We talk endlessly about the hard cases—rape, incest, life and health of the mother—and it's important to remind people about them, because

anti-choicers want to ban those abortions too. At the same time, those represent maybe 10 percent of the more than 1 million abortions that take place every year. My thesis in a nutshell: we need to talk about abortion as a normal part of reproductive life, and access to it as a positive social good. It's a good thing that women don't drop out of school or work because a condom broke or they forgot their pill; that they plan and time their pregnancies; that they stop having kids when they've had as many as they feel they can raise well. It's outrageous that women are expected to be at the mercy of a stray sperm.

Similarly, we need to complicate the way we talk about the abortion decision. Sometimes it's difficult, sure, but a lot of the time it's simple. Women shouldn't be made to feel guilty if they don't agonize over whether they should have a baby just because they happened to get pregnant.

CJ: Give us your reflections on the 2012 elections, especially with respect to the issues that most preoccupy you in your writing, such as reproductive politics, and the "war on women" more generally. Do you agree with those writers, such as Maureen Dowd, who, in response to the Democratic victories, have proclaimed that "the cultural wars are over"?

KP: Don't you hate it that what we call "the culture wars" is actually a struggle over social justice, civil rights and civil liberties? It's like the way news about breast cancer or domestic violence goes in the "style" section, just because it's about women. Birth control is not some frill. It is as much health care as any other medicine or medical device—a lot more important than some of them! Abortion rights and access are totally bound up with women's equality, including women's economic equality, which is not a cultural issue. Gay marriage is about equality for sexual minorities, about social inclusion, and about redefining marriage away from the old patriarchal/religious model. What music to play at the gay wedding—that's a cultural issue.

The 2012 election was a real rebuke to the Tea Party ultra-right and to the flagrant misogyny of the Republican "war on women." But let's not go overboard: Claire McCaskill [of Missouri] might well have lost to a more circumspect anti-choice right-winger than Todd "legitimate rape" Akin; she might even have lost had he not made that much-publicized unfortunate remark. The same was true in conservative Indiana, where a Democrat given little chance of winning took the senate seat after Republican Richard Mourdock said pregnancy from rape was part of God's plan. For the presidential contest, the gender gap was the biggest ever. But let's not forget Republicans still control the House and enough

Senate seats to filibuster and otherwise block much legislation. Just the other day Senate Republicans, led by Rick Santorum, blocked confirmation of the UN treaty on disability rights on the nonsensical grounds that it might someday prevent home schooling.

On abortion rights, as you recently wrote [see huffingtonpost.com/carole-joffe/culture-wars_b_2121578.html], much of the action is in the states. Anti-choicers have done a very good job of making abortion hard to get in much of the South and Midwest: in five states there is only one abortion clinic. Republicans did well at the state level in 2012. They now control 24 state legislatures and 30 governorships. Where they control both, they can really go to town.

In the long run, I think liberal social policies will win. Young people are less racist, less religious, more gay-tolerant, and even, according to some polls, more pro-choice—although not as much as you would expect, given that it is mostly young women who have abortions and young men who impregnate them. The country is becoming more diverse: a party that caters to older White Christian men and their wives may do fine in Wyoming, but it's going to be shut out of national power. Of course the Republicans know that—they are having battle royales behind the scenes as they try to figure out how they let victory slip from their grasp in 2012. They will surely try to jigger their image and modify their policies around the edges to appeal to Latinos, single women, young people and that famous 47 percent of the nation that relies on government programs to survive. Not Black people though—I think they've given up on them. The problem is, the Republican base—rightwing evangelicals and fundamentalists, anti-choicers, extreme right-wingers, and xenophobes—may not let them move in a more centrist direction.

CJ: Finally, can you speak about the range of reactions you get from readers? As was evident from your appearances in two sessions at the ASA, you clearly have a very devoted group of followers—one might even say "groupies"—but obviously not all your mail is positive. In one of your books, you mention the amount of negative responses you got to an essay in which you explained your hesitation to fly the American flag after 9/11. What else has provoked your readers besides that essay?

KP: It's very sad. These days I don't get a lot of hate mail. What am I doing wrong?

family portraits

overview

What do real families look like? The articles in this section suggest that many families are not the ones we're accustomed to seeing in popular culture, whether it's popular television shows *Leave It to Beaver* or *Modern Family*. For instance, whose doing most of the work these days?

Despite the fact that in 2008 seven out of every ten mothers were employed, mothers are still faced with what Arlie Hochschild defined as a "second shift" when they come home. Expectations for mothers' "second shift" in large part include cooking fresh and healthy meals for their families. Sarah Bowen, Sinikka Elliott, and Joslyn Brenton expose this cultural expectation in their article "The Joy of Cooking?"

Food and sharing a meal is not only a central tenet to the family dynamic it is also an important way that interracial and international families negotiate cultural differences. Grace M. Cho, writes about her own experience with the delicate and complicated intersections of food, family, and militarism in her article "Eating Military Base Stew."

Sinikka Elliott and Megan Reid explore the notion of the superstrong Black mother. As a cultural stereotype and a double standard for Black mothers across America, these women must be strong and protective of their children while at the same time protecting herself and her children from institutional racism.

For families, specifically single mothers across America the "second shift" has become a third, fourth, or fifth shift to adequately sustain their family. The complications that come from working multiple low-paying and/or part-time jobs while maintaining a growing family is explored by Lisa Dodson and Wendy Luttrell in their article "Families Facing Untenable Choices."

A growing trend across the U.S. is the presence of stay-at-home fathers (SAHF). Nazneen Kane finds that among this growing contingent of SAHF, some of whom are electing to stay home and raise their children while others do so due to unemployment, men still face negativity due to social stigmas surrounding masculinity and employment status.

things to consider

- Think about how often you had a sit-down dinner with your family unit growing up. What did the act of sharing a meal offer you and your family? What other ritual activities contribute to the experience of family?
- If you could take a family portrait of your blood and/or chosen family, whom would you include and why? What would the backdrop be, and would any family members be holding certain objects or performing different tasks?
- How do you define family in your life?

the joy of cooking?

sarah bowen, sinikka elliott, and joslyn brenton

summer 2014

It's a hot, sticky Fourth of July in North Carolina, and Leanne, a married working-class Black mother of three, is in her cramped kitchen. She's been cooking for several hours, lovingly preparing potato salad, beef ribs, chicken legs, and collards for her family. Abruptly, her mother decides to leave before eating anything. "But you haven't eaten," Leanne says. "You know I prefer my own potato salad," says her mom. She takes a plateful to go anyway.

Her 7-year-old son takes medication for ADHD and often isn't hungry until it wears off, usually right before bedtime. Leanne's 1-year-old daughter gets fussy when her mom cooks, and looks for attention. Her husband doesn't offer much help; his contribution involves pouring barbecue sauce on the ribs, which Leanne calls "working his magic." Leanne wipes her brow and mutters to herself about the $80 she spent on ingredients. By the time she's finished cooking, she says, "I don't want to eat!"

In the fight to combat rising obesity rates, modern-day food gurus advocate a return to the kitchen. Michael Pollan, author of *Cooked*, and America's most influential "foodie-intellectual," tells us that the path to reforming the food system "passes right through the kitchen." *New York Times'* food columnist Mark Bittman agrees, saying the goal should be "to get people to see cooking as a joy rather than a burden." Magazines such as *Good Housekeeping* and television personalities like Rachael Ray offer practical cooking advice to get Americans into the kitchen, publishing recipes for 30-minute meals and meals that can be made in the slow-cooker. First lady Michelle Obama has also been influential in popularizing public health messages that emphasize the role that mothers play when it comes to helping children make healthy choices.

The message that good parents—and in particular, good mothers—cook for their families dovetails with increasingly intensive and unrealistic standards of "good" mothering. According to the sociologist Sharon Hays, to be a good mom today, a woman must demonstrate intense devotion to her children. One could say that home-cooked meals have become the hallmark of good mothering, stable families, and the ideal of the healthy, productive citizen.

Yet in reality, home-cooked meals rarely look this good. Leanne, for example, who held down a minimum-wage job while taking classes for an associate's degree, often spent her valuable time preparing meals, only to be rewarded with family members' complaints—or disinterest. Our extensive observations and interviews with mothers like Leanne reveal something that often gets overlooked: cooking is fraught.

feeding the family

Over the past year and a half, our research team conducted in-depth interviews with 150 Black, White, and Latina mothers from all walks of life. We also spent over 250 hours conducting ethnographic observations with

> *Cooking is at times joyful, but it is also filled with time pressures, tradeoffs designed to save money, and the burden of pleasing others.*

12 working-class and poor families. We observed them in their homes as they prepared and ate meals, and tagged along on trips to the grocery store and to their children's check-ups. Sitting around the kitchen table and getting a feel for these women's lives, we came to appreciate the complexities involved in feeding a family.

While Pollan and others wax nostalgic about a time when people grew their own food and sat around the dinner table eating it, they fail to see all of the invisible labor that goes into planning, making, and coordinating family meals. Cooking is at times joyful, but it is also filled with time pressures, tradeoffs designed to save money, and the burden of pleasing others.

Wanda and her husband Marquan, working-class Black parents of two young girls, were constantly pressed for time. Both were employed by the same fast food chain, but in different rural locations 45 minutes apart. They depended on Wanda's mother, who lived 30 minutes away, for childcare. During the five weeks we spent with them, their car was broken down and since they did not have enough money to repair it, they relied on a complex network of friends and family members for rides. Their lives were further complicated by the fact that they didn't know their weekly schedules—what hours, shifts, or even days they would be working—until they were posted, sometimes only the night before. Once they learned their shifts, they scrambled to figure out transportation and childcare arrangements.

> *While some wax nostalgic about a time when people grew their own food and sat around the dinner table eating it, they fail to see the invisible labor that goes into family meals.*

Wanda liked her job, but her unpredictable schedule made it difficult to cook regular meals the way she wanted to. This time dilemma was also hard for Leanne, who worked for the same fast food corporation as Wanda and Marquan, but in an urban area that lacked reliable public transportation. Sometimes, Leanne would take a taxi to work only to find out that business was slow and she was not needed. At other times, she was asked to work late. Because of this, Leanne and her family had no set meal time: cooking and eating were often catch-as-catch-can.

Wanda and Leanne's situation is increasingly common. As real wages have stagnated, many households depend on every adult family member working, sometimes in multiple jobs and jobs with nonstandard and unpredictable hours, to make ends meet. Since the 1960s, working women have cut back on household tasks, including cooking and cleaning, according to sociologist Liana Sayer. Even so, balancing paid work and unpaid work at home, women today have less free time than they did a generation ago; and, in line with heightened expectations of motherhood, they now report spending more time engaged in childcare than did mothers in the 1960s. It's not surprising that they struggle to find time to cook.

And, of course, cooking isn't just about the time it takes to prepare the meal. It also involves planning ahead to be sure the ingredients are on hand, and it means cleaning up afterwards. Samantha, a single White mother of three, was blunt when we asked her if she liked cooking. "Not really," she said. "I just hate the kitchen . . . having to come up with a meal and put it together. I know I can cook but it's the planning of the meal, and seeing if they're going to like it, and the mess that you make. And then the mess afterwards . . . If it was up to me, I wouldn't cook."

Though the mothers we met were squeezed for time, they were still expected to produce elaborate meals cooked from scratch. Even the middle-class women we talked with, who enjoyed regular work hours and typically shared the household work with a partner, said they lacked the time to cook the way they felt they should. Most got home from work around six o'clock, and then attempted to cook meals from scratch (as the experts advise) while their children clamored for their attention.

between time and money

Greely, a married middle-class White mother of one child, had recently started her own catering company. She was working long hours during the week to get her business off the ground, and reasoned that taking time on the weekend to prep vegetables and lunches would help her create ideal meals. She explained, "I feel [that] when I have the time I enjoy cooking. And when it's so compressed and after a stressful day, it's kind of horrible. I feel like, because I'm not able to spend as much time with Adelle now, I don't want to spend an hour cooking after I pick her up from school every day. You know, like it's fine sometimes, but I want to be able to sit down and help her with her homework or help her finish her Valentines for her classmates or whatever that may be. I was supposed to soak black-eyed peas last night and I forgot."

The mothers we met who were barely paying the bills routinely cooked—contrary to the stereotype that poor families mainly eat fast food—because it was more economical. Isis, a poor single Black mother, told us that she got tired of cooking, but continued to do so to save money. "If I don't cook then they'll go get something out to eat," she said. "But then that's wasting money."

Yet being poor makes it nearly impossible to enact the foodie version of a home-cooked meal. The ingredients that go into meals considered to be healthy—fresh fruits and vegetables, whole grains, and lean meats—are expensive. A recent study of food prices around the globe found that it costs $1.50 more per day—or about $550 a year per person—to eat a healthier diet than a less healthy diet.

The cost of healthy ingredients is not the only barrier. Many of the poor mothers we met also lacked reliable transportation, and therefore typically shopped just once a month. As a result, they avoided buying fresh produce, which spoiled quickly. Mothers also struggled to prepare meals in small trailers or apartments with minimal space. We observed homes without kitchen tables or functional appliances, infested by bugs and rats, and lacking basic kitchen tools like sharp knives, cutting boards, pots and pans.

The idea that home cooking is inherently ideal reflects an elite foodie standpoint. Romantic depictions of cooking assume that everyone has a home, that family members are home eating at the same time, and that kitchens and dining spaces are equipped and safe. This is not necessarily the case for the families we met.

During the month we spent with Flora, a poor Black mother who was currently separated from her husband, she was living with her daughter and two grandchildren in a cockroach- and flea-infested hotel room with two double beds. They prepared all of their food in a small microwave, rinsing their utensils in the bathroom sink. Many of the families we met lived in trailers or homes with thin walls that provided little protection from the outside elements. Some homes had holes in the floor or walls, making it nearly impossible to keep pests out. Claudia, a married Latina mother of four, was battling a serious ant invasion in her home. She watched in horror as the ant poison her 12-year-old son was scattering around the trailer's perimeter drifted through an open window and settled on the food she was preparing at the kitchen counter.

Still mothers felt responsible for preparing healthy meals for their children and keenly experienced the gap between the romanticized version of cooking and the realities of their lives. When asked what an "ideal world" would look like for her, Ruth, a widowed Black mother of two, said she would like to have a bigger house that included a "bigger stove, and kitchen, and refrigerator so I can cook a little more and do what I need to do to cook healthier. Give me the money to provide for them a little healthier." With more money and space, Ruth could cook the elaborate meals she loves.

To our surprise, many of the middle-class mothers we met also told us that money was a barrier to preparing healthy meals. Even though they often had household incomes of more than $100,000 a year, their membership in the middle-class was costly. While they did not experience food shortages, they were forced to make tradeoffs in order to save money—like buying less healthy processed food, or fewer organic items than they would like. For low-income mothers, the tradeoffs are starker: they skipped meals, or spent long hours in line at food pantries or applying for assistance, to make sure their children had enough to eat.

food fights

"I don't need it. I don't want it. I never had it," exclaimed 4-year-old Rashan when his mom served him an unfamiliar side dish. Rashan's reaction was not uncommon. We rarely observed a meal in which at least one family member didn't complain about the food they were served. Some mothers coaxed their children to eat by playing elaborate games or by hand-feeding them. One middle-class mother even set a timer, telling her son that he had to eat as much of what was on his plate as he could before the time ran out. Feeding others involves taking multiple preferences into consideration, and balancing time and money constraints.

Rather than risk trying new and expensive foods that might prove unpopular, many low-income mothers opted to cook the same foods again and again. They reasoned that it was better to stick with foods (often processed) that they knew their families would eat, rather than risk wasting money and food.

Giselle, a single Black mother of two, worked two part-time jobs to make ends meet. There was little room in the food budget to experiment with new or expensive foods. When it came to decide what to make for supper, Giselle played it safe. She explained, "Because I don't want to cook something [they won't like] because I'll like waste the food. Right? Waste the food."

Low-income mothers tended to avoid using recipes, because the ingredients were expensive and they weren't sure if their families would like the new dishes. Instead, they continued to make what was tried and true, even if they didn't like the food themselves. Sandy, a White mother of two, tried hard to cook around her boyfriend's preferences. She liked fish, but her boyfriend didn't. So she ignored her food interests in order to "do something for my whole house." Sociologist Marjorie DeVault also found in her book *Feeding the Family* that women considered men's needs, sometimes above all others, when it came to preparing meals.

> *Being poor makes it nearly impossible to enact the foodie version of a home-cooked meal.*

For middle-class mothers, cooking was about more than negotiating preferences for certain foods. They felt that offering new foods was crucial for developing their kids' palates—even if the process sometimes led to food fights. Their stories suggest that cooking like Pollan and other experts prescribe is time-consuming and stressful. Some spent significant amounts of time reading the literature on the latest and best healthy foods, seeking out and trading new healthy recipes, and reworking the food budget to include more organic food—leading to greater anxiety about cooking and serving food.

For Elaine, a married White mother of one child, cooking involved high stakes. She and her husband worked full-time, and Elaine's efforts to make meals from scratch rarely ended happily. She spent time prepping food on the weekends in order to cook ideal meals during the week. She explained, "When we get home it's such a rush. I just don't know what happens to the time. I am so frustrated. That's why I get so angry! I get frustrated 'cause I'm like, I wanna make this good meal that's really healthy and I like to cook 'cause it's kind of my way to show them that I love them, 'This is my love for you guys!' And then I wind up at the end just, you know, grrr! Mad at the food because it takes me so long. It's like, how can it take an hour for me to do this when I've already cut up the carrots and the celery and all I'm doing is shoving it into a bowl?"

Even the extensive prep work that Elaine did on the weekends didn't translate into a relaxing meal during the weekday. Instead, like so many mothers, Elaine felt frustrated and inadequate about not living up to the ideal home-cooked meal. Their stories suggest that utopian family meals are nearly impossible to create, no matter how hard mothers try.

thinking outside the kitchen

The vision of the family meal that today's food experts are whipping up is alluring. Most people would agree that it would be nice to slow down, eat healthfully, and enjoy a home-cooked meal. However, our research leads us to question why the frontline in reforming the food system has to be in someone's kitchen. The emphasis on home cooking ignores the time pressures, financial constraints, and feeding challenges that shape the family meal. Yet this is the widely promoted standard to which all mothers are held. Our conversations with mothers of young children show us that this emerging standard is a tasty illusion, one that is moralistic, and rather elitist, instead of a realistic vision of cooking today. Intentionally or not, it places the burden of a healthy home-cooked meal on women.

So let's move this conversation out of the kitchen, and brainstorm more creative solutions for sharing the work of feeding families. How about a revival of monthly town suppers, or healthy food trucks? Or perhaps we should rethink how we do meals in schools and workplaces, making lunch an opportunity for savoring and sharing food. Could schools offer to-go meals that families could easily heat up on busy weeknights? Without creative solutions like these, suggesting that we return to the kitchen en masse will do little more than increase the burden so many women already bear.

recommended resources

Alkon, Alison, Block, Daniel, Moore, Kelly, Gillis, Catherine, DiNuccio, Nicole, and Chavez, Noel. 2013. "Foodways of the Urban Poor," *Geoforum 48*: 126–135. Argues that cost, not lack of knowledge or physical distance to food stores, is the primary barrier to healthy food access, and that low-income people employ a wide variety of strategies to obtain the foods they prefer at prices they can afford.

Cairns, Kate, Johnston, Josée, and MacKendrick, Norah. 2013. "Feeding the 'Organic Child': Mothering Through Ethical Consumption," *Journal of Consumer Culture 13*: 97–118. These authors coin the term "organic child," and find that middle-class mothers preserve the purity and safety of their children through the purchase of organic foods.

DeVault, Marjorie. 1991. *Feeding the Family: The Social Organization of Caring as Gendered Work*. Chicago, IL: University of Chicago Press. Argues that cooking (and "food work" more generally) is a form of care work that helps to maintain class and gender divisions.

Guthman, Julie. 2007. "Can't Stomach It: How Michael Pollan et al. Made Me Want to Eat Cheetos," *Gastronomica 7*(2): 75–79. Critiques proponents of the local food movement for reinforcing apolitical and elite values, while offering no suggestions for how to change the food system in an inclusive way.

Hays, Sharon. 1996. *The Cultural Contradictions of Motherhood*. New Hewaven, CT: Yale University Press. An important book on the expectations modern mothers face to spend intensive amounts of time and energy raising their children.

Sayer, Liana. 2005. "Gender, Time, and Inequality: Trends in Women's and Men's Paid Work, Unpaid Work, and Free Time," *Social Forces 84*: 285–303. Uses nationally representative time use data from 1965, 1975, and 1998 to analyze trends and gender differences in time use.

eating military base stew

grace m. cho

summer 2014

Today, a stew called *budae jjigae*, **a spicy hodgepodge of Korean vegetables and American processed meats that translates literally as "military base stew," has become a mainstay at restaurants in Korea and is especially popular in college neighborhoods among young people who have little cultural memory of the stew's dark past. It is the only dish in the Korean culinary lexicon to name its origins so explicitly—as a product of a foreign military intervention and the collision of two cultures.**

The story of the origins of *budae jjigae* (also spelled *boodae chigae*) that circulates in Korean American communities begins during the Korean War, when most Koreans were starving. Word spread that American soldiers stationed there had an endless supply of food, with portions so big that they could afford to throw food away. The bases became destinations for hungry Koreans, who scavenged or purchased the remnants. As some survivors recalled, this food was not exactly palatable; it was often a mélange of various food scraps mixed with inedible things, such as cigarette butts. They recalled that though the food was sometimes disgusting, it kept them alive. Some people would sort through the scraps and find a perfectly intact pink slab of jellied ham and put it in a stew. What the Americans didn't finish, Koreans used to make the first iterations of budae jjigae.

I first came to know budae jjigae as a kind of cultural icon circulating among Korean diasporic artists in the United States, who regarded it as both a culinary travesty and an iconic symbol of U.S. imperialism. I listened to the oral histories of Korean War survivors living in the United States, who spoke about the days during and after the war when they sought food outside U.S. Army bases. They recalled waiting in long lines outside the mess halls to buy bags of "leftovers," though some of them referred to the bags plainly as "garbage." They'd say things like, "Americans have the best food and throw it away, and then Koreans buy that garbage," their voices filled with humiliation, resentment, and gratitude all at once.

The stew had long been the stuff of my nightmares. A stew gone wrong. A stew so laden with Spam, hotdogs, American cheese and other "food products" that it had become a perversion of Korean cuisine, indeed, a perversion of real food. Since it represented both the U.S. military occupation of Korea, and my own hidden past, I never thought I could bring myself to eat it. It was only later that I came to reconcile with that past enough to try budae jjigae, and doing so revealed new layers of what it means to be Korean American.

a stew of family memories

There was a time in my life when I knew almost nothing about my family history. I grew up in the rural Pacific Northwest with a Korean mother and American father, in my father's hometown. Although small town life was conducive to gossip, and my family was often the subject

321

of such talk, I never thought to question my own origins. I never thought to ask the kinds of questions my neighbors asked about how my parents met and whether or not my father was my "real" father. It wasn't until I was in graduate school that I began to interrogate the circumstances of my life, and that was also when I began to understand the mechanisms of silence that operated in my family about my family history, my mother's experience in Korea, and the violent relationship between the United States and Korea that made up the societal context in which my parents met.

As an adult I learned that my mother had worked at a bar at a U.S. naval base, and that her line of work was so unsavory to "normal" Koreans that she was considered a "Yankee whore" and shunned from Korean society.

> **Budae jjigae is a cultural icon, culinary travesty, and symbol of U.S. imperialism.**

But what I remember of my childhood is that my mother strived to be "normal" again in this little xenophobic town where I grew up, and before she became mentally ill, she was somewhat successful in that endeavor. She prided herself on her domestic skills, and cooking well was important to her. She mastered the kind of American cooking my father and his relatives expected and maintained a decent repertoire of Korean dishes for her own enjoyment. Budae jjigae was not part of that repertoire.

Although I grew up eating my mother's Korean cooking and spent some time living among my mother's relatives, I had never heard of budae jjigae until I began working with other diasporic Korean artists and writers. Maybe because my mother once worked at a military base, it was too close to home, or maybe, as part of the earliest wave of Korean immigrants to the United States, my mother had internalized an American view of Spam as a poor person's meat. My guess is that she wanted to dissociate from the meat's stigmas, both Korean and American, so Spam never once made its way into our house.

Hotdogs, on the other hand, with their cultural cachet as an all-American food, were one of my mother's

> **The stew represents both the U.S. military occupation of Korea, and my own hidden past, and I never thought I could bring myself to eat it.**

favorite things to add to rice or noodles. Her version of a quick meal was ramen noodle soup with ketchup, scallions and sliced hotdogs. If one considers the basic components of budae jjigae—broth, noodles, Korean vegetables, American processed meat and other food products—I realize now that this was my mother's

simplified rendition of budae jjigae, using the ingredients that were available in a rural American town with a Korean population of three. At the time, however, I had no awareness of budae jjigae and its complex meanings—and my mother did not encourage such awareness. She merely called it "*ramyeon* with hotdogs."

a dangerous dish

During the postwar era, budae jjigae transcended its association with mess hall trash and became a fixture of Korean cuisine. Koreans were still reeling from the aftermath of a war that left 10 percent of the civilian population dead and civilian life in ruins, and meat continued to be scarce. The most coveted items from U.S. military bases were Spam, hotdogs, and ham—meats that would not spoil quickly and whose saltiness complemented other Korean foods. These meats became the ideal protein base for a stew.

The fact that American products were not legally available to Koreans meant that a thriving black market for American foods developed between the "post exchange" (PX), or retail stores for American soldiers and Korean society that surrounded them. A November 9, 1959 *Time* article titled "The PX Affair," implied that "Korean girls" who had access to the PX through their associations with American soldiers—husbands, boyfriends, or johns—were largely responsible for this illegal trade.

Demand for processed meats soared as political battles over PX privileges broke out between the U.S. Army and the South Korean government. A few years later, *Time* reported on the crackdown on black market trading under the Pak Chung-Hee dictatorship, when Spam smuggling became an offense punishable by death. It gave an element of intrigue to the dish whose main ingredients one could only acquire illegally.

One night over burgers and beer, I met two friends in Brooklyn who had grown up in South Korea during the 1970s and '80s to speak with them about the black market for American goods. Both of them had vivid childhood memories of Spam smuggling. One friend spoke of a smuggler who made clandestine deliveries to her mother before the days when Spam was available in stores. The other friend's mother was a smuggler herself. She'd go to the base and meet with "a woman in heavy makeup" and return with bags full of American food products, which she then resold in Busan's wealthiest neighborhoods.

Listening to them speak, I realized that my own mother could have been one of the suppliers for the illegal distribution of Spam. Though she never admitted as much, my mother was "a woman in heavy makeup" and one of those Korean girls who had PX privileges, by virtue of being married to my American father. When I went back to Korea in 2002, my mother asked me to take a suitcase full of Hershey's chocolate to my relatives, but fretted endlessly that I would "get into big trouble" for carrying such large quantities of American products. "They'll think you're going to sell it on the black market," she admonished. I told her there was no longer a black market for things like that, and a lot had changed since the '70s. I imagine that she had had a few run-ins with the military police. The black market for Spam and other American products continued to be a dangerous business until 1987 when South Korea's pro-democracy movement finally prevailed.

camp stew

When I toured Korea with a group of Korean American activists in 2007, we visited members of the "ban-mi," or anti-U.S. base movement, who are concerned about the long-term impact of U.S. military presence on South Korean society. The site of the former town, whose name means "Great Harvest Village," in a reference to the rice it once produced, is now called Camp Humphreys. At the gate drawing the line of demarcation between Korea and the United States there were daily protests against the expansion of the base. Members of a labor union sat in front of the gate in ponchos chanting for U.S. troop withdrawal. Camp Humphreys' expansion plans spanned 60 years into the future, and the daily gatherings at the border not only opposed the violence done to the surrounding communities, but also the fact that U.S. presence in Korea had become so unabashedly permanent.

In 2003, the U.S. Army, in a document called the Global Posture Review, justified this permanent presence, not to defend South Korea, but to further U.S. military "strategic flexibility" and extend its reach into China. The newly appropriated piece of American territory was not so easily won, however. The daily protests outside Camp Humphreys continued a struggle that began between farmers and the military in 2005 when the Republic of Korea (ROK) government approved the U.S.'s planned seizure of the surrounding villages of Daechuri and Doduri.

As anti-U.S. activists joined forces with the farmers, a series of violent clashes between civilians and riot police broke out. Although a few of the farmers withdrew before the battle ended, most of them stayed to fight. The farmers' refusal to give up their ancestral lands culminated in a full-scale military operation, in which a battalion of 14,000 armed riot police, military paratroopers, and private security forces were deployed to squash the protests, demolish the villages, and eject the farmers from their homes. In the end, only one-third of Doduri remained, while all of Daechuri was subsumed by the base expansion.

Outside Camp Humphreys, the boundary between Korea and the United States, erected in 2006, still bore traces of this violence: there were irrigation ditches filled with cement, spaces made empty by the force of bulldozers, and barbed wire around overgrown rice fields. And in the nearby city of Pyeongtaek, many elders had taken jobs picking up trash from city streets and were living in leftover U.S. military housing. In front of the apartment complex was a sign out of time and place that read "Daechuri"—a town that no longer exists.

The grandmothers fed us a meal that was kind of an "anti" budae jjigae: bowls of local rice they had grown themselves and traditional side dishes, devoid of American influences. It was a last meal of sorts. The Great Harvest rice, like the village that was its namesake, would soon disappear, too.

the first taste

Thirty years after I first tasted my mother's rudimentary version of it, I finally tasted military base stew. The day after our visit with the displaced elders of Daechuri, we went to Uijeongbu, where budae jjigae is a local specialty. In Uijeongbu, like most Korean cities surrounding U.S. military bases, the boundary between the base and the town is porous, with the effects of militarism spilling into everyday life. This community was still recovering from the deaths of two junior high school girls who had been run over by a U.S. military tank a few years earlier, while they were on their way to a friend's birthday party. Violence against women and girls was nothing out of the ordinary in areas near the bases, though most incidents were not nearly as dramatic nor were their victims as innocent, thus rendering the violence part of the invisible fabric of life in Uijeongbu.

> *For me, no other dish provoked such ambivalent feelings, and was so layered with meaning.*

We toured the area immediately surrounding Camp Stanley, which is home to a myriad of bars and brothels that cater to American servicemen. There was little to see in the daytime except for closed storefronts and flyers stapled to telephone poles advertising club jobs for foreign entertainers.

Since the early camptown life of the 1950s, over a million Korean women have sold their sexual labor to Americans. Today the militarized sex industry in Korea is populated by a new generation of women, mostly

Filipina and Russian migrants, alongside an older generation of Korean women who are neither able to make a living inside the camptown nor to return to life outside of it. Historically, the corps of military sex workers were women already marginalized in one way or another—as those who were escaping poverty, abusive families, or the stigma of having become "fallen" women, while others were performing their filial duty as income earners to support their brothers' educations. This commercialized sexual relationship between Korean women and American men also formed one of the most important yet least known conditions of possibility for Korean migration to the United States.

We walked up the hill through winding roads, to a restaurant that served both American servicemen and camptown workers, having witnessed the literal and symbolic violence of U.S. military presence in Korea. The program coordinator ordered a family-size pot of budae jjigae.

"Really?" I asked, trying to gauge the level of irony in his gesture.

"Haven't you ever tried budae jjigae before? It's delicious," he said with a big grin.

It was in fact my first direct and conscious experience of budae jjigae.

There was a Korean woman there, a former sex worker who had aged out of the profession and had little possibility of reintegrating into "normal" Korean society, so she became an *ajumma* who did odd jobs in camptown establishments such as this one. She brought out a bubbling pot of clear noodles, cabbage, onion, scallions, mushrooms, chrysanthemum leaves, hot dogs and Spam, in a spicy *gochu-jang* broth, topped off with a few slices of American cheese that somehow retained their shape through the scalding heat. She sat down with us for a moment and I studied her slightly distant countenance and verbal quirks, and wondered if she, like my mother, was mentally ill. I thought of my mother and wondered what would have become of her—of us—had she not married my father and moved to the United States. I wondered what budae jjigae meant to the people of Uijeongbu, who claimed the dish as part of their regional culinary identity, yet resented the U.S. military for the collateral damage done to their community.

Budae jjigae symbolizes many things. It is a reminder of a brutal "Forgotten War" that has not yet ended. It represents the creativity that emerged from devastation, a legacy of the complicated relationship between Koreans and Americans. Indeed, it is a culinary metaphor for my own personal history. I could think of no other dish that provoked such ambivalent feelings, no other dish as layered with meaning. I tasted the stew. It was flavorful and satisfying, and oddly comforting. There was nothing to do for the moment but eat.

recommended resources

Hohn, Maria, and Moon, Seungsook (eds.). 2010. *Over There: Living with the U.S. Military Empire from World War Two to the Present.* Durham, NC: Duke University Press. Provides a historical analysis of American military base relations with local communities in South Korea, Japan and Germany, paying close attention to issues of gender.

Ku, Robert Ji-Song, Manalansan, Martin, and Mannur, Anita (eds.). 2013. *Eating Asian America: A Food Studies Reader.* New York: New York University Press. Examines the meanings of Asian American foods and foodways for Asian American identities, paying particular attention to social inequality and U.S. imperialism.

Lutz, Catherine (ed.). 2009. *Bases of Empire: The Global Struggle against U.S. Military Posts.* New York: New York University Press. Provides a comprehensive overview of the impact of U.S. bases around the world and local responses to them.

Moon, Katharine. 1997. *Sex Among Allies: Military Prostitution in U.S.- Korea Relations.* New York: Columbia University Press. The first study to examine the institution of militarized prostitution in South Korea and its influence on the geopolitical relationship between the United States and South Korea.

Yuh, Jiyeon. 2004. *Beyond the Shadow of Camptown: Military Brides in America.* New York: New York University Press. An oral history-based study of the experiences of Korean women married to American servicemen, including an analysis of the ways in which the struggle to maintain Korean foodways symbolizes an unequal U.S.-Korea relationship.

the superstrong black mother

sinikka elliott and megan reid

winter 2016

Baltimore mother Toya Graham became a viral video sensation after being filmed yelling at and hitting her teen son. Graham, who is Black, was trying to stop her son from joining the protests following Freddie Gray's death in police custody in Baltimore in April 2015. Dubbed "mother of the year," news outlets applauded Graham for her fierce determination to keep her son out of harm's way by any means necessary. The media and ensuing public response to the video are illuminating for what they say about cultural notions of Black motherhood: the good Black mom should be superstrong to protect her children, but she is also responsible for controlling her children and preventing them from getting into trouble. In celebrating Graham, the media was implicitly condemning all the other mothers whose children participated in the protests—that is, the mothers who did not prevent their children from "senseless" rioting against institutional racism in policing.

According to the social theorist Patricia Hill Collins, the superstrong Black mom has long been a stereotypical image of Black mothers. Initially emerging from Black communities' valorization of Black mothers' intensive efforts to raise their children and shield them from the dangers of living with racism and poverty, the superstrong Black mother image now dictates the terms of good mothering for Black women: be strong and be solely responsible. The modern emphasis on individual responsibility as a solution to structural problems reinforces this idea. This context presents extraordinary challenges for Black mothers as they attempt to protect their children from the dangers of institutionalized racism. The nearly 50 low-income urban Black mothers of teenagers we interviewed in North Carolina and New York described the multiple strategies they use to insulate their children from danger—strategies that also bring stress and hardship to the mothers themselves. About half the mothers we spoke with are partnered but we focus exclusively on the mothers' parenting experiences here. Their stories reveal the staggering odds they are up against as they and their children confront the realities of historical and ongoing racial discrimination.

mothers' common grief

Raising kids is hard, but raising children who face daily assaults on their very being is especially hard. In a study tracking a nationally representative group of mothers of children from kindergarten to third grade, researchers Kei Nomaguchi and Amanda House found that only Black mothers experienced

> *The long-held superstrong Black mother image, Patricia Hill Collins argues, now dictates the terms of good mothering for Black women: be strong and be solely responsible.*

heightened levels of parenting stress as their children grew older and mothers' concerns about their safety and survival increased. Recent analyses by statistician Nate Silver underscore how dangerous the U.S. is for Black Americans, who are almost eight times as likely as White Americans to be homicide victims.

Malaya, a New York mother of three, is a heartbreaking example of this reality. When asked in an interview about recent major events in her life, she said her 26 year-old son had been murdered three weeks ago while trying to break up a fight at a house party. "My son passed away at the same age as his father. He passed away two blocks from where his father got murdered," she somberly related. Malaya's son's death has made her even more worried about the safety of her two younger children.

The day before her son was murdered, Malaya joined a community gym with plans to lose weight because she was experiencing some health problems she wanted to manage: stress, diabetes, and high blood pressure. Since she received the late night phone call about her son's death, she has not returned to the gym. Instead, she has been focused on getting justice for her dead son and insulating her two remaining children from danger. Especially since her son's death, Malaya tries to teach her 16-year-old daughter Nina to keep to herself and not to trust anyone. "I be just so afraid with my daughter outside now, even around friends. And she is like 'Ma, would you want me to be in the house forever?' No I just, I don't even know how to even put it like. . . . Friends are friends, but your life is more important."

Malaya encourages Nina to avoid becoming too close to anyone. Her personal philosophy is "go to work, come home, take care of the house, do what you've got to do. All that mingling in the streets is only going to cause trouble." She takes this approach in her own life: "I can't even trust my own friends. I don't have nothing against them, but I don't know what's their motive. I want Nina to understand it. Because when you came out of my womb you came out alone. So there's always a boundary that you got to know." Malaya instructs Nina to avoid all unnecessary social contact and stay inside their apartment, hoping this will save her life.

Malaya's third child is a 3-year-old son. Even prior to her older son's murder, Malaya was concerned about the safety of her youngest son. To insulate him from danger, Malaya spoke of her interest in homeschooling: "I was really scared to let him out. I'm like that because I've seen what happens when someone gets out." A social worker convinced Malaya to enroll her son in public preschool, but she is strict about his socializing: "I don't have him with no friends. He goes to school on the bus, he comes home on it."

Malaya's story captures several aspects of the unfortunately common experiences of low-income Black mothers: losing a child, living in unsafe neighborhoods owing to subsidized housing policies which intensified poverty and racial segregation, deep social distrust and disenfranchisement, and profound efforts to insulate and protect their children. Her story also demonstrates the impact stress and self-sacrifice can have on mothers' health. Reflecting on how her son's murder affected her life, she said: "And me, all I just wanted is just to live a normal life and just be normal. I want to go to the gym."

safety from the streets, safety from the law

Not only do Black Americans have high homicide rates, they are also disproportionately arrested and incarcerated, leading legal scholar Michelle Alexander to argue that Black incarceration rates reflect a legacy of discriminatory laws and policies, such as racial profiling, the heavy police presence in low-income Black neighborhoods, and the war on drugs, which involved higher prison sentences for possession of crack cocaine (more common among Blacks) than cocaine (more commonly used by Whites) though there is no chemical difference between them.

With one in nine Black men behind bars, Black mothers worry about their children, especially their sons, ending up on the wrong side of the criminal justice system. Vivian, a New York mother of two boys, worried that her 17-year-old son Dixon would end up in jail or dead. Her fears led her to ask him: "Which one do you want to be, a name or a number? What I mean by that is, like, what do you want? A job or you want to go to jail?" Likening Dixon's social environment to crabs trapped in a bucket, Vivian said she had to pull him out and separate him from his friends: "You ever saw like a bucket of crabs, and you pull the crabs up, what is the other crab doing? Yeah, they are holding on. It's always going to be somebody that's going to try to pull you down you know, but if you have a strong family behind you, they're going to break that arm. You know what I'm saying? And that's what the hell I did, I broke that arm. Yeah, and pushed those friends away from him. And look at him now, he's out there working." Vivian intervened to end her son's relationship with friends she worried would expose him to the long arm of the law, and Vivian's brother offered her son a job in his moving company, an option not available to many low-income urban Black youth who face bleak employment prospects.

> **"**
>
> *Raising kids is hard, but raising children who face daily assaults on their very being is especially hard.*

Like Malaya, Vivian keeps to herself and encourages the same for her children, sending them away from the neighborhood as frequently as possible to "show my kids there's a different world out of this place. I know it's nothing but poverty up and down here, but if you can choose to walk outside of this, you will see a different world. I take my kids to 42nd Street, to do things upstate, somewhere out the house, things like that. To Virginia to go see my brothers. . . ." One in four Black Americans live in neighborhoods marked by extreme poverty thanks to a host of federal, state, and local housing policies that concentrate poverty in pre-existing low-income areas. Moreover, these policies are racially-based: Poor Blacks are much more likely than poor Whites to live in neighborhoods characterized by extreme poverty, crumbling infrastructure, and minimal job opportunities. When they are at home, Vivian tries to ensure her sons' safety by keeping them inside and occupied with video games. "If the [video] game keeps them from out of the street, they can play it all day, you know. Hey, if they keeps them under me, under my eye watch, go right ahead. I'm not saying all day, but it keeps them here, you know." Vivian's awareness that too much screen time is unhealthy for children is tempered by her fears for her sons' safety outside and away from her watchful eye.

Adrianna also worries about her children's safety outside their home. We interviewed Adrianna in North Carolina following her move from the northeast in the hopes of finding a safer place to raise her children. The mother of three explained that even so she is vigilant: "I keep very close eyes on my children. They can't be wandering the neighborhood. I need to know where my kids are at. If they're going somewhere with other children, I need to talk to the parents. Who's gonna be supervising them?" Only half-jokingly, Adrianna went on to say that she won't let her children leave the house without the "phone numbers, addresses, and social security numbers" of their friends' parents.

In addition to being vigilant to insulate their children from neighborhood dangers, Black mothers also find themselves advocating for their children in racist institutional contexts such as schools. Adrianna recounted the forms of racial discrimination her three children have faced in school since their move to North Carolina. A recent analysis of federal school data by researchers at the University of Pennsylvania found that, even as Black children represent less than a quarter of the student body in North Carolina and 12 other southern states, they make up about half of all expulsions and suspensions. At the time of her interview, Adrianna's 11-year-old son was facing a possible suspension for violating the dress code with his Mohawk hairstyle, which Adrianna defended as "a part of who we are as a people." In her frustration with

the school system, Adrianna, like Malaya, is considering taking her children out of school to homeschool them. Their interest in homeschooling mirrors a larger trend of homeschooling becoming more popular among Black families as they try to insulate their children from discriminatory treatment.

blaming mothers

"I'm not one of those parents who is laxaditty," emphasized Adrianna, distancing herself from the stereotype of the bad mother. "I have always been a mother first. I don't put anything above my children's lives," she said. Black mothers across the income spectrum have to deal with the negative connotations of stereotypes about them as mothers and the stress of raising Black children in a racist society. In separate works, sociologists Dawn Dow and Karen McCormack found that the controlling images of Black women, such as the welfare queen and the strong Black woman, influence how both poor *and* middle-class Black mothers make parenting decisions, and create a sense of exclusion from White motherhood.

In her book on racial bias in the child welfare system, Dorothy Roberts, an eminent scholar of race, gender, and the law, argues that stereotypes of poor Black women as bad mothers mean that they are more heavily monitored by the state and their mothering is treated with suspicion. Racial bias can infuse even teachers' perceptions of Black mothers. A 2012 study by Susan Dumais and her colleagues found that elementary school teachers viewed Black parents' involvement in their children's schooling negatively, while interpreting White parents' involvement positively. Similarly, the Black mothers we spoke with whose children were involved with state institutions—including public schools and the criminal justice system—discussed the ways their mothering was assumed to be inadequate by institutional practices.

Several of the mothers spoke of their sons' entanglement with the court system in particular. As researchers Victor Rios, Nikki Jones, and others have observed, the institutions that surround Black children are eager to discipline and lock them up; when they do, their mothers also come under the authority of the criminal justice system. Tiana "felt like I was the one that committed the crime," when she recounted the things she had to do in order to meet the conditions of her 14-year-old son's probation for kicking a motorcycle, such as

Vivian's awareness that too much screen time is unhealthy for children is tempered by her fears for her sons' safety outdoors and away from her watchful eye.

attending Saturday morning classes and advocating for him in the system. When a judge threatened to put her son on probation for another six months, Tiana said, "I was like, what? Uh-uh. I had to take him to all them little, you know, classes and it was cutting out time for my other kids." Tiana agreed to attend even more classes with her son, however, to demonstrate her commitment as a mother and to keep him from receiving an additional sentence.

When Mariah's 15-year-old son was caught trying to steal a moped, a condition of his probation was that Mariah had to take weekly parenting classes. She explained, "They send a guy over here to do a parenting class with us every Saturday. He shows us some videos of other parents and their children, going through probably the same things [and teaches us] maybe the different things that maybe I can do instead of yelling and screaming." Mariah described the classes as "sometimes" helpful but noted that they don't address what to do when she tells her son "don't go or you can't go outside today. Soon as you turn your back, he's out the door, like you didn't tell him nothing."

All too often the mothers' stories underscored how state institutions and policies positioned mothers as suspect parents *but also* solely responsible for their children's behavior. Tiffany's 16-year-old son Corey was in trouble for skipping school, for which the school blamed Tiffany. "I don't understand how they want to blame the parents for the kids when you send them out there to go to school," she said, explaining that both the school and the law punished her for Corey's truancy even though she made sure he was out the door with his school clothes and backpack every day. "I get like a phone call telling me that it is mandatory that I makes the school meeting . . . . Basically they were telling me [the principal] was going to call ACS (Administration for Child Services) on me because Corey is not coming to school. I was like, I have a seven year old and you can check, he has perfect attendance. So you cannot fault me for his mistakes." They did however fault her, subjecting her to an embarrassing 30-day investigation involving multiple home visits by ACS workers.

Stereotypes of poor Black women as bad mothers mean that they are more heavily monitored by the state and their mothering is treated with suspicion, even by their kids' teachers

praise and punishment

Highly publicized recent incidences of police brutality have highlighted persistent racism and the ongoing challenges of being Black in America. Black mothers not only fear for their children each time they step outside the door, they also encounter gender, class, and racial discrimination of their own, including stereotypes about them as mothers. The women we interviewed proudly spoke of their strength and the sacrifices they have made to insulate their children from the surrounding dangers, but as their stories demonstrate, these efforts stem from living in impossible conditions created by state policies and practices, and they are often not enough. Praising mothers for being superstrong also makes it easy to lay the blame for children's hardships at mothers' feet.

The US welfare state is shrinking while an emphasis on small government grows, inspired and perpetuated by inaccurate understandings of the causes of poverty and by racist stereotypes about those who use social programs. State and institutional supports for poor families that do exist tend to focus on what mothers are doing wrong and how they could be better parents. This reflects a larger trend of shifting responsibility onto the individual, illustrated in the stories we presented above. The mothers we interviewed described how state involvement in their lives was at best neglectful and at worst exacerbated the parenting challenges and stress they faced. It's no surprise then that they see little choice but to be hypervigilant, separating their children from their peers, keeping them inside, and trying to get them away from the surrounding dangers, including discriminatory treatment.

Time and again sociological research has revealed that mothers like Malaya, Vivian, Adrianna, and others we spoke with face many challenges raising children, and that the vast majority do everything they can to protect and nurture their children. The adverse conditions these mothers and their children find themselves in are created by inadequate and racist past and current social policies, yet mothers are told it is up to them alone to remedy them, to be superstrong. This is a losing proposition that puts undue pressure on low-income Black mothers and blames them when their children falter.

As for Toya Graham, six months after she was filmed determinedly trying to keep her son from joining the Baltimore protests against police brutality, Graham described her life to a CBS reporter as a constant struggle. Speaking of her 16-year-old son, Graham said, "I know there's nothing out there but harm. But I'm going to protect him . . . I know a lot of mothers out here understand where I'm coming from. We're struggling, we're just trying to make sure we keep food on our table for our children, keep them out harm's way, keep them out of danger." On being dubbed a hero, Graham responded, "I just don't feel like a hero. This is a real struggle. When the cameras is gone, the reality of life is still there. It's still there."

recommended resources

Charlton, T.F. 2013. "The Impossibility of the Good Black Mother," In *The Good Mother Myth*. New York: Seal Press. Explores the negative stereotypes that Black mothers face in their everyday lives through a combination of personal essay and gender and race theory.

Collins, Patricia H. 2000. *Black Feminist Thought: Knowledge, Consciousness, and the Politics of Empowerment*. New York: Routledge. Explores the uniqueness of Black women's perspectives and develops an accessible critical social theory.

Ferguson, Ann A. 2000. *Bad Boys: Public Schools in the Making of Black Masculinity*. Ann Arbor, Michigan: University of Michigan Press. Offers a rich account of students' and teachers' daily interactions to demonstrate the ways racialized gender stereotypes lead schools to disproportionately punish Black boys.

Levine, Judith. 2013. *Ain't No Trust: How Bosses, Boyfriends, and Bureaucrats Fail Low-Income Mothers and Why It Matters*. Berkeley, CA: University of California Press. Documents low-income women's interactions with untrustworthy actors and how they contribute to further lack of trust.

Roberts, Dorothy. 2002. *Shattered Bonds: The Color of Child Welfare*. New York: Basic Civitas Books. Examines the racist underpinnings of the child welfare system and the consequences for Black families and communities.

neoliberal mothering
melissa brown
winter 2015

In 2008, actress Jenny McCarthy created a media frenzy when she rejected the use of vaccines for children, citing what she believed to be a link between vaccines and her son's autism. She asserted that providing a healthy diet and safe, clean environment for her son would protect his health as well as any vaccine. Apparently, a lot of middle- and upper-class parents agree.

The majority of parents who seek and obtain vaccine exemptions for their children in the U.S. are White and middle- and upper-class. Writing in *Gender & Society*, Jennifer Reich describes vaccine-refusing mothers as displaying "neoliberal mothering." They assert their individual choice to manage their children independently of the influence of medical institutions and government. For these mothers, good parenting rests on the ability to intervene between children and external institutions.

Reich thus suggests that vaccine refusal is an elite process in which mothers embrace and replicate privilege in order to advocate for their children against state public health standards.

She interviewed 25 mothers who obtained vaccine exemptions for their children. The majority of the women were married, heterosexual, White, and middle- to upper-class. The interviews uncovered the three factors that contributed to the mother's decisions: the perception of vaccine risk and necessity, feeding as health promotion, and the management of risk from imagined gated communities. These women demonstrate neoliberal mothering by investing primarily in their own children's health, whose non-immunity comes at the expense of other children, who are exposed to more pathogens when fewer children are vaccinated. Ultimately, neoliberal mothers exercise their own agency regarding their child's health, while poor mothers experience constraints because they lack similar resources.

families facing untenable choices

lisa dodson and wendy luttrell

winter 2011

Miss Corey is sympathetic to the boys' single mom who works tirelessly to provide for her children, and so she reluctantly stretches school rules to accommodate the situation. She feels it isn't fair to punish the boys because of their mother's work demands. A single mom herself, Miss Corey explains that, were it not for the fact that her own children are on an "early school schedule" that allows her to drop them off on her way to work, she doesn't know how she would manage. Miss Corey is grateful for her job; even though she "pinches pennies at the end of each month," she has health insurance, paid sick days, vacation days, and, if need be, she can always get someone to "cover for" her in the office if one of her children gets sick at school. In contrast, Antonio's mom couldn't be reached when he got a fever. "We called her employer (she works at a nursing home across town) but they didn't give her the message, and the poor child sat in the nurse's office all day. It breaks my heart."

Antonio's mom and Miss Corey are part of an important and expansive group within the labor force: working mothers. According to the Bureau of Labor Statistics, in 2008, seven out of ten mothers were employed. Based on the growth of the service, retail, and carework job sectors, many mothers—disproportionately women of color, immigrants, and single women—are working in low paying, demanding jobs.

For decades, sociologists have studied women's increased labor force participation, focusing on women's lost career opportunity related to family care needs. Arlie Hochschild famously coined the term "second shift" for women's juggling of family care with work demands. The gendered division of household labor that Hochschild reported years ago continues largely unaltered, with women responsible for family care whether they provide it themselves or organize and schedule others to do so. In light of this second shift, sociologist Pam Stone describes how some professional women may feel compelled to "opt out" of high-powered professions to take care of family needs.

Our focus is the dynamic of the second—or more accurately, *multiple*—shifts faced by low wage mothers with few (if any) opting-out choices. Service, retail, and care work jobs pay $8–$12 per hour, so workers are hard-pressed to cover their basics: rent, food, transportation, heat, healthcare, and utilities. Further, these kinds of jobs are more likely to encroach on routine family time, before and after school, or in the evenings and on weekends. The work often involves irregular schedules and unpredictable hours, leaving little flexibility to take care of everyday family life, and employment in these sectors offers few benefits or career ladders that might mean sacrifice today, but bring better times tomorrow. Perhaps most startlingly, taking one of these jobs can also mean taking immediate losses. Economist Randy Albelda calls this the "cliff effect" of post-welfare policy: even the smallest wage increase can result in steep losses in essential public benefits such as housing, healthcare, and food stamps.

What are the particular conditions—material and social—that moms and children face in the real world of low wage work and family? Across the scholarship on low-income families, we find three themes that stand out. First, research points out how inflexible and often unpredictable work schedules undermine mothers' abilities to provide family care. While higher earnings could offset some of this dilemma, a "market solution" is out of reach for these families. The second theme is the stigma faced by low-income mothers and children when they don't meet the middle class norms of work and school in order to put family care first. Finally, we explore a theme infused throughout low-income work/family scholarship: how the norms of major social institutions (employment and education) operate according to rules that demand untenable choices from mothers and children. This angle on the work and family dilemma tends to be ignored or, if highlighted, used as evidence of personal irresponsibility and failed families. Recognizing the true conditions facing tens of millions of families is crucial for reformulating work, family, and educational policy.

inflexibility at work

In 2004, Norma described her job loss this way: "My company is a big corporation, and there are no exceptions. . . . I had attendance problems because of my son's illness . . . but I went ahead. . . . I pushed it and made a choice for family. No matter what it took, I was going to be there sacrificing a risk of attendance problems. So I had no flexibility with work at my employment. . . ." For Norman, "pushing it" meant taking two extra days off until her son, who had been gravely ill, was in stable condition. She lost her job for "abusing" the company's sick day policy.

Research on work schedules in retail, service, and care work jobs reveals a wide spectrum of inflexibilities. Schedules may change with little notice, overtime work may suddenly become mandatory, and productivity (often involving direct contact with customers) may be constantly monitored. The face-to-face nature of much of the retail, personal care, and service labor markets makes small accommodations like breaks, adjustments to start and stop time, or phone calls all but impossible. Work and family scholars Julie Henly and Elaine Waxman, researching retail workers, reported that employees may learn of their work schedule with only a few days notice. They wrote, for these workers, "Everything is open. Nothing is consistent." Just as Norma described, employees find almost no room for negotiation, regardless of the gravity of a family need.

In the past, the rigidity and unpredictability of these jobs led many mothers who had no savings, family money, or higher-earning spouse to turn to welfare if their children needed more intensive care. But by the late 1990s, the policy for low-income moms became "work first." Mothers had to negotiate family care based on the hard terms set by the low-wage labor market.

Deborah spoke of how she once used welfare to navigate family and job demands, believing children "should be with someone who's about raising them." By 2002, new welfare regulations meant Deborah saw no choice but to take a low-wage job, even though her childcare arrangements were "sub par."

This is a hidden layer of risk that arises when inflexible work is coupled with insufficient income to buy good childcare. According to the National Center for Children in Poverty, only 8 percent of infant/toddler care and 24 percent of preschool care is considered high quality. Thus, like many parents, Deborah could find no affordable and decent childcare so she left

> **The interplay of low pay, inflexible work, and school design, coupled with social stigma, create hardship for millions of families.**

them in "self care," which is to say, on their own. But she says, "I'm always afraid. I'm afraid they will say something at school [about her absence] and I'm afraid that something will happen to them." Deborah isn't alone. Federal research reveals that, nationally, only 17 percent of eligible children receive publicly subsidized childcare. Many parents, then, are living with twin fears: they're terrified by both the possibility of harm that could come to children left alone and the possibility that they'll face investigation by state children's services for child neglect.

Tayisha discovered something else that plagues other parents: childcare cheap enough for her budget can be substandard. Cleaning out her daughter Amy's bag she found " . . . all these notes in the bottom of her backpack. She hated it [the after school program]. These kids were picking on her, and the teacher told her she had to work it out. So she would write me notes about being shoved around, spat at . . . " Trying to handle the abuse on her own, Amy had apparently written down what was happening to her, but didn't pass along the notes in order to protect her mother. Coming upon these frequent, painful, but hidden moments in her daughter's life led Tayisha to quit her job. She had little else to fall back on and nothing in the bank. But Tayisha said, "I don't care what . . . I am not going to have her be in a situation like that." Tayisha knew that her job supervisor regarded the abrupt quit a confirmation of her poor work ethic.

Pointedly, the growing demand for all kinds of care work draws low wage mothers' caring labor out of the family and into the labor market. Antonio's mom and so many others like her face this paradox. One nurse's aide said the supervisors in her nursing home workplace "kind of make you feel like 'We're first and your family's second.'"

Inflexible, family-unfriendly, low-paid jobs create a minefield of bad options for millions of families. Yet, it gets worse because mothers and children find that the strategies they design to try to handle these tough conditions can lead to multiple layers of stigma. Studying workplace discrimination, legal scholar Joan Williams notes, "professional women who request a flexible schedule find themselves labeled as uncommitted. Low-wage mothers, for whom no flexibility is available, find themselves stigmatized as irresponsible workers when they need time off in order to be responsible mothers."

stigma

"They (teachers) see it as we aren't being responsible if we don't attend [meetings] and all that."

Low-wage working mothers find that while they are fencing with inflexible work demands, they must also contend with the contemporary standards of "good mothering." Numerous sociological studies have documented class differences in the meaning of good mothering. Poverty researchers Kathryn Edin and Maria Kefalas have written, "Ask a middle-class woman if she's a good mother, and she'll likely reply, 'Ask me in twenty years,' for then she will know her daughter's score on the SAT, the list of college acceptances she has garnered, and where her career trajectory has led. . . . Ask a poor woman whether she's a good mother, and she'll likely point to how clean and well-fed her children are, or how she stands by them through whatever problems come their way."

"It's yours to take care of, and that means your kids come first. That's it, there's no other way. . . . In the end you got to choose."

Middle-class working moms are operating in the world of *hurried* childhood, aimed at creating early academic and social wins. The standard for them requires countless extracurricular activities and skill enhancement to give children a competitive edge throughout life. Family sociologist Annette Lareau describes the demands that this intense schedule places on both children and parents, primarily mothers. By contrast, low-income moms are operating in the world of *adultified* childhood, in which children join the "heavy lifting" in the service of family survival. In these conditions, "girls' family labor" has long been a critical, if largely ignored, alternative source of family work. Family and poverty scholar Linda Burton's work on youth in low income families explores how the *adultification* of children is a critical family coping strategy, yet is out of sync with contemporary expectations of intense and early achievement for future success.

This is the world that Antonio, Cesar, and their mother inhabit. They know their "out of sync" care strategies are stigmatized. Low-income school children, perhaps very involved in family care that pulls them out of school, can easily run into conflict with authorities, attitudes, and regulations in their schools. Indeed, a U.S. Department of Education survey of drop-out rates indicates that shouldering family responsibilities plays a major role in kids' decisions to leave school. Importantly, low-income youth recognize the stigma that surrounds their families' ways of getting by; they're attuned to social judgment. Sociologist of childhood Barrie Thorne has documented that children hear adult talk at home and at school, and they learn how to listen for and read signs of anxiety and stigma. Antonio heard the sympathetic Miss Corey describe how he was "covering for his mother." Her words were a kindness, but one tinged with implications of maternal deficiency. Very early in their lives, children sense the public scrutiny that their working poor mothers face and will attempt to protect them (as Amy did when she hid the notes that would upset her mother). Or children may actively duplicate the stigmatized family ethic, treating the immediate care needs of siblings, parents, even extended family as immediate priority. Yet, just as job supervisors regard mothers engaging in such behavior as "abusing" the system, teachers and school authorities may regard children as uncooperative with school rules and uninterested in getting an education.

Mothers may also find themselves regarded as uncommitted to their children's education by those pointing to their lack of parental participation in school activities. Focusing on the hidden work of mothers, researchers Alison Griffith and Dorothy Smith argue that unequal educational opportunities are built into the contemporary institution of schooling that expects "mothering for schooling," or maternal involvement, to be integral to children's progress. No-show mothers (and their kids) are known by school authorities. Studying urban schools, Michelle Fine quotes a mother who recognizes this attitude, "Society says you're supposed to know what your children are doing at all time. It's not so. I take 2 hours to travel to work, 2 hours to travel back and I'm on my feet 10 hours a day."

We heard the same story in our research. For example, Atlanta, a mother of three in Denver, described a 19-hour day. First she gets one child off to school, and then "I get back and get my older daughters off to their school. So then I can do . . . any extra jobs [under the table manicuring] and then pick her up and later her sisters can watch her and then I go to work at 5PM. I do cleaning office buildings at this point; it starts late so I can spend a little time before." She works until midnight. "I don't even think about ever getting sick."

Cultural critic Joan Morgan describes the "strong-Black-woman" image (which extends its cultural reach to ethnic minority, immigrant, and even working class White women) as one that celebrates a capacity to endure hardship and pain. It's true that, in the face of such challenges, Atlanta took pride in her child-rearing accomplishments and her older daughters took pride in their skills as substitutes when their mother needed them. Yet, these are hardly recognized as essential capabilities or remarkable achievements in most work and family and schooling discourse. In fact, these caring strategies may even be turned into their opposite, treated as signs of negligent parenting and inappropriately adultified children, stigmatizing both mothers and children.

untenable choices

"Don't expect 'them' to get it cause 'they' don't . . . and they don't matter . . . in the end you got to choose."

Mothers and children, trying to manage inflexible work and school demands, without sufficient income to purchase help, face untenable choices. Mothers are pulled to spend more time at work to meet supervisors' expectations and to bring in more sorely needed income. They may turn to children to manage daily household needs and younger children's care. But, in the intensified world of high stakes schooling and extracurricular engagement, siphoning off young people's time and attention to provide family care can cost them dearly. Youngsters are aware of the stakes; they hear talk about achievement and failure all the time and are constantly advised to focus on scoring and winning. In both work and school cultures, the focus on individual effort and personal gain is primary. Yet, in a context in which keeping a family intact may depend on practices that include consciously putting self aside for family needs, mothers and children who put care first may find that themselves viewed as deficient, even deviant.

The sociologist Judith Hennessey describes a "moral hierarchy" that guides low-income mothers as they try to manage their choices; mothers commonly say, "children come first." In our research, this language of priority comes up often. We believe that this assertion of primacy of caring for others reflects extreme work, family, and education conditions. It is, ultimately, about survival. Social theorist Patricia Hill Collins, describing how women of color approach family care, asserts, "Without women's motherwork, communities would not survive." Choosing children (and in the children's case, sometimes choosing family care) "first" can be seen as an assertion of the family's right to continue to even be a family tomorrow.

The interplay of low pay, inflexible work, and school design, coupled with social stigma, create untold hardship for millions of low-income families. These forces also set the stage for the people who live in and care for these families to question the priorities of major social institutions. Reflecting this, in a low-income mothers' group discussion in 2005, we heard a woman offer advice: "It's yours to take care of, and that means your kids come first. That's it, there's no other way. Don't expect 'them' to get it cause 'they' don't . . . and they don't matter . . . in the end you got to choose." All the other mothers nodded as if they knew who "they" were.

private troubles, collective responsibilities

Echoes of the private troubles these difficult care choices create, the structural barriers that must be overcome, and a call for "them" to "get it" are heard from wage-poor, working mothers throughout sociological literature. If "they" are government entities, responsible for the good of the people, establishing a sustainable wage and also providing subsidies to reach it would make a significant difference. If "they" are employers, whose market success rests on the larger society, investing in families by providing work flexibility would go a long way to support that society. If "they" are public education leaders who oversee the route to social mobility, then integrating the real conditions of low-income youth into school policies and practices would help provide equity. But, for now, none of these powerful social institutions demonstrates a commitment to address the real conditions facing low-wage families.

Taking care of family remains a private enterprise in the U.S. Antonio's mother must rely on working multiple shifts, self-care by Antonio and his brother, and self-styled flexibilities, while other families can purchase services to take care of family needs. Yet, the focus on private strategies for untenable choices, some stigmatized and others affirmed, diverts us from the collective responsibility we share for the care of all families.

recommended resources

Chaudray, Ajay. 2004. *Putting Children First: How Low-Wage Working Mothers Manage Childcare*. New York: Russell Sage Foundation. A revealing ethnography describing mothers' daily work and family dilemmas.

Hochschild, Arlie, and Ehrenreich, Barbara (eds.). 2003. *Global Woman: Nannies, Maids, and Sex Workers in the New Economy.* London: Granata Books. Illustrates global market reliance on women's low-wage labor and its eroding effects on families and societies.

Glenn, Evelyn N. 2010. *Forced to Care: Coercion and Caregiving in America.* Cambridge, MA: Harvard University Press. A critical view of the organization of care labor and how it persistently reproduces gender and racial inequality.

Meyer, Madonna H. 2000. *Care Work: Gender Labor and the Welfare State.* London: Routledge. A wide-ranging volume revealing the clash of market demands, private care responsibilities, and the retreat of social welfare.

Hertz, Rosanna, and Marshall, Nancy (eds.). 2001. *Working Families: The Transformation of the American Home.* Berkeley, CA: University of California Press. Cutting-edge essays exploring issues in work and family from scholarly, business, and children's perspectives.

69

mothering while disabled

angela frederick

fall 2014

When she was just two days old, Mikaela Sinnett of Kansas City, Missouri, became a ward of the foster care system. The local social services agency took her away from her parents before the family left the hospital. What horrible crime, one might ask, did Mikaela's parents commit to result in the loss of custody of their newborn daughter? Mikaela's parents were not guilty of abuse or neglect. Rather, they were blind.

Responding to Mikaela's mother's difficulty breast-feeding, a nurse reported the parents to a hospital social worker, setting in motion the bureaucratic machinery of the state's protective services.

Mikaela's parents cooperated with the social worker, answering questions about the care they would provide for their newborn. They could take their daughter's temperature with a talking thermometer; they had access to transportation; and they could take Mikaela to the hospital if she needed immediate medical attention. The one response the social worker wanted, which the parents could not provide, was that someone with sight would be with the child at all times.

According to Erika, Mikaela's mother, the social worker declared "I can't in good conscience send this baby home with blind parents." Erika and her partner were not even allowed to hold their daughter before she was taken into foster care.

It took Mikaela's parents 57 days to get their daughter back. During this time, Erika and her partner were only allowed to spend two to three hours with their daughter each week, and only with supervision. After two months of court hearings and legal action, child protective services closed the case.

Mikaela is now four years old, but the incident, and the associated trauma, will always be a part of her family history.

I too am a mother—of a two-year-old girl. And I am blind. I followed this story closely as it unfolded. What agony this mother must have endured, I thought, as I read the reportage.

From the moment I contemplated becoming a mother, I began collecting resources and advice on how I would care for my child without sight. As I spoke to other blind mothers, I learned the tricks of the trade: how to track toddlers by pinning bells to their clothes; how to wear babies and pull rather than push strollers to accommodate white canes and guide dogs; how to place tactile markings on syringes to measure medicine.

And I learned much more: that as a mother with a disability, the chance of being investigated by social services is ominously high. "Be prepared," these women warned me, "You will be visited by a hospital social worker after childbirth." As a mother, these warnings

> *As a mother with a disability, the chance of being investigated by social services is ominously high.*

made me anxious. But as a sociologist I was curious. How much training do social workers and medical professionals receive about disability? What measures are in place to protect mothers with disabilities from discrimination?

People with disabilities must frequently confront stigmatizing attitudes challenging their right to be in the world, which can have devastating consequences for them and their families.

legacies of exclusion

We tend to think of disability as an issue facing a very small segment of the population. In actuality one in five Americans lives with some kind of disability, and one in ten has a severe disability that limits one or more major life activities. Approximately 2.3 million U.S. mothers caring for children have a disability, and almost 10 percent of American children are currently being cared for by a parent with a disability. As historian Kim Nielsen argues, "Disability is not the story of someone else. It is our story, the story of someone we love, the story of who we are or may become, and it is undoubtedly the story of our nation."

Impairments come in many forms, from physical limitations that limit mobility or stamina, to sensory impairments like blindness or deafness, to cognitive and social disabilities. Some disabilities are easy to identify through one's appearance or the tools and technology one uses. Other impairments, such as learning or psychiatric disabilities, are invisible, and are not immediately noticeable. Some disabilities involve significant pain or illness. Others do not. Individuals can experience the same impairment in very different ways.

In the 1960s, Americans with disabilities began to cultivate a shared political identity as members of an oppressed group. Activists in the disability rights movement demanded recognition as full citizens with rights to live independently outside of institutions, to access quality education and employment, and to participate fully in their communities free from structural and attitudinal barriers. They argued that disabled people, not professionals or charity organizations, should speak on behalf of their communities.

Armed with new political identities and with the civil rights protections guaranteed by the 1990 Americans with Disabilities Act, disabled Americans are more fully participating in their communities than ever before. Yet, despite this progress, public recognition of the right of people with disabilities to parent has yet to be realized. In fact, Through the Looking Glass, an advocacy organization for parents with disabilities, claims that securing the rights of disabled Americans to parent

without unreasonable interference is "the last frontier in disability rights."

This form of prejudice has been particularly insidious for women with disabilities. During the twentieth century eugenics movement, the state subjected disabled people to forced institutionalization, marriage restriction laws, and compulsory sterilization. Eugenicists primarily targeted women in their efforts to purify the genetic make-up of the population. Justifying their work as necessary to eliminate the danger posed by the "feeble-minded," the state authorized the forced sterilization of women with a range of disabilities, women believed to be sexually impure, and Black, Native-American, and immigrant women.

The legacy of the eugenics movement persists today. Women with disabilities still encounter the widely held belief that they cannot perform motherhood competently and that they will spread "defective genes" by passing their impairments to their children. New cultural values about motherhood, which sociologist Sharon Hays has termed "intensive mothering," pose particular dilemmas for disabled mothers. Women are now expected to create child-centered homes that shield children from responsibility and hardship.

Mothers are expected to devote ample amounts of money, time, and energy to nurturing and overseeing their children's development. Disabled women pose a threat to the intensive mothering ethos as they can make visible the realities of imperfection, risk, and even pain and suffering—the very hardships from which mothers are now expected to shield their children.

the child welfare system and disability

Safety is the word most often used to question the rights of disabled mothers. After all, how can the human rights of people with disabilities stack up against the public concern for children's safety? Mothers with disabilities come from all walks of life. They have the same wide range of parenting skills and personal strengths and weaknesses found in the broader community. They experience the same wide range of privileges and hardships as the general population. Some are model parents. Some are not. And, yes, some do abuse and neglect their children.

In cases in which the mother has a disability, however, her status is often used as a proxy for real evidence that she cannot adequately care for her children. Disability communities and advocacy organizations like Through the Looking Glass have a wealth of knowledge about the strategies parents with various disabilities employ to successfully care for children. Frequently, however, the state launches investigations and makes custody determinations without considering these options.

Parents with disabilities often do face barriers, including higher rates of unemployment and poverty, lack of access to transportation, and diminished access to quality healthcare.

Yet, despite these challenges, research shows that these parents are still no more likely to harm their children than parents without disabilities. In other words, parents' disability status is a poor predictor of child maltreatment. According to Paul Preston, anthropologist and director of the National Center for Parents with Disabilities and Their Families, "The vast majority of children of disabled parents have been shown to have typical development and functioning and often enhanced life perspectives and skills."

While we can be deeply moved by media accounts of extreme cases of child abuse and child welfare system's failure to protect children from harm, it is important to remember that these severe cases of abuse actually represent only a small proportion of child welfare cases. Most parents who are involved with child protective services are accused of neglect rather than abuse, and decisions about their cases often entail highly subjective assessments.

In her book *Fixing Families*, sociologist Jennifer Reich presents findings from observations of child welfare investigations and court hearings. She found that parents' attitude toward state workers had the biggest impact on case determinations, not the severity of abuse or neglect. Those who acknowledged their shortcomings, and who expressed remorse and deferred to social workers, were more likely to be permitted to keep their children than those who displayed anger and resistance.

Reich reflects on how this research changed her. "Rather than feeling outrage and disgust with bad parents, I instead can more easily imagine how it would feel as a parent to have the state's gaze upon me," she says. "I have learned what the public gaze feels like through my own experience with pregnancy and have seen it deployed as I walked into houses with the authority of the state, silently thinking that they were only a little worse than my own."

In other words, middle-class, married women who meet normative prescriptions of "good mothers" are less likely to experience the gaze of the state.

misunderstanding disabled mothers

The subjective determinations that must be made about children's welfare create moments of misunderstanding that place the rights of disabled mothers in jeopardy.

Social workers, judges, and other professionals have considerable authority to claim expertise about parents and children, and are in fact required to do so. The state asks social workers and medical professionals to make judgments about parental fitness, even though these professionals don't often know much about disability and are likely to hold the same negative attitudes, which pervade the broader culture. Many mothers with disabilities report living with a sense of fear that they will be scrutinized by medical authorities. At times, when members of the public see a disabled woman out with her children and become concerned, they report the family to child protective services. Mothers with disabilities are at particular risk, as cultural beliefs suggest that mothers rather than fathers are still primarily responsible for their children.

They encounter the belief that they cannot perform motherhood competently, or that they will pass their impairments to their children.

Disability becomes even more daunting for families who have an open case with child protective services. In 37 states, a disability can be legal grounds for termination of parental rights. The focus of child welfare and custody cases in these states easily shifts from considering the actual signs of neglect or abuse, to speculating about potential parenting deficiencies the mother's disability might pose. In fact, disability is one of the few instances in which parental rights can be terminated on the basis of parents' identity status rather than their actions. According to advocates from Through the Looking Glass, words such as "obviously" and "clearly" are often used to draw conclusions about disabled individuals' capacity to parent, and negative language such as "wheelchair-bound" or "afflicted with a disability" often shore up negative assumptions about parents' capacity to care for their children.

Instead of asking whether or not disabled mothers should have children, we should be asking how we can help their families thrive.

When child welfare agencies remove children from their homes, parents with disabilities have fewer opportunities to reunify their families. These agencies offer disabled parents few supports to ease the effects of structural barriers such as lack of access to transportation and quality housing, and they rarely offer parents the opportunity to acquire the adaptive training and equipment that might help them care for their children.

The Safe Families and Adoption Act, signed into law in 1997, marked a dramatic shift in focus for the child welfare system, as the law now requires agencies to prioritize "permanency" for children over reunification with their parents. The new time limits for reunification, as well as emphasis upon adoption, has created even steeper barriers for parents with disabilities seeking to reunify with their children.

Finally, custody decisions in family courts are often particularly difficult for parents with disabilities, as the "best interest of the child" standard for custody determinations in family court leaves even greater room for judges to make decisions based on negative attitudes about disability. Three years ago, a Durham, North Carolina judge awarded full custody of Alaina Giordano's two children to Giordano's ex-husband, acknowledging that Giordano's stage IV breast cancer was a determining factor in her decision. The judge cited the testimony of forensic psychiatrist Helen Brantley, who argued, "Children want a normal childhood, and it is not normal with an ill parent." Giordano died the following year. She was able to spend the last few weeks of her life with her children only after her lawyer filed an emergency motion in family court.

protecting the rights of mothers with disabilities

Disabled mothers are more likely to experience unwarranted investigations from social service agencies. They are more likely to have their parental rights terminated, and when children are removed these families receive fewer supports for reunification.

A handful of states have passed legislation to address these problems. In 2011, partly in response to the Mikaela Sinnett case, Missouri passed legislation that prohibits the child welfare system from discriminating against parents with disabilities. Several states now require that courts consider testimony from disability communities, and include information about adaptive equipment and alternative skills that parents with disabilities employ. Other states now mandate that courts must establish a clear causal relationship between a parent's disability and child maltreatment before disability can be used as grounds for termination of parental rights. Idaho has passed the most comprehensive legislation protecting the rights of disabled parents.

The National Association of Social Workers now recommends that the federal government establish a national fellowship program to train a "disability specialist" from every local and state child welfare agency, who would then participate in investigations and decisions made in cases involving parents with disabilities. A similar model has been used to improve the handling of cases of domestic violence. Other states, including Tennessee, are implementing training programs to educate state workers about disability and parenting, and offer them information about how they can best support struggling parents.

Mikaela Sinnett's story illuminates the devastating consequences families can endure when stigmatizing attitudes about disability influence child welfare decisions. Despite the gains of the disability rights movement, disabled women's still receive undue scrutiny about their right to mother. Instead of asking whether or not disabled mothers should have children, we should be asking how we can help their families to thrive.

recommended resources

Carey, Allison. 2010. *On the Margins of Citizenship: Intellectual Disability and Civil Rights in Twentieth-Century America.* Philadelphia, PA: Temple University Press. Sociological analysis of the fight for civil rights for people with intellectual disabilities throughout the twentieth century.

Kuttai, Heather. 2010. *Maternity Rolls: Pregnancy, Childbirth, and Disability.* Black Point, NS: Fernwood Publishing. The author, who was paralyzed in an automobile accident in childhood, shares her journey through pregnancy and childbirth, powerfully weaving relevant feminist and critical disability theory into her personal accounts.

National Council on Disability. 2012. "Rocking the Cradle: Insuring the Rights of Parents with Disabilities." http://www.ncd.gov/publications/2012/Sep272012/. Documents the pervasive discrimination parents with disabilities experience in the child welfare system, family courts, and reproductive and adoption services.

Nielsen, Kim. 2013. *A Disability History of the United States.* Boston, MA: Beacon Press. Argues that disability has been a central organizing principle of American society.

Reich, Jennifer. 2005. *Fixing Families: Parents, Power and the Child Welfare System.* London: Routledge. Presents findings from a sociological study of the child welfare system in a California county.

stay-at-home fatherhood

nazneen kane

spring 2015

I was the only mom at the park, outnumbered not by nannies and babysitters but by stay-at-home fathers. Unlike my Washington, D.C. neighborhood, where privileged children were customarily tended by European *au pairs* and stay-at-home mothers, the children at this park in Cincinnati, Ohio were hanging out with their dads while mom acted as the primary breadwinner.

One set of dads was primarily comprised of White, college-educated, middle-upper class men *choosing* at-home fatherhood. Another group was primarily Black, unemployed men fathering at or below the poverty line with few, if any, alternatives. Stay-at-home fathers are diverse and their family lives are deeply unequal; there are multiple stay-at-home fatherhoods.

who are stay-at-home fathers?

The Pew Research Center estimates that 2 million stay-at-home fathers comprise 16% of all at-home parents in the United States. Among men who live with their children, Black fathers are most likely to stay-at-home (13%), while White fathers are least likely (6%). Lower educational attainment is also correlated with men's being at-home, with those men lacking a high school diploma most likely to stay at home with their children. Many of these fathers live below the poverty line.

Recently though, other types of fathers are staying at home. In fact, Pew and others have found that men with higher levels of educational attainment account for the greatest increase in stay-at-home fatherhood. This trend accounts for the bifurcation in fatherhoods and families I noticed in Cincinnati, with the primarily White, affluent fathers and the Black, lower income fathers at the park.

diverse motivations for stay-at-home fatherhood

The greatest increase in stay-at-home fatherhood (SAHF) is among men who appear to have some degree of choice and who decide to stay at home to care for their family. According to Pew's analysis of large-scale survey data, the percentage of SAHFs who report their reason as "caring for home and family" grew from 5% in 1989 to 21% in 2012.

However, according to Noelle Chesley's 2011 study, economic and pragmatic factors continue to play a large role in the rise of SAHF. Her in-depth interviews with 21 at-home fathers across the country reveal that the underlying motivation for transitioning into the role of stay-at-home father is largely centered on financial considerations. Chesley notes that even among fathers who reported a desire to be an at-home father, their decision was often simultaneously influenced by their wife's greater income or professional potential.

> *The greatest increase in stay-at-home fatherhood is among men who decide to stay at home to care for their family. Of course, economic and pragmatic factors figure in, too.*

Some at-home fathers, however, would prefer to work for pay. Current Population Survey estimates report that

339

almost a quarter (23%) of SAHFs nationwide are unable to find work. Indicators of economic instability include wage stagnation, the disappearance of manufacturing work, and the recent economic recession. The global economy has displaced many of the jobs previously performed by U.S. men, heavily impacting the working class and those men without college experience. The decline of job opportunities has driven many families to rearrange their work-family lives.

> *In general, when men (and, surely, women) have a high-earning partner and a peer group of other stay-at-home parents, they have less stress and higher role-related satisfaction.*

In the Rust Belt, these socio-economic forces are at work. The Cincinnati neighborhood I studied was once supported by the manufacturing industry. And, while White men are also affected by economic recessions, the socio-economic history of the neighborhood meant that these unemployed fathers were primarily men of color. Rick, a father of three, reported applying for more than 30 minimum wage jobs in the prior month, and complained that each demanded a college degree even though "any dummy can do it." Similarly, Edmond, a SAHF with a GED who cared for his partner's three children while she worked a $10/hour job cleaning a nearby hospital, told me that government assistance kept them afloat. He deeply regretted the felony charge that impeded his employability.

> *Drawbacks to stay-at-home parenting include stigma, social isolation, boredom, loss of professional networks, and a need to justify their role to outsiders.*

John, an African-American SAHF of four children, had a similar story. He talked about his inability to find work due to an "extensive" criminal record. His wife worked full-time at Wal-Mart earning minimum wage. Within a few short weeks of meeting John, he and his family moved out of their Section 8 housing to live with extended family in Chicago, hoping for better job prospects. The perspectives of Rick, Edmond, and John illustrated how men who report frustration with the job market also are less satisfied with SAHF.

perceptions of stay-at-home fatherhood

My interviews with Cincinnati fathers and previous sociological research have both revealed that men experience stay-at-home fatherhood in diverse ways. Men differ greatly in their satisfaction with SAHF; satisfaction often hinges on men's motivation for staying at home. In general, when men's partners had high earnings and when they had social interactions with other SAHFs, they reported significantly less stress and more role-related satisfaction. Brad Harrington, Fred Van Deuson, and Iyar Mazar's interviews with 31 at-home men highlights numerous benefits for this demographic. In their 2012 study, men reported less adherence to a breadwinning ideology, the development of a greater range of parenting skills, a deeper recognition of the importance of care work, strong bonds with children, greater paternal sensitivity, and greater satisfaction in spending time with children and family.

Conversely, men tend to experience SAHF negatively when the transition to at-home fatherhood is due to unemployment, lack of job opportunity, and/or disability. Stigma experienced with friends or family and a man's perception that he is not fulfilling his masculine or fatherly role can contribute to a negative perception of SAHF. This was especially true of Edmond, who expressed feelings of inadequacy and boredom, and did not particularly enjoy caring for his stepchildren. Edmond's situation was particularly discouraging because he held little hope of finding a steady job. He said he was frequently criticized by his closest family and friends.

Regardless of motivation and satisfaction, most SAHFs continue to report stigmatizing experiences. In a 2010 study, Aaron Rochlen and his colleagues found that half of the 207 at-home fathers in their study reported a stigmatizing experience; the majority of the incidents involved derogatory commentary from stay-at-home mothers. Higher status men also report social isolation, boredom, loss of professional networks, and a need to justify their role to outsiders.

Despite these drawbacks, SAHFs generally report positive social interactions with neighbors and friends and satisfaction with their status. Jeremy Smith's *The Daddy Shift* eloquently lays out some of the triumphs and tribulations of SAHF and the ways it is helping to transform the American family.

in my experience

When I began meeting stay-at-home dads at the park, I never considered that my own husband might soon be among them. Unable to find work in Cincinnati, we found that the best alternative to unemployment was for him to work as a touring sound engineer.

This job would involve frequent transitions in and out of stay-at-home fatherhood.

Personal experience with these transitions would soon demonstrate to me another layer of complexity to SAHF—not only are men's motivations and levels of satisfaction with SAHF diverse, their movement into and out of SAHF is situational. Patterns of entry and exit vary across men's lives. While these transitions are challenging, I have found my partner's SAHF rewarding in unexpected ways. My husband and daughter have forged strong bonds of attachment, and I have learned to never underestimate the importance of fathers in the lives of their children.

father schools and promise keepers
nicole bedera
fall 2015

In many countries, women have gained greater access to education, the right to work with fair compensation, and protection from violence. These all reflect changing norms of femininity (what it means to be a girl or a woman), but it's debatable whether the global spread of gender equality represents "Western" femininity. Further, what about masculinity? In a recent *Gender & Society* article, "Taming Tiger Dads," Allen Kim and Karen Pyke explore American norms of masculinity in education programs intended to make Korean men better fathers.

The Father School movement is a response to a "masculinity crisis" in South Korea. During the 1990s, many men lost their jobs and their claim to the breadwinning role as divorce and women's participation in the labor force rose. Programs like the Father School advocated for a new type of masculinity that emphasized men's more involved and loving emotional family connection and the rise of the "New Man."

The system is based on an American program for evangelical men called Promise Keepers, so the Korean Father School uses rhetoric that glorifies American fatherhood norms. What is more surprising is how blatantly American masculinity is built up while Korean masculinity is portrayed as a problem. Participants in the study used phrases like "typical Korean father" as markers of paternal inability, while "American father" indicated paternal success.

Kim and Pyke argue that the framing of American fathers as admirable and Korean fathers as inadequate reflects a larger trend of Western hegemonic masculinity. The Father School movement, then, reflects a combination of capitulation and bargaining, trying to maintain a Korean identity while adapting to the dominant American model.

picturing the self

my mother's family photo albums

robert zussman

fall 2006

Photo albums don't simply represent but celebrate, in an idealized form, individuals in their relationships with family and friends.

The picture on the page was one of my mother's favorites. Taken some 50 years ago, in January 1955, it shows my mother with my father, both now deceased, my then eleven-year-old brother playing the violin, and me, then six at the piano. The picture, as I will explain, is a very much idealized representation of my family. It is altogether conventional. Indeed, each of the women in the Western Massachusetts retirement home where I have also looked at family photo albums has a similar portrait, showing herself with her family, most often limited to husband and children.

I have chosen to write here about my own mother's photo collection more than about the albums of the other women I interviewed. It is a way to avoid many issues of confidentiality and anonymity (particularly difficult with photographs, which prevent any easy substitution of pseudonyms), and it allows me to draw on the dense knowledge I have of my own family to identify what would otherwise be unrecognizable scenes and people. Yet my mother's photo collection is not different in kind or purpose from the photo albums I have seen that belong to other women of roughly the same age as my mother, who died last winter at 89.

I should not exaggerate how deeply either my mother or the other women I interviewed cherish these photographs. My mother's collection included almost 2,500 photos—a number just smaller than the 3,000 that Richard Chalfen estimated two decades ago as the average number of photographs in an American household and probably significantly smaller than the number found today after the advent of digital photography. Yet, while my mother's collection of photos is organized neatly, each placed in an envelope labeled carefully with the year it was taken, beginning with "1940 and before" and stretching through 2005, she had no photos at all on display in her apartment and only two small albums, both stuck away in the far reaches of a storage closet.

Similarly, although all the residents I met in the retirement home (including a few who are blind), display at least a few photographs, most, faced with moving all their possessions into a single room, chose not to save numerous albums. Nonetheless, for the minority of residents who chose to keep their albums, like my mother, the pictures provide a way to remember. All of the women look through their albums at least occasionally and use them to stimulate memories of family, friends and, in at least one instance, a therapist.

albums as narratives of the self

I would go one step further. As a highly selective record of a life, each album tells a story and makes a set of claims about who and what one was and is. In this sense, the assembly and display of photo collections is not simply a way to remember but an autobiographical occasion. By this I mean one of those socially structured moments—including applications for employment, credit, and school; confessions, both religious and criminal; reunions of various sorts; and therapies of various sorts—at which people are encouraged and, at times, even required to provide accounts of themselves. Most important, these accounts do not simply represent the self but constitute it. The self, as many sociologists, psychologists, and philosophers recognize, is not an entity, not a thing, but a story (or stories) we and others tell about ourselves. The notion of autobiographical occasions calls attention to the ways in which the stories we tell about ourselves are socially structured. As on all autobiographical occasions, such stories are often less about finding freedom or agency, less about giving voice to the self, than they are about the regulation of that self.

About the narrative character of photo albums there can be no mistake. All of the collections I have seen are, like my mother's neatly labeled photos, organized chronologically. Of the older women I have talked to, each has a few pictures of parents taken near the turn of the century and, in a few cases, even of grandparents, taken earlier and passed on. These pictures are invariably placed at the beginning of the album, which then proceeds, often over several albums (or in my mother's case many envelopes), through childhood, early adulthood, marriage, and parenthood, typically ending with a display of grandchildren and great grandchildren.

Photo albums totter uncomfortably between mere "chronicles" and full-blown narratives. As straightforward and conventional chronologies, photo albums and collections could easily be mistaken for chronicles, simple listings of events without beginnings or endings, without the connecting threads that give them moral meaning. But the narrative character of the albums—with beginnings, ends, principles of selection, principles of connection, and at least implicit moral meanings—becomes apparent when we think of them as stories of the self. As such, photo albums are highly selective. Most document the lives of children, especially young children, far more insistently than the lives of adults. In my mother's case, her collection peaks at an average of more than 120 pictures per year between 1948, the year I was born, and 1955, the year my brother turned eleven.

From 1961, my brother's senior year in high school, to 1966, my senior year in high school, the total number of pictures is only 42.

Most albums show little of the workplace and only a little more of workmates. In my mother's collection, 14 pictures, all taken at my father's 1976 retirement party from the chemical company where he had worked for more than 30 years, account for more than half the total. Contained in a small album given to my father by his co-workers, the special placement of the photos represents not the specialness of work but its nearly complete segregation from family.

Most albums understate daily activities in favor of special occasions: occasional pictures of travel and more frequent pictures of weddings and graduations (but, notably, not funerals) vastly outnumber pictures of houses or schools, of daily meals, or of families simply sitting together and talking. In my mother's collection, I can find hundreds of pictures of the large Thanksgiving gatherings she hosted for the better part of two decades, with occasional pictures of an elaborately set table interspersed with far more pictures of the day's guests, but only a single picture of my mother in the kitchen.

Most fundamentally, the photo albums I have seen are thoroughly peopled. They include few pictures of places or things and seemingly endless pictures of family and friends. In my mother's collection, 2,275 of her 2,416 photographs include at least one person. Some, mostly friends, appear only once or twice. Others, mostly family, appear often, their presence documented across

Photo albums are thoroughly peopled with seemingly endless pictures of family and friends.

different ages and circumstances. The complexity of the content comes not in configurations of subject matter but in the reconfiguration of specific subjects in varying combinations: a brother shown as a young boy, then with his wife, then with his children; a group of friends shown together and then in pairs, all accompanied in my interviews with running commentary about who got along with whom, about the formation and dissolution of marriages and friendships.

Photo albums are a peculiar kind of autobiographical statement in which the autobiographer—the woman whose album it is—is pictured only occasionally by herself, more often with someone else, and in the majority of pictures not at all. In her own collection, my mother appears in only one of every eight photographs, and in two-thirds of those she appears with someone else. Even the exceptions to the peopled character of albums are instructive. Travel pictures, probably less common in my mother's collection and in the albums of the

Massachusetts women I talked to than in the albums of a younger population, are documents less of the places visited than of the traveler and her companions, posed in the front of the picture with landmarks in the background. The focus, a term I mean here literally, on the person rather than the place makes the picture a testimony to the primacy of the relationship. So, too, occasional pictures of presents piled up at a wedding or baby shower, always still unwrapped, celebrate the group that has come together far more than they celebrate the presents themselves. "This must be boring to you," one woman told me. "You see, it's all about relationships." Indeed, it is.

fact and fiction in celebrations of the self

Photo albums are selective in another sense as well. In particular, they are often fictions. In some cases, these fictions are explicit, as they were in the earliest photo studios of the mid-19th century, which allowed studio clients to pose in borrowed clothes or in front of elaborate backdrops of exotic locations—a practice echoed in comical style in occasional contemporary travel pictures of children posing with their heads through stockades at historical sites.

In other cases, the fictions are subtler. Most important, the pictures that appear in albums and on mantels tend to put their subjects in an idealized light. For example, consider the picture of my family sitting around the piano. Although my mother did play the violin, and my brother took lessons for many years, I took piano lessons for only a few months (much later than 1955), before discovering that I had neither talent nor inclination. My father played neither piano nor violin. I remember no occasions when the four of us sat by the piano, playing, singing, or doing much of anything else. My mother herself was altogether aware of the fictional character of the photo: "It's a farce," she said, as we were looking through her album. But the fictional character of the pose makes the photo no less valuable to her. It is not a picture of my family as it was, but a picture of my family as my mother might have liked it to be, as she would have liked to remember it, as she would like to present it to others and to herself. So, too, if we look at a picture [bottom right, previous page] taken at a cousin's wedding in 1987 of, from left to right, my brother, my mother, the woman who is now my wife, and myself, we see what looks at first glance like a close and coherent family—but with no reference to my father's death four years earlier or my brother's then-recent divorce. Only my brown

shoes, barely visible in the black and white reproduction here, even hint at the infrequency with which I dressed in anything more formal than chino pants and a shirt with no tie. But the picture, taken by itself, shorn of the context that I bring to it, represents nothing so much as an imposing unity of family.

The self represented in photo albums is, then, a celebration and idealization of what might be called the self-in-relation. These albums belong not only to women but to women born in the early part of the twentieth century. Nonetheless, what we find in photo albums is a self portrayed in a style in which American individualism, much excoriated by generation after generation of cultural critics, is virtually absent. Rather, we find a self expressed in relationships, stories of a life told through ceremonial occasions and always in relation to families and friends. It is a self in which the "I" is virtually always subordinate to a "we," albeit a constantly shifting "we."

It is tempting to argue that we should somehow privilege this self-in-relation—that we should recognize it as an unencumbered, more or less free, more or less natural expression of what contemporary Americans wish the self to be, even in the face of pressures that push them in the direction of different types of self-expression. To put the matter differently, we might be tempted to argue that the photo album is a deeply democratic form in which men, and especially women, who are often otherwise silenced, find their own voices.

Indeed, as part of a larger project in which I am looking at autobiographical occasions of various sorts, my original reason for including photograph albums was that, second perhaps only to diaries, they appear to be one of the occasions for storytelling that are mostly free from regulation and from extraneous concerns beyond pure self-expression. Neither jobs nor loans are at stake in photo albums, as they are in accounts of the self like those provided in resumés, job interviews, and credit applications. There is no sense of sin and contrition of the sort that priests, prepared to withhold absolution, or probation officers, prepared to withhold parole, are likely to insist on in confessions both religious and criminal. There is no requirement for a commitment to self-improvement of the sort that both therapists and self-help groups are likely to demand before accepting an account as adequate.

regulating the self

If photo albums are highly conventionalized, there seem to be, at first glance, few sanctions to enforce those conventions. Photo albums appear to be unencumbered by the social structures that elsewhere regulate how we tell stories about ourselves. But this view is too simple. Photo albums are not the creation of individual women and men but of the very families they celebrate. In addition, albums take on an authority—a putative truth—that belies what we can recognize as their fictional character.

In part, photo albums are commercial creations. Film and camera companies have long advertised themselves as being in the service of creating memories ("Kodak moments" from "America's Storyteller") and, although their effectiveness is hard to document, these advertising campaigns have surely contributed to the sense that possession of a photo album or at least a few snapshots is somehow essential to a well-led life. So, too, commercial portrait photographers contribute powerfully to the sort of conventions apparent in the poses they prefer.

Dependent on referrals from satisfied customers, they pose their subjects in ways that show them at their best and thus contribute to the idealization of the family that I have already noted. Neither film and camera companies nor commercial portrait photographers, however, exercise the most powerful effects on family photo albums; rather, it is families themselves and, to a lesser extent, friends that do so.

Family members are the primary audience for photo albums, which, my respondents report, are often pulled out as a stimulus for reminiscence during visits from children and grandchildren. More important, family and friends produce albums together. In a few instances, family members have quite literally produced the albums: The most elaborate album I have seen, belonging to "Florence Ryan," is organized in a carefully bound book with sections first for Florence as a girl with her parents, then for her as a young woman with her husband, and finally for each of her five children, ordered from oldest to youngest, along with their children. It was prepared for Florence by one of her daughters and her son-in-law, who solicited photos from their relatives, and presented it to Florence, with great fanfare, on the occasion of her ninetieth birthday.

In other cases, the social processes involved in the production of albums are only slightly more subtle. Although I have not systematically counted, and while albums do vary, many of the photos in every album I have seen are of gifts, or they are photos sent by relatives and friends of themselves, sometimes posed with the album's owner, more often without. My mother, for example, includes in her collection annual cards sent to her by a nephew and his wife, photos taken by family and friends while traveling, and an assortment of other shots, posed and unposed. "How this got here, I don't know," she repeated several times, gazing at pictures of my brother and me posed with friends—friends I often recognized but my mother seems never to have met.

If the photo album is a repository of memories, we should recognize that many of the memories (at least for the album's owner) exist only in those photographs. Like the family meal and the holiday celebration, the photo album becomes a means not only to commemorate the family but also to create it. When we consider, too, that every picture involves both a subject and a photographer, the very distinction between autobiography and biography begins to collapse. As a narrative of the self-in-relation, the photo album is a product of the same social circles it celebrates. It is a moment in the regulation of selfhood by the family and for the family.

But this is not all there is to the regulation of selfhood in photo albums. Although art historians and literary critics point to the interpretive qualities of photographs, and although I have myself insisted on the selectivity of photo albums, both my mother and the other women I spoke to hold firmly to another tradition that insists on the photograph's authoritative realism. As I suggested, the women whose albums I examined knew that their photos idealized their subjects. Nonetheless, this recognition of idealization coexists happily with an even more powerful insistence on the reality of what the photos represent. Perhaps the best evidence for this is the manifest absence of photographic authorship. By this, I mean first that the photographs in the albums I saw lack distinctive styles. They are almost all taken as either candids or direct shots, with subjects posed in the middle of the picture, without angles, with little play of light and shadow. Nowhere is there the kind of distinctiveness that makes a Diane Arbus or an Ansel Adams photograph, for example, quickly identifiable to those in the know about such things.

Second, and more important, the women I spoke to were both unaware of and lacked interest in their photographs' authors. In a few instances, they were able to remember that a picture had been taken by a studio photographer and, in a very few of these, even the name of the studio photographer. More often, they said they had no idea who had taken the picture, surmised that it had been taken, in the words of one, by "whoever was around," or suggested, in a frequently repeated phrase, much favored by my mother as well, that "it must have been taken" by a particular member of the family absent from the photograph itself. In treating authorship as irrelevant, the women who look at the photographs are, in effect, denying their interpretive elements and stressing their objectivity: the author does not matter because the photographs do not express a particular point of view. In the absence of authorship, photographs take on an appearance of objectivity.

Although the albums are clearly selective, representing only a fraction of all the photographs that have passed through their owners' hands, neither my mother nor anyone else I spoke to could articulate either a principle or a practice of selectivity. Many shrugged their shoulders and said they had simply put in whatever they could find or whatever they had room for. One woman insisted that she had included every photograph she had: "You have to put them in," she said, implying that otherwise she would somehow have made an inaccurate record. In short, regardless of the fictions and artistry that are fundamental to every photograph, the albums become authoritative. They are, at least in the women's understanding, an unmediated representation of reality. They are simply the way things were. Photo albums become not a form of voice but a form of regulation.

autobiographical occasions

The rise of photography is one of the most important events in the democratization of self-representation. The appearance of studio photography in the mid-19th century extended the possibilities of self-memorialization beyond those who could afford to commission a portrait painter to people of a middling sort. The appearance of hand-held cameras toward the end of the 19th century and the progressive simplification of these cameras over the course of the 20th not only put such self-commemoration within the financial reach of virtually every American but also freed the process from professional photographers. Today, nearly as many households—well over 90 percent—have some sort of camera as have television. But the democratization of self-commemoration is not the same as its liberation. As a type of autobiographical account, photo albums are distinctive in their portrayal of a self-in-relation, for their emphasis on networks of kin and friends rather than on morality, as in confession, or self-development, as in therapy, or individual achievement, as in job and credit applications.

This is not because the self-in-relation is an expression of an unencumbered self, a straightforward expression of more or less natural preferences. It is because the democratization of photography means the delivery of this particular type of self-commemoration into the hands of the very family those albums celebrate.

Photo albums are only one example of the more general phenomenon of autobiographical occasions—and an atypical example at that, because they lack formal, organizational, or professional controls. Nonetheless, precisely because they are atypical, photo albums reveal the general characteristics of autobiographical occasions—moments when narratives of the self meet social structure. The narratives produced on those occasions allow for significant choice in self-presentation, but they are also the products of considerable constraint. On other autobiographical occasions—credit and job applications, therapy, confession—an insistence on the presentation of a continuous self, a refusal to exempt any behavior from what is included in the person, is fundamental to a process of social control. So too is an insistence on most of those occasions (a few forms of therapy are partial exceptions) on individual responsibility. The photo album is different. It allows for omissions, as other autobiographical occasions do not, and speaks more in a "language" of relationships than of individualism. Still, even the photo album is deeply implicated in the regulatory process fundamental to any notion of selfhood.

recommended resources

Chalfen, Stuart. 1987. *Snapshot Version of Life.* Bowling Green, OH: Bowling Green State University Press. An excellent sociological study, based on interviews, survey research, and the examination of 200 photograph collections, of what Americans do when they take photographs and look at albums.

Hoffman, Katherine. 1996. *Concepts of Identity: Historical and Contemporary Images and Portraits of Family and Self.* New York: HarperCollins. An art historian's analysis of how 20th century portraits and photographs have represented families.

Hirsch, Marianne. 1997. *Family Frames: Photography, Narrative and Postmemory.* Cambridge, MA: Harvard University Press. Analyzes the use of photography in the autobiographies of Mark Twain, August Strindberg, Walter Benjamin, and Christa Wolf, with implications for the ways men and women claim control over the narratives of their own lives.

ABOUT THE EDITORS

Jodi O'Brien is Professor of Sociology and Women and Gender Studies at Seattle University. She is the editor of the *Encyclopedia of Gender and Society* and co-editor of the "Contemporary Sociological Perspectives" book series. Her books include *The Production of Reality, Social Prisms,* and *Everyday Inequalities.* Her courses and research focus on difference, power and discrimination, and religion and sexuality.

Arlene Stein is a Professor of Sociology and Women's and Gender Studies and the director of the Institute for Research on Women at Rutgers University. She teaches courses on the sociology of gender and sexuality, culture, self and society. She is the author of four scholarly books; the recipient of the Simon and Gagnon Award for career contributions to the study of sexualities and the Ruth Benedict Book Award; and has served on the editorial boards of the journals *Social Problems, SIGNS,* and *Sexualities.*

Jodi and Arlene served as co-editors of *Contexts* magazine from 2011 through 2014.